COBOL:
An Introduction to Structured Logic and Modular Program Design

WILLIAM S. DAVIS
RICHARD H. FISHER
Miami University, Oxford, Ohio

COBOL:
An Introduction to Structured Logic and Modular Program Design

ADDISON-WESLEY PUBLISHING COMPANY
Reading, Massachusetts • Menlo Park, California
London • Amsterdam • Don Mills, Ontario • Sydney

Copyright © 1979 by Addison-Wesley Publishing Company, Inc. Philippines copyright 1979 by Addison-Wesley Publishing Company, Inc.

All rights reserved. No part of this publication may be reproduced, stored in a retrieval system, or transmitted, in any form or by any means, electronic, mechanical, photocopying, recording, or otherwise, without the prior written permission of the publisher. Printed in the United States of America. Published simultaneously in Canada. Library of Congress Catalog Card No. 78-68773.

ISBN 0-201-01431-9
CDEFGHIJKL-AL-89876543210

to Hannah

---

to Judy

Preface

Axiom: the only way to learn to program *is* to program. In one form or another, most computer programming instructors accept this basic premise. The more programs students have opportunity to write, the more they learn about programming.

What, however, does the phrase "to program" mean? All too often, especially to the uninitiated, programming means simply writing instructions in some computer language. There is much more to it; programming is an exercise in logic. The student who fails to see the difference between programming and merely writing instructions is much like the student who, due to excessive concentration on the mechanics of algebra, fails to see the point of calculus, or another who, believing that a grammatically correct paper is necessarily a good one, misses the whole point of effective writing.

Invariably, some students seem almost immediately to grasp the distinction between programming and coding and are able to handle almost anything the instructor assigns. At the other extreme are those students who can't seem to get even a simple program to "run" without help. Why? Can we simply attribute this apparent variation in skill to natural ability? If that is the case, what is the teacher's function. Why do so many intelligent students have so much trouble with something as simple (really) as computer programming?

Perhaps the problem lies with the student's perception of programming. Like mathematics, programming is a problem solving tool. Before a problem can be solved, that problem must be understood. Once understood, the problem can be solved; once solved, a solution can be implemented. Coding, that phase of programming concerned with writing grammatically correct instructions in a programming language, is an implementation step that, ideally, should be undertaken only after the problem has already been understood and solved. Programming is not a tedious exercise in t-crossing and i-dotting; programming is an exercise in logic.

Thus we return to our axiom: the only way to learn to program is to program. For an experienced programmer learning a second or third language, the axiom is easy to interpret. A grasp of the programming process can be assumed. The instructor can quickly introduce the basic syntax rules of the new language and almost immediately start the students working on their first programming assignments, introducing numerous other, more complex problems as the term progresses.

But what about the first time programmer? Will the same approach work for students who have never before written a program? For some, yes it will—many students seem almost to intuitively grasp programming logic. For most beginners, however, we feel that the best way to teach programming is to concentrate on the entire process, emphasizing logic and not mechanics. Thus we have organized this textbook in a rather unconventional manner. Each chapter begins by describing a problem. A solution to that problem is then developed using such language-independent tools as flow diagrams and psuedo code. Finally, only after the problem has been completely understood and solved, the solution is coded in COBOL. We still feel that the only way to program is to program; when working with beginners, however, it is very important that the full meaning of the phrase "to program" be clearly conveyed.

The book emphasizes problem solving; COBOL is treated as a tool for solving problems. Each chapter is organized as a small case study, with a single problem introduced, solved, and coded. We begin with a simple problem, the computation of an average, and build to more and more complex problems. The basic idea is to explain one or two new logical functions in each chapter, with the COBOL language introduced as it is needed to solve a specific problem. The problem, not the features of the language, controls the pace of the book.

Given that the language is COBOL, the COmmon Business Oriented Language, the problems have been taken from the world of business. We have tried to select the most familiar business data processing applications—payroll, inventory, billing, and report generation—for our examples; students do not grasp basic concepts when those concepts are presented in the context of an application they cannot understand. We have also tried to be realistic, and realistic data processing applications are often quite complex. Even a complex problem becomes relatively easy to solve, however, if it is first broken into a series of simple problems and attacked in modular fashion.

We have, therefore, used a modular approach to program development throughout the text, starting with a general program mainline and adding the computational details as a series of independent modules tied together by the mainline.

Given our emphasis on problem solving, we have clearly not been able to cover all of COBOL; the instructor may well discover that certain features he or she considers to be very important are missing. We would consider extra examples from the instructor's own experience, presented either through lecture or handouts, an excellent addition to the course—the more examples of program development the student sees, the better the course becomes.

A well-written program is easy to read, easy to debug, and easy to maintain, and much of what is called "structured" programming has these objectives in mind. We share these objectives. While we have at times deviated from some of the common rules of structured programming (using an occasional GO TO, for example), we have done so only when, in our opinion, such deviation significantly simplified the program.

What students might benefit from a problem solving approach to programming? Clearly we are aiming this text at those who have never programmed before. Many schools are today offering a service course in COBOL programming exclusively (or primarily) for non-majors. Very few of these students will become professional programmers; their interests lie elsewhere. They are looking to improve their understanding of the computer, and we feel that the approach used in this text will help them to do exactly that.

COBOL is often the first programming language taken by a major, particularly in a business data processing curriculum. The major will study other programming languages as well; frequently advanced COBOL programming is required. The program development process is an invaluable tool to such students. Also, the fact that the examples presented in this book are non-trivial will help minimize the problem of the very bright student who, finding elementary programming exercises to be too simple, develops bad habits and then encounters difficulty in future, more advanced courses.

A growing trend in schools of business administration is to include one or more computer-related courses in the core curriculum, often a computer concepts course followed by COBOL programming. Programming is certainly an objective of the latter course, but not the prime objective. Schools of business are training managers, not technicians. The future manager, either as the administrator or the user of computer resources, will have to know something about the process of developing and implementing a computer program, which is exactly what this textbook is designed to illustrate.

The authors share a total of almost 25 years of business programming experience. Mr. Fisher has been teaching COBOL to college students since 1965; Mr. Davis since 1971.

WSD   RHF

Oxford, Ohio

Acknowledgments

The following information, taken from a U.S. Government Printing Office publication and written by the Conference on Data Systems Languages (CODASYL) is presented in acknowledgement of the source of the COBOL language:

> "Any organization interested in reproducing the COBOL report and specifications in whole or in part, using ideas taken from this report as the basis for an instruction manual or for any other purpose is free to do so. However, all such organizations are requested to reproduce this section as part of the introduction to the document. Those using a short passage, as in a book review, are requested to mention 'COBOL' in acknowledgement of the source, but need not quote this entire section.
>
> "COBOL is an industry language and is not the property of any company or group of companies, or of any organization or group of organizations.

"No warranty, expressed or implied, is made by any contributor or by the COBOL Committee as to the accuracy and functioning of the programming system and language. Moreover, no responsibility is assumed by any contributor, or by the committee, in connection therewith.

"Procedures have been established for the maintenance of COBOL. Inquires concerning the procedures for proposing changes should be directed to the Executive Committee of the Conference on Data Systems Languages.

"The authors and copyright holders of the copyrighted material used herein

> *FLOW-MATIC (Trademark of Sperry Rand Corporation), Programming for the UNIVAC (R) I and II, Data Automation Systems copyrighted 1958, 1959, by Sperry Rand Corporation; IBM Commercial Translator, Form No. F28-8013, copyrighted 1959 by IBM; FACT, DSI 27A5260-2760, copyrighted 1960 by Minneapolis-Honeywell*

have specifically authorized the use of this material in whole or in part, in the COBOL specifications. Such authorization extends to the reproduction and use of COBOL specifications in programming manuals or similar publications."

More specifically, most of the examples in this text are coded using IBM's version of standard COBOL. Our two primary references were *IBM OS Full American National Standard COBOL* (IBM publication number GC28-6396), and *IBM OS Full American National Standard COBOL Compiler and Library, Version, 2, Programmer's Guide* (IBM publication number GC28-6399). Our choice of IBM does not imply an endorsement of IBM products or services; for our purposes the version of COBOL supplied by any of the computer manufacturers or independent software suppliers would have served just as well. IBM's COBOL was chosen simply because, in our opinion, more potential students have access to IBM's COBOL than to a version supplied by any other source.

Mr. Edward K. Montgomery, Assistant Professor of Art, Miami University did much of the artwork in the text. Dr. S. Allison McCormack, an Assistant Professor of English at Miami, helped tremendously by copy editing our manuscript. The text was prepared in camera-ready form by Ms. Venis V. Torge using an IBM Electronic Selectric Composer. The authors are, of course, responsible for the accuracy of the finished product.

Abridged Contents

Part I: THE PROGRAM DEVELOPMENT PROCESS

1. Defining and Planning a Problem Solution — 3
2. Basic COBOL: Language Structure, the IDENTIFICATION DIVISION, and the ENVIRONMENT DIVISION — 27
3. Basic COBOL: The DATA DIVISION and the PROCEDURE DIVISION — 41
4. Getting the Program onto the Computer — 63
5. Controlling the Logical Flow of a Program — 83

Part II: MODULAR PROGRAM DESIGN

6. Developing a Program Mainline — 133
7. Adding Functions to the Mainline — 155
8. Table Handling — 177
9. Systems of Programs — 217

Part III: SEQUENTIAL FILE PROCESSING

10. Sequential Files and Sorting — 257
11. A Single-Level Control Break Problem — 281
12. A Double Control Break Problem — 317
13. The Sequential Master File Update Application — 351

Part IV: DIRECT ACCESS

14.	Direct Access File Processing	389
15.	Updating a Direct Access File	423
16	Creating an Indexed File	445
17	Indexed File Processing	465

Contents

PART I: THE PROGRAM DEVELOPMENT PROCESS

1. **DEFINING AND PLANNING A PROBLEM SOLUTION**

A Cautionary Note Before We Begin	4
Defining the Problem	4
Planning a Manual Solution	5
The Computer	8
Planning a Computer Solution	14
Converting Our Plan to a Computer Program	21
Summary	21

2. **BASIC COBOL: LANGUAGE STRUCTURE, THE IDENTIFICATION DIVISION AND THE ENVIRONMENT DIVISION**

COBOL: Some General Comments	28
The COBOL Coding Form	29
The Basic Structure of a COBOL Program	30
Summary	38

3. **BASIC COBOL: THE DATA DIVISION AND THE PROCEDURE DIVISION**

The DATA DIVISION	42
The PROCEDURE DIVISION	48
Summary	59

4. GETTING THE PROGRAM ONTO THE COMPUTER

Preparing a Machine-Readable Version of the Program	64
The Compilation Process	64
Communicating with the Computer System: the Command Language	66
Job Control Language (Optional)	67
The Command Language and Job Submission	72
The Data Cards	73
Putting the Pieces Together	74
Computer Output	76
Summary	81

5. CONTROLLING THE LOGICAL FLOW OF A PROGRAM

The Problem: Adding Interest to Savings Accounts	84
Writing the COBOL Program	89
Defining Headers and the Page Format	105
Some Final Comments on the Planning Process	119
Summary	119

PART II: MODULAR PROGRAM DESIGN

6. DEVELOPING A PROGRAM MAINLINE

Payroll Processing: Problem Definition	134
Planning a Broad, General Solution	134
Detailed Planning	135
Structured, Modular Program Design	136
Summary	150

7. ADDING FUNCTIONS TO THE MAINLINE

State Tax Computations	156
Planning a Computer-Level Solution	157
Coding a Solution in COBOL	160
Testing the New Version of the Program	168
Summary	172

8. TABLE HANDLING

Another Approach to Table Look-Up	178
Setting up a Table in COBOL	183
Accessing the Fields in a Table	184
Table Initialization	194
Testing the New Version of the Payroll Program	204
Adding Other Functions	204
Summary	204

9. SYSTEMS OF PROGRAMS

Failure is Intolerable	218
Edit Checking the Data	220
Tying Together a System of Programs	227
Planning the Edit Check Program	231
Coding the Edit Program	241
Combining the Data Edit and Payroll Programs into a Single Job	250
Summary	251

PART III: SEQUENTIAL FILE PROCESSING

10. SEQUENTIAL FILES AND SORTING

Sequential Files	258
The File Update Application	259
Generating Regular Management Reports	261
Sort Utility Programs	261
The Internal COBOL Sort Feature	269
Systems of Programs	276
Summary	276

11. A SINGLE-LEVEL CONTROL BREAK PROBLEM

The Problem: Generating Student Grade Reports	282
The Program Logic	286
Error Handling	295
COBOL: The IDENTIFICATION and ENVIRONMENT DIVISIONs	297
The DATA DIVISION	297
The PROCEDURE DIVISION	302
Summary	310

12. A DOUBLE CONTROL BREAK PROBLEM

The Basic Problem: Preparing Customer Activity Reports	318
Defining the Major Logical Functions	321
The DATA DIVISION	330
The PROCEDURE DIVISION—the Mainline	332
A Slightly Different Approach	345
Summary	346

13. THE SEQUENTIAL MASTER FILE UPDATE APPLICATION

The Problem: Updating a Master File	352
Program Logic—Getting Started	354
Implementing the Solution	368
The Master File Update Application	378
Summary	379

PART IV: DIRECT ACCESS

14. DIRECT ACCESS FILE PROCESSING

Direct Access	390
Direct Access Techniques	395
Simple Direct Access Using the Division/Remainder Method	397
Creating a Direct Access File Using COBOL	399
Using a Direct Access File	405
User Involvement in the Planning Process	419
Summary	419

15. UPDATING A DIRECT ACCESS FILE

The Nature of the Direct Access File Update	424
Updating the Product File	424
Direct Access File Update Operating Procedures	425
The Program Structure	428
File Backup	439
Programming—The Building Block Approach	440
Summary	441

16. CREATING AN INDEXED FILE

Indexed files	446
Indexed Sequential Files	447
Creating an Indexed Sequential File	448
Reorganizing an Indexed-Sequential File	460
Summary	461

17. INDEXED FILE PROCESSING

Query Applications	466
Writing the Order Status Program in COBOL	467
Updating the Customer Master File	478
Why Direct Access?	490
Direct vs. Indexed Sequential Access	493
Summary	493

APPENDIX:

    A. The IBM 029 Keypunch   499
    B. DOS Job Control and File Linkage   509
    C. COBOL Reserved Words   515
    D. COBOL Ready Reference   521

INDEX: 545

The Program Development Process

Defining and Planning a Problem Solution

OVERVIEW

In this chapter, we will follow, step-by-step, the process of developing a solution to a problem suitable for submitting to a computer. The problem we've chosen is very general: computing an average. We'll begin by carefully defining the problem to be solved. Next, we'll structure a human-level solution, using such generally accepted and understood everyday tools as a pocket calculator and a counter. Having specified a fairly complete human-level solution, we'll briefly discuss a few basic computer concepts and then restructure our solution to fit the requirements of these machines, developing a flowchart and a very precise description of the data to be processed. Finally, we'll show you a COBOL program written to solve this problem.

A CAUTIONARY NOTE BEFORE WE BEGIN

Computers are fascinating machines. But they are just machines, capable of doing nothing without detailed instructions provided by some human being. The fact that you are reading this book indicates that you are interested in learning how to write these detailed sets of instructions, called programs. You must remember, however, that the computer can do *nothing* that you do not yourself know how to do. In other words, the responsibility for solving the problem is yours, and not the computer's. Yes, the computer is very accurate, but "accuracy" may not mean exactly what you think it does. Computers are considered accurate because the results they generate are highly predictable. If you tell a computer to add 2 and 2, it will invariably get 4. If the programmer didn't really mean to have the computer add 2 and 2, it will *still* get 4. The wrong instructions will produce the wrong answer with perfect "accuracy".

A computer is programmed in a programming language; the language we've chosen for this text is COBOL. Anyone can learn to write instructions in COBOL—it's just a matter of practice. There is, however, much more to programming. Before a problem solution can be coded in COBOL (or any other language), there must be a problem solution. The primary purpose of this book is to show you how to develop such solutions. We'll be using a very methodical, structured approach, the top-down approach, to program development. As you begin to learn more about COBOL, the temptation will be to skip planning and careful preparation, and immediately begin coding a solution. Don't. As you move more deeply into COBOL, the problems will become more and more difficult; the need for careful planning *never* disappears. *Think!* Then do.

DEFINING THE PROBLEM

Let's start with a very common problem: computing an average. Undoubtably, you have computed your grade point average, your batting average, your freethrow percentage, or some other average at some time in the past. What does it mean to compute an average? If you had to perform this task, what would you do?

Your view of the problem is probably going to be shaded somewhat by your background. If you are a mathematician, your basic definition of this problem is simply

$$\bar{X} = \frac{\sum_{i=1}^{n} X_i}{n}$$

For most people, the mathematical definition isn't very useful. More likely, your view of the problem consists of the following two steps:

1. add together all the values you wish to average,
2. divide by the total number of values.

The result, in either case, will be an arithmetic average (or mean).

In technical terms, we have just defined an **algorithm**, a set of rules which, if followed precisely, will lead to a correct solution. Note that both the mathematical version and the English language version are valid algorithms; the use of mathematical conventions is *not* essential.

We now know, in very general terms, what has to be done. The question that remains is, "How do we do it?". Let's move along to the planning stage, where we will attempt to answer that question.

PLANNING A MANUAL SOLUTION

If you had to compute an average, precisely how would you go about it? We've already developed an algorithm; looking at that list of two steps, you might feel mildly insulted by the question. It seems obvious. Just

1. add all the values,
2. divide by the number of values.

It is obvious. You are, after all, a human being. Having stated the algorithm, you know how to solve the problem.

True. But that really doesn't help us bring the problem solution down to the computer's level. We must be a bit more precise. A useful technique for introducing this added detail is to set up a straw person (formerly, straw man). Assume that this straw person is unbelievably dense, and is capable of doing only what he or she is told to do. Instructions must be in the form of simple sentences—one verb. Each instruction must specify one and only one very specific action; this person literally cannot chew gum and walk at the same time. Now, tell this person how to compute an average. (You might even get your roommate to play the role.)

We might add a bit of structure to this technique by giving our straw person a pocket calculator (after all, everyone has a pocket calculator). We are now ready to begin instructing this imaginary individual as to exactly how to go about computing an arithmetic average.

What's wrong with simply saying, "Add all the numbers together"? How many numbers are there? If we assume there are 50 numbers, we are asking our straw person to do 50 things. The limit is 1! Our imaginary person can do only 1 thing at a time. We must be more precise.

Breaking this part of the problem into individual steps might produce the following list:

1. Enter the first number.
2. Push the ADD button.
3. Enter the second number.
4. Push the ADD button.

5. Enter the third number.

6. Push the ADD button, and so on.

The pattern should be obvious. Note that each instruction is a simple sentence telling the straw person to perform one and only one very specific function.

How many instructions would we need? If we wanted to find the average of 50 numbers, we would need 50 "Enters" and 50 "Adds". One thousand numbers would require 1000 sets of instructions. Defining a solution in this way would become very tedious. Chances are, you would consider taking a shortcut. Consider, for example, the following:

1. Enter a number.

2. Push the ADD button.

3. Are there any more numbers?

4. If yes, go back to step 1.

How many numbers would this little block of logic add together? How many numbers do we have? Our straw person, following these four instructions, would accumulate values until there were no more values to accumulate. In programming terminology, we'd call this a **loop**.

We might try this logic just to see if, in fact, it works. Take a handful of numbers: 3 + 5 + 2 for example. We know that the correct sum is 10. Let's see if our logic produces that sum. Pick up your pocket calculator and do exactly what the instructions say. Don't clear it; where did you read an instruction that says "Clear the calculator"? Now add 3 + 5 + 2 and get 1347 or some other equally ridiculous answer. Why didn't your logic work? Obviously because you forgot to clear your calculator. By actually trying your solution, you are going through a process known as **desk checking**. It is an invaluable step. No matter how well you think you know what you are doing, there are always going to be little details that you will overlook. The only sure way to catch these oversights is by actually trying your logic. In fact, try it twice; the calculator just might have been cleared by the previous user and you might have missed this problem completely.

Adding the initialization step leads to the following five steps:

1. Clear calculator.

2. Enter a number.

3. Push the ADD button.

4. Are there any more numbers?

5. If yes, go back to step 2.

Now, desk checking should clearly indicate that if we follow the instructions "to the letter" we will successfully add any number of values.

What next? What do we do after there are no more numbers? It's time to divide the accumulated sum of values by the number of values to get the average. We might add step 6, as follows:

6. Divide sum by number of values to get average.

There is only one problem. We know the sum, but how many values were there? Before computing the average, we must count the values. Basically, we have two choices. We can go through our list of values all over again, this time counting instead of accumulating, or we can count values as we go along. The first choice might be reasonable if we have only a few values to average. If we are dealing with hundreds of data points, however, it makes sense to count as we go along. You might imagine yourself making a mark on a paper after adding each number to the accumulator, as in (卌 卌 IIII), or you might use a mechanical counter. Adding this logic to our developing solution, we now have:

1. Clear calculator.
2. Set counter to 0.
3. Enter a number.
4. Push the ADD button.
5. Add 1 to counter.
6. Are there any more numbers?
7. If yes, go back to step 3.
8. Divide accumulator by counter to get average.
9. Copy average onto a sheet of paper.

That last step was added to make certain that a copy of the answer is saved.

We now have a pretty complete average program. The logic should work; desk check it with three or four values to be sure. Try it out on a classmate. Without describing the objective of the program, simply read the instructions, one at a time, and have your friend do exactly what you say. If the answer turns out to be correct, you will *know* that your program works.

Do professional programmers really do this? In many cases, yes. Perhaps the experienced problem solver wouldn't go into quite as much detail, but the basic idea of structuring a human-level solution before trying to tackle the computer-level solution is a technique used by a surprising number of professional programmers. As for reading a program to another person, many programming shops have actually formalized this procedure. The technique, called a **structured walkthrough**, consists of one programmer describing the step by step logic of his or her program to other programmers.

Our objective up to this point was simply to define a problem solution in sufficient detail so that we can actually say that we know how to solve the problem. Now that we know what to do, we can begin to discuss how we might adapt this solution to the computer. Before doing this, we must discuss a few very basic computer concepts.

THE COMPUTER

What exactly is a **computer**? Perhaps the best way to answer that question, without getting into details we really don't need at this point, is to compare a computer to its first cousin, the calculator. Imagine actually implementing the problem solution described above on a calculator. Each time the instruction said "Enter a number," you would key in the value and press the "ENTER" button. Each time the instruction said "Push the ADD button," you would press the "ADD" or "+" button. Each step requires you, the human being, to decide what button is to be pressed, and then to press it. The precise steps may be a bit different with a different calculator, but the basic idea of the need for human participation at each and every step is still valid.

Imagine that you have a special machine which automatically pushes the proper buttons in the proper sequence. Given such a machine, calculations could be performed without human intervention. We'd have an automatic calculator. Of course, all the steps would have to be carefully thought out and "programmed" ahead of time, but if a particular set of computations had to be performed over and over again, many many times, the task of preparing the program would be worth the cost. Such an automatic calculator would be, essentially, a computer.

The basic difference between a computer and a calculator is that a computer is designed to function automatically, under control of a **program**, while a calculator is designed to require step by step human intervention. Bascially, a computer is composed of two primary components (Fig. 1.1), a processor and memory. Programs are stored in the computer's memory. The processor performs two basic functions. First,

Fig. 1.1: *The primary components of a computer.*

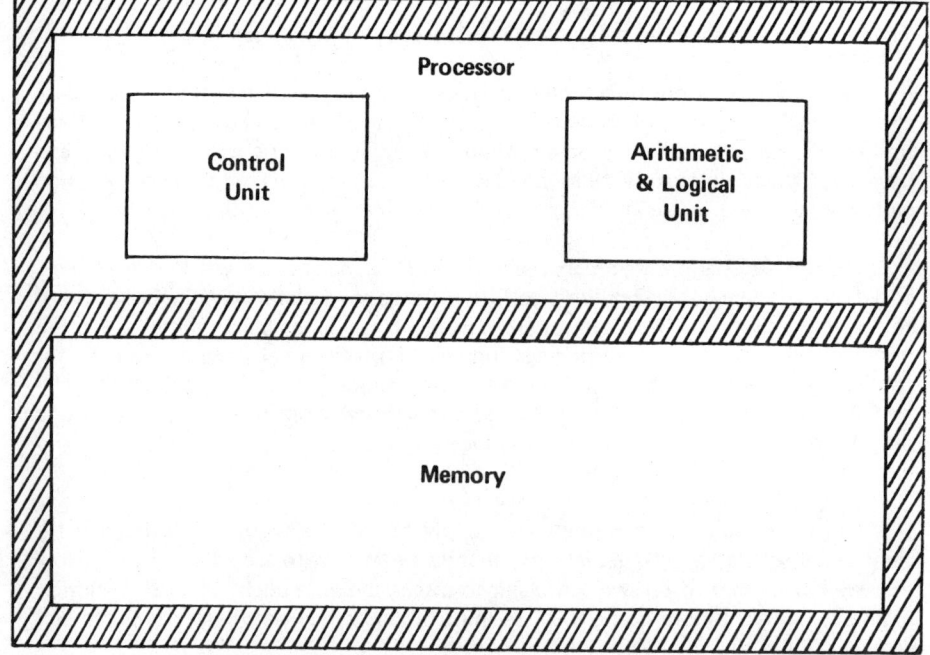

it fetches a single instruction from memory and decodes the instruction, figuring out which specific operation is to be performed; this function is carried out by the control unit portion of the processing unit. Once the control unit has figured out what must be done, it turns control over to an arithmetic and logical unit (Fig. 1.1 again), which does what the instruction says to do. The same thing happens on a calculator, only you provide the control. At some point, you must decide which button to push, performing the function of the control unit. When you make up your mind, you push the button, thus performing the function of the arithmetic and logical unit.

A computer is capable of executing a very limited set of instructions. Most computers can:

1. add two numbers,
2. subtract one number from another,
3. multiply two numbers,
4. divide one number into another,
5. copy data from one memory location to another,
6. perform simple yes/no logic,
7. request the input of some data,
8. request the output of some data.

That's about it. A computer program is nothing more than a series of these very simple operations. Of course, they had better be the right operations, and they had better be in the right sequence, but basically that's all a program is.

A few of the computer's instructions need a bit more explanation. Addition, subtraction, multiplication, and division are obvious, so no additional detail is needed, but what is the copy function? Computers are not restricted to numeric data; they can process letters of the alphabet, punctuation marks, and numerous other forms of data as well. Imagine rearranging your manager's scribbles into attractive tables and well-spaced prose. The computer, acting under control of the copy or "move" instruction, can do much the same thing, preparing attractive, well-spaced computer printouts.

What about the computer's yes/no logic capability? Look back at our human-level solution to the average problem. In step 6, we asked, "Are there any more numbers?". Step 7 said, "If yes, go back to step 2". That's yes/no logic. The computer can do much the same thing, checking to see if one number is bigger than another or if one letter comes before another in the alphabet. As we get into the COBOL language, we'll begin to discover just how powerful this skill really is.

Input and output may well be new concepts to many of you. Let's once again return to our calculator analogy and see if we can develop a parallel. One of the early steps in our average program called for us to enter a number. What does this step entail? Basically, as you can probably imagine, you key in a number one digit at a time and, when you're finished, you hit a button. That's input. You are providing the calculator with an element of data that it does not already have. After computing the average, you probably copy the answer onto a sheet of paper. That's output; you are

Fig. 1.2: *A Terminal.*

Courtesy of Anderson Jacobson, Inc.

Fig. 1.3: *A Typical Card Reader.*

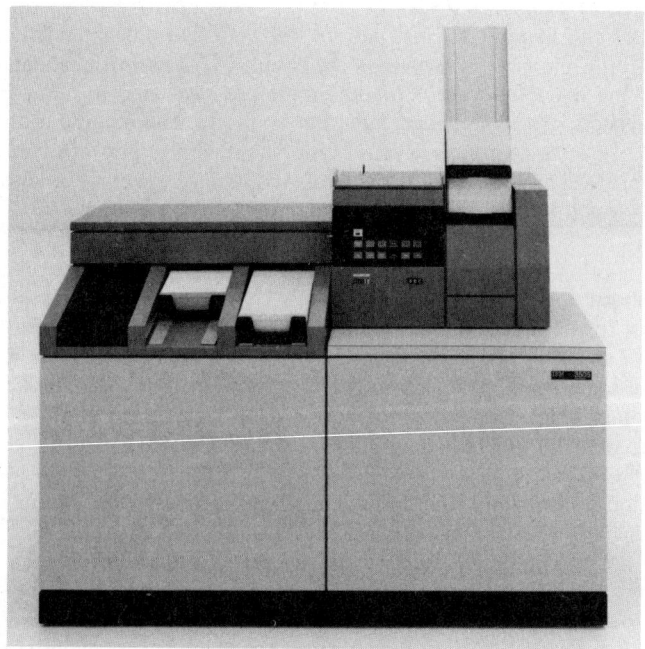

Courtesy of IBM.

transferring information from the calculator to some other medium. Input implies data going into the device; ouput implies answers or other results coming out from the device.

One piece of equipment that is frequently used for getting data into and out from a computer is a terminal (Fig. 1.2). Imagine that you are a terminal operator. As the computer goes through its program (it is, don't forget, working automatically, under control of a pre-supplied program) it eventually encounters an instruction that says, "Read input data." At this point, you, the terminal operator, would be asked to type a number or some other data (depending on the problem being solved) on your terminal and hit the RETURN key, thus sending the data into the computer. Later, when the computer encountered an instruction that told it to write output, the results would be printed on your terminal.

One of the best known of all the computer input devices is the card reader. A card reader (Fig. 1.3), as the name implies, reads punched cards (Fig. 1.4). As we'll see later, data is stored in a card by punching a pattern of holes that stand for letters, digits, and punctuation marks. With a card reader as the input device, when the computer encounters an input instruction, it tells the card reader to transfer one cardfull of data into the computer and store it in memory.

The printer (Fig. 1.5) is perhaps the best known computer output device. A printer is used to prepare printed reports under control of the computer. When the computer encounters an output instruction, it normally sends one full line of output information to the printer.

Fig. 1.4: *A Punched Card.*

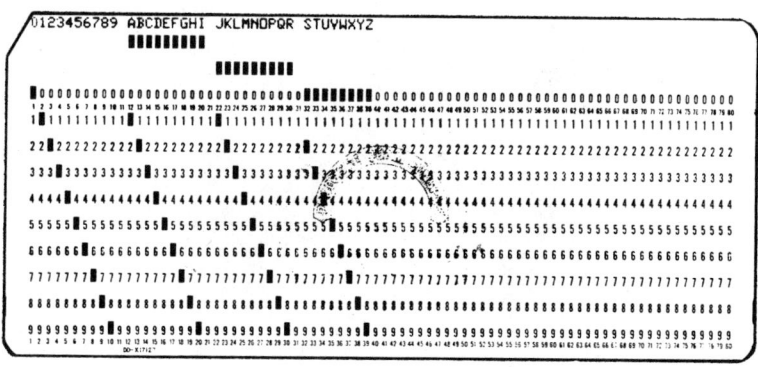

We can now expand our view of a typical computer installation a bit. We still have the computer itself in the middle (Fig. 1.6), but notice that we've added input and output devices. Typically, the computer accepts input data from its input device or devices, processes or manipulates this data, and sends output information to its output devices. That's the normal data processing sequence.

There are many other input and output devices available, of course. Later in the text, we'll consider the use of magnetic tape as a medium for storing intermediate results, and for maintaining vast amounts data in permanent machine-readable storage. Magnetic disk, also to be covered later, gives us even greater flexibility in data storage. For now, however, we'll stay with the card reader and the printer; the first several chapters of this text will discuss programming examples for which these two devices will be adequate.

Storing the Program

Several times in the above discussion, we've mentioned that the computer acts under the control of a program. Where is this program found? How does the program get into the computer?

Let's deal with the first of these questions first. The program is normally found in the computer's memory (Fig. 1.7). The control unit portion of the main processor, as you may recall, fetches an instruction from main memory and decodes it, passing control on to the arithmetic and logical unit, which executes the instruction. Then,

Fig. 1.5: *A line printer.*

Courtesy of Dataproducts Corporation, Woodland Hills, California.

Fig. 1.6: *A computer with input and output devices attached.*

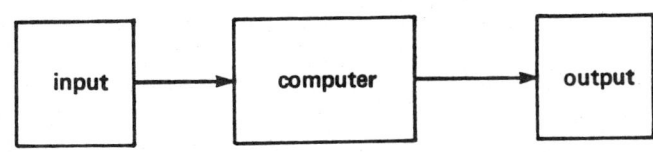

Fig. 1.7: *A computer with a program and data in main memory.*

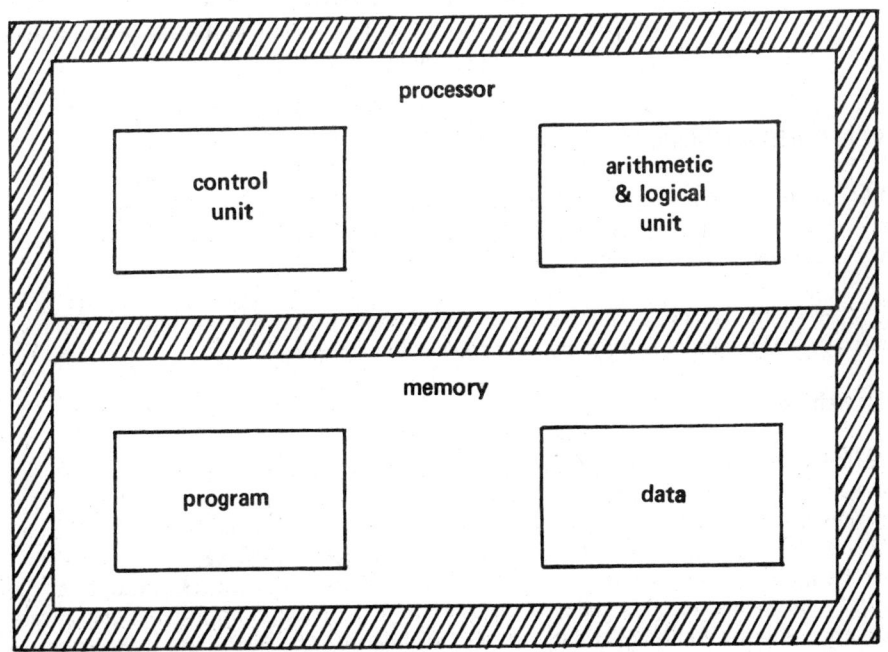

it's back to the control unit, where another cycle begins. For this cycle to work, the program *must be* in main memory.

How does it get there? This question is not quite so easy. Imagine, to over simplify things a bit, that you have very carefully typed your program, making a copy on a tape cassette. You load this cassette into the computer's tape reader, push a button on the computer's control console, and the program is copied into main memory.

Some smaller computers work exactly this way. On larger computers, programs are stored on high-speed magnetic disk devices, and access is controlled by professional operators and special control programs, but the basic idea is the same. We'll consider this process in more detail later.

Storing the Data

What about the data? Where is it stored? Generally, what happens is that, on input, the data is also stored in main memory (Fig. 1.7). While in main memory, the data is processed; in other words, the data is moved around and arithmetic is performed on it. When output is called for, the results are transferred from main memory to an output device.

The Computer: a Summary

In brief, that's what a computer is. It's a machine capable of performing a number of logical functions—arithmetic, copying, simple yes/no logic, input, and output. More importantly, it is possible for a human being to write a program consisting of a series of these logical functions and to introduce this program into the computer's main memory; once this has been done, the machine is capable of following the instructions of the program without further human intervention. In effect, given a program to provide control, a computer becomes an automatic machine. For any well defined, highly repetitive task, it's a very valuable machine, indeed.

PLANNING A COMPUTER SOLUTION

We now know how to compute an average by hand. We also know a little bit about the computer. The next step is to develop a plan for implementing our solution on the computer.

Programmers use a number of different tools to aid in this detailed planning step. One of the more commonly used tools is flowcharting.

Flowcharting

A flowchart is a graphical representation of a program. Program logic (in other words, the arithmetic, the copy steps, the yes/no logic, and the input and output steps) is defined by using a few standard symbols (Fig. 1.8). These symbols are connected by lines to indicate the flow of logic through the program. Let's say, for example, that we want to read a card containing two numbers, to add the numbers, and to print the sum. A flowchart for this logic is illustrated in Fig. 1.9. Note that the flowchart very clearly defines two things. First, the symbols identify the individual logical steps in

Fig. 1.8: *Flowcharting Symbols.*

Symbol	Meaning	Explanation
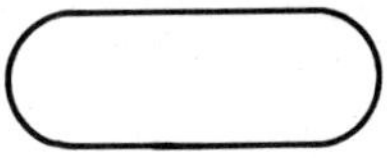 ⬭	Terminal point	Marks the beginning or end point of a program.
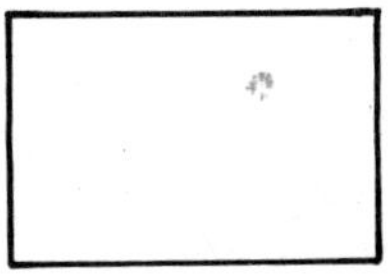 ▭	Process	Used to indicate any addition, subtraction, multiplication, division, or copy operation.
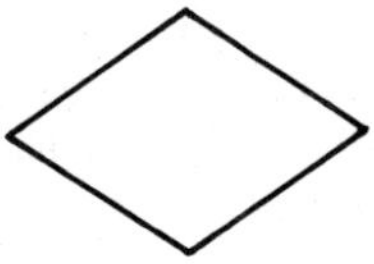 ◇	Decision	Used to indicate any yes/no decision to be made by the program.
 ▱	Input/Output	Used to indicate any input or output operation.

Fig. 1.9: *A simple flowchart.*

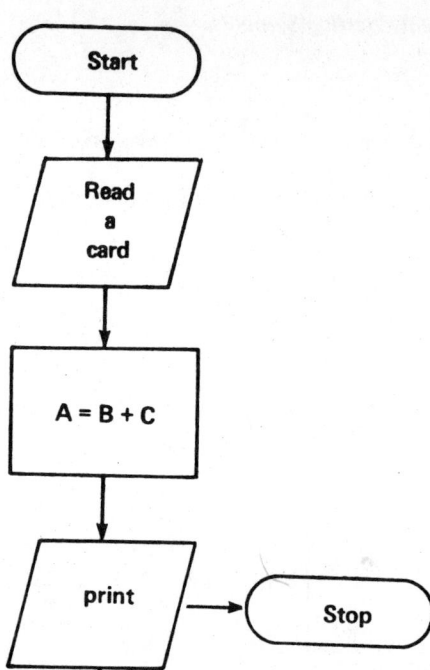

the program. Second, by following the lines connecting the symbols, the sequence of these steps is clearly defined. In other words, in addition to telling what must be done, a flowchart also defines the order in which these steps must be performed.

There are a few simple, generally accepted rules governing the flowlines. The normal direction of flow is from top to bottom or from left to right; arrowheads are used if the direction of flow is anything else. Flowlines should not cross. In general, the idea is to keep things as simple and as straightforward as is possible. In fact, to improve the readability of our flowcharts, we will follow the practice of always using arrowheads to indicate the direction of flow.

Look back at the manual solution we developed. Most of the instructions in that solution are pretty straightforward. "Enter a number" is obviously an input operation. "Push the ADD button" just as obviously calls for the execution of an addition operation. Almost without exception, the manual instructions have a direct match with the list of computer instructions presented on page 9.

There is, however, one exception. Manual instruction 6 asks the question, "Are there any more numbers?". How do you know that there are no more numbers to be processed? Simple, says the human being, there are no more numbers to be processed. It's not that easy for a computer. The computer, don't forget, gets its data through an input device. The "no more data" condition occurs when, for example, there are no more cards in the card reader.

A human being would recognize the fact that there is no more data *before* trying to enter that data. The only way a computer can tell that there is no more data is by asking the card reader to supply some, only to discover that there are no more cards. In other words, the computer cannot look ahead. Instead, it discovers that there is no more data only *after* trying to read that data. This simple fact forces us to change our view of the problem solution.

Let's flowchart how a computer would have to make the "no more data" decision (Fig. 1.10). Our flowchart begins with an input instruction. Following input, we ask a question: Is this the last of the data cards? There are two possible responses: yes or no. If the answer is "no," we process the data. If the answer is "yes," we perform end of data processing.

How can the computer tell that it has in fact encountered the last of the data cards? To avoid any possibility of ambiguity, the programmer is normally required to place an **end-of-data marker** at the end of each deck of data cards. Typically, this end-of-data marker consists of a few unusual characters such as /*, or //, or $EOJ. Essentially, the question, "Is this the last of the data cards?", really means, "Does this card contain the end-of-data marker?".

Fig. 1.10: *A flowchart of end-of-data logic.*

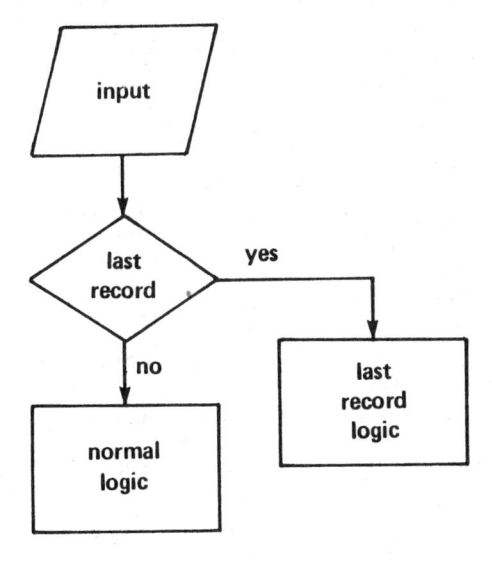

Fig. 1.11: *A flowchart of the Average Problem.*

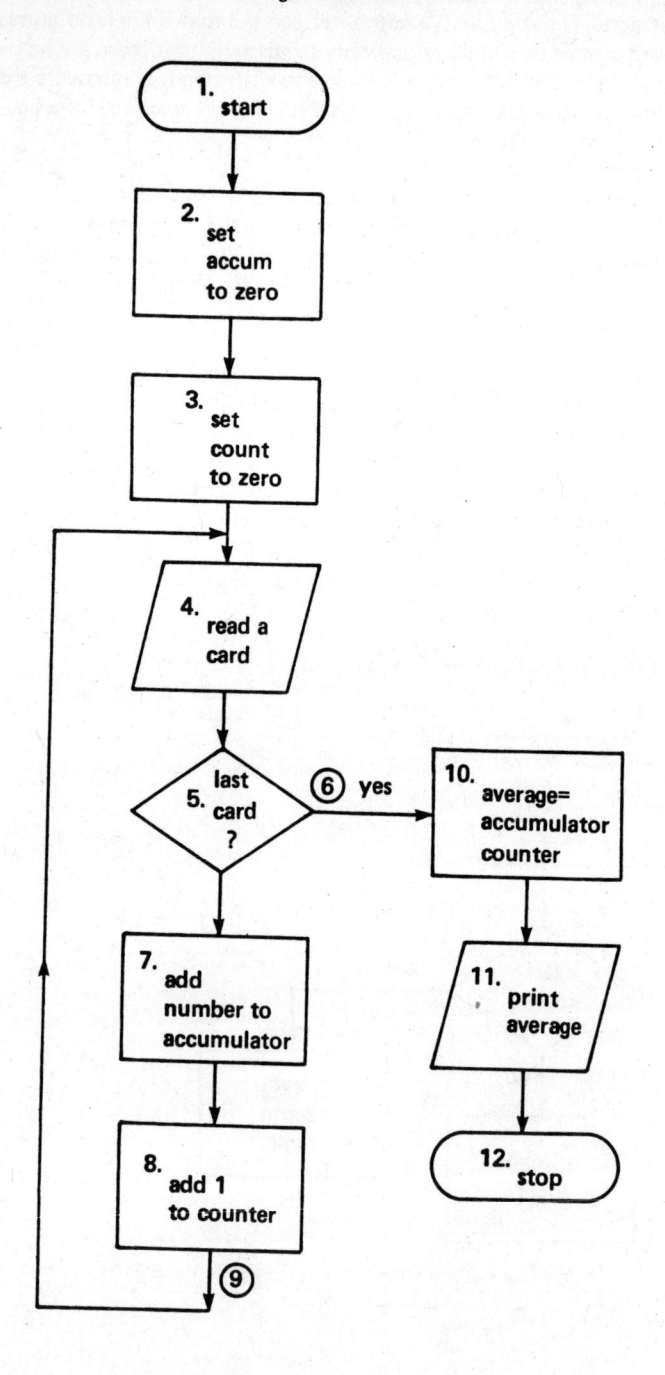

1. start
2. set accum to zero
3. set count to zero
4. read a card
5. last card ?
6. yes
7. add number to accumulator
8. add 1 to counter
9.
10. average = accumulator counter
11. print average
12. stop

Now we're ready to convert the human-level solution to the average problem into flowchart form. The finished flowchart might look like Figure 1.11. Let's go through it step by step; the steps have been numbered to aid in this process. Follow the flowchart carefully as we move through the program, and be sure that you understand exactly what happens in each and every step. The steps are as follows:

1. This is the start of the program.

2. The accumulator is set to zero.

3. The counter is set to zero.

4. Read a card.

5. Test for last card. Why do we test for the last card before accumulating and counting? Do we want to count the card containing this special end-of-data marker? No.

6. If this is the last card, skip to instruction 10, where we will compute the average.

7. If it's not the last card, add the number to the accumulator.

8. Add 1 to the counter.

9. Go back and read another card (return to step 4).

10. Divide the accumulator by the counter to get the average. We reached this point, don't forget, only after the end-of-data card had been encountered.

11. Send a line of output to the printer.

12. Terminate the program.

Our flowchart defines in a very formal way the logic of the soon-to-be-written payroll program. We have used flowcharting as a planning aid, but its formality allows it to serve another important function. At some time in the future when we want to look back at our program and perhaps make some modifications, the flowchart serves as a reference document, clearly describing the logical flow of the program in an easy to follow form. Most programs, particularly business programs, will change over time. Thus, **documentation** is essential, and the flowchart is a very valuable documentation tool.

Defining the Data

The flowchart defines the logical flow of the program, but if a computer is actually to execute this program, additional information must be made available. Remember the diagram of Fig. 1.7 which showed both the program and the data being stored in main memory? To this point, we have worked only with the program side. What exactly does the data look like? Given that we are going to be reading a card in this first program, exactly where on each card can the critical elements of data be found? Given that we are going to be sending output to the printer, exactly what is to be the content of each output line? The computer is going to have to set up memory space to hold an accumulator and a counter; what kind of data are these intermediate fields going to hold? Computers can handle alphabetic data and numeric data. They can handle big numbers and small numbers. Defining the data precisely is a programmer responsibility.

Let's assume that, for our average program, the input data is going to be punched into cards. A card is divided into 80 columns, and each column holds exactly one character of data. If we are dealing with a series of five digit numbers, each with two digits to the right of the decimal point, the contents of each input card might be as follows:

columns	contents
1-5	a number with two digits to the right of the decimal point
6-80	unused

Note that, since every number is going to have exactly two digits to the right of the decimal point, we do not have to actually punch the decimal point; instead, the computer can assume it. We have defined the format of the input card.

Now we can turn our attention to the output line. Our printer works with an output line of 133 characters. We want to print the computed average somewhere on this line. We might use the following format for our program output:

positions	contents
1-15	blank
16-23	the computed average to 4 decimal places
24-133	blank

Where did this format come from? We made it up. We wanted a margin on the left of the line, so we set aside 15 spaces. We then set aside the space needed to print the computed average. Note that we want to actually print the decimal point, and that it takes up one print position. Why do we want to print the decimal point; we didn't keypunch it? The computer can be instructed to assume the location of the decimal point on input. Human beings will be reading the output, and it is *not* reasonable to assume that they will know where the decimal point belongs.

What about the intermediate results? We know that the accumulator and the counter will be holding numbers, but how big do these numbers have to be? Let's assume that we know there will never be more than 100 values to average. The counter, clearly, will never be more than 3 digits in length. As for the accumulator, what is the biggest input number we can possibly have? The answer is **999.99**. There can be no more than 100 of these. Thus, if we multiply 999.99 by 100, we get the biggest possible value the accumulator will ever have to hold; the answer is **99999.00**. We have now completely defined our data.

Defining Input and Output Devices

Only one thing remains to be done before we can begin to convert our plan to a computer program; we must explicitly define all our input and output devices. We have already implicitly done this for the average program; throughout this discussion, we have mentioned the fact that we are going to be reading cards and printing output lines, so our input device must be a card reader, and our output device must be a printer. Still, it is wise to take a few minutes to compile a list of the input and output devices required by the program. Later, when we move on to more difficult problems, the wisdom of this little step will become more clear.

For our average problem, we plan to use the following devices:

    Input: card reader.

    Output: printer.

CONVERTING OUR PLAN TO A COMPUTER PROGRAM

Finally, we are ready to begin coding our program. At this stage, we know three things. All the input and output devices required by our program have been carefully specified. The precise format of all input and output data and all intermediate data elements (the accumulator and the counter in our example) has been defined. The logic of the program has been spelled out in a flowchart. Until the input/output devices, the data formats, and the program logic have been defined, we are not really ready to begin writing a program. Once these factors have been defined, coding a program becomes little more than an exercise in translation.

Chapter 2 will be devoted to the topic of actually coding this program in a language known as COBOL, which stands for the **CO**mmon **B**usiness **O**riented **L**anguage. Before we move on to Chapter 2, try a little experiment. Take a look at Fig. 1.12; it summarizes just about everything we've discussed thus far. On the left hand page, you will see the list of input and output devices, the data formats, and the flowchart developed in this chapter. On the right hand page, you will see a COBOL program written to implement the plan. Read the program, comparing each part of the program to the equivalent part of our plan. Don't worry about the specific rules, and ignore such things as an unusual spelling or the precise punctuation used in the program. Concentrate instead on relating the COBOL logic to our plan; you should find the program relatively easy to read. If you can do it, then you are ready to begin learning the rules of the COBOL language.

SUMMARY

The intent of this chapter was to illustrate a reasonable approach for developing a computer-level solution to a problem. We began by carefully defining the problem to be solved. Next, we set up a straw person and planned a manual solution designed to tell this individual how to solve the problem. Throughout this discussion, we emphasized the value of desk checking.

Fig. 1.12: *The planning steps and the equivalent COBOL code.*

```
IDENTIFICATION DIVISION.

PROGRAM-ID. AVERAGE.
AUTHOR.     DAVIS & FISHER.

REMARKS.    THIS PROGRAM READS A SERIES OF DATA CARDS,
            COUNTS THE CARDS, ACCUMULATES THE VALUES
            PUNCHED ONE TO EACH CARD, AND, AFTER THE
            LAST CARD HAS BEEN READ, COMPUTES THE
            AVERAGE VALUE.

ENVIRONMENT DIVISION.

CONFIGURATION SECTION.

SOURCE-COMPUTER.  IBM-370-148.
OBJECT-COMPUTER.  IBM-370-148.

INPUT-OUTPUT SECTION.

FILE-CONTROL.
    SELECT CARD-FILE  ASSIGN TO UT-S-CARDFILE.
    SELECT PRINT-FILE ASSIGN TO UT-S-PRTFILE.

DATA DIVISION.

FILE SECTION.

FD  CARD-FILE
    LABEL RECORD IS OMITTED.
01  INPUT-CARD.
    05  I-VALUE                     PIC 999V99.
    05  FILLER                      PIC X(75).

FD  PRINT-FILE
    LABEL RECORD IS OMITTED.
01  OUTPUT-LINE.
    05  FILLER                      PIC X(15).
    05  O-AVERAGE                   PIC 999.9999.
    05  FILLER                      PIC X(110).

WORKING-STORAGE SECTION.

77  COUNTER                         PIC 999.
77  ACCUMULATOR                     PIC 99999V99.
```

Definition of I/O Devices:
Input : card reader
Output : printer

Data Formats:

Input:

columns	contents
1-5	a number
6-80	unused

Output:

positions	contents
1-15	blank
16-23	computed average
24-133	blank

Work: accumulator: 99999.99 max.
      counter : 999 max.

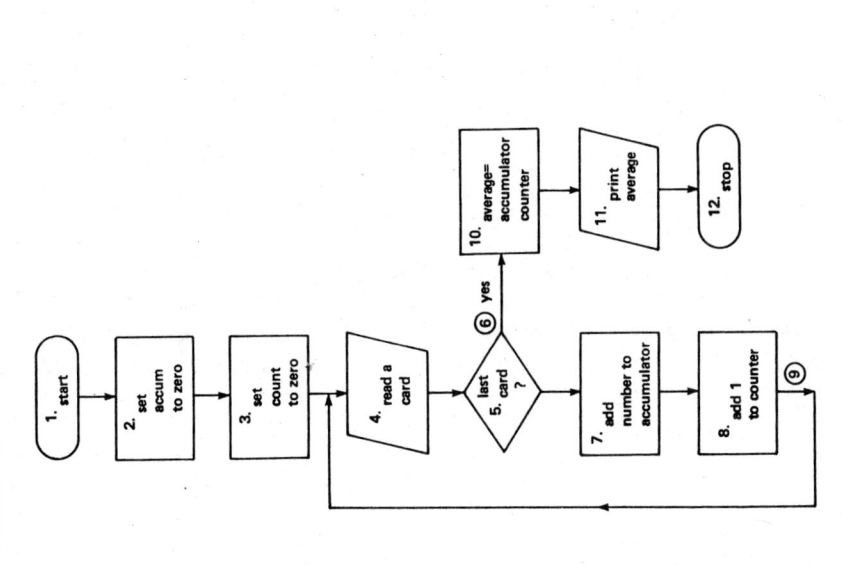

```
PROCEDURE DIVISION.

BEGIN.
    OPEN INPUT CARD-FILE.
    OPEN OUTPUT PRINT-FILE.
    MOVE ZEROS TO COUNTER, ACCUMULATOR.

GET-A-VALUE.
    READ CARD-FILE
        AT END GO TO FIND-AVERAGE.
    ADD 1-VALUE TO ACCUMULATOR.
    ADD 1 TO COUNTER.
    GO TO GET-A-VALUE.

FIND-AVERAGE.
    MOVE SPACES TO OUTPUT-LINE.
    DIVIDE ACCUMULATOR BY COUNTER GIVING D-AVERAGE.
    WRITE OUTPUT-LINE
        AFTER ADVANCING 3 LINES.

END-OF-JOB.
    CLOSE CARD-FILE.
    CLOSE PRINT-FILE.
    STOP RUN.
```

Fig. 1.12: *continued*.

Having solved the problem at a human level, we were ready to move along to a computer-level solution. First, however, we found it necessary to describe a few basic computer concepts. A computer is capable of performing arithmetic, copying data from one memory location to another, performing simple yes/no logic, asking for input, and asking for output. What makes the computer a unique device is that it performs these functions automatically, under the direct control of a program stored in the computer's memory. A program is nothing more than a series of instructions, written by a programmer, designed to guide the computer through some logical function. One of the primary objectives of this text is to teach you how to write such programs. Various input and output devices can be attached to a computer; we concentrated on card readers and printers.

In moving from a manual solution to a computer program, we went through a number of detailed planning steps. First, using flowcharting as a planning aid, we carefully defined the logic of the program. Of particular interest was the way in which a computer recognizes the fact that the last of the data has been read. Once the logic was defined, we moved along to the data, laying out the position-by-position contents of the input data, the output data, and any intermediate work fields. Finally, we made certain that we had a complete list of the input and output devices required by the program. Having defined the input/output devices, the data format, and the program logic, we were ready to begin coding a solution in COBOL.

The chapter ended with a two page figure (Fig. 1.12) showing, on the left, all our planning steps and, on the right, a COBOL program written to implement this plan. Go over the figure carefully. You should be able to see how each planning step is actually implemented in COBOL. Don't worry about punctuation rules, spellings, and strange names; we'll get to that in Chapter 2. At this stage, you should simply be able to read the COBOL program and make sense of it. Once the program has been properly defined and a careful plan has been prepared, actually coding the solution is, after all, little more than an exercise in translation.

KEY WORDS

algorithm	**documentation**	**loop**
computer	**end-of-data-marker**	**program**
desk checking	**flowchart**	**structured walkthrough**

EXERCISES

1. An instructor would like to apply a grade curve to an exam so that the class average comes out to exactly 78. This means that if the actual class average is greater than 78, points will be deducted from every student's score and, if the actual average is less than 78, points will be added to every student's score. The easiest way to do this is to find the actual average and then to compute the difference between this figure and the target of 78. How would you modify the problem solution developed in this chapter to implement the extra computa-

tion? Add the new computation to the flowchart and expand the description of output data to include this new field.

2. A baseball player's batting average is computed by dividing the number of times at bat into the number of hits. Since hits cannot possibly exceed times at bat, this statistic will always be a fraction (exception: 1.000); usually it's computed correct to three decimal places. Plan a computer-level solution, including a flowchart, data formats, and a list of needed input and output devices, to produce a list of the player number, times at bat, hits, and computed batting average of each of the 25 players on a team.

3. An instructor has indicated that each student's final grade will be computed according to the following formula:

>   exam no. 1 . . . . 25%
>
>   exam no. 2 . . . . 25%
>
>   homework 20%
>
>   final exam 30%

Assume that your actual grades for each of these four grade factors have been keypunched into a single card (actual grades are on a scale of 0-100). Plan a computer-level solution to read this card, compute the percentage value of each of these factors, sum the factor values, and print this final "total grade points" value.

4. A very common computer application involves the printing of address labels for mailings. Assume that you have a series of names and addresses written on a deck of 3x5 cards, one name and address per card. Assume that the straw person of this chapter is your secretary, and prepare a set of instructions telling this individual how to prepare properly addressed envelopes from these cards. Once you have completed the human-level instructions, expand your planning to a computer-level solution, based on the assumption that one address will be keypunched on each input card.

5. Every student knows how his or her school computes a grade point average. Plan a computer-level solution to the problem of computing your own. Your solution should be sufficiently general that you can reasonably expect it to work for any future term in college; in other words, do *not* assume that the list of courses and associated credit hours and grades are known before the computation begins. If your school uses letter grades, you may convert to a numerical equivalent on input, replacing A's with 4's, B's with 3's, and so on.

2

Basic COBOL: Language Structure, the IDENTIFICATION DIVISION and the ENVIRONMENT DIVISION

OVERVIEW

Chapter 1 was concerned with developing a solution to a problem—a solution independent of any specific computer programming language. Our intent is to convert this plan into a COBOL program; thus in Chapter 2, we begin our study of the COBOL language. In this chapter, we will concentrate on the basic structure of a COBOL program, introducing the COBOL coding form and describing some of the more general features of the language. Near the end of the chapter, the first two divisions of a COBOL program, the IDENTIFICATION DIVISION and the ENVIRONMENT DIVISION, will be introduced. Chapter 3 will cover the other two divisions of a COBOL program, while Chapter 4 will deal with the process of actually getting a program onto a computer.

COBOL: SOME GENERAL COMMENTS

COBOL is a language—an artifical language to be sure, but still a language. Like any language, COBOL has its rules of grammar, spelling, punctuation, usage, and style. Like any language, if you want to learn to use COBOL, you will have to become familiar with many of these rules. Realistically, the only way to learn to program in COBOL *is* to program in COBOL; there are no shortcuts.

There is a very significant difference between a natural language (English, for example) and an artificial language such as COBOL. A natural language must support communication on virtually every topic imaginable. An artificial language, on the other hand, can be restricted in scope. COBOL is designed to deal with a very specific class of problems, a class that can be summarized under the general heading of **business data processing**. Typical examples include such problems as payroll, inventory, accounts receivable, accounts payable, general ledger, billing, order entry, and many many more.

These problems have a number of common characteristics. All involve the processing of significant amounts of data—everyone's paycheck or every customer's amount due. Generally, the amount of computation that must be perfomed on each element of data is quite limited; on inventory, for example, the program logic consists of little more than adding all arrivals to and subtracting all deletions from the old inventory balance to arrive at a new inventory balance. This typical business data processing problem is in direct contrast with scientific computation, where vast numbers of computations are performed on relatively little data.

Another common characteristic of business data processing problems is their relatively long life. A payroll program is not written to be used once and thrown away; instead, the basic idea is to write the program once and then to use it over and over again, week after week. Given this long life, parts of the program almost certainly will change; on payroll, for example, new income tax withholding rates are expected every few years. Thus, it is highly desirable that a program written to solve a business data processing problem be relatively easy to modify.

Finally, business data processing applications tend to be somewhat universal—there are only so many ways to compute a payroll, and every business must perform this function. Why not write a program in such a way that it can easily be moved from one computer to another with a minimum of recoding? Such compatibility is highly desirable on a business data processing application.

COBOL was designed with exactly these objectives in mind. The language is at its best when performing input and output; in fact, there are numerous instances where, given a choice between internal computer efficiency and input/output efficiency, the language designers opted for the latter. One of the most important factors in making a program easy to modify or maintain is the level of program **documentation**, a term that describes a collection of flowcharts, program listings, and other documents used to explain the function of a program. In keeping with the objective to make COBOL programs easy to maintain, the language is, at least to a certain extent, **self documenting**. (Remember this objective when you are complaining about all the writing you have to do when coding a COBOL program.) Finally, it was the intent of the designers of COBOL to make the language as machine independent as was possible, meaning that a COBOL program written to solve a given problem should look pretty much like another COBOL program written to solve the same problem on another manufacturer's computer.

Let's now turn our attention to the specific rules of the language. Before we begin, remember a few key points. First, COBOL was designed with a specific class of application in mind, and many of the language's features are rooted in the characteristics of this class of applications. Second (and this is perhaps the most important comment of all), the only way to learn to program *is* to program.

THE COBOL CODING FORM

Perhaps the best place to start our study of the COBOL language would be with the **COBOL coding form** (Fig. 2.1). This form provides a framework against which to write COBOL statements. Typically, each of these statements is converted into punched card form; thus, each line contains 80 spaces, one for each card column.

Near the top of the form, you will see space set aside to identify such things as the program name, the programmer's name, and the date the program was written. Near the top right of the form is a spot for numbering pages. This top block also includes space for writing "punching instructions". The professional programmer rarely does his or her own keypunching, but leaves this task to a keypunch operator. The fact that this second person is involved can lead to misunderstandings—for example, is the coded character 0 the letter "O" or the digit "O"? Standard practice is to draw a slash (/) through one of these characters; throughout this text, Ø will represent a zero on our coding forms, and a note to this effect will be written in the "punching instructions" section. The "card form   " is another bit of communication to the keypunch operator; often, the operator's job can be simplified by using a special program card allowing for such things as the automatic skipping of unused fields.

The heart of the coding form lies below this top section, under the heading "COBOL Statement". Each line on the form is divided into 80 vertical columns, one for each column of a punched card; you can see the numbers of selected columns at both the top and the bottom of the form. One character—a letter, a digit, a punctuation mark, or a blank—is printed in each column. After the program has been coded on one or more forms, each horizontal line is converted into a single punched card through a process known as keypunching. For those of you who do not know how to keypunch, detailed instructions can be found in Appendix A.

Let's now turn our attention to an individual line. The first six spaces, corresponding to the first six columns of a data processing card, are set aside to hold a sequence number. Often COBOL programs become very lengthy. Imagine yourself, having just finished keypunching several hundred cards, watching a clumsy operator drop your deck. It can happen (and often has). Sequence numbers make it relatively easy to put the deck back into proper order.

Column 7 is labeled "Cont."; it is used to indicate the continuation of certain types of COBOL statements beyond a single card. On many versions of COBOL, an asterisk (*) in column 7 can be used to indicate a **comment** card, a special card that is not really a part of the program but is added to explain a key point of logic, the contents of a field of data, or any other potentially confusing part of the program.

The actual COBOL statement is coded between columns 8 and 72. This area is itself subdivided into two sections labeled A and B—columns 8 through 11 and 12 through 72 respectively. Certain major breakpoints in a COBOL program *must* begin in section A; other code *may not* begin in section A. The reason for this is really quite simple. One of the intentions of the developers of COBOL was self documentation. By requiring key lines to begin in section A and lesser lines to begin in section B, these key lines will literally stick out like a sore thumb, making it easy to find these key breakpoints while reading the program.

The final section of the COBOL coding form is labeled "identification". As a general rule, this section is unused. It can be used to provide additional optional program identification.

Before leaving the topic of the COBOL coding form, it might be wise to point out that its use is not universal. Perhaps, your school has a small computer system and uses a credit-card sized 96-column card. Another growing trend is toward the use of cassettes or diskettes as the programmer's storage medium, with COBOL statements entered through a keyboard device equipped with a small television (CRT) screen. Perhaps you use standard 80-column cards, but coding forms are just not available in your bookstore. The coding form is simply a means to an end, putting COBOL statements in a form convenient for keypunching or other keyboard entry; it is not only possible but quite common to write valid COBOL programs without using a coding form. Just remember that column 7 is used for certain types of continuation cards or a comment indicator; section A begins in column 8 and runs to column 11; section B includes columns 12 through 72; and that your punched card or magnetic record must follow these rules, and any style of paper can be used. Still, the coding sheet does make it easier; do take advantage of this form if at all possible.

THE BASIC STRUCTURE OF A COBOL PROGRAM

Every COBOL program is divided into four major **divisions**, which are:

1. IDENTIFICATION DIVISION.
2. ENVIRONMENT DIVISION.
3. DATA DIVISION.
4. PROCEDURE DIVISION.

The **IDENTIFICATION DIVISION**, as the name implies, is used to identify the program and the programmer and, in a very general way, to explain the purpose and approach of the program. Its purpose is documentation.

The **ENVIRONMENT DIVISION**, clearly spells out the environment in which the program is designed to run, including such information as the name of the manufacturer and the model number of the computer for which the program was written,

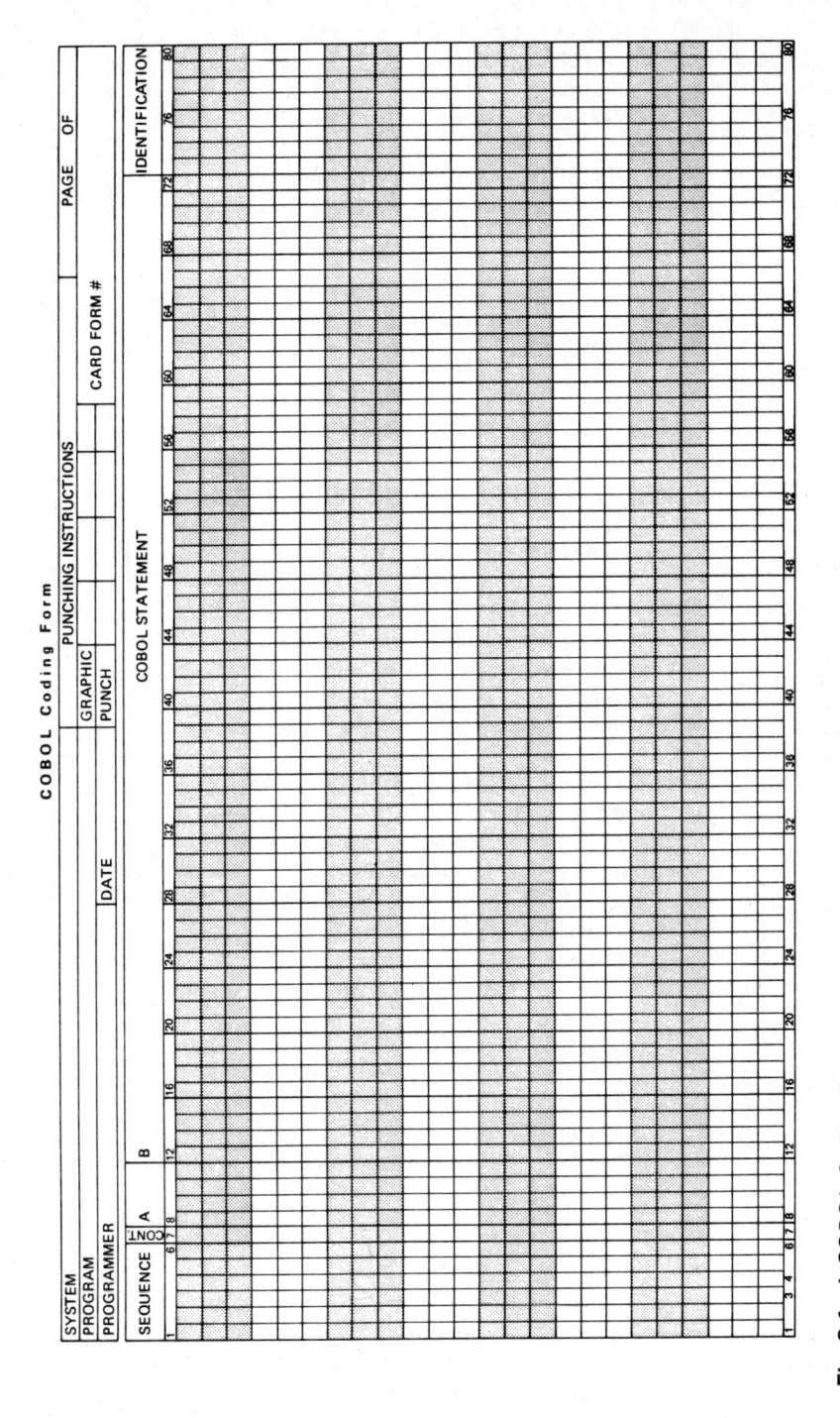

Fig. 2.1: *A COBOL Coding Form.*

and a complete listing of all the input and output devices required by the program. Back in Chapter 1, we developed a list of input and output devices; it's in the ENVIRONMENT DIVISION that this information will be coded. Ideally, the ENVIRONMENT DIVISION contains all installation dependent code, in other words, all parts of the program that might cause a problem when the program is moved from one computer to another.

In the **DATA DIVISION**, the data is described. When, in Chapter 1, we developed formats of our input, output, and work data fields, we were preparing ourselves to code the DATA DIVISION.

The final division is the **PROCEDURE DIVISION**. It is here that the actual logic of the program—the arithmetic, copy, yes/no logic, input, and output steps—is coded. It is here that we will actually implement the logical plan developed in our flowchart.

All four divisions *must be* present in *every* COBOL program; there are no exceptions. They must be coded in the given order, with the IDENTIFICATION DIVISION, followed by the ENVIRONMENT DIVISION, followed by the DATA DIVISION, followed by the PROCEDURE DIVISION. Since these are the major breakpoints in the program, they *must* begin in section A, columns 8 through 11. Finally, each division name *must be* followed by a period.

Each division of the program is further subdivided into **sections** which are themselves subdivided into **paragraphs**. Each is assigned a name, and, as is the case with the division headers, section and paragraph names must begin in section A. Grouped within a paragraph are the COBOL **statements** that actually describe data formats or program logic. In the PROCEDURE DIVISION, one or more statements form what is called a **sentence**, beginning with a verb and ending with a period. If paragraphs and sentences sound a bit like the English language to you, that's a very reasonable observation. The developers of COBOL, don't forget, were trying to design a self-documenting language, and it's hard to imagine a clearer, more generally understood model (at least in the United States) than English.

Let's now consider each of COBOL's divisions one at a time, describing some of the key statements that can be coded as part of each. The first two will be described in this chapter; the DATA and PROCEDURE divisions will be left for Chapter 3.

The IDENTIFICATION DIVISION

Every COBOL program must begin with an IDENTIFICATION DIVISION. The primary function of this division is documentation. An IDENTIFICATION DIVISION for our average program has been coded in Fig. 2.2; we'll be referring to this figure throughout the discussion that follows.

The only paragraph that *must* be included in the IDENTIFICATION DIVISION is the **PROGRAM-ID**. Note carefully the punctuation; there is a **hyphen** or dash character (-) in the paragraph name. Within COBOL, a paragraph name is a single entity, meaning that blanks cannot be buried in the name; thus PROGRAM ID is illegal, and would be interpreted as two separate names. In this case, however, using PROGRAMID would not convey our meaning nearly as well as PROGRAM-ID. The

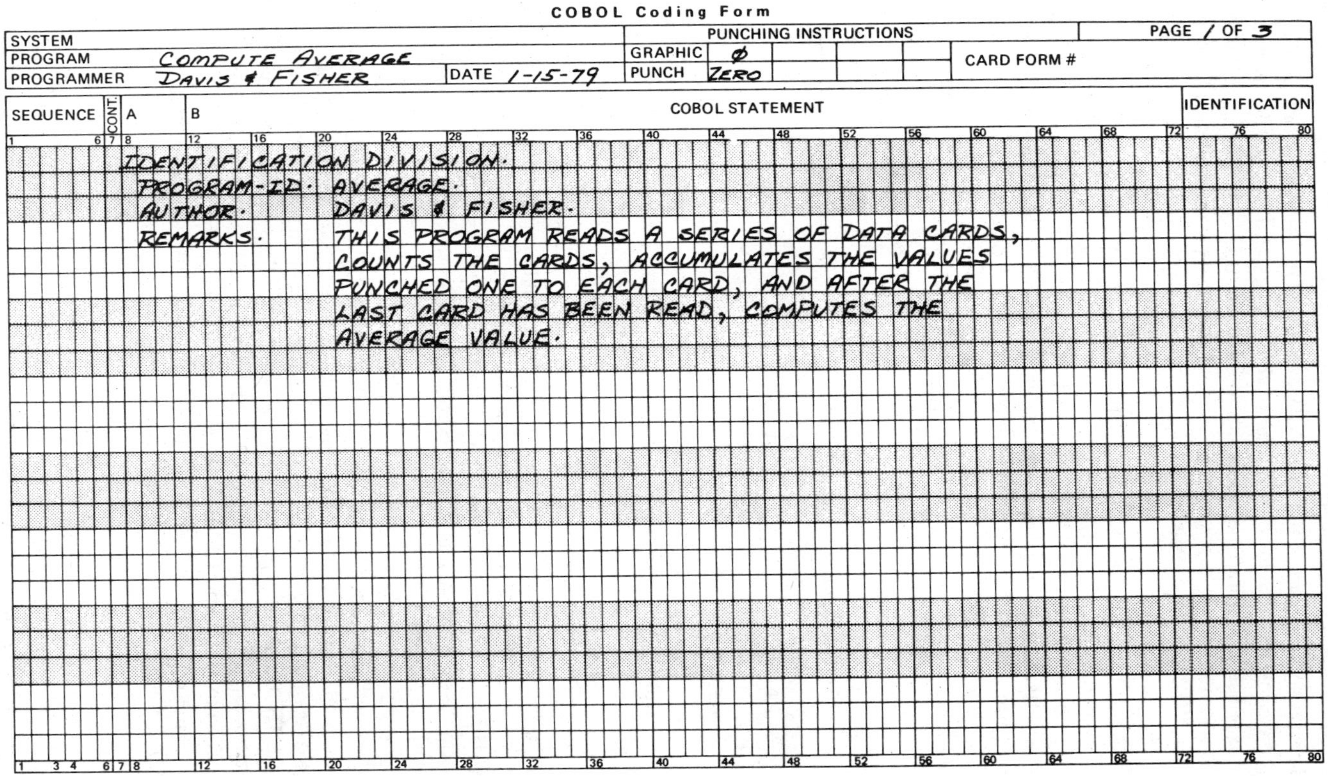

COBOL Coding Form

SYSTEM	COMPUTE AVERAGE		PUNCHING INSTRUCTIONS		PAGE 1 OF 3
PROGRAM	COMPUTE AVERAGE		GRAPHIC		
PROGRAMMER	DAVIS & FISHER	DATE 1-15-79	PUNCH ZERO	CARD FORM #	

```
IDENTIFICATION DIVISION.
PROGRAM-ID. AVERAGE.
AUTHOR.  DAVIS & FISHER.
REMARKS.  THIS PROGRAM READS A SERIES OF DATA CARDS,
          COUNTS THE CARDS, ACCUMULATES THE VALUES
          PUNCHED ONE TO EACH CARD, AND AFTER THE
          LAST CARD HAS BEEN READ, COMPUTES THE
          AVERAGE VALUE.
```

Fig. 2.2: *The IDENTIFICATION DIVISION*

dash or hyphen allows us to break up names into meaningful parts, making them easier to read.

The paragraph name PROGRAM-ID is a COBOL **reserved word**. It has a very special meaning to COBOL, clearly identifying the start of this particular paragraph; thus, this specific spelling and punctuation must be used. The first letter, "P", must be coded somewhere in section A, columns 8 through 11. Immediately following the last letter, "D", you must have a period.

Within the PROGRAM-ID paragraph, the programmer can code virtually any program name he or she wishes. There are a few restrictions, of course. A program name is a special type of COBOL **word**. COBOL words cannot exceed 30 characters. Only the letters of the alphabet, the digits 0 through 9, and the hyphen (-) can be used to form a word. The hyphen cannot be the first or last character in the word. Except for these rather minor restrictions, the programmer has almost complete freedom. Valid program names for our average program would include:

AVERAGE

PROGRAM-1

X

HARRY

C3PO

123456789

Of course, some names are better than others. An ideal program name gives the reader an idea of what the program is designed to do; thus, in Fig. 2.2, we have chosen AVERAGE as our program name. The computer really doesn't care what you use, but it is highly likely that several human beings will, at some time, be reading your program, and they do care.

All other paragraphs in the IDENTIFICATION DIVISION are optional, at least as far as COBOL is concerned. We have chosen to use two additional paragraphs to provide extra (and very important) documentation. The first begins with the reserved word **AUTHOR**. As the paragraph name clearly implies, this paragraph provides a mechanism for identifying the author of the program. The final paragraph shown in Figure 2.2 has the name **REMARKS**. In this paragraph, the programmer can code a concise explanation of the function of the program. We consider these three paragraphs to be essential for minimum documentation; your instructor may well require more.

On many versions of COBOL (yes, there are different versions) the paragraphs in the IDENTIFICATION DIVISION must be coded in the order given. Other IDENTIFICATION DIVISION paragraphs allow the programmer to specify such things as the computer installation, the date the program was written, the date the program was compiled, and various security procedures.

The ENVIRONMENT DIVISION

The second division of a COBOL program must be the ENVIRONMENT DIVISION. The primary purpose of the division is to describe the environment in which the program is designed to run. This includes such factors as the make and model number of the computer used, and a complete list of all the input and output devices required by the program. Actually, we need much more than just a simple list. A typical computer center has numerous input and output devices. It is essential that the program be tied to one or more specific pieces of equipment, and it is in the ENVIRONMENT DIVISION that this relationship is defined.

An ENVIRONMENT DIVISION for our average program is coded in Fig. 2.3. The first entry in the division reads **CONFIGURATION SECTION**. A COBOL **section** is a major subdivision of a division that can contain more than one paragraph. Note that the section name begins in section A (columns 8 - 11) and terminates with a period. Within this section are two paragraphs, **SOURCE-COMPUTER** and **OBJECT-COMPUTER**. The SOURCE-COMPUTER paragraph defines the computer for which the program was written; the OBJECT-COMPUTER paragraph defines the computer on which the program was actually run. Generally, both identify the same computer, but this does not have to be the case. The authors have access to an IBM System/370 Model 148, thus the entries on Fig. 2.3; your school may use a different computer, so your entries may vary.

Note the punctuation used in the section and paragraph names. No hyphen or dash was found between the word CONFIGURATION and the word SECTION. Why? These are two different words. SECTION defines this as a section; CONFIGURATION is the name of this section. There is, however, a hyphen in SOURCE-COMPUTER and OBJECT-COMPUTER. Again, why? Because these are paragraph names, and a COBOL paragraph name must be a single COBOL word.

Let's move along to the next section of the division, the **INPUT-OUTPUT SECTION**. Why is the hyphen needed here? The section name, INPUT-OUTPUT, must be a single COBOL word.

Within the INPUT-OUTPUT SECTION is the FILE-CONTROL paragraph (note the hyphen again; a paragraph name is a single COBOL word). It is in this paragraph where the actual linkages to the input and output devices are defined. A few very basic concepts are necessary before we begin to discuss these linkages. The real point of a computer program is to process data. The basic building block of data is the **character**—a letter, digit, punctuation mark, blank, and so on. Characters are grouped to form **fields**; in a telephone book, for example, an individual's name would form on one field, his or her address would form a second field, and the telephone number, a third. A field is simply a collection of characters that has meaning. Fields are grouped to form **records**; once again using a telephone book as an example, a single record would be one individual's name, address, and telephone number. A record is simply a collection of logically related fields. Finally, we have a **file**. A file is a collection of logically related records; the complete telephone book is a good example.

Later, in the DATA DIVISION, we'll see how the programmer defines each file, the individual records within each file, and the individual fields within each record.

Here in the ENVIRONMENT DIVISION, our concern is one of providing a link between a file as defined within our program and the actual physical device that will provide input data or accept output information. This link is provided through the **SELECT** and **ASSIGN** clauses.

A SELECT... ASSIGN is part of the FILE-CONTROL paragraph; thus, it begins in section B of the COBOL coding form (columns 12 through 72). Following the word SELECT, the programmer codes a **file name**; this is the name by which the file is known *within* the program, and it must match the file name used in the DATA DIVISION. A file name must contain at least one alphabetic character; otherwise, the 30-character limit and the restriction to letters, digits, and the hyphen hold just as they did with paragraph names. We strongly recommend, however, that you use a file name that clearly describes the content of your file; in Fig. 2.3, for example, we've used CARD-FILE and PRINT-FILE.

The purpose of the ASSIGN clause is to assign this file to an external input or output device. The precise mechanism for making this assignment varies significantly from computer to computer. On an IBM System/370 Model 148 running under a control program known as VS1, the ASSIGN clause would, generally, be coded as follows:

ASSIGN TO class-organization-name.

For the class (Fig. 2.3), we have used UT, which stands for utility. Basically what this means is that we are willing to utilize the computer system's standard operating procedures; in other words, we plan on doing nothing exotic. On many smaller computers, our program will directly access a card reader or a printer; if this is the case, UR (for unit record) would be used as the class. Later, we'll be discussing a number of more advanced file processing applications which require the use of a mass storage device; here, we may have to use DA as the class.

Following the device class is the file organization. For the first several chapters, we will be discussing only files having a sequential organization; this means that the records in the file must be processed in a fixed sequence, from first to last, with no possibility of skipping over any records. The letter S is used to designate a sequential organization. Later we'll discuss direct access, where an individual record can be selected from anywhere on the file without first going through all the records that preceed it; a D would be used to designate a direct access organization.

The final part of the ASSIGN clause is an external name; this is the name by which the file is known *outside* the program. On the computer currently being discussed, this is a 1 to 8 character name which must begin with a letter and which can contain only letters and digits. The rules for this name are not imposed by COBOL; rather they are imposed by the job control language used on this computer to allow the programmer to communicate with the system control program. More about job control language later.

We have now defined the linkages to the input and output devices needed by our program. The SELECT and ASSIGN clauses are:

COBOL Coding Form

SYSTEM		PUNCHING INSTRUCTIONS	PAGE 1 OF 3
PROGRAM	COMPUTE AVERAGE	GRAPHIC: Ø	CARD FORM #
PROGRAMMER	DAVIS & FISHER	DATE 1-15-79	PUNCH: ZERO

```
       IDENTIFICATION DIVISION.
        PROGRAM-ID.  AVERAGE.
        AUTHOR.      DAVIS & FISHER.
        REMARKS.     THIS PROGRAM READS A SERIES OF DATA CARDS,
                     COUNTS THE CARDS, ACCUMULATES THE VALUES
                     PUNCHED ONE TO EACH CARD, AND AFTER THE
                     LAST CARD HAS BEEN READ, COMPUTES THE
                     AVERAGE VALUE.


       ENVIRONMENT DIVISION.
        CONFIGURATION SECTION.
         SOURCE-COMPUTER.   IBM-370-148.
         OBJECT-COMPUTER.   IBM-370-148.
        INPUT-OUTPUT SECTION.
         FILE-CONTROL.
             SELECT CARD-FILE  ASSIGN TO UT-S-CARDFILE.
             SELECT PRINT-FILE ASSIGN TO UT-S-PRTFILE.
```

Fig. 2.3: *An ENVIRONMENT DIVISION for the Average Program.*

SELECT CARD-FILE ASSIGN TO UT-S-CARDFILE.

SELECT PRINT-FILE ASSIGN TO UT-S-PRTFILE.

Refer to Fig. 2.3 for the coding format of these two statements.

Once again, we must stress that these clauses are very installation dependent. If you are not using an IBM System/360 or System/370 computer running under an OS or VS operating system, your SELECT and ASSIGN clauses will be different. Appendix B presents examples of the SELECT and ASSIGN clauses and the job control statements used on an IBM computer running under DOS or DOS/VS. If you are using a computer other than an IBM System/360 or System/370, see your instructor for specific guidelines on coding this section for your installation.

SUMMARY

In Chapter 1, we developed a solution to a problem. In this chapter, we begin the process of translating the solution into COBOL, starting with a brief discussion of the difference between a natural and an artificial language, and explaining how COBOL was developed specifically with the characteristics of typical business data processing problems in mind. The COBOL coding sheet was introduced, followed by the basic structure of a COBOL program—divisions, sections, paragraphs, sentences, and statements.

The IDENTIFICATION DIVISION was then covered in some detail, with three key paragraphs being introduced: PROGRAM-ID, AUTHOR, and REMARKS. The idea of a reserved word, the rules for defining regular COBOL words, and the value of defining meaningful words were among the more important topics. The IDENTIFICATION DIVISION exists primarily for documentation purposes.

The function of the ENVIRONMENT DIVISION is to define the environment in which the program is designed to run. In the CONFIGURATION SECTION, the SOURCE-COMPUTER and OBJECT-COMPUTER are defined. In the INPUT-OUTPUT SECTION, the input and output devices are specified, with one set of SELECT and ASSIGN clauses being coded for each device. We spent some time discussing the relationship among characters, fields, records, and files, a topic that will become even more relevant in Chapter 3.

KEY WORDS

ASSIGN clause	comment
AUTHOR paragraph	CONFIGURATION SECTION
business data processing	DATA DIVISION
COBOL coding form	division
character	documentation

ENVIRONMENT DIVISION	**REMARKS paragraph**
field	**reserved word**
file	**section**
file name	**section A (coding form)**
hyphen character	**section B (coding form)**
IDENTIFICATION DIVISION	**SELECT clause**
INPUT-OUTPUT SECTION	**self documenting**
OBJECT-COMPUTER paragraph	**sentence**
paragraph	**SOURCE-COMPUTER paragraph**
PROCEDURE DIVISION	**statement**
PROGRAM-ID paragraph	**word**
record	

EXERCISES

1. Briefly explain the difference between a natural language and an artificial language. COBOL is an artificial language designed with a specific application in mind—business data processing. Discuss the typical characteristics of this particular class of computer applications.

2. Explain the basic function of each of the four divisions of a COBOL program.

3. A COBOL program is subdivided into divisions, sections, paragraphs, sentences, and statements. Explain how these pieces are related. Compare the structure of a COBOL program to a standard term paper outline.

4. Explain the function of each of the following IDENTIFICATION DIVISION paragraphs: PROGRAM-ID, AUTHOR, and REMARKS.

5. What is a COBOL reserved word?

6. Explain the rules imposed by COBOL for programmer-defined words. What is the difference between a programmer-defined word and a COBOL reserved word?

7. What is the function performed in the ENVIRONMENT DIVISION, CONFIGURATION SECTION?

8. What function or functions are performed in the INPUT-OUTPUT SECTION? Explain what SELECT and ASSIGN clauses are used for.

9. Chapter 1, exercise 1 asked you to add a feature to the solution to the average program. Code an IDENTIFICATION DIVISION and an ENVIRONMENT DIVISION for a COBOL program to implement this modified solution. Would you expect these two divisions to change significantly? Why or why not?

10. Code an IDENTIFICATION DIVISION and an ENVIRONMENT DIVISION for the baseball program described in Chapter 1, exercise 2.

11. Code an IDENTIFICATION DIVISION and an ENVIRONMENT DIVISION for Chapter 1, exercise 3.

12. Code an IDENTIFICATION DIVISION and an ENVIRONMENT DIVISION for Chapter 1, exercise 4.

13. Code an IDENTIFICATION DIVISION and an ENVIRONMENT DIVISION for Chapter 1, exercise 5.

3

Basic COBOL:
the DATA DIVISION
and the PROCEDURE DIVISION

OVERVIEW

In this chapter, we continue with an introduction to basic COBOL, concentrating on the DATA and PROCEDURE divisions. In the DATA DIVISION, our objective is to define each file, each record within each file, and each field within each record, right down to the character level. In the PROCEDURE DIVISION, we will code the actual logical steps to be followed by our program.

THE DATA DIVISION

We've just finished describing the link between our program and its external input and output devices. During the process of developing these ideas, we discussed the relationship between characters, fields, records, and files. In the **DATA DIVISION**, we will actually define our files, describe all the records found in each file, lay out each of the fields in each record, and provide a character by character description of each field. Once we've finished working with our files, we'll move along to the intermediate work fields. The DATA DIVISION for our average program is coded in Fig. 3.1.

The FD Entry

The first section in the DATA DIVISION is the **FILE SECTION**. It is here that all input and output files are defined along with the precise format of all input and output records.

The first entry in the FILE SECTION is an **FD entry**, which defines a file. The FD is coded beginning in section A of the coding form; the rest of the file description (which is what FD stands for) is coded in section B. On the same line as the FD is the file name. Note that CARD-FILE, the name of our first file, exactly matches the file name used in a SELECT and ASSIGN clause (see the ENVIRONMENT DIVISION), while PRINT-FILE matches the file name in the other SELECT and ASSIGN. This match *must* exist; it's the only way a reference to a file within a program can be linked with an external device.

An Optional DATA DIVISION Note

In an attempt to improve system efficiency, many computer systems use a technique called spooling. When spooling is used, input coming from a slow device such as a card reader is first read to a high speed device such as disk or tape before being read into the program; coming the other way, output is first spooled to disk or tape and then, later dumped to the printer.

Most spooling systems are designed to be transparent to the programmer. Occasionally, however, the programmer will encounter a system or a version of COBOL where the spooling system can make a difference; this usually occurs when the system programmer, again in the name of efficiency, stores several records in a single block on the spooled file (we'll discuss blocking in more detail later). Should this problem occur on your IBM system, you can usually get around it by coding

BLOCK CONTAINS 0 RECORDS

as an extra clause associated with your FD entry.

COBOL Coding Form

SYSTEM
PROGRAM: COMPUTE AVERAGE
PROGRAMMER: DAVIS & FISHER
DATE: 1-15-79
PUNCHING INSTRUCTIONS — GRAPHIC: Ø — PUNCH: ZERO
PAGE 2 OF 3
CARD FORM #

SEQUENCE | CONT. | A | B | COBOL STATEMENT | IDENTIFICATION

```
       DATA DIVISION.
        FILE SECTION.

           FD  CARD-FILE
               LABEL RECORD IS OMITTED.
           Ø1   INPUT-CARD.
                Ø5   I-VALUE               PIC 999V99.
                Ø5   FILLER                PIC X(75).

           FD  PRINT-FILE
               LABEL RECORD IS OMITTED.
           Ø1   OUTPUT-LINE.
                Ø5   FILLER                PIC X(15).
                Ø5   O-AVERAGE             PIC 999.9999.
                Ø5   FILLER                PIC X(11Ø).

        WORKING-STORAGE SECTION.
           77   COUNTER                    PIC 999.
           77   ACCUMULATOR                PIC 99999V99.
```

Fig. 3.1: *The DATA DIVISION for the Average Program.*

Both files coded on Fig. 3.1 contain a

LABEL RECORD IS OMITTED.

clause. Later, when we are discussing magnetic tape and disk, we'll discover that labels are extremely important in identifying a file. There are, however, no labels on punched cards or printer paper. COBOL assumes that labels are present; therefore we must tell COBOL that they are not.

Record Descriptions

Our files are defined; we now move on to the records contained in those files. Associated with the card file is a record that we have chosen to call INPUT-CARD. Associated with the output files is a record named OUTPUT-LINE. Both are preceeded by the digits 01, beginning in the A section of the coding form. A **01-level** entry identifies a record.

Beneath this record identifier is a series of 05-level entries identifying the fields contained within this record. Actually, any **level number** above 01 and less than 50 could have been used; we chose 05 because that is our habit. A higher number represents a field which is part of a preceeding lower-numbered field. If, for example, we were interested in structuring someone's street address as part of a record, we might code

```
05      ADDRESS   ...
        10 STREET  ...
        10 CITY    ...
        10 STATE   ...
        10 ZIP-CODE...
```

The level numbers clearly show that the field called ADDRESS includes the STREET address, the CITY, the STATE, and the ZIP-CODE, while the label ZIP-CODE refers only to the zip code and to no other part of the record.

Following the level number is a **data name** or field name. Data names must contain at least one letter; otherwise, the usual limitations of a maximum of 30 characters consisting of letters, digits, and the hyphen character still hold true. As before, however, it is definitely to the programmer's advantage to select data names that make sense in the context of the program being written.

The 01-level entry defines an input record; generally the record name is followed by a period. To the right of each of the field names you will see (Fig. 3.1) a **PICTURE clause**. The function of the PICTURE clause (PIC is an acceptable abbreviation) is to describe the field character by character. Each position in the field that can hold an **alphanumeric** character (essentially anything), is represented by an X. Each position that can hold only a **numeric** character is represented by a 9. Alphanumeric fields cannot be used in arithmetic; numeric fields can.

In some programming languages, the programmer is allowed to keypunch an actual physical decimal point as part of his or her input data. This is *not* the case in COBOL; a decimal point buried in the middle of an input data field *will* cause your program to terminate. In COBOL, we almost always use an **implied decimal point**. A capital V is used to indicate where implied decimal point is located in the input field.

In Chapter 1, we laid out the contents of our input and output records. Let's return to these informal descriptions and relate them to the coding in Fig. 3.1. To avoid excessive page-flipping, we'll repeat this portion of the DATA DIVISION in Fig. 3.2.

Our input record was formatted as follows:

columns	contents
1-5	a five digit number with two digits to the right of the decimal point.
6-80	unused

First, we need names for the record and for the individual fields. INPUT-CARD would seem to be a reasonable name for the input card. VALUE would seem reasonable for the number punched into the first 5 columns. We have prefixed this data name with the letter I, meaning Input, yielding a data name I-VALUE. This is merely a technique that allows us to distinguish clearly between input fields and other types of fields when we begin to process the data. We'll be following this practice throughout the book; while not required by COBOL, it is a very nice and easily implemented documentation aid.

The other field on our input card, columns 6 through 80, is unused. It seems silly to try to create a data name for a field we are not even planning to use. In COBOL, the reserved word **FILLER** can be assigned as a data name to all unused data fields.

Fig. 3.2: *The input record to the average program.*

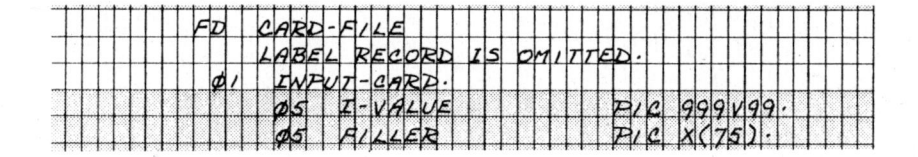

```
FD  CARD-FILE
    LABEL RECORD IS OMITTED.
01  INPUT-CARD.
    05  I-VALUE        PIC 999V99.
    05  FILLER         PIC X(75).
```

Let's talk about reserved words for a minute. Several times in the discussion above and in Chapter 2, we've mentioned the existence of these things. A reserved word is simply a word that has a unique meaning to COBOL. A division name means that a division is starting. The word SECTION means that a section is starting. FILLER identifies an unused data field. Since a reserved word has a special meaning, the programmer cannot use a reserved word as a data name, file name, or paragraph name. That is why, for example, we did not choose NUMBER as a data name for the number on our input card; NUMBER is a reserved word. So, for that matter, is VALUE; avoiding the accidental use of reserved words is another good argument for using "I" as a prefix for all input fields. For a complete list of COBOL reserved words, see Appendix C.

We now have data names for our two input fields. Let's assign the PICTURE clauses. Our objective is to describe each field, character by character. The first field, I-VALUE, is composed of 5 digits; thus we need five 9's (Fig. 3.2). The implied decimal point has two positions to its right; thus the PICTURE clause is 999V99, with the V showing where the decimal point belongs. Note that the decimal point is not really present; rather, it's *implied*. Data cards must match this implied format; the number 1, for example, would be keypunched as 00100, while 1.75 would be keypunched as, 00175. If your data cards are not so keypunched with, in this example, the first number to the right of the decimal point *always* falling in column 4 of the card, your program will produce incorrect results (if it runs at all).

The balance of the card is called FILLER. We need 75 positions. Since we really don't care what these card columns hold, we'll use the X-character as a PICTURE. It would take us half the afternoon to write 75 X's. Fortunately, X(75) achieves the same objective; the number in parenthesis defines the number of times the character is to be repeated. Fig. 3.2 is a description of our input record.

We can describe the fields of the output record in similar fashion. First, we need a record name; OUTPUT-LINE seems logical. The first 15 positions of the output line are to be blank; thus, FILLER and PIC X(15). (See Fig. 3.3). Next, we have the computed average. AVERAGE is a perfect data field name; the O prefix clearly identifies

Fig. 3.3: *The output record from the average program.*

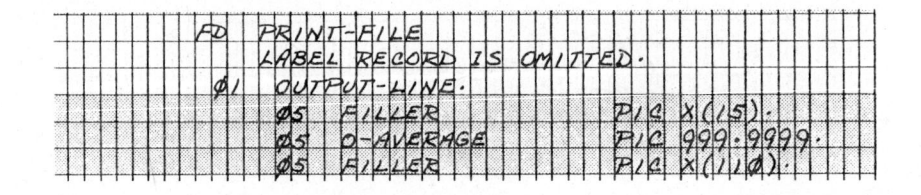

```
        FD   PRINT-FILE
             LABEL RECORD IS OMITTED.
        01   OUTPUT-LINE.
             05   FILLER              PIC X(15).
             05   O-AVERAGE           PIC 999.9999.
             05   FILLER              PIC X(110).
```

this as an output field, yielding the name O-AVERAGE. Since the input data is to have 3 digits to the left of the decimal point, and since the average must lie somewhere between the highest and lowest input values, the computed average can have no more than 3 digits to the left of the decimal point. On input, we supplied data having 2 fractional digits; on output, we can have as many as we want (although our answer really can't be accurate to any more than 2 places). In this case, we chose to print 4 digits to the right of the decimal point, producing 999.9999 as our PICTURE clause (Fig. 3.3). Note that the decimal point has actually been coded; this is *not* an implied decimal point, it's a real one. We want the decimal point to print; therefore it must be coded. Note also that the decimal point *does* take up one print position. This is an example of an **edit character**; more about them later.

The final field of our output record (Fig. 3.3) covers the remaining unused portion of the output line. On our computer, the standard output line is 133 characters long. We've already accounted for 23 with the first two fields; thus, we have 110 left. If your computer system works with a line of 120 characters, to cite a different example, your final PICTURE clause would be X(97).

The WORKING-STORAGE SECTION

We have now provided a detailed description of all the input and output records. We still must describe any **work fields** used in this program. A work field is not part of either an input record or an output record. Rather, it is a field used to hold the intermediate results of computations performed within the computer. In the average problem, we must accumulate and count our values; the accumulator and the counter are neither read into the program nor written as output, but they must exist just the same. Work fields are defined in the second section of the DATA DIVISION, the **WORKING-STORAGE SECTION**. Note once again the spelling; there *is* a hyphen in WORKING-STORAGE. This is a section name, and a section name must be a single COBOL word.

The WORKING-STORAGE SECTION for this program was first described in Fig. 3.1; it is repeated in Fig. 3.4. The data names are obvious—COUNTER and ACCUMULATOR. The PICTURE clauses are also obvious if you look back at our

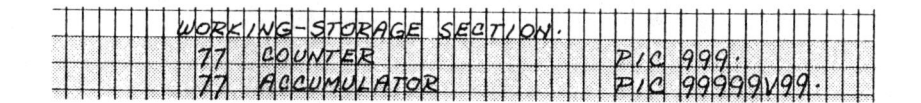

Fig. 3.4: *The WORKING-STORAGE SECTION.*

```
       WORKING-STORAGE SECTION.
       77  COUNTER                      PIC 999.
       77  ACCUMULATOR                  PIC 999999V99.
```

estimate of the biggest possible number we could have in these fields as developed in Chapter 1: 100 for the counter and 99999.00 for the accumulator. Just write the biggest possible 3-digit number, 999, and the biggest possible 7-digit number with two digits to the right of the decimal point, 99999V99, and you have the proper PICTURE clauses. Note that we've used the implied decimal point again; the only time a *real* decimal point is used is on output when we want it printed.

These work fields are assigned level number **77**, a level explicitly reserved for work fields in the WORKING-STORAGE SECTION. The 77 always begins in the A section of the coding form, columns 8 through 11.

Later in the book, we will, of course, be describing more of the features of the data division. For now, however, we've covered enough, and it's on to the PROCEDURE DIVISION.

THE PROCEDURE DIVISION

Finally, we come to the **PROCEDURE DIVISION**, where the actual logic of the program is coded. When most people think of a computer program, this is the part they usually visualize. It is here that the computer is told to add, subtract, multiply, divide, copy, perform simple yes/no logic, request input, and request output.

The basic building block of the PROCEDURE DIVISION is the COBOL **statement**. A statement tells the computer to perform one specific function: add two numbers, for example. One or more statements can be combined to form a COBOL **sentence**, which is terminated by a period. Sentences can be grouped to form paragraphs, and paragraphs can be grouped to form sections.

Rather than continuing to discuss vague generalities, let's move along to a number of specific examples; the PROCEDURE DIVISION for the average program is coded in Fig. 3.5, and, for purposes of comparison, the flowchart of the average program has been repeated in Fig. 3.6.

Basically, the average program can be divided into four major modules:

1. certain functions, such as initializing the counter and the accumulator to zero, that must be performed before we begin;

2. the loop that accumulates and counts input values;

3. the instructions that actually compute and print the average;

4. other functions that must be performed at end of job.

In recognition of these four major subdivisions, we have divided our program into four **paragraphs** labeled START, GET-A-VALUE, FIND-AVERAGE, and END-OF-JOB, respectively. Each paragraph will serve to group the statements that perform one

COBOL Coding Form

SYSTEM		PUNCHING INSTRUCTIONS	PAGE 3 OF 3
PROGRAM	COMPUTE AVERAGE	GRAPHIC Ø	CARD FORM #
PROGRAMMER	DAVIS & FISHER	DATE 1-15-79	PUNCH ZERO

SEQUENCE | CONT. | A | B | COBOL STATEMENT | IDENTIFICATION

```
       PROCEDURE DIVISION.

        BEGIN.
           OPEN INPUT  CARD-FILE.
           OPEN OUTPUT PRINT-FILE.
           MOVE ZEROS  TO COUNTER, ACCUMULATOR.

        GET-A-VALUE.
           READ CARD-FILE
                    AT END GO TO FIND-AVERAGE.
           ADD  I-VALUE TO ACCUMULATOR.
           ADD      1     TO COUNTER.
           GO TO GET-A-VALUE.

        FIND-AVERAGE.
           MOVE    SPACES TO OUTPUT-LINE.
           DIVIDE ACCUMULATOR BY COUNTER GIVING O-AVERAGE.
           WRITE   OUTPUT-LINE
                   AFTER ADVANCING 3 LINES.

        END-OF-JOB.
           CLOSE   CARD-FILE.
           CLOSE   PRINT-FILE.
           STOP RUN.
```

Fig. 3.5: *The PROCEDURE DIVISION for the Average Program.*

Fig. 3.6: *A Flowchart of the Average Problem.*

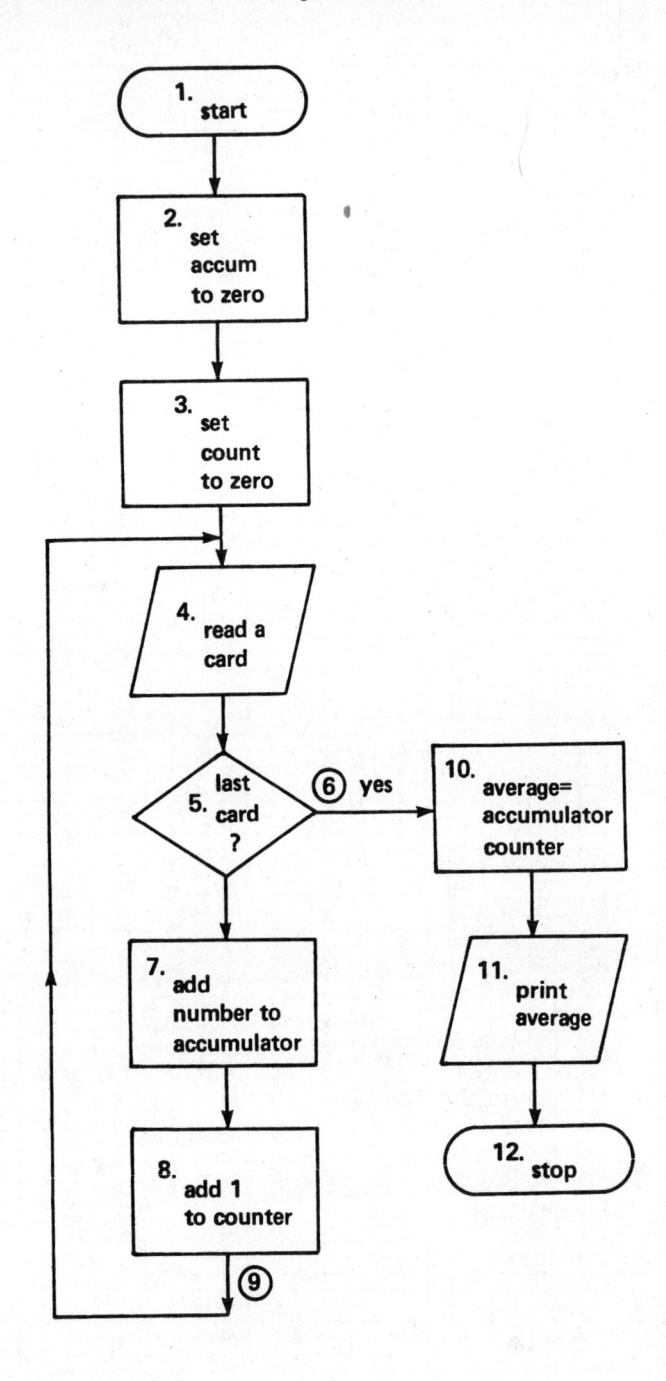

1. start
2. set accum to zero
3. set count to zero
4. read a card
5. last card ?
6. yes
7. add number to accumulator
8. add 1 to counter
9.
10. average = accumulator / counter
11. print average
12. stop

of these four primary functions. The rules for defining a paragraph name are the same as they were in other divisions: any combination of letters, digits, and the hyphen character numbering 30 characters or fewer is legal. Again as before, it makes a great deal of sense to pick paragraph names that identify the function to be performed.

Housekeeping Functions

Let's turn our attention to the first paragraph, named BEGIN (Fig. 3.5). The first two statements in this paragraph are

OPEN INPUT CARD-FILE.

OPEN OUTPUT PRINT-FILE.

The function performed by these two instructions is to make sure that the input and output devices are ready to support the program; it would make little sense, for example, to start the program if the operator had not yet loaded the cards into the card reader. All files *must* be opened before they can be used.

Note carefully how the file name serves to connect the PROCEDURE DIVISION with the DATA DIVISION and the ENVIRONMENT DIVISION (Fig. 3.7). We OPEN a file using the same name we used previously, in the DATA DIVISION, in an FD entry. This name must, in turn, be the same one used in a SELECT clause back in the ENVIRONMENT DIVISION.

Fig. 3.7: *The file name links the three COBOL divisions.*

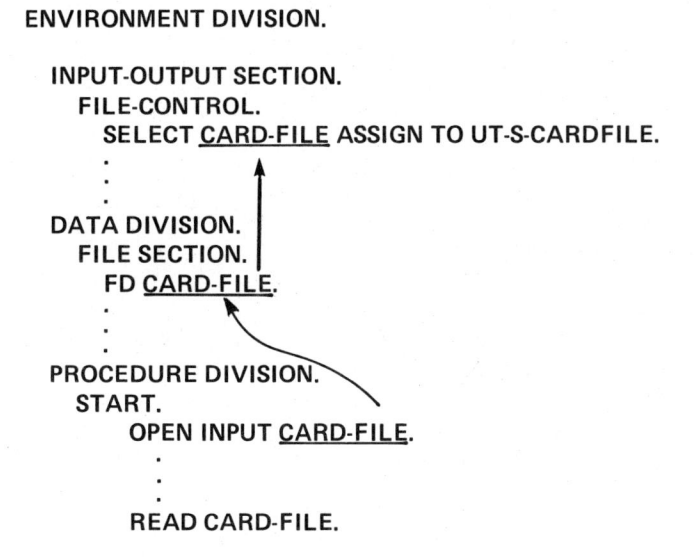

```
ENVIRONMENT DIVISION.
    INPUT-OUTPUT SECTION.
        FILE-CONTROL.
            SELECT CARD-FILE ASSIGN TO UT-S-CARDFILE.
               .
               .
DATA DIVISION.
    FILE SECTION.
        FD CARD-FILE.
           .
           .
PROCEDURE DIVISION.
    START.
        OPEN INPUT CARD-FILE.
        .
        .
        READ CARD-FILE.
```

The other function that must be performed before we can begin is to initialize the counter and the accumulator to zero. To perform this function, we can take advantage of the COBOL **MOVE** verb. The general form of this instruction is

$$\text{MOVE} \begin{Bmatrix} \text{identifier-1} \\ \text{or} \\ \text{literal} \end{Bmatrix} \text{TO identifier-2 identifier-3} \ldots$$

The identifier-1, identifier-2, and identifier-3 refer to data names that have been defined in the DATA DIVISION. Rather than using a data name, we can code a constant.

Our objective is to move the value zero into the accumulator and the counter. There are several ways in which we could achieve this objective. Let's start with a very simple case:

MOVE 0 TO COUNTER.

The word MOVE is a COBOL reserved word. What it means is that whatever is found in the first identifier or literal position is to be copied into the field associated with the second identifier. The first field holds the **constant** 0. The second field is the data name COUNTER, which we previously defined in the DATA DIVISION. As a result of this statement, the value 0 will be copied into the field called COUNTER.

Note very carefully that *every* part of this instruction *must be* fully defined *before* the instruction can be executed (Fig. 3.8): MOVE and TO are COBOL reserved words, 0 is a constant and constants are self-defining and COUNTER was defined in the DATA DIVISION.

We can now

MOVE 0 TO ACCUMULATOR.

Fig. 3.8: *All components of an instruction must be known before the instruction can be executed.*

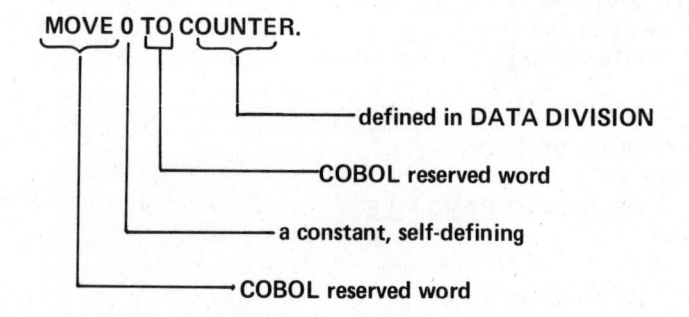

```
MOVE 0 TO COUNTER.
 │    │ │    └──── defined in DATA DIVISION
 │    │ └───────── COBOL reserved word
 │    └─────────── a constant, self-defining
 └──────────────── COBOL reserved word
```

finishing the initialization step. Rather than code two instructions, COBOL allows us to combine two steps into one, as in

>MOVE 0 TO COUNTER, ACCUMULATOR.

This instruction says that the same constant, 0, is to be copied to both COUNTER and ACCUMULATOR. Note once again that all parts of this instruction are fully defined.

Zero is a commonly used constant. As an aid to documentation, there is a COBOL reserved word, **ZEROS**, that allows us to

>MOVE ZEROS TO COUNTER, ACCUMULATOR.

and that is how we've coded the instruction.

It is not essential that a constant be involved. Consider, for example, the following sequence of two instructions:

>MOVE ZEROS TO COUNTER.

>MOVE COUNTER TO ACCUMULATOR.

While not really good coding form, this sequence of instruction would achieve our objective of initializing the two work fields. Note that at the time we MOVE COUNTER TO ACCUMULATOR, the *value* of COUNTER is known to be zero as a direct result of the prior instruction. What we are moving *must be* known if the instruction is to be expected to produce valid results.

Our sample program deals exclusively with numeric data. Both COUNTER and ACCUMULATOR are numeric fields, defined using only a pattern of 9's and the implied decimal point (V). ZEROS is a numeric constant, as is 0. The MOVE instruction is not, however, restricted to numeric data.

We already know how to tell the difference between a numeric field and a nonnumeric field; 9's are used for the numeric PICTURE and X's are used for the nonnumeric PICTURE. Numeric constants are simply written as numbers: 0, or 1.5, or 13457.63 for example. (The fact that a string of digits represents a numeric constant is why data names must contain at least one alphabetic character.) Nonnumeric constants are enclosed within a set of quote marks or apostrophes, depending on the version of COBOL being used. An example of a valid nonnumeric constant is

>'THIS IS AN EXAMPLE OF A NONNUMERIC CONSTANT.'

Anything that can be punched into a card or entered into the computer via other means can be contained between the set of quote marks, forming a valid nonnumeric **literal** constant.

Normally, only numeric fields or numeric constants are moved to a numeric field, and only nonnumeric fields or literal nonnumeric constants are moved to a nonnumeric field. Failure to follow this simple rule is a very common source of error to the beginning programmer.

One final point before we leave the MOVE instruction. Note the punctuation used in this first paragraph; each and every COBOL statement ends with a period. You can almost visualize your program as a series of simple sentences, beginning with a verb and ending with a period. Many beginners find this English language analogy useful. Later, as you become more adept in coding COBOL statements, we'll discuss how related statements can be combined to form compound sentences.

The Accumulation and Counting Loop

Having finished the necessary start-of-job functions, often called **housekeeping** functions, we can move along to the paragraph that reads our data cards and accumulates and counts our values. The paragraph name we have chosen for this group of instructions is GET-A-VALUE. The first statement in this paragraph tells the computer to read a record from the CARD-FILE (Fig. 3.9). As a result of this instruction being executed, we would expect the computer to get a single card from the card reader.

Our flowchart (Fig. 3.6) tells us that we are to add the value on this card to the accumulator and add 1 to the counter, but only if this is *not* the last data card. In Chapter 1, we discussed the use of a special last card indicator (a /*, or //, or $EOD card, for example) to indicate the end of data. Thus, associated with the READ statement is an **AT END clause** that tells the program what to do if this last card indicator is encountered.

```
        READ CARD-FILE

            AT END GO TO FIND-AVERAGE.
```

tells the computer to read a record from the CARD-FILE and, if the last record indicator is encountered, to go directly to the paragraph named FIND-AVERAGE. An AT END clause *must be* associated with a READ statement for all sequential files.

Fig. 3.9: *The GET-A-VALUE paragraph.*

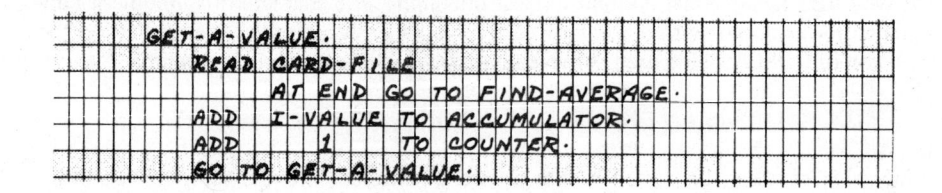

```
    GET-A-VALUE.
        READ CARD-FILE
            AT END GO TO FIND-AVERAGE.
        ADD   I-VALUE TO ACCUMULATOR.
        ADD   1       TO COUNTER.
        GO TO GET-A-VALUE.
```

This sentence is really composed of two statements, one beginning with the verb READ, and the other beginning with the verb **GO TO**. In programming terminology, a GO TO statement is a **branch**. A program normally executes in straight sequence, with instruction following instruction in the order in which they are coded. The GO TO allows the program to deviate from this fixed sequence, branching instead to the first statement in the paragraph named as the target of the GO TO. (You can only branch to a paragraph or section name coded in the PROCEDURE DIVISION.) In the case of the AT END clause, we have a **conditional branch** which is taken if (and only if) the last record is actually encountered.

There is one other GO TO statement used in this paragraph (Fig. 3.9); it's found at the bottom of the paragraph, and it sends the program back to the top, thus setting up a **loop** that will repeat over and over again until such time as the last record is encountered. The statement

GO TO GET-A-VALUE.

is an **unconditional branch**; every time this statement is encountered during normal processing of the program, control will go back to the first statement in the GET-A-VALUE paragraph.

A word about the GO TO statement before we move on. This is perhaps the most misused programming statement ever invented. Excessive use can lead to extremely poor programs. There are those who sincerely believe that the GO TO statement should not be used at all. While not being willing to go quite this far, your authors do recognize the potential dangers inherent in using this instruction, and we intend to restrict its use. Assuming that the readers of this book are probably beginners, an in-depth analysis of these dangers would not, at the present time, be relevant; for now, just remember the following caution:

CAUTION: PROGRAMMING EXPERTS HAVE DETERMINED THAT THE GO TO STATEMENT MAY BE HAZARDOUS TO PROGRAM HEALTH.

The other two statements in this paragraph (Fig. 3.9) add the input value to the accumulator and add 1 to the counter respectively.

There are two basic forms of the ADD statement:

$$\text{ADD} \quad \begin{Bmatrix} \text{data-name-1} \\ \text{or} \\ \text{constant} \end{Bmatrix} \quad \text{TO data-name-1}$$

or

ADD   data-name-1   data-name-2   ...   GIVING   data-name-n.

Both ADDs in the paragraph follow the first general form.

What exactly does the statement

ADD 1 TO COUNTER.

mean? Back in the DATA DIVISION, we defined a field called COUNTER. By defining this field, what we really did was to set aside space in the computer's memory to hold a 3-digit number, assigning the data name COUNTER to this space. More recently, in the first paragraph of the PROCEDURE DIVISION, we initialized this field to zero. Let's assume that we have just read our first data card. The instruction

ADD 1 TO COUNTER.

tells the computer to take whatever value is currently stored in the memory location identified by the data name COUNTER (the "current value is zero), add 1 to this value, and put the answer back into the storage space identified as COUNTER. After reading the second card, COUNTER, which now has the value 1, will, once again, have the value 1 added to it, producing a new count of 2. Each additional card adds another 1 to the COUNTER; in this way, the total number of cards actually processed can be counted. The field called ACCUMULATOR is used in exactly the same way, except that the value read from each input card, rather than the constant 1, will be added.

The other form of the ADD instruction works just a bit differently. For example, the statement

ADD FIRST-NUMBER SECOND-NUMBER GIVING THEIR-SUM.

tells the computer to take whatever value is found in the field called FIRST-NUMBER and whatever value is found in the field called SECOND-NUMBER, add these two values, and place the answer in the field THEIR-SUM. Neither FIRST-NUMBER nor SECOND-NUMBER is changed by the execution of this instruction; both fields maintain their initial values.

The COBOL **SUBTRACT** verb is quite similar to the ADD verb. Again, there are two basic forms:

SUBTRACT FIRST-NUMBER FROM SECOND-NUMBER.

and

SUBTRACT FIRST-NUMBER FROM SECOND-NUMBER.
GIVING THEIR-DIFFERENCE.

Both forms have a meaning that directly parallels the roughly equivalent form of the ADD instruction.

Before moving on to the next paragraph, we should at least mention how a COBOL statement can be continued beyond the limits of a single card. Break at any natural breakpoint, usually after completing a COBOL word or a constant, and simply continue the statement on the next card (or the next line of your coding sheet). The only exception to this rule involves the continuation of a nonnumeric literal constant; we'll cover this exception in a later chapter. What could be simpler than breaking where you would normally code a blank anyway? Basically, with the single exception mentioned above, that's the rule for a COBOL continuation line.

Of course, getting beyond the strict rules of COBOL, there are intelligent breakpoints and not so intelligent breakpoints. In the SUBTRACT statement coded above, we chose to put the numbers to be subtracted on one line and the place where the answer was to be stored on another. We didn't have to do it that way, but grouping the logic of a statement into meaningful related pieces helps make the program easier to read. It's another one of those techniques that requires very little effort but pays off significantly in improved program documentation.

The FIND-AVERAGE Paragraph

Once the last card has been encountered, it's time to compute and print the average; the steps required to perform these operations are grouped in the paragraph called FIND-AVERAGE. Consider that paragraph name for a moment. What exactly is done here? Well, basically, we find the average. Do you see how the very careful selection of a paragraph name gives a real clue as to its function? Once again, a little extra effort during program coding can pay documentation dividends.

The first instruction in this paragraph (Fig. 3.10) is another MOVE instruction. This one,

MOVE SPACES TO OUTPUT-LINE.

is a nonnumeric MOVE. OUTPUT-LINE is the record we defined for our output file. **SPACES** is a reserved word representing, as you may have guessed, blank spaces. The instruction tells the computer to blank out the entire output line.

Fig. 3.10: *The FIND-AVERAGE paragraph.*

```
FIND-AVERAGE.
    MOVE    SPACES TO OUTPUT-LINE.
    DIVIDE ACCUMULATOR BY COUNTER GIVING O-AVERAGE.
    WRITE   OUTPUT-LINE
            AFTER ADVANCING 3 LINES.
```

Why is this necessary? Your program is not the only one using the computer; in fact, the chances are very good that someone else used the space your program is occupying within the computer before you did. This other program left data behind. You have no way of knowing what this data might be; in programming terminology, we call it **garbage**. By blanking the output line, we are making certain that someone else's garbage will not be printed in the middle of our output.

The next instruction (Fig. 3.10) reads

DIVIDE ACCUMULATOR BY COUNTER GIVING 0-AVERAGE.

What it does should be pretty obvious—just read the instruction. Once again, note that every part of the instruction is defined by the time the program encounters it. **DIVIDE** is a COBOL reserved word. ACCUMULATOR and COUNTER are fields that we defined in the DATA DIVISION. BY and GIVING are COBOL reserved words. 0-AVERAGE was also defined in the DATA DIVISION. Everything must be known before an instruction can be executed.

As long as we're discussing the DIVIDE verb, we may as well spend a few lines on the **MULTIPLY** too. The most commonly used form of the MULTIPLY instruction is

MULTIPLY FIRST-NUMBER BY SECOND-NUMBER GIVING THEIR-PRODUCT.

Either FIRST-NUMBER or SECOND-NUMBER (or both) can be a numeric constant.

Finally, the computed average is written to the printer under control of the last instruction in the FIND-AVERAGE paragraph (Fig. 3.10)

WRITE OUTPUT-LINE

AFTER ADVANCING 3 LINES.

Once again, what the instruction does should be fairly clear. The **AFTER ADVANCING clause** tells the printer how many lines to skip before it prints the line. OUTPUT-LINE is defined in the FILE SECTION of the DATA DIVISION and, if you check back (Fig. 3.1), you will see that it contains the computed average, 0-AVERAGE.

There is one potential point of confusion on an AFTER ADVANCING clause; the word LINES is always plural. If, for example, you wanted to skip one line before printing, you would code AFTER ADVANCING 1 LINES.

Note that the output statement refers to a record (the 01-level entry, OUTPUT-LINE), while the input statement

READ CARD-FILE . . .

refers to the file name (the FD entry, CARD-FILE). COBOL reads files but writes records. Perhaps the best explanation for this phenomenon is to remind you of the fact that COBOL was developed by a committee. As a programmer, just remember that that's the way it works, and you should have little trouble.

The END-OF-JOB Paragraph

The last paragraph in our program is named END-OF-JOB, for obvious reasons. This paragraph houses all those functions that must be performed just before the program finishes. The computer, don't forget, is a shared device, being used by many many different programmers. In addition to any functions our program might require, there are a number of system functions that must be handled in preparation for subsequent programs.

Perhaps the key system function is to signal the computer system that we are finished with our input and output devices, and that it can therefore allocate them to some other program. We do this by coding a **CLOSE** statement (Fig. 3.11). Basically, all this statement consists of is the word CLOSE followed by a list of the file names used in the program.

The final statement in the program is **STOP RUN**. This instruction clearly signals the computer system that our program is finished.

Fig. 3.11: *The END-OF-JOB paragraph.*

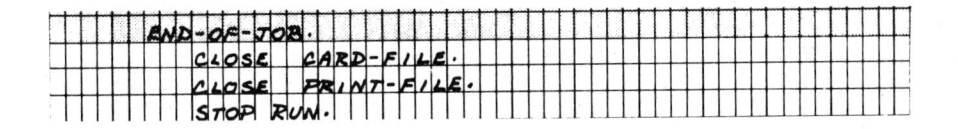

```
        END-OF-JOB.
            CLOSE   CARD-FILE.
            CLOSE   PRINT-FILE.
            STOP RUN.
```

SUMMARY

Continuing with the introduction to basic COBOL, this chapter concentrated on the DATA AND PROCEDURE DIVISIONs. In the DATA DIVISION, the precise format of all files, records, fields, and work fields is defined. In the FILE SECTION, an FD-entry is used to identify each file accessed by the program, with the file name matched with a name previously defined in a SELECT clause in the ENVIRONMENT DIVISION. A 01-level entry is then used to define a record within this file; higher-numbered entries are assigned to each of the fields within this record. A PICTURE clause is used to specify the character-by-character contents of each field. In the WORKING-STORAGE SECTION, work fields are defined using 77-level entries.

The PROCEDURE DIVISION is where the logical data manipulation instructions are coded. We considered the idea of breaking a program into at least three major parts: start of job routines, a mainline, and end of job routines. Specific instructions covered included OPEN, CLOSE, READ, WRITE, GO TO, MOVE, ADD, SUBTRACT, MULTIPLY, DIVIDE, and STOP RUN. A special caution was attached to the GO TO instruction, warning against over use. The idea that every part of a COBOL statement must be defined, either as a reserved word, a constant, or in the DATA DIVISION, before it is used was stressed.

KEY WORDS

ADD	implied decimal point
AFTER ADVANCING clause	level number
alphanumeric data	literal
AT END clause	loop
branch	MOVE
CLOSE	MULTIPLY
conditional branch	numeric data
constant	OPEN
DATA DIVISION	paragraph
data name	PICTURE clause
DIVIDE	PROCEDURE DIVISION
edit characters	READ
FD-entry	sentence
FILE SECTION	SPACES
FILLER	statement
garbage	STOP RUN
GO TO	SUBTRACT
housekeeping	unconditional branch

work field	ZEROS
WORKING-STORAGE SECTION	01-level entry
WRITE	77-level entry

EXERCISES

1. Explain how a file name is used to link the ENVIRONMENT DIVISION, the DATA DIVISION, and the PROCEDURE DIVISION.

2. Explain the function of a PICTURE clause.

3. What is an implied decimal point? Explain the difference between an implied decimal point and a real decimal point.

4. What is the difference between the FILE SECTION and the WORKING-STORAGE SECTION?

5. Cite some examples of housekeeping functions. Why are these functions necessary?

6. Every word in a COBOL statement must be defined before that statement can be coded. Explain what this means.

7. In the text, a cautionary note was included with the description of the GO TO statement. Why?

8. Plan and code a program to read a card containing your name and social security number; reverse the order of these two fields, and then print your social security number followed by your name.

9. Plan and write a complete COBOL program to read a card containing two numbers, compute the sum, difference, product, and quotient of these two numbers, and then print the numbers and the results of the four computations.

10. Write the DATA and PROCEDURE DIVISIONs for Chapter 1, exercise 1.

11. Write these two divisions for Chapter 1, exercise 2.

12. Write these two divisions for Chapter 1, exercise 3.

13. Write these two divisions for Chapter 1, exercise 4.

14. Write these two divisions for Chapter 1, exercise 5.

4

Getting the Program onto the Computer

OVERVIEW

In Chapter 1, we developed a solution to a problem. Chapters 2 and 3 were concerned with converting that solution into COBOL. We now have a set of coding sheets representing the COBOL program; our next task is to get this program into a form the computer can accept. In this chapter we'll start with the coding forms and discuss the preparation of a machine readable version of the program. Since no computer can directly execute COBOL statements, additional translation is necessary; we'll discuss this translation, concentrating on the key steps in the compilation process.

In addition to writing COBOL instructions and providing data, the programmer must also issue commands to the computer system; these commands tell the system such things as the specific type of compiler program to be used, and the specific physical input and output devices required. The mechanism for issuing these commands is a command language or job control language. Finally, having discussed program preparation and the basics of job control, we'll put the pieces together and illustrate a complete program deck, explaining how the computer handles it. The output generated by the computer will be shown, and a few typical varieties of programmer errors will be illustrated.

PREPARING A MACHINE-READABLE VERSION OF THE PROGRAM

Having completed Chapters 2 and 3, we now have a COBOL program written on coding sheets to solve the average problem. The next step is to convert these statements into machine-readable form. Perhaps someday, optical character recognition devices capable of electronically scanning and reading coding sheets will be generally available; unfortunately, this day has not yet arrived. The most common means of preparing a machine-readable version of a program is to enter the program one character at a time through a keyboard device.

The most commonly used keyboard device is the **keypunch**. On a keypunch, the objective is to convert each character into a pattern of holes in a single column of a punched card; later, this pattern of holes can be electronically sensed, allowing the computer to "read" the card's contents. To the keypunch operator, the process of preparing a deck of cards is analogous to typing, with each line from the COBOL coding form being converted to a single punched card. A complete set of instructions for using the IBM 029 keypunch has been included in Appendix A; other keypunches are operated in similar fashion.

The use of a keypunch is not universal; in recent years, many installations have switched over to magnetic diskette or cassette. Generally, one character at a time, keyboard entry is standard operating procedure for cassette or diskette devices too; in fact, the only real difference is that instead of producing a punched card, each line of your coding form is converted to a single record on the cassette or diskette. Your instructor will probably be able to provide detailed instructions for the use of such devices.

THE COMPILATION PROCESS

The program now exists in machine-readable form, but it still isn't quite ready for the computer. *No* computer can directly execute COBOL instructions—additional translation is necessary. The computer is an electronic device. The electronic nature of this device requires that its instructions and data be converted into a simple two-state code that can be represented by the presence or absense of an electric current, in other words, by an on/off condition. Without going into unnecessary details, this on/off code (similar in many ways to the dot/dash code developed by Samuel F.B. Morse for the telegraph) is used inside almost all modern computers. The code is based on the binary number system. The computer is a binary device and, before a program can be executed, it must be converted to binary form. It may be helpful to view the process as a simple translation into a "foreign" language, "computerese".

Fortunately, the programmer does not have to perform this conversion. Special programs called **compilers** have been developed to do this job for us. From the programmer's point of view, the program as written in COBOL *is* the program; the additional translation step we are now discussing is just for the benefit of the computer. Still, this translation does take place, and it is important that you know something about it.

A compiler is a special program. Very simply, its function, is to accept program statements written in a programming language, COBOL for example, and to convert these statements into binary form suitable for execution on the computer. The program as written by the programmer is called a **source module** or source program. The compiler reads these source statements, converting them to machine-level binary language. As its output, the compiler generates what is called an **object module**.

Given the need for this special translation program, the task of actually getting a program on the computer becomes a two-step operation (Fig. 4.1). First, the compiler program must be loaded onto the computer; this program reads the source statements and generates an object module. After the object module has been generated, it (the object module) can be loaded onto the computer and executed. The two steps, in summary, are 1.) the translation or compilation of the application program's source module into an object module by a compiler program; and 2.) the loading and execution of this object module.

On many computer systems, a third intermediate step is required; this extra program is often called a linkage editor. For the beginning programmer, the distinction between a linkage editor and a compiler really isn't critical, as both are involved in the preparation of a valid machine-level program from a source program; thus we will do nothing more than mention the existence of this extra step.

Fig. 4.1: *The compilation process.*

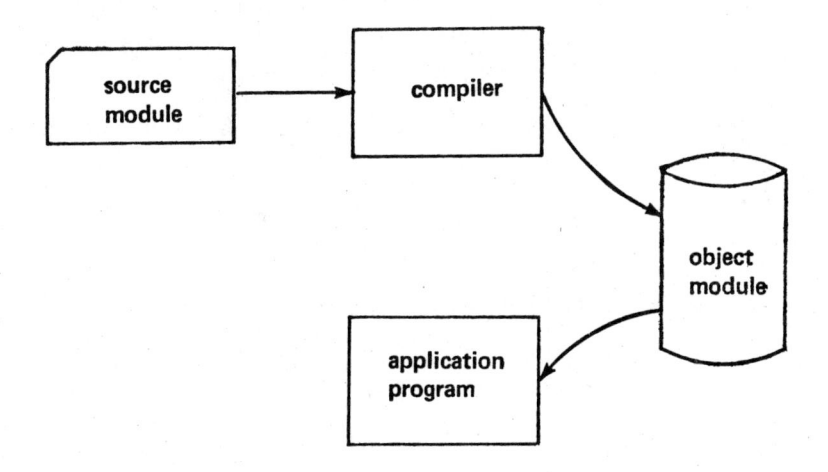

COMMUNICATING WITH THE COMPUTER SYSTEM: THE COMMAND LANGUAGE

COBOL is not the only compiler program available on a modern computer; others you may have heard about include FORTRAN, BASIC, RPG, PL/1, assembler language, and many more. Our program is written in COBOL. How is the computer system to know that we want the COBOL compiler, rather than some other compiler? If you think about it for a minute, it's obvious that someone must in some way tell the computer system which compiler program to use.

Another potential point of misunderstanding involves the allocation of input and output devices. A typical large computer system has a number of card readers and printers, several tape drives and disk drives, and a myriad of other physical devices. As a beginning programmer, the specific card reader or printer used by your program probably doesn't make much difference to you, but to the more experienced programmer, it might. There must be some mechanism that allows the programmer to specify physical device requirements to the system.

A third major problem involves program separation and program identification. If yours is a typical batch processing installation, you will probably submit your program deck along with those of dozens of other programmers; these programs are all stacked together and read into the computer as one big deck. How can the computer system possibly separate your program from all the others? Perhaps more to the point, how can the computer operator possibly separate all those decks and get your program back to you?

Even if your installation does not use traditional batch processing, allowing you instead to enter your program through a terminal, the system must still have a mechanism for identifying each program; it cannot, after all, afford to give its exclusive attention to your program, but instead works concurrently on several different ones. How can the system maintain the identity of yours?

Every computer system faces these three basic problems; it *must* have a mechanism for

1. providing a unique identification for each program on the system,

2. clearly identifying the specific program to be run,

3. clearly identifying the specific input and output devices needed to support the program.

Although the specific mechanism varies significantly from computer system to computer system, every system has some form of **command language** or **job control language.**

The programs in this book have all been written on an IBM System/370 Model 148 computer running under control of an operating system known as VS1. Over the next several pages, we will illustrate the job control language needed to execute a

COBOL program on this system. Anyone having access to an IBM System/360 or System/370 computer running under any of the OS or VS operating systems will encounter a need for similar job control statements. For those of you who have access to an IBM computer running under DOS or DOS/VS, Appendix B contains a summary of typical DOS job control. For those of you who use some other computer system, much of the material in the next several paragraphs will be irrelevant and thus it has been clearly marked as being optional; your instructor or an experienced programmer should be able to fill you in on the details of job control in your installation.

JOB CONTROL LANGUAGE (OPTIONAL)

The JOB Card

The first task of any command language is job identification. Under IBM's job control language, this function is performed by a JOB card.

Every IBM job control language card, except for the end-of-data marker, begins with slashes (//) in columns 1 and 2. There are three key fields on each card (Fig. 4.2): a name, an operation identifying the type of job control card, and operands.

On a JOB card, the job name begins in column 3, immediately following the two slashes (Fig. 4.3). This job name provides the unique

Fig. 4.2: *The general format of an IBM Job Control Language Statement.*

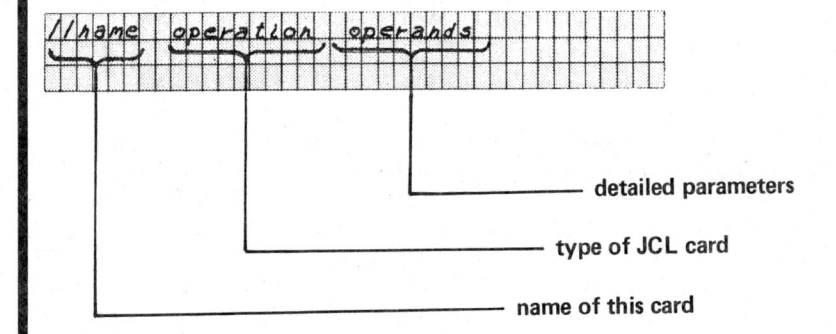

```
//name   operation   operands
            │           │           │
            │           │           └──── detailed parameters
            │           └──────────────── type of JCL card
            └──────────────────────────── name of this card
```

67.

Fig. 4.3: *A typical JOB statement.*

```
//JOB3/4    JOB    (0,EDP/02),'FISHER',CLASS=G
```

identification needed by the job, thus meeting the first requirement of any command language. Following the job name and separated from it by one or more blanks is the word JOB (Fig. 4.3), identifying this as a JOB card. Finally, separated from the word JOB by one or more blanks, is a series of operands. In the example shown in Fig. 4.3, the operands consist of an account number identifying the account to be charged with the cost of running this program, the name of the programmer submitting the job (personal identification), and the job's class, which determines its priority. The precise format of the operands used on a JOB card is completely installation-dependent; this is only an example. In some installations, the programmer doesn't even prepare a JOB card, but is assigned one by the operator as the job is submitted. In other cases, only a partial JOB card is prepared. Follow your local standards; your instructor or an experienced programmer should be able to provide the details.

The EXEC Card

The second function of any command or job control language is to identify the specific program to be loaded onto the computer and executed; in the case of the average program, we want the COBOL compiler. The job control card that identifies the program to be executed is the EXEC or execute card.

Even on an IBM computer, there are several different versions of the COBOL compiler available. Most of the programs in this book were compiled under the control of a procedure known as COBVCG, a version that bypasses some of the more exotic services of a linkage editor routine and thus supports, at a relatively low cost, the type of program typically submitted by beginners. An EXEC card for this procedure is shown in Fig. 4.4; note that there is no name coded on this job control card. Other commonly used procedures include

Fig. 4.4: *A typical EXEC statement.*

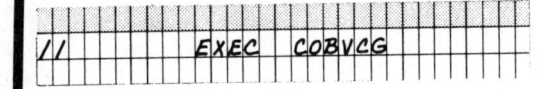

```
//        EXEC  COBVCG
```

    //   EXEC COBOL

and

    //   EXEC COB4CLG

In spite of the fact that the meaning of every letter in the procedure name may not be obvious to you, the function performed by this card should be. Very simply,

    //   EXEC COBVCG

tells the computer system to load and begin the execution of a COBOL compiler. Once again, your instructor or an experienced programmer should be able to show you the EXEC card to be used in your installation.

The DD Card

The final function of a job control or command language is to identify specific input and output devices. Under IBM's job control language, this function is performed by the DD card.

  We already spent some time on the linkage between a program and its I/O devices in Chapters 2 and 3. A file name was defined in a SELECT clause in the ENVIRONMENT DIVISION; this same file name was subsequently used as an FD entry in the DATA DIVISION and as a file name in OPEN, CLOSE, and READ or WRITE statements in the PROCEDURE DIVISION (Fig. 4.5). This linkage defines the file within the program. The only remaining piece to the puzzle is to tie the file to a specific physical input or output device.

  On the one hand (Fig. 4.5) we have a program. On the other hand we have a physical device. The function of the DD card is to link the logical file as defined within the program to a physical device. In the example

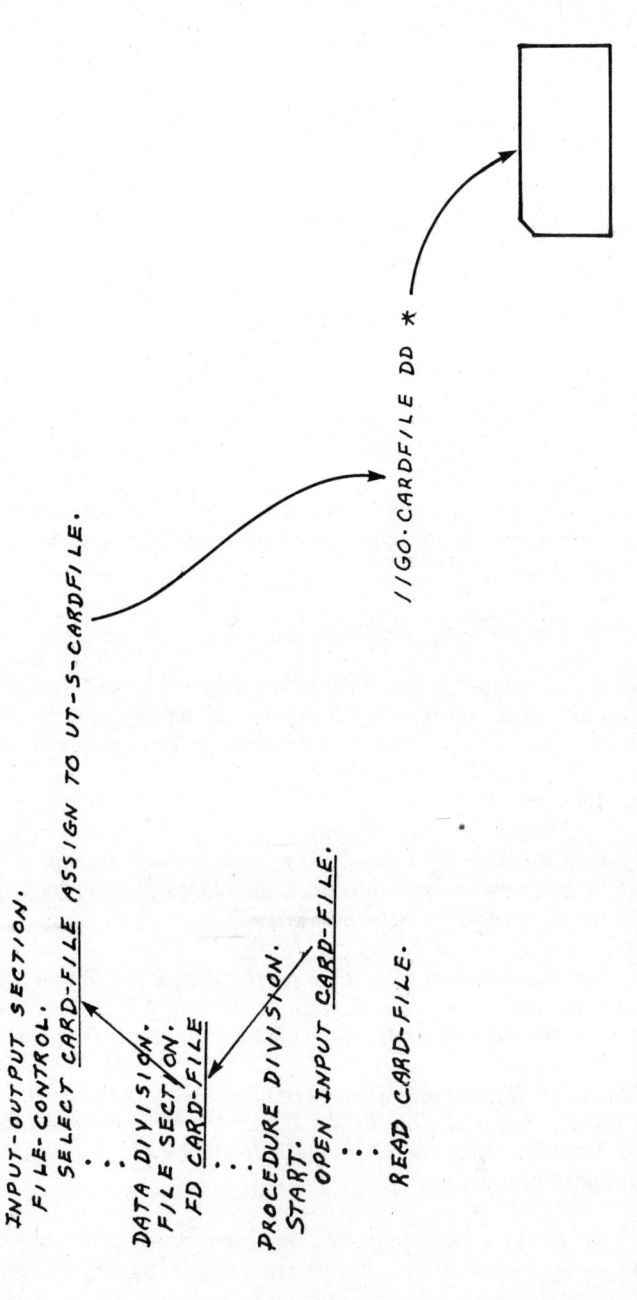

ENVIRONMENT DIVISION.
INPUT-OUTPUT SECTION.
FILE-CONTROL.
SELECT CARD-FILE ASSIGN TO UT-S-CARDFILE.
....
DATA DIVISION.
FILE SECTION.
FD CARD-FILE
....
PROCEDURE DIVISION.
START.
OPEN INPUT CARD-FILE.
....
READ CARD-FILE.

//GO.CARDFILE DD *

Fig. 4.5: *The DD Card Provides a Link between the Program and a Specific Physical Input or Output Device.*

shown in Fig. 4.5, the SELECT clause for the file known as CARD-FILE is tied to an ASSIGN clause that refers to external name CARDFILE. CARDFILE is, in turn, the name of a job control language card. To the right of the DD operation code on this card, a specific physical device is identified; in this case, we have coded an asterisk (*) meaning that we are willing to accept whatever the standard system input device may be. If we had wanted a specific card reader, a 2501 for example, we would have coded

//CARDFILE   DD   UNIT=2501

By following the path outlined in Fig. 4.5, it is possible to go from the definition of a file within the program to a specific physical device.

In the first several chapters of this book we'll be working almost exclusively with card input and printer output. In every case the standard system input or output device will suit our purposes. On most IBM systems, the standard system input device is designated by an asterisk (*) and the standard system output device is designated by SYSOUT=A. A set of job control language cards to link these two devices is shown in Fig. 4.6. The "name" field must, of course, match the external name defined in an ASSIGN clause. The punctuation is simple: // in columns 1 and 3, the name beginning in column 3, one or more blanks following the name, DD following the blank or blanks, one or more blanks following the DD, and the SYSOUT=A or the *.

A final comment before we move on. Frequently, you will see these job control language cards coded as follows

    //COB.SYSIN   DD   *

    //GO.name   DD   SYSOUT=A

    //GO.name   DD   *

Fig. 4.6: *DD Cards for Linking with the Standard System Input and Output Devices.*

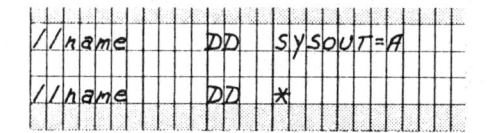

```
//name      DD   SYSOUT=A
//name      DD   *
```

> The COB. and GO. are merely qualifiers. The compilation process is a 2-step process; COB. identifies a DD card as belonging to the compilation step, while GO. identifies the card as belonging to the GO step, which is the step where the translated application program is executed.
>
> **The End-of-Data Marker**
>
> Remember how, as part of the READ statement, we coded an AT END clause? The function of this clause is to tell the computer what to do when the last record indicator is encountered. Under IBM's job control language, the last record or end-of-data indicator is a card with the characters /* punched into the first two columns.

THE COMMAND LANGUAGE AND JOB SUBMISSION

The function of any command language is to support job submission. Fig. 4.7 shows an example of the typical commands needed to support a COBOL compilation and execution on an IBM computer. Imagine yourself issuing these commands to a human operator, one at a time. First, you would identify yourself: this is job number JOB314, charge it to account number EDP102, my name is DAVIS, and run the job under class G priority. That is exactly what the JOB card in Fig. 4.7 says. Having identified yourself, you would now tell the operator to load and start the COBOL compiler, performing the function of the EXEC card. Next, you would tell the operator that input source statements to the COBOL compiler should be entered through the card reader, which is what the "//COB.SYSIN DD *" card says.

Now your program is being compiled. As it finishes, your newly generated object module is loaded into the computer and begins executing. It's time for you to issue two more commands: use the standard system output device for output and the standard system input device for input. These last two functions are handled by the PRTFILE and CARDFILE DD cards. If your system does not use IBM job control language, substitute commands from your own command language for the statements in Fig. 4.7: you should find reasonably close agreement. Perhaps the most significant difference is the fact that, on many systems, if you choose to use the standard input and output devices, no equivalent to a DD card is needed.

It would be unreasonable to expect any computer center to actually allow all its programmers access to the computer room so that conversations such as the one imagined above could take place. The function of a command language or a job control language is to provide the programmer with a mechanism for issuing these commands ahead of time. Once coded, the commands can be intermixed with the program deck, allowing the operator or the computer's control program to react at the appropriate time.

Still, the analogy of a conversation with the computer operator is a valuable one because it very clearly illustrates that the command language is not a part of the program. Instead, these statements and commands perform a support function, telling

Fig. 4.7: *Job control language provides a network of commands to support the submission of a job to the computer.*

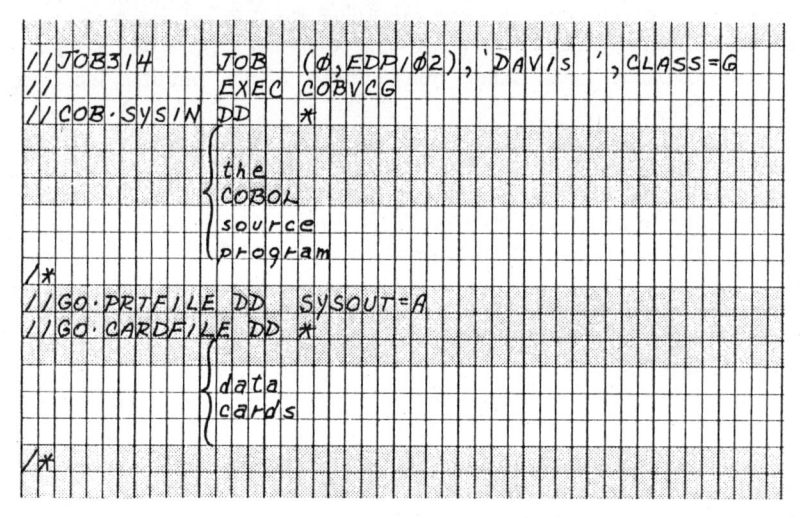

```
//JOB3114      JOB   (0,EDP,102),'DAVIS  ',CLASS=G
//             EXEC  COBVCG
//COB.SYSIN    DD    *
                    ⎧ the
                    ⎪ COBOL
                    ⎨ source
                    ⎩ program
/*
//GO.PRTFILE   DD    SYSOUT=A
//GO.CARDFILE  DD    *
                    ⎧ data
                    ⎨ cards
                    ⎩
/*
```

the computer system what specific major steps should be taken and in what physical order they should be taken.

THE DATA CARDS

COBOL statements are keypunched or otherwise prepared according to the rules of COBOL. Job control language statements or other commands are prepared according to a different set of rules. There is one more part to this puzzle that must be defined before we can submit our program to the computer, and that is the data cards.

The rules of the COBOL language do *not* control the format of the data cards. Instead, the programmer controls this format. Well before we even started writing the average program in COBOL, the content of the data cards was defined as follows:

columns	contents
1-5	a 5-digit number with 2 digits to the right of the decimal point
6-80	unused.

The fields that made up the input record in the DATA DIVISION were carefully structured to match this data format exactly. Likewise, our data cards must precisely match this data format. We must provide a number of data cards each containing a 5-digit number punched into the first five columns.

The only potentially tricky part about preparing these data cards is the fact that the data must be right justified in this five column field. The temptation when, for example, the value 5 is to be keypunched, is to punch the 5 in column 1 and to leave the remaining 4 positions in the field blank. This is incorrect. When you write a number, it is permissible to have leading, nonsignificant blanks, but it is incorrect to have trailing blanks.

Let's be more specific. When we defined the field called I-VALUE as having a PICTURE of 999V99, what we meant was that the digit in the hundreds position would be punched in column 1, the digit in the tens position would be punched in column 2, the units digit would be punched in column 3, column 4 would contain the digit in the 1/10 position, and column 5 would contain the digit in the 1/100 position. Thus, the value 5 would become 00500, while the number 342.75 would be punched as 34275. No decimal point is actually punched, but the data *must* be lined up with the assumed or implied location of the decimal point. Normally, leading zeros can be dropped and replaced by blanks, but the rightmost position in the field, in this case column 5, *must* contain a valid digit.

PUTTING THE PIECES TOGETHER

We now have a fully defined COBOL program, a list of the job control language statements needed to support this program, and a set of data cards. Once these cards have been keypunched, the pieces can be put together and the job submitted to the computer. A fully keypunched and collated job deck is reproduced in Fig. 4.8. Note that the job control statements shown in Fig. 4.8 are for an IBM System/360 or System/370 computer running under the control of an OS or VS-level operating system, and that the job control for your system may vary. Even so, this job deck should be a fairly close reflection of the one you will actually submit to the computer.

The first card in the deck (Fig. 4.8) is the JOB card, which serves to identify the job. Next comes an EXEC card, which tells the computer's control program to load the COBOL compiler into main memory. Next comes a DD card, which tells the COBOL compiler that its source statements are coming from the system input device. The COBOL program itself follows these three control cards; the computer is now in the process of translating the COBOL source statements into machine-level object code under control of the COBOL compiler program. At the end of the COBOL source deck is a /* card, marking the end of data; to the compiler program, these COBOL source statements are its input data, and the standard end-of-data marker is a reasonable way to tell it that there are no more statements to be compiled.

Once compilation is finished, the newly created machine-level application program can be loaded into main memory. As it begins processing, the first DD card provides the link to a physical output device, and the second DD card sets up a physical input link. The data cards can now be read one at a time. (Note that program statements are read during the first, or compilation, step, and the data cards are read during the second step. The program cards and the data cards are two different things.) An end-of-data marker (/*) follows the data cards.

Fig. 4.8: *A Complete Job Deck.*

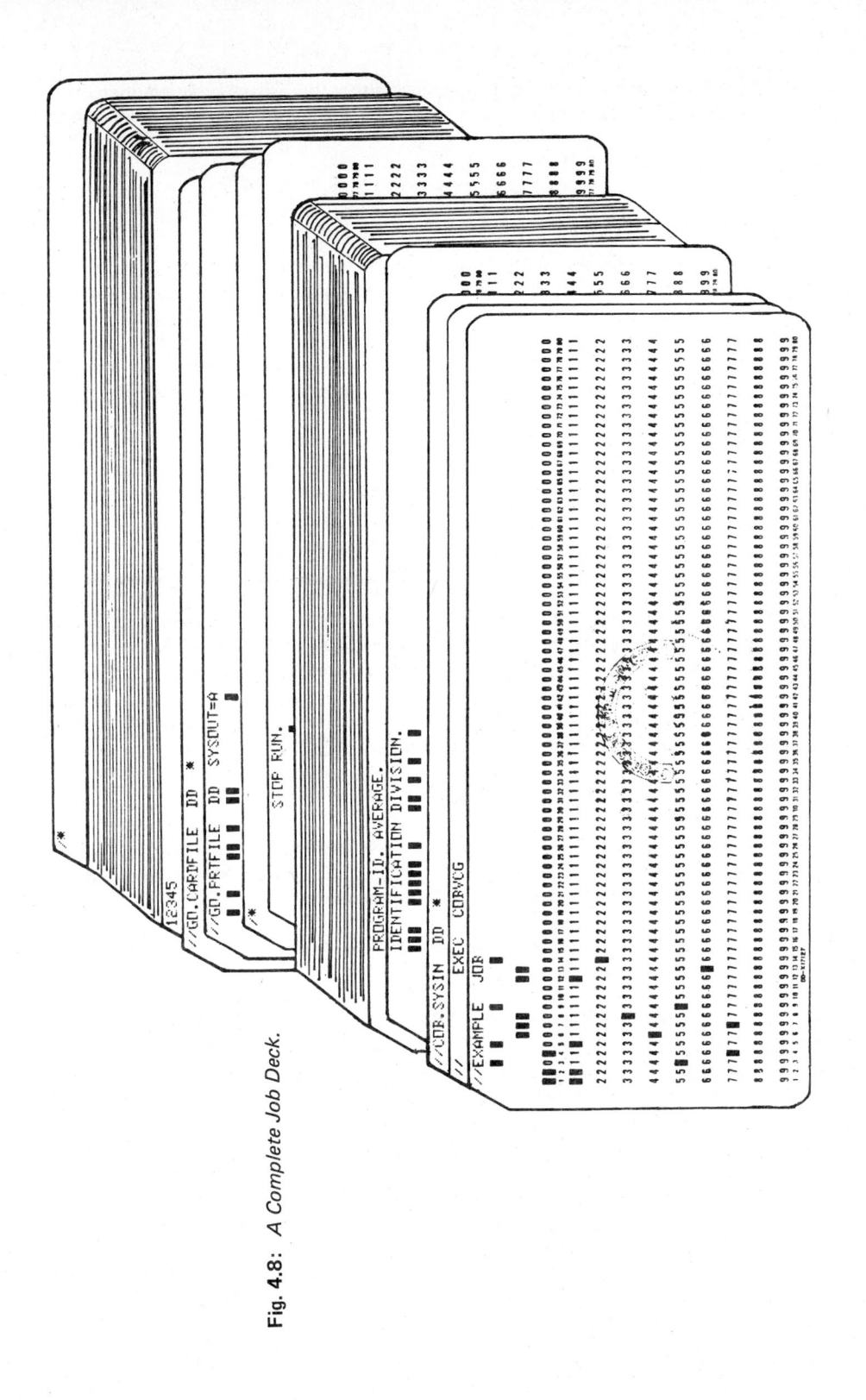

By this time you should have keypunched either the average program or an original solution to a similar problem. If you have not already done so, submit this job to the computer.

COMPUTER OUTPUT

Having submitted your program to the computer, what can you expect in return? In most cases, what you will get will be a computer listing of your program, showing such things as the job control language statements you submitted, the actual COBOL statements contained in your deck (usually numbered sequentially), a list of the data names used in the program, a list of any errors encountered in compiling the program, and, if all goes well, the actual results sent to the printer by your program.

To illustrate the kind of output you can expect from the computer, selected pages from a typical output **listing** of the average problem have been reproduced as Fig. 4.9. To add a bit of interest to this discussion, we have intentionally introduced some of the more typical errors made by beginning COBOL programmers; the **error messages** associated with the listing of Fig. 4.9 are shown in Fig. 4.10.

Let's begin with the listing itself (Fig. 4.9). At the top, you will usually see a header identifying the version of COBOL used, the date of compilation, and any of several other things; since the header information can vary widely from version to version, we have intentionally dropped it from our listing to avoid possible confusion.

Beneath the header is a line-by-line listing of the statements in the program. Near the left margin, each line is assigned a **line number**; for example,

        00001   IDENTIFICATION DIVISION.

represents the very first card in the program. The line numbers provide a mechanism for referring to a specific statement in the program. They are added by the COBOL compiler; the programmer need not assign line numbers.

There are several mistakes in this program. Fig. 4.10 is a list of messages identifying each error. Consider the first message in the list:

     24   IKF1004I-E   INVALID WORD SLECT. SKIPPING.....

The message begins with a number, in this case, 24. The number identifies the line number from the program listing that contains the error; there is something wrong with statement number 24.

What is the problem? A code, in this case IKF1004I, is the number of an error message in a COBOL reference manual; a full explanation can be found there. To save the programmer the trouble of looking it up in another source, the message,

    INVALID WORD SLECT. SKIPPING TO NEXT RECOGNIZABLE WORD.

provides a pretty clear indication of what is wrong. The correct word is SELECT; the

```
    1              12.37.14      SEP 16,1978

00001         IDENTIFICATION DIVISION.


00004         PROGRAM-ID. AVERAGE.
00005         AUTHOR.     DAVIS & FISHER.

00007         REMARKS.    THIS PROGRAM READS A SERIES OF DATA CARDS,
00008                     COUNTS THE CARDS, ACCUMULATES THE VALUES
00009                     PUNCHED ONE TO EACH CARD, AND, AFTER THE
00010                     LAST CARD HAS BEEN READ, COMPUTES THE
00011                     AVERAGE VALUE.


00013         ENVIRONMENT DIVISION.

00015             CONFIGURATION SECTION.

00017                 SOURCE-COMPUTER.    IBM-370-148.
00018                 OBJECT-COMPUTER.    IBM-370-148.

00020             INPUT-OUTPUT SECTION.

00022                 FILE-CONTROL.
00023                     SELECT CARD-FILE  ASSIGN TO UT-S-CARDFILE.
00024                     SLECT  PRINT-FILE ASSIGN TO UT-S-PRTFILE.


00026         DATA DIVISION.

00028             FILE SECTION.

00030                 FD  CARD-FILE
00031                     LABEL RECORD IS OMITTED.
00032                 01  INPUT-CARD.
00033                     05  I-VALUE        PIC 999V99.
00034                     05  FILLER         PIC X(75).

00036                 FD  PRINT-FILE
00037                     LABEL RECORD IS OMITTED.
00038                 01  OUTPUT-LINE.
00039                     05  FILLER         PIC X(15).
00040                     05  O-AVERAGE      PIC 999.9999.
00041                     05  FILLER         PIC X(110).


00043             WORKING-STORAGE SECTION.

00045                 77  COUNTER            PIC 999.
00046                 77  ACCUMULATOR        PIC 99999V99.
```

Fig. 4.9: *A listing of the average program.*

```
2         AVERAGE         12.37.14         SEP 16,1978

00048           PROCEDURE DIVISION.
00050           BEGIN.

00052                 OPEN          CARD-FILE.
00053                 OPEN OUTPUT PRINT-FILE.
00054                 MOVE ZEROS   TO  COUNTR,  ACCUMULATOR.


00056           GET-A-VALUE.

00058                 READ CARD-FILE
00059                       AT END GO TO FIND-AVERAGE.
00060                 ADD I-VALUE TO ACCUMULATOR.
00061                 ADD     1    TO COUNTER.
00062                 GO TO GET-A-VALU.


00064           FIND-AVERAGE.

00066                 MOVE    SPACES TO OUTPUT-LINE.
00067                 DIVIDE ACCUMULATOR BY COUNTER GIVING O-AVERAGE.
00068                 WRITE   OUTPUT-LINE
00069                         AFTER ADVANCING 3 LINES


00071           END-OF-JOB.

00073                 CLOSE   CARD-FILE.
00074                 CLOSE   PRINT-FILE.
00075                 STOP RUN.
```

Fig. 4.9: *Continued.*

Fig. 4.10: *The error messages associated with the program listing of Fig. 4.9.*

```
     4        AVERAGE          12.37.14        SEP 16,1978

    CARD     ERROR MESSAGE
     24      IKF1004I-E       INVALID WORD SLECT . SKIPPING TO NEXT RECOGNIZABLE WORD.
     23      IKF2049I-C       NO OPEN CLAUSE FOUND FOR FILE.
     37      IKF1056I-E       FILE-NAME NOT DEFINED IN A SELECT. DESCRIPTION IGNORED.
     52      IKF1017I-E       CARD-FILE INVALID IN OPEN CLAUSE. SKIPPING TO NEXT CLAUSE.
     53      IKF3001I-E       PRINT-FILE NOT DEFINED. DELETING TILL LEGAL ELEMENT FOUND.
     53      IKF4002I-E       OPEN STATEMENT INCOMPLETE. STATEMENT DISCARDED.
     54      IKF3001I-E       COUNTR NOT DEFINED. DISCARDED.
     62      IKF3001I-E       GET-A-VALU NOT DEFINED. STATEMENT DISCARDED.
     66      IKF3001I-E       OUTPUT-LINE NOT DEFINED. DISCARDED.
     67      IKF3001I-E       O-AVERAGE NOT DEFINED. STATEMENT DISCARDED.
     68      IKF3001I-E       OUTPUT-LINE NOT DEFINED. STATEMENT DISCARDED.
     71      IKF1043I-W       END OF SENTENCE SHOULD PRECEDE END-OF-JOB . ASSUMED PRESENT.
     74      IKF3001I-E       PRINT-FILE NOT DEFINED. DELETING TILL LEGAL ELEMENT FOUND.
     74      IKF4002I-E       CLOSE STATEMENT INCOMPLETE. STATEMENT DISCARDED.
```

programmer has coded SLECT—probably a simple keypunching error. SELECT is a reserved word; SLECT is not; thus the COBOL compiler doesn't know what you mean. As a result, it simply ignores the unknown word, and moves on.

The one part of the message that we have not considered is the letter E which follows the coded error message. There are basically three kinds of compilation errors. True **errors**, identified by an E, represent problems that the compiler just does not know how to handle; as a result it is impossible to produce a valid machine-level program. A **warning**, designated by a W, represents a *possible* error. For example, let's say that your program multiplies two 3-digit numbers and stores the answer in a 5-digit field. The product of two 3-digit numbers *could* be a 6-digit number, which would not fit in the 5-digit field you have defined for it. You may know that the answer will be no more than 5 digits in length, but the compiler assumes the worst and tells you, through a warning, that a possible error has been encountered. A machine-level program will be generated and executed in spite of warnings; this is just COBOL's way of telling you to watch out.

The final type of error message is a **conditional** error, designated by the letter C. A level-C error indicates that the compiler has encountered something that is not quite right, but has made an assumption in an attempt to correct the error. In Fig. 4.10, for example, the second error message tells us that there is no open clause for the file defined in statement 23. That might or might not be significant; the compiler has no way of knowing. It is merely telling you that something is strange; in this case, it is assuming that you, the programmer, really defined an unused field. If only conditionals or warnings are found in the error list, a program will be generated and executed. Is the conditional error significant? That question must be answered by the programmer (in this case, yes it is). Sometimes the compiler will make the correct assumption, and sometimes it won't.

One of the more confusing aspects of compiler error messages is the fact that one error may lead to several others, and some of these subsequent errors may occur on perfectly valid instructions. Let's illustrate. In statement 24, the word SELECT was misspelled; as a result, there is no SELECT clause for the PRINT-FILE. There is nothing wrong with statement number 37, but because there is no SELECT statement associated with the PRINT-FILE (because of the earlier error), this FD description is ignored. Statement 53 is, by itself, perfectly valid, but, since there is no SELECT clause, which in turn means that there is no FD entry, it is impossible to open this file. Statements 66, 67, and 68 are all correct, but, since the file description was ignored by the compiler, the fields OUTPUT-LINE and O-AVERAGE are undefined, making the otherwise correct statements wrong. Finally, in statement number 74, the PRINT-FILE cannot be closed because, due to an earlier error, it has not been defined. All these error messages are generated by a single real error! By correcting the spelling of SELECT (one wrong letter!), all these errors disappear. Your job, as the programmer, is to simply keypunch a corrected card to replace the bad one.

There are other, unrelated errors in the program too. In statement 52, for example, the CARD-FILE cannot be opened. Why? Because the word INPUT (or OUTPUT) has not been coded. Statement 54's error message says "COUNTER NOT DEFINED. DISCARDED". In the WORKING-STORAGE SECTION we used a field named COUNTER, not COUNTR. A programmer must be consistent. COUNTR is just as good a field name as is COUNTER, but the same spelling must be used in both places. Statement number 62 says

GO TO GET-A-VALU.

but the paragraph name is GET-A-VALUE; basically, this is the same mistake. Replace the incorrect cards with new, corrected versions.

Most errors made by the beginning programmer are of this variety—simply keypunching or coding errors; obviously we cannot illustrate all possible errors, but these are representative. Do regular programmers have similar problems? Of course they do, although not as often. Such errors must be corrected if the program is to be successfully compiled; you can reasonably expect at least one and probably two test runs just to remove the keypunching and coding errors, so plan for it. After the trivial errors have been removed, you can turn your attention to the real problem—correcting errors in logic. Eventually, you will discover that even a "perfect" program can fail (or produce unacceptable output) if it is given bad data.

Do you get the feeling that programming is a very exacting activity? Good, because it is. If a program is to work, it must be perfect. Almost isn't good enough. Even 99% right isn't good enough; it must be perfect. Some people find such attention to detail tedious, dull, and more than a little mind-bending; such individuals rarely become professional programmers. Others, however, find such activities uniquely challenging and more than a little exciting.

Eventually, all keypunching and compilation errors will be corrected, and the program will run, producing valid output. It's an exciting moment when, for the very first time, you have successfully guided an expensive piece of electronic equipment through some logical process. You have forced yourself to understand the process in detail, and you have successfully communicated your understanding. That's not easy; it's a real intellectual challenge. Perhaps that's what makes it so exciting.

One final comment before we move on: The most difficult program you will ever write is the first one. There are no shortcuts. Copying from a friend simply postpones the day when your instructor discovers that you are having problems. Write it, and do it yourself.

SUMMARY

Chapters 1 through 3 were concerned with defining a problem solution and converting that solution into a computer program. This chapter discussed the process of getting the program onto a computer.

We began with a general discussion of the compilation process, explaining how the programmer's source code must be translated into machine-level language before the program can be executed. Since a computer cannot do anything without explicit instructions, we turned our attention to the job control language or other command language, a tool that allows the programmer or computer operator to specify such things as which compiler is to be loaded and executed and which physical input and output devices are to be used. An optional section on job control language for the IBM System/360 and System/370 series computers explained these concepts in somewhat more detail.

The chapter ended with a discussion of a typical output listing. The average program was keypunched and compiled. The listing showed several keypunching errors; the format of a number of typical errors was described and the action to be taken by the programmer in correcting these errors was spelled out.

KEYWORDS

command language	error message	listing
compiler	job control language	object module
conditional error	keypunch	source module
error	line number	warning

EXERCISES

1. Briefly explain the compilation process. What happens? Why is this important?
2. What is the function of a command language or job control language?

3. Briefly explain the process of correcting a keypunching error that has been discovered during the compilation process.

4. Keypunch and execute Chapter 1, exercise 2.

5. Keypunch and execute Chapter 1, exercise 3.

6. Keypunch and execute Chapter 1, exercise 4.

7. Keypunch and execute Chapter 1, exercise 5.

8. Write a program simply to read and print a deck of cards. Use the input data prepared for any of the programs described in Chapter 1. On output, separate the input fields from each other by inserting a few blanks.

9. Write a program to read a card containing two 5-digit numbers. Compute and print their sum, difference (first minus second), product, and quotient (first divided into second).

10. Keypunch a card containing the name and address of a friend (you may want to use the format of the earlier exercise on address label preparation, although this is not necessary). Write a program to read this card and prepare a single address label listing the name on the first line, street address on the second line, and the city, state, and zip code on the third line.

11. Simply keypunch and run the textbook problem.

5

Controlling the Logical Flow of a Program

OVERVIEW

This chapter begins with the development of a solution to another business data processing problem—adding interest to savings accounts. As part of this solution, the computer's ability to perform simple yes/no logic will be discussed, and the COBOL IF statement introduced. Proof totals or summary totals and counts will be introduced, along with the WRITE FROM form of the COBOL WRITE statement. Once the mainline of the program has been fully developed, page controls will be added, and page headers printed. The PERFORM verb will be introduced as the mechanism for implementing these page controls.

THE PROBLEM: ADDING INTEREST TO SAVINGS ACCOUNTS

At regular intervals, every bank must add interest to all its savings accounts. The rule for adding interest is quite simple:

1. multiply the old balance in an account by the current interest rate to get interest due;

2. add this interest to the old balance to get the new balance.

Once again, we have verbally defined an algorithm for solving this problem, and we can begin developing a computer-level solution.

Before we continue, let's make this problem a bit more realistic. First, most banks have a "minimum balance" rule for computing interest. Often, what this rule says is that no interest will be paid unless the amount in the account exceeds some minimum balance, typically $10.00 for a regular savings account. This restriction changes our algorithm. We might restate step 1 as follows:

1. If the old balance is greater than $10.00, multiply the old balance by the interest rate to get interest due; otherwise, interest due equals zero.

A second factor usually encountered in a typical business data processing application is the need for **summary totals** or **proof totals**. In computing interest, we are computing an amount of money our organization owes its customers. These computations must be correct (that goes almost without saying), but, almost as importantly, clear trails must be left to allow accounting or an auditor to quickly check on this accuracy. To compile proof totals, a set of running totals of each of the primary monetary fields is maintained and printed at the end of the savings account update activity. Given such figures as the total value of all old balances, the total amount of interest actually paid on all accounts, and the total value of all computed new balances, accounting or an auditor can quickly check to make certain that at least the gross totals balance. Often, a simple count of the number of accounts processed is also included; if this number does not match the number of accounts known to exist *before* the account update program was run, additional effort can be expended to find the discrepancy. Such auditing features are a critical part of most business data processing applications; in our problem solution we'll include proof totals for the old balance, interest earned, new balance, and a count of accounts processed.

We now have a rough idea of what the program is to do, and are ready to begin the process of setting up our human-level solution. In very rough terms, we must

1. get the old account balance;

2. compute interest due, if any;

3. compute the new balance for the account;

4. write the new balance;

    5. accumulate old balance, interest, and new balance;

    6. add 1 to the accounts counter.

These basic steps must be repeated for each account.

    A few questions before we bring our straw person into play. Obviously, the first three steps described above must be performed in the prescribed order. Can you see why? Is it possible to do anything before the basic input data is available? No. Can we compute the new balance before we have computed the interest due? Again, no. What about those last three steps, however? Does it really make any difference in what order we accumulate, count, and write? No it doesn't; the steps do not depend upon each other. Among these three instructions, any order will do. They must, however, follow the first three instructions. Why?

    Now, let's get our human-level instructions for that imaginary straw person. Remember the need to initialize key fields before starting the mainline of the routine. Assuming an interest rate of 5%, we might imagine the following set of instructions as reasonable:

    1. set old balance accumulator to zero;

    2. set interest accumulator to zero;

    3. set new balance accumulator to zero;

    4. set counter to zero;

    5. get account old balance; at end go to step 14;

    6. if old balance is greater than $10.00, multiply old balance by 0.05 to get interest; else interest equals zero;

    7. add old balance and interest to get new balance;

    8. write new balance;

    9. add old balance to old balance accumulator;

    10. add interest to interest accumulator;

    11. add new balance to new balance accumulator;

    12. add 1 to counter;

    13. go back to step 5;

    14. write accumulators and counter.

    15. quit.

Once again, desk check the solution with a handful of data records; make sure it works.

Given a reasonable human-level solution, we can now develop a flowchart as pictured in Fig. 5.1. Note that now that we have covered some of the basics of COBOL, the human-level instructions shown above can be seen to bear a clear resemblance to COBOL instructions. This is not surprising; after all, COBOL was designed specifically for business data processing problems and, after a little practice, the language begins to seem almost "natural" for describing solutions to such problems. As a direct result of this naturalness, it can be argued that COBOL has achieved at least a measure of the self documentation desired by those who developed the language. As an added advantage, the programmer gains a bit of a head start toward coding while simply planning a solution.

There is also a danger. Because this human-level **psuedo code** does resemble COBOL, the temptation is immediately to begin coding finished COBOL, skipping all the intermediate steps. Don't! We still have a great deal to define before coding can begin, and it is much easier, both physically and emotionally, to change rough-penciled psuedo code than to change hard instructions on a coding pad, or a pattern of holes in a series of cards.

Input and Output Devices

As before, the input device used in this program will be the card reader or the system input device, and the output device the printer or standard system output device.

Data Formats

The data formats needed to support this program will be more complex than those of the problem covered in the earlier chapters. We need more than simply a single value coming into the program. Unless this is a very unusual bank, there are many accounts, and each one must maintain its personal identity. Almost invariably, this involves an account identification number of some type. As a minimum, each input record must contain this identification number and the old balance. Thus, we'll assume the following format for our input cards:

columns	contents
1-8	account number
9-15	old balance, correct to 2 decimal places
16-80	unused

All input data cards must be prepared to match this format.

Where did that format come from? In all honesty, the authors simply made it up. In a more realistic situation, a master file will exist, and the format of this master file will dictate the format of your program's input records.

Fig. 5.1: *A Flowchart of the Savings Account Program.*

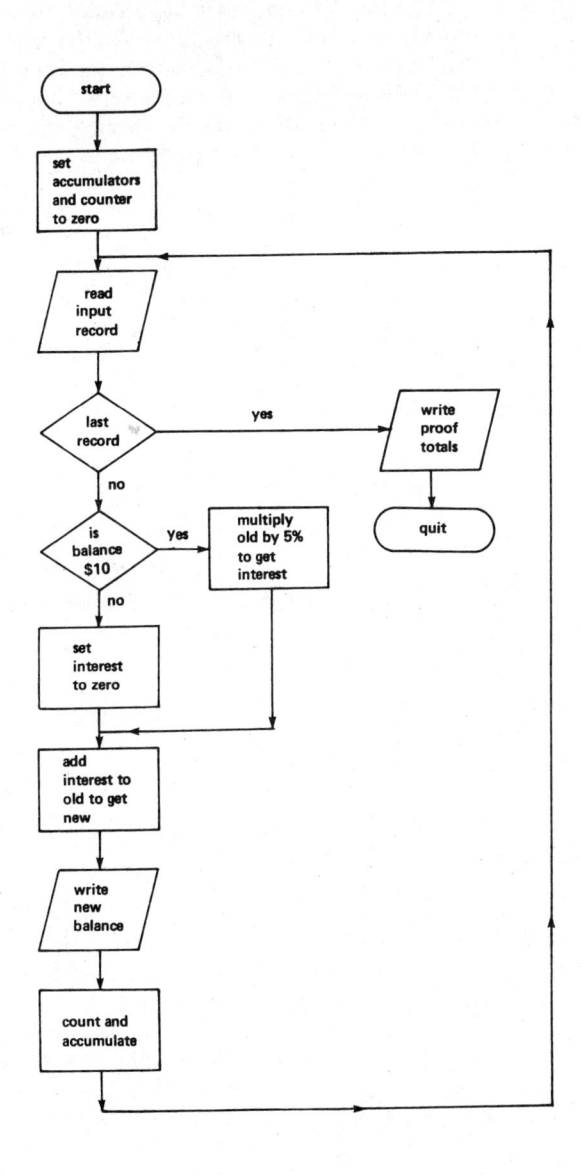

On output, we wish to list on a single line the account number, old balance, interest earned, and new balance. We know that the account number is 8 characters long. The old balance contains 7 digits; for clarity, we will almost certainly want to insert a decimal point and a comma to identify the thousands position, bringing the total up to 9 characters. The new balance will be the same number of characters as the old balance.* Interest is less than 10% of the old balance, so we can safely assume that we need a 6-digit number; allowing for a comma and a decimal point yields 8 print positions.

The definition of output format is rather arbitrary; we'll examine this in more detail later in the chapter. Let's just lay out a rough line in which the fields are separated by a reasonable number of blanks, as follows:

positions	contents
1-5	blank
6-13	account number from input record
14-17	blank
18-26	old balance (99,999.99) from input
27-32	blank
33-40	interest (9,999.99); computed
41-47	blank
48-56	new balance (99,999.99); computed
57-133	blank

Note that we've added a few things. The format of each field has been described in the manner of a COBOL PICTURE clause by simply writing the maximum possible value using all 9's, a decimal point, and commas. This is a very reasonable and clear way to describe data format. Also, to the right of each field, we have indicated the source of the information to be printed in that field—either input or computed. This is nothing but a little memory jog; by going through this exercise, we are clearly indicating that we know the exact source of each field.

Having defined the input and output records, we can now turn our attention to the work fields. We need fields to hold interest and new balance; these fields are 6-digits and 7-digits respectively. We also need fields to hold the required proof

---

*Note: 99,999.99 times 5% is 5000.00. Adding this interest to the old balance would, of course, generate a new balance in excess of 7 digits. We are assuming (based on past records, perhaps) that this cannot occur.

totals. These are accumulators, and their size is dependent on the number of values to be accumulated; obviously, we need a bigger accumulator for a thousand values than would be needed for ten or twelve. Thus it is necessary to make some assumptions in deciding on the size of the accumulators needed to hold the proof totals. We might assume a maximum of 1000 records, for example. With no more than 1000 records possible, the maximum value of any one old balance, 99,999.99, would dictate a maximum value of 99,999,999.99 (again, using 9's, a decimal point, and commas) for the old balance accumulator. As a result of our deliberations, we might come up with the following work fields:

Field name	Maximum value
interest	9999V99
new balance	99999V99
count of accounts	9999
old balance accumulator	99999999V99
interest accumulator	9999999V99
new balance accumulator	99999999V99

WRITING THE COBOL PROGRAM

Having defined the input and output devices, the data formats, and the program logic, we are ready to begin coding a solution in COBOL.

The IDENTIFICATION DIVISION (Fig. 5.2) is essentially as it was before. Only the program name and the REMARKS are different. This is a different program and the name and remarks should reflect its function. The ENVIRONMENT DIVSION is also similar to the one we used in the average program; once again, however, the programmer-defined names have been customized to this new program (Fig. 5.3).

The structure of the DATA DIVISION is also similar to that of the program developed in Chapters 1 through 4. Note that the PICTURE clauses used in both the FILE SECTION and the WORKING-STORAGE section closely match the data formats described on preceeding pages (Fig. 5.4).

There is one major difference in the DATA DIVISION of this program, however. Look at the data structures following the FD entry for the output file. There are *two* 01-level entries, each with its own lower level entries. That's because there are two different kinds of output records. The first type, coded first, is a **detail record**, and is printed during each program cycle. This detail record is designed to hold the results of computations on a single account; in more general terms, one detail record will be written for each and every input record read by the program.

The second 01-level entry marks the beginning of a **summary line**, in this case, the line that holds the values of all the accumulators and counters maintained in this

COBOL Coding Form

SYSTEM	SAVINGS ACCOUNTS	PUNCHING INSTRUCTIONS		PAGE 1 OF 6
PROGRAM	INTEREST EARNED	GRAPHIC	∅	CARD FORM #
PROGRAMMER	DAVIS & FISHER — DATE 1-20-79	PUNCH	ZERO	

```
       IDENTIFICATION DIVISION.
        PROGRAM-ID.  INTEREST.
        AUTHOR.      DAVIS & FISHER.
        REMARKS.     THIS PROGRAM COMPUTES AND PRINTS THE INTEREST
                     EARNED ON A NUMBER OF SAVINGS ACCOUNTS. INTEREST
                     IS COMPUTED AT 5%. NO INTEREST IS ADDED UNLESS
                     THE ACCOUNT BALANCE IS AT LEAST $10.00.


       ENVIRONMENT DIVISION.
        CONFIGURATION SECTION.
         SOURCE-COMPUTER.   IBM-370-148.
         OBJECT-COMPUTER.   IBM-370-148.
         SPECIAL-NAMES.     C01 IS NEW-PAGE.
        INPUT-OUTPUT SECTION.
         FILE-CONTROL.
             SELECT CUSTOMER-FILE   ASSIGN TO UT-S-CUSFILE.
             SELECT CUSTOMER-REPORT ASSIGN TO UT-S-CUSREPT.
```

Fig. 5.2: *The IDENTIFICATION DIVISION.*

Fig. 5.3: *The ENVIRONMENT DIVISION.*

COBOL Coding Form

SYSTEM	SAVINGS ACCOUNTS	PUNCHING INSTRUCTIONS	PAGE 2 OF 6
PROGRAM	INTEREST EARNED	GRAPHIC Ø / PUNCH ZERO	CARD FORM #
PROGRAMMER	DAVIS & FISHER	DATE 1-20-79	

```
       DATA DIVISION.
        FILE SECTION.

         FD  CUSTOMER-FILE
             LABEL RECORD OMITTED.
           Ø1  CUSTOMER-RECORD.
               Ø5  I-ACCOUNT-NUMBER         PIC  X(8).
               Ø5  I-OLD-BALANCE            PIC  99999V99.
               Ø5  FILLER                   PIC  X(65).

         FD  CUSTOMER-REPORT
             LABEL RECORD OMITTED.
           Ø1  REPORT-LINE.
               Ø5  FILLER                   PIC  X(5).
               Ø5  O-ACCOUNT-NO             PIC  X(8).
               Ø5  FILLER                   PIC  X(4).
               Ø5  O-OLD-BALANCE            PIC  ZZ,ZZ9.99.
               Ø5  FILLER                   PIC  X(6).
               Ø5  O-INTEREST-EARNED        PIC  Z,ZZ9.99.
               Ø5  FILLER                   PIC  X(7).
               Ø5  O-NEW-BALANCE            PIC  ZZ,ZZ9.99.
               Ø5  FILLER                   PIC  X(77).
```

Fig. 5.4: *The DATA DIVISION*

COBOL Coding Form

SYSTEM	SAVINGS ACCOUNTS		PUNCHING INSTRUCTIONS		PAGE 3 OF 6
PROGRAM	INTEREST EARNED		GRAPHIC Ø		
PROGRAMMER	DAVIS & FISHER	DATE 1-20-79	PUNCH ZERO	CARD FORM #	

```
Ø1  SUMMARY-PRINT-LINE.
    Ø5  FILLER                    PIC X(13).
    Ø5  S-OLD-BALANCES            PIC ZZ,ZZZ,ZZ9.99.
    Ø5  FILLER                    PIC XX.
    Ø5  S-INTEREST-EARNED         PIC Z,ZZZ,ZZ9.99.
    Ø5  FILLER                    PIC X(4).
    Ø5  S-NEW-BALANCES            PIC ZZ,ZZZ,ZZ9.99.
    Ø5  FILLER                    PIC X(4).
    Ø5  S-NO-OF-ACCOUNTS          PIC ZZZ9.
    Ø5  FILLER                    PIC X(69).

WORKING-STORAGE SECTION.
77  INTEREST                      PIC 9999V99.
77  NEW-BALANCE                   PIC 9999V99.
77  SUM-OF-OLD-BALANCES           PIC 999999V99.
77  SUM-OF-NEW-BALANCES           PIC 999999V99.
77  SUM-OF-INTEREST               PIC 999999V99.
77  NUMBER-OF-ACCOUNTS            PIC 9999.
```

Fig. 5.4: *The DATA DIVISION*

program. A summary line is *not* printed during every program cycle. In this example, the summary line is printed only once, just before the program terminates. Later, we'll see examples of other summary lines printed at major program break points.

Why code both output lines as part of the same FD-entry? Both lines go to the same file. It makes sense to code them together.

Finally, we come to the PROCEDURE DIVISION (Fig. 5.5). Since most of the instructions have already been fully described in Chapter 3, you should have very little trouble following the logic. The program begins with a paragraph named HOUSEKEEPING. In this paragraph, files are opened and the accumulators and counter are set equal to zero. As before, the HOUSEKEEPING paragraph contains all those functions that must be performed once, before the program can begin.

The second paragraph holds the program's **mainline**, the real heart of the program. These instructions are executed over and over again to accomplish the primary function of this program—in this case, to update savings accounts. Secondary functions such as the start-of-job housekeeping and end-of-job cleanup tasks are needed to support this mainline; they are not themselves primary. Typically (not always, but typically), the mainline is composed of an input operation, the processing of the data in this record, the writing of a detail output record, and a branch back to the beginning of the mainline.

Note that the idea of structure has been imposed within the mainline too, with the steps to update a current account balance and the steps which accumulate and count totals treated as two separate functions. The idea of grouping related functions seems intuitively obvious, is very easy to implement, and pays immeasurable documentation dividends.

There is one new instruction in the mainline (Fig. 5.5), the **IF** statement. It is through the IF statement that the programmer implements the computer's yes/no logic capability. The general form of this instruction is

    IF condition   THEN statement-1   ELSE statement-2.

The IF statement revolves around a **condition**. This condition involves the comparison of two fields—two data fields as defined in the DATA DIVISION, or one data field and a constant. Let's say, to cite an example, that we have two fields called A and B. Some of the conditions we can set up include

    IF A IS EQUAL TO B ...

    IF A IS NOT EQUAL TO B ...

    IF A IS LESS THAN B ...

    IF A IS NOT LESS THAN B ...

    IF A IS GREATER THAN B ...

    IF A IS NOT GREATER THAN B ...

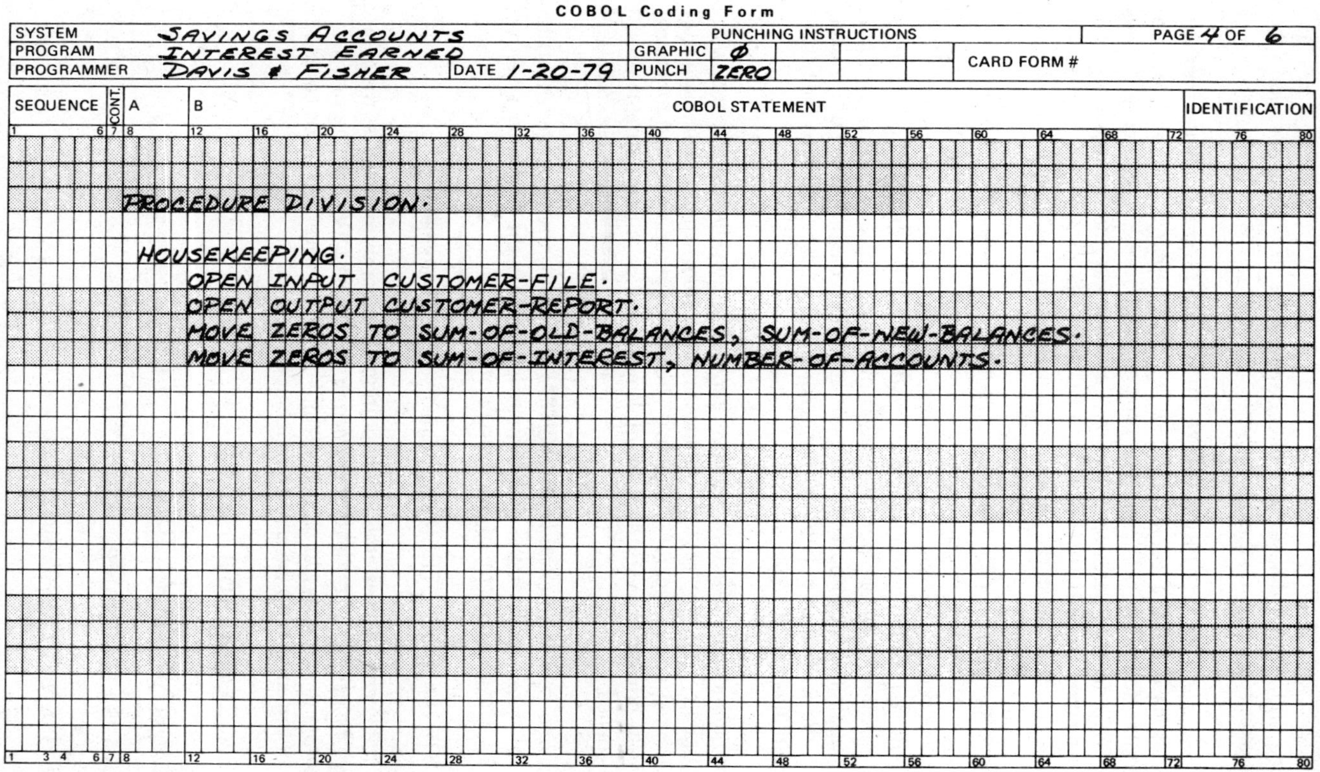

COBOL Coding Form

SYSTEM SAVINGS ACCOUNTS — PROGRAM INTEREST EARNED — PROGRAMMER DAVIS & FISHER — DATE 1-20-79

PUNCHING INSTRUCTIONS: GRAPHIC Ø — PUNCH ZERO — PAGE 4 OF 6 — CARD FORM #

SEQUENCE | CONT. | A | B | COBOL STATEMENT | IDENTIFICATION

```
       PROCEDURE DIVISION.

        HOUSEKEEPING.
           OPEN INPUT  CUSTOMER-FILE.
           OPEN OUTPUT CUSTOMER-REPORT.
           MOVE ZEROS TO SUM-OF-OLD-BALANCES, SUM-OF-NEW-BALANCES.
           MOVE ZEROS TO SUM-OF-INTEREST, NUMBER-OF-ACCOUNTS.
```

Fig. 5.5: *The PROCEDURE DIVISION.*

```
SYSTEM      SAVINGS ACCOUNTS
PROGRAM     INTEREST EARNED
PROGRAMMER  DAVIS & FISHER      DATE 1-20-79
GRAPHIC
PUNCH  ZERO Ø
PAGE 5 OF 6

    START-OF-MAINLINE.
        READ CUSTOMER-FILE
            AT END GO TO END-OF-JOB-ROUTINE.
        ADD 1 TO NUMBER-OF-ACCOUNTS.
        IF I-OLD-BALANCE IS GREATER THAN 10.00
        THEN
            MULTIPLY I-OLD-BALANCE BY 0.05 GIVING INTEREST
        ELSE
            MOVE ZERO TO INTEREST.
        MOVE SPACES TO REPORT-LINE.
        MOVE INTEREST TO O-INTEREST-EARNED.
        ADD INTEREST TO SUM-OF-INTEREST.
        ADD I-OLD-BALANCE TO SUM-OF-OLD-BALANCES.
        ADD I-OLD-BALANCE, INTEREST GIVING NEW-BALANCE.
        ADD NEW-BALANCE TO SUM-OF-NEW-BALANCES.
        MOVE I-ACCOUNT-NUMBER TO O-ACCOUNT-NUMBER.
        MOVE I-OLD-BALANCE TO O-OLD-BALANCE.
        MOVE NEW-BALANCE TO O-NEW-BALANCE.
        WRITE REPORT-LINE
            AFTER ADVANCING 2 LINES.
        GO TO START-OF-MAINLINE.
```

Fig. 5.5: *The PROCEDURE DIVISION, continued.*

COBOL Coding Form

SYSTEM	SAVINGS ACCOUNTS	PUNCHING INSTRUCTIONS	PAGE 6 OF 6
PROGRAM	INTEREST EARNED	GRAPHIC Ø	CARD FORM #
PROGRAMMER	DAVIS & FISHER — DATE 1-20-79	PUNCH ZERO	

```
       END-OF-JOB-ROUTINE.
           MOVE SPACES                  TO SUMMARY-PRINT-LINE.
           MOVE SUM-OF-OLD-BALANCES     TO S-OLD-BALANCES.
           MOVE SUM-OF-NEW-BALANCES     TO S-NEW-BALANCES.
           MOVE SUM-OF-INTEREST         TO S-INTEREST-EARNED.
           MOVE NUMBER-OF-ACCOUNTS      TO S-NO-OF-ACCOUNTS.
           WRITE SUMMARY-PRINT-LINE
                       AFTER ADVANCING 2 LINES.
           CLOSE CUSTOMER-FILE.
           CLOSE CUSTOMER-REPORT.
           STOP RUN.
```

Fig. 5.5: *The PROCEDURE DIVISION. (Con't.)*

It is also possible to code complex conditions, such as

    IF A IS EQUAL TO B OR A IS LESS THAN B . . .

As a beginning programmer, however, you might want to stay away from complex conditions until after you have mastered the basic ones.

    All these conditions have one thing in common; the condition either is or is not met. Either A is equal to B, or it isn't. Either A is less than B, or it isn't. In most reference manuals, the condition is said to be either true or false.

    Let's now return to the general form of an IF statement

    IF condition THEN statement-1   ELSE statement-2.

Statement-1 and statement-2 are simply COBOL statements—ADD, SUBRACT, MULTIPLY, DIVIDE, MOVE, READ, WRITE, even another IF. If the condition is true, statement-1 is executed and statement-2 is skipped. If the condition is false, statement-1 is skipped and statement-2 is executed.

    Look at the IF statement in Fig. 5.5 as an example. It says

    IF I-OLD-BALANCE IS GREATER THAN 10.00

        THEN

            MULTIPLY OLD-BALANCE BY 0.05 GIVING INTEREST

    ELSE

        MOVE ZERO TO INTEREST.

The IF statement means exactly what it says. If the condition (I-OLD-BALANCE IS GREATER THAN 10.00) is true, then interest is computed at a 5% rate. Else, if the condition is false, the value zero is moved to interest. In this way, the bank's rule, "Pay interest only if the old balance exceeds $10.00.", can be implemented.

    This particular block of logic is sometimes called an **IF. . . THEN. . . ELSE** block. In the flowchart of Fig. 5.6, we begin with the program mainline. A condition is encountered. If the condition is true, logic continues down the THEN path. If the condition is false, logic moves to the right over the ELSE path, rejoining the mainline after the THEN logic. A good way to remember how this logic block works is to remember the following statement:

    IF condition is true then do this;

        else do this instead.

Although it is possible to structure a COBOL IF statement in ways that do not follow this IF. . . THEN. . . ELSE model, our usual practice will be to follow the model.

Fig. 5.6: IF...
THEN...
ELSE...
logic block.

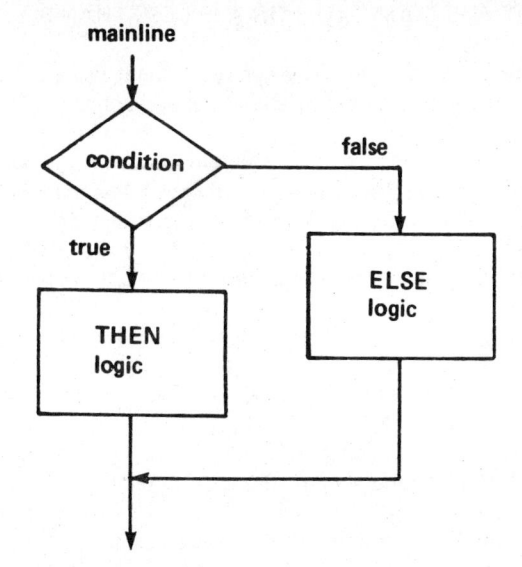

We have consistently used the word THEN in coding our IF statements; not all versions of COBOL support the use of the word THEN. If yours does not, simply skip the word. By clearly identifying the action to be taken when a condition is true, THEN improves documentation.

Following the mainline is a paragraph containing a number of functions that are to be followed at the end of the job. All accumulators and the counter are moved from WORKING-STORAGE into the output line as defined in the FILE SECTION, and the summary line is sent to the printer. Once this has been done, the files can be closed and the program can be ended.

Editing Output Data

You may have noticed a slight difference between the way the output was handled on the average program and the way we just handled it here. On the average program, the computed average was defined as part of the output line; we simply computed it, placing the answer in the output line as part of the divide instruction, and then issued a WRITE. In this program, interest, the new balance, and the accumulators were first set up in WORKING-STORAGE and then moved to the output line following all the computations. Why was it necessary to use these intermediate fields? Why couldn't the interest, new balance, and accumulators be simply set up as part of the output line, with this field being used in computations?

Look closely at the PICTURE clauses of the interest, new balance, and accumulator fields as coded in the DATA DIVISION, FILE SECTION. They contain commas and actual decimal points. These are known as **edit characters**. To add clarity to the output, it is desirable that these characters be included in the printed output—commas and a decimal point do make it much easier to read numeric quantities. Once these edit characters have been added to a field, however, that field can no longer be used in computations. The result of a computation can be assigned to an edited field, but that field cannot itself be used in arithmetic.

In this program, the computed interest will subsequently be used in finding the new balance. Thus the computed interest must be stored in a field containing *only* 9's and the implied decimal point (V) as a PICTURE clause. (There is also an implied sign, an S, to be covered later.) This field has been set up in WORKING-STORAGE. It is also desirable to print this field with proper punctuation; thus the field as defined for output contains commas and a decimal point, and the value is moved from WORKING-STORAGE to the output line prior to printing. A similar argument could be made for any of the other fields, in that all are involved in one or more computations prior to output. On the average program, the computed average was simply printed, participating in no other computations after it was found; thus we were not concerned about keeping it in an unedited state.

These edit characters are very easy to use. Let's say that we have to print an eight digit number with two digits to the right of the decimal point. Begin by writing the eight digits

$$99999999$$

as a pattern of 9's—this is simply the biggest possible 8-digit number. Now, add a decimal point where it belongs:

$$999999.99$$

The standard rule for punctuating a number is to break that number into groups of 3 digits each; following this standard rule, we get

$$999,999.99$$

The result is a properly punctuated COBOL PICTURE clause. There is really no secret. Just write the biggest number you could possibly have, punctuate it properly, and the PICTURE clause is finished.

Don't forget that the commas and the decimal point will be physically printed, and that space will be consumed in the output line; in other words, the 8-digit number 999,999.99 will take up not 8 but 10 print positions. Also, don't forget that no field containing edit characters may be used in computations.

There is one more PICTURE edit character that we should discuss at this time. Consider the number 250. Using the PICTURE clause described above, this number would be printed as 000,250.00. Almost never are those leading, insignificant zeros printed. Ideally, the computer should print   250.00, with blanks replacing the leading zeros and the comma. By using a **zero surpression** character, a Z, we can cause the computer to do exactly this. The PICTURE clause

```
         1                    12.35.57        SEP 16,1978



00003            IDENTIFICATION DIVISION.

00005                PROGRAM-ID.   INTEREST.
00006                AUTHOR.       DAVIS & FISHER.

00008                REMARKS.    THIS PROGRAM COMPUTES AND PRINTS THE INTEREST
00009                            EARNED ON A NUMBER OF SAVINGS ACCOUNTS. INTEREST
00010                            IS COMPUTED AT 5%.  NO INTEREST IS ADDED UNLESS
00011                            THE ACCOUNT BALANCE IS AT LEAST 10.00.


00014            ENVIRONMENT DIVISION.

00016                CONFIGURATION SECTION.

00018                SOURCE-COMPUTER.   IBM-370-148.
00019                OBJECT-COMPUTER.   IBM-370-148.
00020                SPECIAL-NAMES.     C01 IS NEW-PAGE.

00022                INPUT-OUTPUT SECTION.

00024                FILE-CONTROL.
00025                    SELECT CUSTOMER-FILE    ASSIGN TO UT-S-CUSFILE.
00026                    SELECT CUSTOMER-REPORT  ASSIGN TO UT-S-CUSREPT.
```

Fig. 5.7: *A listing of the interest program.*

```
   2        INTEREST       12.35.57       SEP 16,1978


00029           DATA DIVISION.
00031           FILE SECTION.
00033              FD  CUSTOMER-FILE
00034                  LABEL RECORD OMITTED.
00035              01  CUSTOMER-RECORD.
00036                  05  I-ACCOUNT-NUMBER       PIC X(8).
00037                  05  I-OLD-BALANCE          PIC 99999V99.
00038                  05  FILLER       .         PIC X(65).

00040              FD  CUSTOMER-REPORT
00041                  LABEL RECORD OMITTED.
00042              01  REPORT-LINE.
00043                  05  FILLER                 PIC X(5).
00044                  05  O-ACCOUNT-NUMBER       PIC X(8).
00045                  05  FILLER                 PIC X(4).
00046                  05  O-OLD-BALANCE          PIC ZZ,ZZ9.99.
00047                  05  FILLER                 PIC X(6).
00048                  05  O-INTEREST-EARNED      PIC Z,ZZ9.99.
00049                  05  FILLER                 PIC X(7).
00050                  05  O-NEW-BALANCE          PIC ZZ,ZZ9.99.
00051                  05  FILLER                 PIC X(77).
00052              01  SUMMARY-PRINT-LINE.
00053                  05  FILLER                 PIC X(13).
00054                  05  S-OLD-BALANCES         PIC ZZ,ZZZ,ZZ9.99.
00055                  05  FILLER                 PIC XX.
00056                  05  S-INTEREST-EARNED      PIC Z,ZZZ,ZZ9.99.
00057                  05  FILLER                 PIC X(4).
00058                  05  S-NEW-BALANCES         PIC ZZ,ZZZ,ZZ9.99.
00059                  05  FILLER                 PIC X(4).
00060                  05  S-NO-OF-ACCOUNTS       PIC ZZZ9.
00061                  05  FILLER                 PIC X(69).


00064           WORKING-STORAGE SECTION.

00066              77  INTEREST                   PIC 9999V99.
00067              77  NEW-BALANCE                PIC 99999V99.
00068              77  SUM-OF-OLD-BALANCES        PIC 99999999V99.
00069              77  SUM-OF-NEW-BALANCES        PIC 99999999V99.
00070              77  SUM-OF-INTEREST            PIC 9999999V99.
00071              77  NUMBER-OF-ACCOUNTS         PIC 9999.
```

Fig. 5.7: *Program listing for the interest problem. (Con't.)*

```
3          INTEREST        12.35.57        SEP 16,1978


00074              PROCEDURE DIVISION.
00076              HOUSEKEEPING.
00078                  OPEN INPUT   CUSTOMER-FILE.
00079                  OPEN OUTPUT  CUSTOMER-REPORT.
00080                  MOVE ZEROS TO SUM-OF-OLD-BALANCES, SUM-OF-NEW-BALANCES.
00081                  MOVE ZEROS TO SUM-OF-INTEREST, NUMBER-OF-ACCOUNTS.

00083              START-OF-MAINLINE.

00085                  READ CUSTOMER-FILE
00086                        AT END GO TO END-OF-JOB-ROUTINE.
00087                  ADD  1  TO NUMBER-OF-ACCOUNTS.
00088                  IF I-OLD-BALANCE IS GREATER THAN 10.00
00089                  THEN
00090                        MULTIPLY I-OLD-BALANCE BY 0.05 GIVING INTEREST
00091                  ELSE
00092                      MOVE ZERO TO INTEREST.

00094                  MOVE SPACES    TO REPORT-LINE.
00095                  MOVE INTEREST TO O-INTEREST-EARNED.

00097                  ADD  INTEREST       TO SUM-OF-INTEREST.
00098                  ADD  I-OLD-BALANCE TO SUM-OF-OLD-BALANCES.
00099                  ADD  I-OLD-BALANCE, INTEREST GIVING   NEW-BALANCE.
00100                  ADD  NEW-BALANCE    TO SUM-OF-NEW-BALANCES.

00102                  MOVE I-ACCOUNT-NUMBER TO O-ACCOUNT-NUMBER.
00103                  MOVE I-OLD-BALANCE       TO O-OLD-BALANCE.
00104                  MOVE NEW-BALANCE         TO O-NEW-BALANCE.
00105                  WRITE REPORT-LINE
00106                         AFTER ADVANCING 2 LINES.
00107                  GO TO START-OF-MAINLINE.

00109              END-OF-JOB-ROUTINE.

00111                  MOVE SPACES                TO SUMMARY-PRINT-LINE.
00112                  MOVE SUM-OF-OLD-BALANCES TO S-OLD-BALANCES.
00113                  MOVE SUM-OF-NEW-BALANCES TO S-NEW-BALANCES.
00114                  MOVE SUM-OF-INTEREST      TO S-INTEREST-EARNED.
00115                  MOVE NUMBER-OF-ACCOUNTS  TO S-NO-OF-ACCOUNTS.

00117                  WRITE SUMMARY-PRINT-LINE
00118                        AFTER ADVANCING 2 LINES.
00119                  CLOSE CUSTOMER-FILE.
00120                  CLOSE CUSTOMER-REPORT.
00121                  STOP RUN.
```

Fig. 5.7: *Program listing for the interest problem. (Con't.)*

11111111	500.00	25.00	525.00	
22222222	6,000.00	300.00	6,300.00	
33333333	50,000.00	2,500.00	52,500.00	
44444444	100.00	5.00	105.00	
55555555	15,000.00	750.00	15,750.00	
66666666	75.00	3.75	78.75	
77777777	9,000.00	450.00	9,450.00	
	80,675.00	4,033.75	84,708.75	7

Fig. 5.7: *A listing of the interest program—program output.*

ZZZ,ZZ9.99

would cause leading zeros to be surpressed; as soon as the first significant digit is encountered, however, the Z's begin to work just like 9's. Why was a 9 placed just in front of the decimal point? Because 0.25 is easier to read than .25, and, on some versions of COBOL, 0.25 would be printed as 25 if the programmer had not clearly indicated (by coding a 9 in front of the decimal point) that this units position digit is to be printed no matter what its value. Note that, when using zero surpression, nothing (including leading commas or decimal points) is printed until the first "9" or the first significant digit is encountered.

There are a number of other edit characters available in COBOL. Several will be introduced in subsequent chapters when we encounter a need for them.

A Summary of the Savings Account Program

To this point in Chapter 5, we have defined, planned, and written a program to update a set of savings accounts. It's time to keypunch our solution and submit it to the computer; a program listing and sample output data are shown in Fig. 5.7.

Look at the output for a moment. If you hadn't just finished reading about how the program had been developed and what the output line was to contain, would you have any way of knowing what the output means? Of course not, it's just a collection of unidentified numbers. Real computer output is almost never presented in such an unclear form. Invariably, a **header** at the top of each page clearly identifies the subject of the information on the page, and a set of **column headers** clearly identifies the content of each column of figures. The report shown in Fig. 5.8 is much better. How can we cause the computer to print such neat, easy to follow reports?

Neat, well-designed reports can be printed under computer control if (and only if) the programmer, through program instructions, tells the computer to set up and print these headers. Over the next several pages, we'll be describing just how the programmer might go about doing this.

Fig. 5.8: *A formatted report with column headers.*

	CUSTOMER ACCOUNTS		
ACCOUNT NO.	OLD BALANCE	INTEREST EARNED	NEW BALANCE
11111111	500.00	25.00	525.00
22222222	6,000.00	300.00	6,300.00
33333333	50,000.00	2,500.00	52,500.00
44444444	100.00	5.00	105.00
55555555	15,000.00	750.00	15,750.00
66666666	75.00	3.75	78.75
77777777	9,000.00	450.00	9,450.00
88888888	100.00	5.00	105.00
99999999	500.00	25.00	525.00
12222222	25,000.00	1,250.00	26,250.00
13333333	12,000.00	600.00	12,600.00

DEFINING HEADERS AND THE PAGE FORMAT

As is the case with any phase of programming, the programmer must know exactly what must be done before he or she can tell the computer how to do it. This means careful planning—planning that *preceeds* actual coding. Often, the programmer uses a page spacing chart similar to the one shown in Fig. 5.9, carefully laying out the position of each field and its corresponding header. Are there any rules for laying out such headers as the ones shown in Fig. 5.9? No. It's basically a matter of personal choice, with the only real rule: If it looks good, it is. Designing the format of an output page is more an art than a science.

There are some guidelines, of course. The top-of-page header is normally centered over the individual column headers. A margin an inch or so wide (8-10 spaces) is normally used on the left edge of the form, with the right margin as large or as small as necessary. Four or five spaces are normally left between columns; if there are only a handful of columns, it is not essential that the entire width of the form be used. Ideally, a column header and the information to be written in that column (write the biggest possible value, or the PICTURE clause under the header) are roughly the same size, with lengthy headers being spread over two or more lines. These are, however, just guidelines. The acid test is the appearance of the output page. Is it attractive? Is it easy to read? If not, it's wrong.

The output format for the savings account report has been laid out in Fig. 5.9. Note that a page header, coded at the top of the form, clearly identifies the subject of the information printed on the form. Individual column headers identify the content of each column. Under the header, a number or a pattern of X's has been written; this is the PICTURE clause used within the COBOL program to describe the field. By writing the biggest possible value beneath the header, the relationship between the header and the data is clearly established. Finally, note that (last line) the format for the summary line has also been clearly defined; since the fields are bigger than their counterparts in the main body of the report, the field definitions are bound to be different.

Defining Headers in the DATA DIVISION

We now know exactly what the headers are going to look like, and its time to begin coding them in COBOL. Obviously, the header is a form of output data. Output data records are defined in the DATA DIVISION.

There is, however, something different about a header. In a regular data record, the structure of the record is defined, and the actual values of each of the fields are filled in by input, as the result of a computation, or through a MOVE verb. A header, however, is composed mostly of constants; in other words, almost all the characters are fully known before the program ever begins. Otherwise the format of a header is similar to the format of any other output line: a structure beginning with a 02-level entry, followed by associated fields having higher numbers. The fact that each field must be given an initial value means that a header cannot be defined in the FILE SECTION of the DATA DIVISION. Instead, a structure must be set up in the WORKING-STORAGE SECTION.

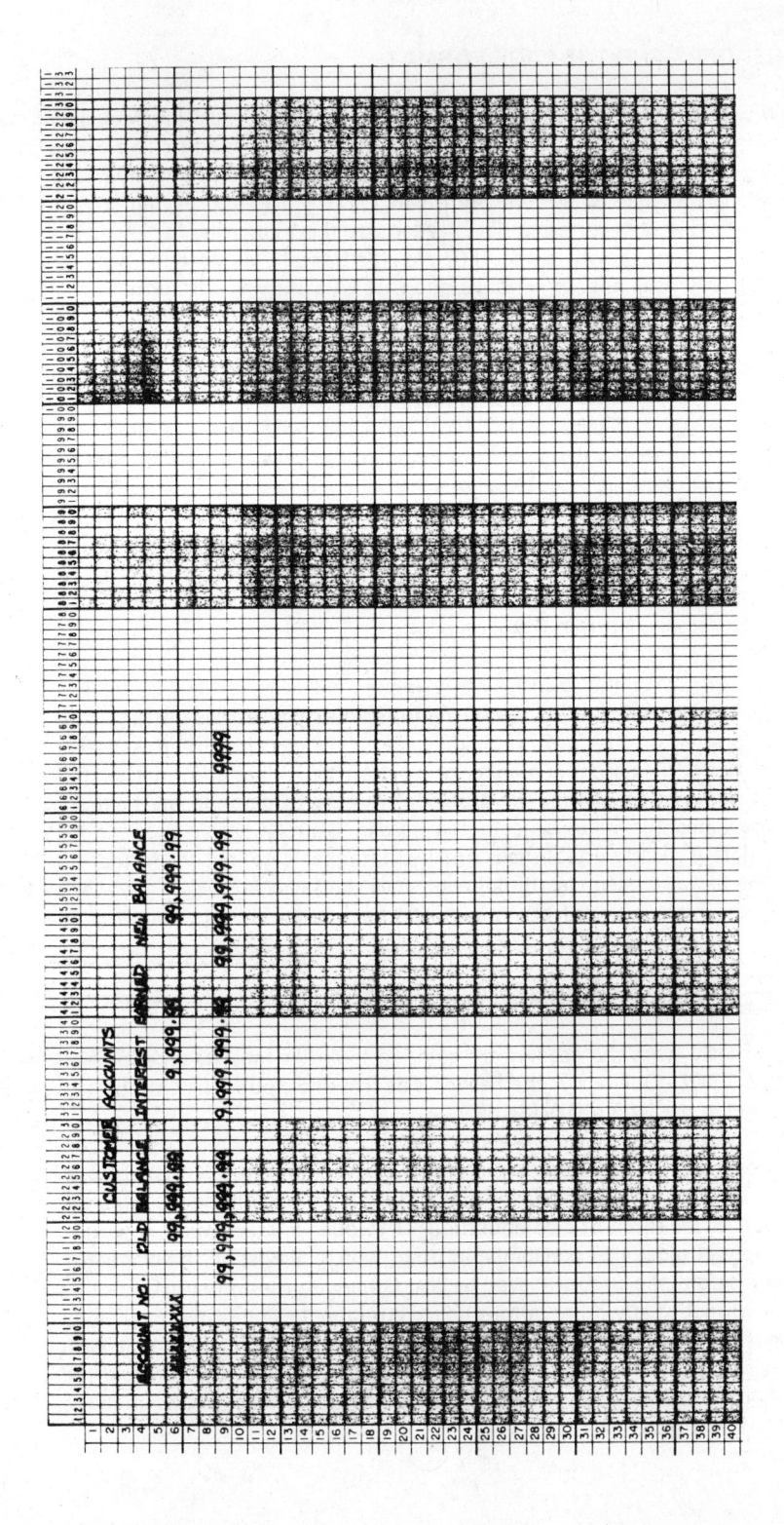

Fig. 5.9: *Output format for a savings account report.*

COBOL Coding Form

SYSTEM	SAVINGS ACCOUNTS		PUNCHING INSTRUCTIONS		PAGE 4 OF 7
PROGRAM	INTEREST EARNED		GRAPHIC	Ø	CARD FORM #
PROGRAMMER	DAVIS & FISHER	DATE 1-25-79	PUNCH	ZERO	

```
       WORKING-STORAGE SECTION.
           77  INTEREST                PIC 9999V99.
           77  NEW-BALANCE             PIC 99999V99.
           77  SUM-OF-OLD-BALANCES     PIC 99999999V99.
           77  SUM-OF-NEW-BALANCES     PIC 99999999V99.
           77  SUM-OF-INTEREST         PIC 9999999V99.
           77  NUMBER-OF-ACCOUNTS      PIC 9999.
           77  LINE-COUNT              PIC 99.

           Ø1  REPORT-HEADER.
               Ø5  FILLER      PIC X(22)   VALUE SPACES.
               Ø5  FILLER      PIC X(17)   VALUE 'CUSTOMER ACCOUNTS'.
               Ø5  FILLER      PIC X(94)   VALUE SPACES.

           Ø1  COLUMN-HEADERS.
               Ø5  FILLER      PIC X(4)    VALUE SPACES.
               Ø5  FILLER      PIC X(11)   VALUE 'ACCOUNT NO.'.
               Ø5  FILLER      PIC X(2)    VALUE SPACES.
               Ø5  FILLER      PIC X(11)   VALUE 'OLD BALANCE'.
               Ø5  FILLER      PIC X(2)    VALUE SPACES
               Ø5  FILLER      PIC X(15)   VALUE 'INTEREST EARNED'.
               Ø5  FILLER      PIC X(2)    VALUE SPACES.
               Ø5  FILLER      PIC X(11)   VALUE 'NEW BALANCE'.
               Ø5  FILLER      PIC X(75)   VALUE SPACES.
```

Fig. 5.10: *A New Version of the WORKING-STORAGE SECTION with Header Fields Coded.*

A complete set of headers corresponding to those defined in Fig. 5.9 has been coded in Fig. 5.10. Note that each header line is defined as a single, independent structure, beginning with a 01-level entry. These header lines are given names that correspond to their function or position on the page.

Within each of these structures, the individual fields are defined. What exactly does "field" mean when referring to a header? Basically, the header consists of a series of words or phrases separated by blanks. The simplest and surest way to define the content of the header is to treat each word or phrase as if it is a field, and to treat each set of blank characters as if it is a separate field. In Fig. 5.10, this procedure has been followed. Each piece of the header line is defined in a separate line of code. It doesn't have to be done this way; it is possible to define an entire header as a single COBOL statement by actually counting and inserting the proper number of blanks between the words in the header. However, trying to define too much in one statement invariably leads to error, makes it difficult to match the format of related lines, and complicates the process of modification, should changes to the format of a line be necessary.

The PICTURE clauses associated with each part of the header are all X's; no part of these fields will be used in any computation. The actual value or content of each part of the header is inserted by using a **VALUE IS** clause. The VALUE IS clause is simply a mechanism for indicating the value of constant information. By coding

    05 FILLER PICTURE X(7) VALUE IS 'ACCOUNT'.

the letters ACCOUNT are placed in this field during the compilation step, before the program actually begins to execute. The clause

    VALUE IS SPACES.

causes blanks to be inserted into the lines where indicated.

In the clause VALUE IS 'ACCOUNT', the word ACCOUNT is enclosed in a set of apostrophes or single quote marks (some versions of COBOL use the regular quote mark). This is an alphanumeric literal constant. Previously we discussed the difference between a numeric constant, a simple number, and a nonnumeric literal constant which must be enclosed between apostrophes; this is an example of the latter type of constant. With an X-type picture, the value must be an alphanumeric literal.

What if we were to code

    ... PICTURE X(8) VALUE IS 'ACCOUNT'.

The field is defined as being 8 characters in length, but the constant is only 7 characters long. No problem. Alphanumeric literal constants are padded to the right with blanks whenever a field as defined is bigger than the constant.

What if we were to define

    ... PICTURE X(5) VALUE IS 'ACCOUNT'

Now, the field is too short for the constant. Most versions of COBOL handle this problem by truncating the rightmost characters of the constant, storing, in this example, only ACCOU in the field. In coding headers, be very careful about matching field lengths and constant lengths, and if you must err, err on the "field too long" side.

Note (Fig. 5.10) that the COBOL reserved word FILLER is used as the data name for each of the fields in each of the headers. It is not our intent to refer to an individual header field. We will, of course, write the complete header, so the record must have a reasonable name, but the only reason for breaking the header into fields is to simplify coding and program maintenance. Almost never do we change the content of the header through a MOVE or computational instruction in the PROCEDURE DIVISION, so individualized data names are not needed.

It is important that each header line up with its associated column of data. The real purpose of the printer spacing form (Fig. 5.9) is to simplify the task of achieving this match. Once headers have been structured on such a form, the task of converting them to COBOL form is simply one of counting (feel free to use your fingers). Although it requires a bit more care, it is certainly possible to plan an ideal output page on plain, unlined paper; just take your time and be careful.

To achieve a balanced appearance, it may be necessary to go back and change the initial spacing of the detail and summary data lines. The fact that these were already coded is beside the point; the only thing that really counts is the appearance and correctness of the final output. If what you have coded is not right, then your code must change.

Designing and coding headers is tedious and time consuming, but it is not difficult. Except for the minor "artistic" challenge of designing a visually appealing format, there is no intellectual challenge to this task. Beginning students have a bad habit of assuming that "nothing can be that easy," and waste a great deal of time looking for the catch. There isn't any. The only secret to designing "good" output formats is to sit down and design formats, changing them if they don't look right. It's hard work, and there are no shortcuts. But there aren't any hidden catches either.

One final comment before we move on. The VALUE IS clause was coded in the WORKING-STORAGE SECTION. Why wasn't it coded in the FILE SECTION? In COBOL, a VALUE IS clause has no meaning in the FILE SECTION. The reasons for this are quite technical; given the assumption that students reading this text are beginners, a detailed explanation is beyond the scope of this book. Thus we'll simply say that the VALUE IS clause won't work in the FILE SECTION and, therefore, headers must be defined in WORKING-STORAGE.

Controlling Spacing on the Printer

It's not enough simply to define the headers; the exact position where each is printed on a paper form must be controlled too. The page header should be printed at the top of a page. Normally, two or three spaces will be skipped before printing the column headers. Perhaps two or three more spaces will be skipped before the printing of the detail lines begins. The number of lines printed on a page must be carefully controlled so as to leave a bottom margin, and a new set of headers must be printed at the top of each new page.

How can we control printer spacing? We've already encountered a certain amount of printer control, coding an AFTER ADVANCING clause as part of a WRITE statement, but more control is needed. Before we can understand how the programmer can control printer spacing, it is first necessary to have at least a basic understanding of the mechanism for physically controlling a printer.

Many printers are equipped with a special **carriage control tape**; the function of this tape is to control printer spacing. The tape is formed into a continuous loop; typically, the size of this loop corresponds (or is proportional) to the length of paper used in the printer. The tape is normally divided into 12 channels, numbered 1 through 12 respectively. Channel 1 is usually set aside for top of page controls. Other channels of the carriage control tape represent other spacing conditions. Channel 2, for example, might represent a "skip 1 line" condition, while channel 3 might hold a "skip 2 lines" condition. It is even possible to design a special carriage control tape to handle a special or unusual printing job, and this is often done.

Many modern printers have done away with the idea of a carriage control tape entirely, replacing this mechanism with a cassette or a special, programmable microcomputer. The basic idea, however, remains the same. Generally, to avoid problems of incompatibility, these newer control devices still allow the programmer to refer to channels, as if the old mechanism were still in place.

Defining Printer Controls in COBOL

You've already seen the AFTER ADVANCING clause. This clause automatically sets up the proper communication with the printer control mechanism for certain standard spacing requirements. The AFTER ADVANCING clause works well when a spacing of 1, 2, or 3 lines is needed. The clause, AFTER ADVANCING 0 LINES, at least on most systems, means exactly what it says: print without skipping; this clause is sometimes used to allow for the underlining of a header. On some systems, however, AFTER ADVANCING 0 LINES is used to send the printer to the top of a page, so be careful.

What if we want something other than a standard skip of 1, 2, or 3 lines? Then it becomes the programmer's responsibility to tell the printer what carriage control channel to skip to. The printer control mechanism is external to the program. All external linkages are defined in the ENVIRONMENT DIVISION.

In the ENVIRONMENT DIVISION, as part of the CONFIGURATION SECTION, is a paragraph called **SPECIAL-NAMES**. Within this paragraph the link between the program and the carriage control channels is established (Fig. 5.11). The names CO1 through C12 represent channels 01 through 12 respectively. By coding CO1 IS NEW-PAGE, we have indicated that, when NEW-PAGE is part of an AFTER ADVANCING clause in the program, we want the printer to skip to carriage control channel 1.

COBOL Coding Form

SYSTEM SAVINGS ACCOUNTS	PUNCHING INSTRUCTIONS		PAGE 1 OF 7
PROGRAM INTEREST EARNED	GRAPHIC Ø		CARD FORM #
PROGRAMMER DAVIS & FISHER	DATE 1-25-79	PUNCH ZERO	

```
SEQUENCE |CONT.| A   B                    COBOL STATEMENT                                IDENTIFICATION
1       6  7   8   12  16  20  24  28  32  36  40  44  48  52  56  60  64  68  72  76  80

       IDENTIFICATION DIVISION.
        PROGRAM-ID. INTEREST.
        AUTHOR.         DAVIS & FISHER.
        REMARKS.        THIS PROGRAM COMPUTES AND PRINT THE INTEREST
                        EARNED ON A NUMBER OF SAVINGS ACCOUNTS. INTEREST
                        IS COMPUTED AT 5%. NO INTEREST IS ADDED UNLESS
                        THE ACCOUNT BALANCE IS AT LEAST $10.00. CONTROLS
                        HAVE BEEN ADDED TO PRINT PAGE HEADINGS AT THE
                        TOP OF EACH PAGE.



       ENVIRONMENT DIVISION.
        CONFIGURATION SECTION.
         SOURCE-COMPUTER.   IBM-370-148.
         OBJECT-COMPUTER.   IBM-370-148.
         SPECIAL-NAMES.     C01 IS NEW-PAGE.
        INPUT-OUTPUT SECTION.
         FILE-CONTROL.
           SELECT CUSTOMER-FILE   ASSIGN TO UT-S-CUSFILE.
           SELECT CUSTOMER-REPORT ASSIGN TO UT-S-CUSREPT.
```

Fig. 5.11: *The CONFIGURATION SECTION with a SPECIAL-NAMES paragraph.*

PROCEDURE DIVISION Considerations

Following our usual practice of carefully defining what must be done before attempting to do it, the first step in integrating the printing of page headers into the PROCEDURE DIVISION is to determine exactly when this action should be taken. Obviously, we want headers printed at the top of the first page of output. The ideal time to do this would be as part of the housekeeping functions. The first page, however, is not the only place where headers must be printed; a typical report consumes many pages, and the identifying information contained in the headers belongs at the top of each page.

How do we decide when to skip to a new page? The answer seems obvious: Skip to a new page when the page you are currently working on is full. Don't forget, however, that we are dealing with a computer and not a human secretary. Define "full."

By far the surest way to control paging is to count the actual number of lines written on a page, and to skip to a new page when this count reaches a critical value. Your instructor or an experienced programmer can probably tell you how many lines per page are standard for the printer in your computer center; 66, 60, and 55 are common.

Once the need for a new page has been established, we are still faced with the problem of actually printing the headers. Obviously, WRITE instructions must be executed. But, where do these instructions fit? The headers at the top of the first page can be predicted and printed as part of the housekeeping functions, but subsequent headers are printed only as a result of a condition that can be tested as part of the program's mainline. The new page logic exists in two places (Fig. 5.12), once within the housekeeping section and once within the mainline.

There is another consideration beyond the problem of duplicate coding. The mainline of a program is the heart of that program. It contains the essential instructions executed on each program cycle. The housekeeping and cleanup functions have consistently been coded separate from the mainline, as these secondary functions perform a support role. Clearly defining and isolating the mainline is extremely important to good program design.

Page controls are not part of the mainline. Granted that this logic is executed in response to a condition detected as part of the mainline, but headers are not printed

---

On some smaller computer systems where the programmer communicates directly with the printer, one of the carriage control channels, usually channel 12, is set aside to indicate an end-of-page condition. As it nears the end of a page, the printer senses a hole in channel 12 and sends a message back to the computer. By coding an END-OF-PAGE clause as part of a WRITE statement, the programmer can instruct the program to take a specific course of action when this condition is encountered.

Fig. 5.12: *The new page logic appears in two places.*

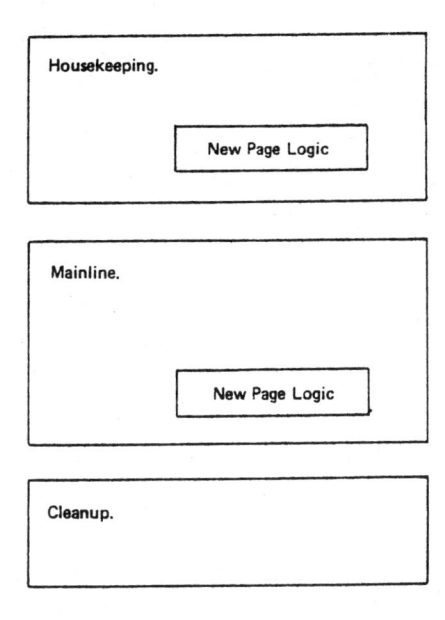

```
┌─────────────────────────────────────────────┐
│ Housekeeping.                               │
│                                             │
│                      ┌──────────────────┐   │
│                      │ New Page Logic   │   │
│                      └──────────────────┘   │
└─────────────────────────────────────────────┘

┌─────────────────────────────────────────────┐
│ Mainline.                                   │
│                                             │
│                                             │
│                      ┌──────────────────┐   │
│                      │ New Page Logic   │   │
│                      └──────────────────┘   │
└─────────────────────────────────────────────┘

┌─────────────────────────────────────────────┐
│ Cleanup.                                    │
│                                             │
└─────────────────────────────────────────────┘
```

as part of each program cycle—they are printed only sometimes. Good programming practice suggests that we remove these instructions from the mainline, and yet they must be executed under control of a mainline instruction. How can we achieve this objective?

The PERFORM Verb

The problem of code duplication and the problem of removing non-critical code from the mainline can both be handled by using the COBOL **PERFORM** verb. In Fig. 5.13, two PERFORM statements and a new TOP-OF-PAGE-ROUTINE paragraph have been added to the PROCEDURE DIVISION of the savings account update program. Probably the best way to illustrate how the PERFORM statement works is by explaining it in the context of this specific application.

The PROCEDURE DIVISION now has four key paragraphs. The first three contain the housekeeping, mainline, and cleanup functions respectively. The fourth, just added to the division, is the TOP-OF-PAGE-ROUTINE. Housekeeping, the mainline, and the cleanup routines form the basic core of the program. The TOP-OF-PAGE-ROUTINE is outside this structure. This relationship is shown graphically in Fig. 5.14.

Let's start with the housekeeping paragraph. After files are opened and the accumulators and counter set to zero, the statement

    PERFORM TOP-OF-PAGE-ROUTINE

    THRU END-TOP-OF-PAGE-ROUTINE.

```
SYSTEM     SAVINGS ACCOUNTS
PROGRAM    INTEREST EARNED
PROGRAMMER DAVIS & FISHER    DATE 1-25-79
PUNCHING INSTRUCTIONS: GRAPHIC Ø  PUNCH ZERO
PAGE 5 OF 7
```

```
PROCEDURE DIVISION.

HOUSEKEEPING.
    OPEN INPUT CUSTOMER-FILE.
    OPEN OUTPUT CUSTOMER-REPORT.
    MOVE ZEROS TO SUM-OF-OLD-BALANCES, SUM-OF-NEW-BALANCES.
    MOVE ZEROS TO SUM-OF-INTEREST, NUMBER-OF-ACCOUNTS.
    PERFORM TOP-OF-PAGE-ROUTINE
        THRU END-TOP-OF-PAGE-ROUTINE.

START-OF-MAINLINE.
    READ CUSTOMER-FILE
        AT END GO TO END-OF-JOB-ROUTINE.
    ADD 1 TO NUMBER-OF-ACCOUNTS.
    IF I-OLD-BALANCE IS GREATER THAN 1Ø.ØØ
    THEN
        MULTIPLY I-OLD-BALANCE BY Ø.Ø5 GIVING INTEREST
    ELSE
        MOVE ZERO TO INTEREST.
```

Fig. 5.13: *The PROCEDURE DIVISION with PERFORM statements and a TOP-OF-PAGE routine.*

COBOL Coding Form

SYSTEM: SAVINGS ACCOUNTS
PROGRAM: INTEREST EARNED
PROGRAMMER: Davis & Fisher
DATE: 1-25-79
PUNCH: ZERO
PAGE 6 OF 7

```
       IF LINE-COUNT IS GREATER THAN 24
       THEN
           PERFORM TOP-OF-PAGE-ROUTINE END-TOP-OF-PAGE-ROUTINE
       ELSE
           NEXT SENTENCE.
       MOVE SPACES TO REPORT-LINE.
       MOVE INTEREST TO O-INTEREST-EARNED.
       ADD  INTEREST    TO SUM-OF-INTEREST.
       ADD  I-OLD-BALANCE TO SUM-OF-OLD-BALANCES.
       ADD  I-OLD-BALANCE, INTEREST GIVING NEW-BALANCE.
       ADD  NEW-BALANCE  TO SUM-OF-NEW-BALANCES.
       ADD  I-OLD-BALANCE, INTEREST TO SUM-OF-NEW-BALANCES.
       MOVE I-ACCOUNT-NO TO O-ACCOUNT-NO.
       MOVE I-OLD-BALANCE TO O-OLD-BALANCE.
       MOVE NEW-BALANCE   TO O-NEW-BALANCE.
       WRITE REPORT-LINE
             AFTER ADVANCING 2 LINES.
       ADD  1 TO LINE-COUNT.
       GO TO START-OF-MAINLINE.
```

Fig. 5.13: *The PROCEDURE DIVISION, continued.*

COBOL Coding Form

SYSTEM: SAVINGS ACCOUNTS
PROGRAM: INTEREST EARNED
PROGRAMMER: DAVIS & FISHER
DATE: 1-25-79
PUNCHING INSTRUCTIONS — GRAPHIC: ∅   PUNCH: ZERO
CARD FORM #:
PAGE 7 OF 7

```
TOP-OF-PAGE-ROUTINE.
    WRITE REPORT-LINE FROM REPORT-HEADER
        AFTER NEW-PAGE.
    WRITE REPORT-LINE FROM COLUMN-HEADERS
        AFTER ADVANCING 2 LINES.
    MOVE ZERO TO LINE-COUNT.
END-TOP-OF-PAGE-ROUTINE.
    EXIT.

END-OF-JOB-ROUTINE.
    MOVE SPACES TO SUMMARY-PRINT-LINE.
    MOVE SUM-OF-OLD-BALANCES TO S-OLD-BALANCES.
    MOVE SUM-OF-NEW-BALANCES TO S-NEW-BALANCES.
    MOVE SUM-OF-INTEREST TO S-INTEREST-EARNED.
    MOVE NUMBER-OF-ACCOUNTS TO S-NO-OF-ACCOUNTS.
    WRITE SUMMARY-PRINT-LINE
        AFTER ADVANCING 2 LINES.
    CLOSE CUSTOMER-FILE.
    CLOSE CUSTOMER-REPORT.
    STOP RUN.
```

```
┌─────────────────────────┐
│                         │
│  TOP-OF-PAGE-ROUTINE.   │
│                         │
│  END-TOP-OF-PAGE-ROUTINE.│
│      EXIT.              │
│                         │
└─────────────────────────┘
         ↑        ↑
         │        │
┌──────────────────┐   ┌──────────────────────────┐   ┌──────────┐
│ Housekeeping.    │   │ Mainline.                │   │ Cleanup. │
│                  │→  │                          │ → │          │
│ PERFORM TOP-OF-  │   │ IF LINE-COUNT IS EQUAL   │   │          │
│ PAGE-ROUTINE.    │   │ TO 50                    │   │          │
│ THRU END-TOP-OF- │   │ PERFORM TOP-OF-PAGE-     │   │          │
│ PAGE-ROUTINE.    │   │ ROUTINE                  │   │          │
│                  │   │ THRU END-TOP-OF-PAGE-    │   │          │
│                  │   │ ROUTINE.                 │   │          │
└──────────────────┘   └──────────────────────────┘   └──────────┘
```

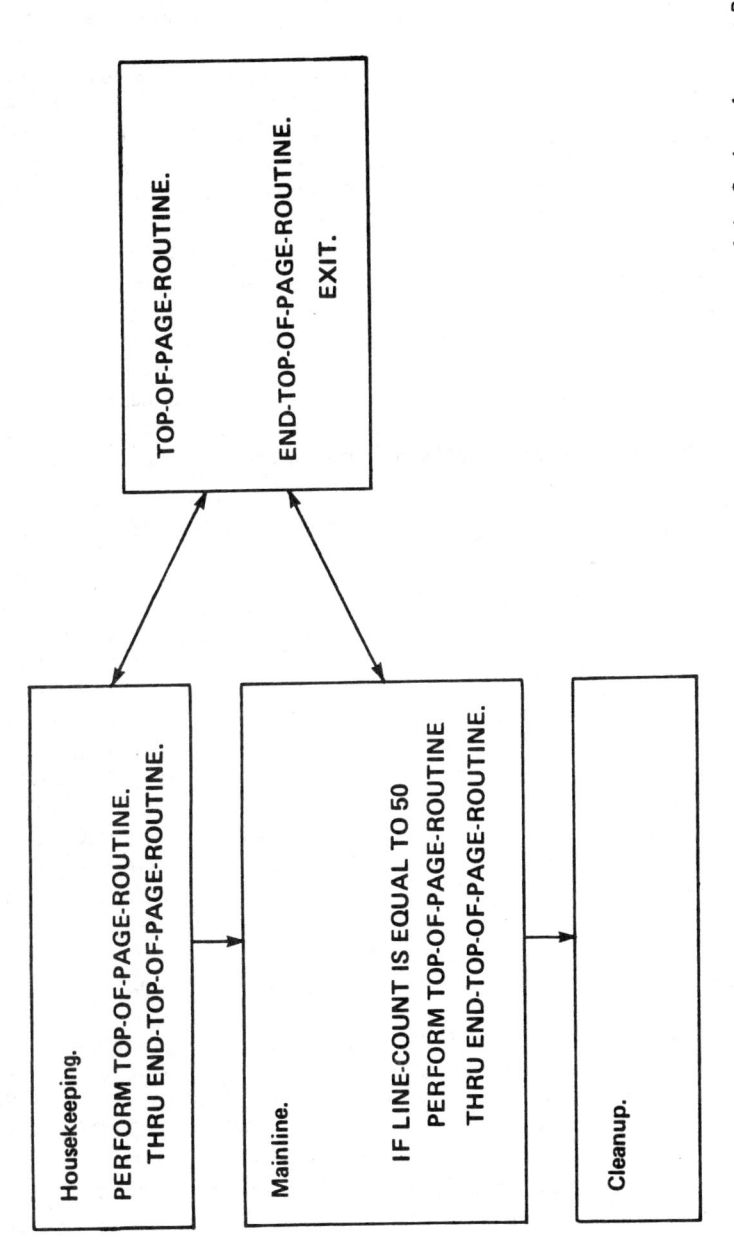

Fig. 5.14: *The New Structure of the Savings Account Program and the Function of the PERFORM Verb.*

is coded. As a result of this statement, the program branches to the first instruction in the TOP-OF-PAGE-ROUTINE paragraph, executes each of the instructions contained in this paragraph, and then, entering the paragraph named END-TOP-OF-PAGE-ROUTINE, encounters an **EXIT** statement and returns to the mainline.

Further down, in the program mainline, another PERFORM can be found. Once again, the program branches to the TOP-OF-PAGE-ROUTINE paragraph, executes the instructions in the routine, and returns to the place where logical flow left the mainline. The PERFORM verb sends control to the named paragraph, allowing the instructions beginning with that paragraph to be executed. Following the execution of these instructions, control is returned to the instruction immediately following the PERFORM. This procedure allows the same routine to be accessed from two or more different places in the program. It also allows complex but non-critical logic to be removed from the mainline.

Note carefully (Fig. 5.13) that the second PERFORM statement is executed only if the condition, LINE-COUNT IS GREATER THAN 24", is true. What if the condition is *not* true? We have not yet filled a page; headers should not be printed at this time; the PERFORM statement should simply be skipped and control should pass on to the next sentence. The phrase ELSE **NEXT SENTENCE** is a formal way of saying exactly that. In COBOL, NEXT SENTENCE is a reserved word meaning exactly what it says: skip on to the next sentence.

The logic of the TOP-OF-PAGE-ROUTINE is basically simple (Fig. 5.13). Naturally, the headers are printed. Look carefully at the WRITE statements, however; they are different. Output cannot be written directly from WORKING-STORAGE; all input and output must take place through the FILE SECTION of the DATA DIVISION. But, the headers must be defined in WORKING-STORAGE because the VALUE IS clause has no meaning in the FILE SECTION. There are two possible solutions to this quandry. One is to MOVE the header as defined in WORKING-STORAGE into a record defined in the FILE SECTION and then to issue a WRITE. We have chosen a second alternative, the WRITE FROM option. Using this option, the programmer instructs the computer to WRITE a record, as defined in the FILE SECTION, from a field or structure defined in the WORKING-STORAGE SECTION. The result is identical to that of the first option, in that the data is moved from WORKING-STORAGE to the FILE SECTION and then written. The only real difference is that the programmer does not have to code two instructions.

The last instruction in the TOP-OF-PAGE-ROUTINE paragraph sets a LINE-COUNT on each program cycle. The LINE-COUNT is then compared to a critical value which represents the desired number of lines per page of output. If the LINE-COUNT is equal to this critical value (in this example, 24), the TOP-OF-PAGE-ROUTINE is PERFORMed. If not, the program simply moves on to the next input record. Remember that, each time the TOP-OF-PAGE-ROUTINE is performed, the LINE-COUNT is reset to zero, thus allowing a new count to start for a new page.

Following the TOP-OF-PAGE-ROUTINE paragraph is another paragraph called END-OF-TOP-OF-PAGE-ROUTINE. Clearly this paragraph marks the end of the routine. The paragraph contains only a single statement, an EXIT. The EXIT statement, in fact this whole paragraph, is not required in this program; why then did we use it? This paragraph very clearly marks the end of a routine. While not really crucial in this program, the value of clearly identifying the beginning and end points of all secondary routines will become obvious as we progress to more complex problems requiring more such routines.

In Fig. 5.15 you will find a program listing for a COBOL program containing these new functions. The output generated by this program was illustrated in Fig. 5.8. Compare this output to the results obtained before headers and page controls were added (Fig. 5.7).

SOME FINAL COMMENTS ON THE PLANNING PROCESS

Planning is crucial; we've made this point many, many times throughout the text, and will make it again. In this chapter, however, we seemed to plan and implement a partial solution, adding page controls after the fact. Is this a violation of the planning standards we have so carefully built up? Not really.

Planning actually takes place in stages. The first step is to plan a solution to the problem. This solution can then be implemented in the form of a fairly simple program composed of housekeeping functions, a mainline, and cleanup functions. Once this basic, core program has been written and debugged, we can begin to consider the addition of other secondary functions such as page controls and error handling routines. Later, we'll also consider the handling of critical but very complex portions of the program in exactly the same way, ignoring the details of implementation on our first cut, and adding this detailed logic later, almost as if it were another, separate problem to be solved.

The objective of this step-by-step approach to planning is not to complicate things; on the contrary, the goal is simplification. A well-written program is constructed almost as if the program logic were composed of a set of building blocks, with each block of logic designed to perform a single function. If this practice is followed, these single-function blocks of logic tend to be quite simple. By combining blocks, a very complex program can be developed from a collection of very simple pieces. This is the basic idea behind **modular, structured programming**, and as the programs covered in this book become more and more complex, the significant advantages of this approach should become more and more obvious.

SUMMARY

The chapter began with a definition of the problem to be solved—computing interest for savings accounts. A human-level solution to the problem was developed, a flowchart drawn, input and output devices identified, and the format of all input, output, and work fields defined. Having completed the planning stage, we began the task of coding the program in COBOL.

One new feature of the interest computation program was a need to keep track of total values for the old balance, interest, and new balance fields; these totals were to be printed at the end of the program; as a result, it became necessary to distinguish

1   20.34.56   SEP 23,1978

00003   IDENTIFICATION DIVISION.
00005   PROGRAM-ID. INTEREST.
00006   AUTHOR.   DAVIS & FISHER.
00008   REMARKS.   THIS PROGRAM COMPUTES AND PRINTS THE INTEREST
00009   EARNED ON A NUMBER OF SAVINGS ACCOUNTS. INTEREST
00010   IS COMPUTED AT 5%. NO INTEREST IS ADDED UNLESS
00011   THE ACCOUNT BALANCE IS AT LEAST $10.00. CONTROLS
00012   HAVE BEEN ADDED TO PRINT PAGE HEADINGS AT THE
00013   TOP OF EACH PAGE.

00017   ENVIRONMENT DIVISION.
00019   CONFIGURATION SECTION.
00021   SOURCE-COMPUTER. IBM-370-148.
00022   OBJECT-COMPUTER. IBM-370-148.
00023   SPECIAL-NAMES.   C01 IS NEW-PAGE.
00025   INPUT-OUTPUT SECTION.
00027   FILE-CONTROL.
00028   SELECT CUSTOMER-FILE   ASSIGN TO UT-S-CUSFILE.
00029   SELECT CUSTOMER-REPORT ASSIGN TO UT-S-CUSREPT.

Fig. 5.15: *A listing of the interest program with headers and page controls.*

```
00034            DATA DIVISION..
00036            FILE SECTION.
00038                FD  CUSTOMER-FILE
00039                    LABEL RECORD OMITTED.
00041                    01  CUSTOMER-RECORD.
00042                        05  I-ACCOUNT-NO         PIC X(8).
00043                        05  I-OLD-BALANCE        PIC 99999V99.
00044                        05  FILLER               PIC X(65).

00046                FD  CUSTOMER-REPORT
00047                    LABEL RECORD OMITTED.
00049                    01  REPORT-LINE.
00050                        05  FILLER               PIC X(5).
00051                        05  O-ACCOUNT-NO         PIC X(8).
00052                        05  FILLER               PIC X(5).
00053                        05  O-OLD-BALANCE        PIC ZZ,ZZ9.99.
00054                        05  FILLER               PIC X(7).
00055                        05  O-INTEREST-EARNED    PIC Z,ZZ9.99.
00056                        05  FILLER               PIC X(7).
00057                        05  O-NEW-BALANCE        PIC ZZ,ZZ9.99.
00058                        05  FILLER               PIC X(75).

00060                    01  SUMMARY-PRINT-LINE.
00061                        05  FILLER               PIC X(14).
00062                        05  S-OLD-BALANCES       PIC ZZ,ZZZ,ZZ9.99.
00063                        05  FILLER               PIC X(3).
00064                        05  S-INTEREST-EARNED    PIC Z,ZZZ,ZZ9.99.
00065                        05  FILLER               PIC X(3).
00066                        05  S-NEW-BALANCES       PIC ZZ,ZZZ,ZZ9.99.
00067                        05  FILLER               PIC X(6).
00068                        05  S-NO-OF-ACCOUNTS     PIC ZZZ9.
00069                        05  FILLER               PIC X(69).
```

Fig. 5.15: *Program listing, continued.*

```
3         INTEREST        20.34.56        SEP 23,1978


00074              WORKING-STORAGE SECTION.
00076              77  INTEREST                    PIC 9999V99.
00077              77  NEW-BALANCE                 PIC 99999V99.
00078              77  SUM-OF-OLD-BALANCES         PIC 99999999V99.
00079              77  SUM-OF-NEW-BALANCES         PIC 99999999V99.
00080              77  SUM-OF-INTEREST             PIC 9999999V99.
00081              77  NUMBER-OF-ACCOUNTS          PIC 9999.
00082              77  LINE-COUNT                  PIC 99.


00085              01  REPORT-HEADER.
00086                  05  FILLER          PIC X(22)   VALUE SPACES.
00087                  05  FILLER          PIC X(17)   VALUE 'CUSTOMER ACCOUNTS'.
00088                  05  FILLER          PIC X(94)   VALUE SPACES.


00091              01  COLUMN-HEADERS.
00092                  05  FILLER          PIC X(4)    VALUE SPACES.
00093                  05  FILLER          PIC X(11)   VALUE 'ACCOUNT NO.'.
00094                  05  FILLER          PIC X(2)    VALUE SPACES.
00095                  05  FILLER          PIC X(11)   VALUE 'OLD BALANCE'.
00096                  05  FILLER          PIC X(2)    VALUE SPACES.
00097                  05  FILLER          PIC X(15)   VALUE 'INTEREST EARNED'.
00098                  05  FILLER          PIC X(2)    VALUE SPACES.
00099                  05  FILLER          PIC X(11)   VALUE 'NEW BALANCE'.
00100                  05  FILLER          PIC X(75)   VALUE SPACES.
```

Fig. 5.15: *Program listing, continued.*

```
     4       INTEREST        20.34.56       SEP 23,1978


00103           PROCEDURE DIVISION.
00105              HOUSEKEEPING.
00107                  OPEN INPUT   CUSTOMER-FILE.
00108                  OPEN OUTPUT  CUSTOMER-REPORT.
00109                  MOVE ZEROS TO SUM-OF-OLD-BALANCES, SUM-OF-NEW-BALANCES.
00110                  MOVE ZEROS TO SUM-OF-INTEREST, NUMBER-OF-ACCOUNTS.
00111                  PERFORM TOP-OF-PAGE-ROUTINE
00112                      THRU END-TOP-OF-PAGE-ROUTINE.

00114              START-OF-MAINLINE.

00116                  READ CUSTOMER-FILE
00117                       AT END GO TO END-OF-JOB-ROUTINE.
00118                  ADD  1   TO NUMBER-OF-ACCOUNTS.

00120                  IF I-OLD-BALANCE IS GREATER THAN 10.00
00121                  THEN
00122                       MULTIPLY I-OLD-BALANCE BY 0.05 GIVING INTEREST
00123                  ELSE
00124                       MOVE ZERO TO INTEREST.

00126                  IF LINE-COUNT IS GREATER THAN 24
00127                  THEN
00128                       PERFORM TOP-OF-PAGE-ROUTINE THRU END-TOP-OF-PAGE-ROUTINE
00129                  ELSE
00130                       NEXT SENTENCE.

00132                  MOVE SPACES    TO REPORT-LINE.
00133                  MOVE INTEREST TO O-INTEREST-EARNED.

00135                  ADD  INTEREST           TO SUM-OF-INTEREST.
00136                  ADD  I-OLD-BALANCE TO SUM-OF-OLD-BALANCES.
00137                  ADD  I-OLD-BALANCE, INTEREST GIVING    NEW-BALANCE.
00138                  ADD  NEW-BALANCE    TO SUM-OF-NEW-BALANCES.
00139                  ADD  I-OLD-BALANCE, INTEREST TO SUM-OF-NEW-BALANCES.

00141                  MOVE I-ACCOUNT-NO  TO O-ACCOUNT-NO.
00142                  MOVE I-OLD-BALANCE TO O-OLD-BALANCE.
00143                  MOVE NEW-BALANCE   TO O-NEW-BALANCE.

00145                  WRITE REPORT-LINE
00146                       AFTER ADVANCING 2 LINES.
00147                  ADD  1   TO LINE-COUNT.
00148                  GO TO START-OF-MAINLINE.
```

Fig. 5.15: *A listing of the interest program with headers and page controls. (Con't.)*

```
5          INTEREST        20.34.56        SEP 23,1978


00152             TOP-OF-PAGE-ROUTINE.
00154                 WRITE REPORT-LINE FROM REPORT-HEADER
00155                     AFTER NEW-PAGE.
00156                 WRITE REPORT-LINE FROM COLUMN-HEADERS
00157                     AFTER ADVANCING 2 LINES.
00158                 MOVE ZERO TO LINE-COUNT.

00160             END-TOP-OF-PAGE-ROUTINE.

00162                 EXIT.


00165             END-OF-JOB-ROUTINE.
00167                 MOVE SPACES TO SUMMARY-PRINT-LINE.
00168                 MOVE SUM-OF-OLD-BALANCES TO S-OLD-BALANCES.
00169                 MOVE SUM-OF-NEW-BALANCES TO S-NEW-BALANCES.
00170                 MOVE SUM-OF-INTEREST     TO S-INTEREST-EARNED.
00171                 MOVE NUMBER-OF-ACCOUNTS  TO S-NO-OF-ACCOUNTS.

00173                 WRITE SUMMARY-PRINT-LINE
00174                     AFTER ADVANCING 2 LINES.
00175                 CLOSE CUSTOMER-FILE.
00176                 CLOSE CUSTOMER-REPORT.
00177                 STOP RUN.
```

Fig. 5.15: *A listing of the interest program with headers and page controls. (Con't.)*

between detail and summary output lines. The IF statement was introduced, along with the basic idea of an IF... THEN... ELSE logic block. The editing of output data was discussed, with the edit characters 9, Z, the comma, and the period being used in writing the program.

Once the basic program had been written, we turned our attention to improving the results, introducing the idea of page and column headers. The headers were defined and coded in the WORKING-STORAGE SECTION, using the VALUE IS clause. We then turned our attention to page controls, discussing the carriage control tape available on many computers and introducing the SPECIAL-NAMES paragraph as the place for defining page controls in COBOL. Counting output lines is a common mechanism for controlling paging within the COBOL program.

The fact that the writing of page headers had to be done at two different places in the program created a problem. We solved it by writing the top-of-page routine as a separate routine, using the PERFORM statement to execute it from various places in the program.

The idea of modular, structured programming was the last topic of this chapter. In the chapter, a program was developed in careful stages. First, a basic solution was planned and implemented. Once this basic solution had been successfully tested, details such as page controls were added to the framework. Such a step-by-step approach to developing a complex program is highly recommended for both the new and experienced programmer.

Chapters 1 through 4 dealt with the development and implementation of a single program. Chapter 5 compresses the ideas presented in the first four chapters into one, taking you through the complete program development process all over again.

KEY WORDS

carriage control tape	**mainline**
column header	**modular programming**
condition	**NEXT SENTENCE**
detail record	**PERFORM**
edit characters	**proof totals**
EXIT	**psuedo code**
header	**SPECIAL-NAMES paragraph**
IF... THEN... ELSE logic	**structured programming**
IF	**summary line**

summary totals

VALUE IS clause

zero supression

EXERCISES

1. Explain the difference between a detail and a summary line.

2. Explain the basic idea of IF... THEN... ELSE logic.

3. Why is the ability to edit output data so valuable? What does zero suppression mean?

4. Why is it necessary to define headers in the WORKING-STORAGE SECTION?

5. Why was the top of page logic implemented through a separate, secondary routine?

6. Explain how the PERFORM statement works.

7. Explain the basic idea of structured or modular programming.

8. In Chapter 1, you were asked to prepare a plan for computing a grade point average; this problem was subsequently developed through Chapters 2, 3, and 4. Since the IF statement had not yet been introduced, you were allowed to enter numeric values for the grades, substituting 4 for an A, 3 for a B, and so on. You now know how to code an IF statement. Modify the program developed over the first 4 chapters to accept a letter grade and, by using a series of IF tests, convert this letter grade to the proper numerical value before computing grade points for the course.

9. Plan and write a program to balance a checking account. The input records to this program will be checks and deposit slips (as simulated on cards). Contents of each input record are:

positions	contents
1-8	account number
9	record type (C=check;D=deposit;B=balance)
10-15	amount (9999V99)

The "B" record represents the old balance in the account; there must be exactly one old balance card in your data deck. Your program should read each transaction, test for type and either add or subtract the amount. After all the records have been processed, print the new balance of the account. The individual transactions should be used to generate detail output lines; the new balance will be printed in a summary line.

Once the basic program has been written and tested, add the code needed to maintain running totals for checks and deposits. Your output summary line should now show the account number, the old balance, the total value of all checks, the total value of all deposits, and the new balance.

10. Plan and write a program to compute gross pay for a number of employees. Input cards to this program contain the following fields:

positions	contents
1-6	employee number
7-20	employee name
21-24	hours worked (99V9)
25	employee classification

    The employee classification field has the following meaning:

If classification is	pay rate is
A	10.50 per hour
B	6.25 per hour
C	4.30 per hour

    Gross pay is computed by multiplying the proper hourly pay rate by the number of hours worked. The proper pay rate can be determined by testing the employee classification code on the input record. Your program should read a series of input records, computing gross pay for each and printing detail lines showing the employee number, employee name, hours worked, and gross pay. A summary line should show the total amount of gross pay paid to all employees.

    For extra credit, add a series of counters to keep track of the number of employees falling into each category. Print these counts as a summary line at the end of the program.

11. Plan and code a program to compute the amount of commission due salespersons. Each sale has been keypunched to cards containing the following fields:

positions	contents
1-6	salesperson number
7-13	amount of sale (99999V99)

The rule for computing commission due is as follows: If the sale is less than $100.00, the commission is 5%; if the sale is between $100.00 and $1000.00, the commission is 10%; if the sale exceeds $1000.00, the commission is 12%. Compute the commission due on each sale. Maintain a running total of both sales and commissions, printing these totals in a summary line at the end of the program output.

12. In Chapter 1, you were asked to plan a solution to a problem involving the printing of address labels. This program was subsequently written over the course of Chapters 2-4. Modify this basic program so that address labels are printed only when the zip code on the input record is a certain, pre-selected value. Design your program so that the first input record identifies the zip code for which address labels are desired. Subsequent input records can be compared against the zip code of this first record, and the decision to prepare or not to prepare a label can be made.

    Add to this basic program a set of counters to keep track of the number of labels actually printed and the number of input records that were skipped because the zip code did not match. Print these counts as a summary line at the end of the job.

13. As a check on the accuracy of a payroll processing program, we have been asked to write a program to read payroll earnings cards and compute a series of "proof-totals". Input cards contain the following data:

columns	contents
1-4	employee number
5-7	type of earnings
8-12	amount of earnings

There are four types of earnings cards in the deck: regular (REG), Overtime (OVR), extra-shift (XTR), and bonus (BON). Count the total number of each type of record and accumulate the total earnings for each type. If any other type of record is found, count it but don't bother with the amount. Print a report showing your counts and totals.

Sample Data	Employee	Type	Earnings
	0001	REG	85.50
	0001	OVR	14.65

Sample Data	Employee	Type	Earnings
	0002	REG	67.60
	0002	BON	10.00
	0003	REG	55.30
	0003	OVR	5.10
	0003	XTR	6.00
	0003	SPC	50.00

Sample data output

REGULAR	3	208.40
OVERTIME	2	19.75
EXTRA-SHIFT	1	6.00
BONUS	1	10.00
OTHER	1	

14. An individual borrows $1,000.00 and agrees to pay it back in a series of $50.00 payments. Interest is to be charged at a rate of 1 and ½ percent per month on the unpaid balance; i.e., the amount yet to be repaid at the beginning of a month. The first few payments might be summarized as follows:

Month	Beginning Balance	Total Payment	Interest	Principle	Ending Balance
1	1000.00	50.00	15.00	35.00	965.00
2	965.00	50.00	14.48	35.52	929.48
3	929.48	50.00	13.94	36.06	893.42

Note that the beginning balance is the same as the ending balance of the preceeding month and that interest is always 0.015 times the beginning balance.

Write a program to read the original balance and an interest rate and produce a similar table. Continue the table until the remaining balance is zero. Note that this program is asking for a general solution to a general interest table problem; the table developed above is for illustrative purposes only.

15. According to tax laws, a business cannot deduct the cost of a large piece of equipment or furniture as a business expense during the year it is purchased.

Instead, recognizing the fact that the piece of equipment will be used for several years, the cost must be spread over several years. This is done through a process known as depreciation.

The simplest form of depreciation is known as straight line depreciation. When using this approach, the initial cost is simply divided by the number of years of expected life, and this quotient becomes the amount of depreciation per year. If for example, a $5000 piece of equipment is expected to last for 5 years, the annual depreciation would be $1000. Annual depreciation for the expected life of the equipment might be described in a table, as follows:

year	start of year	depreciation	end of year
1	5000	1000	4000
2	4000	1000	3000
3	3000	1000	2000
4	2000	1000	1000
5	1000	1000	0

Write a program to read the initial value of a piece of equipment and the expected number of years of life and generate a depreciation schedule similar to the one shown above.

16. Another technique for computing depreciation is the sum-of-the-years-digits technique. The input is the same as that of exercise number 15. In computing depreciation for any given year, however, a different technique is used. The base, as the name implies, is a computation of the sum-of-the-years-digits; if, for example, the estimated life were 5 years, the sum-of-the-years-digits would be 5+4+3+2+1, which is 15 (simply start with 1 and keep adding integers until you reach the estimated life).

Once the sum has been computed, it can be used as a divisor for computing depreciation. The idea is to shift the bulk of the depreciation into the first few years. Again, using 5 years as an example, the depreciation for the first year would be 5/15 of the initial cost. The second year's depreciation would be 4/15, followed by 3/15 in the third, 2/15 in the fourth, and 1/15 in the fifth year. The rule is simple. Start by computing the sum-of-the-years-digits. Compute the first year's depreciation by starting with the expected life, dividing it by the sum, and multiplying by the initial cost of the equipment. In each subsequent year, reduce the dividend (the number you are dividing the sum-of-digits into) by 1 each year, until all depreciation has been accounted for.

Modify the program of exercise 15 to produce a depreciation table using the sum-of-the-years-digits approach.

Modular Program Design

6
Developing a Program Mainline

OVERVIEW

This is the first of four interrelated chapters. The ultimate objective of these chapters is to develop a solution to a very realistic (and hence very complex) business data processing problem. By far the best way to attack such problems is by solving them in levels, breaking the complex into a series of relatively simple pieces. Here in Chapter 6, we'll discuss the nature of this problem (a payroll system has been chosen for this example), and develop the program mainline. In Chapter 7, a routine to compute the actual income state tax due will be added to the mainline; in Chapter 8, a federal income tax computation routine will be added, using tables. Finally, Chapter 9 discusses the addition of still more functions, and points out the possibility of solving a business data processing problem by using a series of separate but interrelated programs.

    Very few new COBOL concepts are presented in this chapter; the key idea is the modular, step-by-step approach to developing and implementing a solution to a problem. (In fact, the major reason for breaking this process into four separate chapters is to emphasize this modular, step-by-step approach.) The word **kludge** is popular in data processing circles; it refers to a massive program or system that more or less evolved in an unplanned manner and, as a result, is very difficult to understand and to follow. The modular approach to planning and implementing large programs is very simply the best way to avoid writing kludges. It is a prescription for developing intelligently structured, easy to follow programs. This concept is important!

PAYROLL PROCESSING: PROBLEM DEFINITION

Every business organization must pay its employees; thus payroll is one of the most common of all business data processing activities, and also one of the easiest to define. The objective of any payroll system must be to prepare and deliver on time, correct paychecks to all employees. The word "correct" in this context, implies correct with respect to existing federal, state, and local tax laws, current union contracts, and company policies. The words "on time" are equally well-defined, meaning something as simple as "no later than 3:30 p.m. on Friday". Very little is left to chance. It is within the context of this problem definition that the payroll program must be written.

PLANNING A BROAD, GENERAL SOLUTION

The essential rules for computing an individual's pay are well known; chances are, if you have ever held a job, you're familiar with them. The first step involves the computation of gross pay. For hourly employees, gross pay is the product of hours worked and an hourly pay rate; for salaried employees, gross pay is, essentially, a constant; for salespeople, it may be based on commissions.

Gross pay is, as we all know, not the same as take-home or net pay. Before net pay can be computed, the amount of money to be deducted for such things as federal, state, and local taxes, union dues, loan repayments, and other things must first be found. These deductions are then subtracted from gross pay to get net pay. In very broad and general terms, the computation of payroll always involves the following steps:

1. compute gross pay;

2. compute the value of all deductions;

3. subtract deductions from gross pay to get net pay.

Although the list of steps described above may seem, at first glance, oversimplified, it does serve a useful purpose by describing the general structure that any payroll program must follow. Gross pay must be found first, followed by all deductions, followed, in turn, by the computation of net pay. It is important that this general structure be firmly in mind before we begin the process of more detailed planning.

Before moving along we might want to provide just a bit more detail, perhaps identifying some of the deductions. A slightly expanded version of a program outline might include:

1. compute gross pay;

2. compute value of deductions, including:

    a. federal income tax,

    b. state income tax,

c. local income tax,

d. social security tax,

e. union dues,

f. bond-of-the-month club,

g. credit union loan repayment,

h. credit union savings,

i. stock purchase plan payments,

j. any other deductions;

3. subtract deductions from gross pay to get net pay.

We now have a reasonably solid outline of the program we will eventually write, showing the major steps and defining the sequence in which these steps must be executed. This broad, general outline is the objective of the first planning step.

DETAILED PLANNING

As a direct result of the broad, general planning step outlined above, we now know what the program will be expected to do. The only question that remains is exactly how each of these steps is to be implemented. It is here in the detailed planning phase that the complexity of our problem becomes apparent, and it is here that many programmers begin to bog down.

Consider, for example, gross pay. The computation of this figure seems simple enough: multiply hours worked by the hourly pay rate. But, what about salaried em employees? Their gross pay is different, essentially a constant amount. And, what about overtime? Often, all hours over 40 in any given week are paid at time and a half. Sometimes, hours exceeding 8 in any day are considered overtime, no matter what the total hours for the week may be. Shift premiums represent another complication; often second and third shift employees are paid a bonus for working the off-prime shift. Are Sunday and holiday hours paid at still another rate? And what about the employee who works at several different jobs during a pay period, earning perhaps $4.50 per hour most of the time, but jumping to an occasional $25.00 per hour for performing some particularly dangerous or undesirable task?

We have just begun to scratch the surface in discussing the complications of this one number—gross pay. The problem facing the programmer is that once payroll computations have been turned over to the computer, the controlling program must be capable of handling everyone's payroll, and not just the normal or standard ones. Before the programmer can tell the computer how to solve a problem, he or she must know how to solve it. What this means is that the programmer must be familiar with *all* the rules for computing gross pay.

Within an organization, where can the programmer find this information? Generally, the rules for computing gross pay will be carefully spelled out in a union contract, employee agreement, or company policy statement. Often, a complete department, the payroll department, is dedicated to the development, documentation, and interpretation of rules having to do with payroll; if such an organization exists in the programmer's firm, this is an obvious place to start.

The important point is that this seemingly simple and well defined task is really quite complex when all the special cases are taken into account. Just computing gross pay, a relatively small piece of the payroll program, is a much more difficult programming task than either of the two programs we developed and wrote over the first five chapters.

Let's move on to the deductions. The first is federal income tax. The rules for withholding federal income tax are carefully spelled out in an Internal Revenue Service publication known as Circular E, the *Employer's Tax Guide*. The publication begins by defining a number of terms and clearly spelling out who must pay tax and on what types of income. The real heart of Circular E, however, is a set of tables that indicate, given an amount of earnings, exactly how much tax is to be withheld.

State and local taxes are similar to federal income tax, usually representing a percentage tax that varies with the level of income. The equivalent of Circular E can be obtained from state or local authorities.

Often, the withholding of state and local taxes is complicated by the fact that many employees live and work in different states or municipalities. The problem arises when tax rates differ. If, for example, state A collects 1.5% of gross pay as an income tax, while state B collects 2%, what happens to the employee who works in state A but lives in state B? Often, the employer is held responsible for collecting the state A tax *and* for sending 0.5% of the employee's gross pay to the state B tax collector. If this problem isn't complex enough, consider the employer who must deal with differing local tax rates and who employs people who live in 100 or more different cities, towns, and villages.

We could make a similar argument for almost all of the deductions, but by now our point should have been made. Each of these steps is itself a significant data processing problem. It is easy to get lost in any one of them. Attempting to handle all these problems at the same time is a prescription for disaster. Unless this problem is broken into reasonable pieces, it is almost insoluble.

STRUCTURED, MODULAR PROGRAM DESIGN

There is an obvious basis for breaking this problem into more-manageable pieces. Back in the general planning stage, an outline of the major steps in the program was developed. Each of these steps represents one major, uniquely identifiable, component of the program. Each of these **modules** can, essentially, be written as a separate entity, almost independent of all the others.

If these primary functions are to be treated as separate entities, there must be a mechanism for tying them together. This mechanism is the program **mainline**. Essen-

Fig. 6.1: *A Flowchart for a Structured Payroll Program.*

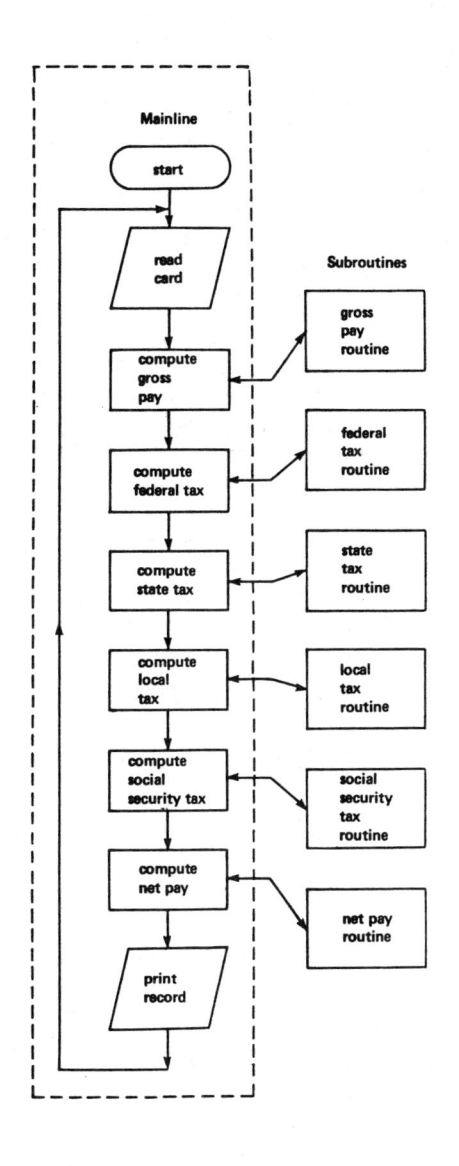

137.

tially, it is possible to structure a program along the lines shown in Fig. 6.1, with a mainline providing the primary control and linking, in turn, to the various logic modules that perform detailed computations. In COBOL, this program structure can be implemented by using the PERFORM statement.

There are many advantages to structuring a program as a collection of detailed computational modules tied together by a mainline. The program is easy to follow, easy to document, easy to debug, and easy to maintain. A change to one routine, a new set of federal income tax withholding rates for example, can be implemented by changing only the affected module, leaving the others unchanged. Should an error occur, its source can be easily isolated to the module in which the incorrect value was computed. Complex problems are often beyond the ability of a single individual, and the modules represent an obvious basis for dividing the work.

An often overlooked but equally important advantage of the modular approach to programming is the fact that it allows the program to be written and implemented in easily tested stages. We might, for example, begin with nothing but the skeleton of a mainline, with key deductions being simply computed at a constant rate and gross pay being defined as simply hours worked times the hourly pay rate. This skeleton program can be tested and debugged. Now, the real federal income tax routine can be added. Once again, the program can be tested. If the results are incorrect, the problem almost certainly lies with the newly added income tax routine; having isolated the probable source of the error, debug is greatly simplified.

Each of the other computational routines can now be added, one at a time, in turn. Following the addition of each new routine, the program can once again be tested. As before, any new errors can probably be attributed to the newly added module, thus isolating the most likely source of the error and greatly simplifying program debugging. Eventually, after all the routines have been integrated into the program, the complete system will be ready to go. This step-by-step approach makes sense, and it works!

Planning a Skeleton Mainline

In the modular, structured approach pictured in Fig. 6.1, the function of the mainline was to tie together all the other computational modules. Looking at it from another perspective, each of the detailed logic routines is concerned with performing one and only one function, giving absolutely no consideration to what might happen in any other part of the program. The only module that is in any way concerned with the *entire* program is the mainline. Thus, it is only reasonable that the mainline be the first program module written.

Picture the flowchart of Fig. 6.1 with no detailed logic modules. If we were to define each of the steps in the mainline as a simple add, subtract, multiply, divide, or move instruction, we could develop the **skeleton** of a **mainline**. This skeleton program could be coded, keypunched, and tested, thus allowing us to prove that the right steps have been coded in the right order. Later, when an actual computational module is ready for testing, one of these simple instructionscould be replaced by a PERFORM statement, and the newly coded routine could be added to the program deck, allowing the income tax, gross pay, or other affected value to be computed by the correct procedure, rather than by the skeleton instruction. The important point is that this substitution would impact only one portion of the program; everything else would remain unchanged. That makes for relatively easy debugging.

The mainline portion of the structured flowchart (Fig. 6.1) provides a pretty good plan for the logic of this skeleton program, but we still need a list of input and output devices and the format of each input and output record and each data item. We'll stay with a card reader and a printer as the input and output devices for this program. Data formats require a bit more discussion.

Almost invariably, the programmer has little or no choice when it comes to defining the input record for a payroll program. Usually, the organization will already be using some form of labor record, often a time card, which becomes the input record. We'll assume that the time card contains the following fields:

columns	contents
1-9	Social Security number
10-25	employee's last name
26-27	employee's initials
28-30	employee's department number
31-33	hours worked, to nearest 1/10
34-37	hourly pay rate (99V99)
38-39	number of dependents
40	marital status (M=married; S=single)
41-80	unused

The output will be a pay check. We probably have little control over the format of this pay check, either. Let's assume that we are expected to print the following fields:

positions	contents
1-20	blank
21-36	employee's last name (from input)
37	blank
38-39	employee's initials (from input)
40-60	blank

61-68	net pay (computed:$9999.99)
69-133	blank

If you look closely, you'll see that this line resembles a check; to avoid complicating this example needlessly, we are intentionally ignoring printing of a check stub listing all deductions.

We need intermediate fields to hold the computed gross pay, federal income tax, state income tax, Social Security tax, any other deductions computed in the program, the total of all deductions, and, undoubtedly, a host of other intermediate fields that we are not even aware of yet. How can we estimate the size of these fields? Basically, all we must do is to compute the worst possible (or biggest) value of each.

Where should we start? Since gross pay is the key to most payroll computations and since, almost by definition, no deduction can possibly exceed gross pay, the best place to start is to estimate the biggest possible value of gross pay. This figure is computed by multiplying the hours worked by the hourly pay rate. On the input card, hours worked is a 3-digit number having a maximum value of 99.9, and the hourly pay rate is a 4-digit number having a maximum value of 99.99; thus, the biggest possible gross pay is the product of 99.9 and 99.99, which is 9989.00. A PICTURE clause for this number would be 9999V99.

Having defined the worst case for gross pay (perhaps best case would be more descriptive), we can now define the worst case for our other fields. A quick glance at the tax tables in Circular E indicates that the withholding rate never exceeds 36%, and 36% of 9999.99 is roughly 3600.00. Converting this to a PICTURE clause, we get 9999V99. State and local tax rates generally run below 10%; thus 999V99 is reasonable. Social Security tax is withheld at a 6.05% rate; again, 999V99 would seem to be reasonable. By performing such rough computations, a reasonable PICTURE clause for each of the work fields can be developed. Staying with the deductions described in the flowchart of Fig. 6.1, we can define the following fields:

gross pay	9999V99
federal income tax	9999V99
state income tax	999V99
local income tax	999V99
Social Security tax	999V99
total deductions	9999V99
net pay	9999V99

Coding a Skeleton Mainline

We now have a list of input and output devices, a complete set of data formats, and a flowchart of the program logic, and can begin the task of coding this program.

COBOL Coding Form

SYSTEM	PAYROLL	PUNCHING INSTRUCTIONS		PAGE 1 OF 5
PROGRAM	COMPUTE HOURLY PAYROLL	GRAPHIC	Ø	CARD FORM #
PROGRAMMER	DAVIS & FISHER	DATE 2-1-79	PUNCH	ZERO

```
       IDENTIFICATION DIVISION.
        PROGRAM-ID.  PAYROLL.
        AUTHOR.      DAVIS & FISHER.
        REMARKS.     THIS PROGRAM COMPUTES THE NET PAY
                     FOR HOURLY EMPLOYEES.


       ENVIRONMENT DIVISION.
        CONFIGURATION SECTION.
         SOURCE-COMPUTER.   IBM-37Ø-148.
         OBJECT-COMPUTER.   IBM-37Ø-148.
         SPECIAL-NAMES.     CØ1 IS NEW-PAGE.
        INPUT-OUTPUT SECTION.
         FILE-CONTROL.
           SELECT TIME-CARD-FILE      ASSIGN TO UT-S-TIMECRDS.
           SELECT PAYROLL-CHECK-FILE ASSIGN TO UT-S-PAYCHEKS.
```

Fig. 6.2: *A skeleton version of the mainline for a payroll computation program.*

COBOL Coding Form

SYSTEM: PAYROLL
PROGRAM: COMPUTE HOURLY PAYROLL
PROGRAMMER: Davis & Fisher DATE: 2-1-79
PUNCHING INSTRUCTIONS — GRAPHIC: ∅ PUNCH: ZERO
PAGE 2 OF 5

```
DATA DIVISION.
FILE SECTION.
FD  TIME-CARD-FILE
    LABEL RECORD OMITTED.
01  TIME-CARD.
    05  I-SOCIAL-SECURITY-NO    PIC 9(9).
    05  I-LAST-NAME             PIC X(16).
    05  I-INITIALS              PIC XX.
    05  I-DEPARTMENT-NO         PIC 999.
    05  I-HOURS-WORKED          PIC 99V9.
    05  I-HOURLY-PAY-RATE       PIC 99V99.
    05  I-NO-OF-DEPENDENTS      PIC 99.
    05  I-MARITAL-STATUS        PIC X.
    05  FILLER                  PIC X(40).
FD  PAYROLL-CHECK-FILE
    LABEL RECORD OMITTED.
01  PAYROLL-CHECK.
    05  FILLER                  PIC X(20).
    05  O-LAST-NAME             PIC X(16).
    05  FILLER                  PIC XX.
    05  O-INITIALS              PIC XX.
    05  FILLER                  PIC X(21).
    05  O-NET-PAY               PIC $9999.99.
    05  FILLER                  PIC X(65).
```

Fig. 6.2: *continued.*

COBOL Coding Form

SYSTEM: PAYROLL
PROGRAM: COMPUTE HOURLY PAYROLL
PROGRAMMER: DAVIS & FISHER   DATE: 2-1-79
GRAPHIC:
PUNCH: ZERO
PAGE 3 OF 3

```
       WORKING-STORAGE SECTION.
   77  GROSS-PAY                PIC 9999V99.
   77  FEDERAL-INCOME-TAX       PIC 9999V99.
   77  STATE-INCOME-TAX         PIC 999V99.
   77  LOCAL-INCOME-TAX         PIC 999V99.
   77  SOCIAL-SECURITY-TAX      PIC 999V99.
   77  TOTAL-DEDUCTIONS         PIC 9999V99.
   77  NET-PAY                  PIC 9999V99.
```

Fig. 6.2: *continued.*

COBOL Coding Form

SYSTEM	PAYROLL	PUNCHING INSTRUCTIONS		PAGE 4 OF 5	
PROGRAM	COMPUTE HOURLY PAYROLL	GRAPHIC	Ø	CARD FORM #	
PROGRAMMER	DAVIS & FISHER	DATE 2-1-79	PUNCH	ZERO	

SEQUENCE	CONT.	A	B	COBOL STATEMENT	IDENTIFICATION

```
       PROCEDURE DIVISION.

        HOUSEKEEPING.
           OPEN INPUT  TIME-CARD-FILE.
           OPEN OUTPUT PAYROLL-CHECK-FILE.
           MOVE SPACES TO PAYROLL-CHECK.
```

Fig. 6.2: *continued.*

COBOL Coding Form

SYSTEM	PAYROLL	PUNCHING INSTRUCTIONS: GRAPHIC Ø / PUNCH ZERO	CARD FORM #	PAGE 5 OF 5
PROGRAM	COMPUTE HOURLY PAYROLL			
PROGRAMMER	DAVIS & FISHER	DATE 2-1-79		

```
       START-OF-MAINLINE.
           READ TIME-CARD-FILE
               AT END GO TO END-OF-JOB.
           MULTIPLY I-HOURLY-PAY-RATE BY I-HOURS-WORKED GIVING GROSS-PAY
           MULTIPLY GROSS-PAY BY Ø.2Ø   GIVING FEDERAL-INCOME-TAX.
           MULTIPLY GROSS-PAY BY Ø.Ø15  GIVING STATE-INCOME-TAX.
           MULTIPLY GROSS-PAY BY Ø.Ø2   GIVING LOCAL-INCOME-TAX.
           MULTIPLY GROSS-PAY BY Ø.Ø6Ø5 GIVING SOCIAL-SECURITY-TAX.
           SUBTRACT FEDERAL-INCOME-TAX, STATE-INCOME-TAX,
               LOCAL-INCOME-TAX, SOCIAL-SECURITY-TAX FROM GROSS-PAY
                   GIVING NET-PAY.
           MOVE I-LAST-NAME TO O-LAST-NAME.
           MOVE I-INITIALS  TO O-INITIALS.
           MOVE NET-PAY     TO O-NET-PAY.
           WRITE PAYROLL-CHECK
               AFTER ADVANCING 2 LINES.
           MOVE SPACES TO PAYROLL-CHECK.
           GO TO START-OF-MAINLINE.


       END-OF-JOB.
           CLOSE TIME-CARD-FILE.
           CLOSE PAYROLL-CHECK-FILE.
           STOP RUN.
```

Fig. 6.2: *concluded.*

Sheets for each of the four divisions are illustrated in Fig. 6.2 as no new features have been added, you should have little difficulty following this program.

The only thing that you have not seen before is the dollar sign ($) which appears as a part of the PICTURE clause of the O-NET-PAY field of the output record in the FILE SECTION of the DATA DIVISION. The dollar sign is a valid edit character; when it is coded as part of an edit PICTURE clause the result is the printing of a dollar sign.

As an alternative, we might have coded

        05 O-NET-PAY PICTURE $$$$9.99.

The result would be a **floating dollar sign**, with the actual dollar sign printed to the left of and adjacent to the first significant digit. The following examples show the difference between these two PICTURE clauses:

value of data	$9999.99	$$$$9.99
1325.50	$1325.50	$1325.50
125.45	$0125.45	$125.45
5.25	$0005.25	$5.25
.50	$0000.50	$0.50

The use of a floating dollar sign makes the task of changing the amount of a check very difficult, thus cutting down on the forgery problem; as a result, floating dollar signs are commonly used in business data processing applications.

Note the instructions in the program mainline. All deductions are simply defined as the product of a constant and gross pay. Eventually, all these instructions will be replaced.

Preparing Test Data

Simply preparing a skeleton solution to the payroll problem is not enough; this solution must be tested. The best way to test a program is to allow it to read realistic data, process this data, and produce real output. These results can then be compared with the expected results and, if variations are noted, corrections can be made.

Where does this **test data** come from? Someone, often the programmer but preferably the user, must create it. How does one go about creating reasonable test data?

The objective of the testing process is to evaluate the program's performance on realistic data. Take a look at the input record for this program. What is a realistic Social Security number? Essentially, any 9 digits will do. What about names? Again, almost anything will do, since the program really does nothing but read the name field, move it to the output line, and print it. On the Social Security number and name fields, the only real test is whether or not the program is capable of reproducing what it is given. The department number field is similar.

Hours worked is different, however. This is one of the fields that will be used in computations. Its value can vary from a low of 00.1 hour to a high of 99.9 hours, although most real time cards can be expected to show something in the neighborhood of 40.0 hours. Prepare some of the test data cards with extremely high values, using low values on others. The balance should reflect a more typical number of hours worked.

The hourly pay rate is another critical field, and it too should be given a distribution of high, low, and intermediate values. Try to design at least one test data card with both the hours worked and the pay rate at or near the upper extreme, and another card with these two values both near the lower extreme. Include records with a high hours worked and a low pay rate, and others with a low hours worked and a high pay rate. Still others should be intermediate in every respect.

The number of dependents is another variable field. It can range from a low of zero to a high of 20 or so (think of the biggest family you have every known, and add a few dependents). Once again, include test data with high, low, and intermediate values. Ideally, test data cards should exist that have every field at or near the upper limit, every field at or near the lower limit, and every possible combination of high and low values in each field. Marital status is either an S for single or an M for married; distribute these codes fairly equally throughout your test data.

The whole point is to prepare test data that exercises all the parts of the program. It is very important that extremes, both high and low, be tested, as these extreme conditions are a frequent cause of program failure. Typical or normal data configurations should also be tested, as these results are likely to be the ones that make the most sense to an individual attempting to evaluate the results of a program.

How many test data records are needed? That depends on the application. The only really accurate answer is: Enough to test the program fully. A more complex program might require hundreds, perhaps even thousands. If page control were important to this program, we'd certainly want enough test data to generate more than a single page of output. For this program, perhaps 10 to 15 records will do.

Once the test data has been prepared, use it to desk check the skeleton program. Pretend that you are a computer, and follow the instructions in the program. Actually use a pocket calculator, and perform all computations. Prepare a mock-up of the expected output report. This exercise achieves two primary purposes, allowing you to check the program before submitting it to the computer, and providing you with a set of expected results to compare against the actual output the computer generates.

Testing the Skeleton Program

We're now ready to actually test the skeleton of the payroll program against our test data; the results are shown in Fig. 6.3. The answers are exactly as we had expected; the logic of this program seems correct.

```
1                     2.42.05        SEP 12,1978

00001           IDENTIFICATION DIVISION.
00002           PROGRAM-ID. PAYROLL.
00003           AUTHOR.       DAVIS & FISHER.
00004           REMARKS.      THIS PROGRAM COMPUTES THE NET PAY
00005                         FOR HOURLY EMPLOYEES.

00007           ENVIRONMENT DIVISION.
00008           CONFIGURATION SECTION.
00009             SOURCE-COMPUTER.  IBM-370-148.
00010             OBJECT-COMPUTER.  IBM-370-148.
00011             SPECIAL-NAMES.     C01 IS NEW-PAGE.
00012           INPUT-OUTPUT SECTION.
00013             FILE-CONTROL.
00014               SELECT TIME-CARD-FILE      ASSIGN TO UT-S-TIMECRDS.
00015               SELECT PAYROLL-CHECK-FILE ASSIGN TO UT-S-PAYCHEKS.

00017           DATA DIVISION.
00018           FILE SECTION.
00019             FD  TIME-CARD-FILE
00020                 LABEL RECORD OMITTED.
00021             01  TIME-CARD.
00022                 05   I-SOCIAL-SECURITY-NO   PIC 9(9).
00023                 05   I-LAST-NAME            PIC X(16).
00024                 05   I-INITIALS             PIC XX.
00025                 05   I-DEPARTMENT-NO        PIC 999.
00026                 05   I-HOURS-WORKED         PIC 99V9.
00027                 05   I-HOURLY-PAY-RATE      PIC 99V99.
00028                 05   I-NO-OF-DEPENDENTS     PIC 99.
00029                 05   I-MARITAL-STATUS       PIC X.
00030                 05   FILLER                 PIC X(40).
00031             FD  PAYROLL-CHECK-FILE
00032                 LABEL RECORD OMITTED.
00033             01  PAYROLL-CHECK.
00034                 05   FILLER                 PIC X(20).
00035                 05   O-LAST-NAME            PIC X(16).
00036                 05   FILLER                 PIC X.
00037                 05   O-INITIALS             PIC XX.
00038                 05   FILLER                 PIC X(21).
00039                 05   O-NET-PAY              PIC $9999.99.
00040                 05   FILLER                 PIC X(65).

00042           WORKING-STORAGE SECTION.
00043             77   GROSS-PAY                  PIC 9999V99.
00044             77   FEDERAL-INCOME-TAX         PIC 9999V99.
00045             77   STATE-INCOME-TAX           PIC 999V99.
00046             77   LOCAL-INCOME-TAX           PIC 999V99.
00047             77   SOCIAL-SECURITY-TAX        PIC 999V99.
00048             77   TOTAL-DEDUCTIONS           PIC 9999V99.
00049             77   NET-PAY                    PIC 9999V99.
```

Fig. 6.3: *A skeleton payroll program.*

```
00053           PROCEDURE DIVISION.

00055              HOUSEKEEPING.

00057                  OPEN INPUT    TIME-CARD-FILE.
00058                  OPEN OUTPUT PAYROLL-CHECK-FILE.
00059                  MOVE SPACES TO PAYROLL-CHECK.


00061              START-OF-MAINLINE.

00063                  READ TIME-CARD-FILE
00064                      AT END GO TO END-OF-JOB.
00065                  MULTIPLY I-HOURLY-PAY-RATE BY I-HOURS-WORKED GIVING GROSS-PAY
00066                  MULTIPLY GROSS-PAY BY 0.20    GIVING FEDERAL-INCOME-TAX.
00067                  MULTIPLY GROSS-PAY BY 0.015   GIVING STATE-INCOME-TAX.
00068                  MULTIPLY GROSS-PAY BY 0.02    GIVING LOCAL-INCOME-TAX.
00069                  MULTIPLY GROSS-PAY BY 0.0605 GIVING SOCIAL-SECURITY-TAX.

00071                  SUBTRACT FEDERAL-INCOME-TAX, STATE-INCOME-TAX,
00072                      LOCAL-INCOME-TAX, SOCIAL-SECURITY-TAX FROM GROSS-PAY
00073                          GIVING NET-PAY.
00074                  MOVE I-LAST-NAME TO O-LAST-NAME.
00075                  MOVE I-INITIALS   TO O-INITIALS.
00076                  MOVE NET-PAY      TO O-NET-PAY.

00078                  WRITE PAYROLL-CHECK
00079                      AFTER ADVANCING 2 LINES.
00080                  MOVE SPACES TO PAYROLL-CHECK.
00081                  GO TO START-OF-MAINLINE.


00084              END-OF-JOB.

00086                  CLOSE TIME-CARD-FILE.
00087                  CLOSE PAYROLL-CHECK-FILE.
00088                  STOP RUN.
```

Fig. 6.3: *continued.*

The content of this skeleton program is *intentionally* sketchy. It is designed to be more of an outline than a true program. Look back at the list of "things to be done" developed during the very first stage of planning, and compare this list to the program mainline; you should see a very close resemblance. This is not an accident. Quite simply, the function of the mainline is to define, briefly and generally, the things which must be done and the order in which they must be done, with few if any details as to exactly how these functions are to be carried out. From the standpoint of the general functions, however, the program is complete. We can now begin to add the details.

Adding the Details

In the ensuing chapters, routines will be added to perform each of the major functions of the program, thus putting flesh on the skeleton. Although it may be necessary to add a few fields to WORKING-STORAGE, you will discover that the IDENTIFICATION, ENVIRONMENT, and DATA DIVISIONs are remarkably complete, allowing us to concentrate on the logic of the computational modules. Almost without exception, the instructions currently making up the mainline of this skeleton program will be replaced, but this should not surprise you; the skeleton program was, after all, never designed with permanence in mind.

Our approach in attacking the detail modules will be simple. Just as if we were starting from scratch, the first step will be planning, eventually leading to a flowchart. The data fields needed in this module will then be listed. Most should already appear in the DATA DIVISION of the skeleton program; if not, we'll add new fields. Finally, the routine will be coded, the old psuedo-instruction in the mainline will be replaced by a PERFORM referencing this new logic module, and the new version of the program will be tested. If that sounds like the program development process starting all over again, you are absolutely correct, because that is exactly what we will be doing. In effect, each module of logic in this program will be treated as if it is a separate program in its own right. The mainline will tie all these small programs together to form one big one. In this way, a massive, complex data processing application can be broken down into a set of little problems, and little problems are easy.

There are many different names for what we are doing: modular programming, structured programming, and top-down programming are three. Although many consider this a new programming approach, it isn't. Looking beyond programming, this technique is very old. Read any good English composition book, and you'll find a sur surprisingly similar set of guidelines for writing a paper: define your topic, outline your entire paper, develop detailed outlines of the individual sections of your paper, and then begin writing. It's a proved approach to writing good English, and it works with COBOL, too.

SUMMARY

The chapter began with the definition and development of a broad plan for a program to compute payroll. As we moved into the detailed planning stage, it became obvious that each of the major functions involved in computing payroll—gross pay computation, income tax computation, and so on—was itself a highly complex operation calling for careful planning and programming. In fact, the individual steps were themselves so complex that the idea of trying to write the whole program as a single routine was almost impossible.

As an alternative to developing a kludge, we turned to the idea of modular, structured programming, developing the program in easy to follow stages. Our intent became one of carefully defining and developing the program mainline and then adding the complex logic associated with each major computational step as a series of separate modules.

Having decided to attack the program in pieces, we developed a skeleton mainline complete with fully defined input and output records, a reasonable set of work fields, and simple, representative computations. This skeleton program was written, keypunched to cards, and tested. In subsequent chapters, the computational details will be added, one major function at a time.

KEY WORDS

floating dollar sign	mainline	skeleton mainline
kludge	module	test data

EXERCISES

1. What is a "kludge"? What are some of the problems associated with a "kludge"?

2. On many realistic computer applications, each of the major steps is itself so complex that the idea of writing the program as one massive routine becomes almost unworkable. When you are faced with such complex problems, the structured modular approach to program development becomes highly desirable. Describe the nature of this approach. What are some of the advantages?

3. Good test data is essential to proper program implementation. Describe some of the characteristics of good test data.

4. Keypunch and test the skeleton payroll program developed in this chapter. In later chapters, we will be asking you to add computational routines to the skeleton.

5. Over the past several chapters, a program to compute a grade point average has been developed. Consider how you might go about adding the logic to handle such complex special conditions as grades for incompletes, successful progress on an independent project, no grade submitted by the instructor, pass/fail, and audit. Once again, you will be asked to add the detailed logic modules in later chapters.

6. University billing can become quite complex. To the full-time student, tuition is simply a fixed charge of so many dollars per term, but the part-time student sees a variable charge of so many dollars per credit hour. Room and board

charges can vary too, with special plans for full room and board, board only, room only, no weekend meals, and several other possible combinations. Activity charges vary from the fixed fee for full-time students to a cost per credit hour for the part-timer.

In this chapter, you are to develop a simple skeleton mainline for preparing university bills. Input records contain the following fields:

positions	contents
1-9	student identification number
10-25	student name
26-27	credit hours registered
28	room classification
29	board classification
30	activities code
31-80	unused but available for other fields as needed

Your skeleton program should simply read input records and prepare bills based on the assumption that all students are standard full-time students with full room, board, and tuition; use the rates currently used by your own school. Later, we'll be adding the routines needed to handle the unusual situations.

7. Input records to a bill preparation program are:

positions	contents
1-6	customer number
7-20	customer name
21-28	part number of product purchased
29-35	description of product purchased
36-42	selling price (99999V99)
43	sales tax code
44	shipping weight code
45	shipping zone code

Basically, the program is very simple, with state sales tax being computed at a 4% rate and shipping costs being free (local service area). Occasionally, however, out of state customers make it necessary for our store to compute sales tax at a different rate, and shipping costs for customers outside our area are computed as a function of both the shipping weight and the shipping distance (the zone).

In developing this program, start by writing a skeleton routine designed to handle only local customers. In a later chapter, the additional logic needed to handle distant customers will be added.

8. Rate structures for computing the amount due on an electric bill can get very complex, with different rates being applied to regular household customers, total electric customers, industrial customers, government installations, educational institutions, hospitals, industrial concerns that are willing to accept a cutback in the event of a shortage of power, and many others. Given this vast array of different rate structures, it is virtually impossible to write an electric bill program as a single large routine; modular programming is almost essential on this application.

Here in Chapter 6, you are to develop a skeleton mainline for an electric bills computation program. Input records contain the following fields:

positions	contents
1-2	rate code
3-10	user or customer number
11-17	kilowatt hours used (nearest hour)

The rate code identifies the type of customer and, later, will be used to determine which rate structure module should be utilized; ignore it for now. The skeleton mainline should simply read input records and compute the amount due using a simple algorithm such as 1 cent per kilowatt hour used. Take the time to design a reasonable format for the output data and print something resembling an electric bill. Keypunch data cards for several different customers.

In subsequent chapters you will be asked to add a number of routines to compute the amount due following several different rate structures.

9. In mid-April of each year, most American citizens are required to pay their income tax. Typically, this involves filling out a number of forms. Most people use only a small subset of the available forms, entering their wages earned and their number of dependents, and then consulting a series of tax tables using the standard deduction to compute the amount of tax due. Others, however, must use a far more complex approach, reporting income from interest, royalties, dividends, a small business, a farm, and any of dozens of other sources. Many taxpayers itemize their deductions, thus calling for additional computations and the use of a different set of tax tables.

In this chapter, you are to plan and write a simple income tax computation program. Input records contain:

positions	contents
1-9	social security number
10-25	taxpayer name
26-33	wages earned (999999V99) as reported on W-2 forms.
34-35	number of dependents
36	filing status (a code)

Other positions are available for other fields as needed later. For now, the filing status can be ignored, as we'll use a very simple algorithm for computing tax due.

Write the skeleton mainline to read input records and compute income tax due as a straight 10% of taxable income, where taxable income is simply wages earned minus $750 for each dependent claimed. Print an output report listing all the input data and the computed amount of tax due. As with the other programs in this chapter, we will be asking you to add the detailed computational routines in subsequent chapters.

7

Adding Functions to the Mainline

OVERVIEW

In this chapter, a routine to compute state income tax will be planned, coded, and added to the mainline developed in Chapter 6. The procedure we will follow will resemble the general program development process described, for complete programs, in past chapters: a careful definition, followed by planning, followed by coding, and ending with testing and implementation.

Several very important points are stressed during the development of this tax computation routine. First, and perhaps foremost, is breaking a complex problem into simple pieces and solving it a piece at a time. Closely related to this general idea is the more concrete concept of modular programming. Within COBOL, a specific technique, the use of nested IF statements, will be introduced.

STATE TAX COMPUTATIONS

In Chapter 6, a skeleton mainline of a payroll program was developed. We are now ready to begin adding meat to these bones by implementing a series of routines to perform the actual detailed computations. Computation of state income tax will be the first detailed logic module added.

Many states collect an income tax. Most are modeled after the federal income tax system, with the amount to be paid computed as a percentage of actual income. Rather than select the actual income tax rate structure used by any one state, we have invented an imaginary representative table (Fig. 7.1).

Briefly, the algorithm for using the table is:

1. compute the amount of gross pay;

2. using gross pay, enter the tax table and find three numbers: the base tax, a percentage tax, and the lower limit for this percentage tax:

3. using these numbers, compute the amount of tax due.

Fig. 7.1: *A Typical State Tax Table.*

for gross pay between:	the amount of tax is:
$0 and $50	$0.00
$50 and $100	1% of excess over $50
$100 and $150	$0.50 plus 1½% of excess over $100
$150 and $200	$1.25 plus 2% of excess over $150
$200 and above	$2.25 plus 2½% of excess over $200

Perhaps an example would help. Assume that an individual earns $125.00 in weekly gross pay. Reading down the first column of the table, we find that $125.00 lies between $100 and $150, thus defining the tax bracket. The amount of tax due is $0.50 plus 1½% of the excess over $100. The excess over $100 (125 minus 100) is $25, and 1½% of this excess is $0.38. Added to the base tax of $0.50, the amount of tax due can be computed as $0.78.

Let's generalize this example into a set of steps. To compute the amount of state income tax due,

1. compute gross pay;

2. find the income range in which this taxpayer fits by locating a line in the tax table where the computed gross pay lies between the upper and lower limits;

3. subtract from gross pay the low limit of the selected table entry, giving excess earnings;

4. multiply excess earnings by the percentage associated with the selected table entry, giving the proportional tax;

5. add the base tax and the proportional tax giving the total tax due.

This set of steps is roughly equivalent to the human-level solution developed during the planning stage of earlier programs.

PLANNING A COMPUTER-LEVEL SOLUTION

For the most part, each of the psuedo-instructions described above converts directly to a single COBOL instruction. There is, however, one exception. The second step says to find the proper income range in a tax table. This is not a simple IF test. The table in question (Fig. 7.1) contains a total of 5 lines, and the only way the computer, limited as it is to simple yes/no logic, can possibly determine which line is correct for a given individual's level of income is by performing a *series* of IF tests. An example of this logic for the tax table shown in Fig. 7.1 can be seen in the flowchart of Fig. 7.2.

Carefully follow the logic of this flowchart, moving from top to bottom and from left to right. The tax table of Fig. 7.1 identifies a first tax bracket, individuals earning $50 or less. The first test compares gross pay with this fifty dollar limit; if gross pay is less than or equal to (the $\leq$ symbol) 50, the routine computes the amount of tax due ($0.00) and then drops to the end of the block of logic. If, on the other hand, the amount of gross pay is greater than $50, the logical flow moves to the second test, where gross pay is compared with $100, the upper limit on the second bracket of the tax table. Basically, each test defines the upper limit of one tax bracket. Program logic drops through the table, step by step, comparing taxable income to each upper limit until such time as an upper limit exceeds gross pay; this event defines the proper tax bracket. Once the bracket is located, logic moves to the right where the amount of tax due is computed, after which the flow of control moves beyond the table look-up module.

Once again an example might help; we'll stay with the $125 income. Start at the upper left of the flowchart of Fig. 7.2, and begin to ask the questions defined in the diamond symbols. Is gross pay less than or equal to $50? No. Move down. Is gross pay less than or equal to 100? No. Once again, move down. Is gross pay less than or equal to 150? Yes! Clearly, 125 is less than 150. We have found the proper tax bracket, so we begin to move to the right. The excess portion of income is computed (125 - 100 = 25), and 1½% of this value is found (1½% of 25 is 0.375, which rounds to 0.38). Finally, the base tax for this bracket, $0.50 or fifty cents, is added to the tax on excess income, and the total amount of tax due, $0.78, is the result. Having computed the state income tax, program logic can now move on to other things, bypassing the remaining logical tests.

Modular Program Development

We have now defined the logic needed to compute state income tax. How shall we integrate this module into the skeleton mainline developed in Chapter 6? Basically we have two choices: we can add the logic to the mainline, or we can write a separate detailed logic module and PERFORM it from the mainline. Both approaches will work, producing programs that generate correct values for state income tax, but which approach is better?

For a number of reasons, it is preferable to design a complex program as a collection of independent computational routines tied together by a relatively small mainline than to design a single, massive mainline. The most obvious advantage of the modular approach is that each major logical function will be housed in its own easily located block of code. While perhaps not of obvious value just yet (we are, after all, about to add only our first module), try to picture the payroll program after all the detailed logic for gross pay and all the deductions is in place. Imagine that an improper value for state income tax is discovered in testing or in actually running the program. With the modular approach, the programmer can concentrate on the routine that computes state income tax, ignoring the rest of the program. With the massive mainline approach, however, the programmer might have to plow through a good part of the program before even finding the relevant code. The modular approach makes program **debugging** easier.

The modular approach also simplifies program **testing**. With a massive mainline housing all program logic, essentially the entire program must be written and tested at one time. With the modular approach, one detailed logic module can be added at a time, and the program can be tested and debugged in stages. In this example, we are about to add a state tax computation routine to an existing skeleton mainline. The mainline has already been tested. If, after adding the detailed logic module and replacing the simple state tax computation statement with a PERFORM, the program doesn't work, it is probably reasonable to assume that the problem lies with the code we have just added. Later, after the state tax routine has been successfully debugged, another logic module (federal income tax, for example) can be added to the program. Again, any errors can probably be isolated to the new routine.

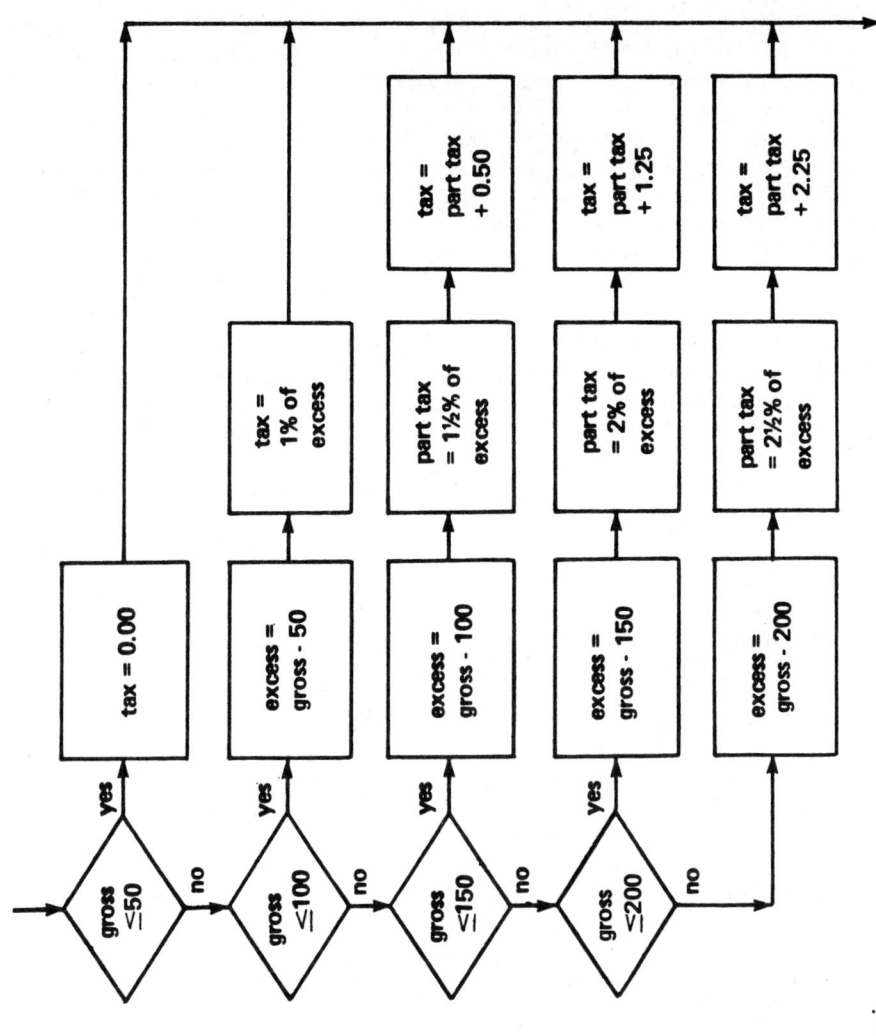

Fig. 7.2: *An example of table look-up logic.*

Program **documentation** is also helped by a modular approach. In a well-designed program, the mainline will read much like an outline or overview of the entire program, giving the reader a quick grasp of the objective and the logical flow. Details are grouped away from this mainline, allowing the reader to concentrate only on those that are of interest. The problem with the massive mainline approach is that the reader often becomes so bogged down in the computational details that he or she cannot see the forest for the trees. Modular programs are simply easier to follow and the whole point of documentation is to make a program easy to understand. Modular design is a significant aid to good program documentation.

Finally, there is the question of program **maintenance**. A program like payroll will almost certainly be used for a number of years. During this time, changes will definitely occur. Income tax rates will change. New Social Security laws will be passed. Unusual conditions will bring previously undetected program bugs to light. A modular program is easy to modify; for example, a new income tax rate structure calls for only a new income tax computation routine, with no other changes needed. If, on the other hand, everything has been included in a massive mainline, it is very easy to miss a key instruction or two when making a change.

We will be using a modular approach in developing this payroll program, adding the major detailed computations as independent logic modules, and using a series of PERFORM statements in the program mainline to tie these pieces together.

Defining the Data Fields

The logic for computing state income tax is defined. Since the mainline is responsible for all input and output, we can bypass the step of defining devices; thus the only thing that remains is to define the data fields.

The best way to go about defining the data fields is often simply to work through the necessary computations, step by step, listing each of the participating fields. Gross pay is the starting point; this field is computed in the mainline. Gross pay will be compared with a series of constants to find the tax bracket. Once the bracket has been located, we can begin the process of computing the tax. The first step is to find the excess income, another needed data field. Using the excess income, the proportional portion of the tax can be found; the proportional tax is another field. Finally, this proportional tax can be added to a constant, the base tax, to get state income tax. A summary of the participating data fields can be seen in Fig. 7.3. Several of these data fields were not defined in the skeleton mainline; thus it will be necessary to add a 77-level entry for each of the new ones.

CODING A SOLUTION IN COBOL

We are now ready to begin coding a solution in COBOL. The mainline developed in Chapter 6 will serve as a base. The IDENTIFICATION and ENVIRONMENT DIVISIONs are fine just the way they are. Since the logic we are about to add requires no new input or output, the FILE SECTION of the DATA DIVISION also remains unchanged. Several new entries must be made to the WORKING-STORAGE SECTION, which has been done in Fig. 7.4.

Fig. 7.3: *A list of the data fields used in computing state income tax.*

field name	source
gross pay	computed in mainline
excess income	computed in tax routine
proportional tax	computed in tax routine
state income tax	computed in tax routine

The real changes are concentrated in the PROCEDURE DIVISION. First, the dummy reference to the state tax computation as coded in the skeleton mainline must be replaced by a PERFORM statement referencing the new detailed logic module (Fig. 7.5). Finally, the routine to compute state income tax can be added (Fig. 7.6).

The word **subroutine** is sometimes used to describe such independent logic modules. A subroutine is a routine that is part of another routine, and a module such as the state income tax computation routine certainly qualifies. We have been careful to avoid using "subroutine" in describing our logic modules because, many computer scientists and data processing professionals restrict the term to a particular type of program module, coded according to a number of very specific rules. We are (loosely) coding internal subroutines but, to eliminate any possibility of misunderstanding, we will continue to avoid using the word.

Before we continue, a little hint on coding technique. *Don't* try to conserve paper. Instead, as you are developing these routines, have several coding sheets in front of you. One should contain the WORKING-STORAGE 77-level entries, your work fields. A second should contain the developing logic. Other sheets containing the mainline and the FILE SECTION of the DATA DIVISION should be available for reference. Carefully check each new PROCEDURE DIVISION instruction, making certain that *all* data names are defined in the DATA DIVISION; if a new one is encountered, create a 77-level entry as you go.

Nested IF Statements

At the heart of the state income tax computation routine (Fig. 7.6) is a table look-up operation designed to locate the proper tax bracket. How can such complex logic be implemented in COBOL? One answer is by using **nested IF statements**.

COBOL Coding Form

SYSTEM	PAYROLL	PUNCHING INSTRUCTIONS	PAGE 3 OF 7
PROGRAM	COMPUTE HOURLY PAYROLL	GRAPHIC: Ø	CARD FORM #
PROGRAMMER	DAVIS & FISHER — DATE 2-1-79	PUNCH: ZERO	

```
       WORKING-STORAGE SECTION.

           77  GROSS-PAY                      PIC 9999V99.
           77  FEDERAL-INCOME-TAX             PIC 9999V99.
           77  STATE-INCOME-TAX               PIC 999V99.
           77  LOCAL-INCOME-TAX               PIC 999V99.
           77  SOCIAL-SECURITY-TAX            PIC 999V99.
           77  TOTAL-DEDUCTIONS               PIC 9999V99.
           77  NET-PAY                        PIC 9999V99.
           77  EXCESS-INCOME                  PIC 9999V99.
           77  PART-TAX                       PIC 9999V99.
```

Fig. 7.4: *The WORKING-STORAGE SECTION.*

COBOL Coding Form

SYSTEM: PAYROLL
PROGRAM: COMPUTE HOURLY PAYROLL
PROGRAMMER: DAVIS & FISHER DATE 2-1-79
PUNCHING INSTRUCTIONS — GRAPHIC: Ø PUNCH: ZERO
PAGE 5 OF 7

```
START-OF-MAINLINE.
    READ TIME-CARD-FILE
        AT END GO TO END-OF-JOB.
    MULTIPLY I-HOURLY-PAY-RATE BY I-HOURS-WORKED
        GIVING GROSS-PAY.
    MULTIPLY GROSS-PAY BY Ø.2Ø GIVING FEDERAL-INCOME-TAX.
    PERFORM STATE-TAX THRU END-STATE-TAX
    MULTIPLY GROSS-PAY BY Ø.Ø2 GIVING LOCAL-INCOME-TAX.
    MULTIPLY GROSS-PAY BY Ø.Ø6Ø5 GIVING SOCIAL-SECURITY-TAX.
    SUBTRACT FEDERAL-INCOME-TAX, STATE-INCOME-TAX,
        LOCAL-INCOME-TAX, SOCIAL-SECURITY-TAX FROM GROSS-PAY
        GIVING NET-PAY.
    MOVE I-LAST-NAME TO O-LAST-NAME
    MOVE I-INITIALS TO O-INITIALS
    MOVE NET-PAY TO O-NET-PAY
    WRITE PAYROLL-CHECK
        AFTER ADVANCING 2 LINES
    MOVE SPACES TO PAYROLL-CHECK.
    GO TO START-OF-MAINLINE.
END-OF-JOB.
    CLOSE TIME-CARD-FILE
    CLOSE PAYROLL-CHECK-FILE
    STOP RUN.
```

Fig. 7.5: *A PERFORM statement is added to the mainline.*

COBOL Coding Form

SYSTEM	PAYROLL	PUNCHING INSTRUCTIONS		PAGE 6 OF 7
PROGRAM	COMPUTE HOURLY PAYROLL	GRAPHIC	Ø	CARD FORM #
PROGRAMMER	DAVIS & FISHER — DATE 2-1-79	PUNCH	ZERO	

```
      ******************************************************************
      **                                                              **
      **       THIS ROUTINE COMPUTES THE STATE INCOME TAX             **
      **                                                              **
       STATE-TAX.

           IF GROSS-PAY IS LESS THAN 5Ø OR EQUAL TO 5Ø
           THEN
               MOVE ZEROS TO STATE-INCOME-TAX
           ELSE
               IF GROSS-PAY IS LESS THAN 1ØØ OR EQUAL TO 1ØØ
               THEN
                   SUBTRACT 5Ø FROM GROSS-PAY GIVING EXCESS-INCOME
                   MULTIPLY EXCESS-INCOME B Ø.Ø1
                       GIVING STATE-INCOME-TAX ROUNDED
               ELSE
                   IF GROSS-PAY IS LESS THAN 15Ø OR EQUAL TO 15Ø
                   THEN
                       SUBTRACT 1ØØ FROM GROSS-PAY GIVING EXCESS-INCOME
                       MULTIPLY EXCESS-INCOME BY Ø.Ø15
                           GIVING PART-TAX ROUNDED
                       ADD PART-TAX, Ø.5Ø GIVING STATE-INCOME-TAX
                   ELSE
```

Fig. 7.6: *The state income tax routine.*

```
SYSTEM    PAYROLL
PROGRAM   COMPUTE HOURLY PAYROLL
PROGRAMMER DAVIS & FISHER           DATE 2-1-79
GRAPHIC  Ø
PUNCH    ZERO
PAGE 7 OF 7
```

```
        IF GROSS-PAY IS LESS THAN 200 OR EQUAL TO 200
        THEN
            SUBTRACT 150 FROM GROSS-PAY
                GIVING EXCESS-INCOME
            MULTIPLY EXCESS-INCOME BY Ø.Ø2
                GIVING PART-TAX ROUNDED
            ADD PART-TAX, 1.25 GIVING STATE-INCOME-TAX
        ELSE
            SUBTRACT 200 FROM GROSS-PAY
                GIVING EXCESS-INCOME
            MULTIPLY EXCESS-INCOME BY Ø.Ø25
                GIVING PART-TAX ROUNDED
            ADD PART-TAX, 2.25 GIVING STATE-INCOME-TAX.
    END-STATE-TAX.
        EXIT.
**
**********************************************************************
```

Fig. 7.6: *continued.*

The general form of an IF statement begins with a condition. If that condition is true, a first conditional statement is executed; if, on the other hand, the condition is false, a second conditional statement is executed. What if one of these conditional statements is itself another IF? Assume, for example, the following simple set of code:

```
IF VARIABLE IS EQUAL TO 0

    THEN

            MOVE 0 TO FIELD

    ELSE    IF VARIABLE IS GREATER THAN 0

            THEN

                    MOVE 10 to FIELD

            ELSE    MOVE -10 TO FIELD.
```

What is the value of FIELD? The answer to this question, of course, depends on the value of VARIABLE. If the condition "VARIABLE IS EQUAL TO 0" is true, FIELD is set equal to 0, and that's the end of it. If the condition is false, the second IF is executed; in fact, the *only* way for the second IF to be executed is if the first condition is false. These IF statements are said to be **nested**.

Perhaps the best way to visualize how nested IF statements work is by comparing them with an equivalent flow diagram (Fig. 7.7). Note that the logical flow through this construct begins with a test, a COBOL condition. If the condition is true, an action is taken and we rejoin the flow of logic after the end of this nested IF block. If the condition is false, a second condition is encountered, leading again to one of two paths.

Note that as soon as a true condition is encountered, an action is taken and the logic module ends. Imagine that, rather than having only two IF's, several were nested in this way. As soon as a true condition were encountered, an action could be taken and the program could move on beyond the nest. Such nested IFs provide a mechanism for implementing a table look-up operation.

Table Look-up in COBOL

Earlier in the chapter a flow chart of the table look-up operation for the state tax table was developed (Fig. 7.2). Except for the fact that there are more tests and more steps surrounding each test, the flowchart of Fig. 7.2 is similar to the one in Fig. 7.7. State income tax computations can be implemented using a set of nested IF statements.

Consider the code of Fig. 7.6. It shows a complete routine for computing state income tax. The instructions have been carefully indented to show where each new tax bracket begins. As you read down the program logic, you will encounter a series of IF statements, each testing to see if gross pay is less than the upper limit of one

IF VARIABLE IS EQUAL TO 0
    THEN MOVE 0 TO FIELD

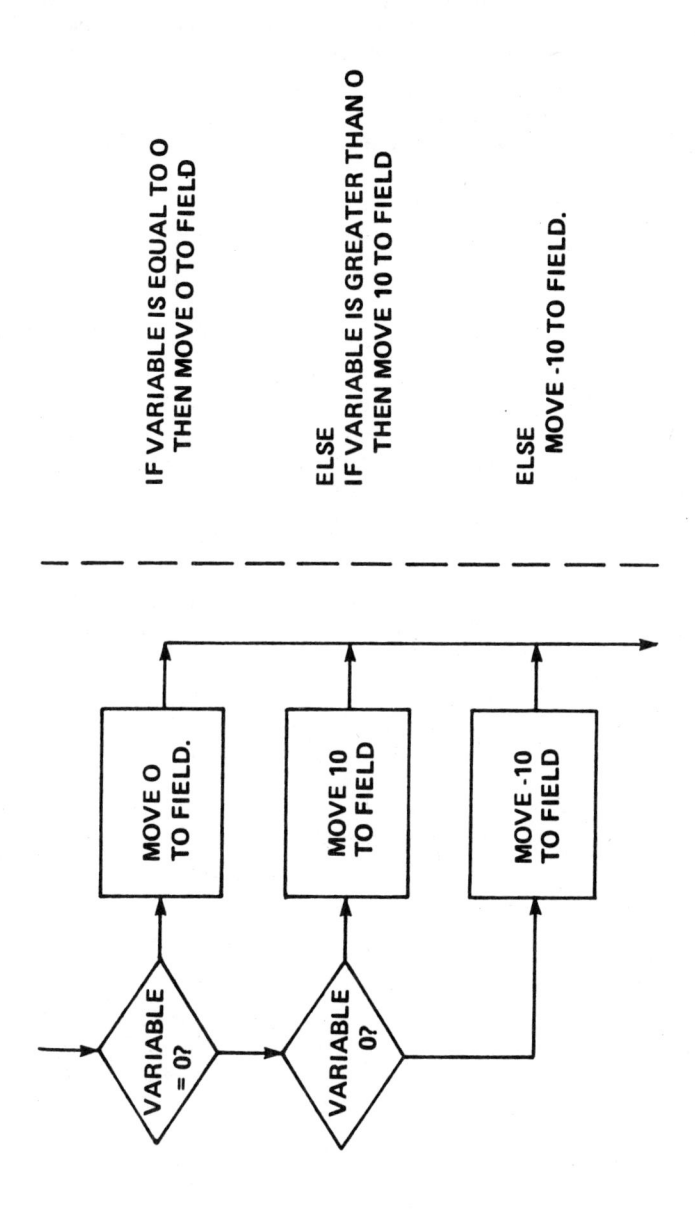

ELSE
IF VARIABLE IS GREATER THAN 0
    THEN MOVE 10 TO FIELD

ELSE
    MOVE -10 TO FIELD.

Fig. 7.7: *Nested IF Statements.*

bracket. In this way, the proper tax bracket can be located; when it is, the tax can be computed and logical flow can proceed to the end of the routine.

A few things may look a bit different in this routine. Consider first the descriptive information found at the beginning of the module. These statements are **comments**. On the version of COBOL being used by the authors, a comment is designated by the presence of an asterisk (*) in column 7 of the instruction card. Comments are not actually part of the program, being added to the code by the programmer as an optional aid to documentation. Some versions of COBOL do not use an asterisk to denote a comment; on these systems, the NOTE statement can be used instead.

Another unusual characteristic of the code shown in Fig. 7.6 is an almost complete absense of periods. To this point, we have been terminating each COBOL statement with a period. Technically, this is unnecessary; groups of COBOL statements may be combined to form a COBOL **sentence** (which must end with a period). This allows the programmer to group related instructions into a single sentence. Within the nested IFs, the action to be taken in the event of a true condition normally involves three distinct steps: compute excess income; compute the percentage amount of tax due on this excess; and then add the base tax for the bracket. These three steps are obviously related, and thus should be part of the same sentence. On a much broader scale, *all* the instructions contained in this nest are related. Note that the only period in this entire mass of code is found at the end of the last statement. It must be done this way, as the use of a period terminates the IF... THEN... ELSE block.

Note also that a **ROUNDED** option has been added to each multiply statement. With it, a computed tax of $0.375 will be rounded to $0.38. Without it, the same result will be truncated to $0.37.

Read through the instructions of Fig. 7.6 carefully. Make up some test data and use the logic to compute state income tax. Does it work? It should.

TESTING THE NEW VERSION OF THE PROGRAM

Since the instructions needed to compute state income tax have been coded, it's time to keypunch these statements, incorporate them into the COBOL program, and run a test. The results are shown in Fig. 7.8.

This is a pretty good-sized program. Imagine how difficult it would have been had we simply started trying to do the entire thing, rather than deciding to attack it in parts. Modular programming makes sense, not only for beginners but for experienced programmers as well. The idea is simple. If the problem is at all difficult, break it into little pieces that are easy to solve and then put the pieces together.

In Chapter 8, we'll be developing a routine to compute federal income tax. The key idea of these chapters is the methodical, step-by-step approach to building a problem solution.

```
  1                     2.42.39       SEP 12,1978
00001           IDENTIFICATION DIVISION.
00002           PROGRAM-ID. PAYROLL.
00003           AUTHOR.     DAVIS & FISHER.
00004           REMARKS.    THIS PROGRAM COMPUTES THE NET PAY
00005                       FOR HOURLY EMPLOYEES. THE STATE
00006                       INCOME TAX MODULE HAS BEEN ADDED.

00008           ENVIRONMENT DIVISION.
00009               CONFIGURATION SECTION.
00010               SOURCE-COMPUTER.  IBM-370-148.
00011               OBJECT-COMPUTER.  IBM-370-148.
00012               SPECIAL-NAMES.    C01 IS NEW-PAGE.
00013               INPUT-OUTPUT SECTION.
00014               FILE-CONTROL.
00015                   SELECT TIME-CARD-FILE     ASSIGN TO UT-S-TIMECRDS.
00016                   SELECT PAYROLL-CHECK-FILE ASSIGN TO UT-S-PAYCHEKS.

00018           DATA DIVISION.
00019           FILE SECTION.
00020           FD  TIME-CARD-FILE
00021               LABEL RECORD OMITTED.
00022           01  TIME-CARD.
00023               05  I-SOCIAL-SECURITY-NO    PIC 9(9).
00024               05  I-LAST-NAME             PIC X(16).
00025               05  I-INITIALS              PIC XX.
00026               05  I-DEPARTMENT-NO         PIC 999.
00027               05  I-HOURS-WORKED          PIC 99V9.
00028               05  I-HOURLY-PAY-RATE       PIC 99V99.
00029               05  I-NO-OF-DEPENDENTS      PIC 99.
00030               05  I-MARITAL-STATUS        PIC X.
00031               05  FILLER                  PIC X(40).
00032           FD  PAYROLL-CHECK-FILE
00033               LABEL RECORD OMITTED.
00034           01  PAYROLL-CHECK.
00035               05  FILLER                  PIC X(20).
00036               05  O-LAST-NAME             PIC X(16).
00037               05  FILLER                  PIC X.
00038               05  O-INITIALS              PIC XX.
00039               05  FILLER                  PIC X(21).
00040               05  O-NET-PAY               PIC $9999.99.
00041               05  FILLER                  PIC X(65).

00043           WORKING-STORAGE SECTION.
00044           77  GROSS-PAY               PIC 9999V99.
00045           77  FEDERAL-INCOME-TAX      PIC 9999V99.
00046           77  STATE-INCOME-TAX        PIC 999V99.
00047           77  LOCAL-INCOME-TAX        PIC 999V99.
00048           77  SOCIAL-SECURITY-TAX     PIC 999V99.
00049           77  TOTAL-DEDUCTIONS        PIC 9999V99.
00050           77  NET-PAY                 PIC 9999V99.
00051           77  EXCESS-INCOME           PIC 9999V99.
00052           77  PART-TAX                PIC 9999V99.
```

Fig. 7.8: *The payroll program with a state tax computation module.*

```
00056           PROCEDURE DIVISION.
00058               HOUSEKEEPING.
00060                   OPEN INPUT  TIME-CARD-FILE.
00061                   OPEN OUTPUT PAYROLL-CHECK-FILE.
00062                   MOVE SPACES TO PAYROLL-CHECK.

00064               START-OF-MAINLINE.
00066                   READ TIME-CARD-FILE
00067                       AT END GO TO END-OF-JOB.
00068                   MULTIPLY I-HOURLY-PAY-RATE BY I-HOURS-WORKED
00069                       GIVING GROSS-PAY.
00070                   MULTIPLY GROSS-PAY BY 0.20    GIVING FEDERAL-INCOME-TAX.
00071                   PERFORM  STATE-TAX THRU END-STATE-TAX.
00072                   MULTIPLY GROSS-PAY BY 0.02    GIVING LOCAL-INCOME-TAX
00073                   MULTIPLY GROSS-PAY BY 0.0605 GIVING SOCIAL-SECURITY-TAX

00075                   SUBTRACT FEDERAL-INCOME-TAX, STATE-INCOME-TAX,
00076                       LOCAL-INCOME-TAX, SOCIAL-SECURITY-TAX FROM GROSS-PAY
00077                       GIVING NET-PAY
00078                   MOVE I-LAST-NAME TO O-LAST-NAME
00079                   MOVE I-INITIALS  TO O-INITIALS
00080                   MOVE NET-PAY     TO O-NET-PAY

00082                   WRITE PAYROLL-CHECK
00083                       AFTER ADVANCING 2 LINES
00084                   MOVE SPACES TO PAYROLL-CHECK
00085                   GO TO START-OF-MAINLINE.

00087               END-OF-JOB.

00089                   CLOSE TIME-CARD-FILE
00090                   CLOSE PAYROLL-CHECK-FILE
00091                   STOP RUN.
```

Fig. 7.8: *continued.*

```
00096      ************************************************************
00097      **                                                         **
00098      **         THIS ROUTINE COMPUTES THE STATE INCOME TAX      **
00099      **                                                         **
00100        STATE-TAX.

00102            IF GROSS-PAY IS LESS THAN 50 OR EQUAL TO 50
00103            THEN
00104                 MOVE ZEROS TO STATE-INCOME-TAX
00105            ELSE
00106                 IF GROSS-PAY IS LESS THAN 100 OR EQUAL TO 100
00107                 THEN
00108                      SUBTRACT 50 FROM GROSS-PAY GIVING EXCESS-INCOME
00109                      MULTIPLY EXCESS-INCOME BY 0.01
00110                           GIVING STATE-INCOME-TAX ROUNDED
00111                 ELSE
00112                      IF GROSS-PAY IS LESS THAN 150 OR EQUAL TO 150
00113                      THEN
00114                           SUBTRACT 100 FROM GROSS-PAY GIVING EXCESS-INCOME
00115                           MULTIPLY EXCESS-INCOME BY 0.015
00116                                GIVING PART-TAX ROUNDED
00117                           ADD PART-TAX, 0.50 GIVING STATE-INCOME-TAX
00118                      ELSE
00119                           IF GROSS-PAY IS LESS THAN 200 OR EQUAL TO 200
00120                           THEN
00121                                SUBTRACT 150 FROM GROSS-PAY
00122                                     GIVING EXCESS-INCOME
00123                                MULTIPLY EXCESS-INCOME BY 0.02
00124                                     GIVING PART-TAX ROUNDED
00125                                ADD PART-TAX, 1.25 GIVING STATE-INCOME-TAX
00126                           ELSE
00127                                SUBTRACT 200 FROM GROSS-PAY
00128                                     GIVING EXCESS-INCOME
00129                                MULTIPLY EXCESS-INCOME BY 0.025
00130                                     GIVING PART-TAX ROUNDED
00131                                ADD PART-TAX, 2.25 GIVING STATE-INCOME-TAX.

00133        END-STATE-TAX.

00135           EXIT.
00136      **                                                         **
00137      ************************************************************
```

Fig. 7.8: *continued.*

Some Final Comments on Nested IF Statements

Earlier in the chapter, an example of the use of nested IF statements was presented. In this example, IFs following the first one were executed only if the tested condition were false. To clear up a possible misunderstanding, a subsequent IF can be associated with a true condition, too. Later, perhaps, we'll have reason to use this structure in an example.

SUMMARY

In Chapter 6, a skeleton version of the payroll computation mainline was planned and coded. In this chapter, the first of the major computational routines (state income tax) was added to the mainline.

Computation of state income tax involves entering a table to find the proper amount of tax for a given level of income. We began by carefully defining the algorithm to be used, illustrating how the standard tables are used. A flow diagram of the table look-up process was developed. Next, we discussed a number of alternatives for placing the income tax computation logic, considering the massive mainline approach and contrasting it with the modular approach to program development. We decided to treat each logically complete function as a separate routine, emphasizing that this tends to simplify the tasks of program maintenance, testing, documentation, and debugging.

Having discussed the logical content and placement of the state income tax routine, we turned our attention to the problem of actually coding this logic. (Note that, once again, the coding begins only after the problem has been essentially solved.) The use of nested IF statements as a means for performing a table look-up function was introduced. The ROUNDED option was briefly discussed. The use of comments to clearly identify the function of a program module was stressed, as was the need to adequately test each routine.

KEY WORDS

comments	maintenance	sentence
debugging	nested IF statement	subroutine
documentation	ROUNDED option	testing

EXERCISES

1. One key point of discussion in this chapter involved the proper placement of a routine. Several alternatives were discussed, with each one being technically correct; in other words there was more than one "correct" way to solve the problem. How does this fact relate to the argument that programming is still somewhat of an art? Why was the modular approach preferred?

2. An important criterion for designing programs is ease of maintenance. Why do you suppose this is so important in business data processing?

3. Explain what happens with a set of nested IF statements. How can nested IF statements be used for table look-ups?

4. Why are comments valuable?

5. Assuming that your state has an income tax, add a routine to the payroll program to compute state income tax due using the rate structure of your own state.

6. Add to the skeleton payroll mainline a routine to compute gross pay according to the following rules:

   a. Any hours worked over 40 are to be paid at 1½ times the normal hourly rate.

   b. A shift premium of 5% is to be paid for all second shift work; a premium of 8% is paid for third shift. What this means is that after regular gross pay has been computed, 5% extra is to be added for second shift and 8% is to be added for third shift. Assume that the shift is punched in column 41.

   c. Any hours worked on Sundays or holidays are to be paid at double the normal rate. If the Sunday/holiday hours are worked on second or third shift, the normal shift premium is to be added to this double pay. The number of Sunday/holiday hours worked is punched in columns 42 through 44 (99V9). These hours are not included in the regular hours worked. To avoid the possibility of data error leading to program termination, punch zeros in any test data cards (columns 42-44) for which there are no Sunday/holiday hours.

7. In Chapter 6, you were asked to develop the outline of a university billing program. The following table represents the university's tuition charges:

	in-state	out of state
full-time	$500	$850
part-time	$50/credit	$85/credit
part time over 65	$25/credit	$85/credit
part time audit	$25/credit	$25/credit

A part time student is defined as anyone taking 10 or fewer credit hours. Incorporate this tuition table into your university billing program; if you would prefer, use the actual tuition charges for your own school. You may have to add fields to the input record, so take your time in planning a solution.

8. Another routine to be added to the unversity billing program involves computation of certain non-tuition charges, including such things as laboratory fees, activity fees, parking fees, and athletic fees. The following table describes the fee structure of a hypothetical college:

fee	required	amount
student activity	yes	$50
student activity	yes	$5/credit part time
laboratory fee	no	$10 if lab course
parking fee	no	$25 if requested
athletic fee	no	$50 if requested

Student activity fees are required of all students; all other fees are charged only if the student has indicated an interest in taking advantage of a particular university resource. Your program should generate a single value of the total of all student fees. Once again, new fields may have to be added to the input records. Once again, feel free to use your own school's fee structure in place of the one outlined above.

9. In Chapter 6, you were asked to develop a bill computation program (exercise number 7). Shipping costs are based on the shipping weight and the shipping zone, both of which are identified by a code. The codes have the following meanings:

zone	factor	weight code	cost
A	0	1	$0.50
B	1.00	2	$0.75
C	1.25	3	$0.95
D	1.50	4	$1.25
E	2.00	5	$1.75
F	5.00	6	$2.50
		7	$5.00

To interpret these tables, assume that a product with weight code 4 is to be shipped to zone D. Weight code 4 carries a shipping cost of $1.25. Zone D has a factor of 1.5. Multiplying the shipping cost by the zone factor (1.25 times 1.5) yields a shipping cost of $1.88. Note that zone A, with a factor of zero, is our free zone.

Add this routine to your program.

10. Another factor in the bill preparation program was the state sales tax rate. Our state charges 4%, and this is the amount normally charged. Surrounding states and their associated sales tax rates are identified by code in the following table:

code	tax rate
blank	4%
A	2.5%
B	3.0%
C	3.5%
D	4.5%
E	5.0%

Add this table to your program.

11. Another program in Chapter 6's exercises involved computing the amount due on an electric bill. The table below lists three rate structures:

code	meaning	base charge	variable	limit
1	household	$3.00	$0.045	50
		7.50	0.035	150
		11.00	0.030	250
2	total elect	7.50	0.030	150
		13.50	0.025	350
		30.00	0.020	1000
3	factory	30.00	0.020	1000
		110.00	0.015	5000
		335.00	0.010	20000

To interpret the table, assume that a regular household customer uses exactly 200 kilowatt hours of power. The first line in the table calls for a charge of $3.00 plus $0.045 for each hour over 50. But the second line calls for $7.50 and only $0.035 for each hour over 150; since the charge per kilowatt hour is less, this is a better rate. Can we use the third line? No; the actual usage is less than 250 kilowatt hours. Thus, the second line is used. The actual charge is $7.50 (the base charge) plus 0.035 (the variable charge per kilowatt hour) of all hours over 150 (200 - 150 = 50), which is 7.50 plus 1.75 or $9.25.

Of course, your program should be able to distinguish regular household customers, total electric customers, and factory customers. In each case, the actual rate used (there are three for each) should be the lowest to which the customer is entitled by virtue of actual usage.

12. Problem number 9 in Chapter 6 asked you to set up a skeleton mainline for a program to compute the amount of annual federal income tax due. The gross pay used on the federal income tax forms is also used for computing several state income taxes. If your state has an income tax based on gross pay, get a copy of last year's income tax tates and write a routine to compute the amount of state tax due. If your state does not have an income tax or if you cannot find the rates, use the following rate table from the state of Ohio:

income	tax
0-5000	½% of income
5000-10,000	$25 plus 1% of excess over $5000
10,000-15,000	$75 plus 2% of excess over $10,000
15,000-20,000	$175 plus 2½% of excess over $15,000
20,000-40,000	$300 plus 3% of excess over $20,000
over $40,000	$900 plus 3½% of excess over $40,000

13. Federal income tax can also be computed from tables. Unfortunately, the tables are quite long, much too long for the nested IF approach to table look-up. In the next chapter, we will be considering another approach to table lookup that is much more convenient for handling large tables.

There are four standard federal income tax tables; each one contains 25 or more entries. Why would you think that the nested IF approach would be a less than idea way to handle such large tables? What problems would you anticipate?

8

Table Handling

OVERVIEW

In this chapter we will investigate a number of techniques for handling tables in COBOL. The procedure for setting up a table using an OCCURS clause will be discussed. Two versions of a federal income tax computation routine, one using subscripting and the other using indexes and the COBOL SEARCH statement, will be written. A number of alternatives for initializing the contents of a table will also be covered.

ANOTHER APPROACH TO TABLE LOOK-UP

Chapter 7 concentrated on the use of nested IF statements to find an entry in a table. Nested IFs represent a reasonable way of solving this problem, as long as the number of elements in the table is relatively small. As the table increases in size, however, nesting begins to create almost as many problems as it solves. Don't forget, there must be one IF statement for each table entry. As the number of levels of nesting grows, the module becomes more and more difficult to follow until the logic eventually becomes lost in a veritable "rat's nest".

Fortunately, COBOL has a number of features that facilitate table handling, making it relatively easy to work with even very large tables. We'll be considering these features over the balance of this chapter.

Federal Income Tax Computations

In Chapter 7, a routine for computing state income tax was added to the skeleton mainline developed in Chapter 6. In this chapter, we will be adding the logic needed to compute federal income tax. Since federal law specifies the procedures that must be followed, much of the preliminary problem definition and general planning practiced on earlier programs is beside the point.

The government publishes tables that show the amount of tax due as a series of percentages varying with the level of income. Briefly, the algorithm for using these tables is:

1. compute the amount of taxable income;

2. using this taxable income, enter the tax table and find three numbers, the base tax, a percentage tax, and the lower limit for this percentage tax;

3. using these numbers, compute the amount of tax due.

The rules are quite similar to the ones we used for finding state tax; there are, however, a few differences.

Taxable income is not the same as gross pay. Every taxpayer is entitled to a certain amount of nontaxable income for each dependent he or she claims. Before the amount of tax due can be computed, an allowance for each dependent, currently $14.40, must be subtracted from gross pay to get taxable income. This computed taxable income is then used to search the table. The actual tables for a weekly payroll period are reproduced as Fig. 8.1.

Note that there are two tables; one for single persons and one for married persons. Perhaps the best way to understand how these tables work is by looking at an example.

Assume that a single individual claiming only one dependent (himself or herself) earns a total of $125.00 in gross pay. Before we enter the table, the amount of taxable income must be computed. To find the taxable portion of income, $14.40 must

Fig. 8.1: *Tax tables for computing federal income tax.*

Multiply number of dependents by $14.40; subtract this amount from gross pay to get taxable income. Use taxable income to enter the table.

TABLE 1. WEEKLY Payroll Period

(a) SINGLE person—including head of household:

If the amount of wages is:		The amount of income tax to be withheld shall be:	
Not over $25 0			
Over—	But not over—		of excess over—
$25	—$67	16%	—$25
$67	—$115	$6.72 plus 20%	—$67
$115	—$183	$16.32 plus 23%	—$115
$183	—$240	$31.96 plus 21%	—$183
$240	—$279	$43.93 plus 26%	—$240
$279	—$346	$54.07 plus 30%	—$279
$346		$74.17 plus 36%	—$346

(b) MARRIED person—

If the amount of wages is:		The amount of income tax to be withheld shall be:	
Not over $48 0			
Over—	But not over—		of excess over—
$48	—$96	17%	—$48
$96	—$173	$8.16 plus 20%	—$96
$173	—$264	$23.56 plus 17%	—$173
$264	—$346	$39.03 plus 25%	—$264
$346	—$433	$59.53 plus 28%	—$346
$433	—$500	$83.89 plus 32%	—$433
$500		$105.33 plus 36%	—$500

Source: Dept. of the Treasury, IRS Publication 15, *Circular E: Employeer's Tax Guide*, (Nov., 1976).

---

be subtracted from gross pay for each dependent claimed; one dependent times $14.40 is $14.40, and $125.00 minus $14.40 is $110.60. We're now ready to consult the tax table.

Since the individual is single, side (a) is used. The computed taxable income lies between $67 and $115. When we read across this line of the table, we find that the correct tax is $6.72 plus 20% of all earnings over $67. There are three steps involved in computing the tax:

1. find the "excess" portion of income—$110.60 minus $67 equals $43.60;

2. find 20% of this figure—20% of $43.60 is $8.72;

3. add this amount to the base tax—$8.72 plus $6.72 equals $15.44.

The computed income tax for this individual is $15.44.

Now, let's change some of the parameters. Assume that the employee is married and has a child. Now, there are three dependents rather than just one. At $14.40 per dependent, 3 times $14.40 (or $43.20) is subtracted from gross pay to get taxable income; assuming $125 in gross pay, the taxable portion becomes $81.80.

We can now look at the tax table and compute the amount of tax due; this time, however, since the individual is married, table (b) is used. Taxable income lies between $48 and $96. There is no base tax for this table entry; the tax is a straight 17% of all earnings over $48. Computing the excess portion ($81.80 minus $48) yields $33.80, and 17% of this number is $5.75, the amount of tax due.

Let's generalize this example into a set of steps. To compute income tax using the percentage method,

1. multiply the number of dependents claimed by $14.40 to get the amount of non-taxable income;

2. subtract this non-taxable income from gross pay to get taxable income;

3. select either the table for single taxpayers or the table for married taxpayers, depending on the person's marital status;

4. find the income range in which this taxpayer fits by locating a line in the table for which the computed taxable income lies between the upper and lower limits;

5. subtract from taxable income the low limit of the selected table entry, giving excess earnings;

6. multiply excess earnings by the percentage associated with the selected table entry, giving the proportional tax;

7. add the minimum tax and the proportional tax giving the total tax due.

This set of instructions is roughly equivalent to the human-level solution developed during the planning stage of earlier programs.

Table Handling as a Computer Sees It

Before examining the details of COBOL table handling, we should discuss how, in general, a computer can deal with something like a table. We might use the single person tax table as an example (Fig. 8.1). The table is obviously prepared for the use of human beings; the phrase, "If the amount of wages is over $67 but not over $115 the amount of income tax to be withheld shall be $6.72 plus 20% of excess over $67.", reads more like one of our human-level psuedo instructions than a COBOL statement. How can we restructure this table into something more like what a computer can use?

First, all the words (which are really instructions) must be stripped from the table. On a computer, don't forget, the data and the instructions telling the computer how to manipulate that data must be separated. (In COBOL, for example, the data goes in the DATA DIVISION and the instructions are coded in the PROCEDURE DIVISION).

Once the words have been stripped from the table, what numbers should be retained? Except for the first two lines, each table line contains five numbers: the lower limit of the tax bracket, the upper limit of the bracket, the base tax for this bracket, the percentage tax on excess earnings, and the amount to be subtracted from gross pay to get excess earnings. Note that the first and last data items are identical, so we really don't need both. A table holding only the numeric data stripped from the single person tax table is shown in Fig. 8.2.

We now have a computer-level table. How can a computer be instructed to search it?

Look carefully at the way the table (Fig. 8.2) is constructed. Each line contains four data fields; each of these data fields can be assigned a data name and a PICTURE clause describing its contents. The data fields in line 1 are identical to the data fields in line 2; in fact, the fields (not the contents, the fields) are the same in every line of the table. In effect, each line of the table is a repeat of the same basic data structure. The values are different, of course, but the structure doesn't change.

The lines are numbered. If you were told to find the upper limit of the bracket coded in line 4 of the table, would you have any difficulty following instructions? Neither would a computer. This basic idea is at the heart of COBOL's table handling facilities.

Before moving on to the details of COBOL implementation, let's step through some computer-level table look-up logic, and develop a flowchart. The keys to this

Fig. 8.2: *The single person table redefined for computer use.*

line number	bracket base	bracket limit	percentage tax	base tax
1	0	25	0	0
2	25	67	16	0
3	67	115	20	6.72
4	115	183	23	16.32
5	183	240	21	31.96
6	240	279	26	43.93
7	279	346	30	54.07
8	346	9999	36	74.17

Fig. 8.3: *Table Look-up Logic.*

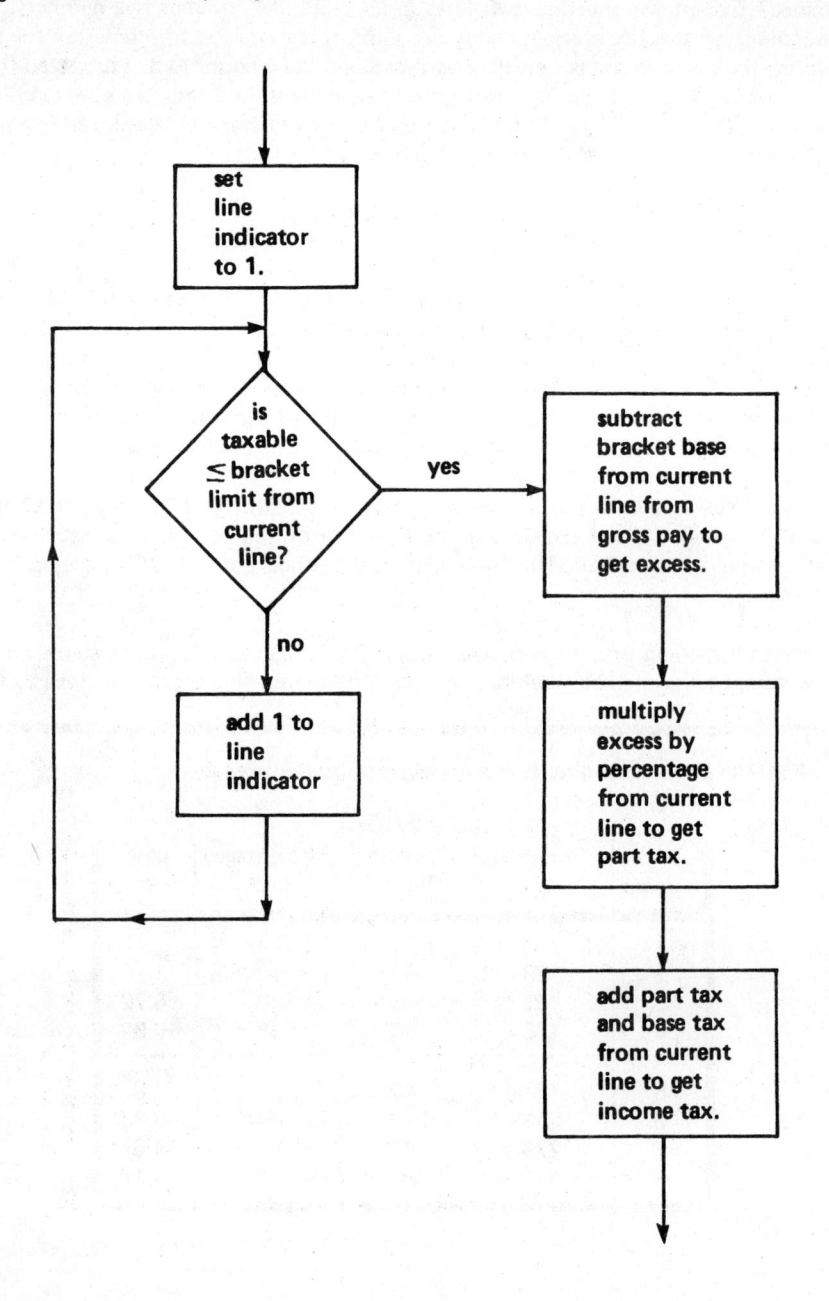

```
              ↓
        ┌───────────┐
        │   set     │
        │   line    │
        │ indicator │
        │   to 1.   │
        └─────┬─────┘
              ↓
    ┌─────────────────┐                 ┌──────────────┐
    │       is        │                 │  subtract    │
    │    taxable      │      yes        │ bracket base │
───→│   ≤ bracket     │───────────────→ │ from current │
│   │   limit from    │                 │  line from   │
│   │    current      │                 │ gross pay to │
│   │     line?       │                 │ get excess.  │
│   └────────┬────────┘                 └──────┬───────┘
│            │ no                              ↓
│   ┌────────┴────────┐                 ┌──────────────┐
│   │    add 1 to     │                 │  multiply    │
│   │      line       │                 │  excess by   │
│   │   indicator     │                 │  percentage  │
│   └────────┬────────┘                 │ from current │
│            │                          │ line to get  │
└────────────┘                          │  part tax.   │
                                        └──────┬───────┘
                                               ↓
                                        ┌──────────────┐
                                        │ add part tax │
                                        │ and base tax │
                                        │ from current │
                                        │ line to get  │
                                        │ income tax.  │
                                        └──────┬───────┘
                                               ↓
```

logic are the line numbers and the data names of each item in the table. Basically, the logic begins by setting the line indicator to 1, the number of the first line. The bracket limit in this first line (it's 25) can be compared with taxable income. If taxable income is less than or equal to this bracket limit, the proper tax bracket has been located, and the actual tax computations can be performed. If, however, taxable income is greater than the upper limit of this first bracket, the line indicator can be reset to 2 and the test can be performed on the second line.

This logic is summarized in Fig. 8.3. Assume that the computed taxable income is $125, and follow the flowchart. The first step is to set the line indicator equal to 1. Having done this, we can now compare the bracket limit for the current line (in line 1, the bracket limit is 25) to taxable income, which is 125. Taxable income is high; therefore the tested condition is false and logical flow continues in a downward direction, where the line indicator is bumped up to 2 (through the simple expedient of adding 1). Next, it's back to the top of the loop, where, once again, the bracket limit for the current line (which is line 2) is compared with taxable income. Since 125 is not less than or equal to 67, the condition is false, so the line indicator is bumped up to 3 and it's on to the next test. The current line is 3; 125 is greater than 115; the condition is false; the line indicator is bumped to 4; and still another test is performed. This time, the taxable income, $125 is less than the bracket limit for the current line, so the condition is true. Flow now proceeds to the right, where the actual tax is computed using fields from the current line.

This form of table look-up logic clearly contains two distinct parts. First, the table is searched, with the program cycling through again and again until the condition being searched for is met (in computer slang, until there is a "hit"). Later, when the sought for table entry has been located, the desired computations can be performed.

SETTING UP A TABLE IN COBOL

Consider the nature of the table we have just been discussing. It consists of a series of identical lines. Each line contains a set of data items. If we could define a structure listing the data items contained in a single line and then, in some way, tell the COBOL compiler that this line is to be repeated several times, we should be able to define the table. This is exactly how it is done in COBOL.

The one new COBOL feature needed to describe a table is the **OCCURS clause**. An OCCURS clause defines how many times a data structure or data element is repeated. A set of income tax tables has been coded in Fig. 8.4. The first line of each table is simply a table identification, included mainly for purposes of documentation; look beyond this 01-level entry and concentrate on the 05-level entry. As before, the presence of a 05-level entry followed by a series of higher numbered entries (the 10s) defines a data structure, meaning that S-BRACKET-BASE, S-BRACKET-LIMIT, S-PERCENTAGE, and S-BASE-TAX are all part of SINGLE-TABLE. An OCCURS clause is attached to the SINGLE-TABLE entry. This means that SINGLE-TABLE (and all fields that are part of SINGLE-TABLE) OCCURS, or is repeated, 8 times.

The MARRIED-TABLE is also shown in Fig. 8.4; both are coded in the WORKING-STORAGE SECTION.

There are a few restrictions on the use of an OCCURS clause. It cannot be coded as part of a 77- or 01-level entry; this is because 77- and 01-level entries require special memory alignment. A maximum of three levels of OCCURS clauses can be coded, yielding, in effect, a three-dimensional table.

ACCESSING THE FIELDS IN A TABLE

Now that you have seen how to set up a table in COBOL, it's time we turned our attention to accessing the data in the table. Obviously, the data name is going to participate in this process. Earlier, when we were discussing how a computer might process a table, we introduced the idea of maintaining a line indicator or counter to keep track of the table line. Essentially, the COBOL programmer does exactly this, using a type of indicator or pointer to identify the table line and then attaching this indicator to a data name to designate a specific table element. This indicator can be either a subscript or an index. We'll concentrate on the use of subscripts first.

Using Subscripts

A **subscript** is a data item or a numeric constant. It must be a positive integer—a whole number with no fractional part having a value of 1 or greater.

The subscript is used to qualify a data name that appears in a table. S-BRACKET-BASE (1), for example, refers to the value stored under the data name S-BRACKET-BASE in the first line of the table, while S-BRACKET-BASE (2) defines the data item stored under the same name but in the second line of the table. The subscript is enclosed in parentheses. The first or left parenthesis is separated from the data name by a blank. The subscript must follow the parenthesis immediately, with no intervening blanks. The right parenthesis immediately follows the subscript, again with no intervening blank.

This technique is valuable because the subscript can be a variable data item rather than a constant. Our objective in the income tax computation subroutine is to find the proper tax bracket, so let's define a 77-level entry called BRACKET:

```
77    BRACKET    PIC 9.
```

Having defined this data item as a positive integer, we can now use it as a subscript. S-BRACKET-LIMIT (BRACKET) can refer to the S-BRACKET-LIMIT in any one of the table lines, depending on the value of BRACKET. If, for example, BRACKET contains the value 1, S-BRACKET-LIMIT (BRACKET) refers to the upper limit of the first tax bracket (the first table line), while, if BRACKET equals 2, the same data name, S-BRACKET-LIMIT (BRACKET), refers to the upper limit of the second tax bracket.

The value of BRACKET can be controlled by the programmer; it is, after all, no different than any other data field. If we were to set up a loop and allow BRACKET to vary from a low of 1 to a high of 8, we could step through the tax table one line at a time. Consider, for example, the loop coded in Fig. 8.5. It begins with the initialization of the data item BRACKET to a value of 1. Entering the TABLE-SEARCH-ROUTINE, TAXABLE-INCOME is compared with S-BRACKET-LIMIT

COBOL Coding Form

SYSTEM	PAYROLL	PUNCHING INSTRUCTIONS: GRAPHIC Ø / PUNCH ZERO	PAGE OF
PROGRAM	COMPUTE HOURLY PAYROLL		CARD FORM #
PROGRAMMER	DAVIS & FISHER	DATE 2-1-79	

```
       01  SINGLE-PERSON-TAX-TABLE.
           05  SINGLE-TABLE                OCCURS 8 TIMES.
               10  S-BRACKET-BASE          PIC 999.
               10  S-BRACKET-LIMIT         PIC 9999.
               10  S-PERCENTAGE            PIC V99.
               10  S-BASE-TAX              PIC 999V99.

       01  MARRIED-PERSON-TAX-TABLE.
           05  MARRIED-TABLE               OCCURS 8 TIMES.
               10  M-BRACKET-BASE          PIC 999.
               10  M-BRACKET-LIMIT         PIC 9999.
               10  M-PERCENTAGE            PIC V99.
               10  M-BASE-TAX              PIC 999V99.
```

Fig. 8.4: *The WORKING-STORAGE SECTION now contains the code to set up married and single tax tables.*

COBOL Coding Form

SYSTEM		PUNCHING INSTRUCTIONS	PAGE OF
PROGRAM		GRAPHIC	CARD FORM #
PROGRAMMER	DATE	PUNCH	

```
       MOVE  1  TO BRACKET.
   S-TABLE-SEARCH-ROUTINE.
       IF TAXABLE-PAY IS NOT GREATER THAN S-BRACKET-LIMIT (BRACKET)
       THEN
           SUBTRACT S-BRACKET-BASE (BRACKET) FROM TAXABLE-PAY
                    GIVING EXCESS-INCOME
           MULTIPLY EXCESS-INCOME BY S-PERCENTAGE (BRACKET)
                    GIVING PART-TAX
           ADD      PART-TAX, S-BASE-TAX (BRACKET)
                    GIVING FEDERAL-INCOME-TAX
       ELSE
           ADD  1  TO BRACKET
           IF BRACKET IS GREATER THAN 8
           THEN
               PERFORM END-OF-JOB
           ELSE
               GO TO S-TABLE-SEARCH-ROUTINE.
```

Fig. 8.5: *A COBOL loop to search a table using subscripts.*

(BRACKET); since BRACKET, the subscript, is currently equal to 1, this implies a comparison with the upper limit of the first table line or the first tax bracket. Assuming that TAXABLE-INCOME is greater than this first bracket limit (thus the condition is false), the logic adds 1 to BRACKET, checks to see that BRACKET does not exceed 8 (there are, after all, only 8 lines in the table), and loops back for another search. This time, BRACKET, the subscript, is equal to 2; thus the comparison is between TAXABLE-INCOME and the upper limit of the second tax bracket. Eventually, the tested condition will be true, the amount of income tax due will be computed, and the loop will terminate.

Why was it necessary to compare BRACKET to 8 before looping back for another test? The OCCURS clause set up only 8 copies of the basic structure pattern; hence there is no S-BRACKET-LIMIT (9). Since this element does not exist, any reference to it is obviously an error. The value of any subscript cannot exceed the number of elements in a table. If it does, program failure is likely. Always be prepared to test for this upper limit.

Is there any other way to ensure that this error condition will not occur? In this program, yes. The basis for computing taxable income is gross pay. We already know the maximum possible value of gross pay: Since hours worked cannot exceed 99.9 and the hourly pay rate has a maximum value of 99.99, the biggest possible value of gross pay is 9989.00. Taxable income can't be any greater. Thus if the upper limit of the eighth and final tax bracket is set to 9999.99, there is no possibility (short of computer failure, which negates all results anyway) that taxable income will not lie in one of the tax brackets. In actually implementing a table look-up version of the income tax subroutine, this is what we'll do, thus eliminating the need for the subscript range test.

Using an Index

A subscript is simply a data item defined in the DATA DIVISION and used to reference a table. Except for being limited to positive integer values, there is nothing special about a subscript.

Instead, the programmer can choose to use an **index**, a special type of data item used strictly for identifying table elements. An index variable is defined as part of the table definition. Fig. 8.6 shows the two tax tables redefined with an index; the index (in this example S-BRACKET and M-BRACKET are used) is not defined anywhere else in the program. It cannot be part of any data structure. The precise format of an index depends upon the computer system being used. Very simply, the form of data that is most efficient on a given computer can be chosen for the index, allowing the computer to perform a table look-up operation in less time.

An index may be modified only by a SET statement, a SEARCH statement, or a special type of PERFORM statement. If we were to rewrite the table look-up routine of Fig. 8.5 using an index, it might look like Fig. 8.7. The new routine begins with a SET S-BRACKET TO 1 instruction. Within the loop, the index is used just as the subscript was used. Before returning to the top of the loop we SET S-BRACKET UP BY 1 rather than ADD 1 to it. Except for these two relatively minor changes, there is no real difference between the two routines.

COBOL Coding Form

SYSTEM	PAYROLL	PUNCHING INSTRUCTIONS	PAGE OF
PROGRAM	COMPUTE HOURLY PAYROLL	GRAPHIC Ø	CARD FORM #
PROGRAMMER	DAVIS & FISHER	DATE 2-1-79	PUNCH ZERO

```
       Ø1  SINGLE-PERSON-TAX-TABLE.
           Ø5  SINGLE-TABLE            OCCURS 8 TIMES
                                       INDEXED BY S-BRACKET.
               1Ø  S-BRACKET-BASE      PIC 999.
               1Ø  S-BRACKET-LIMIT     PIC 9999.
               1Ø  S-PERCENTAGE        PIC V99.
               1Ø  S-BASE-TAX          PIC 999V99.

       Ø1  MARRIED-PERSON-TAX-TABLE.
           Ø5  MARRIED-TABLE           OCCURS 8 TIMES
                                       INDEXED BY M-BRACKET.
               1Ø  M-BRACKET-BASE      PIC 999.
               1Ø  M-BRACKET-LIMIT     PIC 9999.
               1Ø  M-PERCENTAGE        PIC V99.
               1Ø  M-BASE-TAX          PIC 999V99.
```

Fig. 8.6: *A new version of the table definitions with an INDEXED BY option.*

COBOL Coding Form

```
           SET S-BRACKET TO 1
       S-TABLE-SEARCH-ROUTINE.
           IF TAXABLE-PAY IS NOT GREATER THAN
               S-BRACKET-LIMIT (S-BRACKET)
           THEN
               SUBTRACT S-BRACKET-BASE (S-BRACKET) FROM TAXABLE-PAY
                        GIVING EXCESS-INCOME
               MULTIPLY EXCESS-INCOME BY S-PERCENTAGE (S-BRACKET)
                        GIVING PART-TAX
               ADD      PART-TAX, S-BASE-TAX (S-BRACKET)
                        GIVING FEDERAL-INCOME-TAX
           ELSE
               SET S-BRACKET UP BY 1
               IF S-BRACKET IS GREATER THAN 8
               THEN
                   PERFORM END-OF-JOB
               ELSE
                   GO TO S-TABLE-SEARCH-ROUTINE.
```

Fig. 8.7: *A table look-up routine using an index.*

Why then use an index? Computer efficiency is really rather beside the point; what is the advantage to the programmer? If an index is used, the programmer can take advantage of the COBOL **SEARCH** statement.

The general form of a SEARCH statement is:

SEARCH table-name

AT END statement-1

WHEN condition-1

statement-2.

The "table-name" is simply the data name assigned to the DATA DIVISION entry that defines the table to be searched; this entry *must* contain an OCCURS clause. The AT END option tells the program what to do if the end of the table is encountered before the test condition is met. The WHEN option defines a condition to be tested for each line of the table; when this condition is found to be true, the COBOL statements following the WHEN are executed, and the search ends. In Fig. 8.8, the table look-up routine has been rewritten using a SEARCH statement.

What could be clearer? The first part of the instruction tells the computer to search a table. The second major subdivision (initiated by the WHEN option) defines the condition for ending the search, and tells the program what to do when this condition is met. In Fig. 8.8, the phrase NEXT SENTENCE is used in conjunction with the WHEN option. As the phrase implies, it tells the program to move on to the next sentence when the test condition has been met. If the condition is not met, of course, the search continues.

The SEARCH statement initiates what is known as a **serial search**, meaning that the table will be searched from start to finish (or until the condition is met), line by line. An alternate version, SEARCH ALL, sets up a **binary search**, which allows a very large table to be searched quickly. For our 8-entry table a straight sequential search is more than adequate.

Having defined the COBOL table look-up features, we can now write the income tax routines. The SEARCH statement has been chosen for both these modules. (Figures 8.9 and 8.10). The table definitions must, of course, be added to the WORKING-STORAGE SECTION.

We are, however, not quite ready to test the new version of the program. Throughout this discussion, we have assumed that the tables contain the values specified in Fig. 8.2. They don't. Unless the programmer fills these tables with the proper values, there is no way of knowing what they contain. Thus we turn our attention to the topic of table initialization.

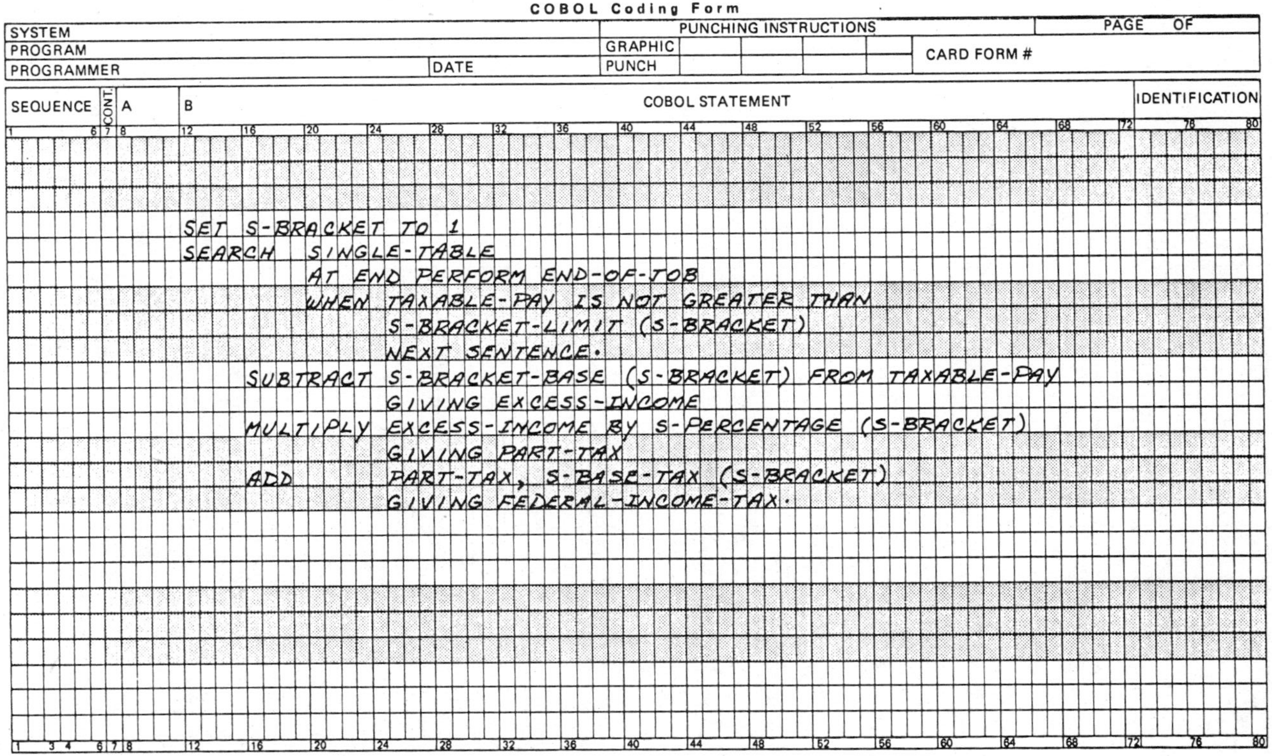

COBOL Coding Form

SYSTEM		PUNCHING INSTRUCTIONS		PAGE OF
PROGRAM		GRAPHIC		CARD FORM #
PROGRAMMER	DATE	PUNCH		

SEQUENCE | CONT. | A | B | COBOL STATEMENT | IDENTIFICATION

```
           SET S-BRACKET TO 1
           SEARCH   SINGLE-TABLE
                   AT END PERFORM END-OF-JOB
                   WHEN TAXABLE-PAY IS NOT GREATER THAN
                        S-BRACKET-LIMIT (S-BRACKET)
                        NEXT SENTENCE.
               SUBTRACT S-BRACKET-BASE (S-BRACKET) FROM TAXABLE-PAY
                        GIVING EXCESS-INCOME
               MULTIPLY EXCESS-INCOME BY S-PERCENTAGE (S-BRACKET)
                        GIVING PART-TAX
               ADD      PART-TAX, S-BASE-TAX (S-BRACKET)
                        GIVING FEDERAL-INCOME-TAX.
```

Fig. 8.8: *A table look-up routine using a SEARCH statement.*

COBOL Coding Form

SYSTEM	PUNCHING INSTRUCTIONS	PAGE OF
PROGRAM	GRAPHIC	CARD FORM #
PROGRAMMER / DATE	PUNCH	

SEQUENCE | CONT. | A | B | COBOL STATEMENT | IDENTIFICATION

```
       FEDERAL-TAX-FOR-SINGLE-PERSON.

           MULTIPLY I-NO-OF-DEPENDENTS BY 14.40 GIVING NON-TAXABLE-PAY
           SUBTRACT NON-TAXABLE-PAY FROM GROSS-PAY GIVING TAXABLE-PAY
           SET S-BRACKET TO 1.
           SEARCH  SINGLE-TABLE
                   AT END PERFORM END-OF-JOB
                   WHEN TAXABLE-PAY IS NOT GREATER THAN
                        S-BRACKET-LIMIT (S-BRACKET)
                        NEXT SENTENCE.
               SUBTRACT S-BRACKET-BASE (S-BRACKET) FROM TAXABLE-PAY
                        GIVING EXCESS-INCOME
               MULTIPLY EXCESS-INCOME BY S-PERCENTAGE (S-BRACKET)
                        GIVING PART-TAX
               ADD      PART-TAX, S-BASE-TAX (S-BRACKET)
                        GIVING FEDERAL-INCOME-TAX

       END-FEDERAL-TAX-FOR-SINGLE.

           EXIT.
```

Fig. 8.9: *The Single Person Income Tax Routine.*

COBOL Coding Form

SYSTEM		PUNCHING INSTRUCTIONS		PAGE OF
PROGRAM		GRAPHIC		CARD FORM #
PROGRAMMER	DATE	PUNCH		

SEQUENCE | CONT. | A | B | COBOL STATEMENT | IDENTIFICATION

```
       FEDERAL-TAX-FOR-MARRIED-PERSON.

           MULTIPLY I-NO-OF-DEPENDENTS BY 14.4Ø GIVING NON-TAXABLE-PAY
           SUBTRACT NON-TAXABLE-PAY FROM GROSS-PAY GIVING TAXABLE-PAY
           SET M-BRACKET TO 1
           SEARCH MARRIED-TABLE
                     AT END PERFORM END-OF-JOB
                     WHEN TAXABLE-PAY IS NOT GREATER THAN
                              M-BRACKET-LIMIT (M-BRACKET)
                              NEXT SENTENCE.
                SUBTRACT M-BRACKET-BASE (M-BRACKET) FROM TAXABLE-PAY
                         GIVING EXCESS-INCOME
                MULTIPLY EXCESS-INCOME BY M-PERCENTAGE (M-BRACKET)
                         GIVING PART-TAX
                ADD      PART-TAX, M-BASE-TAX (M-BRACKET)
                         GIVING FEDERAL-INCOME-TAX.

       END-FEDERAL-TAX-FOR-MARRIED.

           EXIT.
```

Fig. 8.10: *The Married Person Income Tax Routine.*

TABLE INITIALIZATION

Before the values in a table can be used in a computation, the values must be placed in the table. How do they get there? Basically, two approaches are commonly used in COBOL: the values can be defined as DATA DIVISION constants by using the VALUE IS clause, or the values can be read from a table file stored on cards or a magnetic medium.

Let's consider the internal constants approach first. We've used the VALUE IS clause before, primarily as a means of setting up the literal constants that constitute a header. In general, this clause can be attached to any WORKING-STORAGE data field. For example, the data definition

      77   COUNTER   PIC 999   VALUE IS 0.

sets up a three digit counter and gives it the initial value of zero, while the data definition

      05   FILLER   PIC X(15) VALUE IS SPACES.

sets up a 15-character nonnumeric field and initializes it to a series of blank characters.

This would seem an ideal mechanism for initializing a table, but there is one problem. A table is set up by an OCCURS clause which defines the number of times a field or a structure is to be repeated. The whole point of the OCCURS is to save the programmer the trouble of coding all those repetitious fields; thus only the basic pattern and *not* each and every field is coded. The only way to assign a value to a field using a VALUE IS clause is to attach that clause to the specific field. Since only a few of the actual fields are coded, this is impossible.

It is impossible to assign a VALUE IS clause to every element of a table, since most of the elements are not explicitly coded. Why not simply define all the elements? If all the elements are to be defined, there is no need for an OCCURS clause. Unfortunately, if an OCCURS clause is not coded, there is no way that subscripts, indexes, or the SEARCH statement can be used. Our quandry, simply stated, is that if we use an OCCURS clause because we want to take advantage of COBOL's table handling features, we can't use the VALUE IS clause to initialize the table, and if we want to use the VALUE IS clause to initialize our table, we can't use an OCCURS clause, thus eliminating the option of table handling.

The only way to successfully set up a table using an OCCURS clause and initialize that table using internal, DATA DIVISION constants is to actually do it *both* ways. In Fig. 8.11 a table is created, as before, using an OCCURS clause. Below this table is a data structure containing 32 data fields, each representing one element in this table. A VALUE IS clause is used to associate one table value with each of these data items; note that the order is the same as that defined by the OCCURS clause. The table is actually defined twice, once as a table and once as a structure of constants.

01	SINGLE-TABLE-CONTENTS.		
	05 BRACKET-1.		
	10 FILLER	PIC 999	VALUE 0.
	10 FILLER	PIC 9999	VALUE 25.
	10 FILLER	PIC V99	VALUE .00.
	10 FILLER	PIC 999V99	VALUE 0.00.
	05 BRACKET-2.		
	10 FILLER	PIC 999	VALUE 25.
	10 FILLER	PIC 9999	VALUE 67.
	10 FILLER	PIC V99	VALUE .16.
	10 FILLER	PIC 999V99	VALUE 0.
	05 BRACKET-3.		
	10 FILLER	PIC 999	VALUE 67.
	10 FILLER	PIC 9999	VALUE 115.
	10 FILLER	PIC V99	VALUE .20.
	10 FILLER	PIC 999V99	VALUE 6.72.
	05 BRACKET-4.		
	10 FILLER	PIC 999	VALUE 115.
	10 FILLER	PIC 9999	VALUE 183.
	10 FILLER	PIC V99	VALUE .23.
	10 FILLER	PIC 999V99	VALUE 16.32.

Fig. 8.11: *Initializing a table by overlaying a set of constants.*

COBOL Coding Form

Sequence		B	COBOL Statement
		05	BRACKET-5.
		10	FILLER PIC 999 VALUE 183.
		10	FILLER PIC 9999 VALUE 240.
		10	FILLER PIC V99 VALUE .21.
		10	FILLER PIC 999V99 VALUE 31.96.
		05	BRACKET-6.
		10	FILLER PIC 999 VALUE 240.
		10	FILLER PIC 9999 VALUE 279.
		10	FILLER PIC V99 VALUE .26.
		10	FILLER PIC 999V99 VALUE 43.93.
		05	BRACKET-7.
		10	FILLER PIC 999 VALUE 279.
		10	FILLER PIC 9999 VALUE 346.
		10	FILLER PIC V99 VALUE .30.
		10	FILLER PIC 999V99 VALUE 54.07.
		05	BRACKET-8.
		10	FILLER PIC 999 VALUE 346.
		10	FILLER PIC 9999 VALUE 9999.
		10	FILLER PIC V99 VALUE .36.
		10	FILLER PIC 999V99 VALUE 74.17.

Fig. 8.11: *Continued.*

COBOL Coding Form

SYSTEM	PUNCHING INSTRUCTIONS	PAGE OF
PROGRAM	GRAPHIC	CARD FORM #
PROGRAMMER / DATE	PUNCH	

SEQUENCE | CONT. | A | B | COBOL STATEMENT | IDENTIFICATION

```
        01  SINGLE-PERSON-TAX-TABLE    REDEFINES SINGLE-TABLE-CONTENTS.
            05 SINGLE-TABLE            OCCURS 8 TIMES
                                       INDEXED BY S-BRACKET.
               10 S-BRACKET-BASE        PIC 999.
               10 S-BRACKET-LIMIT       PIC 9999.
               10 S-PERCENTAGE          PIC V99.
               10 S-BASE-TAX            PIC 999V99.
```

Fig. 8.11: *Continued.*

All that remains now is to tell the COBOL compiler that the table and the structure of constants, although defined as separate entities, are really the same thing. This is done by using a **REDEFINES clause**. Look at the first line, the 01-level entry, in the structure that creates the table—the data name is SINGLE-PERSON-TAX-TABLE. Immediately following the data name is the clause REDEFINES SINGLE-TABLE-CONTENTS, which is the data name assigned to the 01-level entry for the structure containing the constant values. Imagine lifting all the data fields defined in the structure named SINGLE-PERSON-TAX-TABLE, and dropping them on top of the fields defined in the structure called SINGLE-TABLE-CONTENTS. Essentially, this is what the REDEFINES clause does. It simply tells the COBOL compiler that (in this example) SINGLE-PERSON-TAX-TABLE and SINGLE-TABLE-CONTENTS are two different versions of the same things.

That's a lot of code. Although in many cases this may well be the best way to initialize a table, there is an alternative. We can store the table on punched cards, magnetic tape, or magnetic disk and read the values into the program as one of the housekeeping functions.

This approach involves some extra coding, too. Although the table of 32 constants is no longer needed for each tax table, the fact that extra input and output will be required means that changes must be made to the ENVIRONMENT DIVISION, the DATA DIVISION, and the PROCEDURE DIVISION.

Let's start with the ENVIRONMENT DIVISION. The old version of our program contained SELECT and ASSIGN clauses for a card reader and a printer. The values needed to fill the table will be coming from some other device, so another SELECT and ASSIGN clause has been added (Fig. 8.12).

In the DATA DIVISION, a new FD entry and the associated record and field definitions will be needed (Fig. 8.13). To avoid needlessly complicating this problem, we'll assume that these values will be read from another card reader and define an 80-character record. Each card contains exactly one line of table values, as follows:

columns	contents
1-3	the base value of the tax bracket (999)
4-7	the upper limit of the tax bracket (9999)
8-9	the percentage tax rate (V99)
10-14	the base tax for this bracket (999V99)

Compare this record description to the PICTURE clauses of Fig. 8.13.

The actual reading of this table file is done in the PROCEDURE DIVISION. The table must exist before the mainline of the program can start; thus the table initialization routine must be part of the housekeeping paragraph. The objective of this routine will be to read the first card and move the values to the first line of the income tax table; then to read the second card, moving these values into the second

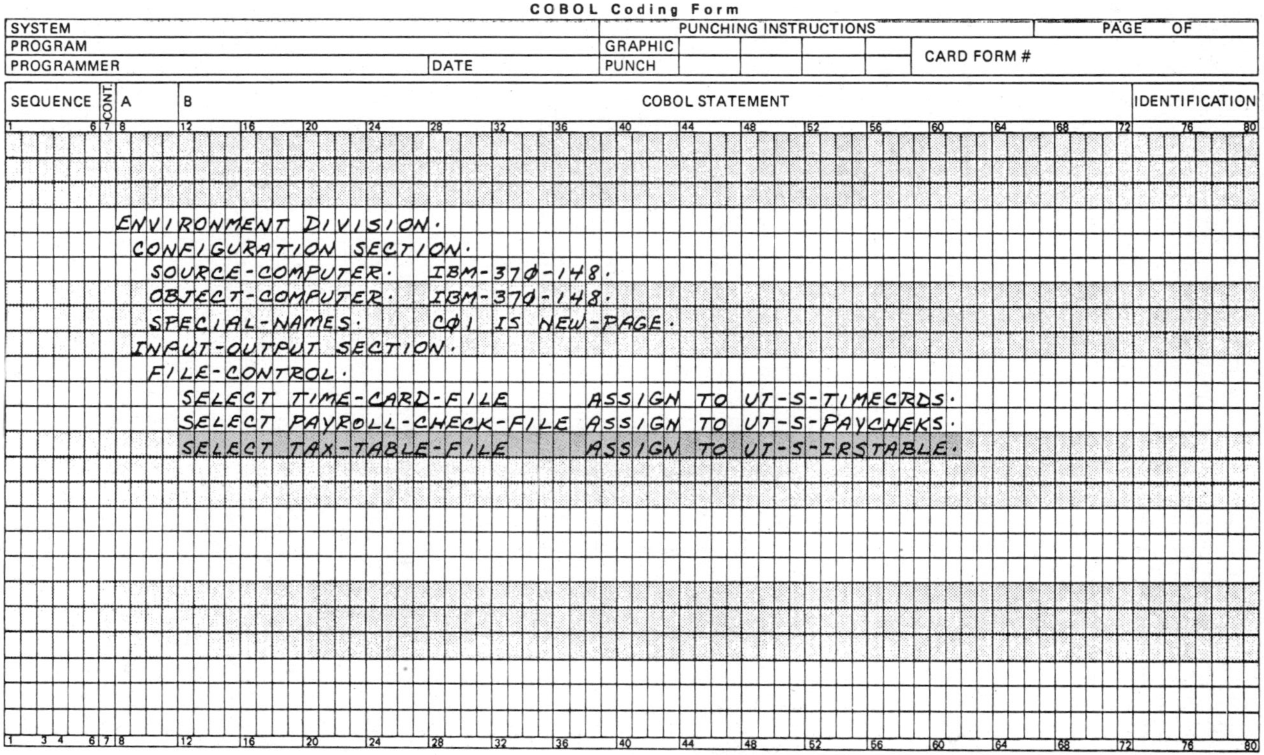
COBOL Coding Form

SYSTEM | PROGRAM | PROGRAMMER | DATE | PUNCHING INSTRUCTIONS | GRAPHIC | PUNCH | PAGE OF | CARD FORM #

SEQUENCE | CONT. | A | B | COBOL STATEMENT | IDENTIFICATION

```
       ENVIRONMENT DIVISION.
        CONFIGURATION SECTION.
         SOURCE-COMPUTER.   IBM-370-148.
         OBJECT-COMPUTER.   IBM-370-148.
         SPECIAL-NAMES.     C01 IS NEW-PAGE.
        INPUT-OUTPUT SECTION.
         FILE-CONTROL.
           SELECT TIME-CARD-FILE      ASSIGN TO UT-S-TIMECRDS.
           SELECT PAYROLL-CHECK-FILE  ASSIGN TO UT-S-PAYCHEKS.
           SELECT TAX-TABLE-FILE      ASSIGN TO UT-S-IRSTABLE.
```

Fig. 8.12: *A new entry to the ENVIRONMENT DIVISION.*

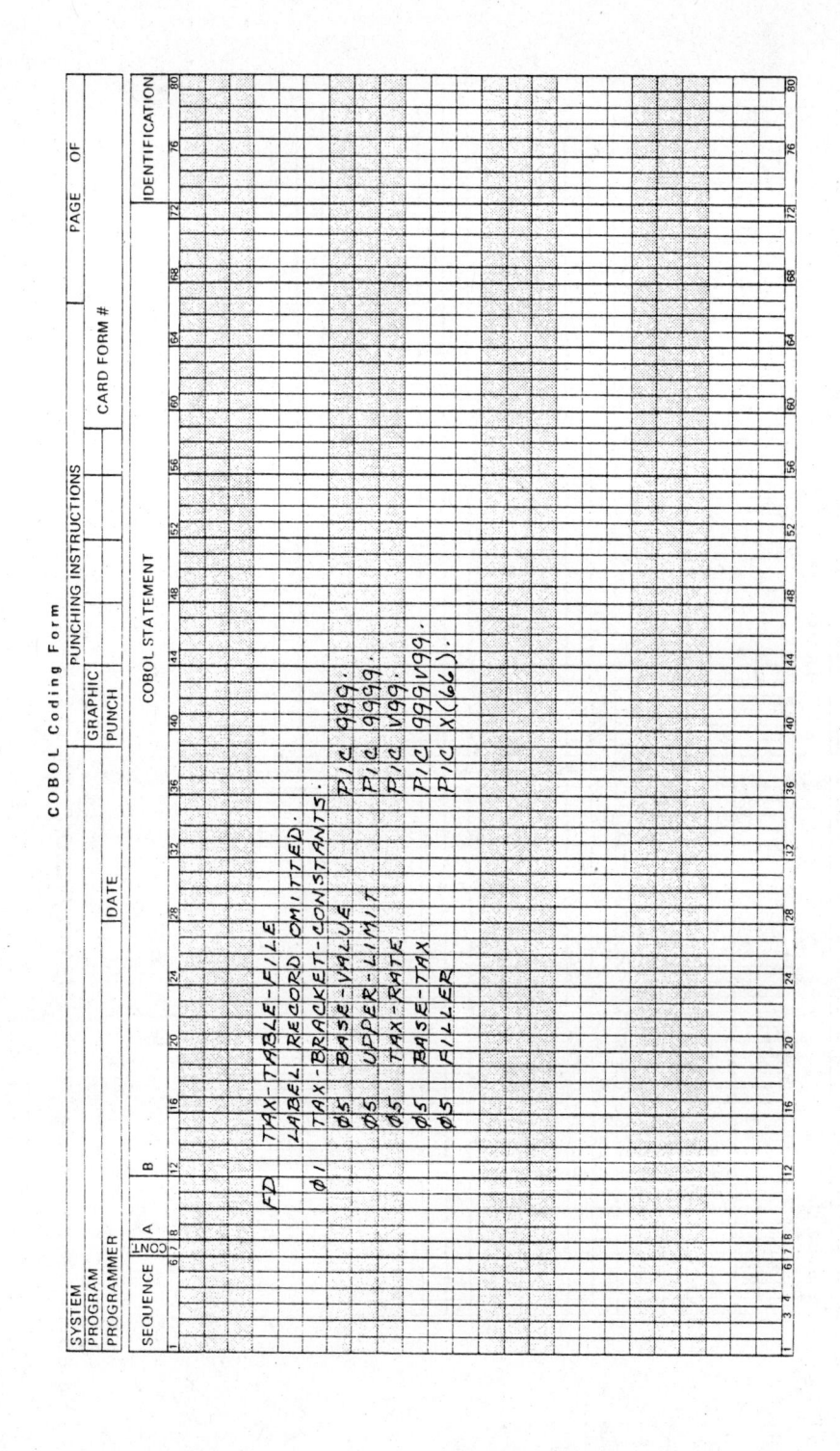

```
FD  TAX-TABLE-FILE
    LABEL RECORD OMITTED.
01  TAX-BRACKET-CONSTANTS.
    05  BASE-VALUE      PIC 999.
    05  UPPER-LIMIT     PIC 9999.
    05  TAX-RATE        PIC V99.
    05  BASE-TAX        PIC 999V99.
    05  FILLER          PIC X(66).
```

Fig. 8.13: *A new DATA DIVISION entry is needed to read the table file.*

line of the table, and so on. We could set up a little loop and vary the index from 1 to 8, reading and moving at each step. There is, however, another way.

A special form of the PERFORM statement is almost perfectly suited to this application. Its general form is

> PERFORM paragraph-names
>
> VARYING index-name
>
> FROM initial-value
>
> BY increment
>
> UNTIL condition-1.

In Fig. 8.14, this general form is implemented twice in the HOUSEKEEPING paragraph, once for each of the two tax tables. The statement

> PERFORM INITIALIZE-SINGLE-TAX-TABLE
>
> VARYING S-BRACKET FROM 1 BY 1
>
> UNTIL S-BRACKET IS GREATER THAN 8.

tells the program to set the index, S-BRACKET, equal to 1 and then PERFORM the paragraph named INITIALIZE-SINGLE-TAX-TABLE (the function of which should be obvious). On the next cycle, S-BRACKET is to be varied BY 1, making it equal to 2, and the paragraph executed once again. This continues, with the value of BRACKET increasing by 1 each time, until S-BRACKET exceeds the value 8.

What happens within the paragraph named INITIALIZE-SINGLE-TAX-TABLE (Fig. 8.15)? One input card is read, and the four table values are moved into a line of the single tax table. The table line to which they are moved is controlled by S-BRACKET, which varies from 1 to 8, allowing the values to be moved to the proper table positions. Note that the secondary routine will not be executed for S-BRACKET equals 9; the PERFORM ends as soon as the specified condition is met.

Which approach is better? Should the contents of a table be defined within the program, or should these constant values be stored on a table file and read in as the program begins executing? The answer to this question depends on the specific application being discussed. Clearly, table size is an important consideration; an extremely large table will not be defined as constants. In this example, because of the history of frequent change to the income tax withholding rates, it makes sense to use a table file and read the values as the program begins. In this way, any changes to the table contents can be implemented by simply changing the external table, without affecting the program itself. As the table handling versions of the income tax computation routines are coded, this is the approach we will use.

COBOL Coding Form

SYSTEM | PUNCHING INSTRUCTIONS | PAGE OF
PROGRAM | GRAPHIC | CARD FORM #
PROGRAMMER | DATE | PUNCH

SEQUENCE | CONT. | A | B | COBOL STATEMENT | IDENTIFICATION

```
       PROCEDURE DIVISION.

        HOUSEKEEPING.

           OPEN INPUT  TAX-TABLE-FILE.
           PERFORM INITIALIZE-SINGLE-TAX-TABLE THRU END-SINGLE-INIT
                   VARYING S-BRACKET FROM 1 BY 1
                   UNTIL S-BRACKET IS GREATER THAN 8.
           PERFORM INITIALIZE-MARRIED-TAX-TABLE THRU END-MARRIED-INIT
                   VARYING M-BRACKET FROM 1 BY 1
                   UNTIL M-BRACKET IS GREATER THAN 8.
           CLOSE TAX-TABLE-FILE.

           OPEN INPUT  TIME-CARD-FILE.
           OPEN OUTPUT PAYROLL-CHECK-FILE.
           MOVE SPACES TO PAYROLL-CHECK.
```

Fig. 8.14: *The housekeeping paragraph with reference to the tax table initialization routines.*

COBOL Coding Form

SYSTEM | PROGRAM | PROGRAMMER | DATE | PUNCHING INSTRUCTIONS: GRAPHIC, PUNCH | CARD FORM # | PAGE OF

SEQUENCE | CONT. | A | B | COBOL STATEMENT | IDENTIFICATION

```
       INITIALIZE-SINGLE-TAX-TABLE.

           READ TAX-TABLE-FILE
               AT END CLOSE TAX-TABLE-FILE
                      STOP RUN.
           MOVE BASE-VALUE  TO S-BRACKET-BASE  (S-BRACKET).
           MOVE UPPER-LIMIT TO S-BRACKET-LIMIT (S-BRACKET).
           MOVE TAX-RATE    TO S-PERCENTAGE    (S-BRACKET).
           MOVE BASE-TAX    TO S-BASE-TAX      (S-BRACKET).

       END-SINGLE-INIT.

           EXIT.
```

Fig. 8.15: *The table initialization routine*

TESTING THE NEW VERSION OF THE PAYROLL PROGRAM

It is now time to put the pieces together and test the new version of the payroll program. The program listing is reproduced as Fig. 8.16. Note that instructions to read the table values from a table file have been included in the housekeeping paragraph of the PROCEDURE DIVISION and that the code needed to support this input operation has been added to the DATA and ENVIRONMENT DIVISIONs.

The program mainline has changed hardly at all; in effect, all we have done is to replace the former dummy income tax computation with a test for marital status and a link (PERFORM) to the proper computational routine. The fact that a new subroutine can be added without impacting the mainline should very clearly demonstrate the ease with which programs can be maintained under the modular approach to program design and development. This is very important. Most experts agree that, at least when it comes to business data processing, program maintenance represents the biggest component of total program cost. Good modular program design helps to minimize this cost by making it easy to make changes.

ADDING OTHER FUNCTIONS

The payroll program pictured in Fig. 8.16 is, of course, incomplete; additional routines to compute gross pay, local income tax, Social Security tax, and numerous other deductions must be added. The key idea of the modular approach to programming is that each of these routines can be developed independently, using the techniques outlined over the past three chapters. In this way, a very complex program can be broken down into a series of relatively simple modules. The mainline ties all these independent computational routines together.

Remember to plan each level of program development carefully. Start by defining, in general terms, what must be done. Develop a skeleton program consisting, at least in the PROCEDURE DIVISION, of little more than an outline-level mainline. Add the details step by step, first planning exactly how a particular detail is to be implemented and then coding a routine to do it. The result of following such a meticulous, step by step approach will be programs that work better, are easier to debug and maintain, and that, at least in the long run, cost less.

SUMMARY

The chapter began with a discussion of the structure of a simple numeric table holding the income tax data. We then described the idea of looping through a table search routine by varying the line number of such a table.

Next, we turned our attention to the task of actually setting up such a table in COBOL. This can be done by using the OCCURS clause in the DATA DIVISION of the program. Accessing individual table entries can be achieved by either of two means: subscripting or indexing. The primary advantage of indexing is that it lets the programmer take advantage of the COBOL SEARCH statement, which greatly simpli-

```
1                      20.36.24        SEP 23,1978

00001           IDENTIFICATION DIVISION.
00002           PROGRAM-ID. PAYROLL.
00003           AUTHOR.       DAVIS & FISHER.
00004           REMARKS.      THIS PROGRAM COMPUTES THE NET PAY FOR HOURLY
00005                         EMPLOYEES.  IT USES TAX TABLES TO COMPUTE
00006                         FEDERAL INCOME TAX.

00008           ENVIRONMENT DIVISION.
00009           CONFIGURATION SECTION.
00010              SOURCE-COMPUTER.  IBM-370-148.
00011              OBJECT-COMPUTER.  IBM-370-148.
00012              SPECIAL-NAMES.       C01 IS NEW-PAGE.
00013           INPUT-OUTPUT SECTION.
00014              FILE-CONTROL.
00015                 SELECT TIME-CARD-FILE      ASSIGN TO UT-S-TIMECRDS.
00016                 SELECT PAYROLL-CHECK-FILE  ASSIGN TO UT-S-PAYCHEKS.
00017                 SELECT TAX-TABLE-FILE      ASSIGN TO UT-S-IRSTABLE.

00019           DATA DIVISION.
00020           FILE SECTION.
00021              FD  TIME-CARD-FILE
00022                  LABEL RECORD OMITTED.
00023                  01  TIME-CARD.
00024                      05  I-SOCIAL-SECURITY-NO   PIC 9(9).
00025                      05  I-LAST-NAME            PIC X(16).
00026                      05  I-INITIALS             PIC XX.
00027                      05  I-DEPARTMENT-NO        PIC 999.
00028                      05  I-HOURS-WORKED         PIC 99V9.
00029                      05  I-HOURLY-PAY-RATE      PIC 99V99.
00030                      05  I-NO-OF-DEPENDENTS     PIC 99.
00031                      05  I-MARITAL-STATUS       PIC X.
00032                      05  FILLER                 PIC X(40).

00034              FD  PAYROLL-CHECK-FILE
00035                  LABEL RECORD OMITTED.
00036                  01  PAYROLL-CHECK.
00037                      05  FILLER                 PIC X(20).
00038                      05  O-LAST-NAME            PIC X(16).
00039                      05  FILLER                 PIC X.
00040                      05  O-INITIALS             PIC XX.
00041                      05  FILLER                 PIC X(21).
00042                      05  O-NET-PAY              PIC $9999.99.
00043                      05  FILLER                 PIC X(65).

00045              FD  TAX-TABLE-FILE
00046                  LABEL RECORD OMITTED.
00047                  01  TAX-BRACKET-CONSTANTS.
00048                      05  BASE-VALUE             PIC 999.
00049                      05  UPPER-LIMIT            PIC 9999.
00050                      05  TAX-RATE               PIC V99.
00051                      05  BASE-TAX               PIC 999V99.
00052                      05  FILLER                 PIC X(66).
```

Fig. 8.16: *The payroll program with federal income tax routines.*

```
     2         PAYROLL         20.36.24         SEP 23,1978



00057              WORKING-STORAGE SECTION.
00059              77   GROSS-PAY                   PIC 9999V99.
00060              77   FEDERAL-INCOME-TAX          PIC 9999V99.
00061              77   STATE-INCOME-TAX            PIC 999V99.
00062              77   LOCAL-INCOME-TAX            PIC 999V99.
00063              77   SOCIAL-SECURITY-TAX         PIC 999V99.
00064              77   TOTAL-DEDUCTIONS            PIC 9999V99.

00066              77   NON-TAXABLE-PAY             PIC 9999V99.
00067              77   TAXABLE-PAY                 PIC 9999V99.
00068              77   PART-TAX                    PIC 9999V99.
00069              77   EXCESS-INCOME               PIC 9999V99.
00070              77   NET-PAY                     PIC 9999V99.

00072              01   SINGLE-PERSON-TAX-TABLE.
00073                   05   SINGLE-TABLE               OCCURS 8 TIMES
00074                                                   INDEXED BY S-BRACKET.
00075                        10   S-BRACKET-BASE        PIC 999.
00076                        10   S-BRACKET-LIMIT       PIC 9999.
00077                        10   S-PERCENTAGE          PIC V99.
00078                        10   S-BASE-TAX            PIC 999V99.

00080              01   MARRIED-PERSON-TAX-TABLE.
00081                   05   MARRIED-TABLE              OCCURS 8 TIMES
00082                                                   INDEXED BY M-BRACKET.
00083                        10   M-BRACKET-BASE        PIC 999.
00084                        10   M-BRACKET-LIMIT       PIC 9999.
00085                        10   M-PERCENTAGE          PIC V99.
00086                        10   M-BASE-TAX            PIC 999V99.
```

Fig. 8.16: *Continued.*

```
00089           PROCEDURE DIVISION.

00091               HOUSEKEEPING.

00093                   OPEN INPUT   TAX-TABLE-FILE.
00094                   PERFORM INITIALIZE-SINGLE-TAX-TABLE THRU END-SINGLE-INIT
00095                       VARYING S-BRACKET FROM 1 BY 1
00096                           UNTIL S-BRACKET IS GREATER THAN 8.
00097                   PERFORM INITIALIZE-MARRIED-TAX-TABLE THRU END-MARRIED-INIT
00098                       VARYING M-BRACKET FROM 1 BY 1
00099                           UNTIL M-BRACKET IS GREATER THAN 8.
00100                   CLOSE TAX-TABLE-FILE.

00102                   OPEN INPUT   TIME-CARD-FILE.
00103                   OPEN OUTPUT  PAYROLL-CHECK-FILE.
00104                   MOVE SPACES TO PAYROLL-CHECK.

00106               START-OF-MAINLINE.

00108                   READ TIME-CARD-FILE
00109                       AT END GO TO END-OF-JOB.
00110                   MULTIPLY I-HOURLY-PAY-RATE BY I-HOURS-WORKED
00111                       GIVING GROSS-PAY

00113                   IF I-MARITAL-STATUS IS EQUAL TO 'M'
00114                   THEN
00115                       PERFORM FEDERAL-TAX-FOR-MARRIED-PERSON
00116                   ELSE
00117                       PERFORM FEDERAL-TAX-FOR-SINGLE-PERSON.

00119                   PERFORM STATE-TAX THRU END-STATE-TAX
00120                   MULTIPLY GROSS-PAY BY 0.02    GIVING LOCAL-INCOME-TAX
00121                   MULTIPLY GROSS-PAY BY 0.0605 GIVING SOCIAL-SECURITY-TAX
00122                   SUBTRACT FEDERAL-INCOME-TAX, STATE-INCOME-TAX,
00123                       LOCAL-INCOME-TAX, SOCIAL-SECURITY-TAX FROM GROSS-PAY
00124                           GIVING NET-PAY

00126                   MOVE I-LAST-NAME TO O-LAST-NAME
00127                   MOVE I-INITIALS  TO O-INITIALS
00128                   MOVE NET-PAY     TO O-NET-PAY

00130                   WRITE PAYROLL-CHECK
00131                       AFTER ADVANCING 2 LINES
00132                   MOVE SPACES TO PAYROLL-CHECK
00133                   GO TO START-OF-MAINLINE.

00135               END-OF-JOB.

00137                   CLOSE TIME-CARD-FILE.
00138                   CLOSE PAYROLL-CHECK-FILE.
00139                   STOP RUN.
```

Fig. 8.16: *Continued.*

```
00142              FEDERAL-TAX-FOR-MARRIED-PERSON.
00144                   MULTIPLY I-NO-OF-DEPENDENTS BY 14.40 GIVING NON-TAXABLE-PAY
00145                   SUBTRACT NON-TAXABLE-PAY FROM GROSS-PAY GIVING TAXABLE-PAY
00146                   SET M-BRACKET TO 1.
00147                   SEARCH    MARRIED-TABLE
00148                             AT END PERFORM END-OF-JOB
00149                             WHEN TAXABLE-PAY IS NOT GREATER THAN
00150                                  M-BRACKET-LIMIT (M-BRACKET)
00151                                  NEXT SENTENCE.
00152                   SUBTRACT M-BRACKET-BASE (M-BRACKET) FROM TAXABLE-PAY
00153                            GIVING EXCESS-INCOME
00154                   MULTIPLY EXCESS-INCOME BY M-PERCENTAGE (M-BRACKET)
00155                            GIVING PART-TAX
00156                   ADD      PART-TAX, M-BASE-TAX (M-BRACKET)
00157                            GIVING FEDERAL-INCOME-TAX.

00159              END-FEDERAL-TAX-FOR-MARRIED.
00161                   EXIT.


00163              FEDERAL-TAX-FOR-SINGLE-PERSON.
00165                   MULTIPLY I-NO-OF-DEPENDENTS BY 14.40 GIVING NON-TAXABLE-PAY
00166                   SUBTRACT NON-TAXABLE-PAY FROM GROSS-PAY GIVING TAXABLE-PAY
00167                   SET S-BRACKET TO 1.
00168                   SEARCH    SINGLE-TABLE
00169                             AT END PERFORM END-OF-JOB
00170                             WHEN TAXABLE-PAY IS NOT GREATER THAN
00171                                  S-BRACKET-LIMIT (S-BRACKET)
00172                                  NEXT SENTENCE.
00173                   SUBTRACT S-BRACKET-BASE (S-BRACKET) FROM TAXABLE-PAY
00174                            GIVING EXCESS-INCOME
00175                   MULTIPLY EXCESS-INCOME BY S-PERCENTAGE (S-BRACKET)
00176                            GIVING PART-TAX
00177                   ADD      PART-TAX, S-BASE-TAX (S-BRACKET)
00178                            GIVING FEDERAL-INCOME-TAX.

00180              END-FEDERAL-TAX-FOR-SINGLE.
00182                   EXIT.
```

Fig. 8.16: *Continued.*

```
5          PAYROLL        20.36.24       SEP 23,1978


00185           INITIALIZE-SINGLE-TAX-TABLE.
00187                READ TAX-TABLE-FILE
00188                     AT END CLOSE TAX-TABLE-FILE
00189                          STOP RUN.
00190                MOVE BASE-VALUE  TO S-BRACKET-BASE   (S-BRACKET).
00191                MOVE UPPER-LIMIT TO S-BRACKET-LIMIT  (S-BRACKET).
00192                MOVE TAX-RATE    TO S-PERCENTAGE     (S-BRACKET).
00193                MOVE BASE-TAX    TO S-BASE-TAX       (S-BRACKET).

00195           END-SINGLE-INIT.

00197                EXIT.

00199           INITIALIZE-MARRIED-TAX-TABLE.
00201                READ TAX-TABLE-FILE
00202                     AT END CLOSE TAX-TABLE-FILE
00203                          STOP RUN.
00204                MOVE BASE-VALUE  TO M-BRACKET-BASE   (M-BRACKET).
00205                MOVE UPPER-LIMIT TO M-BRACKET-LIMIT  (M-BRACKET).
00206                MOVE TAX-RATE    TO M-PERCENTAGE     (M-BRACKET).
00207                MOVE BASE-TAX    TO M-BASE-TAX       (M-BRACKET).

00209           END-MARRIED-INIT.

00211                EXIT.
```

Fig. 8.16: *Continued.*

```
 6         PAYROLL        20.36.24        SEP 23,1978

00213          ***********************************************************
00214          **                                                       **
00215          **        THIS ROUTINE COMPUTES THE STATE INCOME TAX     **
00216          **                                                       **
00217            STATE-TAX.
00219              IF GROSS-PAY IS LESS THAN 50 OR EQUAL TO 50
00220              THEN
00221                  MOVE ZEROS TO STATE-INCOME-TAX
00222              ELSE
00223                  IF GROSS-PAY IS LESS THAN 100 OR EQUAL TO 100
00224                  THEN
00225                      SUBTRACT 50 FROM GROSS-PAY GIVING EXCESS-INCOME
00226                      MULTIPLY EXCESS-INCOME BY 0.01
00227                          GIVING STATE-INCOME-TAX ROUNDED
00228                  ELSE
00229                      IF GROSS-PAY IS LESS THAN 150 OR EQUAL TO 150
00230                      THEN
00231                          SUBTRACT 100 FROM GROSS-PAY GIVING EXCESS-INCOME
00232                          MULTIPLY EXCESS-INCOME BY 0.015
00233                              GIVING PART-TAX ROUNDED
00234                          ADD PART-TAX, 0.50 GIVING STATE-INCOME-TAX
00235                      ELSE
00236                          IF GROSS-PAY IS LESS THAN 200 OR EQUAL TO 200
00237                          THEN
00238                              SUBTRACT 150 FROM GROSS-PAY
00239                                  GIVING EXCESS-INCOME
00240                              MULTIPLY EXCESS-INCOME BY 0.02
00241                                  GIVING PART-TAX ROUNDED
00242                              ADD PART-TAX, 1.25 GIVING STATE-INCOME-TAX
00243                          ELSE
00244                              SUBTRACT 200 FROM GROSS-PAY
00245                                  GIVING EXCESS-INCOME
00246                              MULTIPLY EXCESS-INCOME BY 0.025
00247                                  GIVING PART-TAX ROUNDED
00248                              ADD PART-TAX, 2.25 GIVING STATE-INCOME-TAX.

00250            END-STATE-TAX.

00252                EXIT.
00253          **                                                       **
00254          ***********************************************************
```

Fig. 8.16: *Continued.*

fies the task of table look-up. We briefly discussed the difference between a serial search and a binary search.

Table initialization was the last major topic of the chapter. Basically, there are two ways to initialize a table. A series of constants can be defined in the DATA DIVISION using the VALUE IS clause; then this series of constants can be overlaid on top of the table by using a REDEFINES clause. As an alternative, the table can be created in another program and stored on cards or a magnetic device, with the table values being read from this table file at the beginning of the program.

The chapter ended with brief comments on program testing and on the addition of other functions to the mainline.

KEYWORDS

binary search	**OCCURS clause**	**SEARCH**	**SET**
index	**REDEFINES clause**	**serial search**	**subscript**

EXERCISES

1. Explain how a table can be set up in COBOL. Don't simply say "by using an OCCURS clause". What really happens when the OCCURS clause is used? What is really set up?

2. Explain the differences between subscripting and indexing. What are the advantages of indexing?

3. How can a table be initialized in COBOL?

4. What is a serial search?

5. Problem 5 in Chapter 7 asked you to incorporate a state income tax computation into your payroll program. Implement this table look-up operation using tables rather than nested IF statements.

6. Problem 12 of Chapter 7 was concerned with the computation of the state income tax due at the end of the year. Implement this program using tables.

7. Problem 13 of Chapter 7 discussed the difficulties inherent in using nested IF statements for a table as complex as that used to compute federal income tax at the end of each year. By using tables, however, the problem can be greatly simplified.

Illustrated below is one of the tax tables used in the 1977 federal income tax instructions—this one is the single persons table. Write a subroutine for computing the amount of tax due using this table and incorporate it in the income tax program. The leftmost columns refer to "the amount on Schedule TC, ..." This amount can be computed by multiplying the number of exemptions (or dependents) claimed by $750 and then subtracting the answer from the amount of income input to the program.

As a next step, you might consider combining the routines written in problems 6 and 7 of this chapter as being part of a single COBOL program which computes both the state and local income tax due.

SCHEDULE X—Single Taxpayers Not Qualifying for Rates in Schedule Y or Z

If the amount on Schedule TC, Part I, line 3, is: Not over $2,200............ Enter on Schedule TC, Part I, line 4: —0—

Over—	But not over—		of the amount over—
$2,200	$2,700	14%	$2,200
$2,700	$3,200	$70+15%	$2,700
$3,200	$3,700	$145+16%	$3,200
$3,700	$4,200	$225+17%	$3,700
$4,200	$6,200	$310+19%	$4,200
$6,200	$8,200	$690+21%	$6,200
$8,200	$10,200	$1,110+24%	$8,200
$10,200	$12,200	$1,590+25%	$10,200
$12,200	$14,200	$2,090+27%	$12,200
$14,200	$16,200	$2,630+29%	$14,200
$16,200	$18,200	$3,210+31%	$16,200
$18,200	$20,200	$3,830+34%	$18,200
$20,200	$22,200	$4,510+36%	$20,200
$22,200	$24,200	$5,230+38%	$22,200
$24,200	$28,200	$5,990+40%	$24,200
$28,200	$34,200	$7,590+45%	$28,200
$34,200	$40,200	$10,290+50%	$34,200
$40,200	$46,200	$13,290+55%	$40,200
$46,200	$52,200	$16,590+60%	$46,200
$52,200	$62,200	$20,190+62%	$52,200
$62,200	$72,200	$26,390+64%	$62,200
$72,200	$82,200	$32,790+66%	$72,200
$82,200	$92,200	$39,390+68%	$82,200
$92,200	$102,200	$46,190+69%	$92,200
$102,200	....	$53,090+70%	$102,200

8. In this program, you are to use tables for a quite different purpose. Input records contain the following fields:

columns	contents
1-9	student number
10-25	student name
26	class (1, 2, 3, or 4)
27	sex (M or F)
28-80	unused

The program is to read these records and maintain a set of counts by class and by sex; in other words, what we want is a count of the number of freshman males, freshman females, sophomore males, sophomore females, and so on. You are to create a table with one entry for each count, and maintain the counts in the tables. At the end of the program, the contents of the counters should be moved to an output line and printed.

9. As part of a customer bill preparation program, management has decided that customers should be given an itemized statement that clearly identifies the department where each purchase was made. Input records contain the following:

columns	contents
1-8	customer number
9-20	customer name
21-28	amount of purchase (999999V99)
29-30	department number

As you can see, the department is identified on the input record as a two-digit number. We want these numbers converted to verbal descriptions such as "fine china" or "housewares".

To do this, you are to set up a table consisting of a list of department descriptions; the first several table entries might be:

dept. no.	department name
01	girls' clothing
02	boys' clothing
05	shoes
07	sportswear
10	women's clothing
11	men's clothing
12	housewares
15	fine china

and so on—there are 25 departments (make up your own names). Note that the department numbers, while in sequence, are not consecutive.

Your program should set up a table for the 25 department numbers and names (maximum 20 characters per name), and initialize this table. Following initialization, read the input data cards, look up the department number in the table, and print the customer number and the amount of purchase, followed by the verbal description of the department.

10. This problem uses the elements of a table as work spaces for holding data and performing computations, rather than as a simple table in which information is to be found.

A speciality shop stocks ten items. The current stock on hand for each of the ten items is as follows:

item no.	quantity
1	14
2	28
3	3
4	95
5	12
6	37
7	18
8	9
9	42
10	11

During the current week, all part numbers had activity as follows:

day	item	code	quantity
M	2	2	5
M	5	2	10
M	9	2	23
T	2	2	15
T	1	2	10
T	4	2	15
T	2	2	2
W	8	1	25
W	7	2	8
W	3	1	25
W	7	2	8
T	3	2	12
T	6	2	10
T	8	2	20
F	1	1	25
F	10	2	3
F	4	2	32
F	6	2	10
F	7	1	25

Each transaction is punched on a separate card, with a code of "1" meaning an addition to inventory, and a code of "2" meaning a deletion from inventory.

Initialize an array to hold the current level of inventory for each item, reading the complete "old inventory" from cards at the start of your program. Read individual transaction cards, keeping track of additions and deletions by item number.

Print a report showing, for each item, the beginning inventory, additions to inventory, deletions from inventory, and ending inventory. Place an asterisk (*) to the right of the ending inventory field for any part number having an ending inventory less than ten (10)—this is a reorder flag. Use explicit column headings.

Hint: the item number can be used as a subscript.

11. Test scores on the SAT test are computed using something like the following algorithm:

   a. complete a raw score (number correct, for example) for each person taking the test;

   b. find the average raw score;

   c. compute each individual score by dividing the actual raw score by the average raw score and then multiplying the resulting ratio by 500 (converting scores to a scale with 500 as the average).

The only problem with this algorithm is the fact that all raw scores must first be read and accumulated to find the average, and then, *after* the average has been computed, these actual raw scores must be accessed again to find the SAT score.

One way of solving this problem is to first read all the raw scores (complete with an identification number, of course) into a large table. Then, the table data can be used to compute an average raw score and subsequently used again to compute each individual's actual SAT score. Write a program to do this. Assume that input records contain:

columns	contents
1-9	student identification number
10-14	raw score (99999)

Once the basic program has been written, add logic to make certain that the maximum SAT score is 800 and the minimum score is 200.

9

Systems of Programs

OVERVIEW

Breaking a program into modules is a good idea. It simplifies programming, makes documentation easier, and significantly improves a programs maintainability. Sometimes it is desirable to carry the idea of modularization one step further, breaking the logic needed to support a particular application into two or more programs. In this chapter, we will investigate just such an application, developing a program to edit check payroll data for accuracy before beginning payroll computation.

Intermediate files are often needed to support interrelated programs, and we will investigate the use of such files. As we move into the planning and development of the data edit program, such topics as class tests for a numeric or alphabetic field and range tests for upper and lower limits on a field will be covered. This new program will be tied together with the previously developed payroll program to form a single two-step job.

FAILURE IS INTOLERABLE

Imagine that you are working for a large company. It's payday. At 3:30 p.m. the word comes down that, "Due to program error there will be no checks today." Picture your reaction.

On an application like payroll processing, program failure is intolerable. It goes almost without saying that checks must be distributed on time. And these checks must be reasonably accurate. Oh, an occasional minor error can be tolerated and corrected on a subsequent check, but generally, accuracy is essential.

Computers are accurate, right? Therefore we have nothing to worry about. Right? Wrong! "Accurate" does not necessarily mean what you probably think it does. It definitely does not mean "absolutely correct". On a computer, "predictable" more closely matches the real meaning of "accurate". A computer is accurate simply because, given the same instructions and the same data, it will consistently and predictably generate the same answer. If these instructions and data are correct, then the answers will be correct. If these instructions and data are wrong, then the answer *will be* wrong, with equal certainty.

Of course, the programmer is responsible for the accuracy (perhaps it is better to say for the "correctness") of the instructions in the program. What about data accuracy? Who is responsible for making sure the data is correct? In many firms a timekeeping department is responsible for this. The keypunch operation, of course, bears some of the blame when things go wrong. If, however, a data error leads to program failure, the programmer is at fault. Even if someone else made the data error, the fact that the program failed is still the programmer's fault.

How can a data error lead to program failure? What can go wrong? Plenty. Something as simple as a real decimal point or another nonnumeric character buried in the middle of a numeric field can lead to immediate program termination as soon as this field is used in a computation, or as one of the data items in an IF statement. An incorrect Social Security number or name field can lead to complications for the individual attempting to cash a check. A simple shifting of digits—4 or 400 rather than 40, for example—can lead to an incorrect check.

Naturally, the programmer cannot be expected to catch and eliminate every error. Some mistakes are, however, worse than others. Obviously, anything that could cause program termination would jeopardize the prompt distribution of pay checks, and is intolerable. At a slightly lower level, data errors that could lead to incorrect amounts, while limited to a relatively few checks, still represent a potential loss to the organization and should be eliminated if possible. Finally, there are such things as an occasional misspelling or incorrect Social Security number. Errors on these fields may inconvenience a few employees, although it's equally likely that no one will be inconvenienced at all. Correcting these errors becomes a lower priority item—do what you can.

Incidently, the problem we are now discussing is one of those things that makes programming such a challenging profession. In most fields, 95% correct is satisfactory. In programming, 100% correct is the only acceptable target. The fact that your

Fig. 9.1: *Edit checking as a routine attached to the existing modular payroll program.*

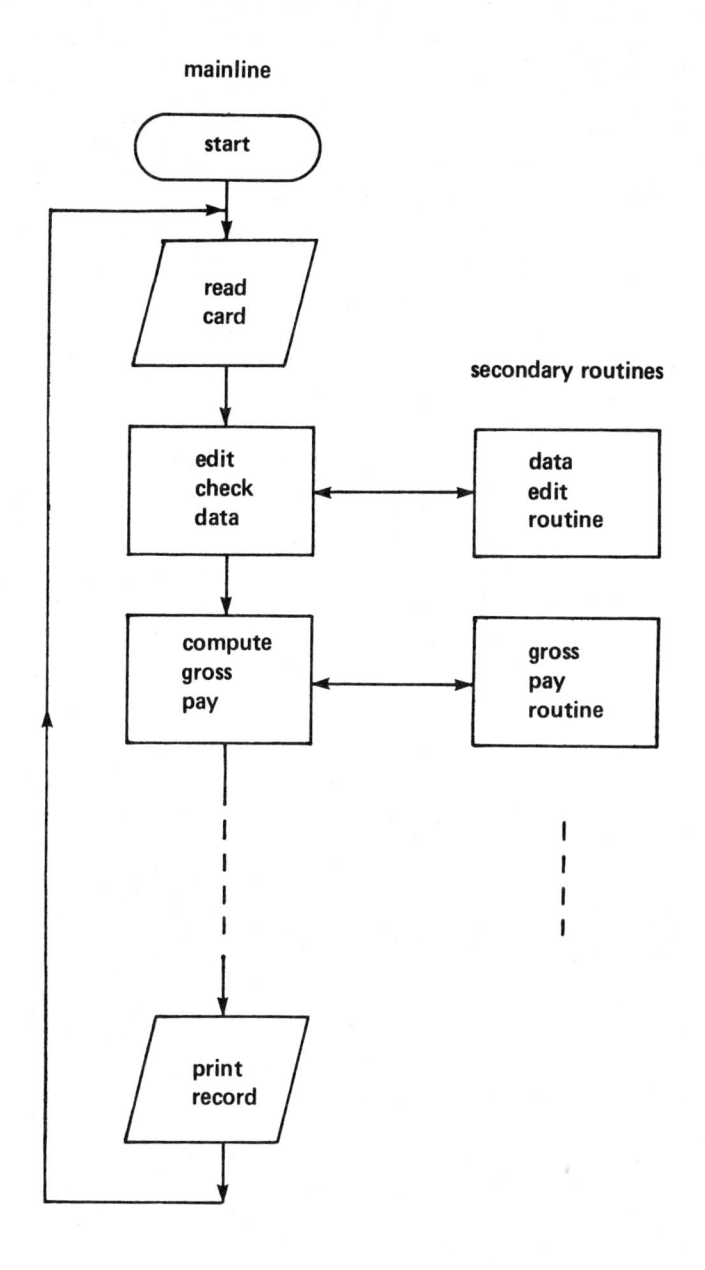

program may have produced millions of perfectly valid paychecks is beside the point when a few bad ones begin coming out.

EDIT CHECKING THE DATA

Although technically the responsibility for data accuracy lies with others, the programmer is held responsible for program failure, no matter what the source. Data error is a common cause of program failure; therefore the programmer really *is* responsible for data accuracy. What steps can the programmer take to ensure the validity of input data?

Fortunately, it is possible to instruct the computer to verify input data before using it. Hours worked can, for example, be compared with an upper limit of perhaps 70 hours and a lower limit of perhaps 10 hours, and rejected if they do not fall within this range. A field that is supposed to be numeric can be tested to see if it really is numeric before any computations are called for. This is called **edit checking** the data, and it is an important part of almost every business computer application.

Obviously, edit checking must be performed before computations using the field or fields in question begin. One option for implementing these functions is outlined in Fig. 9.1; it shows an edit checking routine being added to the existing payroll program, with a link to this routine immediately following the input of a record of data. Often, an edit checking routine is itself quite complex, with significant amounts of code. The danger in this approach is that the program might become too big, too clumsy, too difficult to follow.

As an alternative, edit checking can be performed in a separate program executed before the main payroll program (Fig. 9.2). This new program reads payroll data cards, checks each field for accuracy or reasonability, and then generates two output files—one for good records and one for rejects. The rejects file is simply turned over to the payroll department for manual processing. The "good" records file is written to a high-speed medium such as magnetic tape or disk for subsequent input to the main payroll program.

By separating the edit checking functions into a separate program, we are simply carrying the idea of modularization one step further. And, why not? Edit checking is, after all, a recognizably separate function. It is also a function that must be performed before any actual computations can be taken care of, so it makes sense to check all the data first and then to process it.

Splitting the logic into two independent programs does, however, create one new problem. In the first program, the edit program (Fig. 9.2), the input data comes from punched cards. Where does the input data for the second program come from? The whole point of the edit program was to eliminate data records containing certain errors; since these error records are still in the original data deck, it makes no sense simply to reread this deck into the second program. Instead, the edit check program must create, as its output, a file of data records that can subsequently be read into the payroll program. To repeat, the output generated by the edit program becomes the input for the payroll program. What we are discussing is an **intermediate data file**.

Fig. 9.2: *The data edit function as a separate program.*

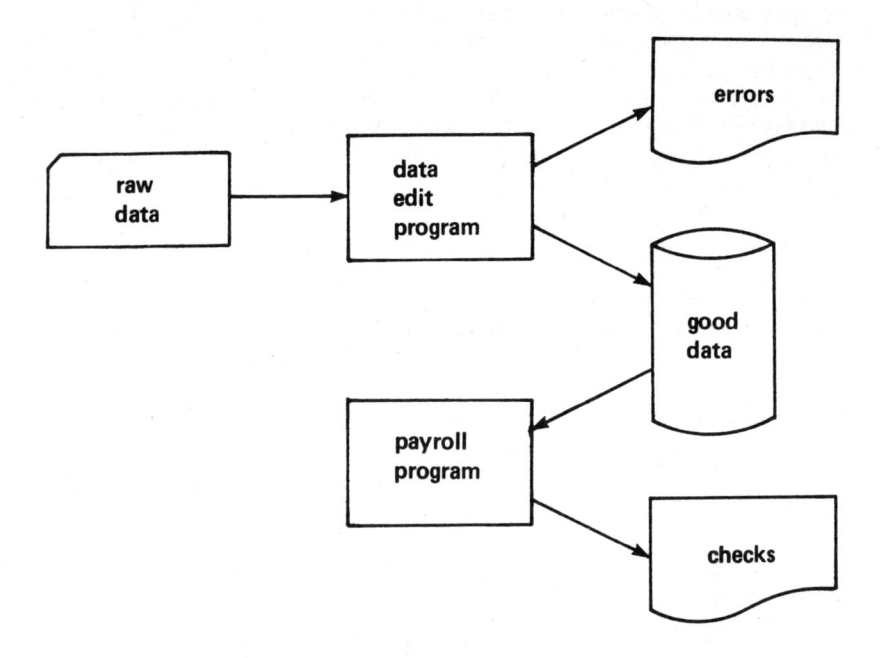

How can this be done? One possibility is to punch a new data deck, under control of the edit program, via a card punch machine. Using this approach, the edit program would read a card from the original data deck and check it for accuracy. If the record were good, the edit program would issue a WRITE instruction, sending a copy of this data card to the card punch, where a new record would be punched. If, on the other hand, something was wrong with the input record, an error message would be sent to the printer, and the card punching step would be bypassed. In this way, a new data deck containing only good records would be produced. This deck could then be read into the payroll program.

There is one major problem associated with using cards to hold the intermediate file. Cards are slow. If you have ever seen a card reader handling as many as 1000 cards per minute, the statement "cards are slow" may seem absurd, but consider the following. A computer, internally, can manipulate as many as 2 million characters per second—on some computers, even more. A rate of 1000 cards per minute, assuming an 80-character card, is 80,000 characters per minute, which converts to only 1333 characters per second. On a comparative scale, we are talking, conservatively, about slightly over 1000 vs. 2,000,000! In other words, the computer is almost 2000 times as fast as a card reader! That's what we mean when we say that a card reader is slow—it is slow relative to the internal speeds of the computer.

It makes a great deal of sense to use, as the medium for an intermediate work file, a device that permits data to be stored and retrieved at rates somewhat comparable with the computer's internal speeds.

Tape and Disk

Magnetic tape and disk are both magnetic storage media, meaning that data is stored on these devices as a pattern of invisible magnetic spots. Both are in common use, and both are relatively fast. Let's consider tape first, as it is probably much more familiar to the average student.

Magnetic computer **tape** works almost exactly like magnetic sound recording tape; in fact, on many smaller computers and some modern terminals, regular cassettes are used as a storage medium. You probably have at least a basic idea of how a tape recorder works. Picture a reel-to-reel machine. As you turn the machine on, the tape begins to move from one reel to the other at a constant rate. Your first words are recorded near the beginning of the tape, with subsequent words strung out along the tape in sequential fashion. Later, when the tape is played back, you get an exact duplication of what was said during the recording phase. The magnetic signals that carry the information cannot, of course, be seen, but that really doesn't matter.

When magnetic tape is used for computer output or input, there is no audio signal to contend with. Instead, electronic signals representing the data to be stored are sent from the computer to the tape's read/write head which records the magnetic signals on the tape surface. Later, when reading the data back into the computer, these magnetic signals are sensed by the read/write heads and converted into an electronic signal which is sent to the computer. As is the case with sound recording tape, what goes back into the computer is a perfect reproduction of the data put on the tape in the first place.

Most programs are designed to write and read a record of data; thus the record is the basic unit of data storage. Sound recording tape is recorded and played back at a constant speed; in fact, the better the tape recorder, the more closely this speed is controlled. A computer tape drive works in similar fashion, recording and reading at a constant speed.

Most sound tapes contain periods of silence separating the various selections on the tape; we can easily interpret the meaning of these gaps. A magnetic tape drive is an electronic device. It does not have a human mind to provide control; thus the mechanism for separating "selections", records on the tape, must be simplier. Normally, a fixed length gap of unused space is left between successive records (Fig. 9.3). As a record is read, the tape is stopped; roughly one half of a gap is used up by the mechanism as it drops from its constant read/write speed to a full stop. Later, as the next record is read or written, the last half of the gap gives the drive the space it needs to come from rest up to normal read/write speed.

These gaps do, of course, represent wasted space. To conserve some of this space, the programmer will often group a number of records together into a single **block** (Fig. 9.4). Without blocking, there is one set of interrecord gaps associated with each logical record; with blocking, one set of gaps can control access to several records. Fewer total gaps means less wasted space.

A tape drive is designed to read or write all the data from one interblock gap to the next interblock gap. Without blocking, one record at a time is transferred between the computer and the device. With blocking, several records are transferred at a time. But, most programs are designed to read or write only one record at a time, not several. By attempting to improve the utilization of the tape, we have created another problem for the programmer.

Fortunately, there is an easy solution. On most systems, the problem of blocking and deblocking data records is handled by special software (an access method) or by the computer hardware, so the programmer can essentially ignore it. Generally, the programmer's only responsibility is to provide a detailed description of the record (by using PICTURE clauses) and to indicate the number of logical records found in a

Fig. 9.3: *Records as stored on magnetic tape.*

| gap | record no. 1 | gap | record no. 2 | gap | record no. 3 | gap |

Fig. 9.4: *Blocked records on magnetic tape.*

| gap | record no. 1 | record no. 2 | record no. 3 | gap | record no. 4 |

single block. This is done through the **BLOCK CONTAINS** clause that is added to the FD-entry for the file in question. For example, the clause

BLOCK CONTAINS 10 RECORDS

clearly indicates that there are ten logical records in each block.

One potential problem with magnetic tape is that all tapes look pretty much alike. If you have a private collection of taped music, the chances are that you carefully label each tape so that you can tell them apart. The same thing is done with computer tapes. In addition to a human-readable stick-on label, most tapes are assigned a header **label** that is actually recorded on the tape surface so that the computer can tell them apart (Fig. 9.5).

If magnetic tape is similar to magnetic sound recording tape, magnetic disk can be compared with a long-playing record album. On the album, information, in this case music or spoken words, is recorded on a spiral groove on the surface of the disk. On a magnetic computer disk, the disk-shaped surface (Fig. 9.6) is coated with a magnetic material similar to that used on magnetic tape, and data or information is stored on a series of concentric circles on this surface called **tracks**.

On a record album it is possible to select a song by picking up and moving the tone arm. On a magnetic **disk**, it is possible to select a specific track by moving the read/write heads either in or out. The movable read/write head gives disk the ability to retrieve data selectively or randomly, without regard for the order in which it was stored; we'll consider some applications that depend on this capacity in later chapters.

Often, several disk surfaces are stacked on a single spindle and accessed by a set of read/write heads mounted together on a single **access arm** (Fig. 9.7). One position of this read/write mechanism allows the heads to access one track on each of several surfaces; in other words, given that a set of several heads moves together, one position of the read/write mechanism defines not one but several tracks, usually one under another (Fig. 9.7 again). This collection of tracks defined by a single position

Fig. 9.5: *Tape Files are Usually Labeled.*

Fig. 9.6: *On disk, data is stored on a series of concentric circles called tracks.*

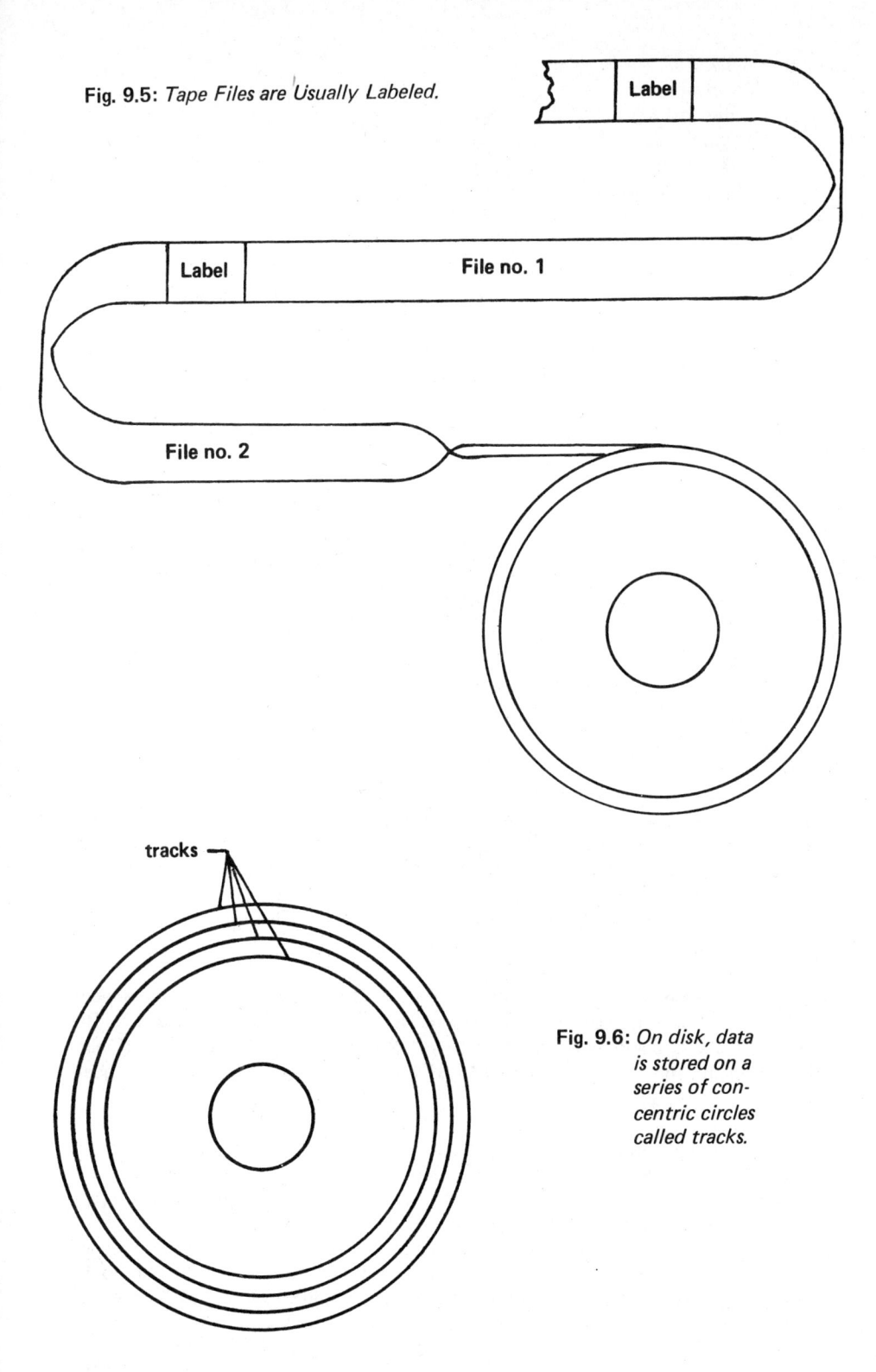

Fig. 9.7: *A Typical Disk Arrangement Showing a Stack of Individual Disks and Movable Read/Write Heads.*

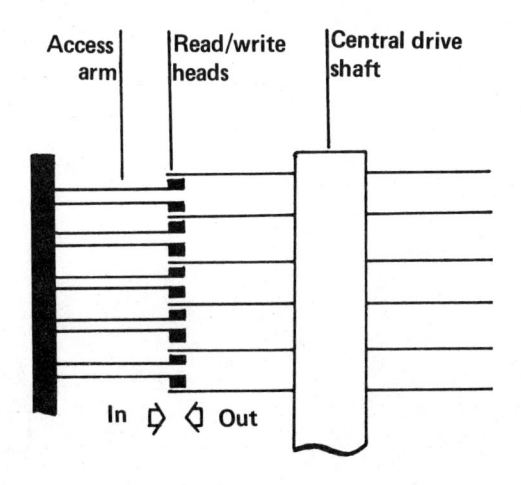

of the access arm is called a **cylinder**. The stack of related disk surfaces is called a disk pack.

Not all manufacturers use the cylinder and track approach for addressing disk space. Some divide the space on a disk surface into **sectors**. Imagine if the disk surface pictured in Fig. 9.6 were divided into a number of pie-shaped slices, each of equal size. As a consequence, each track would be divided into a series of arcs; each arc is one sector. A fixed amount of data could then be stored in each sector. On IBM's System/3 series of computers, for example, each disk sector is designed to hold 256 characters of data.

As is the case with tape, the information stored on disk is not human-readable. This means that, once again, labels are needed for identification purposes. The LABEL RECORD clause in the DATA DIVISION is used to identify the type of label used. Normally, the LABEL RECORD IS STANDARD, meaning that standard labels are used.

For our application, temporarily storing data in an intermediate file, there is not a great deal of difference between tape and disk. Our intent is simply to store the data in sequence and then to retrieve it in the same sequence. Placing the data on tape or disk is achieved by coding a WRITE instruction; later, to retrieve the data, a READ instruction is coded. Earlier, in describing what might happen if we used punched cards for the intermediate file, we indicated that each output record would be punched into a separate card, and that this new deck would be subsequently read into the second program. Using tape or disk, each output record is recorded as a sort of card image, and these images are read back in.

TYING TOGETHER A SYSTEM OF PROGRAMS

The program mainline ties the pieces of a modular program together. We are now discussing the possibility of a wider view of the modular approach, breaking an application into an integrated **system** of programs. These are now separate programs, so the idea of a program mainline serving as the cement to tie all the pieces together is no longer valid. Since these programs are interrelated, however, there must be some mechanism for tying them together. On most computer systems, this objective is achieved through the command or job control language.

A few basic command language concepts were presented in Chapter 4; for those of you who program on an IBM System/360 or System/370 computer, an optional section presented some of the elements of IBM's job control language. The three basic functions of any command language are:

  1. to identify the job,

  2. to identify the specific program or programs that make up the job,

  3. to identify the input and output devices needed by this job.

Without getting into specifics, a rough outline of the job control language needed to support this system of programs might look like Fig. 9.8 (standard IBM job control is used as a rough model for this figure). Note that there is only one JOB card, indicating that this whole thing describes only one job. Within this job are two EXEC cards, each describing one of the programs to be run. This structure clearly indicates the fact that both programs are related (being part of the same job), and that EDIT must be run before PAYROLL. The DD cards serve to define the input and output devices attached to each program or **job step**.

Don't look at the details of the individual job control cards; that is not the point we are trying to make at present. Concentrate instead on the structure and the relationship imposed by these command or control statements. Very simply, their function is to tie together a series of related programs into a single job and to specify the input and output devices used by each of these programs. The command language used on your computer may be different from the example presented above, but the general structure should be similar.

Job Control Language for the IBM System/360 and System/370 (Optional)

For those of you who have access to an IBM System/360 or System/370 computer running under an OS or VS operating system, the job control language cards described below will serve as models for creating and retrieving data from an intermediate file on tape or disk. The job control statements are intended to be typical, and not absolute; check with your instructor or an experienced programmer.

To create a magnetic tape file, you will normally need a DD card containing the following parameters:

```
//filename  DD      UNIT=unit-name,
//                  LABEL=(,SL),
//                  DISP=(NEW,PASS),
//                  VOL=SER=volume-serial-number,
//                  DSNAME=external-name
```

The UNIT parameter defines the physical output device. If, for example, the tape is to be mounted on a 2400 tape drive, this parameter would be coded as UNIT=2400.

The LABEL=(,SL) is a shorthand way of telling the system that the file is the first one on the tape and that it has standard labels. Not all installations use standard labels. In some cases, the use of standard labels has been so strongly implemented that this parameter is automatic, meaning that the programmer need not code it. Once again, check your local standards.

The DISP=(NEW,PASS) parameter identifies this file as one to be created in this job step (NEW) and then passed to a subsequent job step (PASS).

Each reel of magnetic tape has a unique volume serial number associated with it. In order to have the computer operator mount the proper reel or volume, it is necessary to code this serial number, which is the purpose of the VOL=SER parameter. Often, the programmer, especially when creating a nonpermanent, inermediate file, really doesn't care what volume is used. In this case, the parameter VOL=SER=SCRTCH is sometimes coded, telling the operator to mount a scratch tape. The limit on the length of a serial number is 6 characters, accounting for the apparent misspelling of the word scratch.

Fig. 9.8: *An Example of the Typical Job Control Statements Needed to Support a System of Two Programs.*

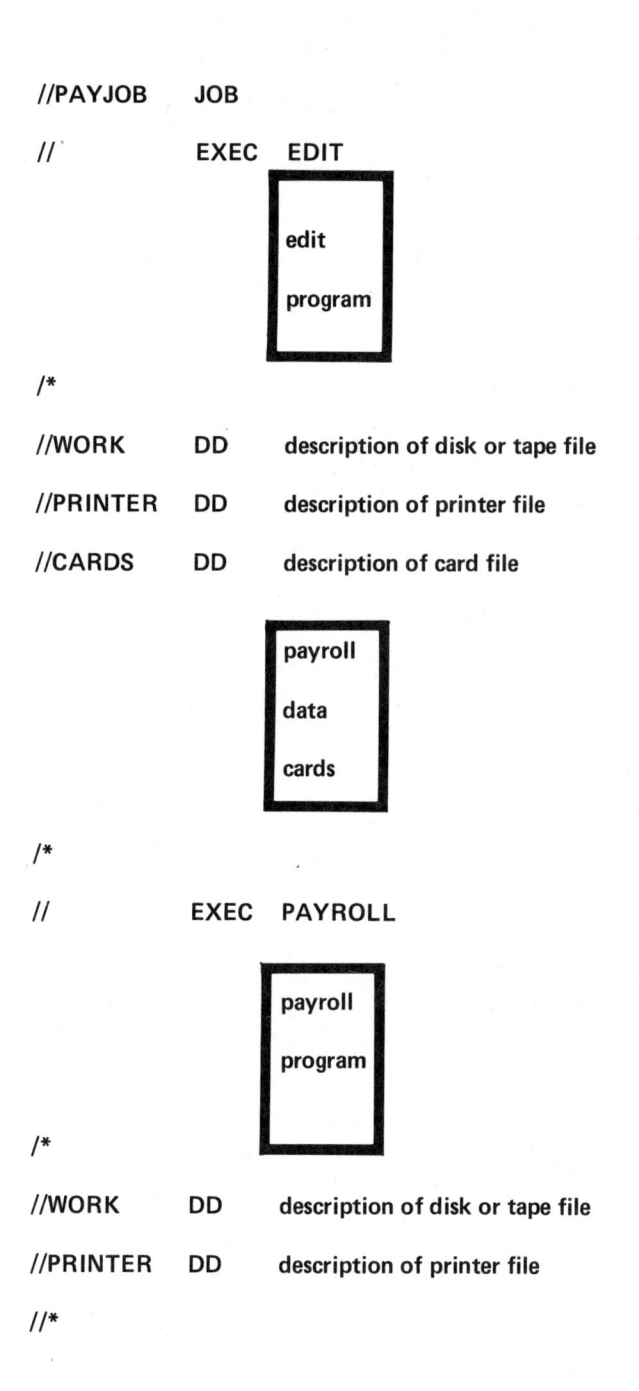

```
//PAYJOB    JOB
//          EXEC   EDIT
                   ┌─────────┐
                   │ edit    │
                   │ program │
                   └─────────┘
/*
//WORK      DD     description of disk or tape file
//PRINTER   DD     description of printer file
//CARDS     DD     description of card file
                   ┌─────────┐
                   │ payroll │
                   │ data    │
                   │ cards   │
                   └─────────┘
/*
//          EXEC   PAYROLL
                   ┌─────────┐
                   │ payroll │
                   │ program │
                   └─────────┘
/*
//WORK      DD     description of disk or tape file
//PRINTER   DD     description of printer file
//*
```

The rules for punctuating this job control language card are simple. Begin with slashes (//) in the first two columns. The file name (which, as you may recall from Chapter 4, must match the name specified in an ASSIGN clause in the program's ENVIRONMENT DIVISION) begins in column 3. Following the file name are one or more blanks, and then the DD operation code. The DD, which defines this as a data definition card, is itself followed by one or more blanks, and then come the parameters. All the parameters may be coded on a single card, if they fit. If not, simply break after any comma, start a new card with the // characters in the first two columns, skip a space or two, and resume coding; the "one parameter per card" approach illustrated in the example cited above is perfectly legal. No blanks, other than the ones described above, may be coded.

A DD card to create a disk file is just a bit different. Normally, such a card will contain the following parameters:

```
//filename  DD      UNIT=unit-name,

//                  DISP=(NEW,PASS),

//                  DSNAME=external-name,

//                  SPACE=(type,amount)
```

When disk is used many installations set aside space specifically for programmers needing temporary intermediate storage. If this is the case, the UNIT parameter often refers to a standard device assignment such as UNIT=SYSDA or UNIT=WORK1. The DISP and DSNAME parameters are no different than they were with magnetic tape. LABEL and VOL parameters are generally not coded.

The only new parameter is SPACE. When you use magnetic tape, the usual rule is that a program has exclusive use of a tape drive. This is not the case on disk. Since disk has a movable access arm, it is possible to allow several different programs to be accessing the device over the same time period. Also, even if concurrent access is not the rule, it is possible to subdivide the disk surface into a number of different areas and place a different file on each. Since a disk can be shared, it is necessary to indicate how much space your program will need, which is the function of the space parameter. A typical request for disk space would be SPACE=(TRK,2), which asks for two tracks.

Once a file has been created on disk or tape, a subsequent job step must be able to retrieve it. This is where the value of the DSNAME parameter can be seen. By coding simply

```
//filename  DD  DSNAME=external-name,DISP=(OLD,DELETE)
```

> the file can be retrieved. As before, the filename must match the name coded in the program ASSIGN clause. The external-name must match the external-name coded in the job control language card that created this file. DISP=(OLD,DELETE) identifies the file as being OLD (it does, after all, already exist) and says that when the job step is finished, the file can be DELETED (it was, after all, just a temporary work file).

PLANNING THE EDIT CHECK PROGRAM

Now that we've discussed the basic idea of intermediate files, let's turn our attention to planning a solution to the edit check problem. The problem definition is quite simple: check input data for accuracy before the payroll program is executed. The problem definition presupposes that there is already a payroll program in existence; in fact, we've spent the last three chapters describing it. Because this edit check program is a support module for the payroll program, much of the planning is already done.

Probably the best place to begin is with the input data. It has been defined; the code is reproduced as Fig. 9.9. Our objective is to check this data for accuracy.

What checks should be performed? Earlier, we discussed the types of errors that could arise from bad data. Of prime importance were those errors that might cause program termination. Obviously, such errors must be eliminated, but before we can eliminate them, we must identify them.

What kinds of errors can cause a program to terminate? The answer requires a knowledge of computer internals beyond the scope of this book, but a few general guidelines can be established. Basically, assuming that the computer is functioning properly, the only thing that can lead to program termination is an illegal arithmetic operation or comparison. Dividing by zero is an example. So is attempting to perform arithmetic on two fields that do not contain numeric data. Trying to compare a numeric and a nonnumeric field can, under certain conditions, cause program termination too.

On most modern computers, there is a significant difference, within the machine, between the way numeric and nonnumeric data is represented. Telling a computer to add two nonnumeric fields is about as absurd as telling you to add Sam and Oscar. You reject such requests as ridiculous. The computer quits.

Note that we were careful to say that the problem occurs when attempting to perform arithmetic on two fields that do not *contain* numeric data. The way the fields are defined is beside the point. If a real decimal point is punched in the middle of an otherwise numeric field, then that field contains nonnumeric data and cannot be used in arithmetic. The most common source of program termination due to data error is the presence of a nonnumeric character in an otherwise numeric field.

Thus, the first objective of the data edit program is clear. Any fields used in computations must be tested to make certain that they contain *only* numeric characters—0, 1, 2, 3, 4, 5, 6, 7, 8, 9. What fields are used in computations? Look at Fig. 9.9. Only hours worked, hourly pay rate, and number of dependents are computational fields. The data edit program will begin with a series of tests to make certain that these fields contain only numeric characters.

Having covered the most crucial type of potential error, we can turn our attention to problems that could cause a financial loss. Too many hours worked or too high a pay rate could lead to computing an inflated amount of gross pay. Too many dependents could lead to an excessively low value for income tax. If the marital status is neither M nor S, no income tax would be computed at all.

The last of these potential problems is the easiest to handle—a simple IF test or two can make sure that either M or S is punched on the card. But what of the other problems? What do we mean when we say that hours worked or the hourly pay rate is too high? How high is too high? What we need are some reasonable limits on these fields.

This kind of question requires some leg work. Who in the organization knows what is reasonable? In this particular case, the payroll department probably knows. Perhaps, following a visit to the manager of this department, the programmer can come back with the following reasonable estimates:

   hours worked must lie between 15 and 65

   hourly pay rate must lie between 3.00 and 12.50

   dependents may not exceed 12.

Any payroll card containing values lying outside these ranges can be assumed to be in error and should therefore be rejected.

Note that this kind of test is not an absolute. Someone might very well have to work 70 hours in a given week. A pay rate in excess of $12.50 per hour is not beyond belief. There are people with more than 12 dependents. The whole idea of these tests is to screen out *potential* errors, perhaps for analysis by the payroll department. It is likely that these limits may have to be changed with time. They represent an attempt to introduce a touch of common sense to the program.

The final type of edit check concerns what might be called convenience items. A Social Security number should contain all digits. If it doesn't, if a stray nonnumeric character should creep in, no real harm is done (except, perhaps, to the ego of the employee). Still, if it is convenient to make sure the data is correct, why not? Another similar check has to do with the employee's name. It should contain all alphabetic characters (we'll ignore names like Fawcett-Majors for this example). Again, no real harm is done if the employee's name is not printed correctly on the check, but it should be. Note that we cannot guarantee that the name or the Social Security number are correct; we can merely eliminate certain obvious errors. There is a saying in the computer field: Garbage in, garbage out. Its meaning is quite simple: If the input data is wrong, the results will be wrong.

COBOL Coding Form

SYSTEM	PAYROLL		PUNCHING INSTRUCTIONS	PAGE 2 OF 15
PROGRAM	EDIT TIME CARDS		GRAPHIC Ø	
PROGRAMMER	DAVIS & FISHER	DATE 2-1-79	PUNCH ZERO	CARD FORM #

SEQUENCE | CONT. | A | B | COBOL STATEMENT | IDENTIFICATION

```
       DATA DIVISION.

        FILE SECTION.

         FD  TIME-CARD-FILE
             LABEL RECORD OMITTED.
          Ø1  TIME-CARD.
              Ø5  I-SOCIAL-SECURITY-NO  PIC 9(9).
              Ø5  I-LAST-NAME           PIC X(16).
              Ø5  I-INITIALS            PIC XX.
              Ø5  I-DEPARTMENT-NO       PIC 999.
              Ø5  I-HOURS-WORKED        PIC 99V9.
              Ø5  I-HOURLY-PAY-RATE     PIC 99V99.
              Ø5  I-NO-OF-DEPENDENTS    PIC 99.
              Ø5  I-MARITAL-STATUS      PIC X.
              Ø5  FILLER                PIC X(4Ø).
```

Fig. 9.9: *The format of the input records.*

The final step that should be completed before moving along to the coding of this plan in COBOL is the definition of input and output devices. Input will come from punched cards. The output will go to two places: a disk file to hold the "good" records, and a printer to list the known errors.

The Output Record to the Intermediate File

One of the output records from this program will be sent to an intermediate file on disk. Bascially, this record should be a copy of the input record, assuming of course that the data is valid. There is, however, one major difference between disk and punched cards that will allow us to make at least one very significant change.

A punched card is a unit record medium. The card is 80 characters long. The fact that all 80 characters may not be needed is beside the point—the card is still 80 characters in length. Card readers are designed to read one card at a time. Card punches are designed to punch one card at a time. The length of a punched card record is determined by the physical nature of the card itself.

This problem does not exist on magnetic disk. Records can be any length. In this example, the original input cards contain useful data in columns 1 through 40, and columns 41 through 80 are not used at all. Thus the output record sent to disk is defined as being only 40 characters in length (Fig. 9.10); why bother storing forty blanks?

Disk records are also frequently blocked (Fig. 9.10); in this example, each block will contain 5 records. How is this blocking factor selected? Ideally, the blocking factor should be selected to make the most effective possible use of storage space on a disk pack. Generally, this is a question for an experienced programmer, and the beginner should not spend too much time worrying about it. For a temporary file, blocking factors of 5 or 10 are usually reasonable.

The Exceptions File

The other output file from this program is a list of all input records that contain one or more errors. The original input data should, of course, be part of this output record, as someone will almost certainly want to review and analyze all errors in an attempt to correct them. Ideally, the output data should be formatted so it will be easy to read. It would also be valuable if each output line contained an error message explaining exactly what the program found to be wrong in the record. The format of these output records is shown in Fig. 9.11. Note that space has been set aside to hold an error message; the actual messages that will be selectively used are spelled out in the WORKING-STORAGE SECTION.

What if a given input record contains more than one error? Are we to list only the first error encountered, or are we to list all errors? Given the intent of this error report, we should list all. Ideally, records having multiple errors should be clearly identified, to minimize the possibility of misunderstanding. We will return to this topic shortly.

COBOL Coding Form

SYSTEM: PAYROLL
PROGRAM: EDIT TIME CARDS
PROGRAMMER: DAVIS & FISHER
DATE: 2-1-79
GRAPHIC: ∅
PUNCH: ZERO
PAGE: 3 OF 15

```
FD  VALID-TIME-FILE
    LABEL RECORD IS STANDARD
    BLOCK CONTAINS 5 RECORDS.
01  VALID-TIME-RECORD.
    05  V-SOCIAL-SECURITY-NO    PIC 9(9).
    05  V-LAST-NAME             PIC X(16).
    05  V-INITIALS              PIC XX.
    05  V-DEPARTMENT-NO         PIC 999.
    05  V-HOURS-WORKED          PIC 99V9.
    05  V-HOURLY-PAY-RATE       PIC 99V99.
    05  V-NO-OF-DEPENDENTS      PIC 99.
    05  V-MARITAL-STATUS        PIC X.
```

Fig. 9.10: *The format of the intermediate file records.*

COBOL Coding Form

SYSTEM: PAYROLL
PROGRAM: EDIT TIME CARDS
PROGRAMMER: DAVIS & FISHER
DATE: 2-1-79
PUNCHING INSTRUCTIONS — GRAPHIC: Ø PUNCH: ZERO
PAGE 4 OF 15

```
FD  TIME-EXCEPTION-REPORT
    LABEL RECORD OMITTED.
Ø1  TIME-EXCEPTION.
    Ø5  FILLER                  PIC X(11).
    Ø5  E-SOCIAL-SECURITY-NO    PIC X(9).
    Ø5  FILLER                  PIC X(3).
    Ø5  E-LAST-NAME             PIC X(16).
    Ø5  FILLER                  PIC X(3).
    Ø5  E-INITIALS              PIC XX.
    Ø5  FILLER                  PIC X(3).
    Ø5  E-DEPARTMENT-NO         PIC 999.
    Ø5  FILLER                  PIC X(3).
    Ø5  E-HOURS-WORKED          PIC 99V9.
    Ø5  FILLER                  PIC X(3).
    Ø5  E-HOURLY-PAY-RATE       PIC 99V99.
    Ø5  FILLER                  PIC X(3).
    Ø5  E-NO-OF-DEPENDENTS      PIC 99.
    Ø5  FILLER                  PIC X(3).
    Ø5  E-MARITAL-STATUS        PIC X.
    Ø5  FILLER                  PIC X(9).
    Ø5  E-MESSAGE               PIC X(40).
    Ø5  FILLER                  PIC X(12).
```

Fig. 9.11: *The format of the exceptions (or error) records.*

COBOL Coding Form

SYSTEM	PAYROLL		PUNCHING INSTRUCTIONS	PAGE 1 OF 15
PROGRAM	EDIT TIME CARDS		GRAPHIC Ø	CARD FORM #
PROGRAMMER	DAVIS & FISHER	DATE 2-1-79	PUNCH ZERO	

SEQUENCE | CONT. | A | B | COBOL STATEMENT | IDENTIFICATION

```
       ENVIRONMENT DIVISION.

        CONFIGURATION SECTION.

         SOURCE-COMPUTER.    IBM-370-148.
         OBJECT-COMPUTER.    IBM-370-148.
         SPECIAL-NAMES.      C01 IS NEW-PAGE.

        INPUT-OUTPUT SECTION.

           SELECT TIME-CARD-FILE        ASSIGN TO UT-S-TIMECRDS.
           SELECT VALID-TIME-FILE       ASSIGN TO UT-S-VALDTIME.
           SELECT TIME-EXCEPTION-REPORT ASSIGN TO UT-S-TIMEXCEP.
```

Fig. 9.12: *The ENVIRONMENT DIVISION showing the SELECT. . . ASSIGN clauses.*

The ENVIRONMENT DIVISION

This program is accessing three files, so there must be three SELECT and ASSIGN clauses. They are shown in Fig. 9.12.

Class Tests

One of the most important types of tests that must be performed in this program is to ascertain that the content of certain key fields is numeric. In another less crucial test, the program will determine if the employee name field is all alphabetic. COBOL supports two **class tests** that simplify the coding of such comparisons.

In the statement

>   IF HOURS-WORKED IS NUMERIC . . .

the programmer is checking to see if the HOURS-WORKED field contains only the numeric characters 0 through 9, with, perhaps, a sign. In the statement

>   IF EMPLOYEE-NAME IS ALPHABETIC . . .

the test is for the alphabetic characters A through Z and the blank character.

Range Tests

A **range test** is designed to make certain that the value of a key field lies within a reasonable range—hours worked between 15 and 65, for example. One way of performing such tests is by using nested IF statements, as in

>   IF HOURS-WORKED IS LESS THAN 15
>
>   THEN PERFORM RANGE-ERROR-ROUTINE
>
>   ELSE IF HOURS-WORKED IS GREATER THAN 65
>
>   THEN PERFORM RANGE-ERROR-ROUTINE
>
>   ELSE NEXT SENTENCE.

An alternative approach involves the use of **compound conditions**, for example

>   IF (HOURS-WORKED IS LESS THAN 15)
>
>   OR (HOURS-WORKED IS GREATER THAN 65)
>
>   THEN PERFORM RANGE-ERROR-ROUTINE
>
>   ELSE NEXT SENTENCE.

Compound conditions require great care, because it is very easy to code something that looks right but isn't; the parentheses, although not really required, are strongly recommended as a mechanism for clearly identifying each of the basic conditions being tested. A compound condition consists of two or more simple conditions connected by the reserved word OR, which means that if either is true the condition is true, or AND, which means that all of the individual conditions must be true for the compound condition to be true.

HOURS-WORKED is a numeric field; thus it is compared with a numeric constant. What if a nonnumeric character were buried in the field? The comparison would cause program failure, but the whole point of this program is to *avoid* program failure. Clearly, it is important that the range test be skipped if the NUMERIC class test is failed. The easiest way to achieve this objective is to attach the range test to the associated class test as part of a nested IF structure.

The test for proper marital status is a special type of range test in that only certain very specific values will do. The marital status must be M or S.

Using a Switch to Control Program Output

One way to design this program would be to test the input fields until the first error was encountered, and then to print an error message and move on to the next record. This program structure would be very easy to implement, but it is not what we want. Instead, our intent is to test all fields no matter how many are in error, printing a separate error message for each error encountered. This implies that there may be several error messages for a given record; ideally, the input data should be printed only once, with just the error message being included in subsequent output lines for this same record (Fig. 9.13). In this way, the person using this listing to correct data errors can easily distinguish between records.

The other output file used by this program is to contain only good records; in other words, any record found to contain one or more errors should *not* be sent to this disk file. Thus we have two problems. Once an error has been encountered, subsequent error output routines must be made aware of this fact so that the error listing can be modified. If an error has been encountered anywhere in the program, the routine that writes good records must be aware of the fact so that output can be skipped. Both problems can be handled by using a **switch**.

A switch is nothing but a simple data item; in this example, it will be defined by coding

```
77  ERROR-SWITCH  PIC  9  VALUE  0.
```

During the processing of the program, if an error is encountered this switch will be "turned on" by moving a value other than 0 to it (1 is commonly used). Following the writing of an output record, the switch will always be turned off (reset to 0) before control is returned to the top of the program for the reading of another input record. If this process is followed, the switch will always have one of two values—0 or 1. An 0, meaning "off", means that no error has yet been encountered on this record. A 1, for "on", means that an error has already been found. By testing the value of this switch, an error routine can modify the content of an error message, and the "good data" output module can decide if a record should or should not be written. We'll be using this switch to control program output.

11110111	XPLTZ	J	101	400	0350	00	M	SOCIAL SECURITY NO. IS NOT NUMERIC
12222222	GREENGIANT .	GR	410	135	5050	00	1	NAME IS NOT ALPHABETIC HOURS WORKED IS NOT WITHIN RANGE HOURLY PAY RATE IS NOT WITHIN RANGE
13333333	KRAZZY	UR	105	450	0675	02	M	MARITAL STATUS CODE IS INVALID
14444444	PRINCE	J	105	146	2000	02	M	HOURS WORKED IS NOT WITHIN RANGE MARITAL STATUS CODE IS INVALID
15555555	SCHABER	TS	105	156	0575	05	M	HOURLY PAY RATE IS NOT WITHIN RANGE
16666666	CROSSWHITE	CP	109	660	0425	02	S	MARITAL STATUS CODE IS INVALID HOURS WORKED IS NOT WITHIN RANGE MARITAL STATUS CODE IS INVALID
17777777	BOOKER	DK	201	400	1550	08	M	HOURLY PAY RATE IS NOT NUMERIC MARITAL STATUS CODE IS INVALID
18888888	MANDT	HO	201	200	0300	04	S	MARITAL STATUS CODE IS INVALID
19999999	SHULMAN	MC	205	400	0600	5	M	NO. OF DEPENDENTS IS NOT NUMERIC MARITAL STATUS CODE IS INVALID
21111111	HARVEY	AT	205	425	0425	13	M	NO. OF DEPENDENTS IS NOT WITHIN RANGE MARITAL STATUS CODE IS INVALID
22222222	FAIRBURN	DC	210	400	2000	05	M	NAME IS NOT ALPHABETIC MARITAL STATUS CODE IS NOT WITHIN RANGE MARITAL STATUS CODE IS INVALID
23333333	GUPTA	NO	301	200	0325	01	X	MARITAL STATUS CODE IS INVALID
24444444	JAIN	AK	500	600	2500	04	M	HOURLY PAY RATE IS NOT WITHIN RANGE MARITAL STATUS CODE IS INVALID

Fig. 9.13: *Output listing showing formatted error messages.*

Some programmers use the letters 'Y' and 'N', for "yes" and "no", in setting a switch. Others use the figurative constants HIGH-VALUE and LOW-VALUE. The choice of switch settings is a matter of personal preference; the concept is the same no matter what constants are used.

CODING THE EDIT PROGRAM

Now that we have described the needed COBOL features, it is time to code the PROCEDURE DIVISION for the edit program (Fig. 9.14 shows the listing). Note that the program mainline contains all the actual tests, while the error routines have been moved out of the mainline and housed in secondary routines. If you assumed that a given record contains no errors, the mainline would represent the complete logical path taken by this record. Since the vast majority of records can be expected to be correct (if this is not the case, something is very wrong), the mainline represents the most common path through the program, and this is as it should be. Errors can be viewed as deviations from a normal cycle, and such deviations should be moved outside the mainline.

You may have noticed that the WRITE statement for the error file is encountered several times, once in each error routine. Many programmers would find such a level of repetition to be undesirable. As an alternative, they might code a common output routine and PERFORM it from the individual error routines. This is the approach we will use.

Read the logic of the data edit program carefully. Note especially how the switch is used. In the mainline, the switch-setting conditions the writing of a record to the intermediate disk file. Within all the error handling routines except the first, the switch is used to determine if the data from the input record will be included in the error message.

The WRITE instruction for the intermediate disk file does not contain an AFTER ADVANCING clause, while the WRITE statements for the error file do. Why? The error file goes to the printer, where line spacing is important. Line spacing has no meaning on disk.

Before moving on, we should discuss the **OPEN** and **CLOSE** instructions. Previously, these two instructions have had little real meaning to us. Chapter 3 explained that the OPEN instruction made sure that the device was ready for use, and the CLOSE instruction told the computer system that the device was now free and ready to be assigned to another program. These explanations were rather weak, but, given our restriction to card input and tape output, additional details would have been meaningless and possibly confusing. Now that we have introduced the basic idea of files, we can provide an explanation of these two statements.

The OPEN statement makes sure that the device is ready for use. On tape, this means sending a message to the computer operator to mount the desired tape. On disk, this means positioning the access arm over the proper track. On an existing file, the label can be checked; on a new file, a label can be created. On many systems, OPEN time is when the first actual input operation takes place; in effect, the computer anticipates the demands of the program.

```
1                    20.35.28       SEP 23,1978


00004          IDENTIFICATION DIVISION.

00006          PROGRAM-ID.    EDITIME
00007          AUTHOR.        DAVIS & FISHER.

00009          REMARKS.       THIS PROGRAM CHECKS EACH FIELD IN THE TIME
00010                         CARD FOR VALID CHARACTERS AND/OR REASONABLE
00011                         DATA.  THOSE TIME RECORDS THAT ARE CORRECT
00012                         WILL BE RECORDED ON A MAGNETIC DISK FILE.
00013                         THOSE THAT ARE INCORRECT WILL BE PRINTED ON
00014                         AN EXCEPTION REPORT.



00017          ENVIRONMENT DIVISION.

00019             CONFIGURATION SECTION.

00021             SOURCE-COMPUTER.   IBM-370-148.
00022             OBJECT-COMPUTER.   IBM-370-148.
00023             SPECIAL-NAMES.     C01 IS NEW-PAGE.

00025             INPUT-OUTPUT SECTION.

00027             FILE-CONTROL.
00028                 SELECT TIME-CARD-FILE        ASSIGN TO UT-S-TIMECRDS.
00029                 SELECT VALID-TIME-FILE       ASSIGN TO UT-S-VALDTIME.
00030                 SELECT TIME-EXCEPTION-REPORT ASSIGN TO UT-S-TIMEXCEP.
```

Fig. 9.14: *A listing of the data edit program.*

```
2          EDITIME          20.35.28          SEP 23,1978


00033           DATA DIVISION.
00035           FILE SECTION.
00037           FD   TIME-CARD-FILE
00038                LABEL RECORD OMITTED.
00039                01   TIME-CARD.
00040                     05   I-SOCIAL-SECURITY-NO PIC 9(9).
00041                     05   I-LAST-NAME          PIC X(16).
00042                     05   I-INITIALS           PIC XX.
00043                     05   I-DEPARTMENT-NO      PIC 999.
00044                     05   I-HOURS-WORKED       PIC 99V9.
00045                     05   I-HOURLY-PAY-RATE    PIC 99V99.
00046                     05   I-NO-OF-DEPENDENTS   PIC 99.
00047                     05   I-MARITAL-STATUS     PIC X.
00048                     05   FILLER               PIC X(40).

00050           FD   VALID-TIME-FILE
00051                LABEL RECORD IS STANDARD
00052                BLOCK CONTAINS 5 RECORDS.
00053                01   VALID-TIME-RECORD.
00054                     05   V-SOCIAL-SECURITY-NO PIC 9(9).
00055                     05   V-LAST-NAME          PIC X(16).
00056                     05   V-INITIALS           PIC XX.
00057                     05   V-DEPARTMENT-NO      PIC 999.
00058                     05   V-HOURS-WORKED       PIC 99V9.
00059                     05   V-HOURLY-PAY-RATE    PIC 99V99.
00060                     05   V-NO-OF-DEPENDENTS   PIC 99.
00061                     05   V-MARITAL-STATUS     PIC X.

00063           FD   TIME-EXCEPTION-REPORT
00064                LABEL RECORD OMITTED.
00065                01   TIME-EXCEPTION.
00066                     05   FILLER               PIC X(11).
00067                     05   E-SOCIAL-SECURITY-NO PIC X(9).
00068                     05   FILLER               PIC X(3).
00069                     05   E-LAST-NAME          PIC X(16).
00070                     05   FILLER               PIC X(3).
00071                     05   E-INITIALS           PIC XX.
00072                     05   FILLER               PIC X(3).
00073                     05   E-DEPARTMENT-NO      PIC 999.
00074                     05   FILLER               PIC X(3).
00075                     05   E-HOURS-WORKED       PIC 99V9.
00076                     05   FILLER               PIC X(3).
00077                     05   E-HOURLY-PAY-RATE    PIC 99V99.
00078                     05   FILLER               PIC X(3).
00079                     05   E-NO-OF-DEPENDENTS   PIC 99.
00080                     05   FILLER               PIC X(3).
00081                     05   E-MARITAL-STATUS     PIC X.
00082                     05   FILLER               PIC X(9).
00083                     05   E-MESSAGE            PIC X(40).
00084                     05   FILLER               PIC X(12).
```

Fig. 9.14: *Continued.*

```
3         EDITIME         20.35.28         SEP 23,1978


00088               WORKING-STORAGE SECTION.
00090               77  ERROR-SWITCH                    PIC 9   VALUE 0.
00092               01  EXCEPTION-REPORT-MESSAGES.
00094                   05  SOCIAL-SECURITY-MESSAGE     PIC X(40)
00095                       VALUE 'SOCIAL SECURITY NO. IS NOT NUMERIC'.
00097                   05  NAME-MESSAGE                PIC X(40)
00098                       VALUE 'NAME IS NOT ALPHABETIC'.
00100                   05  HOURS-RANGE-MESSAGE         PIC X(40)
00101                       VALUE 'HOURS WORKED IS NOT WITHIN RANGE'.
00103                   05  HOURS-NUMERIC-MESSAGE       PIC X(40)
00104                       VALUE 'HOURS WORKED IS NOT NUMERIC'.
00106                   05  RATE-RANGE-MESSAGE          PIC X(40)
00107                       VALUE 'HOURLY PAY RATE IS NOT WITHIN RANGE'.
00109                   05  RATE-NUMERIC-MESSAGE        PIC X(40)
00110                       VALUE 'HOURLY PAY RATE IS NOT NUMERIC'.
00112                   05  DEP-RANGE-MESSAGE           PIC X(40)
00113                       VALUE 'NO. OF DEPENDENTS IS NOT WITHIN RANGE'.
00115                   05  DEP-NUMERIC-MESSAGE         PIC X(40)
00116                       VALUE 'NO. OF DEPENDENTS IS NOT NUMERIC'.
00118                   05  MARITAL-MESSAGE             PIC X(40)
00119                       VALUE 'MARITAL STATUS CODE IS INVALID'.
```

Fig. 9.14: *Continued.*

```
    4        EDITIME        20.35.28        SEP 23,1978


00123            PROCEDURE DIVISION.
00125                HOUSEKEEPING.
00127                    OPEN INPUT  TIME-CARD-FILE
00128                    OPEN OUTPUT VALID-TIME-FILE
00129                    OPEN OUTPUT TIME-EXCEPTION-REPORT
00130                    MOVE SPACES TO TIME-EXCEPTION.

00132                START-OF-MAINLINE.

00134                    READ TIME-CARD-FILE
00135                        AT END GO TO END-OF-JOB.

00137                    IF I-SOCIAL-SECURITY-NO IS NOT NUMERIC
00138                    THEN
00139                        PERFORM SOCIAL-SECURITY-ERROR THRU END-SOC-SEC-ERROR
00140                    ELSE
00141                        NEXT SENTENCE.

00143                    IF I-LAST-NAME IS NOT ALPHABETIC OR
00144                       I-INITIALS IS NOT ALPHABETIC
00145                    THEN
00146                        PERFORM NAME-ERROR THRU END-NAME-ERROR
00147                    ELSE
00148                        NEXT SENTENCE.

00150                    IF I-HOURS-WORKED IS NOT NUMERIC
00151                    THEN
00152                        PERFORM HOURS-NUMERIC-ERROR THRU END-HOURS-NUMERIC-ERROR
00153                    ELSE
00154                        IF    (I-HOURS-WORKED IS LESS    THAN 15)
00155                           OR (I-HOURS-WORKED IS GREATER THAN 65)
00156                        THEN
00157                            PERFORM HOURS-RANGE-ERROR THRU END-HOURS-RANGE-ERROR
00158                        ELSE
00159                            NEXT SENTENCE.
```

Fig. 9.14: *Continued.*

```
    5        EDITIME         20.35.28        SEP 23,1978

00163               IF I-HOURLY-PAY-RATE IS NOT NUMERIC
00164               THEN
00165                     PERFORM RATE-NUMERIC-ERROR THRU END-RATE-NUMERIC-ERROR
00166               ELSE
00167                     IF   (I-HOURLY-PAY-RATE IS LESS      THAN   3.00)
00168                       OR (I-HOURLY-PAY-RATE IS GREATER THAN 12.50)
00169                     THEN
00170                           PERFORM RATE-RANGE-ERROR THRU END-RATE-RANGE-ERROR
00171                     ELSE
00172                           NEXT SENTENCE.

00174               IF I-NO-OF-DEPENDENTS IS NOT NUMERIC
00175               THEN
00176                     PERFORM DEPENDENTS-NUMERIC-ERROR
00177                        THRU END-DEP-NUMERIC-ERROR
00178               ELSE
00179                     IF I-NO-OF-DEPENDENTS IS GREATER THAN 12
00180                     THEN
00181                           PERFORM DEPENDENTS-RANGE-ERROR
00182                              THRU END-DEP-RANGE-ERROR
00183                     ELSE
00184                           NEXT SENTENCE.

00186               IF I-MARITAL-STATUS IS NOT EQUAL TO 'M' OR
00187                  IS NOT EQUAL TO 'S'
00188               THEN
00189                     PERFORM MARITAL-STATUS-ERROR
00190                        THRU END-MARITAL-STATUS-ERROR
00191               ELSE
00192                     NEXT SENTENCE.

00194               IF ERROR-SWITCH IS EQUAL TO 1
00195               THEN
00196                     MOVE 0 TO ERROR-SWITCH
00197                     GO TO START-OF-MAINLINE
00198               ELSE
00199                     MOVE I-SOCIAL-SECURITY-NO TO V-SOCIAL-SECURITY-NO
00200                     MOVE I-LAST-NAME         TO V-LAST-NAME
00201                     MOVE I-INITIALS          TO V-INITIALS
00202                     MOVE I-DEPARTMENT-NO     TO V-DEPARTMENT-NO

00204                     MOVE I-HOURS-WORKED      TO V-HOURS-WORKED
00205                     MOVE I-HOURLY-PAY-RATE   TO V-HOURLY-PAY-RATE
00206                     MOVE I-NO-OF-DEPENDENTS  TO V-NO-OF-DEPENDENTS
00207                     MOVE I-MARITAL-STATUS    TO V-MARITAL-STATUS
00208                     WRITE VALID-TIME-RECORD
00209                     GO TO START-OF-MAINLINE.

00211           END-OF-JOB.
00212               CLOSE TIME-CARD-FILE.
00213               CLOSE VALID-TIME-FILE.
00214               CLOSE TIME-EXCEPTION-REPORT.
00215               STOP RUN.
```

Fig. 9.14: *Continued.*

```
  6         EDITIME        20.35.28       SEP 23,1978

00217            SOCIAL-SECURITY-ERROR.

00219               MOVE 1 TO ERROR-SWITCH
00220               PERFORM  MOVE-TIME-CARD-TO-EXCEPTION
00221               MOVE SOCIAL-SECURITY-MESSAGE TO E-MESSAGE
00222               PERFORM PRINT-EXCEPTION.

00224            END-SOC-SEC-ERROR.
00225               EXIT.

00227            NAME-ERROR.

00229               IF ERROR-SWITCH IS EQUAL TO 1
00230               THEN
00231                   NEXT SENTENCE
00232               ELSE
00233                   MOVE 1 TO ERROR-SWITCH
00234                   PERFORM MOVE-TIME-CARD-TO-EXCEPTION.
00235               MOVE NAME-MESSAGE TO E-MESSAGE
00236               PERFORM PRINT-EXCEPTION.

00238            END-NAME-ERROR.
00239               EXIT.

00241            HOURS-NUMERIC-ERROR.

00243               IF ERROR-SWITCH IS EQUAL TO 1
00244               THEN
00245                   NEXT SENTENCE
00246               ELSE
00247                   MOVE 1 TO ERROR-SWITCH
00248                   PERFORM MOVE-TIME-CARD-TO-EXCEPTION.
00249               MOVE HOURS-NUMERIC-MESSAGE TO E-MESSAGE
00250               PERFORM PRINT-EXCEPTION.

00252            END-HOURS-NUMERIC-ERROR.
00253               EXIT.

00255            HOURS-RANGE-ERROR.

00257               IF ERROR-SWITCH IS EQUAL TO 1
00258               THEN
00259                   NEXT SENTENCE
00260               ELSE
00261                   MOVE 1 TO ERROR-SWITCH
00262                   PERFORM  MOVE-TIME-CARD-TO-EXCEPTION.
00263               MOVE HOURS-RANGE-MESSAGE TC E-MESSAGE
00264               PERFORM PRINT-EXCEPTION.

00266            END-HOURS-RANGE-ERROR.
00267               EXIT.
```

Fig. 9.14: *Continued.*

```
    7          EDITIME        20.35.28        SEP 23,1978

00269              RATE-NUMERIC-ERROR.

00271                  IF ERROR-SWITCH IS EQUAL TO 1
00272                  THEN
00273                      NEXT SENTENCE
00274                  ELSE
00275                      MOVE 1 TO ERROR-SWITCH
00276                      PERFORM MOVE-TIME-CARD-TO-EXCEPTION.
00277                  MOVE RATE-NUMERIC-MESSAGE TO E-MESSAGE
00278                  PERFORM PRINT-EXCEPTION.

00280              END-RATE-NUMERIC-ERROR.
00281                  EXIT.

00283              RATE-RANGE-ERROR.

00285                  IF ERROR-SWITCH IS EQUAL TO 1
00286                  THEN
00287                      NEXT SENTENCE
00288                  ELSE
00289                      MOVE 1 TO ERROR-SWITCH
00290                      PERFORM MOVE-TIME-CARD-TO-EXCEPTION.
00291                  MOVE RATE-RANGE-MESSAGE TO E-MESSAGE
00292                  PERFORM PRINT-EXCEPTION.

00294              END-RATE-RANGE-ERROR.
00295                  EXIT.

00297              DEPENDENTS-NUMERIC-ERROR.

00299                  IF ERROR-SWITCH IS EQUAL TO 1
00300                  THEN
00301                      NEXT SENTENCE
00302                  ELSE
00303                      MOVE 1 TO ERROR-SWITCH
00304                      PERFORM MOVE-TIME-CARD-TO-EXCEPTION.
00305                  MOVE DEP-NUMERIC-MESSAGE TO E-MESSAGE
00306                  PERFORM PRINT-EXCEPTION.

00308              END-DEP-NUMERIC-ERROR.
00309                  EXIT.

00311              DEPENDENTS-RANGE-ERROR.

00313                  IF ERROR-SWITCH IS EQUAL TO 1
00314                  THEN
00315                      NEXT SENTENCE
00316                  ELSE
00317                      MOVE 1 TO ERROR-SWITCH
00318                      PERFORM MOVE-TIME-CARD-TO-EXCEPTION.
00319                  MOVE DEP-RANGE-MESSAGE TO E-MESSAGE
00320                  PERFORM PRINT-EXCEPTION.
00321              END-DEP-RANGE-ERROR.
00322                  EXIT.
```

Fig. 9.14: *Continued.*

```
8          EDITIME        20.35.28        SEP 23,1978


00326            MARITAL-STATUS-ERROR.

00328                IF ERROR-SWITCH IS EQUAL TO 1
00329                THEN
00330                    NEXT SENTENCE
00331                ELSE
00332                    MOVE 1 TO ERROR-SWITCH
00333                    PERFORM MOVE-TIME-CARD-TO-EXCEPTION.
00334                MOVE MARITAL-MESSAGE TO E-MESSAGE
00335                PERFORM PRINT-EXCEPTION.

00337            END-MARITAL-STATUS-ERROR.
00338                EXIT.


00340            PRINT-EXCEPTION.

00342                WRITE TIME-EXCEPTION
00343                    AFTER ADVANCING 1 LINES
00344                MOVE SPACES TO TIME-EXCEPTION.

00346            END-PRINT-EXCEPTION.
00347                EXIT.


00349            MOVE-TIME-CARD-TO-EXCEPTION.

00351                MOVE I-SOCIAL-SECURITY-NO TO E-SOCIAL-SECURITY-NO
00352                MOVE I-LAST-NAME          TO E-LAST-NAME
00353                MOVE I-INITIALS           TO E-INITIALS
00354                MOVE I-DEPARTMENT-NO      TO E-DEPARTMENT-NO

00356                MOVE I-HOURS-WORKED       TO E-HOURS-WORKED
00357                MOVE I-HOURLY-PAY-RATE    TO E-HOURLY-PAY-RATE
00358                MOVE I-NO-OF-DEPENDENTS   TO E-NO-OF-DEPENDENTS
00359                MOVE I-MARITAL-STATUS     TO E-MARITAL-STATUS.

00361            END-MOVE-TIME-CARD.
00362                EXIT.
```

Fig. 9.14: *Continued.*

The CLOSE instruction cleans up at the end of the job. One of its functions is to create an end-of-data marker. Remember how, on cards, a special end-of-data card was placed at the end of the data deck and the AT END clause attached to a READ statement tested for this marker? On disk or tape, during subsequent input of this file, the end-of-data marker created by CLOSE performs this function. Other functions of CLOSE involve assuring the proper dismounting and saving of the file.

COMBINING THE DATA EDIT AND PAYROLL PROGRAMS INTO A SINGLE JOB

The data edit program makes certain that the payroll program receives good data. It is not independent; the data edit program serves in a support role. Once the program has been tested and debugged, the next step should be obvious—the two programs must be combined to form a single job.

As we have already discussed, a command language or job control language can be used to achieve this combination. Once the proper control cards have been set up, the actual execution of these two related programs can proceed. First, the data edit program can read the input cards and create two output files, one containing errors and the other containing good data. When this program has finished processing, the payroll program can be loaded and executed, reading and processing the data from the good records file created by the data edit program. We now have a system of interrelated programs.

Given the fact that the payroll program must now read its input data from a file created by the data edit program rather than from cards, a few minor changes are necessary. The first has to do with the format of each record. Given that a disk file was to be used, the data edit program did not include the 40 characters of unused space from the input card as part of the output record. Our original version of the payroll program contained space for these 40 characters in the input record description, and this must be removed from the program. We also now know the blocking factor actually used in creating the file and can code it in the BLOCK CONTAINS clause (although BLOCK CONTAINS 0 RECORDS would work on an IBM machine, with the actual blocking factor being picked up from the file label). Except for a change to the job control language card describing the input record, however, that's it.

In business data processing, such systems of programs are the rule rather than the exception. Invariably, the interrelationship of programs goes beyond even the single application. The output of a system such as payroll, for example, is part of the input to other systems such as the accounting ledger system, budget vs. actual expenses system, and the firm's financial status reporting system. If you plan to become a business programmer, get used to the idea of using someone else's output as your input.

SUMMARY

In many business data processing applications, program failure cannot be tolerated; payroll is perhaps the most dramatic example. In order to minimize the risk of program failure it is often necessary to add logic to check the data before computations take place. Such data edit routines are clearly not part of the primary function of the program, but the demand for uninterrupted program execution makes such secondary functions essential.

There are two ways of implementing a data edit routine: as a secondary routine attached to the main program or as a separate program. We have taken the second alternative, introducing what is in effect another level of modularization. The basic function of this new program will be to read the input data cards, check certain key fields, and send the record to either an exceptions file or a "good data" file. Subsequently, the real payroll program will read only the data from the "good data" file, thus bypassing potential errors. Using two interrelated programs calls for the use of an intermediate data file; thus we discussed intermediate files, and covered a few basic magnetic tape and disk concepts. The idea of a system of programs was introduced, with a command language such as job control language being used to tie the pieces of the system together. An optional discussion of job control language for the IBM System/360 and System/370 series of computers was included for those having access to an IBM machine.

Various types of edit checks were identified. Certain errors can lead to program failure, and these errors must be screened out. Other checks, called reasonablility checks, are designed to identify potential errors that might lead to an incorrect computation or result. Finally, there are convenience checks which, although not necessarily significant errors, can be easily identified and flagged by the program and, since the program is going to run anyway, "why not?" All three types are incorporated in the program being developed for this chapter.

The format of the intermediate and exceptions files was defined. Class tests for NUMERIC and ALPHABETIC fields were explained. The use of compound conditions as a means for performing range tests was introduced. The use of switches as a mechanism for controlling program flow was covered in some detail. OPEN and CLOSE instructions were covered in greater detail than was the case in earlier chapters.

The chapter ended with a discussion of systems of programs. The possibility of combining the data edit program of this chapter with the payroll program of prior chapters was used to illustrate the essential nature of systems of programs.

KEY WORDS

access arm	class test	cylinder
block	CLOSE	disk
BLOCK CONTAINS clause	compound condition	edit check

intermediate file	OPEN	switch
job step	range test	system
label	sector	track
magnetic tape		

EXERCISES

1. Why is program failure intolerable on business applications such as payroll?

2. Edit checking is a secondary function rather than a primary function. What does this mean?

3. Explain how a system of programs can be linked together by using intermediate files.

4. Explain how a job control language or other command language can be used to tie the components of a system of programs together formally.

5. Three basic types of edit checks were described in the chapter: those designed to eliminate the risk of program failure; those designed to catch potential errors; and those performed largely for convenience. Explain each type.

6. What is a class test?

7. Explain how switch setting can be used to control the logical flow of a program.

8. Explain what the OPEN and CLOSE instructions do.

9. Exercise 7 in Chapter 7 dealt with a university billing program. Write a data edit program to preceed the billing program. The minimum number of credit hours allowable is 3; the maximum is 20. Full-time students are not eligible for audit credit. The student number must be all digits.

    Exercise 8 was essentially an extension of exercise 7; it uses other fields such as the room classification, board classification, and various activities codes. You were invited to develop your own code structure in planning this program; add to the edit routine a number of checks to make certain that the codes are within proper limits.

10. Exercise 9 in Chapter 7 asked you to develop a program for computing shipping costs based on two table entries. Include a set of edit checks to make certain that the codes as entered on the input card are reasonable (in other words, are actually represented in the tables). Would you implement this check as a routine attached to the main program or as a separate program in a system of programs? Why?

11. Exercise 10 in Chapter 7 dealt with sales tax rates which were found in a table. Once again, include an edit check to make sure that the code as entered on the input card is reasonable. Should his be a subroutine or a separate program? Why? Why can we not say that our program will make sure that the tax rate code is *correct*; why must we instead simply claim that we can test only for *reasonability*?

12. Exercise 11 in Chapter 7 was concerned with developing an electric bill preparation program. Input records contained a rate code, a customer number, and the amount of kilowatt hours used. Write either a separate program or a subroutine to check for a reasonable code, to make sure the customer number is numeric, and to make sure kilowatt hours are numeric. Would you choose a subroutine or a separate program? Why? What is the basis for making this decision? Three general types of potential errors were described in the text; what variety is each of the three fields to be tested by this program?

13. As a simple practice exercise in the use of intermediate files and systems of programs, write two COBOL programs. The first should simply read a deck of cards and copy the card images to disk. The second program should read this disk file and dump the contents, record by record, to the printer. The precise format of the data records is not really relevant; in fact, you may find that, with minor modifications, an earlier program written for this course can be used.

14. Most computer installations make a series of special utility programs available to their programmers; common utilities perform such functions as copying a file from one storage medium to another or rearranging the records on a file. One of the more commonly used utility programs (at least by the application programmer) is a print/punch routine that copies a file to the printer or to punched cards (on an IBM system, this utility is named IEBPTPCH). Write a COBOL program to read cards and copy them to a disk file (you might use the same program developed for exercise number 13). After the file has been created, use a print/punch utility to copy it to the printer.

15. Exercise 11 in Chapter 8 asked you to write a program to compute SAT scores using internal tables. Another approach to the problem would be to read the raw data from cards, accumulate the raw scores for eventually computing an average, and then to write the raw data to a work file. Later, after the average had been computed, the raw data could be read back in and SAT scores computed. Revise the program to do this.

Sequential File Processing

10

Sequential Files and Sorting

OVERVIEW

Two common business applications of the computer are maintaining records and generating management reports; Section III concentrates on these two applications. We'll begin with a discussion of sequential files, and then move on to a brief introduction to some of the more common permanent files maintained by a typical business concern. Updating these files and preparing reports based on the data in the files are the primary applications to be covered in Chapters 11 through 14. In this chapter we will consider a number of techniques for sorting records into sequence by a key field, a necessary pre-requisite to these applications. We will briefly cover how a computer sorts, and then spend some time on sort utility programs and COBOL's internal sort routine.

SEQUENTIAL FILES

Chapter 9 introduced the idea of using an intermediate work file to pass data from one program to another. The records on the work file were written, one at a time, by a first program. Later, a second program retrieved these records, again one at a time, by starting at the beginning of the file and working through to the end. The first program created the file in a fixed sequence; the second program processed the records in the same order. There was no skipping of an occasional record, and no attempt to read a record out of sequence. Our intermediate work file was a perfect example of a **sequential file**. A sequential file is simply one that is created and retrieved in a fixed sequence, and only in that fixed sequence.

Clearly, a sequential file is the only kind that can be stored on magnetic tape. A tape is shaped like a ribbon. When data is stored on tape, the first record is followed by the second, which is in turn followed by the third, and so on. The only way to reread the file is by starting at the beginning of the tape and processing the records in a fixed sequence; in other words, the only way to read record number 500 is by first passing through the first 499 records.

On magnetic disk, a sequential file can be created by storing records in adjacent locations along a track or series of tracks, and then retrieving the records in the same order. As we'll see later, there are other options on disk; for now, however, simply remember that a sequential file can be stored on disk.

Temporary and Permanent Files

The file of Chapter 9 was a temporary file used only to pass records from one program to another. When the second program (in our example the payroll program) was finished processing the data, the temporary file was no longer needed and the tape or disk space could be reused for some other application. The file was needed only for the life of the program.

Note all files are so temporary; in fact, most business concerns maintain a large number of permanent or semi-permanent files on tape, disk, or even on cards. Consider, for example, the payroll application. Look at a paycheck. Invariably it contains an attached stub showing year-to-date earnings, deductions, and net pay. (We skipped this part of the payroll program in Chapters 6 through 9 so as to avoid overcomplicating our example.) Where do these year-to-date figures come from? By law, the employer must maintain records of this information for each employee. In most modern business organizations, these records are maintained on magnetic tape or disk.

Accounts receivable is a similar application. Most firms sell at least some of their products on credit. Records must be maintained on how much each customer owes so that accurate bills can be sent. It is essential that the firm keep track of old balances due, any new purchases, and any payments made by each individual customer.

Many other applications could be cited, including:

1. payroll and year-to-date earnings,

2. accounts receivable,

3. accounts payable,

4. accounting ledgers (operating expenses),

5. actual performance vs. quota,

6. actual expenses vs. budget,

7. inventory levels,

8. customer orders,

9. the status of any work in process,

and depending on the nature of the organization, often many more. These records are permanent, not temporary. They must be maintained for weeks, months, even years. In all but the very smallest of firms, they are maintained by computer.

Although these files are said to be "permanent," they do change. On the payroll file, for example, because employees are paid at regular specified times, there will be new data to add to the year-to-date earnings file at regular intervals. Customers will purchase new products and pay their old bills, and this information must be reflected in the accounts receivable files. It is not enough simply to have the files; they must be kept up to date.

THE FILE UPDATE APPLICATION

Imagine that you are a clerk for a small firm, and that you are responsible for keeping track of accounts receivable.

Since the firm is small, there are relatively few customers. Thus it is easy to keep the accounts receivable books up to date by simply accepting each credit memo or payment receipt as it arrives, turning to the page containing the list of purchases and payments made by this customer, and adding or subtracting the new payment or purchase.

What happens, however, as the firm begins to grow? More customers mean more sales, and more sales mean more paperwork. Imagine that you have sitting in front of you several thousand credit memos and payment receipts, all of which must be added to the books. Suddenly, the informal, one-record-at-a-time approach becomes unworkable. How would you handle this problem?

Chances are, you would organize the record keeping task. Imagine how much easier it would be if the master records for all the customers were arranged in a known sequence, perhaps by customer number, or alphabetically by customer name. If this were the case, by simply arranging the transactions (the credit memos and payments) in the same sequence, it would be possible to update the master file by going through the book once, from start to finish, updating each record in sequence.

On a computer, this is how the job is normally done. The ledger book described in the example above becomes a **master file** on magnetic tape or disk (Fig. 10.1). The transactions become a **transactions file**. The master file is normally maintained in sequence by some **key**, usually an identification number such as a Social Security number, a part number, a customer number, or similar identification code. The transactions file is **sorted** into sequence by the same key, and is subsequently used to update the master file under control of the master file update program. The output of this program usually consists of an updated new master file and a printed report showing the status of the master file.

Fig. 10.1: *The Master File Update Application.*

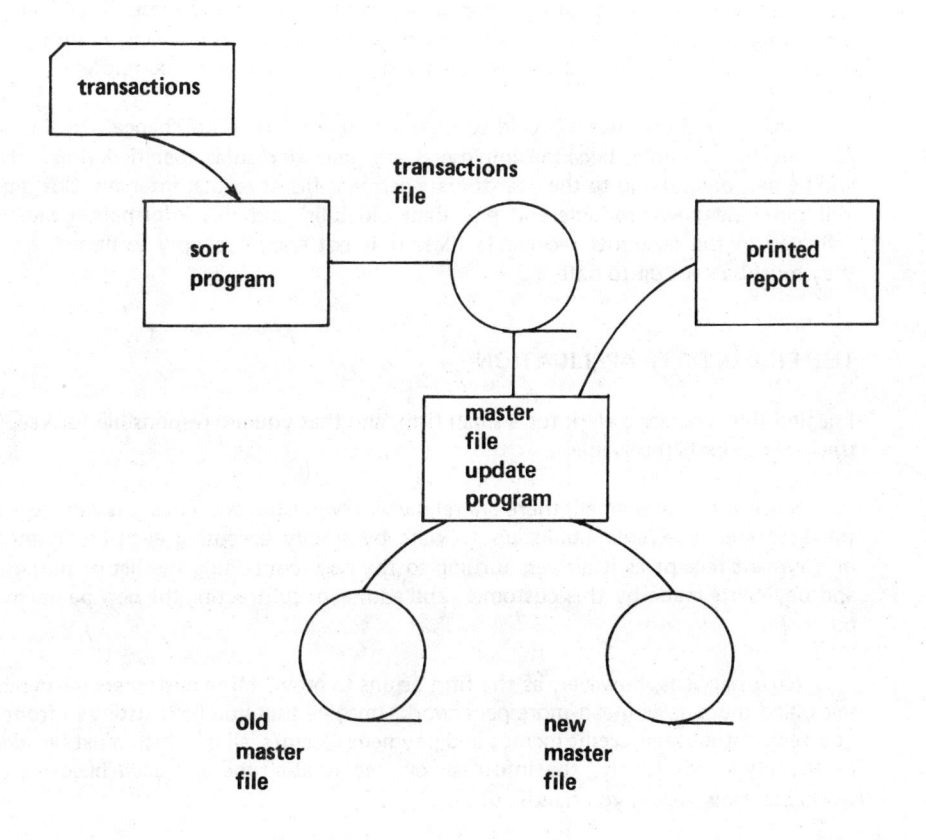

All the files involved in the **master file update application** are sequential files. Note, however, that sorting is not what makes these files sequential. Any file created and retrieved in a fixed order (and only in that fixed order) is, by definition, sequential. The act of sorting simply makes the file easier to use by allowing the programmer to make certain assumptions as to which record comes next.

GENERATING REGULAR MANAGEMENT REPORTS

Another common (and related) computer application is generating various management reports. Consider, as an example, the customer order file. Any organization wants to keep track of its orders; thus a customer order master file will almost certainly exist. As new sales are made, new orders must be added to the file, and old orders must be deleted as they are shipped; thus a master file update application is called for.

In addition to updating the master file, management will almost certainly want to know the status of customer orders. Is the firm running ahead of plan or behind plan? Which sales district is doing the best job? Which salesperson is most successful? Can we identify those relatively few customers who represent the bulk of our sales, so that high level management can concentrate on them? Clearly these questions are important. The best way to answer them is by carefully analyzing the data on the master file and the transactions files. Since we are looking for information summarized by customer, sales district, sales person, or some other specific key, often the easiest way to obtain this information is by first sorting the data into sequence by the desired key. In Chapters 11 and 12 we'll consider two examples of the management report generation application. Once again, sorting is the key.

SORT UTILITY PROGRAMS

If sorting is common to so many applications, it is probably reasonable to assume that many programmers will have a need for sort logic. There are numerous techniques for sorting on a computer, and most professional programmers know one or two; thus it is possible for the programmer to write an original sort routine as part of any program that needs it. Most programmers, however, look at sorting differently. If sorting is so common, it makes sense to assume that certain reasonably efficient techniques have already been coded by someone, somewhere. Why reinvent the wheel? Why not simply buy or lease one of these sort programs and use it? A wide selection of sort **utility programs** is available for almost any model and make of computer.

Such utility programs are commonly used as part of a system of programs. Fig. 10.2, for example, illustrates a system of three programs, an edit routine, a sort, and a payroll program.

As an alternative to the "separate program" approach, many systems support a special sort subroutine, that can be linked with a mainline (Fig. 10.3). Standard ANSI COBOL includes a sort subroutine accessed through a SORT statement; we'll cover this statement later in the chapter.

How a Computer Sorts

Before moving on to a discussion of sort utility programs and the COBOL internal sort feature, it would be useful briefly to consider exactly how a computer sorts data. Perhaps a basic understanding of what actually happens will help you to better understand the need for some of the commands and control cards that must be coded.

Sorting is a logical process. Basically it involves comparing a common field in two records and then moving the record with the higher (or lower, depending on whether ascending or descending order is required) value in this key field to the front of the line. Within the computer, such logical operations are performed by the central processing unit. If the central processing unit is to work on data under control of a program, that data must be in main memory. Because of the relatively high cost of main memory, this computer component is usually in short supply.

Consider the demands of a typical sort application. The transactions used to support payroll often exist as timecards, and every employee in the organization will have one. Payroll processing usually calls for these cards to be sorted into order by the employee number. It is not at all unusual for a large organization to employ 5000 or more people, meaning that 5000 or more cards must be sorted. At 80 characters per card, that comes to 400,000 memory locations for the data alone, and even on a large computer that is a great deal of space. Although it is possible to do the whole job in main memory, the cost of this approach is prohibitive.

Most commercially available sort packages use a combination of main memory space and less expensive secondary storage space on magnetic tape or disk. To get an idea of how this might work, imagine that you are faced with the following problem. You are employed by the college library. Several hundred books have been returned today, and they must be placed in call number sequence for reshelving. How long do you think it would take to do this job all by yourself?

Now, consider how you might do it if several other student assistants are available to help. You might begin by dividing the returned books into piles. Each student could then place the books in his or her pile into proper order. Once this had been done, the properly sorted blocks of books could be merged into a single stack. Wouldn't this combination of sorting and merging be a quicker and easier way to do the job?

On a computer, the **sort/merge** approach to putting records in order makes a great deal of sense. A series of input records representing a fraction of the total records in the file can be read into the computer's main memory and sorted. The resulting block of sorted records can then be written to a secondary storage medium, freeing the main memory space for another set of input records. This process continues, with a block of records being read, sorted, and written to a secondary device, until all the input records have been read. At this time, the presorted blocks can be read from secondary storage and merged with other presorted blocks. Eventually, following a number of merge steps, all the records will have been placed into proper order, and the sorted file can be written to an output device.

Fig. 10.2: *A System of Programs Including a Sort.*

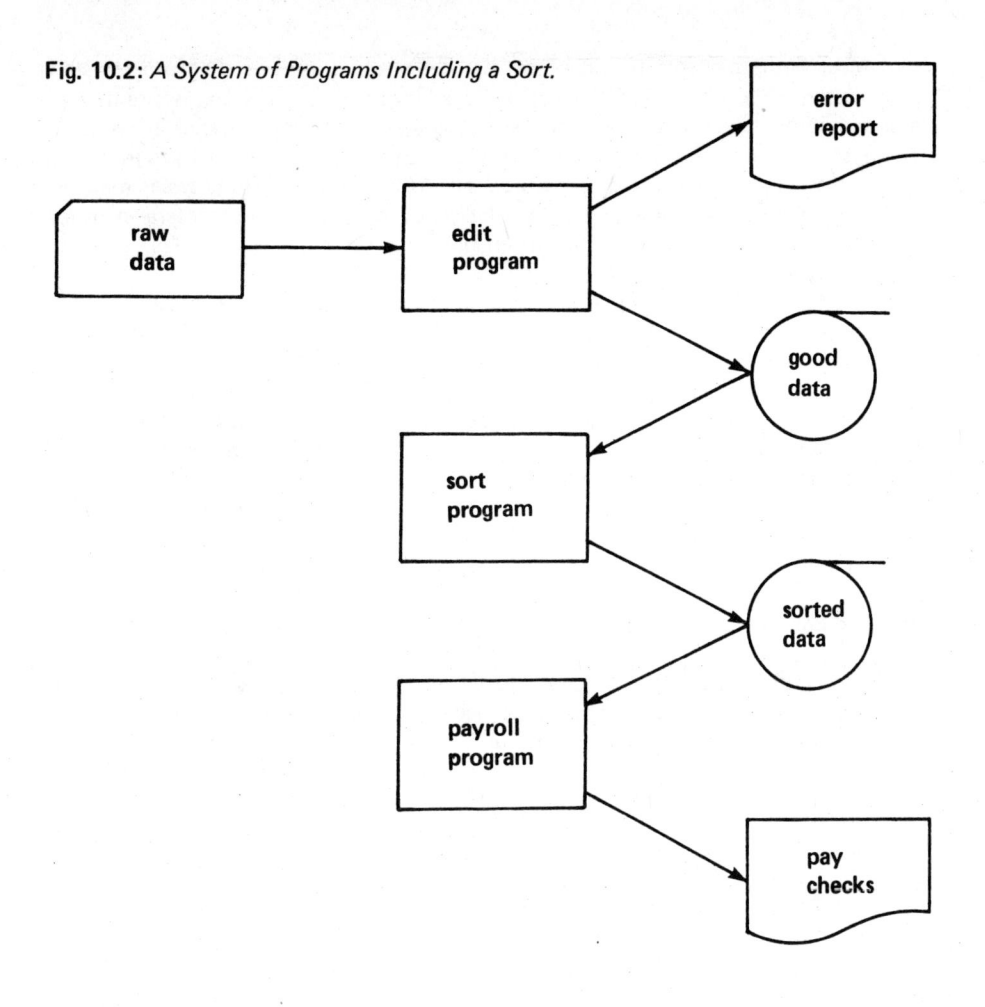

Fig. 10.3: *Sort as a Subroutine.*

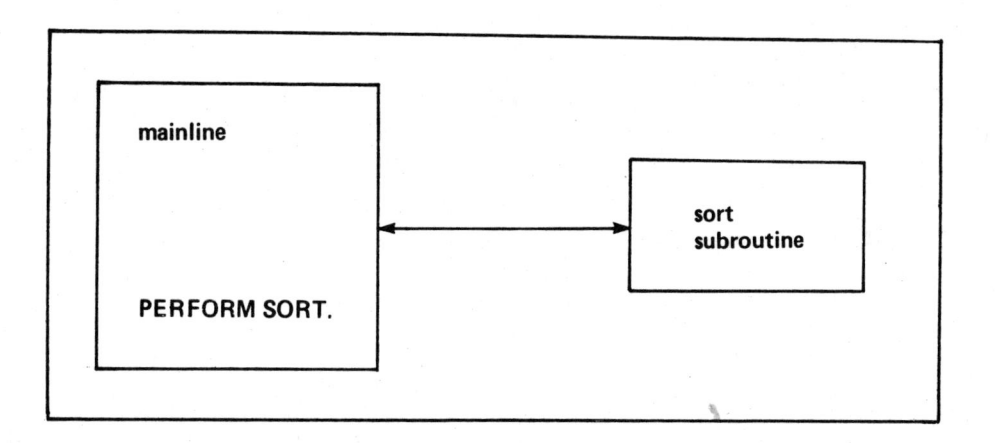

Most computer sort routines use the sort/merge approach. The process starts with an input file (Fig. 10.4). Records are read into the sort program, where they are grouped into blocks, with the records within any given block placed in sequence. These sorted blocks are written to secondary storage. Next, the sort program deals with the secondary files, transferring blocks of data back and forth between main and secondary storage, and merging these blocks. Eventually, all records are in proper sequence, and can be copied to the output file.

What does all this mean to the programmer? The programmer is responsible for defining all input and output devices used by the program. In COBOL, this means that SELECT and ASSIGN clauses will be needed for the input file, the output file, and the sort work files. These three files will also have to be described to the system through the command language or the job control language. Data formats for the sort files as well as the input and output files will have to be provided. It will be necessary to clearly identify the sort key, that field by which the output file is to be sequenced. If you keep in mind these basic characteristics of *any* sort routine, the specific parameters of the routines we are about to cover will be much easier to understand.

Sort and Sort/Merge Utilities

Most computer suppliers or manufacturers market a sort or sort/merge program designed to perform with reasonable efficiency on their own equipment. In addition to these vendor-supplier programs, a number of packages designed and written by

Fig. 10.4: *Steps Involved in the Sort/Merge Operation.*

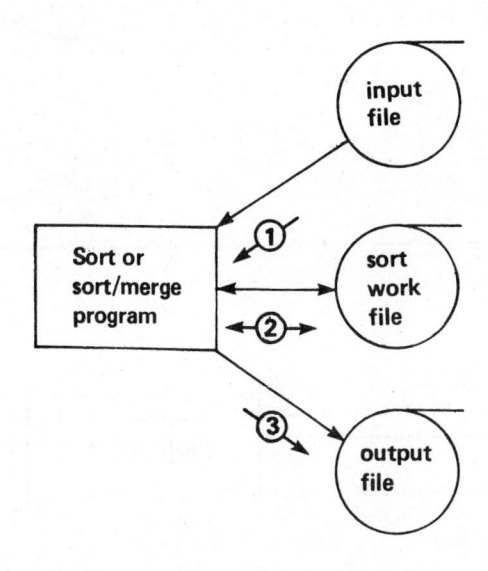

independent software suppliers are commercially available. It is a rare computer installation that does not have a sort utility program.

These utilities are usually designed to be both easy to use and general-purpose in nature (in other words, able to handle a wide variety of sorting tasks). Often, all the programmer must supply is such information as the identity of the input, sort work, and output files, and a description of the record to be sorted, including the location of any sort keys. If the routine is designed to be used as an internal routine to a program written in COBOL or some other language, this information must be conveyed as a part of the program. If the sort utility is designed to be used as an independent program and incorporated into a system of programs, job control or command language statements are used.

The specific procedures for using a sort utility will vary from computer manufacturer to computer manufacturer, and you should follow the practices of your own installation. In the optional section which follows, an example illustrating the use of the standard IBM sort/merge utility will be presented; a parallel example of the use of the sort/merge on a DOS system can be found in Appendix B.

IBM's Sort/Merge Utility (Optional)

The job control language needed to execute IBM's standard System/360 and System/370 sort/merge program is illustrated in Fig. 10.5. The first card shown is an EXEC card; it indicates that a program named SORTD is to be loaded and executed. Actually, SORTD represents a bit more than just the name of a program. In IBM terminology, this is an example of a cataloged procedure, and it defines the actual EXEC statement for the program to be executed, as well as two DD cards—one indicating the location of the program library containing the routine, and the other identifying where sort messages are to be printed. There is another commonly available cataloged procedure named SORT; this one incudes the job control language needed to support the use of another special program, called the linkage editor, that permits the programmer to add special logical modules to the standard sort/merge program.

The input file to the sort routine must be named SORTIN; in the example (Fig. 10.5), SORTIN is an OLD file with an external name PAYFILE. The output file must be named SORTOUT; an external name of PAYSORT has been assigned. The output file is NEW since this program will create it; following the sort operation, the newly created file is to be passed (the PASS) to a subsequent job step. Three tracks of direct access space on the system direct access device (SYSDA) are allocated for the use of this file. Finally, the format of the records in this file is described through a data control block (DCB). In this example, the logical record length (LRECL) is 40 characters, the blocksize (BLKSIZE) is 400 characters (meaning that each block contains 10 records), and the record format (RECFM) is fixed blocked. Data control block parameters must be defined for any NEW file.

Following the SORTOUT statement is a series of three files named SORTWK01, SORTWK02, and SORTWK03. These are the sort work files. Why are there three of them? For reasons of efficiency, it is a good idea to give the sort routine more than one work file so that it can handle several levels of reads and writes concurrently as it moves data back and forth between main memory and secondary storage. Usually, a minimum of three work files is required. On larger sorts even more work files are called for, with six, named SORTWK01 through SORTWK06, being frequently used. It is actually possible (though very unusual) to assign as many as 32 sort work files.

Each of the sort work files (Fig. 10.5) is assigned (in this example) to the system direct access device; magnetic tape or any other direct access device could have been used instead. Three tracks have been requested for each work file. The CONTIG that has been added to the space request indicates that the assigned three tracks must be contiguous. It is possible to assign space on disk in pieces, with one track from here and another from there, and most applications really don't care if the records in a file are spread out all over the pack. The sort program, however, relies on a number of extremely efficient high speed input and output techniques, and contiguous data storage is essential.

Following the definition of the work files is a //SYSIN DD * card, announcing the upcoming sort control card. The asterisk, as before, signifies that input will be coming from a card reader. This input parameter

SORT FIELDS=(1,9,CH,A)

says that the sort key begins in position 1 of the input record, is 9 characters in length, holds character (rather than numeric) data, and is to be sorted in ascending order; this is the Social Security number field of the payroll record. A generalized version of this control card is shown in Fig. 10.6. Notice that following the first set of fields, additional fields can be defined. These are secondary sort fields. If, for example, the department number were made the primary field and the employee number were coded as the secondary field, the resulting output would be in sequence by department number and all the employees within a given department would be listed in employee number sequence.

The last card shown in Fig. 10.5, the /* card, is an end-of-data marker indicating that there are no more sort control cards.

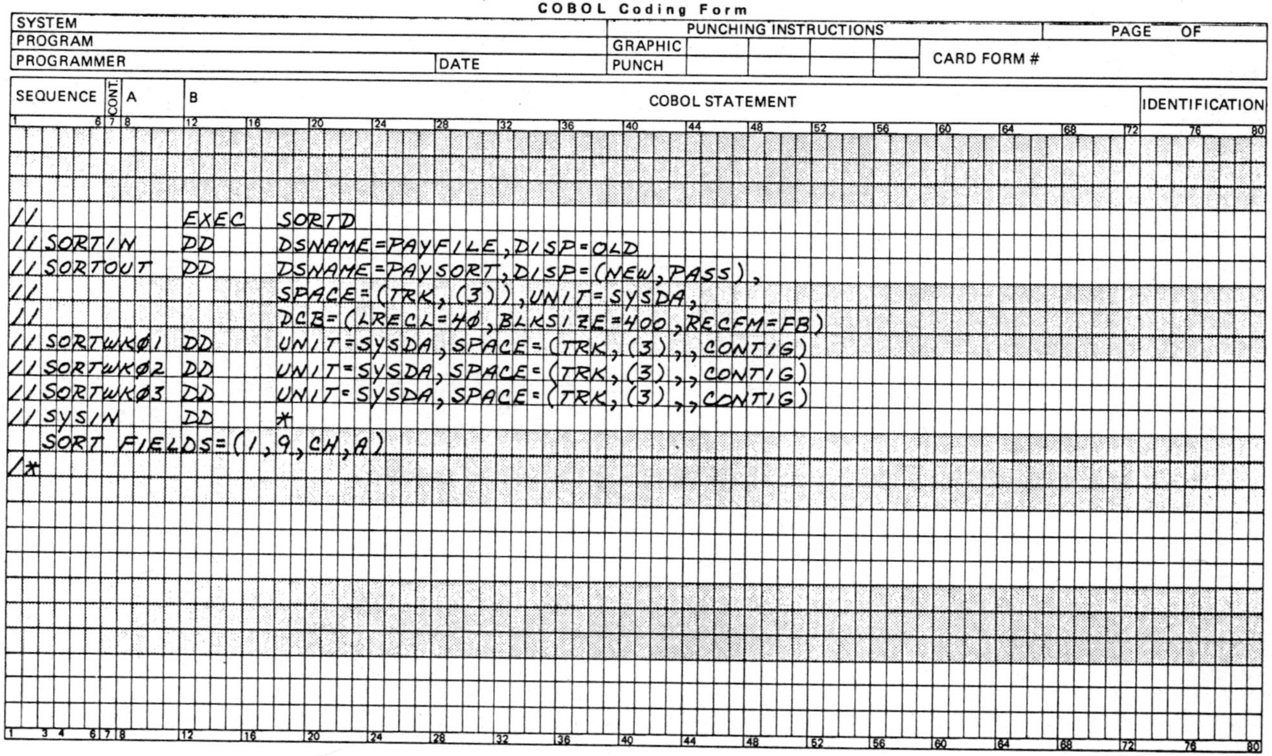

COBOL Coding Form

SYSTEM		PUNCHING INSTRUCTIONS	PAGE OF
PROGRAM		GRAPHIC	CARD FORM #
PROGRAMMER	DATE	PUNCH	

SEQUENCE | CONT. | A | B | COBOL STATEMENT | IDENTIFICATION

```
//            EXEC   SORTD
//SORTIN      DD     DSNAME=PAYFILE,DISP=OLD
//SORTOUT     DD     DSNAME=PAYSORT,DISP=(NEW,PASS),
//                   SPACE=(TRK,(3)),UNIT=SYSDA,
//                   DCB=(LRECL=4Ø,BLKSIZE=400,RECFM=FB)
//SORTWKØ1    DD     UNIT=SYSDA,SPACE=(TRK,(3),,CONTIG)
//SORTWKØ2    DD     UNIT=SYSDA,SPACE=(TRK,(3),,CONTIG)
//SORTWKØ3    DD     UNIT=SYSDA,SPACE=(TRK,(3),,CONTIG)
//SYSIN       DD     *
  SORT FIELDS=(1,9,CH,A)
/*
```

Fig. 10.5: *An Example of a Sort/Merge Utility Program.*

The sort/merge utility program is intended to be used as one of a system of programs. Normally, the output file will be passed to some other program for further processing. The cataloged procedures described above—SORTD and SORT—are very close to being standards and are available on most IBM systems running under an OS or VS operating system. They are not, however, universally available. Check with your instructor or an experienced programmer.

Fig. 10.6: *The SORT Control Statement.*

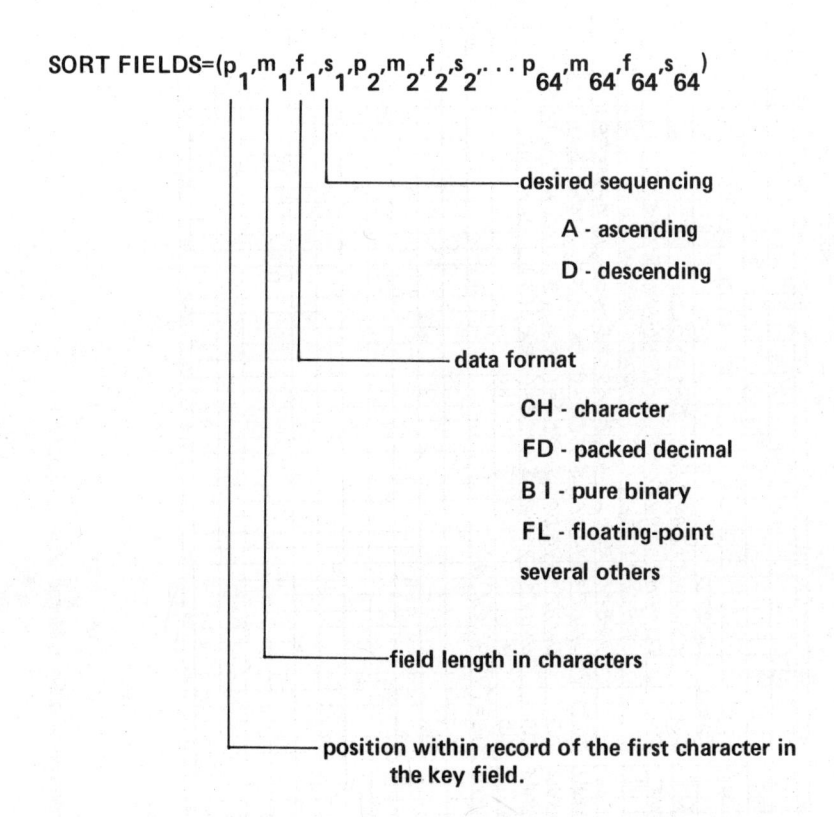

SORT FIELDS=$(p_1, m_1, f_1, s_1, p_2, m_2, f_2, s_2, \ldots p_{64}, m_{64}, f_{64}, s_{64})$

- desired sequencing
  - A - ascending
  - D - descending

- data format
  - CH - character
  - FD - packed decimal
  - BI - pure binary
  - FL - floating-point
  - several others

- field length in characters

- position within record of the first character in the key field.

THE INTERNAL COBOL SORT FEATURE

Standard ANSI COBOL includes a sort feature that allows the programmer to specify a sort operation as part of a larger COBOL program. In effect, the sort or sort/merge routine is treated as a subroutine of the COBOL program, and this subroutine is executed under control of a COBOL SORT statement. Most professional programmers prefer to use the standard sort/merge utility program when it is available, as this utility tends to be more efficient and somewhat easier to use than the COBOL internal sort. Generally, the internal sort is restricted to applications in which a relatively small file or table is manipulated within a routine, making the external sort inconvenient. Our coverage of the COBOL sort feature, given the somewhat restricted real-life utilization, will be brief.

We know that all files accessed by a program must be defined in the ENVIRONMENT DIVISION; thus the input, output, and work files are defined in a series of SELECT and ASSIGN clauses.

The function of the SELECT and ASSIGN clauses is to tie together the program and the physical file. A SELECT clause contains the name of the file as it is known within the program. The associated ASSIGN contains the name of a job control language card or in some other way identifies the input or output device. Fig. 10.7 illustrates a set of SELECT and ASSIGN clauses that might be used to sort the payroll records of the preceeding four chapters. The internal file names associated with the SELECT clauses are programmer defined. In this case, the external names associated with ASSIGN clauses *must be* SORTIN for the input file and SORTOUT for the output file. There must be a SELECT and an ASSIGN clause for the sort work file, but, at least on the IBM system used by the authors, the ASSIGN part is simply treated as comments. Our standard is to associate the name of the very first sort work file with the ASSIGN clause, although virtually any name will do.

The normal COBOL standard is that there be one set of SELECT and ASSIGN clauses for each and every file accessed by the program. There are at least three work files, so it would seem to follow that there must be at least three SELECT and ASSIGN clauses, right? Wrong. Only one SELECT... ASSIGN is needed to cover all the work files no matter how many are actually used.

The format of each of the records in each of the files must be defined in the DATA DIVISION, FILE SECTION. The sort work file is not exception, although it is a bit different from the usual input or output file. The sort work file must be defined in an **SD**, meaning sort description, **entry** (Fig. 10.8). No LABEL RECORD or BLOCK CONTAINS clause may be associated with an SD-entry; in fact, the only two clauses that may be coded with an SD are the RECORD CONTAINS and the DATA RECORDS clauses, both of which serve primarily as documentation. In our example we have simply coded the internal name of the sort file, which must match the name associated with a SELECT clause in the ENVIRONMENT DIVISION.

Except for the SD-entry itself, there is no difference between coding the DATA DIVISION entries for a regular file and a sort work file. A data structure is defined, the fields associated with the record are spelled out, and the content of each field is defined with a PICTURE clause.

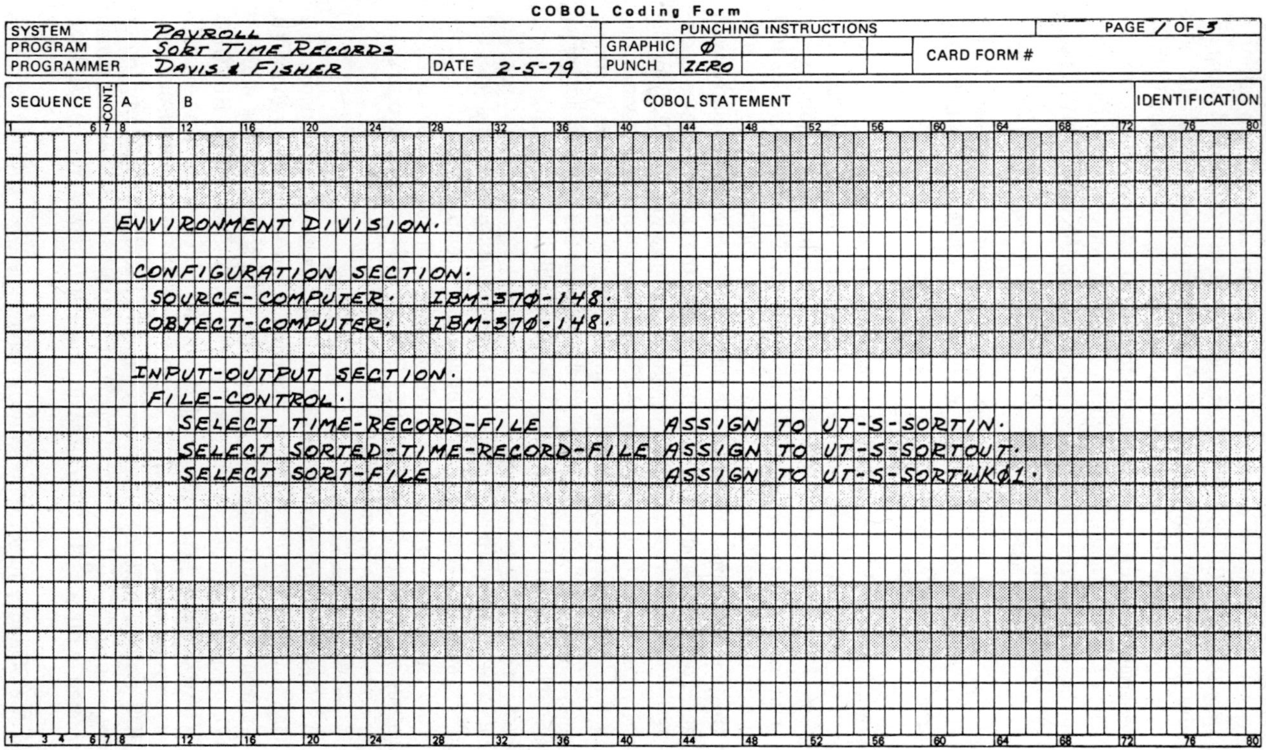

COBOL Coding Form

SYSTEM: PAYROLL
PROGRAM: SORT TIME RECORDS
PROGRAMMER: DAVIS & FISHER
DATE: 2-5-79
PAGE 1 OF 3
GRAPHIC: Ø
PUNCH: ZERO

```
ENVIRONMENT DIVISION.

CONFIGURATION SECTION.
SOURCE-COMPUTER. IBM-370-148.
OBJECT-COMPUTER. IBM-370-148.

INPUT-OUTPUT SECTION.
FILE-CONTROL.
    SELECT TIME-RECORD-FILE        ASSIGN TO UT-S-SORTIN.
    SELECT SORTED-TIME-RECORD-FILE ASSIGN TO UT-S-SORTOUT.
    SELECT SORT-FILE               ASSIGN TO UT-S-SORTWKØ1.
```

Fig. 10.7: The ENVIRONMENT DIVISION for a sample internal sort program. Note the FILE-CONTROL paragraph of the INPUT-OUTPUT SECTION.

```
         DATA DIVISION.
         FILE SECTION.
         SD  SORT-FILE.
         01  S-TIME-RECORD.
             05  S-SOCIAL-SECURITY-NO   PIC X(9).
             05  S-LAST-NAME            PIC X(16).
             05  S-INITIALS             PIC XX.
             05  S-DEPARTMENT-NO        PIC 999.
             05  S-HOURS-WORKED         PIC 99V9.
             05  S-HOURLY-PAY-RATE      PIC 99V99.
             05  S-NO-OF-DEPENDENTS     PIC 99.
             05  S-MARITAL-STATUS       PIC X.
```

Fig. 10.8: *An SD entry.*

In the PROCEDURE DIVISION, the COBOL sort feature is implemented through the **SORT** statement. In its simpliest form, this statement identifies the sort work file to be used, the key, the input file, and the output file; an example is shown in Fig. 10.9. Breaking this example into pieces, the first line

SORT SORT-FILE

identifies the sort work file as defined in an SD-entry and, earlier, in a SELECT clause. The second line

ON ASCENDING KEY S-SOCIAL-SECURITY-NO

identifies the sort key, a field defined as part of the SD-entry, and indicates the order of sort—in this case, ASCENDING implies ascending order, from smallest to biggest. The input file is indicated in the line that reads

USING TIME-RECORD-FILE

while the output file is defined in the line

GIVING SORTED-TIME-RECORD-FILE.

As is the case with any regular COBOL file, the file name used in a USING or GIVING clause must have been defined in an FD-entry in the DATA DIVISION and, previously, in a SELECT clause in the ENVIRONMENT DIVISION.

An output listing for a simple internal sort program is shown in Fig. 10.10. You may note that in the DATA DIVISION the SD-entry is coded first, before any FD-entries. On some versions of COBOL, this order is required; on other versions, the order is optional. Having worked with both varieties, our standard is to always code the SD's first, as this approach works on any system.

Except for the STOP RUN, there is only one statement in the PROCEDURE DIVISION of this program, the SORT statement; the program is really nothing more than a rough equivalent of the sort/merge utility as it might be written in COBOL. What about the OPEN and CLOSE statements for the input, output, and sort work files? They are part of the sort routine; in fact, if you were to code these statements, your program would probably fail to work at all. Do not code the actual OPENs and CLOSEs when the USING and GIVING options are used with a SORT statement.

In a larger program, how would the SORT statement be used? Imagine coding the SORT at or near the beginning of the housekeeping paragraph. After the sort is finished, it is possible to OPEN the SORTOUT file for input, and process these sequential records throughout the remainder of an otherwise normal COBOL program. Didn't we just say that the OPEN should not be used with this type of internal sort? Perhaps we should clarify this point. The problem arises from the fact that the sort routine itself OPENs and CLOSEs the input, output, and sort work files. If the programmer were to issue an OPEN, the sort routine would then try to reOPEN an already OPENed file, and this can cause trouble. After the sort is finished, however, the sort routine, as its final act, CLOSEs all files. Now, the programmer can legally issue an OPEN.

COBOL Coding Form

SYSTEM	PAYROLL	PUNCHING INSTRUCTIONS		PAGE 3 OF 3	
PROGRAM	SORT TIME RECORDS	GRAPHIC	Ø	CARD FORM #	
PROGRAMMER	DAVIS & FISHER	DATE 2-5-79	PUNCH	ZERO	

SEQUENCE | CONT. | A | B | COBOL STATEMENT | IDENTIFICATION

```
       PROCEDURE DIVISION.
        SORT-TIME-RECORDS.
           SORT SORT-FILE
                ON ASCENDING KEY S-SOCIAL-SECURITY-NO
                USING TIME-RECORD-FILE
                GIVING SORTED-TIME-RECORD-FILE.
           STOP RUN.
```

Fig. 10.9: *The PROCEDURE DIVISION, highlighting the SORT statement.*

Using the Internal COBOL Sort on an IBM Machine (Optional)

On an IBM System/360 or System/370 computer running under an OS or VS operating system, the COBOL sort feature is implemented by attaching the standard sort/merge utility program to the COBOL program as a subroutine, an approach that is common to many other systems. As a result, the same job control language or command language statements needed to support the standard utility program must be added to the COBOL module. The control language statements needed to support an internal sort on an IBM computer are summarized in Fig. 10.11.

Those of you who covered the optional material of the last several pages probably recognize these control statements. There are two statements that we did not need before. The statement

//SYSOUT   DD   SYSOUT=A

defines a printer file for listing sort messages. The statement

//SORTLIB   DD   DSNAME=SYS1.SORTLIB,DISP=SHR

defines the library containing the sort programs. The file providing input to the sort routine must be named SORTIN; the output file intended to hold the results of the sort must be named SORTOUT. Sort work files must be named SORTWK01, SORTWK02, SORTWK03, and so on. A minimum of three such files is required. No other file accessed by the COBOL program may use these names.

If your computer is not an IBM machine, the standards for accessing the sort feature will be different, of course. Still, you should encounter the same basic pattern, with input files, output files, work files, and the location of the sort routine being defined in some way.

Input and Output Procedures

The example of the COBOL internal sort presented above is a very elementary example, utilizing only the most basic of available features. It is possible for the programmer to supply input and/or output procedures to replace the USING and GIVING options. When procedures are used, the programmer assumes the full responsibility for input and output, OPENing the files, READing the records, issuing any needed WRITE instructions, and coding CLOSE instructions; only the sort work files are automatically OPENed, CLOSEd, and accessed. Under control of a procedure, an

```
00004        IDENTIFICATION DIVISION.
00005        PROGRAM-ID. SORTIME.
00006        AUTHOR.     DAVIS & FISHER.
00007        REMARKS.    THIS PROGRAM SORTS THE TIME RECORD
00008                    FILE INTO ASCENDING ORDER BY
00009                    SOCIAL SECURITY NUMBER.

00011        ENVIRONMENT DIVISION.
00012        CONFIGURATION SECTION.
00013            SOURCE-COMPUTER.  IBM-370-148.
00014            OBJECT-COMPUTER.  IBM-370-148.
00015        INPUT-OUTPUT SECTION.
00016            FILE-CONTROL.
00017                SELECT TIME-RECORD-FILE         ASSIGN TO UT-S-SORTIN.
00018                SELECT SORTED-TIME-RECORD-FILE  ASSIGN TO UT-S-SORTOUT.
00019                SELECT SORT-FILE                ASSIGN TO UT-S-SORTWK01.

00021        DATA DIVISION.
00022        FILE SECTION.
00023            SD  SORT-FILE.
00024            01    S-TIME-RECORD.
00025                  05  S-SOCIAL-SECURITY-NO  PIC X(9).
00026                  05  S-LAST-NAME           PIC X(16).
00027                  05  S-INITIALS            PIC XX.
00028                  05  S-DEPARTMENT-NO       PIC 999.
00029                  05  S-HOURS-WORKED        PIC 99V9.
00030                  05  S-HOURLY-PAY-RATE     PIC 99V99.
00031                  05  S-NO-OF-DEPENDENTS    PIC 99.
00032                  05  S-MARITAL-STATUS      PIC X.
00033                  05  FILLER                PIC X(40).
00034            FD  TIME-RECORD-FILE
00035                LABEL RECORD IS OMITTED.
00036            01    I-TIME-RECORD             PIC X(80).
00037            FD  SORTED-TIME-RECORD-FILE
00038                LABEL RECORD IS STANDARD
00039                BLOCK CONTAINS 5 RECORDS.
00040            01    O-TIME-RECORD             PIC X(80).

00042        PROCEDURE DIVISION.
00043        SORT-TIME-RECORDS.
00044            SORT SORT-FILE
00045                ON ASCENDING KEY S-SOCIAL-SECURITY-NO
00046                USING TIME-RECORD-FILE
00047                GIVING SORTED-TIME-RECORD-FILE.
00048            STOP RUN.
```

Fig. 10.10: *A program listing featuring an internal COBOL sort.*

input record is read by the programmer's code and then processed (edit checked, for example). Once the input procedure is finished with the record, the programmer codes a RELEASE statement to turn the record over to the sort routine.

This continues until all the records have been read and processed by the input procedure. Once all records have been RELEASEd, the sort routine takes over, putting the records into the desired sequence. When the sort is finished, control is given to the output procedure (if any). Again, the programmer can code any instructions he or she wishes to code, requesting single records from the final sorted file by issuing a RETURN statement.

In this text we do not intend to cover every detail of the sort feature. Sorting is a very common business data processing activity, and subsequent chapters will present specific applications that depend on the sort. We have presented only the basics of this tool in an attempt to lay the groundwork for these subsequent chapters. Examples of a COBOL internal sort that utilizes the full range of available features can be found in most COBOL reference manuals.

SYSTEMS OF PROGRAMS

A sort routine is not intended to be independent. Almost without exception, the purpose of a sort is to structure records into a sequence needed for a subsequent data processing operation; almost never is a simple file of sorted records the ultimate objective. Thus when we speak of a sort, we almost invariably imply the existence of a system of programs, with the sort merely one intermediate step. In the chapters that follow, we will consider several examples of such systems.

SUMMARY

The chapter began with a discussion of sequential files; a sequential file is simply a file that is created and retrieved in a fixed order. The difference between a temporary file and a permanent file was then explained. Record keeping is an important business data processing application; often records are maintained on sequential files. Usually, to simplify the programming task, these records are sorted into sequence by some key field. Updating the files and preparing management reports are two applications that depend on the sequence of the data.

There are basically two ways of implementing a sort: as an internal subroutine, or as a separate program. Most computer installations have a sort or sort/merge utility program that can be incorporated into a system of programs. COBOL has a sort subroutine that can be accessed through the COBOL SORT statement. We spent some time discussing just how a computer performs a sort operation. An optional section covering the IBM sort/merge utility program was included for those who have access to an IBM computer.

COBOL's internal sort feature was then described in some detail. The COBOL sort feature requires an SD-entry in the DATA DIVISION and a SORT statement in the PROCEDURE DIVISION. Job control or command language statements needed

```
//
// COB.SYSIN   EXEC COBVCLG
               DD   *
    { cobol program
/*
//GO.SORTIN    DD   DSNAME=PAYFILE,DISP=OLD
//GO.SORTOUT   DD   DSNAME=PAYSORT,DISP=(NEW,PASS),
//                  SPACE=(TRK,(3)),UNIT=SYSDA,
//                  DCB=(LRECL=40,BLKSIZE=400,RECFM=FB)
//GO.SORTWK01  DD   UNIT=SYSDA,SPACE=(TRK,(3),,CONTIG)
//GO.SORTWK02  DD   UNIT=SYSDA,SPACE=(TRK,(3),,CONTIG)
//GO.SORTWK03  DD   UNIT=SYSDA,SPACE=(TRK,(3),,CONTIG)
//GO.SYSOUT    DD   SYSOUT=A
//GO.SORTLIB   DD   DSNAME=SYS1.SORTLIB,DISP=SHR
    { other files as required by the program
```

Fig. 10.11: *Job Control Language Statements Needed to Support an Internal COBOL Sort on an IBM System/360 or System/370 Computer Running Under Control of an OS or VS Operating System.*

to support the COBOL internal sort can be quite tricky, so be careful. It is possible to code a COBOL program with input and output procedures attached to the internal sort, allowing the programmer to, perhaps, edit check the data and process the sorted records within a single program module; our sample program, however, merely sorted the data to a secondary file.

A sort routine is most commonly used as part of a system of programs. If you have access to a sort/merge utility program, by all means use it in preference to the COBOL internal sort; numerous studies have shown significant inefficiencies associated with the internal version. For those who do not have access to a utility, the use of a "sort only" COBOL program, such as the one developed in this chapter, as one of a system of programs is recommended.

KEY WORDS

key	sequential file	SORT
master file	sort	transaction file
master file update application	sort/merge	utility program
SD entry		

EXERCISES

1. Sorting is one of the most common of all data processing activities. Why do you suppose this is so?

2. What is meant by batch processing?

3. Explain the master file update application. Why is sorting essential to this application?

4. Explain, in very general terms, how a computer sorts. Why are secondary storage devices such as magnetic tape and disk so often used for a sort operation?

5. Explain how a sort operation might fit into a system of interrelated programs.

6. Using the input records first defined as part of the program development process in Chapter 6 (Fig. 6.2), write a COBOL sort routine or use a sort utility program to arrange the data into ascending (smallest first, biggest last) order by Social Security number. Send the sorted output to the printer.

7. Combine the edit program developed in Chapter 9, the payroll program developed over Chapters 6, 7, and 8, and the sort routine developed in exercise 6 of this chapter into an integrated system of three programs to (1.) check the input data for accuracy, (2.) sort the good records, and (3.) compute and print net pay for each employee using the sorted good data.

8. Keypunch a set of bibliography cards using the textbooks or other books found in your personal library. Include, for each book, the following information:

columns	contents
1-15	author's last name (first author only)
16-40	title
41-50	publisher
51-54	year published
55-60	cost (9999V99)
61-72	Library of Congress number or call number if available.

   Write a program to simply read these bibliography cards and generate a formatted listing of the contents complete with column headers. This "file dump" routine will be used in conjunction with a number of later assignments.

9. Using a sort utility or a COBOL internal sort, arrange the bibliography cards into alphabetical order by the author's last name. Use the "file dump" program developed in exercise 8 as a second program in this system of two and list the books in author sequence.

10. Sort the bibliography cards into sequence by title and produce a formatted list using the program of exercise 8.

11. Sort the bibliography cards into sequence by publisher and generate a formatted list. Use the list to identify the publisher who provided the greatest number of your textbooks.

12. Sort the bibliography cards into sequence by cost, with the most expensive book coming first (descending order). Produce a formatted list.

13. Keypunch a series of personal information cards containing such information as:

columns	contents
1-20	student name
21-30	major
31-40	dorm or street where individual lives
41-42	age
43-80	any other information you might like to add.

You might make up your own data; as an alternative, your instructor might assign each member of your class the responsibility for producing multiple copies of personal information, one for each class member. Once these records are combined, each class member can have a set of data records on the entire class for analysis. Write a COBOL program to generate a formatted list of this data.

14. Sort the data records of exercise 13 into alphabetic order by student name and generate a formatted list.

15. Sort the records of exercise 13 into sequence by major and produce a formatted list. Count the number of people who have the same major that you do.

16. Sort the data into sequence by dorm or street and generate a formatted list. How many people live near you? Believe it or not, the procedure you have just followed was actually used to recommend car pools during the energy crisis of a few years ago.

17. Prepare a set of input cards containing player names, numbers, and important statistical information (total points, field goal percentage, foul shooting percentage, batting average, home runs, average gain per carry, etc., depending on the sport) for each player on a real or imaginary team. Write a COBOL program to generate a formatted list of this data. Now, using a sort utility or the COBOL sort, generate listings of the players on the team in whatever order you choose, listing, for example, a table showing points scored from highest to lowest.

18. Go back to the student data generated in support of exercise 13 and the subsequent exercises. Modify the system of programs to generate a list of only those individuals meeting a certain criterion—only these living in a specific dorm or exceeding a certain age, for example.

11

A Single-Level Control Break Problem

OVERVIEW

In this chapter we will examine the report generation application, discussing a program to compute student grade point averages from individual student course records and print a series of student grade reports. As has been our practice, the chapter begins by defining the problem. A complete solution will be planned before the first line of COBOL code is written.

The key to the program logic is the idea of a control break. Student grade records will be in sequence by the student identification number; all the records for a given student will, as a consequence, be grouped together. As long as the identification number (the key) on the "just read" record matches the key that was on the "prior" record, we are working with the same student. If, however, the student identification number changes, we have begun to process the records of another student; this change in the value of the key field is called a control break. The action to be taken by the program will depend on whether or not a control break has occured, and a good part of the chapter is devoted to a discussion of how such control breaks can be recognized and handled.

THE PROBLEM: GENERATING STUDENT GRADE REPORTS

Imagine that you are a programmer working for a university. You have just been assigned the task of writing a new program to compute and print student grade point averages, using the 4.000 scale, for the current academic term. Where would you start?

Chances are, your starting point would be the input data. The initial source of input data is the grade report form each instructor fills out at the end of a term. These forms contain the name, student identification number, and grade of every student in the course. They also contain a course identification code and the number of credit hours the course carries. In raw form, the data is not very useful. Before it can be used to compute grade point averages, individual entries must be stripped from these forms and placed in student (rather than course) sequence. Thus before our grade point average computation program ever gets started, a considerable amount of preprocessing must have taken place. A system of programs is needed.

The first program in this system (Fig. 11.1) strips the individual lines from the instructor's grade report creating a new file of records each containing a student name, student identification number, and the course name, credit hours, and grade earned for a single course taken by one student. This first program also edits the data, eliminating such potential problems as undecipherable or illegal grades before they enter the grade point average program. Following a successful data edit, the resulting raw data records (by this time on magnetic tape) are sorted, by a second program, into student number sequence, producing a sorted data file on tape.

By the time the grade point average program begins processing, these two steps have already taken place. Input data will come from magnetic tape and will have the following format:

positions	contents
1-6	course identification code
7-15	student identification number
16-35	student name
36	credit hours
37	grade earned

Phase I of the planning process is complete.

Unless the school is very unusual, the format of the output record will be similarly constrained. Chances are very good that an administrative department, perhaps with the advice of a faculty committee, has already decided exactly what the grade report is to look like. The programmer will probably be given a sample grade report form and told to create output to fit it. The form might look like the one in Fig. 11.2.

Fig. 11.1: *The Grade Point Average Computation System.*

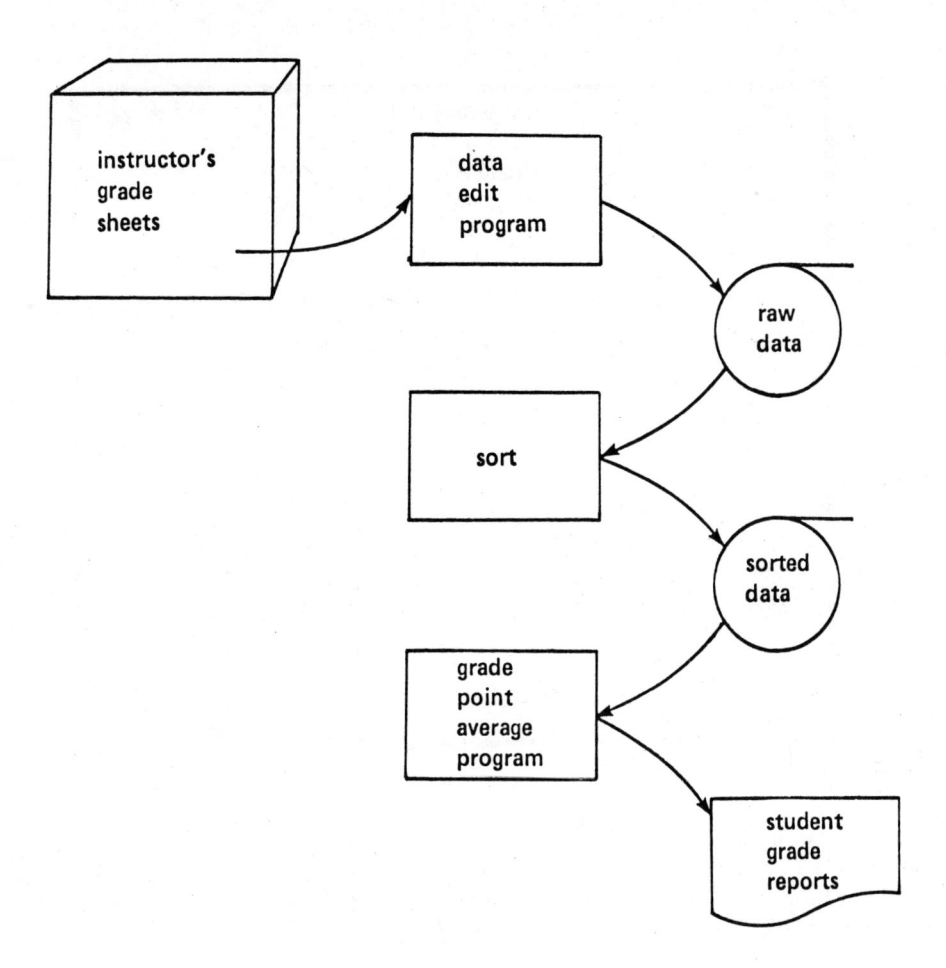

Fig. 11.2: *A Sample Student Grade Report.*

```
┌─────────────────────────────────────────────────────────┐
│                    Mt. Valley College                   │
│                                                         │
│              Student Grade Report, FALL 1980            │
│                                                         │
│   Student name:  JOHN SMITH         Student ID: 123456789│
├─────────────────────────────────────────────────────────┤
│          course      credits     grade    grade points  │
│                                                         │
│          ACC101         4          A          16        │
│                                                         │
│          BOT214         3          B           9        │
│                                                         │
│          ENG111         3          C           6        │
│                                                         │
│          SOC201         3          D           3        │
│                                                         │
│                                                         │
│      credits: 13    grade points: 34    G.P.A.: 2.615   │
└─────────────────────────────────────────────────────────┘
```

With the exception of field identifying the quarter or semester, all the constant headers on this form are preprinted, meaning that the programmer need not set them up in main memory. The student name and student ID must be printed near the top of the form, and this data comes from an input record. For each detail line, the course identification, credits, and grade earned are also taken from the input record; grade points, however, are computed. The final line on the form lists the total number of credits, the total number of earned grade points, and the computed grade point average; these fields are to be printed only after all records for a student have been read and processed.

Clearly, there are three distinct output operations associated with each student. First, as part of the header routine, the name, identification number, and term must be written once on each grade report form. Next, information on each course taken must be written for as many courses as the student has taken, no matter how many that may be. Finally, summary information is printed at the bottom of the form. In programming terminology, the first of these output operations produces what is called a **header line**; the second series of operations produces **detail lines** (one for each input record), and the third, a **summary line**.

Most computer printers can be set to print either 6 or 8 lines per inch; thus a ruler can be used to determine vertical spacing. Most printers print 10 characters per inch across the page, and this knowledge allows the programmer to determine horizontal spacing. Later, we will convert a set of imaginary measurements of the grade report form directly into the structure and PICTURE clauses of a header line, a detail line, and a summary line.

The rules for computing a grade point average are all that remain to be defined. We are not yet ready to begin concerning ourselves with the details of implementation, so it is reasonable to restrict the analysis to a single student at this time. How do we go about computing one student's grade point average?

If your school uses a 4-point system, you probably already know how. As a memory refresher, and for the benefit of those whose schools use some other procedure, let's go through the example shown in Fig. 11.2. Each A is worth 4 points; each B counts 3; C's are valued at 2 points; D's earn only 1; and any F is assigned zero. To get grade points, these point values are multiplied by the number of credit hours for the course. In the example of Fig. 11.2, the first course, ACC101, shows a grade of A and a total of 4 credit hours; the 4 hours multiplied by the value of an A, 4, generates 16 grade points. The second course, BOT214, shows a grade of B for this 3-credit course; the product of 3 and 3 (the value of a B) yields 9 grade points.

Once all the grade point computations have been made, the total number of credits taken (in this example, 13) and the total number of grade points earned (34) are found. Then, grade points are divided by credits earned to give the grade point average.

At this stage, it might be wise to define the algorithm for the benefit of our straw person. We might list the following steps:

1. set credits accumulator to zero;

2. set grade points accumulator to zero;

3. read a record;

4. if last record, go to step 10;

5. add credits to credits accumulator;

6. compute grade points;

7. add grade points to grade points accumulator;

8. write detail line;

9. go to step 3;

10. divide grade points accumulator by credits accumulator
giving grade point average;

11. write summary line.

Some details have been left out. The straw person is, after all, intended to be only an *aid* to planning.

Do we really know all there is to know about this algorithm? Not really. We have assumed, for example, that only the grades A, B, C, D, and F are valid. Is this true? No! How, for example, is an incomplete handled? What about the student who withdrew from the course but whose name still appears on the grade form? How do we handle the special grades designed to cover those students working on multi-term research projects? For purposes of this program, we'll assume that all non-standard grades will be simply ignored in computing a grade point average, with neither the grade nor the credit hours being factored in; chances are that your school uses different rules. All rules must, of course, be known before a valid program can be written.

Although this is not really a business data processing problem, it is typical. The business programmer, especially during his or her first few years of employment, is usually given the format of all input and output records and asked simply to write a program to get from the input to the output. Often, most if not all of the algorithms needed will be similarly prescribed. Working within the bounds of such a well defined problem is quite common in business as well as in university programming.

THE PROGRAM LOGIC

To this point, planning the grade point average program, except for defining input and output records, has stayed at the level of the individual student. The program must be able to deal with many students; thus it is time we expanded our view a bit.

Before we begin more detailed planning, a few hints are in order. At least three distinct types of records exist in every sequential input data file: the first record, the last record, and all the records in between. The first record is unique because no other records preceed it. The last record is unique because no other records follow it. Because these two records are unique a number of problems are created that must be handled by unique code. It is usually a good idea to begin planning program logic in the middle, after the first record and before the last one. The unique start-of-job and end-of-job code can be added later.

One of the very best ways to go about planning the structure of a program is to start with a set of simple set of test data and work through it, making notes of the actions that must be taken. The data need not be elaborate. Since planning is now concerned with the entire program rather than a single individual, the test data must represent more than one student, but otherwise, almost any reasonable set of data will do. In the discussion which follows, the data shown in Fig. 11.3 will be used. Don't forget that we are temporarily ignoring the problems associated with the first and last records.

Fig. 11.3: *Test Data for use in Planning a Problem Solution.*

course	student ID	Student name	credits	grade
ACC101	123456789	SMITH	3	A
BOT202	123456789	SMITH	4	B
CHM303	123456789	SMITH	2	C
EDP121	123458888	JONES	3	D
GER315	123458888	JONES	4	F
HST105	123459999	ANYBODY	3	A
LAT312	123459999	ANYBODY	3	B

Before we do, however, it might be wise to stop and look at our data. The records are clearly in sequence by the student identification number. Imagine that you have the responsibility for manually sorting a group of records, and that you have encountered two or more records with the same value in the key field—Jones, student number 123458888, for example, took two courses (Fig. 11.3). What would you do with these records? Clearly, they all must follow any records in which the student identification number has a lower value; otherwise the records would not be in sequence. Clearly, if sequence is to be maintained, they must all preceed any records in which the student identification number has a higher value. As a result, all records in which the key field has the same value will be grouped together.

Our program will read these records one at a time. As long as the student identification number remains the same, we are working with the same student, and must accumulate grade points and credits. When the student number changes, however, we are working with a different student, and a different set of actions is called for. This is called a **control break**. The logic of our program will depend on our ability to recognize and handle such control breaks.

Let's return to our planning. The first record (student number 123456789) has, don't forget, already been read. The second record is also for student number 123456789. How can we tell? Simple. The student identification number is compared with that of the first record, and the two fields match. What should we do? We are working with the same student, and the problem of computing one student's grade point average has already been solved for the benefit of the straw person. As long as the student identification number remains the same, we

1. accumulate credits,

2. compute grade points,

3. accumulate grade points,

4. write a detail line,

5. go back and get another record.

This block of logic might be labeled the "SAME STUDENT" block, in that it is performed as long as a record for the same student is read.

The third record is also for student 123456789; thus the "SAME STUDENT" logic is performed once again. The fourth record, however, is for student 123458888, and that is a different number. What happens when the number changes? If the data is really in sequence, *every* record for student 123456789 must come before *any* record for student 123458888; thus it is reasonable to assume that there are no more records for 123456789.

A break point has occured. All the records for student number 123456789 have been processed; thus it is time to compute this student's grade point average. A very rough flowchart of program logic as it has been defined to this point is shown in Fig. 11.4.

Note that the break point was recognized as a result of comparing the student identification number fields of *two successive records*. To this point, all our programs have followed a simple linear pattern. A single record was read, the data in that

Fig. 11.4: *Basic Program Logic (Incomplete).*

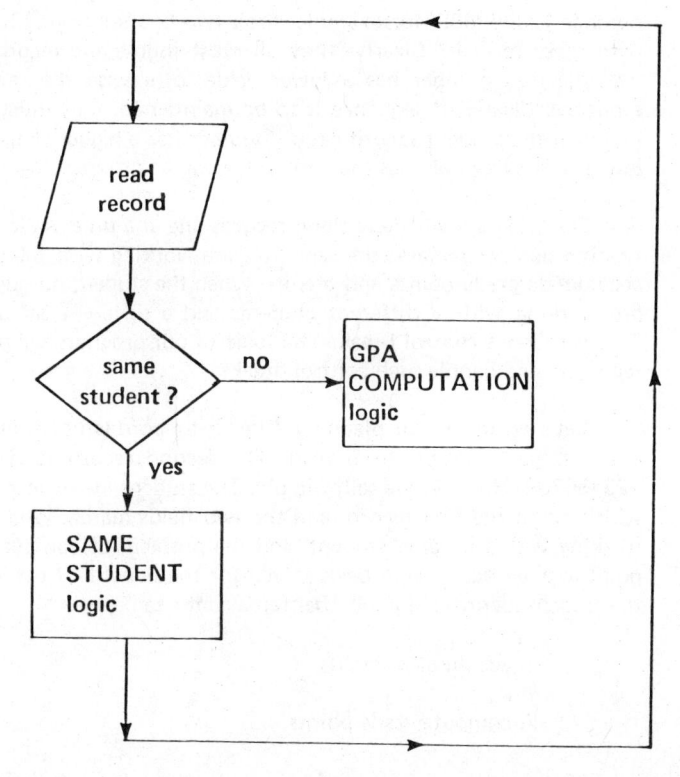

record was processed, and a single record of output was written; then the pattern was repeated. This application is different. The action to be taken depends on the value that was found in the key field of a record read in an *earlier* program cycle. Don't let this subtle difference confuse you.

What happens after the GPA COMPUTATION logic? We have now finished with the first student and are ready to turn our attention to the second. A quick glance at the straw person logic reminds us that accumulators must be set to zero before beginning the new set of computations, so a "RESET ACCUMULATORS" block of logic can be added.

Now what? The obvious answer, looking only at the straw person logic, is to go back and read another record, but we have already read the first record for student 123458888; it supplied the student identification number that allowed us to recognize that there were no more records for 123456789. If we were to read another record now, the data contained in the fourth record (Fig. 11.3) would be lost. If grade point averages are to be computed accurately , the data contained in this record must be processed. There are significant differences between writing a program to perform one set of computations and writing a similar program to perform many sets of the same computations, and the need to remember that the "next" record may have already been read is one of the more important ones.

We cannot return to the top of the mainline and read another record. The proper path, once accumulators have been reset, is to reenter the mainline at the point where the SAME STUDENT logic is coded, accumulating the credits and grade points and writing a detail line before returning to the top and reading another record. The already read record must be handled first (Fig. 11.5).

Carefully consider the flowchart of Fig. 11.5. Note how it refers only to major blocks of program logic. We are following a modular approach to programming. The contents, the specific instructions, of each of these logic blocks can certainly be defined, but we don't need them yet. As we shall see shortly, restricting the program flow to major logic blocks will allow us to spot obvious patterns and duplicate code, an advantage we would not enjoy were a complete detailed flowchart prepared at this time.

The key is the test for "same student". The logical tests from earlier chapters have been concerned with comparing two fields from the same record, fields from two different records, or one field and a constant. This comparison is different, as it tests the relationship between the same field on two successive input records. Consider the implications. The first step after reading record number 2 is to compare its student identification number with that of record number 1. Unfortunately, the act of reading record number 2 destroys record number 1, at least within the computer's main memory, unless, of course, the programmer takes action to avoid the loss of data. All that the programmer must do is copy the student identification number to a work field each time a new student is encountered, a step that can be added to the RESET ACCUMULATORS logic module.

Does the fact that the student numbers on two successive records are not the same necessarily imply that a grade point average is to be computed? As long as the

Fig. 11.5: *The Basic Program Mainline.*

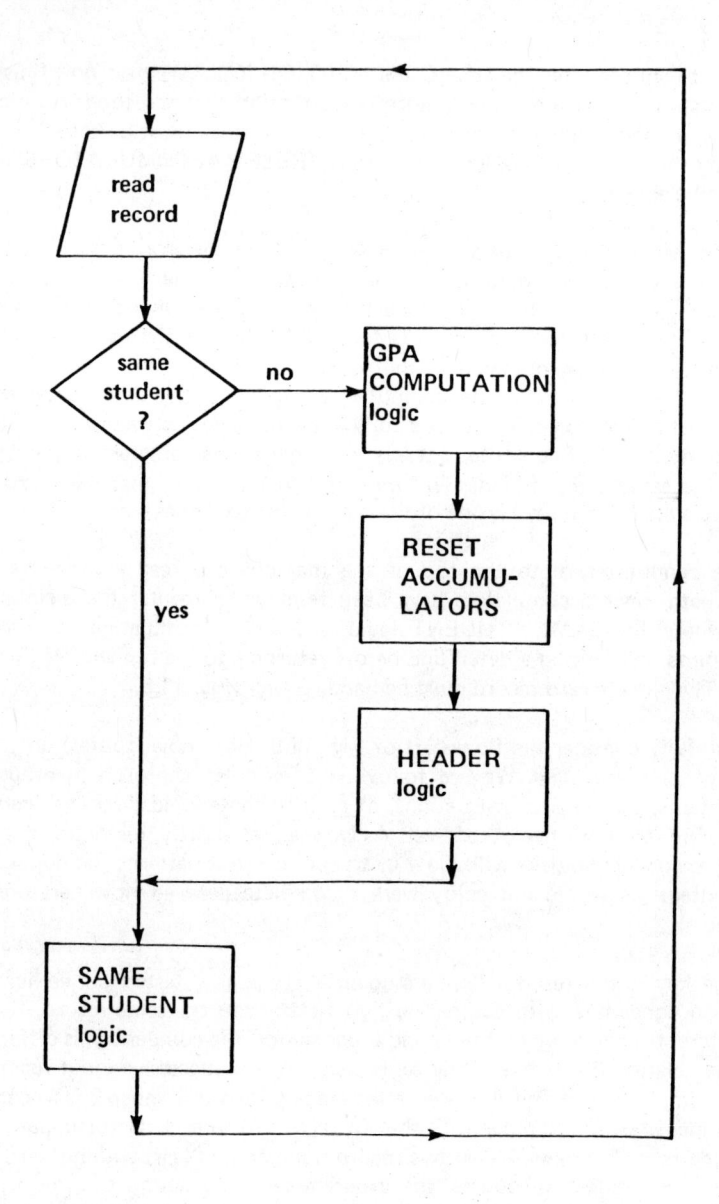

records are in proper sequence, yes it does, but what happens when a stray, out of sequence record is included in the file? The fact that 123456789 is followed by 111111111 does not necessarily prove that there are no more 123456789 records; another one could quite reasonably follow 111111111. An out of sequence record is an error. Our mainline should include a test for an out of sequence condition, perhaps between the "same student" logical test and the GPA COMPUTATION module, and such a test will be added to the finished program. This test should be performed in spite of the fact that an earlier program sorted the data. Murphy's law states that "If anything can possibly go wrong, it will." Ask any experienced programmer to comment on the validity of that law.

Getting Started: First Record Processing

The key to the basic mainline logic of Fig. 11.5 is a comparison between a field in the just read record and the same field in the prior record. The first record in the file is different simply because there is no prior record. The fact that the record is unique means that it must be handled in a unique way.

What exactly must be done with the first record? Obviously, it must be read. Before the second record can be read, all accumulators must be set to their proper values, a set of headers (basically, the student name and identification number) must be printed, and the credit hours and grade points from this new record must be accumulated. The start-of-job logic is illustrated in Fig. 11.6.

Fig. 11.6: *Start of Job Logic.*

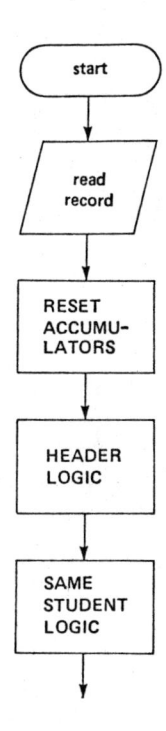

Last Record Processing

Like the first record, the last record is also different, simply because there is no record following it. What must be done when the last record is encountered? If you think about it, it is clear that we must have been in the middle of accumulating the information to compute some student's grade point average when the data ran out, and the grade point average must be computed and printed for this last student. Normally, following the GPA COMPUTATION routine, the program continues with computations for other students. Following the last record, however, there are no more students to be processed, so the program should terminate, (but not, of course, until the average for the last student has been printed). The last record logic is illustrated in Fig. 11.7.

Putting the Pieces Together

We now have modules to handle the first record, the last record, and everything in between. We also know that an error routine of some kind is needed. Let's put the pieces together and evaluate the complete program (Fig. 11.8). Perhaps, missing pieces will be spotted. It is even more likely that common blocks of code will be identified and possibly combined.

A close review of the flow diagram (Fig. 11.8) does reveal a number of interesting things. Each of the major blocks of logic, except for the ERROR routine, is referenced in at least two places, indicating that a separate routine which is PERFORMed from the mainline is probably best. Two blocks of logic, RESET ACCUMULATORS and the HEADER logic always appear together and so can reasonably be combined into one. The read statement for the input file appears in two places, once in the start of job routine and once in the mainline. Many would argue that a common module containing the read statement and the associated end of data test should be coded in a separate routine of its own, with this routine being PERFORMed as needed. We will not take this approach, as it is not particularly advantageous in this case, representing only one statement. Perhaps, the use of a common input routine will be more attractive in a subsequent program.

Fig. 11.7: *End of Job Logic.*

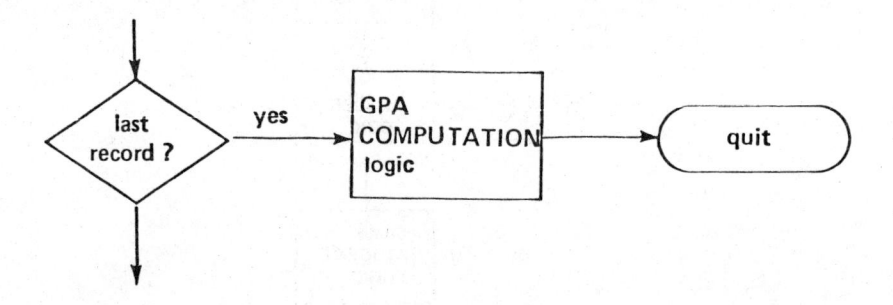

Fig. 11.8: *Complete Program Logic for the Grade Point Average Program.*

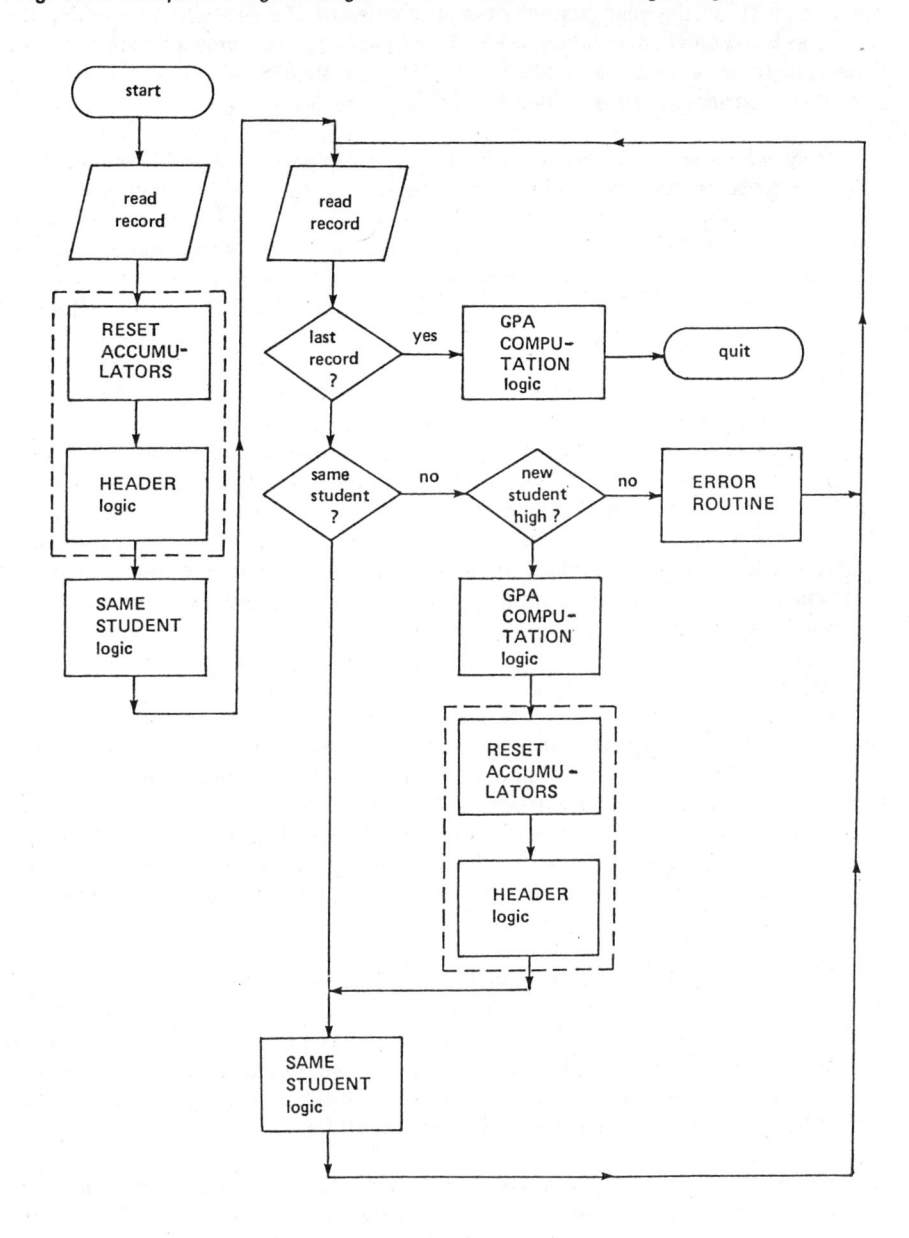

What actual code should be included in the mainline? A minimum mainline would consist of the read statement and a series of IFs designed to identify the condition being handled and then to PERFORM the necessary detailed logic modules. Others might argue that the SAME STUDENT logic should be part of the mainline, since these instructions are executed for each input record.

In deciding what should and should not be included in a given logic module, a key objective is that the module should be easy to follow and to understand. As a rule of thumb, when a logic module exceeds a single page on an output listing (roughly 50 to 60 lines) it becomes more difficult to follow, simply because a page must be turned in order to see the whole thing. We choose not to include the SAME STUDENT routine as part of the mainline because we want to keep all modules as small as possible.

There is, of course, a corollary to this rule of thumb. Excessive modularization just for its own sake is every bit as bad as excessively large modules. Extremely short routines consisting of an instruction or two may be internally easy to follow, but the task of mentally linking from one routine to another is itself a difficult exercise and should be minimized. Thus we combined two related routines into one, and decided not to create a new routine for the read instruction. Some programmers believe that the more levels of modularization, the better, but the whole point of our approach is to simplify the task of writing and maintaining a program, and a certain element of common sense must be applied.

Planning the Detailed Logic

We can now turn our attention to more detailed planning, and lay out the contents of the various detailed logic modules. The first routine is the one to reset accumulators. Obviously, setting the credits accumulator and the grade points accumulator to zero must be part of this routine. Earlier, the chapter described the need to set a WORKING-STORAGE field equal to the student identification number of the "just read" record in order to support the test for a break point; this routine is the obvious place to do it.

The header routine always appears with the reset accumulators routine; thus they can be combined. Basically, two things have to happen. First, the name and date of the current academic term (FALL, 1980) must be printed near the top of the form on the same line as the "Student Grade Report" preprinted header. Next, the student's name and identification number must be printed adjacent to the appropriate titles. The header routine clearly requires two write statements.

Should these two routines be flowcharted? Some programmers argue that complete flowcharts are necessary for documentation. Others state that, given the very clear flowchart of Fig. 11.8, flowcharts of the individual detailed logic modules would do little more than echo the COBOL instructions, thus adding little that could not, just as easily, be derived from the code itself. When only a handful of noncomplex instructions must be coded, a flowchart serves little or no purpose. For a more complex routine, the computation of income tax, for example, a flowchart is essential. As is so often the case, a little common sense must be applied to the question of whether or not a flowchart should be prepared.

The next routine involves the SAME STUDENT logic. Before a detail line can be printed, a number of computations must be done. Credits must be accumulated. Grade points must be computed, which involves substituting a number for a letter grade. If the grade is not A, B, C, D, or F, the data in this record is not to participate in the computation of a grade point average, although a detail line is to be printed; grade points are to be computed and accumulated in all other cases. The logic is sufficiently complex that a flowchart of the subroutine might well be in order (Fig. 11.9). Note that, to avoid the problem of accumulating credits and then discovering a nonstandard grade, the test for grade and the computation of grade points are done first.

The next routine contains the logic needed to compute a grade point average. Following the divide instruction, the computed grade point average and the accumulated credit hours and grade points are moved to the summary line and printed. Certainly no flowchart is needed for such a simple routine.

The last remaining module contains the error handling logic for an out-of-sequence record. How exactly should these errors be handled? An out-of-sequence record belongs somewhere else; in other words, it is almost certainly part of someone's academic effort and should be included on that student's grade report. The only problem is that our program is specifically designed to handle only in-sequence records. At the very least, a list of these errors must be maintained so that someone in the registrar's office can correct the affected student grade reports.

There are several ways that this could be done. The error records can simply be written to the printer (a different printer, of course) as they are encountered. Instead, the errors can be written to a temporary disk file and then sorted into sequence before being printed, thus simplifying the task of correcting the errors. To keep our program as simple as possible, we'll simply write error records to the printer.

ERROR HANDLING

Error handling is a very significant problem to the professional programmer, consuming a great deal of planning and coding time. Very early in their careers, programmers learn to ask, "What could possibly go wrong?" and then to plan and implement error handling routines to deal with these hypothetical situations. For example, what would happen if the sort step had been accidently skipped by the computer operator? Given the error handling routine described above, almost all of the input records would be printed as errors, and the long error list would represent a trememdous waste of paper. A mere handful of out-of-sequence records would be enough to demonstrate that the sort routine had either been bypassed or was unsuccessful; thus many programmers include a counter as part of the error routine, terminating the program as soon as a significant number of sequence errors have been encountered.

Sequence checking is not the only possible source of errors. A nonnumeric entry in the credit hours field could, for example, cause program termination. Many programmers test such fields almost as a matter of course, figuring that the insignificant amount of computer time spent performing the test is more than offset by the

Fig. 11.9: *The SAME STUDENT Routine.*

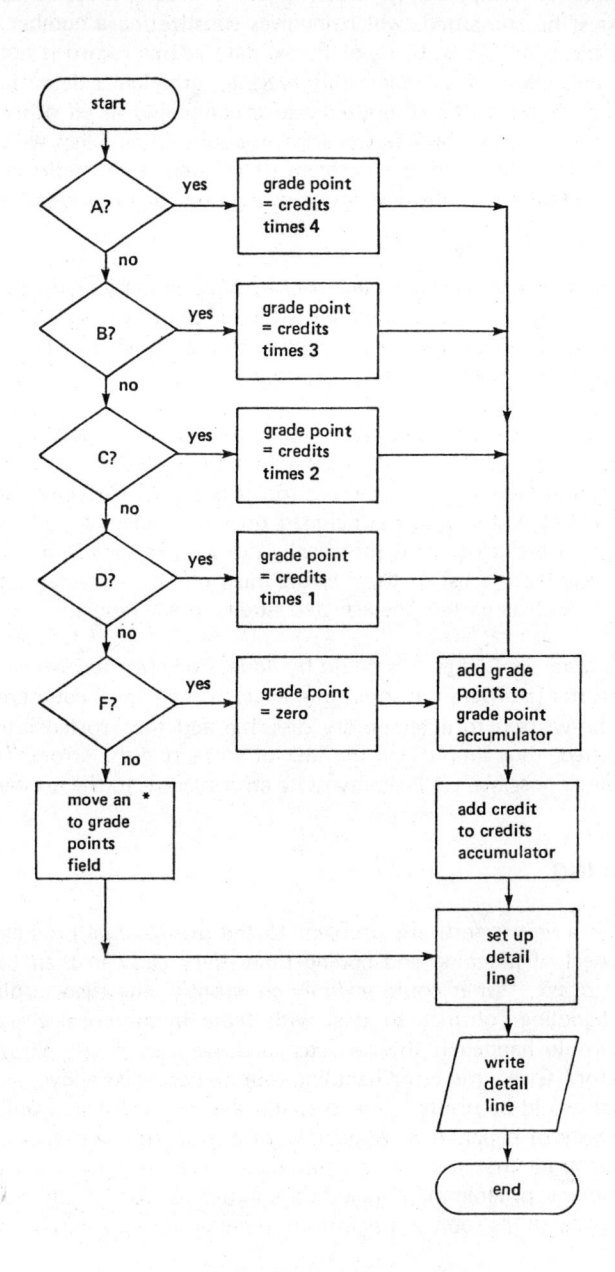

risk of program failure if the test is not made. The fact that the data had previously been edited does help to minimize the problem, but the programmer soon learns to assume that no program is perfect.

Have you ever known a student who, due perhaps to personal or family illness, missed a significant number of classes and thus received the grade of incomplete for all courses? It has happened. What does our program do with grades other than A, B, C, D, or F? They are simply not counted. The student with all incompletes would show a total of zero credit hours earned as the program links to the CPA COMPUTATION routine.

Within this routine, the grade point average is computed by dividing credits into grade points. But, in this example, there are no credits—the value of the field is zero. Division by zero is illegal; it will cause immediate program termination on most computers. To avoid the risk of program shut down due to an unpredictable zero divide, most programmers include a test for a zero divisor, skipping the divide operation if necessary.

There are other areas where the real-life programmer might well add code. Consider nonstandard grade assignments. We have assumed that any grade other than A, B, C, D, or F is valid, and is to be printed as part of the grade report but not considered in computing the grade point average. In a real program, all the other legitimate grades would be identified and tested for, with an "unknown grade" condition calling for another type of error message.

Often, a significant part of the logic of a real program is taken up with error handling. The mainline and primary subroutines represent only a part of the programmer's responsibility. Identifying and designing logic to handle possible errors requires tremendous attention to detail, and it is this attention to detail that separates the outstanding programmer from the average or below average one.

COBOL: THE IDENTIFICATION AND ENVIRONMENT DIVISIONS

The IDENTIFICATION and ENVIRONMENT DIVISIONs for this program are shown in Fig. 11.10. Note that three files are defined in the SELECT and ASSIGN clauses: one for input, one for the normal output, and one for the error output. Note also, in the SPECIAL-NAMES paragraph, the presence of an entry associating the top-of-page condition with carriage control channel 1.

The DATA DIVISION

Fig. 11.11 illustrates the DATA DIVISION. A few new features require some explanation. Whenever a grade other than A, B, C, D, or F is encountered, the results of the course are not counted in computing a grade point average. To indicate this fact, we would like to move an asterisk (*) into the grade points field of the detail line. Unfortunately, the grade points field has a numeric picture (Z9), and it is illegal to move a nonnumeric constant such as * to a numeric field. To get around this problem, the grade points field has been redefined by the COBOL statement

COBOL Coding Form

SYSTEM	STUDENT	PUNCHING INSTRUCTIONS	1 PAGE 1 OF 11
PROGRAM	GRADE REPORT	GRAPHIC Ø	CARD FORM #
PROGRAMMER	DAVIS & FISHER	DATE 3-1-79	PUNCH ZERO

SEQUENCE | CONT. | A | B | COBOL STATEMENT | IDENTIFICATION

```
       IDENTIFICATION DIVISION.

        PROGRAM-ID.  GRADES.
        AUTHOR.      DAVIS & FISHER.

        REMARKS.     THIS PROGRAM COMPUTES AND PRINTS
                     STUDENT GRADE POINT AVERAGES FOR
                     THE CURRENT ACADEMIC TERM.

       ENVIRONMENT DIVISION.

        CONFIGURATION SECTION.

         SOURCE-COMPUTER.   IBM-37Ø-148.
         OBJECT-COMPUTER.   IBM-37Ø-148.
         SPECIAL-NAMES.     CØ1 IS NEW-PAGE.

        INPUT-OUTPUT SECTION.

         FILE-CONTROL.
           SELECT STUDENT-COURSE-GRADE-FILE ASSIGN TO UT-S-CRSEFILE.
           SELECT STUDENT-GRADE-REPORT      ASSIGN TO UT-S-GRDREPT.
           SELECT GRADES-EXCEPTION-FILE     ASSIGN TO UT-S-GREXCEPT.
```

Fig. 11.10: *The IDENTIFICATION and ENVIRONMENT DIVISIONs.*

COBOL Coding Form

SYSTEM	STUDENT	PUNCHING INSTRUCTIONS: GRAPHIC Ø / PUNCH ZERO	PAGE 2 OF 11
PROGRAM	GRADE REPORT		CARD FORM #
PROGRAMMER	DAVIS & FISHER	DATE 3-1-79	

```
       DATA DIVISION.
        FILE SECTION.
         FD STUDENT-COURSE-GRADE-FILE
              BLOCK CONTAINS 1Ø RECORDS
              LABEL RECORD IS STANDARD.
          Ø1 COURSE-GRADE-RECORD.
              Ø5 I-COURSE-CODE            PIC X(6).
              Ø5 I-STUDENT-NUMBER         PIC 9(9).
              Ø5 I-STUDENT-NAME           PIC X(2Ø).
              Ø5 I-CREDIT-HOURS           PIC 9.
              Ø5 I-GRADE-EARNED           PIC X.
```

Fig. 11.11: *The DATA DIVISION.*

```
SYSTEM     STUDENT                                            PAGE 3 OF 11
PROGRAM    GRADE REPORT
PROGRAMMER DAVIS & FISHER    DATE 3-1-79
```

FD	STUDENT-GRADE-REPORT	
	LABEL RECORD IS OMITTED.	
01	REPORT-HEADER-1.	
05	FILLER	PIC X(32).
05	O-TERM	PIC X(6).
05	FILLER	PIC X(20).
01	REPORT-HEADER-2.	
05	FILLER	PIC X(17).
05	O-STUDENT-NAME	PIC X(20).
05	FILLER	PIC X(11).
05	O-STUDENT-NUMBER	PIC 9(9).
05	FILLER	PIC X.
01	REPORT-DETAIL-LINE.	
05	FILLER	PIC X(8).
05	O-COURSE-CODE	PIC X(6).
05	FILLER	PIC X(7).
05	O-CREDIT-HOURS	PIC 9.
05	FILLER	PIC X(8).
05	O-GRADE-EARNED	PIC X.
05	FILLER	PIC X(9).
05	O-GRADE-POINTS	PIC Z9.
05	NON-STANDARD-GRADE-FLAG REDEFINES O-GRADE-POINTS	
		PIC XX.
05	FILLER	PIC X(14).

Fig. 11.11: *Continued.*

COBOL Coding Form

SYSTEM	STUDENT		PUNCHING INSTRUCTIONS		PAGE 4 OF 11
PROGRAM	GRADE REPORT		GRAPHIC	Ø	CARD FORM #
PROGRAMMER	DAVIS & FISHER	DATE 3-1-79	PUNCH	ZERO	

```
       01 REPORT-SUMMARY-LINE.
           05 FILLER                        PIC X(12).
           05 S-TOTAL-CREDIT-HOURS          PIC Z9.
           05 FILLER                        PIC X(19).
           05 S-TOTAL-GRADE-POINTS          PIC Z9.
           05 FILLER                        PIC X(16).
           05 S-GRADE-POINT-AVERAGE         PIC 9.999.
           05 FILLER                        PIC X(2).

       FD GRADE-EXCEPTION-FILE
           BLOCK CONTAINS 10 RECORDS
           LABEL RECORDS OMITTED.
       01 EXCEPTION-RECORD                  PIC X(37).

       WORKING-STORAGE SECTION.

       01 PRIOR-STUDENT-ID                  PIC 9(9).

       01 ACCUMULATORS.
           05 TOTAL-CREDIT-HOURS            PIC 99.
           05 TOTAL-GRADE-POINTS            PIC 99.
           05 GRADE-POINTS                  PIC 99.
```

Fig. 11.11: *Concluded.*

05 NONSTANDARD-GRADE-FLAG REDEFINES O-GRADE-POINTS

PIC XX.

The **REDEFINES clause** allows the same field to be viewed in two different ways. O-GRADE-POINTS is the data name of the field whenever a numeric value such as the computed grade points is to be moved to it. The alternate name (almost an alias) of NONSTANDARD-GRADE-FLAG is used when a nonnumeric move is called for.

The only other unusual entry in the DATA DIVISION is the field set aside to hold the identification number found on the previously read input record. The field will be used to test for a change in student, triggering the printing of a summary line. It can be defined as a 77-level entry, but need not be; in this example, we have used a 01-level entry for the PRIOR-STUDENT-ID. When you are defining space for nonnumeric work fields, using a level indicator other than 77 often saves storage space.

The PROCEDURE DIVISION

Given the program flowchart of Fig. 11.8, the descriptions and flowchart of the logic contained in each of the routines, and the definitions of fields in the DATA DIVISION, the PROCEDURE DIVISION (Fig. 11.12 shows the housekeeping and mainline paragraphs) should present no problems. One COBOL statement is new. Attached to the READ statement in the HOUSEKEEPING-PARAGRAPH is an AT END clause that says

DISPLAY 'NO INPUT DATA' UPON CONSOLE

The **DISPLAY** statement is a special form of WRITE designed for transmitting short, one-time messages from the program to the computer operator or the programmer. If an end of file condition is encountered during an attempt to read the very first input record, there is clearly no input data to be read; should this occur (perhaps because of operator error or some other mix up), the operator is told, through a message displayed on the console, that there is no data, and the program then terminates.

Note that the program mainline fits on a single coding sheet. It consists primarily of a read statement and a series of IF tests that identify the condition being handled and that causes the proper computational routines to be PERFORMed. All complex logic is housed in the secondary routines, and can be seen in Fig. 11.13.

An edit check designed to make certain that the I-CREDIT-HOURS field is numeric before computations take place has been added to the SAME-STUDENT-ROUTINE. Another edit check, this one designed to ensure that the TOTAL-CREDIT-HOURS is not zero, has been added to the GPA-COMPUTATION-ROUTINE. Except for these relatively minor changes, you should be able to follow the program by simply reading it.

COBOL Coding Form

SYSTEM	STUDENT		PUNCHING INSTRUCTIONS		PAGE 5 OF 11	
PROGRAM	GRADE REPORT		GRAPHIC	Ø	CARD FORM #	
PROGRAMMER	DAVIS & FISHER	DATE 3-1-79	PUNCH	ZERO		

SEQUENCE | CONT. | A | B | COBOL STATEMENT | IDENTIFICATION

```
       PROCEDURE DIVISION.

        HOUSEKEEPING-PARAGRAPH.

           OPEN INPUT  STUDENT-COURSE-GRADE-FILE.
           OPEN OUTPUT STUDENT-GRADE-REPORT.
           OPEN OUTPUT GRADES-EXCEPTION-FILE.
           READ STUDENT-COURSE-GRADE-FILE
                AT END DISPLAY 'NO INPUT DATA' UPON CONSOLE
                       PERFORM END-OF-ROUTINE
                       STOP RUN.
           PERFORM INITIALIZATION-AND-HEADER THRU END-INITIALIZATION.
           PERFORM SAME-STUDENT-ROUTINE THRU END-SAME-STUDENT.
```

Fig. 11.12: *The PROCEDURE DIVISION—housekeeping and mainline paragraphs.*

```
TOP-OF-MAINLINE.
    READ STUDENT-COURSE-GRADE-FILE
        AT END PERFORM GPA-COMPUTATION-ROUTINE
                   THRU END-GPA-COMPUTATION
               PERFORM END-OF-JOB-ROUTINE
               STOP RUN.
    IF I-STUDENT-NUMBER IS EQUAL TO PRIOR-STUDENT-ID
        THEN
           PERFORM SAME-STUDENT-ROUTINE THRU END-SAME-STUDENT
        ELSE
           IF I-STUDENT-NUMBER IS GREATER THAN PRIOR-STUDENT-ID
               THEN
                  PERFORM GPA-COMPUTATION-ROUTINE
                       THRU END-GPA-COMPUTATION
                  PERFORM INITIALIZATION-AND-HEADER
                       THRU END-INITIALIZATION
                  PERFORM SAME-STUDENT-ROUTINE THRU END-SAME-STUDENT
               ELSE
                  PERFORM EXCEPTION-ROUTINE THRU END-EXCEPTION.
    GO TO TOP-OF-MAINLINE.
```

Fig. 11.12: *Continued.*

```
     1                    2.28.15      OCT  7,1978

00001          IDENTIFICATION DIVISION.

00003          PROGRAM-ID. GRADES.
00004          AUTHOR.     DAVIS & FISHER.

00006          REMARKS.    THIS PROGRAM COMPUTES AND PRINTS
00007                      STUDENT GRADE POINT AVERAGES FOR
00008                      THE CURRENT ACADEMIC TERM.


00010          ENVIRONMENT DIVISION.

00012          CONFIGURATION SECTION.

00014              SOURCE-COMPUTER.  IBM-370-148.
00015              OBJECT-COMPUTER.  IBM-370-148.
00016              SPECIAL-NAMES.    C01 IS NEW-PAGE.

00018          INPUT-OUTPUT SECTION.

00020              FILE-CONTROL.
00021                  SELECT STUDENT-COURSE-GRADE-FILE  ASSIGN TO UT-S-CRSEFILE.
00022                  SELECT STUDENT-GRADE-REPORT       ASSIGN TO UT-S-GRDREPT.
00023                  SELECT GRADES-EXCEPTION-FILE      ASSIGN TO UT-S-GREXCEPT.
```

Fig. 11.13: *A listing of the grade point average computation program.*

```
 2          GRADES           2.28.15        OCT  7,1978

00025              DATA DIVISION.
00026              FILE SECTION.
00027                 FD STUDENT-COURSE-GRADE-FILE
00028                    BLOCK CONTAINS 10 RECORDS
00029                    LABEL RECORD IS STANDARD.
00030                 01 COURSE-GRADE-RECORD.
00031                    05 I-COURSE-CODE            PIC X(6).
00032                    05 I-STUDENT-NUMBER         PIC 9(9).
00033                    05 I-STUDENT-NAME           PIC X(20).
00034                    05 I-CREDIT-HOURS           PIC 9.
00035                    05 I-GRADE-EARNED           PIC X.

00037                 FD STUDENT-GRADE-REPORT
00038                    LABEL RECORD IS OMITTED.
00039                 01 REPORT-HEADER-1.
00040                    05 FILLER                   PIC X(32).
00041                    05 C-TERM                   PIC X(6).
00042                    05 FILLER                   PIC X(20).
00043                 01 REPORT-HEADER-2.
00044                    05 FILLER                   PIC X(17).
00045                    05 O-STUDENT-NAME           PIC X(20).
00046                    05 FILLER                   PIC X(11).
00047                    05 O-STUDENT-NUMBER         PIC 9(9).
00048                    05 FILLER                   PIC X.
00049                 01 REPORT-DETAIL-LINE.
00050                    05 FILLER                   PIC X(8).
00051                    05 O-COURSE-CODE            PIC X(6).
00052                    05 FILLER                   PIC X(7).
00053                    05 O-CREDIT-HOURS           PIC 9.
00054                    05 FILLER                   PIC X(8).
00055                    05 O-GRADE-EARNED           PIC X.
00056                    05 FILLER                   PIC X(9).
00057                    05 O-GRADE-POINTS           PIC Z9.
00058                    05 NONSTANDARD-GRADE-FLAG REDEFINES O-GRADE-POINTS
00059                                                PIC XX.
00060                    05 FILLER                   PIC X(14).
00061                 01 REPORT-SUMMARY-LINE.
00062                    05 FILLER                   PIC X(12).
00063                    05 S-TOTAL-CREDIT-HOURS     PIC Z9.
00064                    05 FILLER                   PIC X(19).
00065                    05 S-TOTAL-GRADE-POINTS     PIC Z9.
00066                    05 FILLER                   PIC X(16).
00067                    05 S-GRADE-POINT-AVERAGE    PIC 9.999.
00068                    05 FILLER                   PIC X(2).

00070                 FD GRADES-EXCEPTION-FILE
00071                    BLOCK CONTAINS 10 RECORDS
00072                    LABEL RECORDS OMITTED.
00073                 01 EXCEPTION-RECORD            PIC X(37).

00075              WORKING-STORAGE SECTION.
00076              01 PRIOR-STUDENT-ID               PIC 9(9).
00077              01 ACCUMULATORS.
00078                 05 TOTAL-CREDIT-HOURS          PIC 99.
00079                 05 TOTAL-GRADE-POINTS          PIC 99.
00080                 05 GRADE-POINTS                PIC 99.
```

Fig. 11.13: *Continued.*

```
    3         GRADES          2.28.15      OCT  7.1978

00082         PROCEDURE DIVISION.

00084             HOUSEKEEPING-PARAGRAPH.

00086                 OPEN INPUT  STUDENT-COURSE-GRADE-FILE.
00087                 OPEN OUTPUT STUDENT-GRADE-REPORT.
00088                 OPEN OUTPUT GRADES-EXCEPTION-FILE.
00089                 READ STUDENT-COURSE-GRADE-FILE
00090                     AT END DISPLAY 'NO INPUT DATA' UPON CONSOLE
00091                         PERFORM END-OF-JOB-ROUTINE.
00092                 PERFORM INITIALIZATION-AND-HEADER THRU END-INITIALIZATION.
00093                 PERFORM SAME-STUDENT-ROUTINE THRU END-SAME-STUDENT.

00095             TOP-OF-MAINLINE.

00097                 READ STUDENT-COURSE-GRADE-FILE
00098                     AT END PERFORM GPA-COMPUTATION-ROUTINE
00099                            THRU END-GPA-COMPUTATION
00100                         PERFORM END-OF-JOB-ROUTINE.

00102                 IF I-STUDENT-NUMBER IS EQUAL TO PRIOR-STUDENT-ID
00103                 THEN
00104                     PERFORM SAME-STUDENT-ROUTINE THRU END-SAME-STUDENT
00105                 ELSE
00106                     IF I-STUDENT-NUMBER IS GREATER THAN PRIOR-STUDENT-ID
00107                     THEN
00108                         PERFORM GPA-COMPUTATION-ROUTINE
00109                            THRU END-GPA-COMPUTATION
00110                         PERFORM INITIALIZATION-AND-HEADER
00111                            THRU END-INITIALIZATION
00112                         PERFORM SAME-STUDENT-ROUTINE THRU END-SAME-STUDENT
00113                     ELSE
00114                         PERFORM EXCEPTION-ROUTINE THRU END-EXCEPTION.
00115                 GO TO TOP-OF-MAINLINE.

00117             END-OF-JOB-ROUTINE.

00119                 CLOSE STUDENT-COURSE-GRADE-FILE.
00120                 CLOSE STUDENT-GRADE-REPORT.
00121                 CLOSE GRADES-EXCEPTION-FILE.
00122                 STOP RUN.
```

Fig. 11.13: *Continued.*

```
    4         GRADES          2.28.15       OCT  7,1978

00124              SAME-STUDENT-ROUTINE.

00126                  IF I-CREDIT-HOURS IS NOT NUMERIC
00127                  THEN
00128                      PERFORM EXCEPTION-ROUTINE THRU END-EXCEPTION
00129                      GO TO END-SAME-STUDENT
00130                  ELSE
00131                      NEXT SENTENCE.

00133                  IF I-GRADE-EARNED IS EQUAL TO 'A'
00134                  THEN
00135                      MULTIPLY I-CREDIT-HOURS BY 4 GIVING GRADE-POINTS
00136                  ELSE
00137                      IF I-GRADE-EARNED IS EQUAL TO 'B'
00138                      THEN
00139                          MULTIPLY I-CREDIT-HOURS BY 3 GIVING GRADE-POINTS
00140                      ELSE
00141                          IF I-GRADE-EARNED IS EQUAL TO 'C'
00142                          THEN
00143                              MULTIPLY I-CREDIT-HOURS BY 2 GIVING GRADE-POINTS
00144                          ELSE
00145                              IF I-GRADE-EARNED IS EQUAL TO 'D'
00146                              THEN
00147                                  MULTIPLY I-CREDIT-HOURS BY 1
00148                                      GIVING GRADE-POINTS
00149                              ELSE
00150                                  IF I-GRADE-EARNED IS EQUAL TO 'F'
00151                                  THEN
00152                                      MOVE ZERO TO GRADE-POINTS
00153                                  ELSE
00154                                      MOVE '*' TO NONSTANDARD-GRADE-FLAG
00155                                      GO TO SET-UP-DETAIL-LINE.

00157                  ADD  GRADE-POINTS   TO TOTAL-GRADE-POINTS.
00158                  ADD  I-CREDIT-HOURS TO TOTAL-CREDIT-HOURS.
00159                  MOVE GRADE-POINTS   TO O-GRADE-POINTS.

00161              SET-UP-DETAIL-LINE.

00163                  MOVE I-COURSE-CODE  TO O-COURSE-CODE.
00164                  MOVE I-CREDIT-HOURS TO O-CREDIT-HOURS.
00165                  MOVE I-GRADE-EARNED TO O-GRADE-EARNED.
00166                  WRITE REPORT-DETAIL-LINE AFTER ADVANCING 1 LINES.

00168              END-SAME-STUDENT.

00170                  EXIT.
```

Fig. 11.13: *Continued.*

```
   5        GRADES         2.28.15       OCT 7,1978

00172              INITIALIZATION-AND-HEADER.
00174                  MOVE ZEROS    TO TOTAL-CREDIT-HOURS.
00175                  MOVE ZEROS    TO TOTAL-GRADE-POINTS.
00176                  MOVE SPACES TO REPORT-HEADER-1.
00177                  MOVE 'FALL' TO C-TERM.
00178                  WRITE REPORT-HEADER-1 AFTER NEW-PAGE.
00180                  MOVE SPACES          TO REPORT-HEADER-2.
00181                  MOVE I-STUDENT-NAME   TO O-STUDENT-NAME.
00182                  MOVE I-STUDENT-NUMBER TO O-STUDENT-NUMBER.
00183                  WRITE REPORT-HEADER-2 AFTER ADVANCING 3 LINES
00185                  MOVE SPACES TO REPORT-DETAIL-LINE.
00186                  WRITE REPORT-DETAIL-LINE AFTER ADVANCING 5 LINES.
00187                  MOVE  I-STUDENT-NUMBER TO PRIOR-STUDENT-ID.
00188              END-INITIALIZATION.
00189                  EXIT.

00191              GPA-COMPUTATION-ROUTINE.
00193                  MOVE SPACES TO REPORT-SUMMARY-LINE.
00195                  IF TOTAL-CREDIT-HOURS IS EQUAL TO ZERO
00196                  THEN
00197                      MOVE ZERO TO S-GRADE-POINT-AVERAGE
00198                  ELSE
00199                      DIVIDE TOTAL-GRADE-POINTS BY TOTAL-CREDIT-HOURS
00200                          GIVING S-GRADE-POINT-AVERAGE.
00202                  MOVE TOTAL-CREDIT-HOURS TO S-TOTAL-CREDIT-HOURS
00203                  MOVE TOTAL-GRADE-POINTS TO S-TOTAL-GRADE-POINTS
00204                  WRITE REPORT-SUMMARY-LINE AFTER ADVANCING 6 LINES.
00206              END-GPA-COMPUTATION.
00208                  EXIT.

00210              EXCEPTION-ROUTINE.
00212                  MOVE  COURSE-GRADE-RECORD TO EXCEPTION-RECORD.
00213                  WRITE EXCEPTION-RECORD AFTER ADVANCING 2 LINES.
00215              END-EXCEPTION.
00217                  EXIT.
```

Fig. 11.13: *Continued.*

Controlling Printer Spacing on the Program Listing

Throughout this text, the idea of planning program modules small enough to fit on a single page of the output listing has been stressed as a valuable rule of thumb. Such planning, however, does little good if the printer is allowed to control its own destiny, printing the COBOL statements wherever it chooses. If the programmer is really to get full value from the documentation afforded by well-planned routines, he or she must have the ability to control the program listing.

Most versions of COBOL give the programmer this flexibility by providing a number of source listing format control statements. Under IBM's version, for example, an **EJECT** statement causes the printer to advance to the top of a new page, while SKIP1, SKIP2, and SKIP3 tell the printer to skip 1, 2, or 3 extra lines before printing the next line. These format control statements may be written anywhere within area B of the coding form (positions 12 through 72). By placing EJECT statements after the end of each division and each major program subdivision, the programmer can cause such things as the IDENTIFICATION and ENVIRONMENT DIVISIONs, the DATA DIVISION FILE SECTION, the WORKING-STORAGE SECTION, the HOUSEKEEPING paragraph, the program mainline, and each of the computational routines to be printed on a separate page. Within a module, the **SKIPn** statement can be used to provide extra spacing, highlighting key portions of the code. Your version of COBOL may not use EJECT and SKIPn, but a close examination of the reference manual should turn up statements that perform a similar function. Note: use no punctuation (period, etc.) with an EJECT or SKIPn statement.

SUMMARY

The sample problem solved in this chapter involved computing a grade point average for a number of different students. The first step in the planning process, however, concentrated on defining the algorithm for a single student. The basic idea of header, detail, and summary lines was explained, and the computations needed to find an individual's grade point average were clearly defined at a human level.

Next, we turned our attention to the problem of handling similar computations for a large number of different individuals. Since first record and last record handling introduce complications, we decided to postpone these two stages of planning, concentrating instead on handling all those records between the two extremes. The basic logic of the program, given the assumption that the data records have been sorted into sequence by some key, is to perform "same key" logic as long as the key of the record currently being processed matches the key of the previously processed record, but to switch to "new key" logic as soon as a record with a different key is read; this change is known as a break point or a control break. The logic to be followed for the "same key" condition was defined, after which the "new key" logic was carefully structured. Next we turned our attention to first and last record processing.

Before actually coding the program, we discussed the problem of program design. The idea of a mainline containing the logic encountered by all (or almost all) input records with secondary routines housing the logic required only under certain conditions was presented as a general guideline. A few rules of thumb, including such ideas as the value of restricting a block of logic to no more than a single page of the program listing, the desirability of assigning each logically identifiable block of logic to its own routine, and the sometimes conflicting objective of keeping the number of different levels of routines to a reasonable minimum, were introduced. The problem of realistic error handling was also discussed.

Finally, having completely defined the program, we turned our attention to coding it. The REDEFINES clause was used to allow a field to be treated as either numeric or alphabetic, depending on circumstances. The DISPLAY statement was introduced as a mechanism for communicating with the operator or generating a "one time" error message. The compiler instructions for controlling printer spacing on the program listing, the EJECT and the SKIPn instructions, were introduced.

KEY WORDS

control break	**error handling**	**sequence checking**
detail line	**header line**	**SKIPn**
DISPLAY	**REDEFINES clause**	**summary line**
EJECT		

EXERCISES

1. Explain the difference between a header line, a detail line, and a summary line.

2. What is it that makes the first and last records in a file so unique? Why is special logic needed to handle these two records?

3. Explain the basic idea of using control break logic to generate a report such as the grade point average report of this chapter.

4. Several "rules of thumb" for designing a program were presented in the chapter—a few are listed below. Briefly explain what each rule means.

    a. The mainline should contain the logic common to the majority of program cycles.

    b. Each logically identifiable block of logic should be assigned to its own routine.

    c. Avoid designing a program with "too many" levels of routines; when reasonable, combine small routines.

    d. Ideally, all the logic in a given routine should fit on one page of a program listing.

A broader objective of good program design is to make the program as easy to read and to maintain as is possible. How do the rules of thumb expressed above contribute to this objective?

5. Imagine that registration has just been completed and that each student has filled out one card containing the following information for each course he or she wishes to take:

columns	contents
1-9	student identification number
10-25	student name
26-31	course identification code
32	section

Each student has from 1 to 7 different cards depending on the number of courses to be taken. Although the records associated with a given student will generally be grouped together, there is no particular sequence to the raw data.

Begin by sorting the records into course identification code sequence, ideally by using a sort utility program. Now generate a report listing students by course, producing a summary line indicating the number of students registering for the course at the bottom of each course roll. When a new course student list is started, it should begin on a new page.

6. Each week, our sales people submit an expense account. The data from these expense accounts is keypunched to cards containing the following fields:

columns	contents
1-8	salesperson number
9-12	district
13-18	lodging expenses (9999V99)
19-24	meals (9999V99), including business meals
25-30	transportation (9999V99)
31-35	other expenses (999V99)

Each quarter, a summary report is prepared showing, for each salesperson, the actual amounts claimed on each expense account and the total amounts claimed (for each expense category as well as the over all total) on all expense accounts for the entire quarter. Plan and write a program to generate this report.

7. It is not always necessary to print detail lines; in fact, they often get in the way of the manager who wishes to interpret a report. Modify the program written for exercise number 6, eliminating the printing of all detail lines. Instead, print only the summary line showing the quarter totals for each sales person.

8. Go back to the student registration data of problem 5. Use these same data cards to prepare a set of student schedules. Don't forget that the key to this program is the student identification number and not the course identification code.

9. Now combine the programs prepared for exercises 5 and 8 into a system of programs to (a.) sort the raw data into student order, (b.) prepare student schedules, (c.) sort the data into course sequence, (d.) produce lists of students by course.

10. Each week, customer sales orders are collected for processing. Each sale is reported on a card containing the following fields:

columns	contents
1-8	customer number
9-25	customer name
26-31	amount of purchase
32-39	salesperson number
40-43	sales district

    Sales are made on a daily basis, but the data is processed on a weekly basis, meaning that the data cannot be said to be in any particular order.

    Plan and code a program to produce a sales register by customer. Each customer's register should be printed on a separate page. At the top of the page, the customer should be identified by name and number. Each sale should be listed on a single detail line. At the bottom of the page, print a summary line showing the total amount of all purchases made by the customer.

11. Our company sells 5 different products. The identification code and selling price of each is shown below:

product code	selling price
A	$15.95
B	25.30
C	52.50

D	112.98
E	175.00

Following each sale, the sales person fills out a commission slip which eventually is keypunched to cards containing the following fields:

columns	contents
1-6	salesperson number
7	product code
8-10	quantity

You are to write a program to prepare a commission report. Input records must first be sorted into salesperson number sequence. As each card is read, use the product code to look up the selling price in a table; the product of the selling price and the quantity is the revenue produced by this sale. Accumulate all sales by salesperson. The amount of commission due is 10% of total sales.

The report should contain information for each salesperson on a separate page. Page headers should identify the salesperson by number; column headers should identify the produce code, the selling price of that product, the quantity sold on the order, and the revenue produced by that order. The summary line or lines should show totals for quantity and revenue, a count showing the number of sales made, and the computed commission due.

At the very end of the program, a count of total sales generated by all sales persons and an accumulation of total revenue for the period should be printed.

12. It has been called to our attention that there are a number of duplicate entries on our name and address file. Each record in the file contains the following fields:

positions	contents
1-20	name
21-40	street address
41-50	city
51-52	state
53-57	zip code

Start by sorting records into alphabetical order by name. Go through the entire file, copying from the old name and address file to a new one. Skip (do not copy to the new file) any entries with a duplicate name.

Ideally, this program should read an old master file from tape or disk and produce a new master file on a similar magnetic medium. Recognizing the fact that this may not be practical for student assignments, use card input and generate card or printer output. Be aware, however, that a tape-to-tape approach is most common for this program in a real-world environment.

12

A Double Control Break Problem

OVERVIEW

The problem covered in this chapter resembles the one in Chapter 11, except that two levels of summary lines, a minor summary and a major summary, are to be printed. The logic is just a bit more complicated. As before, we will develop a solution step by step, starting with a very general view of the problem and then introducing details one level at a time. Once again the input will be defined by an existing file; this time, however, we will be able to design our own output format.

THE BASIC PROBLEM: PREPARING CUSTOMER ACTIVITY REPORTS

Imagine that you are employed by a commercial bank. A major source of income for your bank is a national credit card system similar to Master Charge® or Visa®. Our customers, the member retail stores, have asked for a special report. Each store wants a list of all purchaes and credit transactions made in that store, summarized by customer. The retailers need this information to allow them to identify regular customers for advertising purposes. The stores are also concerned about the occasional credit abuser, and feel that a summarized list of actual sales and purchases by customer might help them to identify these individuals.

A rough outline of the desired report, prepared by the programming supervisor, is illustrated in Fig. 12.1. Your instructions are simple: Write a program to read the customer transactions and produce a report similar to the supervisor's sketch.

Fig. 12.1: *A sketch of the desired report format.*

```
                    CUSTOMER ACTIVITY REPORT
                  FOR RETAIL MERCHANT NO. 123456
```

CUSTOMER NUMBER	NAME	PURCHASES	CREDITS	NET
0001	SMITH	50.00		
0001	SMITH	100.00		
0001	SMITH		50.00	
CUSTOMER TOTAL		150.00	50.00	100.00
0002	JONES	75.00		
0002	JONES		35.00	
CUSTOMER TOTAL		75.00	35.00	40.00
STORE TOTAL		225.00	85.00	140.00

Any experienced programmer would immediately recognize this assignment as a special case of the control breaks problem introduced in Chapter 11; the only real difference is that two control breaks, one for customer and one for the store, are called for. Carefully note the format of the report. Headers are, of course, called for; it is very unusual to print a business report without them. Each detail line represents a single customer transaction. The first summary level is for the customer, meaning that when the customer number changes, a customer summary line is to be printed. Later, a different summary line will be printed for the store.

It is quite possible, in fact likely, that there will be many customer summary lines for each store. Typically, the report will begin with several detail lines followed by a customer summary line for the first customer. Next will come the detail lines and the summary line for the second customer. This pattern will be repeated until all the customer records for the store have been processed, after which a store summary line will be printed. Then the process will be repeated for the next store. The **major break** is the store; customer number is a **minor break**.

This hierarchy implies something: all transactions for a single store must be grouped together and, within a given store's records, sorted into customer order. In preparing to sort the input data for this application, the store number will be the **primary key** and the customer number the **secondary key**. Once the data has been placed in proper sequence, the logic of the report preparation program will concentrate on looking for changes in these two key fields, printing a customer summary line when a minor break occurs and then printing a store summary when a major break occurs.

The Input Data

Let's turn our attention to the input data. The initial source is the customer transaction card (or sales slip) prepared by the retail merchant at the time of a purchase. The bank collects the transaction cards at regular intervals, turning them over to the keypunch department for data preparation.

At a fixed time each month all the transactions are collected into a batch, and the bill preparation process begins. Since the bills are to be sent to the customers and not to the stores, the transactions are first sorted into customer number sequence.

The sketch of the bill preparation system of programs (Fig. 12.2) shows that our report preparation module is simply a spin-off. The real objective of the system is getting the bills out on time, but if we can take added advantage of the data and use it to prepare extra, useful reports, so much the better. One of the real advantages of automatic data processing is this ability to use the same data in a multitude of different applications.

At any rate, our program gets the data in customer number sequence; thus our first act will be to sort it into store number sequence, with a secondary sort based on the customer number. The format of the input data, given that it does exist and has been used by another program, must, of course, be known; we'll assume that the records contain the following fields:

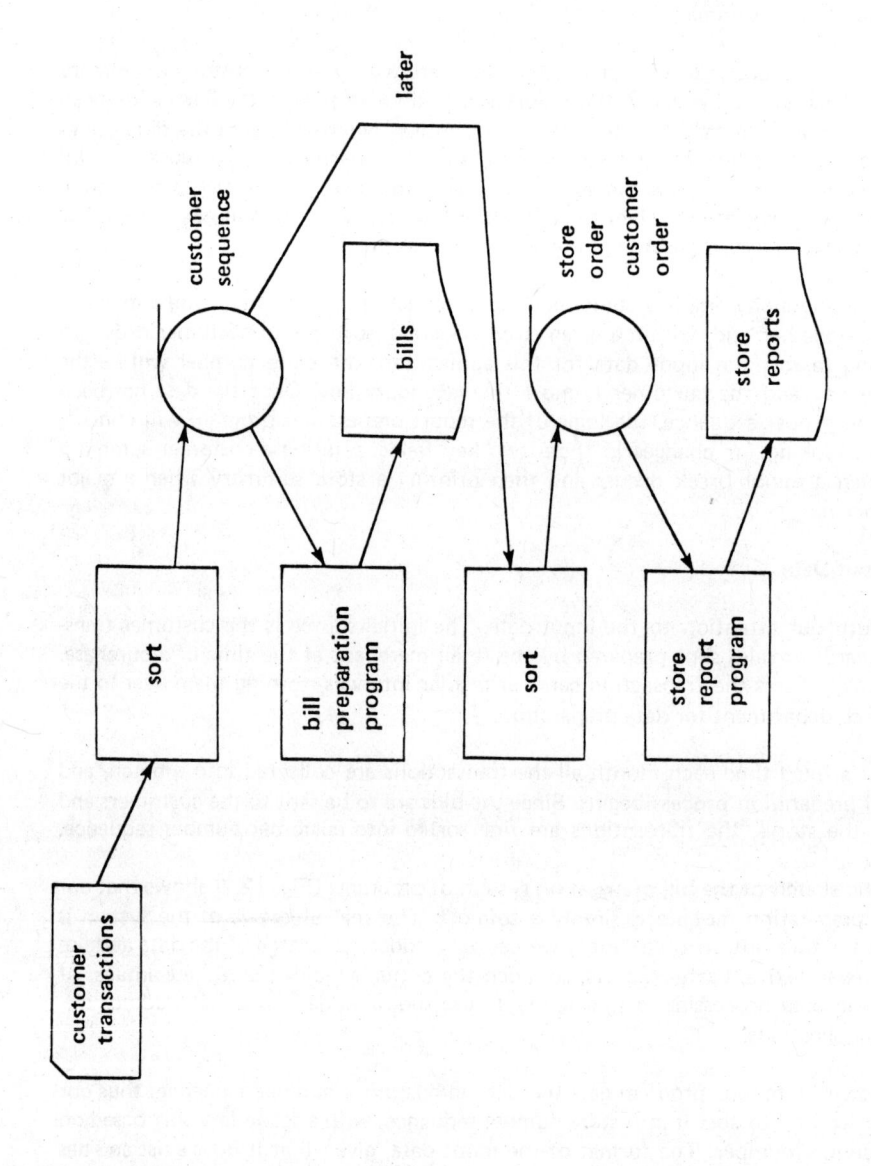

Fig. 12.2: *The System of Which the Report Program is Part.*

320.

positions	contents
1-8	customer account number
9-30	customer name
31-36	store identification number
37-42	amount of purchase or credit (9999V99)
43	transaction type: C=credit

For those who have access to an IBM computer using the standard sort/merge utility, a parameters card for this primary/secondary sort would be:

SORT FIELDS=(31,6,CH,A,1,8,CH,A)

Defining Output

While tightly constrained by existing data structures on input, we do have a somewhat free hand in defining the format of the output line. The programmer, at this stage, would almost certainly reach for a pad of print-chart paper and begin to lay out the various print lines needed by the program. Headers (Fig. 12.3) will grace the top of each page, with column headers identifying the contents of each column of data. A detail line is needed to hold each customer transaction. A summary line is needed to hold customer totals, and a different summary line will be used to hold store totals.

The headers (Fig. 12.3) are as they will appear on the report. In the detail line, customer number 12345678 has been written in to indicate clearly that this is an 8-character field. The customer name is identified as a string of 22 X's, the PICTURE clause that will eventually be used to identify the content of the field. Numeric amounts are shown in the form of a PICTURE clause too, complete with punctuation. The "NET BUSINESS" field, representing the difference between purchases and credits, is not relevant to an individual transaction, being used only in summary lines.

The customer name and number are not printed in the summary lines. PICTURE clauses are used to identify numeric fields. The single asterisk (*) to the right of the customer line and the double asterisk (**) to the right of the store summary line are included to make it easier to spot these summaries in a report.

DEFINING THE MAJOR LOGICAL FUNCTIONS

Since input and output records have been defined, we can now turn our attention to the necessary logical steps. This is not, however, the time to begin writing code. It is always wise to start with a broad, general view of the problem, define the major blocks of logic, and then fill in the details.

This application calls for reading a file in sequence and looking for breakpoints. As was the case in Chapter 11, the first and last records are different; thus we begin

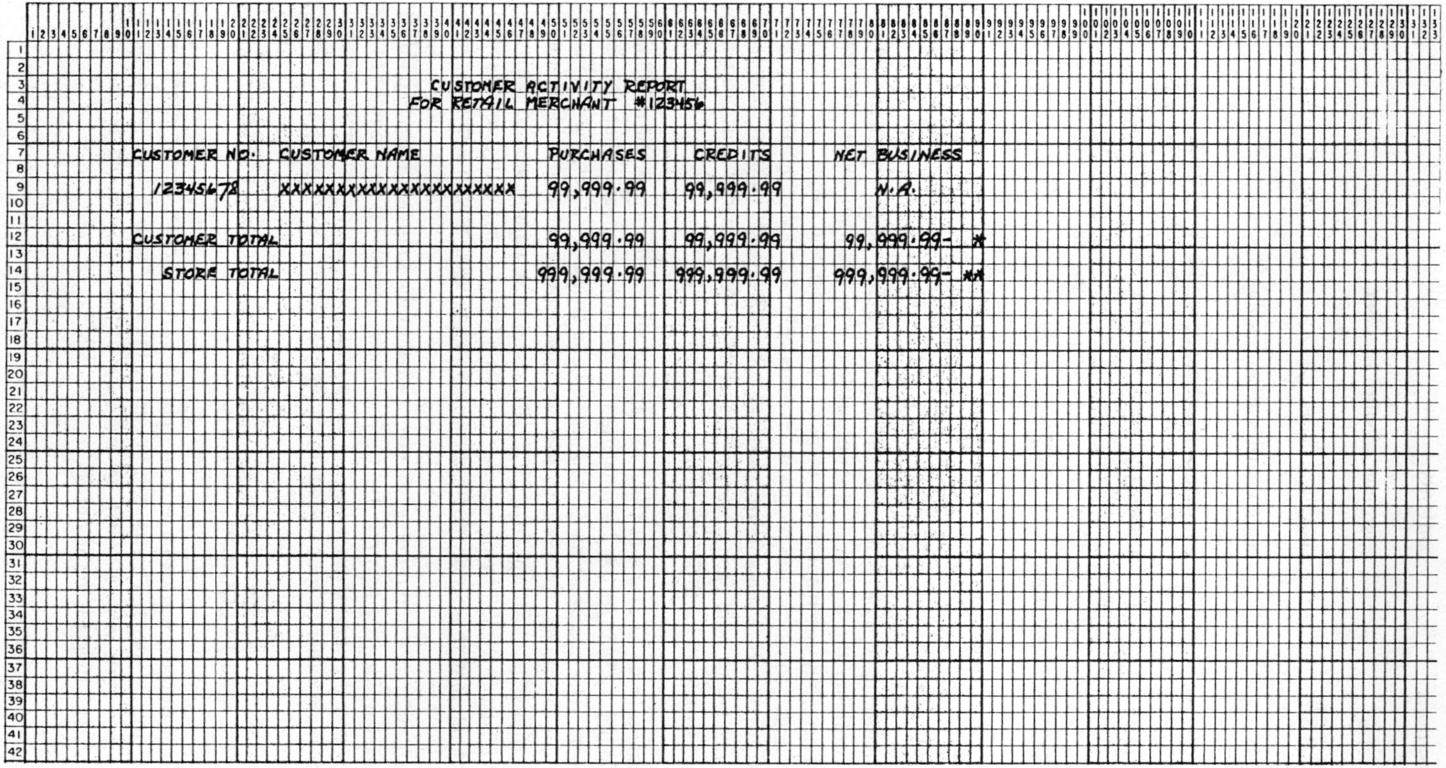

Fig. 12.3: A Layout of the Program Output Lines on Print Chart Paper.

Fig. 12.4: *A Rough Outline of Program Logic.*

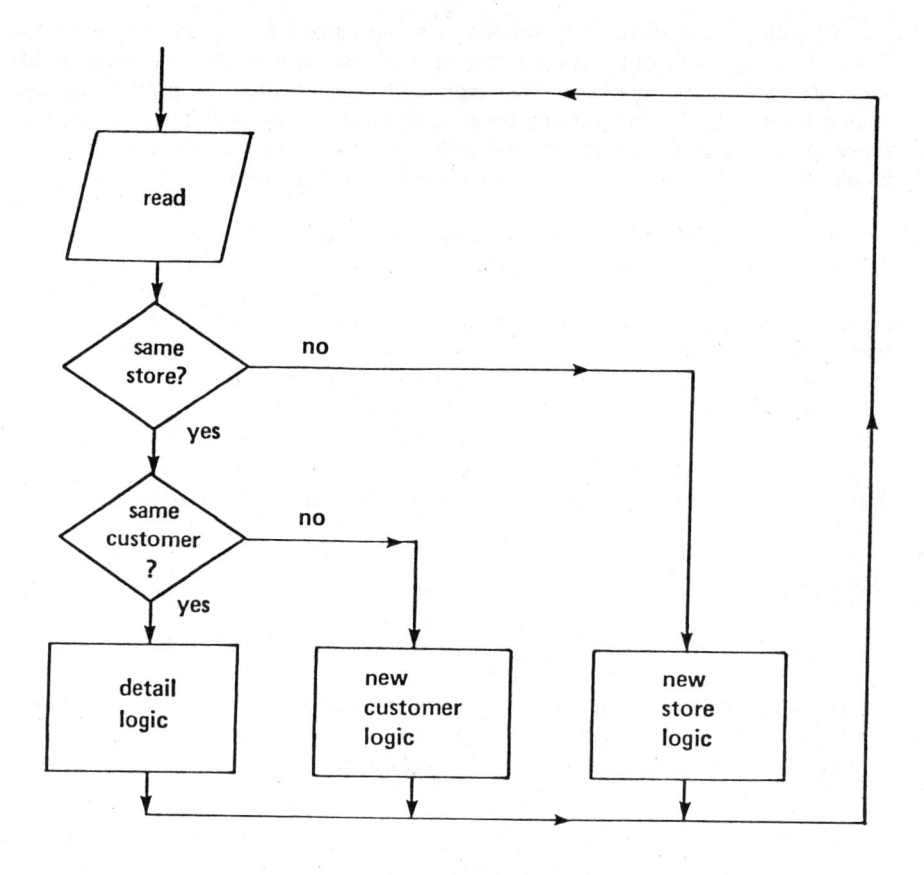

by assuming that the first record has already been read and that start-of-job activities have been completed, allowing us to concentrate on planning the program mainline.

Basically, three distinct operations must take place as this program executes. These three functions can be tied to the three types of output lines; detail, customer summary, and store summary. The main body of the program must distinguish among the conditions for printing these lines; thus, a rough outline of the program showing only a read instruction, the tests, and the logical positions of the detail block, the customer block, and the store block can be developed (Fig. 12.4).

Why (in Fig. 12.4) is the test for same store done first? The store is the primary key. A change in store represents a major break. The customer number is a secondary key or minor break point, and there may be several of them within each major break. Testing for a change in customer first could (and almost certainly would) lead to errors. For example, what if the store number were to change but the customer number were to remain the same? Is it possible that the last customer for store 0001 could also be the first customer for store 0002? It could happen. It isn't very likely, of course, but if anything can possibly go wrong, it will. The result of this unusual set of circumstances would be inclusion, on store 0001's report, of a detail line that really belongs on store 0002's report. Testing for the major control break first eliminates this risk.

Detail Logic

Let's expand these general logic blocks a bit and consider the major functions that must be performed within each. We'll start with the detail logic (Fig. 12.5). Obviously, a key part of the detail logic is to write a detail line. (The "write detail line" block includes the instructions needed to set up the line.) The other major function of detail time logic is to accumulate credits and purchases.

Fig. 12.5: *Detail logic.*

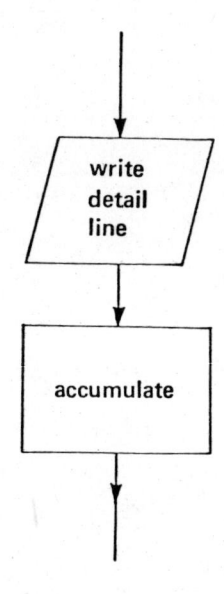

New Customer Logic

The first step in the new customer routine (Fig. 12.6) is to write a customer summary line. Next, customer accumulators must be reset.

Don't forget that this block of logic is reached only after a record with a different customer number is read. Following the write and reset steps, this record is still waiting to be processed; thus, the final step in the new customer logic block is to process the waiting record through the detail logic.

New Store Logic

When the store number changes, the new store logic is implemented. The first major step in this block is to prepare and print a *customer* summary line. Why not start with the store summary? A change in store implies a change in customer, from the last customer for store 0001 to the first customer for store 0002. All customer summaries are to come before the store summary within a given store's report. Thus, the new customer logic comes first (Fig. 12.7). The customer summary line is printed; customer accumulators are reset; the store summary line is printed; store accumulators are reset, and the detail record is written and accumulated. A store change implies a customer change. Also, remember that a new detail record is waiting to be processed.

A change in the store number requires that a new set of headers be printed; after all, the report is designed to be separated and sent to the various stores, and the easiest way to separate a report is to start each major piece on the top of a new page.

Fig. 12.6: *New customer logic.*

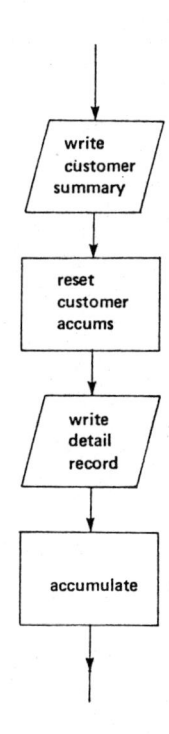

Fig. 12.7: *New Store Logic.*

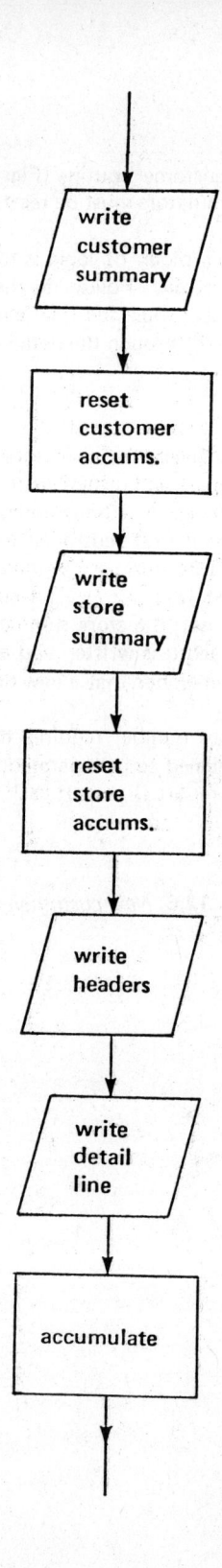

Where should the writing of headers be done? If you consider the meaning of each of the output lines, the answer is obvious. The store summary line is the last line on one part of the report. The detail record waiting to be processed belongs to the next store. Thus, the headers must be printed between the printing of the store summary and the detail line (Fig. 12.7).

Printing Headers When the Store Number Does Not Change

In the grade point average problem of Chapter 11, we didn't have to worry about printing headers except when the student number changed; in most schools, students are restricted in the number of courses they can take at one time, and the grade report form is planned so as to hold the maximum number of courses. There are no such limits on the report being generated by the program of this chapter. It is quite possible that a given store will have several pages of output; thus, provision must be made for printing headers within the primary flow of the program.

Perhaps the easiest way to control printing of headers is to set up a line counter and keep track of the number of lines actually printed on a page. When this counter reaches a critical level, 50 lines, for example, headers are printed and the counter is reset. The value 1 can be added to this counter as part of each of the output routines.

What if the fiftieth line on a page is a customer summary line? Ideally, both summary lines should be printed on the same page. Unless the programmer has selected a line limit which totally fills the page, this is no problem—the store summary can simply be printed without regard for page controls. Typically, the programmer will leave a few lines at the bottom of the page as a margin, choosing, for example, 50 as a critical line count when 55 would really fit. This safety margin allows for unusual conditions.

The Program Mainline

We can now put the pieces together to form a reasonable approximation of the program mainline (Fig. 12.8). Note that page controls have been added. Except for the first and last records, the plan is essentially complete.

First Record Processing

The first record is different simply because there is no prior record to supply a value for the old customer number or the old store number? How should this first record be processed? First, of course, it must be read. Next, both the customer and the store accumulators can be initialized, and the customer number and store number from the first record can be moved to the "prior" fields. A set of headers can be printed. Finally, this first record can be handled as the detail record that it is (Fig. 12.9). Following these first record steps, the program can enter the mainline.

Last Record Processing

When the last record is encountered, it means that there are no more transactions to be processed. We cannot, however, simply terminate the program, as totals for the very last store must have been in the process of being accumulated when the

Fig. 12.8: *The Program Mainline.*

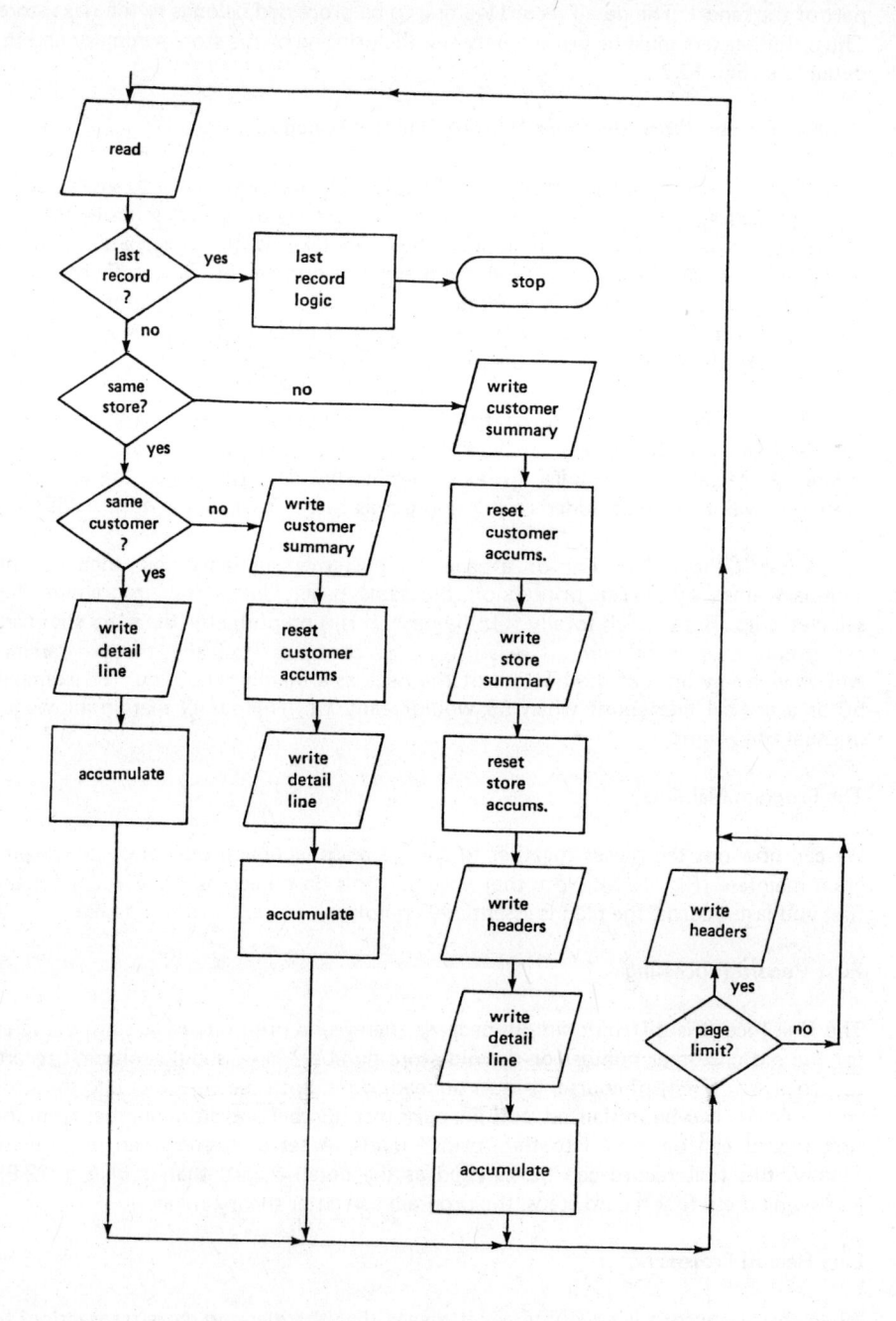

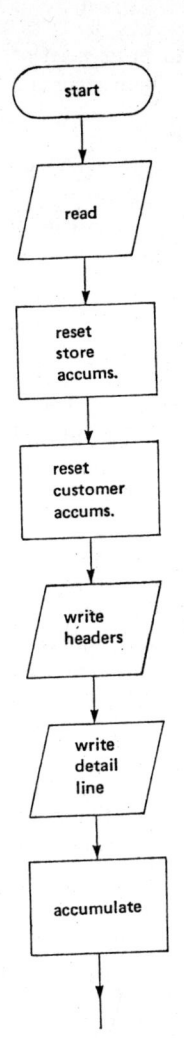

Fig. 12.9: *First record processing.*

Fig. 12.10: *Last record processing.*

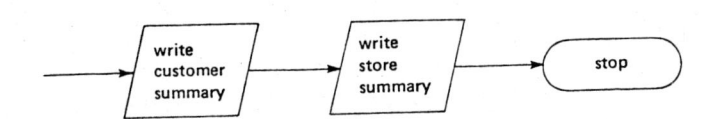

end-of-file marker was read. Thus, the last act of the program is to print a set of customer and store summary lines and then to end the program. These steps are summarized in Fig. 12.10.

Note that there is no need to reset accumulators—there is nothing else to be accumulated. Also, there is no need to print the next detail line, as there is no next detail line. The last record logic is similar to the mainline's new store logic, but there are differences. The last record is unique.

Putting the Pieces Together

Having defined each of the major blocks of logic, we can now put the pieces together and develop a single, key-function flowchart for the entire program (Fig. 12.11). A close review of this flowchart might reveal areas of common logic, allowing some of these basic blocks to be combined. Our objective is to define the mainline and secondary computational routines of the final program.

The steps of writing a detail line and then accumulating always appear together; thus these two steps can be combined. Looking just at the mainline, it might be tempting to combine the steps that write the customer summary line and reset the customer accumulator; a similar argument could be made for the store summary logic. In the start-of-job logic, however, the functions of resetting accumulators are performed without the write operations and, in the end-of-job routine, writing is done without resetting.

There is a way to treat these functions as a single entity and yet retain the ability to refer to specific subfunctions when conditions demand. Basically, the secondary routines can be divided into paragraphs, each containing one of the two major pieces of logic. Later, by using a PERFORM statement without the THRU option, the program can be told to execute only selected paragraphs rather than the entire routine; thus they can be combined.

Note that the flowchart of Fig. 12.11 does not attempt to show every instruction in the program. Instead, it is designed to show key functions, and each function might well represent more than one instruction. This is a planning flowchart. The objective is to show enough detail to define the flow of logic through the program, but not so much that the general flow is hidden. There are no national standards for drawing such flowcharts. The only real test is: does it make sense?

We can now turn our attention to completing our plan at a detailed level and coding the solution in COBOL. As before, we may or may not flowchart the individulal routines, depending on the complexity of the logic.

THE DATA DIVISION

The IDENTIFICATION and ENVIRONMENT DIVISIONs for this program are much like those of earlier programs; thus we will move on to the DATA DIVISION. The first two divisions can be seen in the program listings.

Fig. 12.11: *The Entire Program.*

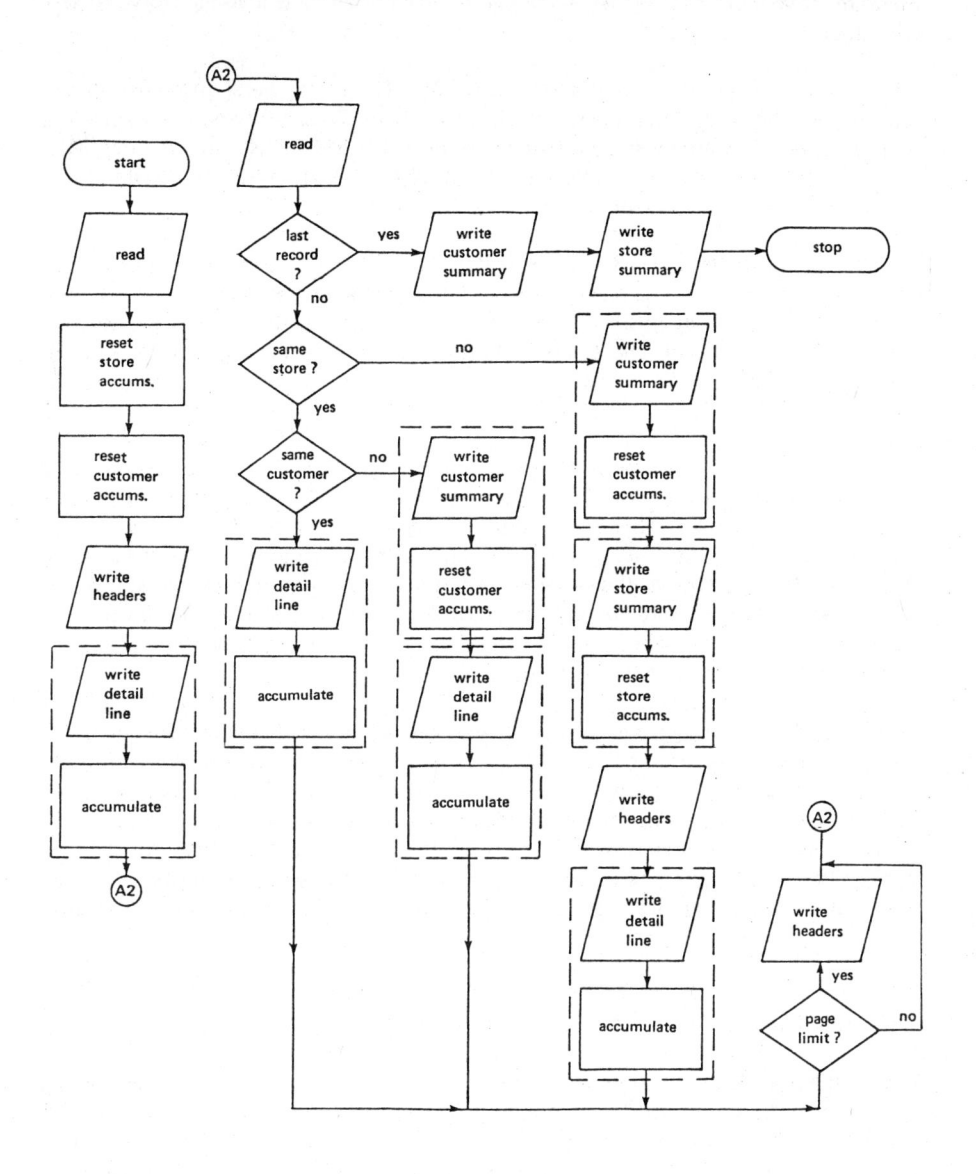

As you may recall, the input file for the program was defined by an earlier program. Given the file format, coding this first FD entry is a straightforward task (Fig. 12.12).

The output file will be written to the printer. There are several different types of output lines: headers, detail lines, and summary lines. To simplify coding the various output formats, a dummy line is defined in the FILE SECTION, with the details of each line shifted to the WORKING-STORAGE SECTION. The WRITE FROM option will be used throughout the program.

In the WORKING-STORAGE SECTION, a number of work fields must also be defined. Accumulators are needed to hold the customer and store totals for purchases, credits, and net business. They are also defined in the output line, but the output fields contain edit characters. Additional fields hold the value of the previous customer number and the previous store number. A line counter is needed to support the logic that controls the printing of headers.

One new feature has been added to the PICTURE clauses of the output summary lines, a negative sign. The field called "net business" is computed by subtracting credits from purchases. This value could be negative—credits could outweigh purchases for any given customer in any given month. If the value is negative, a sign must be printed. By convention, the negative sign, if required, is printed to the right of the affected field. If you were to look at a column of figures, nicely lined up or **right justified**, any negative signs present would "stick out like a sore thumb", which explains the reason for this standard convention.

In COBOL, the negative sign is an edit character just like the comma or the decimal point. It is coded to the right of the PICTURE clause, usually as the last character. If, during program execution, the actual value of the field happens to be negative, the sign will print; otherwise, no sign is printed. As an alternative to using a negative sign, the programmer can use the letters CR for credit or DB for debit in this rightmost positions; the result is the same, with the selected letters being printed only if the value is negative. Again, the idea is to clearly identify the unusual negative result.

THE PROCEDURE DIVISION—THE MAINLINE

The program, as is usual, begins with a housekeeping paragraph in which the files are opened. Moving on to the start-of-job logic (as defined in the flowchart of Fig. 12.11), a record is read and the routines to reset customer accumulators, reset store accumulators, read a customer transaction, write a set of headers, and write a detail line are all either executed or performed. Note that we have used a simple PERFORM statement with no THRU option—only part of the routine is needed (see Fig. 12.13).

The mainline consists of a READ statement followed by a series of IF statements designed to identify the condition to be handled. Once the condition is defined, the proper secondary routine can be performed. Within the main body of the program, the entire detailed logic routine must be performed; thus the mainline PERFORM statements all use the THRU option. At end-of-file, the customer and

COBOL Coding Form

SYSTEM: CREDIT CARD
PROGRAM: CUSTOMER ACTIVITY
PROGRAMMER: DAVIS & FISHER   DATE: 3-15-79
PUNCHING INSTRUCTIONS — GRAPHIC: ∅   PUNCH: ZERO
PAGE 2 OF 11

```
DATA DIVISION.

FILE SECTION.

FD  CUSTOMER-TRANSACTION-FILE
    BLOCK CONTAINS 10 RECORDS
    LABEL RECORDS ARE STANDARD.
01  CUSTOMER-TRANSACTION.
    05  I-CUSTOMER-NO            PIC 9(8).
    05  I-CUSTOMER-NAME          PIC X(22).
    05  I-STORE-NO               PIC 9(6).
    05  I-AMOUNT                 PIC 9999V99.
    05  I-TRANSACTION-TYPE       PIC X.
    05  FILLER                   PIC X(37).

FD  CUSTOMER-ACTIVITY-REPORT
    LABEL RECORDS ARE OMITTED.
01  REPORT-LINE                  PIC X(133).
```

Fig. 12.12: *The DATA DIVISION.*

COBOL Coding Form

SYSTEM: CREDIT CARD
PROGRAM: CUSTOMER ACTIVITY
PROGRAMMER: DAVIS & FISHER
DATE: 3-15-79
PUNCH: ZERO
PAGE 3 OF 11

```
WORKING-STORAGE SECTION.
01  REPORT-HEADER-1.
    05  FILLER              PIC X(39)  VALUE SPACES.
    05  HEADER-1            PIC X(24)  VALUE 'CUSTOMER ACTIVITY REPORT'.
    05  FILLER              PIC X(70)  VALUE SPACES.
01  REPORT-HEADER-2.
    05  FILLER              PIC X(37)  VALUE SPACES.
    05  HEADER-2            PIC X(22)  VALUE 'FOR RETAIL MERCHANT #'.
    05  O-STORE-NO          PIC 9(6).
    05  FILLER              PIC X(68)  VALUE SPACES.
01  COLUMN-HEADER.
    05  FILLER              PIC X(11)  VALUE SPACES.
    05  FILLER              PIC X(14)  VALUE 'CUSTOMER NO.'.
    05  FILLER              PIC X(25)  VALUE 'CUSTOMER NAME'.
    05  FILLER              PIC X(27)  VALUE 'PURCHASES          CREDITS'.
    05  FILLER              PIC X(56)  VALUE 'NET BUSINESS'.
```

Fig. 12.12: *Continued.*

COBOL Coding Form

SYSTEM	CREDIT CARD	PUNCHING INSTRUCTIONS: GRAPHIC Ø / PUNCH ZERO	PAGE 4 OF 11
PROGRAM	CUSTOMER ACTIVITY		CARD FORM #
PROGRAMMER	DAVIS & FISHER	DATE 3-15-79	

```
       01  CUSTOMER-DETAIL.
           05  FILLER                  PIC X(13)      VALUE SPACES.
           05  O-CUSTOMER-NO           PIC 9(8).
           05  FILLER                  PIC X(4)       VALUE SPACES.
           05  O-CUSTOMER-NAME         PIC X(22).
           05  FILLER                  PIC X(3)       VALUE SPACES.
           05  O-PURCHASES             PIC ZZ,ZZ9.99.
           05  FILLER                  PIC X(4)       VALUE SPACES.
           05  O-CREDITS               PIC ZZ,ZZ9.99.
           05  FILLER                  PIC X(61)      VALUE SPACES.

       01  CUSTOMER-SUMMARY.
           05  FILLER                  PIC X(13)      VALUE SPACES.
           05  C-LINE-TITLE            PIC X(14)
                                       VALUE 'CUSTOMER TOTAL'.
           05  FILLER                  PIC X(23)      VALUE SPACES.
           05  C-PURCHASES-SUM         PIC ZZ,ZZZ.99.
           05  FILLER                  PIC X(4)       VALUE SPACES.
           05  C-CREDITS-SUM           PIC ZZ,ZZZ.99.
           05  FILLER                  PIC X(6)       VALUE SPACES.
           05  C-NET-BUSINESS          PIC ZZ,ZZ9.99-.
           05  FILLER                  PIC XX         VALUE SPACES.
           05  C-ASTERISK              PIC X          VALUE '*'.
           05  FILLER                  PIC X(42)      VALUE SPACES.
```

Fig. 12.12: *Continued.*

COBOL Coding Form

SYSTEM	CREDIT CARD	PUNCHING INSTRUCTIONS: GRAPHIC Ø, PUNCH ZERO	PAGE 5 OF 11
PROGRAM	CUSTOMER ACTIVITY		CARD FORM #
PROGRAMMER	DAVIS & FISHER	DATE 3-15-79	

```
       Ø1  STORE-SUMMARY.
           Ø5  FILLER                  PIC X(16)        VALUE SPACES.
           Ø5  S-LINE-TITLE            PIC X(11)        VALUE 'STORE TOTAL'.
           Ø5  FILLER                  PIC X(22)        VALUE SPACES.
           Ø5  S-PURCHASES-SUM         PIC ZZZ,ZZ9.99.
           Ø5  FILLER                  PIC X(3)         VALUE SPACES.
           Ø5  S-CREDITS-SUM           PIC ZZZ,ZZ9.99.
           Ø5  FILLER                  PIC X(5)         VALUE SPACES.
           Ø5  S-NET-BUSINESS          PIC ZZZ,ZZ9.99-.
           Ø5  FILLER                  PIC X            VALUE SPACES.
           Ø5  S-ASTERISK              PIC XX           VALUE '**'.
           Ø5  FILLER                  PIC X(42)        VALUE SPACES.

       Ø1  PRIOR-CUSTOMER-NO           PIC 9(8).
       Ø1  PRIOR-STORE-NO              PIC 9(6).
       Ø1  LINE-COUNT                  PIC 99.

       Ø1  ACCUMULATORS.
           Ø5  CUSTOMER-PURCHASES      PIC 99999V99.
           Ø5  CUSTOMER-CREDITS        PIC 99999V99.
           Ø5  STORE-PURCHASES         PIC 999999V99.
           Ø5  STORE-CREDITS           PIC 999999V99.
           Ø5  CUSTOMER-NET-BUSINESS   PIC S999999V99.
           Ø5  STORE-NET-BUSINESS      PIC S999999V99.
```

Fig. 12.12: *Concluded.*

store summary routines must be executed; once again (Fig. 12.13, the program listing), the simple form of the PERFORM is called for.

Near the bottom of the mainline is an IF test that checks the line counter to see if page headers should be printed. The line counter is incremented within the routines that print a line of output.

The Detailed Logic Modules

The detailed logic modules are basically simple; one required flowcharting. The real planning has already been done, and we are now at that rather nebulous boundary separating planning from implementation. On such straightforward routines, the best way to plan a solution is often to code it in COBOL; the results can be seen in the program listing of Fig. 12.13. A caution: Combining planning and coding is only reasonable when prior planning has brought us to such a well defined point.

Let's start with the single paragraph routines. Headers are written under control of the routine named HEADER-ROUTINE. One of the first steps in this routine is to MOVE the store number from the "just read" input record into the header, which is why the read instruction must preceed the HEADER-ROUTINE. After the headers have been written, the line counter must be reset to zero.

The DETAIL-ROUTINE handles detail records. The key to this routine is a test for the transaction type—the letter C in position 43 designates a credit transaction. Depending on the value of this field, the amount from the input record is moved to either the purchases or credits field, the other field is blanked, and the amount is added to the appropriate accumulator. Note the test for a NUMERIC field; this is the only place where bad data can be introduced. Following the logical test, a line is written and the value 1 is added to the line counter; this counter is the same one that was tested in the program mainline.

The other two secondary routines handle customer control breaks and store control breaks. Both (Fig. 12.13) follow much the same pattern; let's concentrate on the routine called CUSTOMER-SUMMARY-ROUTINE. Note that the routine has been divided into three paragraphs containing, respectively, the instructions needed to set up and print a summary line, the instructions to reset the accumulator and the PRIOR-CUSTOMER-NUMBER field, and an EXIT statement. In the start-of-job routine, only the second paragraph is PERFORMed. In the end-of-job routine, only the first paragraph is PERFORMed. The program mainline, however, refers to the entire three-paragraph routine.

The paragraph concerned with setting up and printing the summary line simply moves the accumulators from WORKING-STORAGE into the output line and then issues a WRITE FROM statement. The paragraph which resets accumulators also moves the customer number (or store number) into the PRIOR-CUSTOMER-NUMBER field. The STORE-SUMMARY-ROUTINE is a direct parallel.

Basically, that's about it. The COBOL statements needed to implement this relatively complex program are no more difficult than those used to implement the average program of Chapters 1 through 4. The mistake most beginning programmers

```
     1                          1.58.30       OCT  7,1978
00001           IDENTIFICATION DIVISION.
00003              PROGRAM-ID.  CUSACT.
00004              AUTHOR.      DAVIS & FISHER.
00006              REMARKS.     THIS PROGRAM PROVIDES A CUSTOMER
00007                           ACTIVITY REPORT FOR EACH STORE IN
00008                           THE CREDIT CARD SYSTEM.

00011           ENVIRONMENT DIVISION.
00013              CONFIGURATION SECTION.
00015                 SOURCE-COMPUTER.   IBM-370-148.
00016                 OBJECT-COMPUTER.   IBM-370-148.
00017                 SPECIAL-NAMES.     C01 IS NEW-PAGE.
00019              INPUT-OUTPUT SECTION.
00021                 FILE-CONTROL.
00022                    SELECT CUSTOMER-TRANSACTION-FILE  ASSIGN TO UT-S-CUSTRANS.
00023                    SELECT CUSTOMER-ACTIVITY-REPORT   ASSIGN TO UT-S-CUSREPT.
```

Fig. 12.13: *A listing of the customer account program.*

```
    2         CUSACT          1.58.30        OCT  7,1978

00025          DATA DIVISION.
00027          FILE SECTION.
00029          FD CUSTOMER-TRANSACTION-FILE
00030             BLOCK CONTAINS 10 RECORDS
00031             LABEL RECORDS ARE STANDARD.
00032          01 CUSTOMER-TRANSACTION.
00033             05   I-CUSTOMER-NO           PIC 9(8).
00034             05   I-CUSTOMER-NAME         PIC X(22).
00035             05   I-STORE-NO              PIC 9(6).
00036             05   I-AMOUNT                PIC 9999V99.
00037             05   I-TRANSACTION-TYPE      PIC X.
00038             05   FILLER                  PIC X(37).

00040          FD CUSTOMER-ACTIVITY-REPORT
00041             LABEL RECORDS ARE OMITTED.
00042          01 REPORT-LINE                  PIC X(133).
```

Fig. 12.13: *Continued.*

```
     3         CUSACT           1.58.30      OCT 7,1978


00045               WORKING-STORAGE SECTION.
00047               01 REPORT-HEADER-1.
00048                  05   FILLER               PIC X(39)   VALUE SPACES.
00049                  05   HEADER-1             PIC X(24)
00050                                            VALUE 'CUSTOMER ACTIVITY REPORT'.
00051                  05   FILLER               PIC X(70)   VALUE SPACES.

00053               01 REPORT-HEADER-2.
00054                  05   FILLER               PIC X(37)   VALUE SPACES.
00055                  05   HEADER-2             PIC X(22)
00056                                            VALUE 'FOR RETAIL MERCHANT #'.
00057                  05   O-STORE-NO           PIC 9(6).
00058                  05   FILLER               PIC X(68)   VALUE SPACES.

00060               01 COLUMN-HEADER.
00061                  05   FILLER               PIC X(11)   VALUE SPACES.
00062                  05   FILLER               PIC X(14)
00063                                            VALUE 'CUSTOMER NO.'.
00064                  05   FILLER               PIC X(25)
00065                                            VALUE 'CUSTOMER NAME'.
00066                  05   FILLER               PIC X(27)
00067                                            VALUE 'PURCHASES       CREDITS'.
00068                  05   FILLER               PIC X(56)
00069                                            VALUE 'NET BUSINESS'.

00071               01 CUSTOMER-DETAIL.
00072                  05   FILLER               PIC X(13)   VALUE SPACES.
00073                  05   O-CUSTOMER-NO        PIC 9(8).
00074                  05   FILLER               PIC X(4)    VALUE SPACES.
00075                  05   O-CUSTOMER-NAME      PIC X(22).
00076                  05   FILLER               PIC X(3)    VALUE SPACES.
00077                  05   O-PURCHASES          PIC ZZ,ZZ9.99.
00078                  05   FILLER               PIC X(4)    VALUE SPACES.
00079                  05   O-CREDITS            PIC ZZ,ZZ9.99.
00080                  05   FILLER,              PIC X(61)   VALUE SPACES.
```

Fig. 12.13: *Continued.*

```
     4       CUSACT        1.58.30        OCT  7,1978


00084           01  CUSTOMER-SUMMARY.
00085               05  FILLER                    PIC X(13)    VALUE SPACES.
00086               05  C-LINE-TITLE              PIC X(14)
00087                                             VALUE 'CUSTOMER TOTAL'.
00088               05  FILLER                    PIC X(23)    VALUE SPACES.
00089               05  C-PURCHASES-SUM           PIC ZZ,ZZ9.99.
00090               05  FILLER                    PIC X(4)     VALUE SPACES.
00091               05  C-CREDITS-SUM             PIC ZZ,ZZ9.99.
00092               05  FILLER                    PIC X(6)     VALUE SPACES.
00093               05  C-NET-BUSINESS            PIC ZZ,ZZ9.99-.
00094               05  FILLER                    PIC XX       VALUE '*'.
00095               05  C-ASTERISK                PIC X        VALUE '*'.
00096               05  FILLER                    PIC X(42)    VALUE SPACES.

00098           01  STORE-SUMMARY.
00099               05  FILLER                    PIC X(16)    VALUE SPACES.
00100               05  S-LINE-TITLE              PIC X(11)    VALUE 'STORE TOTAL'.
00101               05  FILLER                    PIC X(22)    VALUE SPACES.
00102               05  S-PURCHASES-SUM           PIC ZZZ,ZZ9.99.
00103               05  FILLER                    PIC X(3)     VALUE SPACES.
00104               05  S-CREDITS-SUM             PIC ZZZ,ZZ9.99.
00105               05  FILLER                    PIC X(5)     VALUE SPACES.
00106               05  S-NET-BUSINESS            PIC ZZZ,ZZ9.99-.
00107               05  FILLER                    PIC X        VALUE SPACES.
00108               05  S-ASTERISK                PIC XX       VALUE '**'.
00109               05  FILLER                    PIC X(42)    VALUE SPACES.

00111           01  PRIOR-CUSTOMER-NO             PIC 9(8).
00112           01  PRIOR-STORE-NO                PIC 9(6).
00113           01  LINE-COUNT                    PIC 99.

00115           01  ACCUMULATORS.
00116               05  CUSTOMER-PURCHASES        PIC 99999V99.
00117               05  CUSTOMER-CREDITS          PIC 99999V99.
00118               05  STORE-PURCHASES           PIC 999999V99.
00119               05  STORE-CREDITS             PIC 999999V99.
00120               05  CUSTOMER-NET-BUSINESS     PIC S999999V99.
00121               05  STORE-NET-BUSINESS        PIC S999999V99.
```

Fig. 12.13: *Continued.*

```
     5         CUSACT          1.58.30        OCT  7,1978

00123          PROCEDURE DIVISION.

00125              HOUSEKEEPING.

00127                  OPEN INPUT   CUSTOMER-TRANSACTION-FILE.
00128                  OPEN OUTPUT  CUSTOMER-ACTIVITY-REPORT.
00129                  READ CUSTOMER-TRANSACTION-FILE
00130                      AT END PERFORM END-OF-JOB-ROUTINE.

00132                  PERFORM RESET-CUSTOMER-ACCUMULATORS.
00133                  PERFORM RESET-STORE-ACCUMULATORS.
00134                  PERFORM HEADER-ROUTINE
00135                      THRU END-HEADERS.
00136                  PERFORM DETAIL-ROUTINE
00137                      THRU END-DETAIL-ROUTINE.

00139              TOP-OF-MAINLINE.

00141                  READ CUSTOMER-TRANSACTION-FILE
00142                      AT END PERFORM CUSTOMER-SUMMARY-ROUTINE
00143                             PERFORM STORE-SUMMARY-ROUTINE
00144                             PERFORM END-OF-JOB-ROUTINE.

00146                  IF I-STORE-NO IS EQUAL TO PRIOR-STORE-NO
00147                  THEN
00148                      IF I-CUSTOMER-NO IS EQUAL TO PRIOR-CUSTOMER-NO
00149                      THEN
00150                          PERFORM DETAIL-ROUTINE THRU END-DETAIL-ROUTINE
00151                      ELSE
00152                          PERFORM CUSTOMER-SUMMARY-ROUTINE
00153                              THRU END-CUSTOMER-SUMMARY
00154                          PERFORM DETAIL-ROUTINE THRU END-DETAIL-ROUTINE
00155                  ELSE
00156                      PERFORM CUSTOMER-SUMMARY-ROUTINE
00157                          THRU END-CUSTOMER-SUMMARY
00158                      PERFORM STORE-SUMMARY-ROUTINE THRU END-STORE-SUMMARY
00159                      PERFORM HEADER-ROUTINE THRU END-HEADERS
00160                      PERFORM DETAIL-ROUTINE THRU END-DETAIL-ROUTINE.

00162                  IF LINE-COUNT IS GREATER THAN 50
00163                  THEN
00164                      PERFORM HEADER-ROUTINE THRU END-HEADERS
00165                  ELSE
00166                      NEXT SENTENCE.
00167                  GO TO TOP-OF-MAINLINE.

00169              END-OF-JOB-ROUTINE.

00171                  CLOSE CUSTOMER-TRANSACTION-FILE.
00172                  CLOSE CUSTOMER-ACTIVITY-REPORT.
00173                  STOP RUN.
```

Fig. 12.13: *Continued.*

```
   5          CUSACT          1.58.30         OCT  7,1978

00175              HEADER-ROUTINE.

00177                   WRITE REPORT-LINE FROM REPORT-HEADER-1
00178                       AFTER NEW-PAGE.
00180                   MOVE I-STORE-NO TO O-STORE-NO.
00181                   WRITE REPORT-LINE FROM REPORT-HEADER-2
00182                       AFTER ADVANCING 1 LINES.
00183                   WRITE REPORT-LINE FROM COLUMN-HEADER
00184                       AFTER ADVANCING 3 LINES.

00186                   MOVE SPACES TO REPORT-LINE.
00187                   WRITE REPORT-LINE
00188                       AFTER ADVANCING 1 LINES.
00189                   MOVE ZEROS TO LINE-COUNT.

00191              END-HEADERS.
00192                   EXIT.


00194              DETAIL-ROUTINE.

00196                   MOVE I-CUSTOMER-NO   TO O-CUSTOMER-NO.
00197                   MOVE I-CUSTOMER-NAME TO O-CUSTOMER-NAME.

00199                   IF I-AMOUNT IS NOT NUMERIC
00200                      THEN MOVE 0 TO I-AMOUNT
00201                      ELSE NEXT SENTENCE.
00202              *
00203              *** NOTE: FOR SIMPLICITY, WE HAVE NOT ADDED
00204              ***       REALISTIC ERROR HANDLING PROCEDURES.
00205              *

00207                   IF I-TRANSACTION-TYPE IS EQUAL TO 'C'
00208                      THEN
00209                          MOVE I-AMOUNT TO O-CREDITS
00210                          MOVE ZEROS TO O-PURCHASES
00211                          ADD  I-AMOUNT TO CUSTOMER-CREDITS
00212                          ADD  I-AMOUNT TO STORE-CREDITS
00213                          SUBTRACT I-AMOUNT FROM CUSTOMER-NET-BUSINESS
00214                          SUBTRACT I-AMOUNT FROM STORE-NET-BUSINESS
00215                      ELSE
00216                          MOVE I-AMOUNT TO O-PURCHASES
00217                          MOVE ZEROS TO O-CREDITS
00218                          ADD  I-AMOUNT TO CUSTOMER-PURCHASES
00219                          ADD  I-AMOUNT TO STORE-PURCHASES
00220                          ADD  I-AMOUNT TO CUSTOMER-NET-BUSINESS
00221                          ADD  I-AMOUNT TO STORE-NET-BUSINESS.

00223                   WRITE REPORT-LINE FROM CUSTOMER-DETAIL
00224                       AFTER ADVANCING 1 LINES.
00225                   ADD 1 TO LINE-COUNT.

00227              END-DETAIL-ROUTINE.
00228                   EXIT.
```

Fig. 12.13: *Continued.*

```
    7          CUSACT         1.58.30        OCT  7,1978

00230              CUSTOMER-SUMMARY-ROUTINE.

00232                   MOVE CUSTOMER-PURCHASES      TO C-PURCHASES-SUM.
00233                   MOVE CUSTOMER-CREDITS        TO C-CREDITS-SUM.
00234                   MOVE CUSTOMER-NET-BUSINESS TO C-NET-BUSINESS.
00235                   WRITE REPORT-LINE FROM CUSTOMER-SUMMARY
00236                       AFTER ADVANCING 2 LINES.
00237                   ADD 2 TO LINE-COUNT.

00239              RESET-CUSTOMER-ACCUMULATORS.

00241                   MOVE ZEROS TO CUSTOMER-PURCHASES, CUSTOMER-CREDITS,
00242                        CUSTOMER-NET-BUSINESS.
00243                   MOVE I-CUSTOMER-NO TO PRIOR-CUSTOMER-NO.

00245              END-CUSTOMER-SUMMARY.
00246                   EXIT.


00248              STORE-SUMMARY-ROUTINE.

00250                   MOVE STORE-PURCHASES        TO S-PURCHASES-SUM.
00251                   MOVE STORE-CREDITS          TO S-CREDITS-SUM.
00252                   MOVE STORE-NET-BUSINESS TO S-NET-BUSINESS.
00253                   WRITE REPORT-LINE FROM STORE-SUMMARY
00254                       AFTER ADVANCING 2 LINES.

00256              RESET-STORE-ACCUMULATORS.

00258                   MOVE ZEROS TO STORE-PURCHASES, STORE-CREDITS,
00259                        STORE-NET-BUSINESS.
00260                   MOVE I-STORE-NO       TO PRIOR-STORE-NO.

00262              END-STORE-SUMMARY.
00263                   EXIT.
```

Fig. 12.13: *Continued.*

make is to over complicate things. The temptation is simply to jump in and begin coding. Don't! Take the time to break a complex program into interrelated simple ones. Why insist on making an easy task difficult? Think, then act.

A SLIGHTLY DIFFERENT APPROACH

The program written above will almost certainly produce a massive report. How many credit card customers does a large bank have? Perhaps 100,000 or more. How many purchases does the average customer make each month? Probably ten or more. At one detail line per purchase, an almost unbelievable amount of paper would be consumed in producing the store reports.

Is all that detail really necessary? Does a store really want a list of every single purchase made by every single customer? Probably not. In fact, almost certainly not. Most likely, what is really needed is a simple summary report with absolutely no detail lines at all. By making only a few minor modifications to the program developed above, we can implement this new, more realistic program.

What would have to be done? First, the output detail line could be removed from the program, along with all references to this line down in the PROCEDURE DIVISION. Second, the instructions to move the customer name and number into the customer summary line, along with the DATA DIVISION entries needed to support these fields, could be added to the program. Basically, that should do the trick.

Why do we introduce a program change at this time? Why didn't we simply start the chapter with the proper program definition? Lack of foresight? No. A midstream change in program definition is an all too common occurance in the life of the average programmer. The main purpose of this particular midstream change was to illustrate just how easy it is to modify a properly designed program. Modular programs are simply easier to modify and maintain than are nonmodular programs. If for no other reason, the modular approach is the way to go.

Other changes might suggest themselves. For example, what if you were asked to print a customer summary line only if the amount of credit represented at least 25% of the amount of purchase? How would you do it? Given the fact that this qualification is intended to limit the printing of a customer summary line, it would have to be implemented in the module that prints a customer summary line. Where, in the midst of the relative handful of instructions of that subroutine, would you code the instructions needed to make printing conditional? There aren't too many options. You see here another tremendous advantage of modularization—changes are compartmentalized, affecting only a very limited segment of code.

Problems involving multiple breakpoints are quite common in business data processing. By following a step by step procedure for developing a problem solution, such programs become easy to write. The basic pattern really never changes. The contents of the secondary routines will, of course, change with the application, but the mainline stays essentially the same.

SUMMARY

Chapter 12 introduced the idea of a single break point program. Often, the programmer finds it necessary to write programs to generate reports with more than one break point. This chapter was concerned with such multiple break point programs.

The chapter began by describing the basic structure of the desired store activity report. The rough structure of the report was sketched, and the problem definition was stated as "write a program to produce this report". The input data was very clearly defined simply because our application was essentially a spin-off of the primary bill preparation application. We designed the needed output lines on a printer spacing chart and moved on to a consideration of the program logic.

The basic logic of the program is quite simple, consisting of little more than an input statement, a series of tests to identify which break point, if any, has been encountered, and a series of links to the necessary detailed logic routines. The fact that the major break point must be tested first was explained in some depth. Routines for handling a detail transaction, a major break point, and a minor breakpoint were defined and flowcharted. The problem of printing headers at times other than when a break point had occured was considered, and the logic for handling this problem was developed. The pieces were put together to form a mainline and supporting routines, first record and last record processing steps were added, and a complete program flowchart was drawn.

Having finished the planning of a solution, we turned to the task of implementing the solution in COBOL. The mainline and the secondary routines were coded and the program was tested. The chapter ended with a brief discussion of the desirability of reports on which only summary lines are printed.

KEY WORDS

major control break	**primary key**	**secondary key**
minor control break	**right justification**	

EXERCISES

1. Explain the difference between a major control break and a minor control break. Explain the difference between a primary key and a secondary key.

2. When a program with multiple control breaks is written, the major break is normally tested first, followed by the secondary control breaks. Why?

3. When a primary control break occurs it implies that all secondary control breaks have also occured. Why?

4. How can the programmer control printing headers at times other than break points?

5. Exercise 5 in Chapter 11 asked you to prepare a list of students by course. This was not a particularly realistic program, as what would probably be desired would be a list of students by section. Modify the program to treat the course identification code as a primary key and the section number as a secondary key, using the program to generate realistic class lists suitable for the instructor's use.

6. Exercise 6 in Chapter 11 was concerned with preparing a summary report from expense accounts. Of perhaps even greater use would be a report summarizing expense account activity by sales district. Using the same input as you did in the last chapter, plan and write a program listing the totals of all expense accounts by district. Within each district, summary lines showing the total expenses for each employee should be printed; there will be no detail lines. The primary key will be the district number; the secondary key will be the employee number. Don't forget the need for sorting the data into district order and, within a given district, into employee sequence.

7. Exercise 10 in Chapter 11 asked you to prepare a series of sales registers. To simplify distribution of these registers, it is highly desirable that they be generated in sales district sequence. Modify the program so that the sales district becomes the primary key and the customer number becomes the secondary key. Note that it is possible for a given customer to do business with more than one sales district.

8. Exercise 11 in Chapter 11 dealt with a price table and generated sales reports for the purpose of computing sales commissions. Modify the program so that the product code is treated as a secondary key. The new version of the program should accumulate sales for each product, generating exactly five product summary lines showing the total quantity and revenue produced by product code for each salesperson. A summary line, printed when a major break on salesperson number occurs, is to contain total revenue for the salesperson; this line will show the computed commission. There are no detail lines.

9. Refer to exercise 12 in Chapter 11. Treat the name as a primary key, the zip code as a secondary key, and the street address as a third level key. Discard a customer name and address from the file only if a duplicate entry exists for all three fields.

10. Our organization has just conducted a survey of hospitals throughout the country. Data has been collected and keypunched to cards containing the following fields:

columns	contents
1-15	name of city
16-30	county
31-32	state
33-40	number of hospital beds

Prepare a report to list the number of hospital beds by city, by county, by state, and nationally. Note that the national total is the sum of 50 state totals, each state total is the sum of several county totals, and each county total is the sum of several city totals.

11. Every evening, the bank runs a program to update checking accounts. Input records hold the following fields:

positions	contents
1-8	customer account number
9-11	transaction type: CHK=check; DEP=deposit or an old balance transaction
12-18	amount of transaction (99999V99)

    Write the checking account update program. Sort the transactions into account number sequence. Within a given account, the deposits should come first followed by the checks. Print each deposit or check as a separate detail line. Immediately following the list of all deposits, print a summary line showing total deposits; immediately following the listing of all checks, print a summary line showing total checks.

    A final summary line for each account should show total deposits, total checks, and the new balance (deposits minus checks). If the new balance is negative, print a negative sign to the right of the new balance.

12. A complete set of all customer transactions for the current month against our credit card company can be found on a file of punched cards. Individual records are formatted as follows:

positions	contents
1-8	account number
9-30	name
31-36	store number
37-42	amount of purchase or credit
43-45	authorization initials
46	type of transaction: blank for purchase, C for credit

    The data is in random sequence.

Use a sort/merge utility to sort this data into account number sequence and, within this sequence, into store sequence. Write a program to read this data and generate a summary report showing:

1. Total credits and purchases for each customer by store.

2. Total credits and purchases for each customer for all stores.

At the end of the program, show the total number of customers processed and the total value of all purchases and credits.

13

The Sequential Master File Update Application

OVERVIEW

Chapters 11 and 12 concentrated on a common business data processing application: the control breaks problem. Here in Chapter 13, we turn our attention to the sequential master file update application.

The problem begins with a master file that defines the state of an area of the business—inventory, payroll, accounts receivable—as of some closing date. Since the time of the master file's last update, a number of transactions have taken place—additions to or deletions from inventory, for example. The information in the master file must be updated to reflect these changes.

Both files, the master file and the transactions, are sorted into sequence by the same key. The problem then becomes a special case of the control breaks problem, with two input files rather than one. Typically, two output files, a new master file and a summary report, are required. In this chapter, our objective is to build, step by step, a solution to this basic data processing problem; the specific example used to illustrate general concepts will be an inventory application.

THE PROBLEM: UPDATING A MASTER FILE

Assume that you are employed by a manufacturing concern. You have been asked to write a program to maintain a master file of finished goods inventory. What exactly does this problem entail?

First, let's consider why inventory is maintained. Some small organizations don't need an inventory, but instead build specific products to specific customer order; our organization, however, does not enjoy that happy state of affairs. Instead, we operate in a very competitive marketplace. While some customers are sufficiently pleased with past performance that they are willing to wait 3 months for delivery, most are not. Often (or so our salespeople tell us) the fact that we can deliver within a week or two spells the difference between our firm or a competitor getting an order. The only way we can possibly react this quickly is by making products before they are ordered and then storing them in a warehouse. Customer shipments go directly from the warehouse to the customer, with manufacturing subsequently replenishing the warehouse supply.

Obviously, the warehouse approach does absolutely no good if we don't know exactly what is stored there. That's where you, the programmer, come in. Given the size of the warehouse, it is impossible for any human being to mentally keep track of its contents. The volume of business makes manual data processing (on 3x5 cards, for example) totally unacceptable. A computer is essential.

The systems analysis department has already determined the basic structure of the inventory system. The key to this system is the part number assigned to each unique product manufactured by our firm. The inventory **master file** will be created by keypunching the results of the next physical inventory, sorting these cards into part number sequence, and then copying the resulting file to magnetic tape. File creation is not your problem; it will be handled by another programmer.

The program you are to write will update this master file. It will be run on a weekly basis. During the week, inventory clerks will be expected to fill out a form each time material is added to inventory or shipped from inventory. These forms will subsequently be keypunched, and the resulting transaction cards used to update the master file (Fig. 13.1). It will be necessary to sort these transactions into part number sequence; for reasons of efficiency, the output file will be stored on magnetic tape. Once it is created, the transactions tape can be used to update the master file under control of the master file update program. Individual master file entries can be changed to reflect additions to and deletions from inventory, and a new master file can be generated.

A summary report showing the new status of inventory is also required from the master file update program. This report is used by management to make decisions regarding inventory. Production, for example, can be told to schedule a given product if the inventory report shows that the number of units on hand has dropped below some critical level.

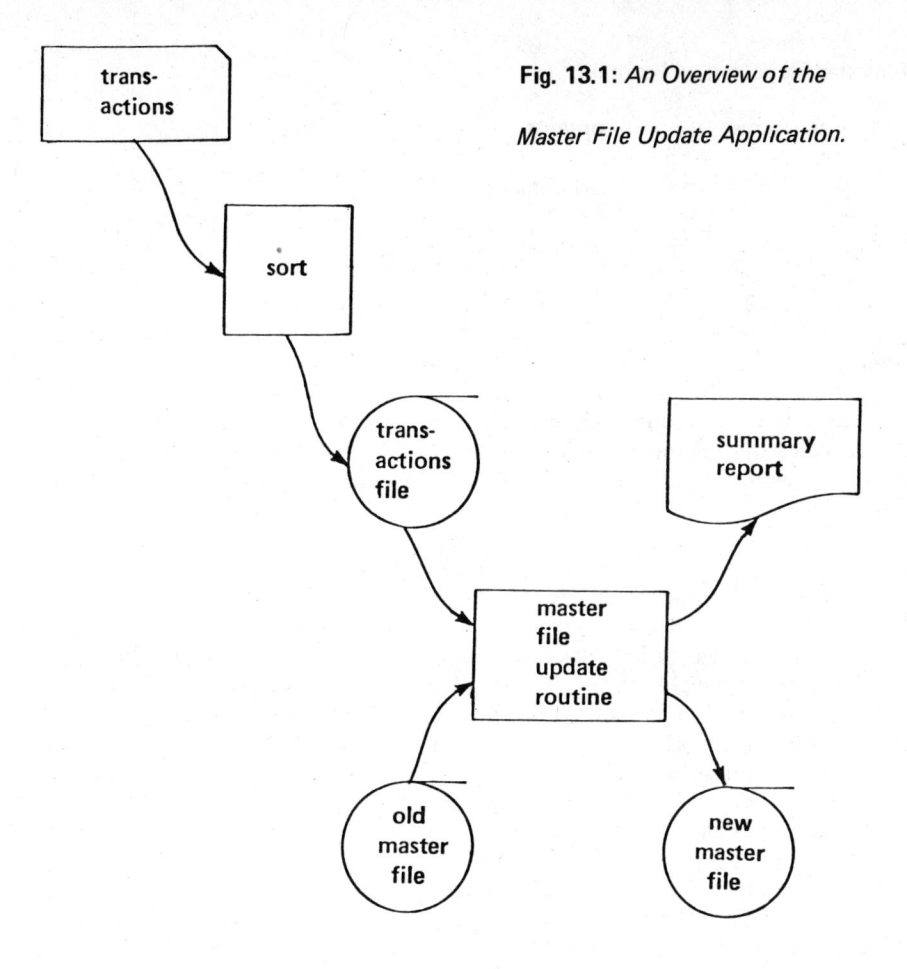

Fig. 13.1: *An Overview of the Master File Update Application.*

Defining Input

Two input files will feed data to the master file update program, a **transaction file** and an **old master file**. The formats of both files have been defined elsewhere. Each transaction record will contain:

positions	contents
1-4	part number
5-8	quantity (number of units)
9-11	transaction type:

        ADD means an addition to inventory

        DEL means a deletion from inventory

Each master file record will contain:

positions	contents
1-4	part number
5-26	description
27-30	stock on hand

Defining Output

It is essential that the output **new master file** have exactly the same format as the input old master file, as the new master produced this week becomes the old master input to next week's master file update. Thus, the format of the new master file is as defined above.

We do have a bit of freedom with respect to the design of the output listing. Obviously, the part number and the new balance for each part number must be shown. The description of the product might prove useful, and should be included. Management might want to consider the trend in stock level for a given product, so it would also help if the old balance, the sum of all additions, the sum of all deletions, and the new balance were all printed for each part. In many cases, the average size of an order can be an important factor in determining the proper inventory level for a product, so a count indicating the number of addition transactions and deletion transactions would be helpful. The format of the necessary output lines is shown on the printer chart of Fig. 13.2.

Incidently, where does the programmer come up with ideas as to what is needed on the printed report? In many firms, the systems analysis department is responsible for forms design. More often, the programmer develops such plans by actually going out and talking to the people who will be using the reports (in this case the inventory clerks) and asking them what they want. Direct user contact is an important part of almost every programmer's job.

PROGRAM LOGIC—GETTING STARTED

After we define the input and output files needed by the master file update program, all that remains is to define the internal logic. In developing a solution to the grade point average problem of Chapter 11, we discovered that using a set of simple test data often helps identify the essential steps of a new program. Let's once again take advantage of this technique. We'll define a number of records for a master file and a transactions file (Fig. 13.3) and process this data manually, making notes as we go along.

The key to this problem is the part number. If the part number of the master file record and the part number of the transaction match, we are looking at the same product and must either add or subtract the quantity (depending on the transaction type). If, on the other hand, the part numbers do not match, other actions are called

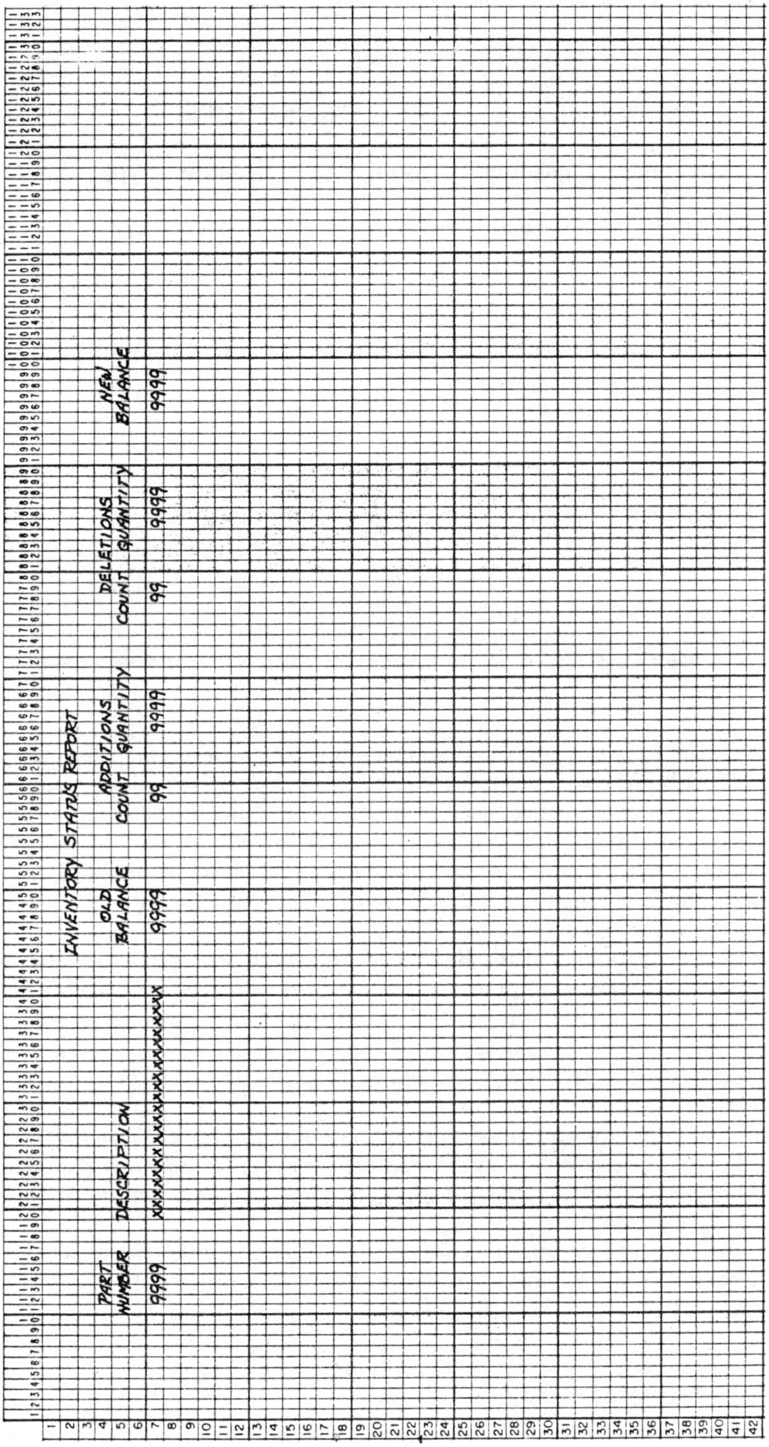

Fig. 13.2: *Summary Report Format.*

Fig. 13.3: *Test Data for the Master File Update Application.*

MASTER FILE		TRANSACTIONS		
part number	quantity	part number	quantity	type
0001	14	0001	5	ADD
0005	92	0001	1	DEL
0006	35	0006	24	DEL
0009	57	0008	50	ADD
0010	104	0009	3	DEL
		0009	14	DEL
		0009	25	ADD

---

for. We have tried to select test data representing all possible occurences—master file equal, master file high, and master file low. Let's see how each condition might be handled. As has been our practice, we'll temporarily postpone consideration of the unique problems associated with first record processing and assume that the first record for each file is in the computer and that all essential accumulators and control fields have been properly initialized.

Thus we begin by looking at the first record from each file. Both have the same part number: 0001. What does this mean? Obviously, since the master file record and the transaction both carry the same part number, they must represent a record for the same part. What should we do? Since the transaction type is ADD, we add the quantity on the transaction record to the quantity on the master file record.

Are there any other transactions against this part number? How can we find out? By reading another transaction. The next transaction is also for part number 0001; since it's a DEL record, we subtract the quantity from the old inventory balance.

Is any other type of transaction record possible? Sure, but if its's not an ADD or a DEL, it must be an error. Whenever the part number (or, in general, the key) of the master file and the transaction file match, we

> 1. add the quantity from the transaction to the old balance if it's an ADD transaction,

  2. subtract the quantity from the transaction from the old balance if it's a DEL transaction,

  3. report an error if the transaction is neither ADD nor DEL,

  4. read another transaction.

These instructions are, of course, for the benefit of our straw person.

  Are there any more transactions against this part number? The only way to find out is to read another transaction. Since our data is in sequence by part number, if there are any other transactions against this same part they must follow in sequence; if the next transaction is for a different part number, we know that there are no more for 0001.

  The third transaction (Fig. 13.3) is a deletion from the inventory of part number 0006, a different number. There are no more transactions against part number 0001; thus we know that all additions have been added to and all deletions have been subtracted from the inventory balance, leaving the new inventory balance for part number 0001. A new master file record can be written.

  Now what? We still have an unprocessed transaction waiting to be handled. We know that it does not belong to part number 0001. If we are to use this transaction to update the master file, a new master file record must be read into the program; the second master record (Fig. 13.3) is for part number 0005. We can now return to the test for same part number.

  To summarize the steps that must be taken when the transaction is greater than the master file, we must

  1. write a new master file record,

  2. read the next old master file record.

  We now have a master file record for part 0005 and a transaction for part 0006. What does this mean? Are there any transactions against 0005? If there were, they would have preceeded the transaction now being handled. Our conclusion: There are no more transactions against 0005. In fact, there are no transactions at all against this part number; we are looking at a product that did not sell. What should we do? Since we still have the product in inventory, we want part number 0005 to be part of our new master file; we can achieve this by simply copying it to the new master file without change. Will the steps described just above accomplish this objective? Certainly. If we haven't added anything to or subtracted anything from the old balance, then we haven't changed the old balance, and the record can simply be copied to the new master file. As long as the part number of the master file record is low, the condition is handled in exactly the same way, and it really doesn't matter if a master file record or a transaction was most recently read.

  Having written a new master file entry for part number 0005, we turn our attention to the next master file record; it's part number 0006 (Fig. 13.3). Again, we have a match. The transaction is a deletion of 14 units; thus we subtract 14 from the old master file balance and go on to the next transaction, an addition of 50 unites of part number 0008. Since the master file entry is now low, it's time to write a new master file entry and turn to the next old master file record.

The next master file record is for part number 0009. We are working with a transaction for part number 0008. They don't match, but this condition is different from the master file low condition encountered earlier. Do we know that there are no more transactions against part number 0009? No; in fact, we haven't even hit the first transaction for this part. We are certainly not yet ready to write a new master file entry. When the transaction is lower than the master file, we know either that there is no master file entry for this part or that the data is out of sequence. In either case, we have an unusual condition that cannot be handled normally. Rather than get into the details of error handling, we'll simply consider each "transaction low" condition to be an error, print an error message identifying the error, and move on to the next transaction.

Basically, that's it. The key to updating the master file is comparing the part number of an old master file record and the part number of a transaction. There are only three possible conditions; master high, master low, and master equal. We have considered how each of these conditions might be handled; we can now begin planning a computer level solution.

The Structure of the Mainline

The mainline of this program is really quite simple. All that must be done is to identify the condition—master high, low, or equal—being handled and then to indicate the proper detailed logic routines. Each of the routines will issue a read against one of the files depending on the condition, so the mainline doesn't even need a read. The structure of the mainline is shown in Fig. 13.4.

The SAME-KEY-ROUTINE

What is to be done when the key of the master file and the key of the transaction match? Basically, if the transaction type is ADD, we add the quantity to the old balance, and if the transaction type is DEL, we subtract. Actually, given the objectives of this program, in particular given the desired output, we might take a slightly different approach (Fig. 13.5), adding the quantity to an additions accumulator or a deletions accumulator as the case may be. The new balance would subsequently be computed in the NEW-KEY-ROUTINE.

Other fields to appear in the output include a counter of the additions for this part number, and a separate count of the number of deletions transactions. The ideal place to count transactions is where they are handled.

Note how, during the process of planning the program logic, we frequently refer to the format of the output data. This should not surprise you. After all, we are, writing the program for the expressed purpose of producing the specified output.

What if the transaction is neither an addition nor a deletion? Then, it's an error. Note, however, that this error is quite different from the sequence error detected as

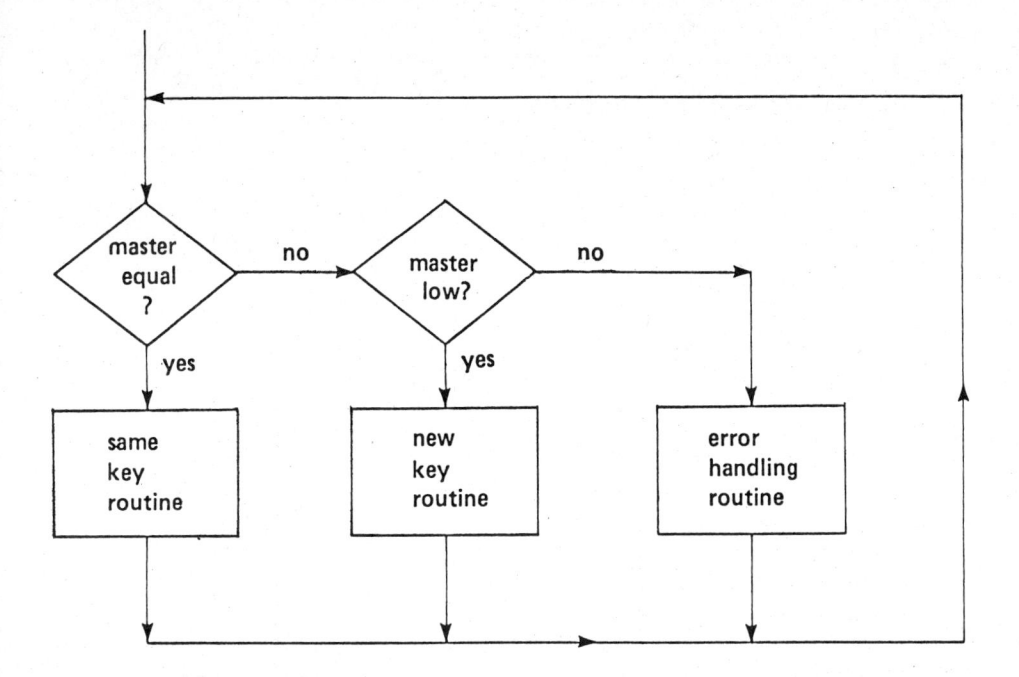

Fig. 13.4: *The Program Mainline.*

part of the program mainline. Consequently, a different error handling routine is referenced—the DATA-ERROR-HANDLING-ROUTINE.

The last action of the SAME-KEY-ROUTINE is always to read a new transaction; the end-of-file condition will be discussed later.

The NEW-KEY-ROUTINE

When the key of the master file record is less than the key of the transaction, there are no more transactions for this part number. Basically, our program must write a record to the new master file and read the next record from the old master file before returning to the mainline. There is a bit more to it, however.

Before a new master file record can be written, the record must be set up in memory. The part number and description appear on the old master file record and can simply be copied. The new balance, on the other hand, must be computed by adding the value of the ADD accumulator to the old balance and then subtracting the value of the DEL accumulator. Once the new master file record has been set up, it can be written (Fig. 13.6).

A summary line must be written at this time too. The new balance has already been computed, so it, the value in the two counters, and the value in the two accumulators can be moved to the output line and a WRITE statement can be executed. Finally, the accumulators and counters can be reset to zero, and the next master file record can be read.

Fig. 13.5: *The SAME-KEY-ROUTINE.*

Program Mainline

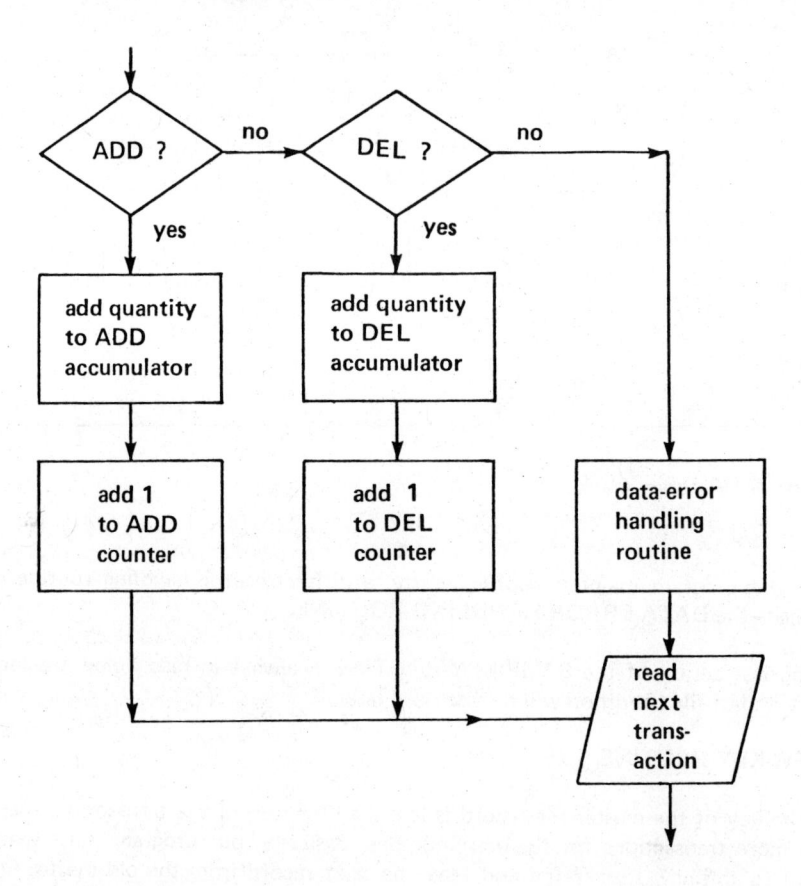

Fig. 13.6: *The NEW-KEY-ROUTINE.*

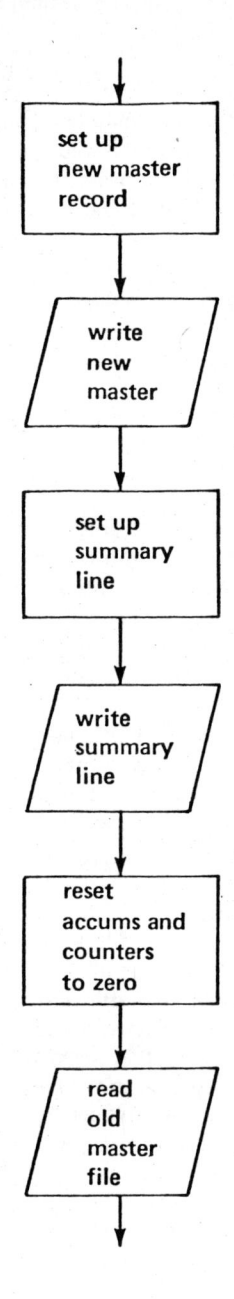

Why read the old master file last? It really could have been read as soon as the new master file record was set up in memory. As we shall see shortly, however, handling two files creates a number of end-of-job problems, and it is wise to finish all possible processing before risking the end-of-data condition.

The ERROR-ROUTINE

If the part number of the master file is neither equal to nor less than the part number of the transaction, an error condition is recognized. How are these errors to be handled? There are many possible answers. Perhaps an ADD transaction can be assumed to represent a new product being placed in inventory for the first time; other explanations are equally possible. For the sake of simplicity, we'll assume that any "master high" condition is a pure error, and that the transaction is simply to be listed on an error report and otherwise skipped.

Thus, the ERROR-ROUTINE contains only two primary functions. First, the error message must be set up and sent to the printer. Once the message has been printed, the next transaction is read.

Processing the First Record

The mainline of the master file update program begins with a comparison between the key field of the master file record and the key field of a transaction file record. If this test is to be executed successfully, there must be a master file record and a transaction in the computer. Thus, the start-of-job routine must include instructions to read a record from each of these files (Fig. 13.7). The initialization of all counters and accumulators to zero is the other major function of the start-of-job routine.

Once the first record from each of the files has been read, control can be given to the mainline. The secondary routines contain instructions to read either a transaction or a master file record; thus, when control returns to the top of the mainline there will always be two records to compare.

End-of-Job Routines

The end-of-job routines for the master file update program are a bit tricky simply because there are two input files. What if all the records in the transactions file have been processed but master file records still remain? Obviously, since there are no more transactions, these remaining master file records will not be changed by any additions or deletions. Basically, all that need be done is to read the master file records and write them, without change, to the new master file (Fig. 13.8). Of course, a line must be written on the summary report for each of these part numbers. If this logic seems familiar, it should be, as we have just described the NEW-KEY-ROUTINE (Fig. 13.6).

On the other hand, what if the master file is to run out of records first? Any remaining transactions will not have matching master file entries, and we have already defined this condition as an error. Errors are simply listed on the error report and otherwise ignored. Thus, if the master file should encounter end-of-file before the transaction file, our program must write each remaining transaction to the error file

Fig. 13.7: *Start-of-Job Routine.*

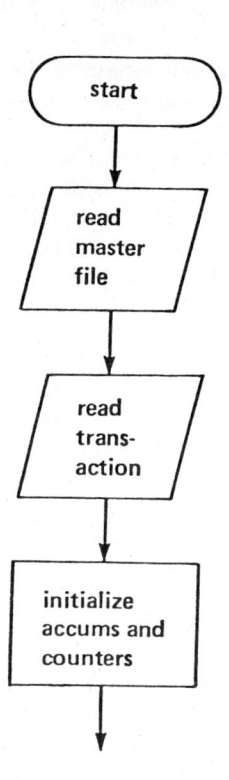

```
         start
           │
           ▼
     ┌──────────┐
    / read      /
   / master    /
  / file      /
 └──────────┘
           │
           ▼
     ┌──────────┐
    / read      /
   / trans-    /
  / action    /
 └──────────┘
           │
           ▼
    ┌────────────┐
    │ initialize │
    │ accums and │
    │ counters   │
    └────────────┘
           │
           ▼
```

and then read the next transaction, repeating this cycle until such time as the end of the transactions file is reached (Fig. 13.9).

Before moving on, we should discuss one other special case of the end-of-data condition. What happens if the end-of-data marker is encountered while attempting to read the very first record? If this happens on the transactions file, there *are no* transactions, and there is no sense wasting time updating the unchanged master file. If the master file hits end-of-data on the first read, we have a very different problem, in that there is no master file to update. In either case, it makes no sense to continue, so the program is simply terminated.

Printing Headers

The summary report should be printed with a reasonable set of page and column headers; the headers to be used were defined on the printer layout sheet pictured in Fig. 13.2. When should the headers be printed? One set, of course, should be printed at the beginning of the job, adding one more function to the start-of-job routine. The decision to print additional headers will be based on the number of summary lines actually printed; thus a line counter and a link to the header routine must be added to the NEW-KEY-ROUTINE, which is the only place where summary lines are actually printed.

Putting the Pieces Together

Now that the logic of each of the primary modules has been defined, it's time we put the pieces together. As in prior chapters, our objective at this stage is to identify common blocks of logic and determine the content of the mainline and the various secondary routines in the final version of the program.

There is, however, one problem we are certain to encounter as we begin to try to develop a general flowchart for this program. The problem is a result of the complex relationship among the modules, and can best be seen in the last-record-processing routines. During the processing of the SAME-KEY-ROUTINE, if the end-of-file condition is encountered on the transactions file, the desired action is to read and dump the rest of the master file. This logic is housed in the NEW-KEY-ROUTINE. If, during the processing of the NEW-KEY-ROUTINE, the end of the master file is encountered, the rest of the transactions file must be dumped to the error listing, and this logic is part of the SAME-KEY-ROUTINE. It is extremely difficult to show such complex interrelationships on a standard flowchart. Even if we were to decide to duplicate the logic for end-of-job processing, creating separate routines and refusing to take advantage of common code, we would still be talking about three levels of interrelated routines, and such complexity is simply beyond understanding when using traditional flowcharting methods.

When faced with such a problem, many programmers choose a slightly different flowcharting approach. We have already developed flowcharts for the start-of-job logic, the program mainline, each of the computational routines, and the two end-of-job conditions. Why not simply spread these individual flowcharts out on a desk top or paste them up on a large sheet of paper (Fig. 13.10)? By placing these routines in their logical positions, we can get a good overall view of the total program logic without forcing things into some arbitrary format. The diagram clearly shows the relationship between the mainline and the various secondary routines, and the logical position of the two end-of-job routines is established without ambiguity. The relationship between the end-of-data routines and the regular processing routines can be quickly spotted, but the differences also remain out in the open. As a program begins to get complex, such **modular flowcharts** can be a tremendous aid, helping the programmer to maintain a grasp of the entire solution. In most cases, the back side of a sheet or two of used computer output paper should be more than adequate.

What can we see on the modular flowchart? Clearly, the logic block that initializes all accumulators and counters appears in two places: within the start-of-job routine and again within the NEW-KEY-ROUTINE. These instructions can be grouped into a single paragraph.

The only other places where significant amounts of common code are encountered is in the end-of-data routines. Here, the action to be taken matches that of either the SAME-KEY-ROUTINE or the NEW-KEY-ROUTINE, but with one notable exception. Consider, for example, the two instructions that read the master file. Within the NEW-KEY-ROUTINE, an end-of-file condition must cause a link to the END-OF-MASTER routine. Within the END-OF-TRANSACTION routine, the other place where this read appears, an end-of-file condition will result in the program's going to END-OF-JOB. The fact that the read instructions are not identical does create problems when we attempt to use the same code in both places. Fortunately, there are techniques that allow the programmer to differentiate between end-of-file conditions. These techniques involve the setting of switches, a topic covered briefly in a prior chapter and to be covered in more detail later in this chapter.

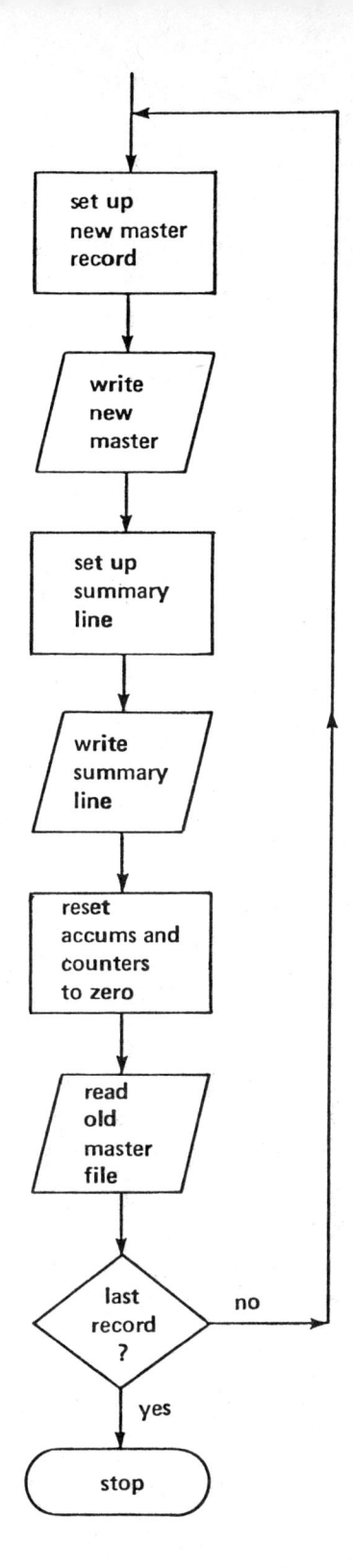

Fig. 13.8: *Program Logic Following the End-of-Data Condition on the Transactions File.*

Fig. 13.9: *Program Logic Following the End-of-Data Condition on the Master File.*

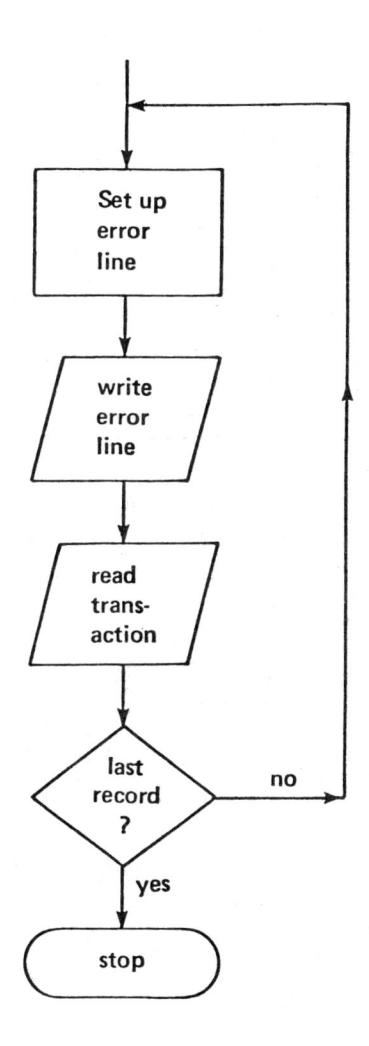

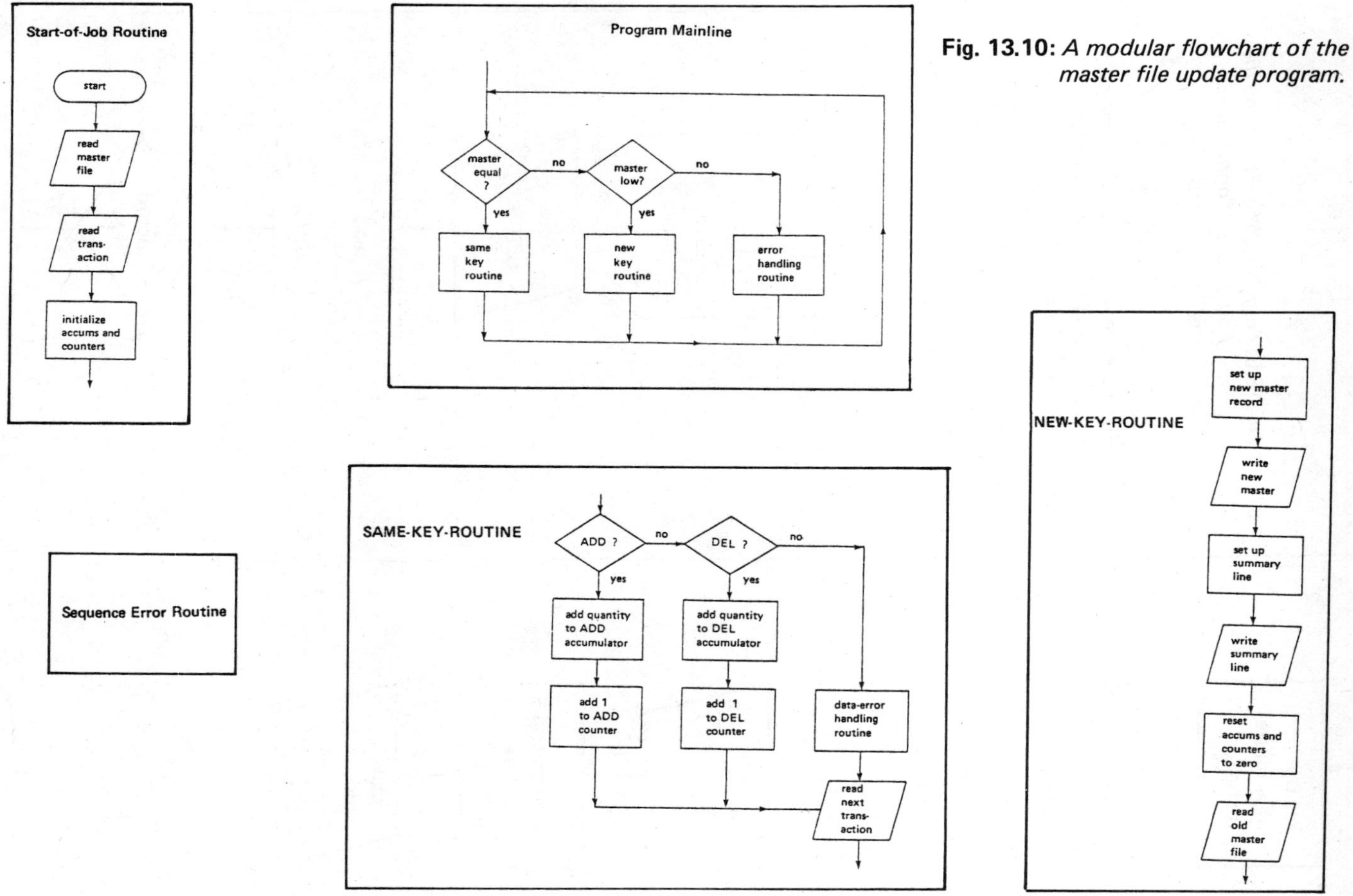

Fig. 13.10: *A modular flowchart of the master file update program.*

Fig. 13.10: *Continued.*

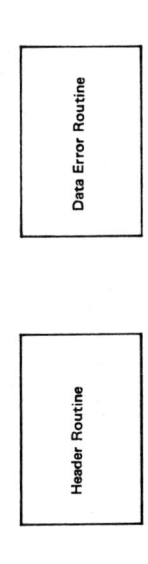

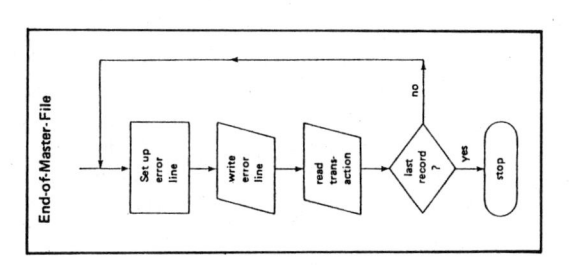

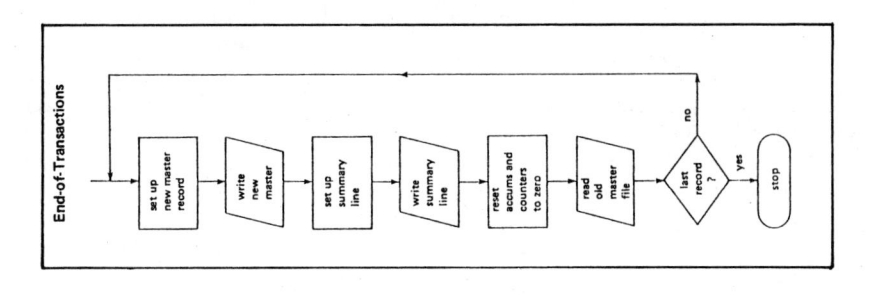

IMPLEMENTING THE SOLUTION

The IDENTIFICATION and ENVIRONMENT DIVISIONs for a COBOL master file update program are much like those found in any other program; thus we'll move right along to the DATA DIVISION. Rather than continuing the practice of showing the actual coding sheets, the discussion that follows will refer to the program listing, Fig. 13.11.

The DATA DIVISION

There is nothing really surprising about the DATA DIVISION (Fig. 13.11) either. There are five FD-entries in the FILE SECTION, one for each file; record formats match the record descriptions presented at the beginning of the chapter. Note that, as in Chapter 12, only a dummy output line for the printed files has been set up in the FILE SECTION; the detailed contents of the various lines can be seen in the WORKING-STORAGE SECTION.

The work fields are predictable too. Accumulators and counters are needed to support the collection of summary data. The line counter supports the logical control over the printing of headers. The two switches will be used to indicate end-of-job conditions.

The PROCEDURE DIVISION

The PROCEDURE DIVISION (Fig. 13.11) begins with the usual OPEN instructions and then reads the first record from each of the two input files; note that an end-of-file condition at this stage will result in program termination. Next, a set of headers is printed and the counters and accumulators are initialized to zero through a PERFORM statement. Having completed the housekeeping functions, it's on to the mainline.

The program mainline is quite short, simply testing the two part numbers, identifying the condition being handled, and linking to the proper detailed logic routine. Read the secondary routines; they are easy to follow too. Actually, this should not surprise you, because we have planned our solution with great care. If the planning is properly done, actually coding the program should consist of little more than simply translating a clean solution into another language.

The only really tricky part to this program involves handling the last record. Depending on which file runs out of data first, end-of-job procedures can differ markedly. Perhaps the cleanest way to handle these unusual conditions is to write two separate and complete logic modules. In the SAME-KEY-ROUTINE and the NEW-KEY-ROUTINE, where the bulk of these files are read, the end-of-file condition would reference the appropriate end-of-file routine, while in these end-of-file routines, the end-of-file condition would reference the end-of-job routine, leading to normal program termination.

These special end-of-file routines would, however, be almost identical to the SAME-KEY-ROUTINE and the NEW-KEY-ROUTINE respectively; the only difference is the statement associated with the AT END clause of the READ. Repeating

```
00004           IDENTIFICATION DIVISION.
00006              PROGRAM-ID. INVUPDAT.
00008              AUTHOR.     FISHER & DAVIS.
00009              REMARKS.    THIS PROGRAM PROCESSES THE INVENTORY
00010                          TRANSACTIONS TO UPDATE THE INVENTORY
00011                          MASTER FILE AND PROVIDE AN INVENTORY
00012                          ACTIVITY REPORT.

00014           ENVIRONMENT DIVISION.
00016              CONFIGURATION SECTION.
00018                 SOURCE-COMPUTER.   IBM-370-148.
00019                 OBJECT-COMPUTER.   IBM-370-148.
00020                 SPECIAL-NAMES.     C01 IS NEW-PAGE.
00022              INPUT-OUTPUT SECTION.
00024                 FILE-CONTROL.
00025                     SELECT OLD-INVENTORY-MASTER-FILE ASSIGN TO UT-S-OLDINV.
00026                     SELECT NEW-INVENTORY-MASTER-FILE ASSIGN TO UT-S-NEWINV.
00027                     SELECT INVENTORY-TRANSACTION-FILE ASSIGN TO UT-S-INVTRANS.
00028                     SELECT INVENTORY-ERROR-FILE      ASSIGN TO UT-S-INVERRS.
00029                     SELECT INVENTORY-REPORT-FILE     ASSIGN TO UT-S-INVREPT.
```

Fig. 13.11: *The master file update program.*

```
2        INVUPDAT      2.59.18       OCT 21,1978


00033           DATA DIVISION.
00035           FILE SECTION.
00037           FD OLD-INVENTORY-MASTER-FILE
00038              BLOCK CONTAINS 10 RECORDS
00039              LABEL RECORDS ARE STANDARD.
00040           01   OLD-INVENTORY-MASTER-RECORD.
00041              05   O-PART-NUMBER              PIC 9(4).
00042              05   O-DESCRIPTION              PIC X(22).
00043              05   O-STOCK-ON-HAND            PIC 9(4).

00045           FD NEW-INVENTORY-MASTER-FILE
00046              BLOCK CONTAINS 10 RECORDS
00047              LABEL RECORDS ARE STANDARD.
00048           01   NEW-INVENTORY-MASTER-RECORD.
00049              05   N-PART-NUMBER              PIC 9(4).
00050              05   N-DESCRIPTION              PIC X(22).
00051              05   N-STOCK-ON-HAND            PIC 9(4).

00053           FD INVENTORY-TRANSACTION-FILE
00054              BLOCK CONTAINS 20 RECORDS
00055              LABEL RECORDS ARE STANDARD.
00056           01   INVENTORY-TRANSACTION-RECORD.
00057              05   T-PART-NUMBER              PIC 9(4).
00058              05   T-QUANTITY                 PIC 9(4).
00059              05   TRANSACTION-TYPE           PIC X(3).

00061           FD INVENTORY-ERROR-FILE
00062              LABEL RECORDS ARE OMITTED.
00063           01   ERROR-PRINT-RECORD.
00064              05   FILLER                     PIC X.
00065              05   ERROR-PRINT-LINE           PIC X(132).

00067           FD INVENTORY-REPORT-FILE
00068              LABEL RECORDS ARE OMITTED.
00069           01   REPORT-PRINT-RECORD.
00070              05   FILLER                     PIC X.
00071              05   REPORT-PRINT-LINE          PIC X(132).
```

Fig. 13.11: *Continued.*

```
3       INVUPDAT       2.59.18      OCT 21,1978


00075             WORKING-STORAGE SECTION.
00076
00077             01  REPORT-HEADER.
00078                 05  FILLER              PIC X(44)    VALUE SPACES.
00079                 05  FILLER              PIC X(23)
00080                                         VALUE 'INVENTORY STATUS REPORT'.
00081             01  COLUMN-HEADER-1.
00082                 05  FILLER              PIC X(11)    VALUE SPACES.
00083                 05  FILLER              PIC X(36)
00084                                         VALUE 'PART       DESCRIPTION'.
00085                 05  FILLER              PIC X(31)
00086                                         VALUE 'OLD               ADDITIONS'.
00087                 05  FILLER              PIC X(21)
00088                                         VALUE 'DELETIONS         NEW'.
00089             01  COLUMN-HEADER-2.
00090                 05  FILLER              PIC X(45)
00091                                         VALUE '                 NUMBER'.
00092                 05  FILLER              PIC X(18)
00093                                         VALUE 'BALANCE    COUNT'.
00094                 05  FILLER              PIC X(19)
00095                                         VALUE 'QUANTITY    COUNT'.
00096                 05  FILLER              PIC X(19)
00097                                         VALUE 'QUANTITY    BALANCE'.
00098             01  INVENTORY-SUMMARY-LINE.
00099                 05  FILLER              PIC X(11)    VALUE SPACES.
00100                 05  D-PART-NUMBER       PIC 9(4).
00101                 05  FILLER              PIC X(4)     VALUE SPACES.
00102                 05  D-DESCRIPTION       PIC X(22).
00103                 05  FILLER              PIC X(5)     VALUE SPACES.
00104                 05  D-OLD-BALANCE       PIC ZZZ9.
00105                 05  FILLER              PIC X(8)     VALUE SPACES.
00106                 05  D-ADDITIONS-COUNT   PIC Z9.
00107                 05  FILLER              PIC X(5)     VALUE SPACES.
00108                 05  D-ADDITIONS-QUANTITY PIC ZZZ9.
00109                 05  FILLER              PIC X(8)     VALUE SPACES.
00110                 05  D-DELETIONS-COUNT   PIC Z9.
00111                 05  FILLER              PIC X(5)     VALUE SPACES.
00112                 05  D-DELETIONS-QUANTITY PIC ZZZ9.
00113                 05  FILLER              PIC X(7)     VALUE SPACES.
00114                 05  D-NEW-BALANCE       PIC ZZZ9.
```

Fig. 13.11: *Continued.*

```
   4       INVUPDAT        2.59.18      OCT 21,1978


00118             01  ERROR-REPORT-HEADER.
00119                 05    FILLER               PIC X(40)      VALUE SPACES.
00120                 05    FILLER               PIC X(22)
00121                                            VALUE 'INVENTORY ERROR REPORT'.
00122             01  ERROR-COLUMN-HEADER-1.
00123                 05    FILLER               PIC X(26)      VALUE SPACES.
00124                 05    FILLER               PIC X(19)      VALUE 'PART'.
00125                 05    FILLER               PIC X(11)
00126                                            VALUE 'TRANSACTION'.
00127             01  ERROR-COLUMN-HEADER-2.
00128                 05    FILLER               PIC X(25)      VALUE SPACES.
00129                 05    FILLER               PIC X(23)
00130                                            VALUE 'NUMBER     QUANTITY'.
00131                 05    FILLER               PIC X(11)      VALUE 'TYPE'.
00132                 05    FILLER               PIC X(13)
00133                                            VALUE 'ERROR MESSAGE'.
00134             01  ERROR-DETAIL-LINE.
00135                 05    FILLER               PIC X(26)      VALUE SPACES.
00136                 05    E-PART-NUMBER        PIC 9(4).
00137                 05    FILLER               PIC X(6)       VALUE SPACES.
00138                 05    E-QUANTITY           PIC 9(4).
00139                 05    FILLER               PIC X(6)       VALUE SPACES.
00140                 05    E-TRANSACTION-TYPE   PIC X(3).
00141                 05    FILLER               PIC X(7)       VALUE SPACES.
00142                 05    ERROR-MESSAGE        PIC X(20).

00144             01  ACCUMULATORS.
00145                 05    ADDITIONS-COUNT      PIC 99.
00146                 05    ADDITIONS-QUANTITY   PIC 9999.
00147                 05    DELETIONS-COUNT      PIC 99.
00148                 05    DELETIONS-QUANTITY   PIC 9999.
00149                 05    NEW-BALANCE          PIC 9999.
00150                 05    LINE-COUNT           PIC 99.
00151                 05    ERROR-LINE-COUNT     PIC 99         VALUE 28.

00153             01  SWITCHES.
00154                 05    LAST-MASTER-SWITCH   PIC 9          VALUE ZERO.
00155                 05    LAST-TRAN-SWITCH     PIC 9          VALUE ZERO.
```

Fig. 13.11: *Continued.*

```
5        INVUPDAT      2.59.18      OCT 21,1978


00159            PROCEDURE DIVISION.

00161                HOUSEKEEPING.
00162                    OPEN INPUT   OLD-INVENTORY-MASTER-FILE.
00163                    OPEN INPUT   INVENTORY-TRANSACTION-FILE.
00164                    OPEN OUTPUT  NEW-INVENTORY-MASTER-FILE.
00165                    OPEN OUTPUT  INVENTORY-ERROR-FILE.
00166                    OPEN OUTPUT  INVENTORY-REPORT-FILE.
00167                    READ OLD-INVENTORY-MASTER-FILE
00168                        AT END DISPLAY 'NO MASTER FILE' UPON CONSOLE
00169                            PERFORM END-OF-JOB-ROUTINE.
00170                    MOVE O-STOCK-ON-HAND TO NEW-BALANCE.
00171                    READ INVENTORY-TRANSACTION-FILE
00172                        AT END DISPLAY 'NO TRANSACTIONS' UPON CONSOLE
00173                            PERFORM END-OF-JOB-ROUTINE.
00174                    PERFORM PRINT-HEADERS THRU END-PRINT-HEADERS.
00175                    PERFORM SET-ACCUMULATORS THRU END-SET-ACCUMULATORS.

00177                TOP-OF-MAINLINE.
00178                    IF O-PART-NUMBER IS EQUAL TO T-PART-NUMBER
00179                    THEN
00180                        PERFORM SAME-KEY-ROUTINE THRU END-SAME-KEY
00181                    ELSE
00182                        IF O-PART-NUMBER IS LESS THAN T-PART-NUMBER
00183                        THEN
00184                            PERFORM NEW-KEY-ROUTINE THRU END-NEW-KEY
00185                        ELSE
00186                            MOVE 'NO MASTER' TO ERROR-MESSAGE
00187                            PERFORM DATA-ERROR-ROUTINE THRU END-DATA-ERROR.
00188                    IF LAST-TRAN-SWITCH IS EQUAL TO 1
00189                    THEN
00190                        PERFORM END-OF-TRANSACTIONS
00191                    ELSE
00192                        IF LAST-MASTER-SWITCH IS EQUAL TO 1
00193                        THEN
00194                            PERFORM END-OF-MASTERS.
00195                    GO TO TOP-OF-MAINLINE.

00197                END-OF-JOB-ROUTINE.
00198                    CLOSE OLD-INVENTORY-MASTER-FILE.
00199                    CLOSE NEW-INVENTORY-MASTER-FILE.
00200                    CLOSE INVENTORY-TRANSACTION-FILE.
00201                    CLOSE INVENTORY-ERROR-FILE.
00202                    CLOSE INVENTORY-REPORT-FILE.
00203                    STOP RUN.
```

Fig. 13.11: *Continued.*

```
00208           SAME-KEY-ROUTINE.

00210               IF T-QUANTITY IS NUMERIC
00211               THEN
00212                   NEXT SENTENCE
00213               ELSE
00214                   MOVE 'QUANTITY NOT NUMERIC' TO ERROR-MESSAGE
00215                   PERFORM DATA-ERROR-ROUTINE THRU END-DATA-ERROR
00216                   GO TO READ-NEXT-TRANSACTION.

00218               IF TRANSACTION-TYPE IS EQUAL TO 'ADD'
00219               THEN
00220                   ADD T-QUANTITY TO ADDITIONS-QUANTITY
00221                   ADD     1         TO ADDITIONS-COUNT
00222               ELSE
00223                   IF TRANSACTION-TYPE IS EQUAL TO 'DEL'
00224                   THEN
00225                       ADD T-QUANTITY TO DELETIONS-QUANTITY
00226                       ADD     1         TO DELETIONS-COUNT
00227                   ELSE
00228                       MOVE 'TRANSACTION INVALID'  TO ERROR-MESSAGE
00229                       PERFORM DATA-ERROR-ROUTINE THRU END-DATA-ERROR.

00231           READ-NEXT-TRANSACTION.

00233               READ INVENTORY-TRANSACTION-FILE
00234                   AT END MOVE 1 TO LAST-TRAN-SWITCH.

00236           END-SAME-KEY.

00238               EXIT.


00240           SET-ACCUMULATORS.

00242               MOVE ZEROS TO ADDITIONS-COUNT, ADDITIONS-QUANTITY,
00243                                DELETIONS-COUNT, DELETIONS-QUANTITY.

00245           END-SET-ACCUMULATORS.

00247               EXIT.
```

Fig. 13.11: *Continued.*

```
   7        INVUPDAT       2.59.18       OCT 21,1978

00249          NEW-KEY-ROUTINE.
00250              IF LINE-COUNT IS EQUAL TO 26
00251              THEN
00252                  PERFORM PRINT-HEADERS THRU END-PRINT-HEADERS
00253              ELSE
00254                  NEXT SENTENCE.
00255              MOVE O-PART-NUMBER        TO D-PART-NUMBER.
00256              MOVE O-DESCRIPTION        TO D-DESCRIPTION.
00257              MOVE O-STOCK-ON-HAND      TO D-OLD-BALANCE.
00258              MOVE ADDITIONS-COUNT      TO D-ADDITIONS-COUNT.
00259              MOVE ADDITIONS-QUANTITY   TO D-ADDITIONS-QUANTITY.
00260              MOVE DELETIONS-COUNT      TO D-DELETIONS-COUNT.
00261              MOVE DELETIONS-QUANTITY   TO D-DELETIONS-QUANTITY.
00262              MOVE O-STOCK-ON-HAND TO NEW-BALANCE.

00264              ADD  ADDITIONS-QUANTITY TO NEW-BALANCE.
00265              SUBTRACT DELETIONS-QUANTITY FROM NEW-BALANCE.
00266              MOVE NEW-BALANCE TO D-NEW-BALANCE.
00267              MOVE INVENTORY-SUMMARY-LINE TO REPORT-PRINT-LINE.
00268              WRITE REPORT-PRINT-RECORD
00269                  AFTER ADVANCING 2 LINES.
00270              ADD 1 TO LINE-COUNT.
00271              MOVE O-PART-NUMBER TO N-PART-NUMBER.
00272              MOVE O-DESCRIPTION TO N-DESCRIPTION.
00273              MOVE NEW-BALANCE      TO N-STOCK-ON-HAND
00274              WRITE NEW-INVENTORY-MASTER-RECORD
00275              PERFORM SET-ACCUMULATORS THRU END-SET-ACCUMULATORS.
00276              READ OLD-INVENTORY-MASTER-FILE
00277                  AT END MOVE 1 TO LAST-MASTER-SWITCH.
00278          END-NEW-KEY.
00279              EXIT.


00281          PRINT-HEADERS.
00282              MOVE   REPORT-HEADER TO REPORT-PRINT-LINE.
00283              WRITE REPORT-PRINT-RECORD
00284                  AFTER NEW-PAGE.
00285              MOVE   COLUMN-HEADER-1 TO REPORT-PRINT-LINE.
00286              WRITE REPORT-PRINT-RECORD
00287                  AFTER ADVANCING 2 LINES.
00288              MOVE   COLUMN-HEADER-2 TO REPORT-PRINT-LINE.
00289              WRITE REPORT-PRINT-RECORD
00290                  AFTER ADVANCING 1 LINES.
00291              MOVE ZEROS TO LINE-COUNT.
00292          END-PRINT-HEADERS.
00293              EXIT.
```

Fig. 13.11: *Continued.*

```
00297           END-OF-TRANSACTIONS.

00299               PERFORM NEW-KEY-ROUTINE THRU END-NEW-KEY
00300                   UNTIL LAST-MASTER-SWITCH IS EQUAL TO 1.
00301               PERFORM END-OF-JOB-ROUTINE.

00303           END-OF-MASTERS.

00305               MOVE 'NO MASTER' TO ERROR-MESSAGE.
00306               PERFORM DATA-ERROR-ROUTINE THRU END-DATA-ERROR
00307                   UNTIL LAST-TRAN-SWITCH IS EQUAL TO 1.
00308               PERFORM END-OF-JOB-ROUTINE.

00310           DATA-ERROR-ROUTINE.

00312               IF ERROR-LINE-COUNT IS EQUAL TO 28
00313               THEN
00314                   PERFORM PRINT-ERROR-HEADER THRU END-PRINT-ERROR-HEADER
00315               ELSE
00316                   NEXT SENTENCE.
00317               MOVE T-PART-NUMBER       TO E-PART-NUMBER.
00318               MOVE T-QUANTITY          TO E-QUANTITY.
00319               MOVE TRANSACTION-TYPE    TO E-TRANSACTION-TYPE.
00320               MOVE ERROR-DETAIL-LINE TO ERROR-PRINT-LINE.
00321               WRITE ERROR-PRINT-RECORD
00322                   AFTER ADVANCING 2 LINES.
00323               ADD 1 TO ERROR-LINE-COUNT.

00325           END-DATA-ERROR.

00327               EXIT.


00329           PRINT-ERROR-HEADER.

00331               MOVE ERROR-REPORT-HEADER TO ERROR-PRINT-LINE.
00332               WRITE ERROR-PRINT-RECORD AFTER NEW-PAGE.
00333               MOVE ERROR-COLUMN-HEADER-1 TO ERROR-PRINT-LINE.
00334               WRITE ERROR-PRINT-RECORD AFTER ADVANCING 2 LINES.
00335               MOVE ERROR-COLUMN-HEADER-2 TO ERROR-PRINT-LINE.
00336               WRITE ERROR-PRINT-RECORD AFTER ADVANCING 1 LINES.
00337               MOVE ZERO TO ERROR-LINE-COUNT.

00339           END-PRINT-ERROR-HEADER.

00341               EXIT.
```

Fig. 13.11: *Continued.*

such large blocks of code is not considered good programming practice (although on a modern, large, paging system, such repetition does not negatively impact program efficiency). Ideally, given the similarity of the code, we should be able to use the same routines for both normal and end-of-job processing. The best way to achieve this objective is to use **switches**.

A switch is simply a data field, defined by the programmer, that can be assigned a unique value depending upon conditions. In this example, two switches, LAST-MASTER-SWITCH and LAST-TRAN-SWITCH, have been defined in the WORKING-STORAGE SECTION. These switches are both given an initial value of zero by using a VALUE IS clause. The zero value will remain constant throughout the program until the last record is encountered. The last statement in the NEW-KEY-ROUTINE is

    READ MASTER-FILE

        AT END MOVE 1 TO LAST-MASTER-SWITCH.

The *only way* LAST-MASTER-SWITCH can be anything but zero is if the last record has been encountered. Similar code can be found in the SAME-KEY-ROUTINE.

Note that it is not essential that the switches be set to 0 or 1. Many programmers prefer to use 'Y' for yes and 'N' for no to indicate if the switch is on or off. Others use the COBOL reserved words HIGH-VALUE and LOW-VALUE. Actually, *any* set of two testable conditions, one representing switch-on and the other representing switch-off, can be used.

The problem with normal end-of-data testing is that, due to the nature of computer input, the only way to test for this condition is as part of the READ instruction. The whole point of the switch-setting technique is to set up another unique condition that can represent the end-of-data condition *and* that can be tested in another part of the program.

Where should the switch be tested? In this program, the only logical place is back in the mainline. Why? The mainline represents the steps involved in normal processing. An end-of-data condition represents an interruption in normal processing. The last official act of the NEW-KEY, SAME-KEY, and error routines is to read (or try to read) a record; if no additional record is present, this fact must be sensed before another normal cycle begins. Thus, the tests for an end-of-data condition must be performed after linkage to a normal detailed logic routine has been performed but before another cycle can begin. The ideal spot is at the bottom of the mainline (Fig. 13.11).

This new block of logic consists of two IF tests. Unless one of the last record switches has previously been set equal to 1, nothing happens. As soon as one of the switches is equal to 1, however, it can be assumed that the associated file has run out of data and that the remaining records in the other file must be handled before the program terminates.

Consider, for example, what must happen if the master file runs out of data first. The remaining transactions have no master file entry and thus are all considered errors. Each of these remaining records must be read and copied to the error report, and the necessary statements are housed in the ERROR-ROUTINE. The statement

>PERFORM ERROR-ROUTINE
>
>UNTIL LAST-TRAN-SWITCH IS EQUAL TO 1

will give control over and over again to the ERROR-ROUTINE until there are no more transactions (which is what LAST-TRAN-SWITCH equal to 1 implies).

The general form of this new version of the PERFORM is

>PERFORM paragraph-1 THRU paragraph-2
>
>UNTIL condition.

The "THRU paragraph-2" portion is optional. The statement sets up a repetitive operation, with the named paragraph or paragraphs being executed over and over again until the condition is met.

A few features that did not appear in the initial planning are present in the code of Fig. 13.11. The quantity fields of both the transaction records and the old master file records have been tested to make sure that they are NUMERIC before arithmetic is performed; this is simply the programmer's normal precaution designed to eliminate the risk of program termination due to bad data. These errors are different from the record type error detected in the program mainline, so a new routine named DATA-ERROR-ROUTINE has been added. Note that this new error routine uses the existing ERROR-ROUTINE to print an error message and read the next transaction.

THE MASTER FILE UPDATE APPLICATION

Every business establishment (and it is very difficult to imagine an exception) must maintain records in the form of master files and must maintain these files in an up-to-date condition. Thus every business establishment uses this master file update application. It is without a doubt the most common application of the computer. If you should ever become a professional programmer, you almost certainly will write, modify, or maintain programs resembling the example presented in this chapter. There is just no question about it; the application is so common that you *will* encounter it. The written report prepared as a spinoff of the master file update is really nothing more than a simple control break report. Many professional programmers make a very good living dealing almost exclusively with these two general classes of applications.

Inventory is but one example of the master file update application. In general terms, the problem involves a master file and a set of transactions, both of which are sorted into sequence by the same key. The master file update program then reads both files, creating a new, updated master file and, usually a summary report. What are some other examples of this class of computer applications?

Consider payroll, with its records on the year-to-date earnings of each employee. The year-to-date file is the master file. The transactions file consists of labor records, perhaps time cards, for the current payroll period, one for each employee. The master file update program reads the transactions and computes the pay due for the current period; this current information is then added to the start-of-period year-to-date information to get the end-of-period year-to-date information, the new master file. Several summary reports, including paychecks (a special case to be sure), accounting reports, and budgeting reports, can be produced.

Accounts receivable can be handled in similar fashion. The master file contains records indicating how much each customer owes at the beginning of the period. The transaction records represent payments and new credit purchases. The master file update program corrects the old master file to reflect payments and new purchases, prepares a new master file, and generates customer bills and accounting reports. Accounts payable is similar, except that the records show how much we owe others.

A business organization's general ledger is a compilation of its income and expenditures. The start-of-period ledger can be viewed as an old master file, records identifying new incomes and new expenditures can be viewed as transactions, and maintaining the ledger can be viewed as still another master file update application. Personnel records can be updated in this way, with transactions representing new employees, employee terminations, and changes in the status of existing employees being viewed as the transactions.

Banks maintain the balance of checking accounts, savings accounts, and customer loans through the master file update procedure. Schools keep track of student records and new student admissions. The government maintains income tax records, Social Security records, voter registrations, driving records, and many other records through, essentially, this same application. Insurance firms keep track of the status of outstanding policies. Law enforcement agencies maintain fingerprint, "modus operandi", and dangerous-criminal files. Libraries track their circulation. Hospitals control their bed inventory and the dispensing of drugs. Publishers keep mailing lists up to date. A list of specific examples of the master file update application could go on and on.

Many believe that, without the computer's record keeping ability as implemented through the master file update application, our society would have long ago drowned in its own paperwork. As society continues to grow in complexity, the need for record keeping can only increase.

SUMMARY

One of the most common of all business computer applications is the sequential master file update. The chapter began with a description of a typical example of this class of program, an inventory update application. The format of the two input files, the master file and the transactions file, was defined in other parts of the system. On output, the new master file must match the format of the old master file; thus it too was predefined. The programmer did have some freedom in structuring the printed report that was to accompany the output, and we planned the format of this report using a printer spacing work sheet.

To help plan the flow of program logic, we made up some test data and actually performed the necessary file update steps at the straw person level. We recognized three key conditions: master file key and transaction key match, transaction key high, and transaction key low. When the keys match, a change is made to the status of the master file record currently being processed. A transaction high condition represents a kind of control break leading to the writing of a new master file entry. If the transaction key is low, an error of some kind has occured.

Having defined the basic program logic, we moved on to more detailed planning, developing flowcharts for the mainline and each of the three primary conditions. Routines to handle the first record and end-of-data conditions were then flowcharted. A modular flowchart of the entire program was developed.

Once all the planning had been finished, we were ready to begin coding the program in COBOL. Although last-record processing was somewhat tricky, calling for the use of program control switches, no new COBOL features were introduced. The chapter ended with a discussion of other similar master file update applications.

KEY WORDS

master file   new master file   switch

modular flowchart   old master file   transaction file

EXERCISES

1. Why is it reasonable to assume that the format of the two input files and the new master file will be defined for the programmer in a master file update application?

2. Relate the "transaction high" condition (as described in the text) to the control breaks of Chapters 11 and 12.

3. Why was the "transaction low" condition (as described in the text) considered to be an error?

4. Why is last record processing so complex on a master file update application?

5. What is a modular flowchart?

6. Plan and write a program to update all of a bank's customer checking accounts. The old master file, containing the current balance in each account, is composed of records having the following fields:

positions	contents
1-7	customer account number
8-30	customer name
31-45	street address
46-65	city
66-67	state
68-72	zip code
73-80	account balance (999999V99)

The new master file will have an identical format. Transactions (checks and deposits) have the following format:

positions	contents
1-7	customer account number
8	transaction type (C=check; D=deposit)
9-15	amount of transaction (99999V99)

Generate a printed report showing, for each customer, the old balance, the total of all checks, the total of all deposits, and the computed new balance. The master file is in sequence by account number; the transactions are in random sequence, so don't forget to sort them.

Ideally, this program should be run with tape or disk master files. Since this is often unrealistic for students, use cards and the printer, or send the new master file to the card punch.

7. Federal law requires every employer to keep track of each employee's year-to-date earnings. Typically, this is done as part of the payroll processing program. Transactions are the same as those first presented in Chapter 6, and contain the following fields:

columns	contents
1-9	Social Secutiry number
10-25	employee's last name

381.

positions	contents
26-27	employee's initials
28-30	employee's department number
31-33	hours worked, to nearest 1/10
34-37	hourly pay rate (99V99)
38-39	number of dependents
40	marital status (M=married; S=single)

The year-to-date earnings master file contains the following:

positions	contents
1-9	Social Security Number
10-25	employee's last name
26-27	employee's initials
28-33	YTD gross pay (99999V99)
34-40	YTD federal income tax (99999V99)
41-47	YTD state income tax (99999V99)
48-54	YTD local income tax (99999V99)
55-61	YTD Social Security tax (99999V99)
62-68	YTD other deductions (99999V99)
69-75	YTD net pay (99999V99)

Plan and write a program to update the master file, adding the computed gross pay, individual deductions, and net pay to the values on the master file. Initially, use the skeleton version of the payroll program as defined in Chapter 6; later, add the detailed computational subroutines.

8. Our company runs a retail credit system similar to the well-known bank systems. Customer transactions contain the following fields:

columns	contents
1-8	customer account number
9-30	customer name
31-36	store number

positions	contents
37-42	amount of purchase or credit (9999V99)
43	type of transaction (C=credit; blank for purchase)

Customer information is kept on a master file containing the following data for each customer:

positions	contents
1-8	customer account number
9-30	customer name
31-45	street address
46-55	city
56-57	state
58-62	zip code
63-68	balance due last month (9999V99)

Write a program to update the master file and produce bills for each customer. The bills should list each purchase or credit transaction on a separate line. A summary line should show the old balance due, new purchases, credits, and the new balance due. Payments on last month's bill will show up as credits. Compute and print (as part of the summary line) the minimum payment due, which is 10% of the balance due or $10, whichever is greater.

9. In addition to collecting money from credit account customers, our firm must pay the retail stores for any purchases made under our credit system. Using the same transactions as used in exercise 8, sort them into store number sequence and prepare an accounts payable report, updating the store master file in the process. The store master file contains:

positions	contents
1-6	store account number
7-26	store name
27-41	street address
42-46	city
47-48	state

positions	contents
49-53	zip code
54-61	old account balance

The old account balance represents funds we owe them but have not yet paid them.

The accounts payable report should show, for each store, the old balance, the sum of all purchases made at that store, the sum of all credit transactions against that store, and the computed new balance (old plus purchases minus credits).

Our service charge, 3% of the computed new balance with a minimum of $25, should be computed and subtracted from the computed new balance to find the amount due the store; it is this amount due that should be stored in the master file.

10. Student master files contain the following fields:

positions	contents
1-9	student identification number
10-25	student name
26-28	credits earned to date
29-31	grade points earned to date
32-35	cumulative grade point average

Grade reports for the current term include:

columns	contents
1-9	student identification number
10-25	student name
26-31	course identification code
32	credit hours
33	grade (A, B, C, D, or F)

Write a program to compute current grade point averages and to recompute cumulative grade point averages for all the students in the school (if your school uses something other than a 4.0 scale, use your own school's rules). Generate complete grade reports for each student, listing each course taken and printing the current and cumulative GPA's in a summary line. Each student should appear on a separate page.

11. Statistics on the point production of the members of our basketball team have been collected and stored in a master file containing the following fields:

positions	contents
1-2	player number
3-15	player name
16-18	field goals attempted
19-22	field goals made
23-25	field goal percentage (V999)
26-29	fouls attempted
30-33	fouls made
34-36	foul shooting percentage (V999)
37-40	total points
38-39	games played
40-42	average points per game (99V9)
43-46	assists
47-50	rebounds
51-53	rebounds per game (99V9)

Following each game, a punched card is prepared for each player containing the player number, field goal attempts, field goals made, foul attempts, fouls made, assists, and rebounds for the just-completed game. These transactions are used to update the master file. The printed output should show the new master file entry for each player.

If basketball is not your game, a similar program can be developed for almost any sport.

IV

Direct Access

14

Direct Access File Processing

OVERVIEW

The applications of Part III were all concerned with processing sequential files. In each case, the objective was to read or write all the records in the file in a fixed sequence; in fact, the logic of the programming examples depended upon this sequence being maintained.

Often it is necessary to access only one record rather than a complete file, thus creating a need for direct access. In this chapter we begin our analysis of direct access file processing, concentrating on one of the easier to use direct access techniques, the division/remainder method. Chapter 15 will consider the updating of such files. We will begin with a brief discussion of underlying concepts of direct access before moving on to the COBOL implementation of these concepts.

DIRECT ACCESS

Sequential access is not always acceptable. Consider, for example, the task of locating several books in the library by using a card catalog. Straight sequential access would involve starting with the very first drawer and reading through the entire catalog until the desired volumes were located. Obviously, no one does it quite this way. Instead, students take advantage of the fact that the catalog is arranged alphabetically, and quickly narrow the search to a relative handful of cards. This is a form of **direct access**. The term direct access relates to the act of retrieving a specific record of data, disregarding its physical position in a file. In effect, direct access means that we go directly (or almost directly) to the desired record without first passing through all the records that preceed it. The term **random access**, which implies processing in no particular order, is synonymous with direct access.

Direct Access Devices

Magnetic tape will not do for such applications; the very nature of tape, a continuous ribbon of material, requires sequential processing. Some other type of mass storage device must be used for direct access.

What if we were to cut a reel of magnetic tape into strips (Fig. 14.1), with each strip containing exactly one hundred records? Assume that the file has been organized sequentially and that there are no "missing" records. Records 1 through 100 would be found on the first strip, records 101 through 200 would be on the second strip,

Fig. 14.1: *The Direct Access Concept Illustrated by a Volume of Magnetic Tape Cut Into Strips.*

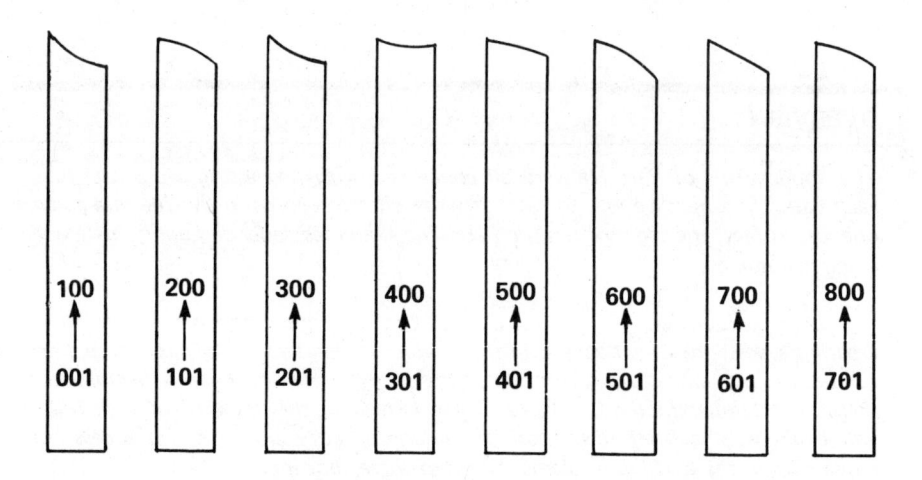

and so on. Let's say that we wanted record 1132. It's a simple matter to figure out which strip holds this record; all we need do is find this strip, mount it on some magnetic I/O device, and search the selected strip for the desired record. It's not quite direct, but we do get pretty close without going through all the intervening records.

Clearly, no one is going to cut a reel of tape into strips and use them for direct access—the individual strips would be just too difficult to handle. Still, the image of tape strips does illustrate the basic idea of direct access.

The first commercially important direct access device was the magnetic **drum**. The name is quite descriptive. Imagine a cylindrical, drum-shaped device with our "strips of tape" wrapped around the outer surface. Replace these strips with a continuous. unbroken coating of the same material that coats magnetic tape and you have a magnetic drum. Data is stored around the surface in a series of circular patterns called tracks.

Today's most commonly used direct access device is the magnetic **disk**. In describing magnetic tape, we used the analogy of reel-to-reel sound-recording tape. A magnetic disk is analogous to a long-playing record album. It's a disk-shaped device with a magnetic coating on the flat surface (Fig. 14.2). Rather than being stored in a spiral pattern as is the case on a record album, data on magnetic disk is stored on a series of concentric circles called **tracks** (Fig. 14.3).

On a long-playing record album, it is possible to play the fourth song on side 1 by simply picking up the tone arm and placing it at the beginning of the desired song. A magnetic disk is equipped with a movable **access mechanism** that houses the **read/write heads** and works in analogous fashion. If, for example, the programmer wants a record that is stored on track number 75, he or she simply instructs the computer to move the access mechanism over track number 75 and then look for the desired record.

Some computer manufacturers, particularly on minicomputer systems, subdivide a track into **sectors**, with one or more records of data stored in each sector. Except for a slight difference in the way the programmer must specify the desired positioning of the access mechanism, the sector approach and the track approach to direct access are similar. When using tracks, the programmer normally specifies a track location. With sectors, the programmer will normally specify a sector number, and the computations needed to convert a sector number to an actual position for the access mechanism are done by the system. Sectors tend to be a little easier for the programmer to use; tracks give the programmer greater flexibility.

The Relative Address Concept

The capacity of a disk pack is usually measured in millions of characters of storage capacity. As a result, a typical pack in a typical installation holds not just one but many different files. This creates a very real problem for the programmer.

Imagine that you are about to create a direct access file. How can you know what tracks or sectors are to be used for your file? On some smaller system, a clerk, sometimes called the data base administrator, will assign specific tracks, and the programmer codes to match this assignment. On a larger system, however, such direct human involvement tends to become very inefficient. Instead, special system programs assign direct access space as it is needed.

How then can the programmer know exactly where a file is to be located? The program must be written in such a way that it tells the computer system to move the access mechanism to a specific track in order to begin a search for a specific record, but space is assigned only after the program has been written.

The programmer gets around this quandry by using **relative addresses** rather than actual addresses. The concept is really very simple; let's consider it first at the record level. The very first record stored in a file is **relative record** 0 (it is 0 records away from the start of the file). The second record is relative record 1; the third record is relative record 2; the 100th record is relative record 99, and so on. These relative locations are valid no matter where the file actually begins; thus the programmer can refer to relative locations without regard for the actual physical starting point of the file. As the space is actually allocated for the file, a record of the file name and the physical location of the beginning of the file can be maintained. Once this has been done, the actual physical location of any record can be obtained by adding the actual location of the beginning of the file and the relative location of the specific record in the file. Relative record 0 would, for example, be found at the start of the file plus zero records, while relative record 99 would be at the start of the file plus 99 records.

On disk, records are typically stored on tracks or in sectors, and it is this physical unit of storage (rather than a specific record) that is accessed; thus a **relative sector** or **relative track** address might be more relevant than a relative record number. Relative track 0 is simply the first track in a file (start of file plus 0 tracks), while the 100th track would be relative track 99; a similar argument could be made for relative sectors. Once again, by adding the relative location to the actual address of the first physical sector or track assigned to the file, it is possible to compute the actual location of the physical unit of storage holding a desired record.

Where can the physical location of the start of a file be found? On most direct access devices, each disk pack (or disk volume) has a table of contents or index of the files stored on that volume; typically this table of contents is stored in an easy to find location, for example on the first track or two. Thus, locating a record normally involves two steps: find the location of the start of the file in the table of contents; then add to the start address the relative address of the desired record to find the actual address of the desired record.

Searching a Track

On disk, the best that can be done is to move the read/write mechanism to the track containing the desired record. Almost certainly there will be numerous other records stored on this track; how can the proper one be found?

Records are typically stored on disk in the format of Fig. 14.4. Preceeding the actual data is a key, a logical key—a part number or employee number, for example.

Fig. 14.2: *A Cross-Section of a Disk.*

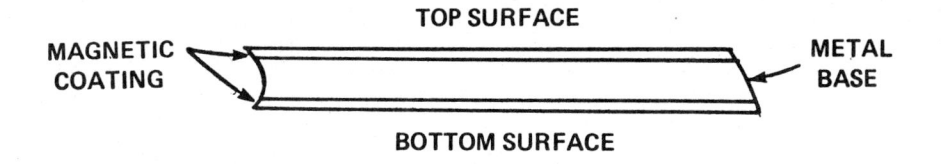

Fig. 14.3: *On a Disk, Data is Stored on a Series of Concentric Circles Called Tracks.*

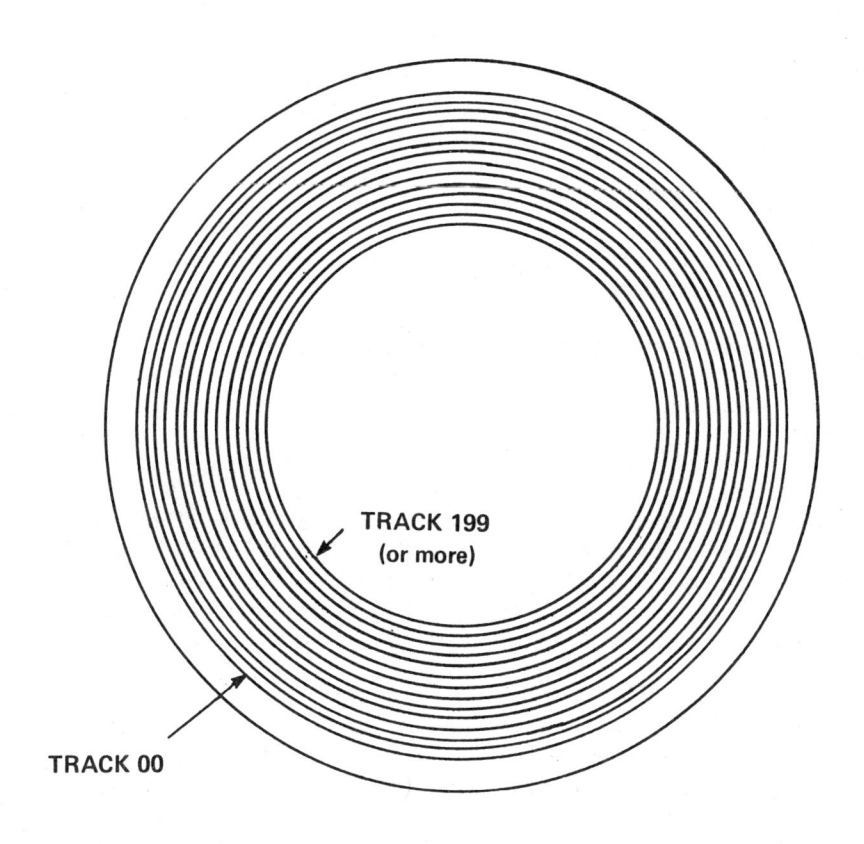

Fig. 14.4: *Data as Stored on a Disk.*

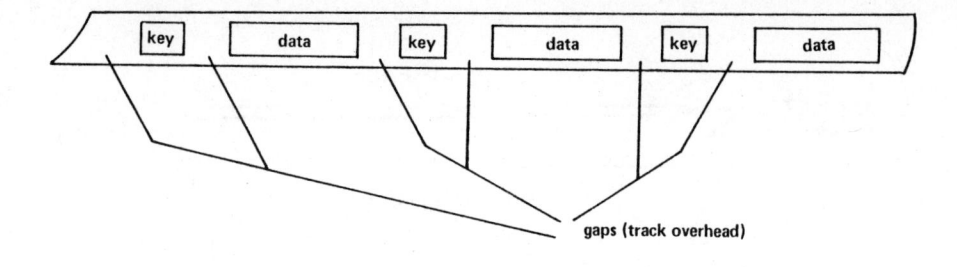

[Figure 14.4: A disk track showing alternating key and data blocks (key, data, key, data, key, data) with gaps (track overhead) between them.]

The task of locating a record for employee number 12345 would thus consist of the following steps:

1. find the start address of the file in the table of contents;

2. add the relative track location of record 12345 to this file start address;

3. locate the read/write mechanism over the computed track;

4. search for a record with the key 12345;

5. read the data record that follows key 12345 into the computer.

Clearly the programmer must provide two distinct pieces of identification if a record is to be located. First is the relative track address (or relative sector). Second is the logical key of the record. To this point we have concentrated on the physical aspects of storing records on a direct access device; we are now about to turn our attention to the logical aspects of direct access—to those things that are the programmer's responsibility.

Before turning our attention to the logic of direct access, we should mention an alternative to the "search by logical key" approach described above. Imagine (Fig. 14.4) if the key portion of each data record was replaced by a simple count. The first record on the file would be assigned count 0; the second record, 1; the third, 2; and so on. Each count would be a relative record number, representing the location of the record relative to the beginning of the file. The search for a specific record would require only the relative record number rather than both the relative track address *and* the logical search key; since only one field would be needed access would seem (to the programmer) to be easier.

The relative record approach is the new American National Standard for COBOL (1972). From a practical standpoint, however, it has yet to be universally implemented. We feel that the old, 1968 standard, which called for relative track addressing, remains the most commonly used direct access technique, and thus we have based the examples in this and the next chapter on the old standard.

DIRECT ACCESS TECHNIQUES

On a sequential file, records are simply written, one after another, until all have been written. Later, when the file is read, processing normally starts at the beginning and proceeds to the end of the file, with each record read in sequence. The position of an individual record is irrelevant. The order in which records are processed is a direct function of the order in which they are created.

On a direct access file, things are different. The whole point of a direct access application is to process individual records, one at a time, disregarding the physical position of the record on the file. If this objective is to be achieved, the exact location of each individual record must be known. How can we possibly know the location of every record on a file? Basically, there are two alternatives:

1. control where each record is placed by using some predictable and repetitive rule, or

2. write records where they fit but keep track, after the fact, of exactly where each one has been written.

The first alternative involves the use of an algorithm. If, for example, the Social Security number is the record key, the last four digits might be used to represent a relative record number. On creation, a record would be stored by simply taking the last four digits, treating them as a single field, and instructing the computer to write the record using this field as the relative record number. Later, when the record is retrieved, the same algorithm can be used, with the system being told to search for a record having a relative record number composed of the last four digits of a Social Security number. If a relative track address is desired, perhaps the last two digits can be used. The key idea is that an algorithm, a consistently applied rule, is used on creating the file and this same rule is used again on retrieving the data.

The most commonly used algorithm is the **division/remainder method**. With this technique, the logical key of the record is divided by a constant, and the remainder is used as a relative address. As long as the same constant is used on both file creation and file retrieval, the computer can, in effect, "remember" where the record was stored, thus allowing direct retrieval.

The algorithm approach is based on controlling the location of individual records. There are some problems associated with this approach. Record keys are not, as a rule, distributed as perfectly as pure theory would have them; instead, record keys tend to cluster. As a result, two or more record keys could generate the same relative record number. (You may, for example, know two people who have the same last four digits in their Social Security numbers.) When two or more logical keys generate the same relative record number, a **synonym** is produced. Ideally, all synonyms should be stored at the same physical location on the disk or other direct access device, but this is impossible.

How do we handle synonyms? The problem cannot be avoided; no matter how good our algorithm may be, synonyms will be generated. The only real solution is to allow extra space for **overflow**. Most computer systems follow a procedure in which

1. an attempt is made to write a record where it belongs;

2. if the spot where it belongs is already occupied (in other words, if a synonym has been generated), the record is placed as close to where it belongs as possible.

The general rule of thumb is a simple one: Allow about 20% for overflow. If, for example, you expect a file of 1000 records, allow for 1200. The extra 20% creates space for overflow records and allows for enough slack throughout the file that localized clusters of synonyms can be accomodated. If relative track addresses are used, allow for extra tracks, again using roughly a 20% overflow factor.

As an alternative to the algorithm approach, it is possible to place records where they best fit and then to keep track of where they have been placed. Consider, for example, the index in the back of this book. The word "synonym" is found in Chapter 14 simply because it fits here; no algorithm has been used to determine its position. By referring to the index, however, it is possible for you to locate every occurrence of the word "synonym". Basically, the word has been written where the flow of the material dictates it be placed, and a separate record has been maintained to indicate its position.

The same thing can be done with data files. A file can be created sequentially. As each record is added to the file, an entry identifying the logical key and the record's physical position on the direct access device can be made in an **index** or table. Later, when the data record is retrieved, the table can be searched for the logical key, the physical position can be extracted from the table, and the record can be retrieved.

Are there any advantages to the table approach? Certainly. Synonyms are no longer a significant problem, since the relative record number or relative track number is a function of the order of creation (rather than the logical key), and no two records can possibly be created at the same time. As a result, the size of the file can be planned to contain the number of records actually anticipated, with overflow space needed only to hold data added after initial file creation.

What about disadvantages? The big one is the index itself. The index must be created and kept up to date. It must be stored, and storage consumes space. Looking up a key in an index is much more complex than simply computing the key using a straightforward algorithm. If the index is lost, the ability to retrieve the data on the file is lost, while an algorithm could simply be recoded.

Fortunately, most suppliers of computer equipment market software that supports the creation and maintenance of indexed files. Essentially, these packages assume responsibility for the index, thus freeing the programmer from this burden and making the indexed technique relatively easy to use.

In this chapter, we will investigate the creation and access of a file using the division/remainder method. In Chapter 15, we will cover the updating of the file. Indexed files will be covered in Chapters 16 and 17.

SIMPLE DIRECT ACCESS USING THE DIVISION/REMAINDER METHOD

We want to create a file of descriptive information on all the products sold by our company. The file will consist of records holding the following information:

positions	contents
1-8	product number
9-30	product description
31-36	current selling price
37-40	shipping cost
41-46	supplier number
47-52	secondary supplier number

The file will be used in preparing bills and advertising copy, evaluating supplier performance, and providing product descriptions on numerous unrelated reports. It will also be accessed by a number of business planning applications.

Our company makes roughly 1000 different products, so the file must contain about 1000 records. Individual records are 52 characters long. Let's estimate how much disk space might be needed for the file. We'll use a specific example to illustrate the process.

On an IBM 3330 direct access system, the capacity of each track is 13,030 characters. When keys are used, each record must be allocated 191 characters for system overhead. Adding the length of the key and the length of the data record to the 191 overhead characters (191 + 8 + 52) yields 251 characters that must be allocated for each record in the file. Given the track capacity of 13,030 characters, division indicates that 51 records can be stored on each track. The statistics used to support these calculations were taken from IBM's *COBOL Programmer's Guide* (IBM publication number GC28-6399); the precise constants used will, of course, vary with the device.

If 51 records can be stored on each track and a total of 1000 records must be stored, slightly over 19 tracks will be needed. Since fractional tracks cannot be allocated, 20 is the correct estimate. But, what about overflow? When an algorithmic approach is used, 20% extra space is normally allocated to handle synonyms; thus 25 tracks should be set aside to hold the file. Actually, there may well be no more than 1000 actual records, but synonyms tend to be clustered rather than evenly distributed and, since it is impossible to predict where these clusters will occur, the extra space must be spread throughout the entire file. In some places, all available space will be utilized. In other places, there will be unused space. There is really no way to beat this problem.

Now what? We know that a total of 25 tracks will be needed to hold the data. Our objective is to spread the 1000 records over these 25 tracks as evenly as possible. How can this be done?

The key is the relative track number. The first track in the file is relative track 0; the second track is relative track 1; the third is relative track 2; and so on through the last track, which is relative track 24. What would happen if we were to divide the logical key of each of the records by 25? Each division operation would generate a quotient and a remainder. There is something very interesting about these remainders: None can be less than zero and none can be more than 24. Why? The remainder cannot be negative, so it must be at least equal to zero. If the remainder is greater than 24, an error must have been made, because 25 would have gone into the dividend at least one more time.

The remainder, following division by 25, must be a number between 0 and 24. Compare this range with the range of relative track addresses in our file. Both ranges are identical! The remainder can simply be used as a relative track number. Later, on retrieval, the same algorithm can be used to generate the same relative track number.

Earlier, we mentioned that the new standard calls for relative record addressing rather than relative track addressing. Our file contains roughly 1000 records; allowing for a 20% overflow means that the file must contain space for 1200 records. What are the possible remainders generated from dividing the logical key by 1200? The remainder must lie between 0 and 1199. What are the relative record numbers that would be assigned to 1200 records? The first would be 0; the second, 1; the last one would be relative record 1199. If we were to use relative record rather than relative track addressing, we would simply divide the logical key by the number of records planned for the file, using the remainder as the relative record number.

Actually, we probably wouldn't use 1200 as a divisor, but would instead choose an odd number close to it. Computer experts have long believed that the divisor used in computing relative record or relative track numbers using the division/remainder method must be a prime number (a number which is divisible only by itself). 25 is not prime because it is evenly divisible by 5; the closest prime to 25 is 23. Clearly, 1200 is not prime, either. It was argued that using a prime number as the divisor would tend to generate relative addresses in a more random fashion, thus

tending to distribute the records more evenly throughout the file. Recent studies*
have shown that, while there may be reason to avoid the use of even numbers, an odd
divisor (25 or 1201, for example) works just as well as a prime number.

CREATING A DIRECT ACCESS FILE USING COBOL

It is easy to create a direct access file using the divisional/remainder method and
COBOL. Only a few new COBOL features are needed; let's cover them division by
division. We will be using relative *track* addressing.

The fact that a direct access file is to be created has no real impact on the
IDENTIFICATION DIVISION. The primary impact is found in the ENVIRONMENT
DIVISION; given the fact that all external factors are described in the ENVIRON-
MENT DIVISION, the need for significant changes here should not surprise you.

Within the ENVIRONMENT DIVISION (Fig. 14.5), SELECT and ASSIGN
clauses are needed for each file accessed by the program. For a direct access file,
two clauses, ACCESS MODE and ACTUAL KEY, must be added. The "system name"
associated with the ASSIGN clause must read, on an IBM machine, **DA-D**-name.

The **ACCESS MODE** clause defines the access mode. If the clause is not coded,
COBOL assumes that ACCESS MODE IS SEQUENTIAL which, on all earlier programs, was exactly what we wanted. If direct access is desired, the programmer must
override this **default** and code

ACCESS MODE IS RANDOM

The keyword RANDOM has, at least in this context, the same meaning as direct.

Having informed the system that random or direct access is to be used, the
programmer must now clearly identify the access key. Thus, an "**ACTUAL KEY** IS
data-name" clause must be coded. The ACTUAL KEY will eventually be defined as
a data item in the DATA DIVISION.

For a direct access file the FD entry of the DATA DIVISION, FILE SECTION
must contain the clause: BLOCK CONTAINS 1 RECORDS. Direct access records
must not be blocked.

The most important addition to the DATA DIVISION is the definition of the
ACTUAL KEY previously mentioned in the ENVIRONMENT DIVISION (Fig.
14.5). Remember how, during our discussion of basic direct access concepts, it was
necessary to provide two pieces of information, a relative track address and a logical
key, in order to directly access a record? The ACTUAL KEY contains *both* parts.
The relative track address must come first, followed by the logical key.

---

*Lum, Yuen, and Dodd, "Key to Address Transform Techniques: A Fundamental
Performance Study on Existing Formatted Files", Communications of the ACM,
April 1971.*

```
IDENTIFICATION DIVISION.
PROGRAM-ID. PRFILCRT.
AUTHOR. FISHER & DAVIS.
REMARKS. THIS PROGRAM CREATES A DIRECT ACCESS
         PRODUCT FILE USING THE DIVISION/REMAINDER
         METHOD.

ENVIRONMENT DIVISION.

CONFIGURATION SECTION.
SOURCE-COMPUTER. IBM-370-148.
OBJECT-COMPUTER. IBM-370-148.

INPUT-OUTPUT SECTION.
FILE-CONTROL.
    SELECT PRODUCT-SEQUENTIAL-FILE ASSIGN TO UT-S-PRDSEQ.
    SELECT PRODUCT-DIRECT-FILE     ASSIGN TO DA-D-PRDDIR
        ACCESS MODE IS RANDOM
        ACTUAL KEY IS ACTUAL-KEY-FIELD.
```

Fig. 14.5: *The IDENTIFICATION, ENVIRONMENT, and DATA divisions of a direct access file creation program.*

COBOL Coding Form

SYSTEM: PRODUCT
PROGRAM: DIRECT FILE CREATION
PROGRAMMER: DAVIS & FISHER
DATE: 4-15-79
PAGE 2 OF 4
PUNCHING INSTRUCTIONS — GRAPHIC: ∅ PUNCH: ZERO
CARD FORM #

```
DATA DIVISION.
FILE SECTION.
FD  PRODUCT-SEQUENTIAL-FILE
    LABEL RECORD IS OMITTED.
01  PRODUCT-SEQUENTIAL-CARD.
    05  PRODUCT-SEQUENTIAL-RECORD.
        10  I-PRODUCT-NUMBER     PIC 9(8).
        10  FILLER               PIC X(44).
    05  FILLER                   PIC X(28).
FD  PRODUCT-DIRECT-FILE
    LABEL RECORD IS STANDARD
    BLOCK CONTAINS 1 RECORDS.
01  PRODUCT-DIRECT-RECORD.
    05  DA-PRODUCT-NUMBER        PIC 9(8).
    05  DA-DESCRIPTION           PIC X(22).
    05  DA-SELLING-PRICE         PIC 9999V99.
    05  DA-SHIPPING-COST         PIC 99V99.
    05  DA-SUPPLIER-CODE         PIC X(6).
    05  DA-2ND-SUPPLIER          PIC X(6).
```

Fig. 14.5: *Continued.*

COBOL Coding Form

SYSTEM: PRODUCT
PROGRAM: DIRECT FILE CREATION
PROGRAMMER: DAVIS & FISHER
DATE: 4-15-79
PUNCHING INSTRUCTIONS — GRAPHIC: ∅ PUNCH: ZERO
PAGE 3 OF 4

```
WORKING-STORAGE SECTION.
77  WORK-FIELD
77  QUOTIENT
01  ACTUAL-KEY-FIELD.
    05  RELATIVE-TRACK     PIC S9(5)   USAGE COMP SYNC.
    05  LOGICAL-RECORD-KEY PIC S9(5)   USAGE COMP SYNC.
                           PIC S9(5)
                           PIC 9(8).   USAGE COMP SYNC.
```

Fig. 14.5: *Continued.*

COBOL Coding Form

SYSTEM	PRODUCT	PUNCHING INSTRUCTIONS	PAGE 4 OF 4
PROGRAM	DIRECT FILE CREATION	GRAPHIC Ø	CARD FORM #
PROGRAMMER	DAVIS & FISHER DATE 4-15-79	PUNCH ZERO	

SEQUENCE | CONT. | A | B | COBOL STATEMENT | IDENTIFICATION

```
       PROCEDURE DIVISION.

        HOUSEKEEPING.
           OPEN INPUT  PRODUCT-SEQUENTIAL-FILE.
           OPEN OUTPUT PRODUCT-DIRECT-FILE.

        FILE-CREATE-LOOP.
           READ PRODUCT-SEQUENTIAL-FILE
               AT END GO TO END-OF-JOB.
           MOVE PRODUCT-SEQUENTIAL-RECORD TO PRODUCT-DIRECT-RECORD.
      ***
      **** CREATE THE ACTUAL-KEY-FIELD
      ***
           MOVE I-PRODUCT-NUMBER TO WORK-FIELD, LOGICAL-RECORD-KEY.
           DIVIDE WORK-FIELD BY 25 GIVING QUOTIENT
               REMAINDER RELATIVE TRACK.
           WRITE PRODUCT-DIRECT-RECORD
                 INVALID KEY PERFORM END-OF-JOB.
           GO TO FILE-CREATE-LOOP.

        END-OF-JOB.
           CLOSE PRODUCT-SEQUENTIAL-FILE.
           CLOSE PRODUCT-DIRECT-FILE.
           STOP RUN.
```

Fig. 14.6: *The PROCEDURE DIVISION.*

The relative track address must be a pure binary integer consisting of exactly 5 digits; thus the PICTURE clause, S9(5). (The S allows for a sign.) The "pure binary" requirement is something we have yet to cover. Computers are designed to be most efficient when working with numbers represented in the binary (or base-2) number system. In COBOL, this objective can be achieved by defining the field as **COMPUTATIONAL**. Further efficiencies can be achieved by defining the data item as **SYNCHRONIZED**, which means aligned on an internal storage boundary.

The second part of the ACTUAL KEY is the logical key as seen by the programmer; if, for example, the application is to search for records by product number, then the second part of the ACTUAL KEY will be the product number. This part may consist of from 1 to 255 characters and the data may be of any type—character, numeric, alphabetic, pure binary, or any other form acceptable to COBOL. Both parts of the ACTUAL KEY must be correct before a record can be successfully read or written.

In the PROCEDURE DIVISION, the only new clause is the **INVALID KEY** clause associated with a READ or a WRITE statement (see Fig. 14.6). The INVALID KEY clause works much like an AT END clause, except that the condition being tested is an unsuccessful completion of the input or output operation rather than the end of data. What can cause unsuccessful completion of an input or output operation? The key might be something other than a pure binary number. On a read, the searched for logical key might not be on the file. The relative track number specified in the first part of the ACTUAL KEY might be outside the range of tracks set aside for the file. In short, anything that would make it impossible to complete the input or output operation is sensed as an INVALID KEY. As was the case with an end-of-file condition, the programmer can code a special routine to deal with the INVALID KEY condition.

Otherwise, the PROCEDURE DIVISION for a direct access program is very straightforward. Basically, all that must be done to create a direct access file is to compute the needed relative track address, move the result into the first part of the ACTUAL KEY, move the logical key into the second half of the ACTUAL KEY, and issue a WRITE instruction (Fig. 14.6) for each record.

Note the algorithm. The search key, in this example the product number, is first moved to a work field that has been defined COMPUTATIONAL SYNCHRONIZED, thus allowing for highly efficient (and accurate) computation. Next, the work field is divided by 25 (remember the objective of spreading the records over 25 tracks). Following division the remainder is placed in the RELATIVE-TRACK portion of the ACTUAL-KEY-FIELD by coding

DIVIDE WORK BY 25 GIVING QUOTIENT

REMAINDER RELATIVE-TRACK.

Next, the product number is moved to the second part of the ACTUAL KEY through a simple MOVE instruction, and a WRITE is issued. Basically, that's all there is to it.

A listing of a complete program to create a direct access file using the division/remainder technique in COBOL is shown in Fig. 14.7.

Incidently, when using relative record addressing, the ACTUAL KEY clause is not used. Instead, the programmer must place a relative record number in a field called the NOMINAL KEY. Relative record direct access references *only* this relative record number; the logical key is not needed to support the search process.

USING A DIRECT ACCESS FILE

There are many different ways the data stored in the direct access product file might be used. In preparing customer bills, for example, the product description might be added to an itemized statement by simply using the part number to access the file and then moving the product description field into the about-to-be-printed detail line. Just prior to shipping an order, the file might be used to provide shipping costs for each of the individual parts composing the order. Another possible application would be in contract bidding, where a salesperson might submit a list of the products being considered by a potential customer; in this application, the product file would be accessed by part number for each different product in the order, the current selling price and shipping cost of the product would be retrieved, and the total cost of the order would be compiled.

These applications all have one thing in common. The data on the file is simply being used without modification. It's much like a table look-up application, except that the table is stored on a secondary storage device. Let's consider a specific example.

Preparing Price Quotations

Preparing accurate price quotations for customer consideration is a long-standing problem in our organization. Prices change, making it difficult to keep a price book up to date. Sales people tend to make errors when using a price book. If a price quotation is too high, we may lose the business; if the quoted price is too low, we may get the order but lose money filling it. As if these reasons were not enough, we recently had a price book fall into the hands of a competitor, causing us very real problems in several competitive bidding situations.

Sales has proposed that we do away with price books, replacing them with a computer file and a program. The product file, the one created earlier using the division/remainder method, holds the current selling price and shipping cost of each product offered for sale by our firm. The price quotation program will read a series of input cards through a remote card reader that has been installed in each sales office. Each card will identify, by part number, a specific product desired by a customer; a complete order may include several cards. Using the product number as a key, the program will find the master record for the product in the file, extract the selling price and the shipping cost, generate a report listing, line by line, each individual product, and then summarize, at the end of the report, the total cost of the entire potential order.

```
1                    0.42.36      NOV 9,1978


00002           IDENTIFICATION DIVISION.

00004           PROGRAM-ID. PRFILCRT.
00005           AUTHOR.     FISHER & DAVIS.
00006           REMARKS.    THIS PROGRAM CREATES A DIRECT ACCESS
00007                       PRODUCT FILE USING THE DIVISION/REMAINDER
00008                       METHOD.

00010           ENVIRONMENT DIVISION.

00012              CONFIGURATION SECTION.
00013              SOURCE-COMPUTER.  IBM-370-148.
00014              OBJECT-COMPUTER.  IBM-370-148.
00015              INPUT-OUTPUT SECTION.
00016              FILE-CONTROL.
00017                 SELECT PRODUCT-SEQUENTIAL-FILE ASSIGN TO UT-S-PRDSEQ.
00018                 SELECT PRODUCT-DIRECT-FILE     ASSIGN TO DA-D-PRDDIR
00019                    ACCESS MODE IS RANDOM
00020                    ACTUAL KEY IS ACTUAL-KEY-FIELD.


00022           DATA DIVISION.

00024              FILE SECTION.
00025              FD PRODUCT-SEQUENTIAL-FILE
00026                 LABEL RECORD IS OMITTED.
00027              01 PRODUCT-SEQUENTIAL-CARD.
00028                 05  PRODUCT-SEQUENTIAL-RECORD.
00029                     10  I-PRODUCT-NUMBER    PIC 9(8).
00030                     10  FILLER              PIC X(44).
00031                 05  FILLER                  PIC X(28).

00033              FD PRODUCT-DIRECT-FILE
00034                 LABEL RECORD IS STANDARD
00035                 BLOCK CONTAINS 1 RECORDS.
00036              01 PRODUCT-DIRECT-RECORD.
00037                 05  DA-PRODUCT-NUMBER       PIC 9(8).
00038                 05  DA-DESCRIPTION          PIC X(22).
00039                 05  DA-SELLING-PRICE        PIC 9999V99.
00040                 05  DA-SHIPPING-COST        PIC 99V99.
00041                 05  DA-SUPPLIER-CODE        PIC X(6).
00042                 05  DA-2ND-SUPPLIER         PIC X(6).


00044              WORKING-STORAGE SECTION.
00045              77 WORK-FIELD                  PIC S9(5)   USAGE COMP SYNC.
00046              77 QUOTIENT                    PIC S9(5)   USAGE COMP SYNC.

00048              01 ACTUAL-KEY-FIELD.
00049                 05 RELATIVE-TRACK           PIC S9(5)   USAGE COMP SYNC.
00050                 05 LOGICAL-RECORD-KEY       PIC 9(8).
```

Fig. 14.7: *A listing for the direct access file creation program.*

```
00055           PROCEDURE DIVISION.
00057               HOUSEKEEPING.
00059                   OPEN INPUT   PRODUCT-SEQUENTIAL-FILE.
00060                   OPEN OUTPUT  PRODUCT-DIRECT-FILE.


00063               FILE-CREATE-LOOP.
00065                   READ PRODUCT-SEQUENTIAL-FILE
00066                       AT END GO TO END-OF-JOB.
00067                   MOVE PRODUCT-SEQUENTIAL-RECORD TO PRODUCT-DIRECT-RECORD.
00068               ***
00069               **** CREATE THE ACTUAL-KEY-FIELD
00070               ***
00071                   MOVE I-PRODUCT-NUMBER TO WORK-FIELD, LOGICAL-RECORD-KEY.
00072                   DIVIDE WORK-FIELD BY 25 GIVING QUOTIENT
00073                       REMAINDER RELATIVE-TRACK.
00074                   WRITE PRODUCT-DIRECT-RECORD
00075                       INVALID KEY PERFORM END-OF-JOB.
00076                   GO TO FILE-CREATE-LOOP.


00079               END-OF-JOB.
00081                   CLOSE PRODUCT-SEQUENTIAL-FILE.
00082                   CLOSE PRODUCT-DIRECT-FILE.
00083                   STOP RUN.
```

Fig. 14.7: *Continued.*

The fact that all prices will be maintained on a single, centralized file makes it relatively easy to keep price information up to date. Computers are more accurate than most human beings, which helps minimize computational error. Finally, the centralized nature of the master file makes data security much easier. All in all, this approach promises very significant improvements over the present price book approach.

Planning a Solution

The price quotation program is a sales department project. Its intent is to provide service to sales. Sales requested it. The obvious place to start the planning process is by going to the sales people and finding out exactly what they want.

Sales is not a technical function. Salespeople probably have no interest in the content of the program we are about to write, viewing the computer as a simple black box that accepts input data in the form of a request for a price quotation and disgorges a written document in a form suitable for presentation to a customer.

While sales probably does not care about the content of the program, they certainly care about the format of the input and output records. They will be required to prepare the input documents. They will use the output. By far the best way of discovering exactly what sales wants is to ask them to help define the input and output record formats. Once these have been defined, a program can be written to generate the desired output from the supplied input.

The output will almost certainly be the first topic of discussion, as this is the sales department's primary concern; the input is really nothing more than a means to the desired end. Without going into the details of this imaginary discussion, let's assume that a report in the form outlined in fig. 14.8 has been developed jointly by programming and sales. The next step is to design the input record.

All that is really needed as input to this program is a product number and the number of units (for example, 4 boxes of product number 22233344); all other information can be taken from the product master file. How are the sales people to input this information? A major part of the decision will, of course be made by the nature of the equipment available to sales. If each office has a terminal, the terminal will be the input device. In our organization, the sales offices have all been equipped with remote card readers and printers, so our input device will be a card reader.

The format of an input card designed to hold two fields should be obvious, as there are only a very limited number of alternatives. Something like

positions	contents
1-8	product number
9-10	units ordered

would make sense.

	PRODUCT DESCRIPTION	UNITS	UNIT PRICE LIST	UNIT PRICE SHIPPING	TOTAL PRICE LIST	TOTAL PRICE SHIPPING
XYZ CORPORATION						
PRODUCT PRICE QUOTATION						
PRODUCT NUMBER						
12345678	xxxxxxxxxxxxxxxxxxxx	99	9999.99	99.99	99,999.99	99.99
99999999	xxxxxxxxxxxxxxxxxxxx	99	9999.99	99.99	99,999.99	99.99
		TOTALS:			999,999.99	999.99
		TOTAL QUOTED PRICE:			$999,999.99	

Fig. 14.8: *The format of the price quotation report.*

What if the customer order is for more than one product? Should the sales office prepare one card for each product, or should they continue punching the same card, putting the second product in columns 11-20, the third in columns 21-30, and so on? Either approach would work. However, punching numerous fields in a single card creates a significantly increased risk of data error, so the one-product-per card approach would seem best.

Knowing how a computer works, we might suggest that the sales people always enter a 2-digit number, such as 01, or 02, or 15 when punching the "units ordered" field. In this way, problems with nonnumeric data can be kept to a minimum. Otherwise, the input and output records make a great deal of sense and can easily be used to support a product price quotation application. Having learned exactly what the sales department wants, we can turn our attention to developing a program to provide it.

Basically, the program logic (Fig. 14.9) is pretty simple. It begins by writing a set of headers. Next, a loop is set up to read the input records, access the direct access product file, prepare a detail line, and print this line. When the end-of-file marker is encountered on the card file, the program branches to an end of job routine which prints two summary lines (the need for summary data implies that several accumulation steps must be added to the mainline loop), closes all files, and terminates the program.

The input and output files have already been defined; thus the only remaining piece to the puzzle is the product file created earlier. The records in this file contain the following fields:

positions	contents
1-8	product number
9-30	product description
31-36	current selling price
37-40	shipping cost
41-46	supplier number
47-52	secondary supplier number

The file was created by using the division/remainder method. The algorithm used to compute a relative track number was to divide the product number by 25, using the remainder as the first part of the ACTUAL-KEY.

The data formats and program logic have now been basically defined, so we can begin the process of coding a solution. Error handling routines will, of course, have to be added; we can do this as the program is being coded.

Fig. 14.9: *Basic logic of the price quotation program.*

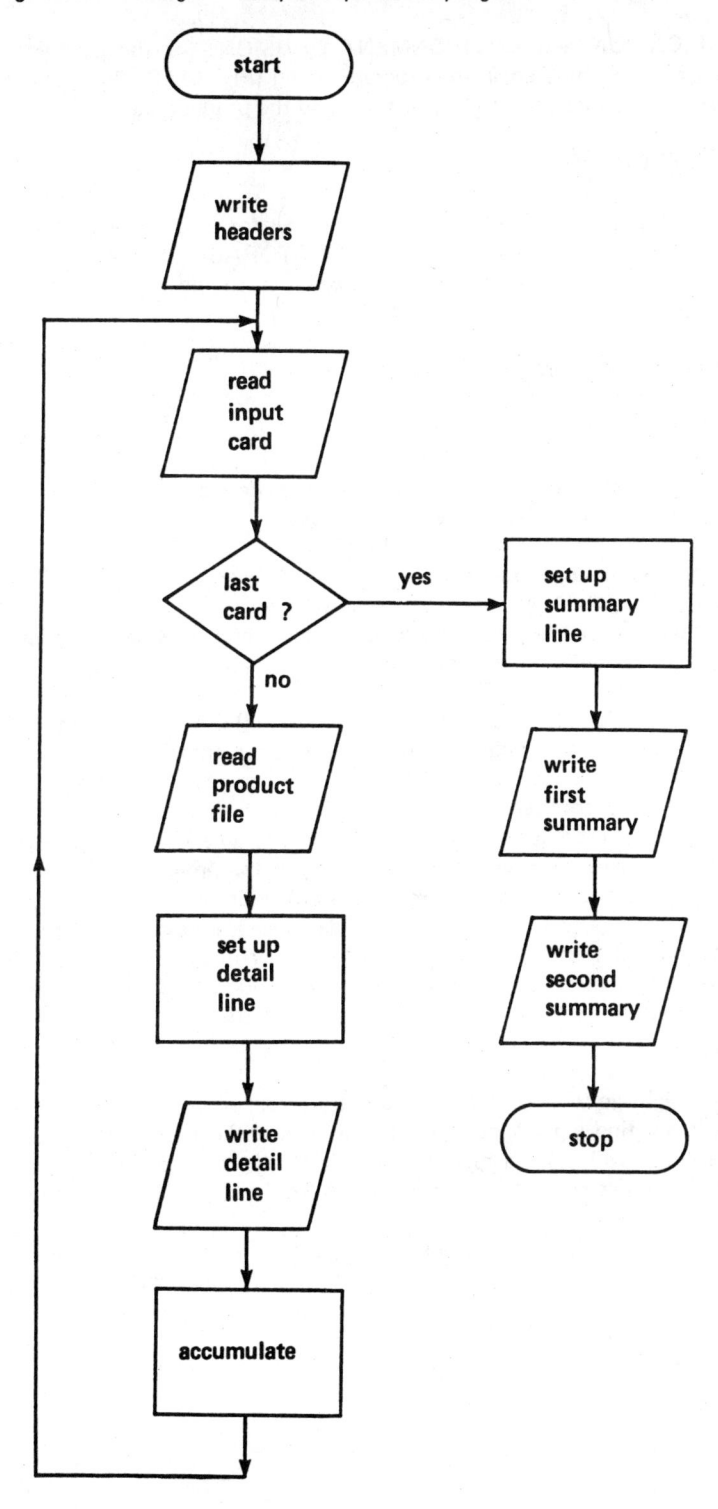

The IDENTIFICATION and ENVIRONMENT DIVISIONs

The IDENTIFICATION and ENVIRONMENT DIVISIONs for the product price quotation program can be seen in the program listing (Fig. 14.10). Note that three files are described—the input file, the output file, and the product master file.

The DATA DIVISION

The DATA DIVISION (Fig. 14.10) contains FD entries for each of the program files. The ACTUAL KEY is defined in the WORKING-STORAGE SECTION as are the contents of the various output lines. At this stage, you should expect no surprises, and there are none.

The PROCEDURE DIVISION

The PROCEDURE DIVISION's mainline (Fig. 14.10) follows the flowchart of Fig. 14.9 very closely. Except for the fact that direct access is involved, this program is no more complex than the simple savings account program developed back in Chapter 5. Read the logic carefully; you should have little trouble.

What Can Go Wrong?—Error Processing

As is the case with most computer programs, things cannot always be expected to work exactly as they should. What errors might we anticipate?

The sales clerk might (and, eventually, probably will) provide bad data in either the product number or units fields, or both, so a test for numeric data is essential. It's even possible that the sales clerk might forget to provide any data at all, so an end-of-file condition encountered on the very first read should be identified as a unique type of error. Probably the easiest way to identify an end-of-data-on-first-read condition is to set a switch to zero at the beginning of the program and then to set it to 1 following the first successful read. If this procedure is followed, the end-of-data routine can test the switch and react if no date has been read. Another possible approach is to have the end-of-data routine test the accumulators, assuming that a zero accumulator implies that no data has been read. (But then a zero accumulator might imply something entirely different.) We will use the switch approach in our program.

What else might go wrong? Due to data entry error, programming error, or file error, we might not find a given input product number in the master file. Should this occur, our program will print a message identifying the error condition and then quit. This condition is associated with an INVALID KEY clause.

Error handling logic and the various error messages can be seen in the program listing in Fig. 14.10. Note that following *any* error, we are simply going to terminate the program.

```
1                   0.43.13       NOV  9,1978


00004           IDENTIFICATION DIVISION.
00006           PROGRAM-ID.  PRICQUOT.
00007           REMARKS.     THIS PROGRAM PREPARES A PRICE
00008                        QUOTATION USING THE PRODUCT FILE.

00010           ENVIRONMENT DIVISION.
00012           CONFIGURATION SECTION.
00013           SPECIAL-NAMES.  C01 IS NEW-PAGE.

00015           INPUT-OUTPUT SECTION.
00016           FILE-CONTROL.
00017               SELECT PRODUCT-ORDER-FILE   ASSIGN TO UT-S-PRODORD.
00018               SELECT PRICE-QUOTATION-FILE ASSIGN TO UT-S-PRICQUOT.
00019               SELECT PRODUCT-FILE         ASSIGN TO DA-D-PRODFILE
00020                   ACCESS MODE IS RANDOM
00021                   ACTUAL KEY IS ACTUAL-KEY-FIELD.


00024           DATA DIVISION.

00026           FILE SECTION.

00028           FD PRODUCT-ORDER-FILE
00029              LABEL RECORD IS OMITTED.
00030           01 PRODUCT-ORDER-RECORD.
00031              05  I-PRODUCT-NUMBER       PIC 9(8).
00032              05  I-UNITS-ORDERED        PIC 99.
00033              05  FILLER                 PIC X(70).

00035           FD PRICE-QUOTATION-FILE
00036              LABEL RECORD IS OMITTED.
00037           01 PRICE-PRINT-RECORD.
00038              05 PRICE-PRINT-LINE        PIC X(80).

00040           FD PRODUCT-FILE
00041              LABEL RECORD IS STANDARD
00042              BLOCK CONTAINS 1 RECORDS.
00043           01 PRODUCT-RECORD.
00044              05  DA-PRODUCT-NUMBER      PIC 9(8).
00045              05  DA-DESCRIPTION         PIC X(22).
00046              05  DA-SELLING-PRICE       PIC 9999V99.
00047              05  DA-SHIPPING-COST       PIC 99V99.
00048              05  DA-SUPPLIER-CODE       PIC X(6).
00049              05  DA-2ND-SUPPLIER        PIC X(6).
```

Fig. 14.10: *A listing of the price quotation program.*

```
2         PRICQUOT      0.43.13      NOV 9,1978


00057              WORKING-STORAGE SECTION.
00059              77  WORK-FIELD            PIC S9(5)   USAGE IS COMP SYNC.
00060              77  QUOTIENT              PIC S9(5)   USAGE IS COMP SYNC.
00061              77  DATA-READ-SWITCH      PIC 9.
00063              01  ACTUAL-KEY-FIELD.
00064                  05  RELATIVE-TRACK    PIC S9(5)   USAGE IS COMP SYNC.
00065                  05  LOGICAL-RECORD-KEY PIC 9(8).
00067              01  ACCUMULATORS.
00068                  05  TOTAL-QUOTED-PRICE  PIC 9(6)V99  VALUE ZERO.
00069                  05  TOTAL-LIST-PRICE    PIC 9(6)V99  VALUE ZERO.
00070                  05  TOTAL-SHIPPING      PIC 999V99   VALUE ZERO.
00071                  05  TOTAL-PRODUCT-LIST  PIC 9(5)V99.
00072                  05  TOTAL-PRODUCT-SHIP  PIC 99V99.
00074              01  HEADER-1.
00075                  05  FILLER            PIC X(32)   VALUE SPACES.
00076                  05  FILLER            PIC X(15)
00077                                        VALUE 'XYZ CORPORATION'.
00079              01  HEADER-2.
00080                  05  FILLER            PIC X(28)   VALUE SPACE.
00081                  05  FILLER            PIC X(23)
00082                                        VALUE 'PRODUCT PRICE QUOTATION'.
00084              01  COLUMN-HEADER-1.
00085                  05  FILLER            PIC XX      VALUE SPACES.
00086                  05  FILLER            PIC X(32)
00087                                        VALUE 'PRODUCT DESCRIPTION'.
00088                  05  FILLER            PIC X(30)
00089                                        VALUE 'UNITS       UNIT PRICE'.
00090                  05  FILLER            PIC X(11)
00091                                        VALUE 'TOTAL PRICE'.
00093              01  COLUMN-HEADER-2.
00094                  05  FILLER            PIC XX      VALUE SPACES.
00095                  05  FILLER            PIC X(41)   VALUE 'NUMBER'.
00096                  05  FILLER            PIC X(19)
00097                                        VALUE 'LIST       SHIPPING'.
00098                  05  FILLER            PIC X(17)
00099                                        VALUE 'LIST       SHIPPING'.
```

Fig. 14.10: *Continued.*

```
3        PRICQUOT        C.43.13        NOV  9,1978


00107          01 PRODUCT-LINE.
00108             05   FILLER                   PIC X         VALUE SPACE.
00109             05   P-PRODUCT-NUMBER         PIC 9(8).
00110             05   FILLER                   PIC X         VALUE SPACE.
00111             05   P-DESCRIPTION            PIC X(22).
00112             05   FILLER                   PIC X(4)      VALUE SPACE.
00113             05   P-UNITS                  PIC Z9.
00114             05   FILLER                   PIC XXX       VALUE SPACES.
00115             05   P-UNIT-LIST-PRICE        PIC ZZZ9.99.
00116             05   FILLER                   PIC XXXX      VALUE SPACES.
00117             05   P-UNIT-SHIP-PRICE        PIC Z9.99.
00118             05   FILLER                   PIC XXX       VALUE SPACES.
00119             05   P-TOTAL-PROD-LIST        PIC ZZ,ZZ9.99.
00120             05   FILLER                   PIC XXXX      VALUE SPACES.
00121             05   P-TOTAL-PROD-SHIP        PIC Z9.99.

00123          01 TOTALS-LINE.
00124             05   FILLER                   PIC X(39)     VALUE SPACES.
00125             05   FILLER                   PIC X(20)     VALUE 'TOTALS:'.
00126             05   T-TOTAL-LIST-PRICE       PIC ZZZ,ZZ9.99.
00127             05 FILLER                     PIC XXX       VALUE SPACES.
00128             05   T-TOTAL-SHIP-PRICE       PIC ZZ9.99.

00130          01 TOTAL-QUOTED-LINE.
00131             05   FILLER                   PIC X(39)     VALUE SPACES.
00132             05   FILLER                   PIC X(19)
00133                                              VALUE 'TOTAL QUOTED PRICE:'.
00134             05   T-TOTAL-QUOTED-PRICE     PIC $ZZZ,ZZ9.99.
```

Fig. 14.10: *Continued.*

```
     4       PRICQUOT         C.43.13        NOV  9,1978



00142          PROCEDURE DIVISION.

00144              HOUSEKEEPING.
00146                  MOVE ZERO   TO DATA-READ-SWITCH.
00147                  OPEN INPUT  PRODUCT-ORDER-FILE.
00148                  OPEN OUTPUT PRICE-QUOTATION-FILE.
00149                  OPEN INPUT  PRODUCT-FILE.
00150                  MOVE ZERO TO DATA-READ-SWITCH.
00151                  PERFORM PRINT-HEADERS THRU END-PRINT-HEADERS.
```

Fig. 14.10: *Continued.*

```
5         PRICQUOT      0.43.13      NOV  9,1978


00159              MAINLINE.
00161                  READ PRODUCT-ORDER-FILE
00162                      AT END GO TO END-OF-JOB.
00163                  MOVE  1   TO DATA-READ-SWITCH.
00165                  IF I-PRODUCT-NUMBER IS NOT NUMERIC OR
00166                     I-UNITS-ORDERED  IS NOT NUMERIC
00167                  THEN
00168                      PERFORM BAD-DATA-ROUTINE THRU END-BAD-DATA
00169                      GO TO END-OF-JOB
00170                  ELSE
00171                      NEXT SENTENCE.
00173                  MOVE   I-PRODUCT-NUMBER TO WORK-FIELD, LOGICAL-RECORD-KEY.
00174                  DIVIDE WORK-FIELD BY 25 GIVING QUOTIENT
00175                         REMAINDER RELATIVE-TRACK.
00177                  READ   PRODUCT-FILE
00178                      INVALID KEY PERFORM BAD-DATA-ROUTINE THRU END-BAD-DATA
00179                             GO TO END-OF-JOB.
00181                  MOVE I-PRODUCT-NUMBER TO P-PRODUCT-NUMBER.
00182                  MOVE DA-DESCRIPTION    TO P-DESCRIPTION.
00183                  MOVE I-UNITS-ORDERED   TO P-UNITS.
00184                  MOVE DA-SELLING-PRICE TO P-UNIT-LIST-PRICE.
00185                  MOVE DA-SHIPPING-COST TO P-UNIT-SHIP-PRICE.
00187                  MULTIPLY I-UNITS-ORDERED BY DA-SELLING-PRICE
00188                           GIVING TOTAL-PRODUCT-LIST.
00189                  MULTIPLY I-UNITS-ORDERED BY DA-SHIPPING-COST
00190                           GIVING TOTAL-PRODUCT-SHIP.
00192                  MOVE TOTAL-PRODUCT-LIST TO P-TOTAL-PROD-LIST.
00193                  MOVE TOTAL-PRODUCT-SHIP TO P-TOTAL-PROD-SHIP.
00194                  MOVE PRODUCT-LINE       TO PRICE-PRINT-LINE.
00196                  WRITE PRICE-PRINT-RECORD AFTER ADVANCING 2 LINES.
00198                  ADD   TOTAL-PRODUCT-LIST TO TOTAL-LIST-PRICE
00199                                              TOTAL-QUOTED-PRICE.
00200                  ADD   TOTAL-PRODUCT-SHIP TO TOTAL-SHIPPING
00201                                              TOTAL-QUOTED-PRICE.
00202                  GO TO MAINLINE.
```

Fig. 14.10: *Continued.*

```
00205      END-OF-JOB.
00206          IF DATA-READ-SWITCH IS EQUAL TO ZERO
00207          THEN
00208              PERFORM NO-DATA-ROUTINE THRU END-NO-DATA
00209          ELSE
00210              PERFORM PRINT-TOTALS THRU END-PRINT-TOTALS.
00211          CLOSE PRODUCT-ORDER-FILE.
00212          CLOSE PRICE-QUOTATION-FILE.
00213          CLOSE PRODUCT-FILE.
00214          STOP RUN.

00217      PRINT-HEADERS.
00218          MOVE   HEADER-1 TO PRICE-PRINT-LINE.
00219          WRITE  PRICE-PRINT-RECORD AFTER NEW-PAGE.
00220          MOVE   HEADER-2 TO PRICE-PRINT-LINE.
00221          WRITE  PRICE-PRINT-RECORD AFTER ADVANCING 1 LINES.
00222          MOVE   COLUMN-HEADER-1 TO PRICE-PRINT-LINE.
00223          WRITE  PRICE-PRINT-RECORD AFTER ADVANCING 2 LINES.
00224          MOVE   COLUMN-HEADER-2 TO PRICE-PRINT-LINE.
00225          WRITE  PRICE-PRINT-RECORD AFTER ADVANCING 1 LINES.
00226      END-PRINT-HEADERS.
00227          EXIT.

00230      NO-DATA-ROUTINE.
00231          MOVE 'NO PRODUCT ORDER RECORDS' TO PRICE-PRINT-LINE.
00232          WRITE PRICE-PRINT-RECORD AFTER ADVANCING 2 LINES.
00233      END-NO-DATA.
00234          EXIT.

00237      BAD-DATA-ROUTINE.
00238          MOVE SPACES TO PRODUCT-LINE.
00239          MOVE I-PRODUCT-NUMBER TO P-PRODUCT-NUMBER.
00240          MOVE I-UNITS-ORDERED  TO P-UNITS.
00241          MOVE 'NON-NUMERIC DATA' TO P-DESCRIPTION.
00242          MOVE PRODUCT-LINE     TO PRICE-PRINT-RECORD.
00243          WRITE PRICE-PRINT-RECORD AFTER ADVANCING 2 LINES.
00244      END-BAD-DATA.
00245          EXIT.

00248      PRINT-TOTALS.
00249          MOVE TOTAL-LIST-PRICE TO T-TOTAL-LIST-PRICE.
00250          MOVE TOTAL-SHIPPING   TO T-TOTAL-SHIP-PRICE.
00251          MOVE TOTALS-LINE      TO PRICE-PRINT-LINE.
00252          WRITE PRICE-PRINT-RECORD AFTER ADVANCING 3 LINES.
00253          MOVE TOTAL-QUOTED-PRICE TO T-TOTAL-QUOTED-PRICE.
00254          MOVE TOTAL-QUOTED-LINE TO PRICE-PRINT-LINE.
00255          WRITE PRICE-PRINT-RECORD AFTER ADVANCING 2 LINES.
00256      END-PRINT-TOTALS.
00257          EXIT.
```

Fig. 14.10: *Continued.*

USER INVOLVEMENT IN THE PLANNING PROCESS

Note the procedure followed in developing the product price quotation program. The requirements of the program users were considered very early in the planning process, and only after we had a good idea of what the user wanted did we begin to plan actual program code. Several programming details and technical programming questions were then explored, but always within the context of the initial definition of user need. Programs do not exist as ends in and of themselves. Programs exist to meet legitimate user needs.

All too often, the programmer will lose sight of this basic fact of life. Programming is fun. It's an intellectual challenge. Besides, it's easy for a bright young programmer simply to assume the user really doesn't know what he or she wants anyway. As a result, a completed program all too often represents the programmer's (rather than the user's) view of the problem. Ask anyone who works for an organization that utilizes computers if each and every application performs a useful function. Probably several wlll be widely regarded as useless or worse—the offspring of poor programmer/user communication. Don't ever forget that programming is a service function.

SUMMARY

The chapter began with a brief introduction to the physical aspects of direct access, covering various direct accsss devices (especially disk), the relative address concept, and the way data is typically stored on a track. We then turned our attention to the logical considerations, introducing a number of commonly used direct access techniques. We concentrated on the division/remainder method in this chapter; updating a file using the division/remainder technique will be covered in Chapter 15. Indexed files will be covered in later chapters.

The division/remainder technique was explained and a file of product information was created. New COBOL features included the ACCESS MODE clause, the ACTUAL KEY clause, the INVALID KEY clause, and COMPUTATIONAL SYNCHRONIZED data.

Having created the file, we then wrote a program to use the data, being very careful to follow our usual procedure of first defining the problem, then planning a solution, and finally coding the solution in COBOL. The importance of including the ultimate user of an application in the early planning stages was emphasized.

KEY WORDS

access mechanism	ACTUAL KEY clause	default
ACCESS MODE clause	COMPUTATIONAL	direct access

disk	random access	relative track
division/remainder method	read/write head	sector
drum	relative address	synonym
index	relative record	SYNCHRONIZED
INVALID KEY clause	relative sector	track
overflow		

EXERCISES

1. What exactly is direct access?

2. Explain briefly how magnetic disk works.

3. Explain the relative address concept.

4. Explain how a record of data can be retrieved "directly" from a disk surface.

5. Explain the division/remainder method for direct access.

6. Draw a parallel between the application cited in this chapter and a table look-up application as described in an earlier chapter.

7. Why is error processing such an important consideration on the product price quotation application?

8. Several different applications within our organization require access to customer names and addresses; thus, we have been asked to create a customer name and address file. Each record should contain:

positions	contents
1-6	customer number
7-20	customer name
21-35	street address
36-45	city
46-47	state
48-52	zip code

positions	contents
53-56	dollar volume last year (in thousands)
57-60	sales district

We have roughly 500 customers. They key for accessing this file will be the customer number. Use the division/remainder method.

9. In an earlier chapter, you were asked to write a simple bill preparation program, listing all transactions for a given customer as detail lines and printing a summary line showing the total amount due. Modify this old program, adding one more step; using the customer number as a key, look up the customer information in the name and address file and prepare a mailing label.

For those of you who did not write the earlier bill preparation program, assume that the customer number and total amount due can be read from a work file, and use this information, along with the name and address file, to prepare addressed customer bills.

10. Another specific function common to many different applications is the addition of alphabetic product descriptions to a report. Normally, only the product number is carried on a given file, with the descriptive information being retrieved from a direct access product description file only when needed. Write a program to create this file. Assume that we have roughly 2500 different products. Use the division/remainder method. Records contain:

positions	contents
1-8	product number
9-30	description

11. As another extension to the bill preparation program, add product description information to the detail lines of the bill using the product description file described in exercise 10.

12. We have been asked to create an on-line inventory system. The basic idea is to have clerks update the level of inventory through a terminal each time a transaction takes place. The system will be supported by a direct access inventory file containing, among other things, the current stock on hand of each of our 5000 products.

Records on the file will contain:

positions	contents
1-6	product part number
7-25	description
26-30	stock on hand

31-35	reorder level
36-40	number of units on order
41-46	expected arrival date of order (mmddyy)
47-52	supplier code number

Use the division/remainder method with the part number as key. The data to create the initial file will be taken from punched cards containing the above information; these cards are generated from our annual physical inventory.

13. A district sales manager would like to be able to get an answer to the question, "What is the current stock on hand of part number 123456?"; such information is extremely useful, as it allows sales to decide if, in fact, a customer can be realistically promised immediate delivery. Write a program to provide this service using the data on the inventory file as described in exercise 12.

14. In preparation for opening day, the local professional baseball team has asked us to write a special program to compute player batting averages. The idea is to display on the scoreboard the current batting average for each player as he steps to the plate, adjusting that average with each time at bat. The scoreboard operator will be given the responsibility for entering each time at bat and whether or not the player got a hit. The batting average is computed by dividing the times at bat into the number of hits; these two statistics will be accumulated in a direct access file.

    Write a program to create the file. There are 25 players on the team; thus there will be 25 entries. Each player record should contain the player number, player name, times at bat, and hits.

15. Write a program to simply compute and display the current batting average of a given player using the information on the file described in exercise 14. The key should be the player number.

15

Updating a Direct Access File

OVERVIEW

As is the case with any file, the data on a direct access file will change over time; thus the file must be updated. The information contained in an existing record might change—a new selling price or a change in order status, for example. New records can be added to the file—new products or new customers. Old records can be deleted from the file. A direct access master file update program must be capable of handling additions, deletions, and changes.

In this chapter, we'll develop a program to update the product file created in Chapter 14. Given the text's card/printer orientation, the program will be written to accept punched card input, printing a confirmation message following each update transaction. After the program has been developed, we'll turn our attention to the topic of modular program development.

THE NATURE OF THE DIRECT ACCESS FILE UPDATE

A direct access file is designed to be accessed one record at a time. Sequence is not an important consideration. Thus it is not surprising that master file updates are normally done one at a time too.

What kind of updates can be expected? The information associated with any given record may well change over time. On the product file, for example, changes in selling price and shipping cost can be anticipated, and suppliers will probably change.

Changes to existing records are not the only kind of transactions that must be processed. New products are added to the company's line, so new records must be added. On the negative side, products become obsolete, so old records must sometimes be deleted from the file.

The direct master file update program must be capable of dealing with all three types of transactions: changes, additions, and deletions. Basically, the program must read transactions, determine the transaction type, and then either add, delete, or read and rewrite the affected record.

UPDATING THE PRODUCT FILE

The product file created in Chapter 14 contains the following fields:

positions	contents
1-8	product number
9-30	product description
31-36	selling price
37-40	shipping cost
41-46	supplier code
47-52	secondary supplier

What kinds of changes might we expect to make to the data on this file?

Our company certainly expects to begin offering new products for sale over the next several months, and records identifying these new products will have to be added. Certain old products will become obsolete, making it necessary to delete them. On existing products, except for the product number, each field is subject to potential change.

The problems of adding, deleting, and updating records on a direct access file are both technical and procedural. Following our usual custom of first defining what must be done and then discussing how to do it, we'll start with the procedural questions. From the viewpoint of the people who will have to do the work, how exactly are we to go about implementing a master file update?

DIRECT ACCESS FILE UPDATE OPERATING PROCEDURES

In the master file update of Chapter 13, a batch of transactions was collected and run against the master file. Typically, each transaction was generated as a result of some well-defined event. Inventory deletions were defined by a formal document of some kind. Inventory additions were similarly defined, possibly by a set of shipping papers. Perhaps the clearest example of a well defined event can be found in the checking account update application, where a physical check or a deposit slip serves as the source record for updating the master file.

The existence of a document serves many purposes. In the event of a dispute over the proper level of inventory or the proper balance of a checking account, these source documents allow the events producing this new balance to be recreated. Fraudulent activity is made much more difficult when a formal document of some kind is used. From an auditing standpoint, using formal source documents provides control, allowing the firm to fully trace the history of each master file entry.

Such control is even more crucial on a direct access file. When sequential files are used, a period of time elapses between successive file updates, allowing for reflection and the possible recognition of errors. On a direct access file, however, it is possible that modified information on a master file record may be used within seconds of the change, making it likely that the erroneous information will be propagated throughout the organization before there is any chance for correction. It is also possible that one update to a given record can be almost immediately followed by another change to the same record, thus burying the effect of the first change and making it very difficult to trace back to the source.

Controlling access to the master file update program is another problem. On a batch processing application, all the transactions and master files are located in a single room under control of the computer operators. Sensitive master file updates (payroll, for example) can be run with the doors to the computer room locked, making unauthorized changes difficult to implement. Direct access files, on the other hand, are often updated through a remote terminal or a remote card reader, making it very difficult to control access.

Given these problems, it is obvious that a number of steps must be taken to ensure the accuracy of any direct access file updates. The source of the transaction must be clearly identified. It is crucial that the accuracy of the change be verified before submission to the computer. Within the program, edit checks and reasonability checks must be performed. Finally, as both a mechanism for correcting errors that do occur and as a means for identifying the source of any errors so that corrective action can be taken, a **transaction log** of all changes made to the file must be maintained.

Direct access file update procedures must begin with the individuals who generate the raw data that will be used to update the file. Often, specialists are assigned the task of reading for accuracy sales orders or other source documents, rejecting anything that seems to be out of line. Frequently, special signoff procedures are instituted, requiring a manager or some other responsible individual to sign or initial the source document before it can be submitted to the computer. The key to ensuring data accuracy is to very clearly establish the responsibility for data accuracy. If one person is accountable for data errors of a particular type, that person will strive to avoid making such errors. If, on the other hand, the actual data entry function is to be simply handed over to a group of low-paid clerks who neither understand the significance of the data nor care about its accuracy, errors are certain to occur.

Note that this first step has absolutely nothing to do with programming. These are human procedures designed to make certain that human beings properly prepare the data that will eventually be read into a computer. If accuracy is an objective, such steps are essential.

In the examples of this chapter, we'll assume that that the clear identification of an individual responsible for data accuracy has been established as a standard procedure. To this end, the initials of the responsible person will be keypunched into each change, add, or delete card. Following keypunching, the cards are returned to the responsible person who is expected to check them visually to make certain that the card and the source document from which the card is prepared match and, more importantly, that the data is correct (it is possible to keypunch incorrect data correctly).

The control over computer access is achieved through the use of special passwords on the job control language or command language cards. Such controls are not part of the program. They are implemented instead by the computer's control program. Passwords are changed at frequent intervals, and are made known only to the authorized remote job entry operators in each sales location. With the responsibility for making change, and the authority to submit jobs split between two people, the risk of one individual acting unilaterally to sabotage the master file is greatly reduced.

Within the program, a number of edit checks will be imposed. Also within the program, a logging procedure will be implemented. In response to every transaction, a copy of the master file record as it was before the change, a copy of the change, and a copy of the new record after the change will be written to magnetic tape; in this way, if anything does go wrong, the old file can be recreated.

Preparing Input Records

On many computer systems, input records to a direct access file update routine are prepared and entered into the system through an on-line terminal. On our system, partly through a desire to maintain tight control over data accuracy and partly as a result of a prior decision to locate card reader/printer terminals in the sales offices, a punched card will be prepared for each change. This does cost us something in terms of response—it takes time to prepare a punched card, and changes cannot be entered as quickly as they might be. Company management has decided, however, that the right control exercised over data accuracy is worth the loss in response time.

What kinds of updates are possible? New records might be added, so an ADD operation is needed. Old records might be dropped from the file, so a DEL operation is necessary. Finally, selected fields might change, so a MOD (for MODify) operation is needed.

For a NEW record, the entire record must be supplied to the program. For a DEL operation, only the product number is needed, although for security purposes other fields might be called for. For a MOD transaction, any one or even all the fields (except for the product number, which is needed to locate the desired record) may change. To avoid the problem of giving the data entry people a different set of procedures for each type of transaction, it has been decided that the input card will always follow the format of the master file, with the first 52 columns holding the same fields in the same relative positions. This leaves columns 53-80 for other use. It has been decided that the transaction type and the initials identifying the individual responsible for the transaction will be right justified on the card, making them easy to spot; thus the transaction type will be punched in columns 75-77 and the initials will be punched in 78-80.

Program Output

The primary output file for the master file update program is, of course, the master file itself. Record formats must match those of the old master file.

A transaction log must also be maintained. When a record is added, the log is to contain a copy of the transaction and a copy of the new master file entry. When a deletion transaction is encountered, both the transaction and the old master file entry are to be logged. Modifications to existing records call for logging the transaction, the old master file entry, and the new master file entry. The log file is to be written to magnetic tape. In addition to holding a record of all updates, the log will also hold a copy of all transactions found to be in errror; it is believed that by logging errors, the weaker data entry people can be identified and corrective action taken.

What about the format of these transaction log records? Master file records are 52 characters long. We can squeeze the transactions to 58 characters by shifting the transaction type and the authorizing initials from columns 75-80 to positions 53-58, but the transaction record is still 6 characters longer than a master file record, and records of both types must be logged. It is possible to create a tape file with variable length records, but rather than complicate things for the programmer who will eventually be writing a log tape analysis program, we'll simply make the message that is to accompany each log entry 6 characters longer when working with a master record.

Finally, we need a written log containing confirmation messages to send back to the individuals responsible for the update transactions. The written log allows for the verification of the accuracy of all changes as *actually* made, thus providing still another opportunity for catching and correcting any errors that may have slipped through. An added feature of this update list might well be a number of computer-generated error messages or warnings telling the responsible person that, for example, a record was updated in spite of the fact that a change was a bit outside normal limits.

THE PROGRAM STRUCTURE

The major structure of a program to update the product file is basically quite simple. The mainline will read a transaction, identify the transaction type, and link to the proper detailed logic routine. Separate routines will be designed to handle additions, deletions, and changes.

In the additions routine, the first step will be to edit-check the data for accuracy. Once accuracy has been determined, a direct access key can be computed and the new master file record can be written.

A change or modification to an existing record is just a bit trickier. It is likely that only selected portions of the record must be changed. Rather than punching a complete card when only a few fields are affected, our standard operating procedure is to have only the changed fields punched; thus the program must first check to see if a field is all blank before checking it for accuracy and getting ready to move it into the updated output record. Basically, the logic of this routine involves reading a master file record, replacing the selected, non-blank fields, and writing the new master file record (see Fig. 15.1).

Deleting a record from the file is not as simple as it might seem. What exactly does it mean to delete a record? It most certainly does not mean that the record is erased and that all other records on the track are shifted into this newly freed space. Instead, the "deleted" record is simply flagged for future use, with the space simply retained as if nothing had happened. On many systems, the next record added to the affected track will replace the "deleted" or flagged record. On other systems, the freed space simply "sits there" until such time as the file is reconstructed.

In either case, the programmer must take specific action to delete a record. Under standard ANSI COBOL, the record must first be read into the computer, just as though a change were planned. Next, the figurative constant **HIGH-VALUE** must be moved into the first character position of the logical key portion of the ACTUAL KEY. Finally, the record is written back to disk. The HIGH-VALUE, a COBOL reserved word representing the highest possible value that can be stored in a single character position, makes it impossible to subsequently retrieve this record; by later system or programmer action, however, the flag can be recognized and the space assigned to another record.

A modular flowchart of the master file update proram is shown in Fig. 15.1. Note that many of the detailed steps are common to several of the routines. The need to edit-check data appears in two places, and will almost certainly be implemented as a separate, third-level module. Writing of records to both the tape and the printed logs appears in all the primary routines, and thus forms an obvious separate routine. Other candidates include reading and writing master file records. Error handling routines, of course, are almost always handled separately.

Is it always a good idea to separate repetitive code into a different routine? Not necessarily. If the primary routines are relatively small, and if the repetitive code represents only an instruction or two, it may be better to actually recode it in several places. Repeating the code is particularly useful on a key function such as a major

Fig. 15.1: *A modular flowchart of the direct access master file update.*

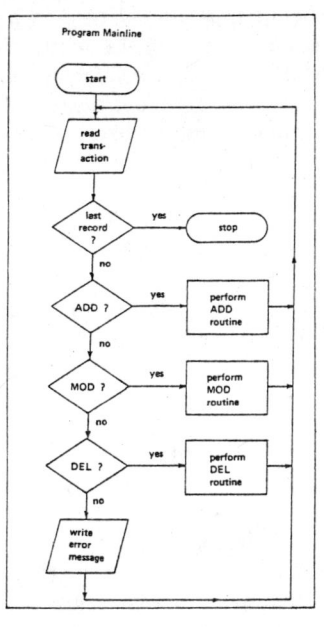

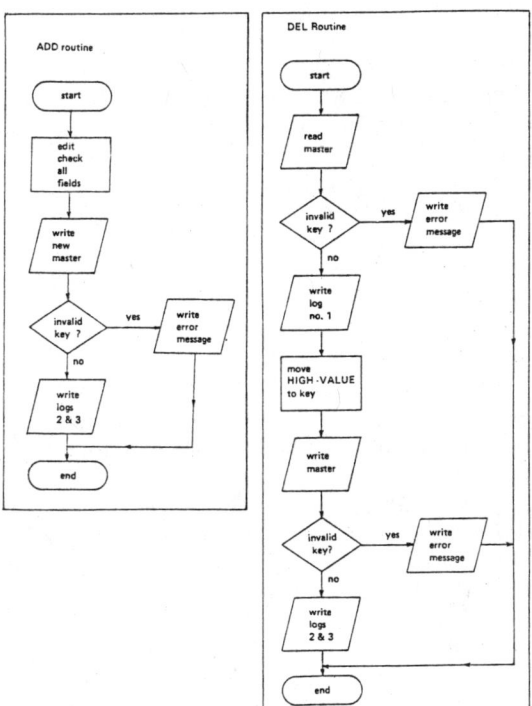

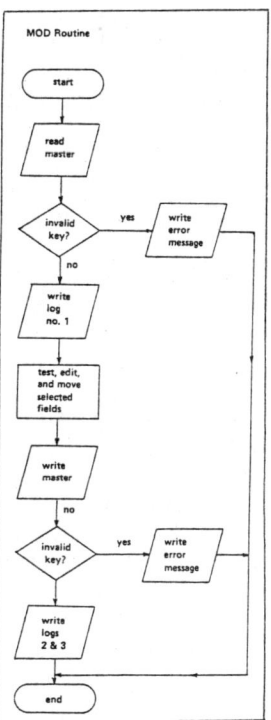

input or output operation; keeping the major instruction as part of the primary routine helps program documentation. In this program, for example, we will be computing and setting up the ACTUAL KEY field in a separate routine, but executing the read or write instruction against the master file in the primary routine. The setting up of an ACTUAL KEY requires several instructions, so a separate routine is desirable. Reading or writing the master file is the whole point of the program, thus justifying keeping these instructions in the primary routine.

The Program—the First Two Divisions

The IDENTIFICATION DIVISION and the ENVIRONMENT DIVISION for the product master file update program can be seen in the program listing, Fig. 15.2. Note that a total of four files have been defined; they are the input card file, the master file, the tape log, and the printer log.

The DATA DIVISION

The DATA DIVISION (see Fig. 15.2) begins with FD entries for each of the four files. The only thing that is a bit unusual in this program is the REDEFINES clauses associated with the first file, the TRANSACTIONS-FILE. Standard operating procedures for making changes to an existing record call for the responsible individual to fill out what is, in effect, a complete record, leaving those fields that are not to be changed blank. This implies that the program will test for a blank field, taking the steps of edit-checking and moving the data only if the field is non-blank. The field T-SELLING-PRICE has a PICTURE of 9999V99, clearly identifying it as being numeric; T-SHIPPING-COST is also numeric. Comparing a numeric field with the nonnumeric constant SPACES will cause program termination on many systems; it is an illegal operation. By using the REDEFINES clause, however, the field can be treated as a nonnumeric field for purposes of the comparison with SPACES, and subsequently treated as a numeric field during later computations. The REDEFINES does *not* create any new storage space, it simply "redefines" existing space.

The PROCEDURE DIVISION

At first glance, the PROCEDURE DIVISION of the master file update program (Fig. 15.2) looks very complex. It isn't; if you have carefully followed the development of the program in this chapter, you should have little or no trouble following it. Just start with the mainline, and then move out to the detailed logic routines. Consider the function to be performed before worrying about how to perform it.

The program mainline is fairly straightforward. It begins by reading a transaction and immediately checking for a valid entry in the T-AUTHORIZATION field. Remember how the individual responsible for a change was required to initial that change? The T-AUTHORIZATION field contains those initials.

If the T-AUTHORIZATION field is blank, nothing is done with the record; an error message is generated, and it's on to the next record. If the authorization is acceptable, the transaction type is identified, and the proper transaction handling routine is started. Finally, it's back for another transaction.

```
1                          0.43.40      NOV  9,1978


00002            IDENTIFICATION DIVISION.
00004            PROGRAM-ID. UPDTPROD.
00005            AUTHOR.      DAVIS & FISHER.
00006            REMARKS.     THIS PROGRAM UPDATES THE DIRECT PRODUCT
00007                         FILE FOR ADDITIONS, CHANGES AND DELETIONS.

00010            ENVIRONMENT DIVISION.

00012            CONFIGURATION SECTION.
00013              SPECIAL-NAMES.  C01 IS NEW-PAGE.

00015            INPUT-OUTPUT SECTION.
00016            FILE-CONTROL.
00017                SELECT PRODUCT-TRANSACTION-FILE     ASSIGN TO UT-S-TRANFILE.
00018                SELECT TRANSACTION-LOG-TAPE-FILE    ASSIGN TO UT-S-TAPELOG.
00019                SELECT TRANSACTION-LOG-PRINT-FILE   ASSIGN TO UT-S-PRTLOG.
00020                SELECT PRODUCT-MASTER-FILE          ASSIGN TO DA-D-PRODMST
00021                       ACCESS MODE IS RANDOM
00022                       ACTUAL KEY  IS ACTUAL-KEY-FIELD.
```

Fig. 15.2: *A listing of the direct access master file update program.*

```
2         UPDTPROD       0.43.40      NOV  9,1978

00024          DATA DIVISION.

00026          FILE SECTION.

00028          FD  PRODUCT-TRANSACTION-FILE
00029              LABEL RECORD IS OMITTED.
00030          01  TRANSACTION-RECORD.
00031              05  T-PRODUCT-NUMBER      PIC 9(8).
00032              05  T-DESCRIPTION         PIC X(22).
00033              05  T-SELLING-PRICE       PIC 9999V99.
00034              05  TX-SELLING-PRICE      REDEFINES T-SELLING-PRICE
00035                                        PIC X(6).
00036              05  T-SHIPPING-COST       PIC 99V99.
00037              05  TX-SHIPPING-COST      REDEFINES T-SHIPPING-COST
00038                                        PIC X(4).
00039              05  T-SUPPLIER-CODE       PIC X(6).
00040              05  T-2ND-SUPPLIER        PIC X(6).
00041              05  FILLER                PIC X(22).
00042              05  T-TRANSACTION-TYPE    PIC X(3).
00043              05  T-AUTHORIZATION       PIC X(3).

00045          FD  TRANSACTION-LOG-TAPE-FILE
00046              LABEL RECORD IS STANDARD
00047              BLOCK CONTAINS 1 RECORDS.
00048          01  LOG-TAPE-RECORD.
00049              05  LOG-RECORD            PIC X(52).
00050              05  L-TYPE-AND-INITIALS.
00051                  10  L-TRANSACTION-TYPE   PIC X(3).
00052                  10  L-AUTHORIZATION      PIC X(3).

00054          FD  TRANSACTION-LOG-PRINT-FILE
00055              LABEL RECORD IS OMITTED.
00056          01  LOG-PRINT-RECORD.
00057              05  FILLER                PIC X.
00058              05  LOG-PRINT-LINE        PIC X(82).
00059              05  LOG-PRINT-MESSAGE     PIC X(50).

00061          FD  PRODUCT-MASTER-FILE
00062              LABEL RECORD IS STANDARD
00063              BLOCK CONTAINS 1 RECORDS.
00064          01  PRODUCT-MASTER-RECORD     PIC X(52).
```

Fig. 15.2: *Continued.*

```
     3          UPDTPROD        0.43.40        NOV  9,1978

00067              WORKING-STORAGE SECTION.

00069                 77 WORK-FIELD                  PIC S9(5)     USAGE COMP SYNC.
00070                 77 QUOTIENT                    PIC S9(5)     USAGE COMP SYNC.

00072                 01 ACTUAL-KEY-FIELD.
00073                    05 RELATIVE-TRACK           PIC S9(5)     USAGE COMP SYNC.
00074                   .05 LOGICAL-RECORD-KEY       PIC 9(8).

00076                 01 WS-PRODUCT-MASTER-RECORD.
00077                    05 M-PRODUCT-NUMBER         PIC 9(8).
00078                    05 MX-PRODUCT-NUMBER        REDEFINES M-PRODUCT-NUMBER
00079                                                PIC X(8).
00080                    05 M-DESCRIPTION            PIC X(22).
00081                    05 M-SELLING-PRICE          PIC 9999V99.
00082                    05 M-SHIPPING-COST          PIC 99V99.
00083                    05 M-SUPPLIER-CODE          PIC X(6).
00084                    05 M-2ND-SUPPLIER           PIC X(6).
```

Fig. 15.2: *Continued.*

```
4          UPDTPROD        0.43.40        NOV  9,1978


00090           PROCEDURE DIVISION.
00092           HOUSEKEEPING.
00094               OPEN INPUT   PRODUCT-TRANSACTION-FILE.
00095               OPEN OUTPUT  TRANSACTION-LOG-TAPE-FILE.
00096               OPEN OUTPUT  TRANSACTION-LOG-PRINT-FILE.
00097               OPEN I-O     PRODUCT-MASTER-FILE.

00100           MAINLINE.
00102               READ PRODUCT-TRANSACTION-FILE
00103                   AT END GO TO END-OF-JOB.
00104               IF T-AUTHORIZATION IS EQUAL TO SPACES
00105               THEN
00106                   MOVE 'INVALID AUTHORIZATION' TO LOG-PRINT-MESSAGE
00107                   PERFORM BAD-TRANSACTION THRU END-BAD-TRANSACTION
00108                   GO TO MAINLINE
00109               ELSE
00110                   NEXT SENTENCE.

00112               IF T-TRANSACTION-TYPE IS EQUAL TO 'ADD'
00113               THEN
00114                   PERFORM ADD-ROUTINE THRU END-ADD
00115               ELSE
00116                   IF T-TRANSACTION-TYPE IS EQUAL TO 'MOD'
00117                   THEN
00118                       PERFORM MOD-ROUTINE THRU END-MOD
00119                   ELSE
00120                       IF T-TRANSACTION-TYPE IS EQUAL TO 'DEL'
00121                       THEN
00122                           PERFORM DEL-ROUTINE THRU END-DEL
00123                       ELSE
00124                           MOVE 'INVALID TRANSACTION TYPE' TO
00125                               LOG-PRINT-MESSAGE
00126                           PERFORM BAD-TRANSACTION THRU END-BAD-TRANSACTION.
00127               GO TO MAINLINE.

00130           END-OF-JOB.
00132               CLOSE PRODUCT-TRANSACTION-FILE.
00133               CLOSE TRANSACTION-LOG-TAPE-FILE.
00134               CLOSE TRANSACTION-LOG-PRINT-FILE.
00135               CLOSE PRODUCT-MASTER-FILE.
00136               STOP RUN.
```

Fig. 15.2: *Continued.*

```
00138        ADD-ROUTINE.
00139            PERFORM EDIT-TRANSACTION THRU END-EDIT-TRANSACTION.
00140            PERFORM CREATE-ACTUAL-KEY THRU END-CREATE-KEY.
00141            MOVE TRANSACTION-RECORD TO WS-PRODUCT-MASTER-RECORD.
00142            WRITE PRODUCT-MASTER-RECORD FROM WS-PRODUCT-MASTER-RECORD
00143                INVALID KEY MOVE 'DUPLICATE PRODUCT NUMBER'
00144                           TO LOG-PRINT-MESSAGE
00145                       PERFORM BAD-TRANSACTION THRU
00146                           END-BAD-TRANSACTION
00147                       GO TO END-ADD.
00148            PERFORM LOG-TRANSACTION THRU END-LOG.
00149        END-ADD.
00150            EXIT.

00153        MOD-ROUTINE.
00154            PERFORM CREATE-ACTUAL-KEY THRU END-CREATE-KEY
00155            READ PRODUCT-MASTER-FILE INTO WS-PRODUCT-MASTER-RECORD
00156                INVALID KEY MOVE 'PRODUCT MASTER NOT FOUND'
00157                           TO LOG-PRINT-MESSAGE
00158                       PERFORM BAD-TRANSACTION THRU
00159                           END-BAD-TRANSACTION
00160                       GO TO END-MOD.
00161            PERFORM LOG-OLD-MASTER.
00162            PERFORM TEST-AND-EDIT-TRANSACTION THRU END-TEST-AND-EDIT.
00163            WRITE   PRODUCT-MASTER-RECORD FROM WS-PRODUCT-MASTER-RECORD
00164                INVALID KEY MOVE 'CANT  REWRITE MODIFIED MASTER'
00165                           TO LOG-PRINT-MESSAGE
00166                       PERFORM BAD-TRANSACTION THRU
00167                           END-BAD-TRANSACTION
00168                       GO TO END-MOD.
00169            PERFORM LOG-TRANSACTION THRU END-LOG.
00170        END-MOD.
00171            EXIT.

00174        DEL-ROUTINE.
00175            PERFORM CREATE-ACTUAL-KEY THRU END-CREATE-KEY.
00176            READ PRODUCT-MASTER-FILE INTO WS-PRODUCT-MASTER-RECORD
00177                INVALID KEY MOVE 'PRODUCT MASTER NOT FOUND'
00178                           TO LOG-PRINT-MESSAGE
00179                       PERFORM BAD-TRANSACTION THRU
00180                           END-BAD-TRANSACTION
00181                       GO TO END-DEL.
00182            PERFORM LOG-OLD-MASTER
00183            MOVE HIGH-VALUE TO MX-PRODUCT-NUMBER.
00184            WRITE   PRODUCT-MASTER-RECORD FROM WS-PRODUCT-MASTER-RECORD
00185                INVALID KEY MOVE 'CANT  REWRITE DELETED MASTER'
00186                           TO LOG-PRINT-MESSAGE
00187                       PERFORM BAD-TRANSACTION THRU
00188                           END-BAD-TRANSACTION
00189                       GO TO END-DEL.
00190            PERFORM LOG-TRANSACTION THRU END-LOG.
00191        END-DEL.
00192            EXIT.
```

Fig. 15.2: *Continued.*

```
00195        BAD-TRANSACTION.
00196            MOVE  TRANSACTION-RECORD TO LOG-PRINT-LINE.
00197            WRITE LOG-PRINT-RECORD AFTER ADVANCING 2 LINES.
00198        END-BAD-TRANSACTION.
00199            EXIT.

00201        EDIT-TRANSACTION.
00202            IF SPACES IS EQUAL TO T-DESCRIPTION OR T-SUPPLIER-CODE
00203                                               OR T-2ND-SUPPLIER
00204            THEN
00205                GO TO MOVE-ERROR-MESSAGE
00206            ELSE
00207                IF T-SELLING-PRICE IS NOT NUMERIC OR
00208                   T-SHIPPING-COST IS NOT NUMERIC
00209                THEN
00210                    GO TO MOVE-ERROR-MESSAGE
00211                ELSE
00212                    GO TO END-EDIT-TRANSACTION.
00214        MOVE-ERROR-MESSAGE.
00215            MOVE 'INVALID OR MISSING DATA' TO LOG-PRINT-MESSAGE.
00216            PERFORM BAD-TRANSACTION THRU END-BAD-TRANSACTION.
00217        ***
00218        **** RETURN TO MAINLINE TO GET ANOTHER TRANSACTION
00219        ***
00220            GO TO MAINLINE.
00221        END-EDIT-TRANSACTION.
00222            EXIT.

00224        CREATE-ACTUAL-KEY.
00225            IF T-PRODUCT-NUMBER IS NOT NUMERIC
00226            THEN
00227                MOVE 'PRODUCT NUMBER IS NOT NUMERIC'
00228                    TO LOG-PRINT-MESSAGE
00229                PERFORM BAD-TRANSACTION THRU END-BAD-TRANSACTION
00230                GO TO MAINLINE
00231            ELSE
00232                MOVE T-PRODUCT-NUMBER TO WORK-FIELD, LOGICAL-RECORD-KEY
00233                DIVIDE WORK-FIELD BY 25 GIVING QUOTIENT
00234                    REMAINDER RELATIVE-TRACK.
00235        END-CREATE-KEY.
00236            EXIT.
```

Fig. 15.2: *Continued.*

```
    7        UPDTPROD       0.43.40        NOV  9,1978


00239           TEST-AND-EDIT-TRANSACTION.
00240               IF T-DESCRIPTION IS EQUAL TO SPACES
00241               THEN
00242                   NEXT SENTENCE
00243               ELSE
00244                   MOVE T-DESCRIPTION TO M-DESCRIPTION.
00245               IF T-SELLING-PRICE IS NOT NUMERIC
00246               THEN
00247                   GO TO MOVE-NUMERIC-ERROR-MESSAGE
00248               ELSE
00249                   IF TX-SELLING-PRICE IS EQUAL TO SPACES
00250                   THEN
00251                       NEXT SENTENCE
00252                   ELSE
00253                       MOVE T-SELLING-PRICE TO M-SELLING-PRICE.

00255               IF T-SHIPPING-COST IS NOT NUMERIC
00256               THEN
00257                   GO TO MOVE-NUMERIC-ERROR-MESSAGE
00258               ELSE
00259                   IF TX-SHIPPING-COST IS EQUAL TO SPACES
00260                   THEN
00261                       NEXT SENTENCE
00262                   ELSE
00263                       MOVE T-SHIPPING-COST TO M-SHIPPING-COST.

00265               IF T-SUPPLIER-CODE IS EQUAL TO SPACES
00266               THEN
00267                   NEXT SENTENCE
00268               ELSE
00269                   MOVE T-SUPPLIER-CODE TO M-SUPPLIER-CODE.
00270               IF T-2ND-SUPPLIER IS EQUAL TO SPACES
00271               THEN
00272                   GO TO END-TEST-AND-EDIT
00273               ELSE
00274                   MOVE T-2ND-SUPPLIER TO M-2ND-SUPPLIER
00275                   GO TO END-TEST-AND-EDIT.
00276           MOVE-NUMERIC-ERROR-MESSAGE.
00277               MOVE 'SELLING PRICE OR SHIPPING COST IS NOT NUMERIC'
00278                   TO LOG-PRINT-MESSAGE.
00279               PERFORM BAD-TRANSACTION THRU END-BAD-TRANSACTION.
00280               GO TO MAINLINE.
00281           END-TEST-AND-EDIT.
00282               EXIT.
```

Fig. 15.2: *Continued.*

```
       8        UPDTPROD        0.43.40        NOV  9,1978


00286              LOG-OLD-MASTER.
00287                  MOVE WS-PRODUCT-MASTER-RECORD TO LOG-RECORD.
00288                  MOVE SPACES TO L-TYPE-AND-INITIALS.
00289                  WRITE LOG-TAPE-RECORD.
00290                  MOVE SPACES TO LOG-PRINT-RECORD.
00291                  MOVE WS-PRODUCT-MASTER-RECORD TO LOG-PRINT-LINE.
00292                  WRITE LOG-PRINT-RECORD AFTER ADVANCING 2 LINES.

00294              LOG-TRANSACTION.
00295                  MOVE TRANSACTION-RECORD TO LOG-TAPE-RECORD.
00296                  WRITE LOG-TAPE-RECORD.
00297                  MOVE SPACES TO LOG-PRINT-RECORD.
00298                  MOVE TRANSACTION-RECORD TO LOG-PRINT-LINE.
00299                  WRITE LOG-PRINT-RECORD AFTER ADVANCING 2 LINES.

00301              LOG-NEW-MASTER.
00302                  PERFORM LOG-OLD-MASTER.
00303              END-LOG.
00304                  EXIT.
```

Fig. 15.2: *Continued.*

Having gained an understanding of the mainline, we can move on to the primary transaction handling routines. In ADD-ROUTINE, a new record is to be added to the master file. Obviously, the data must be edit-checked before being added to the file. Once this step has been accomplished (don't worry about how just yet), the ACTUAL KEY can be set up, the record can be written, and the necessary log entries can be created.

In DEL-ROUTINE, an existing record is to be deleted from the system. Read the routine (Fig. 15.2) carefully.

The last of the primary transaction handling routines is called MOD-ROUTINE; the function of this module is to modify an existing record. Obviously, the routine must start with the reading of the desired master file record and end with the rewriting of the record. In between, the fields to be changed must be identified, edit-checked, and moved. Read the routine carefully, and see how record modification is implemented. Note that each field in the input record is compared against the COBOL constant SPACES, with further action taken only if the field IS NOT EQUAL TO SPACES. Note also that the REDEFINEd versions of the two numeric fields are used in the nonnumeric comparisons. Do professional programmers really think of such details before beginning to code? Not always. That's why most professional programmers code in pencil, not ink. Even so, how can such minor technical details be recognized? Practice.

FILE BACKUP

There is always a risk that, through human error, computer failure, or some other catastrophe, a master file may be destroyed. The loss of a master file can have very serious consequences; thus, **backup** copies are usually maintained and file recreation procedures normally exist. On a sequential master file, backup is most often provided by simply keeping the old master file and the most current transactions file; master file recreation can be achieved by simply rerunning the master file update program with the old data.

No such convenient backup exists on a direct access file. A file update does not involve all the records; usually only a handful are affected. The log tape does provide a form of backup for those records that are updated, but what about all the others? Unless specific steps are taken to protect the data, the loss of a complete file is quite possible.

In most organizations, file backup is handled through the simple expedient of **dumping** all direct access master files to magnetic tape at regular intervals, usually daily. Using the tape copy, and factoring in changes that may have occured since the file was dumped (source: the log tape), the master file can be recreated should disaster strike.

PROGRAMMING—THE BUILDING BLOCK APPROACH

The word **kludge** is quite popular in programming circles; its definition is rather imprecise at best, but every programmer knows what a kludge is. Basically, the term refers to a program that has been written in such an unplanned and unstructured manner that it defies logical interpretation. Even the highly skilled programmer has difficulty following the tortuous twisting and turnings of a true kludge. Often, such programs are the result of random evolution rather than intelligent planning, with "patches" and "fixes" being added here and there in an attempt to solve whatever problem is "currently" encountered.

Most programmers encounter their first kludge when they are assigned to maintain one. More often than not, simple maintenance is impossible, and the programmer decides to scrap the old hulk and start all over again. Scrapping a program representing many months of programming effort may seem wasteful, but if the program really is a kludge, scrapping it may be the best thing to do.

Throughout this text, we have stressed a step-by-step approach to program planning and development. In effect, the objective of our approach is to design a framework for the entire program and then to hang routines housing computational and logical details on this mainline framework. The programmer who carefully follows these principles can actually avoid creating kludges.

Imagine if all programs were planned and developed in such a logical and straightforward manner. Changes to the program would be easy to implement, being restricted to one or two easily identified routines. New features could be added by simply hanging a new routine on the already existing mainline structure.

Perhaps even more importantly, the basic patterns of these programs would begin to emerge. A master file update is, after all, a master file update; why reinvent the wheel every time a new master file must be updated? In the world of the future, programmers may actually follow such a building block approach, identifying the general class of problem to be solved, selecting the general solution to that problem, hanging a few standard secondary routines on the framework of the general solution, and writing a handful of specialized modules to take care of those features that make the problem unique.

Does this mean that the need for computer programmers will eventually disappear? If by "computer programmer" you mean an individual who codes solutions to problems in COBOL or some other language, the answer may well be "yes"; in fact, it is almost certain that the next decade will see such significant changes in the comptuer field that the details of COBOL you have been learning throughout this book will be largely obsolete. The task of identifying the problem to be solved and then planning and implementing a specific solution will, however, remain. If by "computer programmer" you refer to an individual who is responsible for identifying, planning, and implementing a problem solution without regard for the specific language used to achieve these objectives, then the answer to the question posed at the beginning of this paragraph must be "no". In fact, make that a resounding "NO"! The demand for people who can solve specific business problems will never dry up; it can only increase.

Most computer people are very careful to distinguish between the "coder" and the "programmer". A coder is a person who writes instructions in a specific programming language, often following someone else's plan. A programmer is more—much more. A programmer is a problem solver; a coder is a clerk. A true programmer will never become obsolete; a coder almost certainly will. The coder is like a typist; the programmer is like an author.

SUMMARY

The topic of this chapter was the direct access master file update application. Basically, a direct access file is updated in the same way it is accessed—one record at a time. Three types of update transactions can be identified: modifications to existing records, deletions of existing records, and additions of new records.

We turned our attention to planning and coding a program to update the product file. Initially, operating procedures and the need for strict controls on the file update application were discussed in some detail; such controls are crucial in any direct access file update application simply because using a direct access file makes it difficult to identify and correct errors after they have occurred. Input record formats were carefully planned, with a key objective being to make errors as unlikely as possible. The format of a transaction log, a necessary file backup and activity monitoring device, was defined. Finally, the program was written in COBOL. The only new COBOL feature was the use of HIGH-VALUE to indicate a deleted direct access record.

The need for file backup was stressed. Often, file backup procedures include a regularly scheduled dump of the contents of each file. The transactions log, used in conjunction with the dump, can be used to reconstruct a lost file.

Our generalized building block approach to program development was shown to be a tremendous aid to the programmer, allowing previously solved problems to be reapplied to new situations with only a few details to be changed.

KEY WORDS

backup	**HIGH-VALUE**	**transaction log**
dumping	**kludge**	

EXERCISES

1. In any direct access master file update application there are three basic types of transactions. What are they? Describe the characteristics of each.

2. Why is it so important that clear operating procedures be established and intricate controls be implemented on any direct access master file update application?

3. How is a record deleted from a master file? Physically, how is the fact of deletion represented on the direct access device?

4. Why is a REDEFINES clause needed when certain class tests are performed?

5. Why is file backup necessary? Discuss some common procedures for file backup.

6. Describe the building block approach to program development.

7. Write a program to update the customer name and address file of exercise 8 in Chapter 14.

8. In exercise 10 of Chapter 14, a product description file was created. It is a very simple file, with records containing only the product number and a description. Modifications to existing records are thus quite rare, so only deletion and addition transactions are considered necessary to the file update program that you are to write.

9. A number of data entry clerks have been hired to keep the inventory master file created in exercise 12 of Chapter 14 in an up-to-date condition. These clerks will not be given the responsibility for adding new products to or deleting old products from the file; in fact they will be prohibited from such activities. Instead, they will concentrate on the existing products, reporting changes in the stock on hand.

    The data entry clerks will deal with two types of transactions—an addition to inventory and a deletion from inventory. Each transaction will include the product part number, a code identifying the type of transaction, and the quantity (number of units) involved in the transaction. Additions to inventory will be reported as soon as the clerk receives a set of signed papers from the receiving department. Deletions from inventory will be entered when the warehouse manager gives the clerk a signed shipping order. All transactions are to be logged on a transaction tape, with the clerk submitting the transaction being carefully identified and his or her employee number recorded.

10. Changes to other fields in the inventory file, additions to this file, and deletions from the file are much more carefully monitored. Additions and deletions can be made only by engineering. A new value for the reorder level can be computed by the inventory department, and this field may be changed only by that department. The number of units on order, the expected arrival date of an order, and the supplier code number are under the control of purchasing. Finally, the inventory department can, following a physical count, change the stock on hand.

    Each of these departments is required to fill out a special form for any of these changes. The forms are collected daily and keypunched; the resulting small batch is then read into the computer and the file is updated. The only reason why this is not a traditional sequential master file update application is because the activity is so low.

Write a program to update the master file for these transactions. Be sure to generate reports for each of the involved departments clearly listing any changes they may have made.

11, It is often necessary to make changes to the master file described in exercise 14 of Chapter 14. Players are traded, sent to the minor leagues, or retire. Other players are acquired or promoted from the minor leagues. Occasionally, a player will change numbers during the season, necessitating the transfer of his old record to a new record accessed by a new number. Some new players will arrive with no major league record for the current year; others will arrive with a record from some other team or, perhaps, a prior stint with our club. Write a program to allow these changes to be made.

16

Creating an Indexed File

OVERVIEW

As an alternative to the division/remainder technique, the programmer can achieve direct access by maintaining an index showing where each record has been physically stored on the direct access device. Chapter 16 begins with a discussion of the underlying ideas of such indexed files.

The most difficult problem with using indexed files is maintaining the index; thus most computer manufacturers and many independent software suppliers market software packages to support indexed file processing. We will examine one such package, IBM's indexed sequential access method (ISAM), creating and reorganizing a file in this chapter. In Chapter 17 we will access and update the file.

INDEXED FILES

Consider a telephone book. Each of its record consists of an individual's name, address, and telephone number. The records are arranged in alphabetical order by last name. It would be easy to argue that the telephone book is a sequential file, but the records in this file are almost never processed sequentially. Instead, taking advantage of our knowledge of the alphabet and using the names printed at the top of each page as a guide (the first and last names on the page), we quickly locate the page containing the name we are looking for and then search only that page. This is a form of direct access. The names listed at the top of each page serve as an **index**.

A dictionary provides another example. The thumb slots found along the edge of the pages can be used to locate the section containing words beginning with a given letter. Now the guide words at the top of each page can be used to locate the proper page. A search of this page brings us to the desired word.

Many other examples could be cited—a card catalog in a library, the table of contents in a book, the index in a book, the list of selections on a juke box, the headings on folders in a file cabinet, the *Reader's Guide to Periodical Literature*. All these examples have one thing in common: an index is used to simplify the task of finding specific information. Using an index is perhaps the most "natural" of all direct access techniques.

How can we use an index to support direct access on a computer file? The answer is simple. We begin by setting up a table in memory (the use of tables was discussed in Chapter 8). Each table entry contains a key and a relative address. The file can be created sequentially. As each record is added to the file, the logical key of the record and the relative address of the record on the direct access device can be stored in the table. After all the records have been written, the table (actually, an index showing the address where each record has been stored) can itself be written to disk, usually to an easy-to-find location such as the very first track in the file.

Later, when it becomes necessary to retrieve a record, the index can be read into a program. Using the logical key of the desired record, the index table can be searched; once the key has been located in the table, the associated relative address can be used in a READ operation.

There is only one problem: the index is difficult to maintain. As long as nothing changes there is no problem, but things do change. As records are added to and deleted from the file, entries must be added to and deleted from the index. Unless the file is very small, processing efficiencies usually dictate that the index be kept in sequence by the key field, so each change to the file will require a sort operation. As the size of the index begins to grow, merely storing and retrieving it becomes a hassle.

As a result of these problems, few programmers actually go the the trouble of creating and maintaining their own indexes. Instead they use any of a number of commercially available indexing systems. In this chapter we will investigate a typical example, IBM's **Indexed Sequential Access Method (ISAM)**.

INDEXED SEQUENTIAL FILES

ISAM is IBM's version of indexed file support. It is not, we must stress, an industry standard; instead it is a single manufacturer's product. Other suppliers have similar products; many are functionally identical to ISAM. For certain applications, others may well be superior. ISAM is, however, representative.

When an indexed sequential file is created, the data must be in sequence. Records are added to the file one at a time, filling successive locations on a track. Eventually a complete track will be filled. When this happens, the key of the last record added is placed in a **track index**, which contains the key of the *last* record added to the track. Later, on retrieval, if the desired key is less than the key of the last record on this track, then the record must (if it is on the file at all) be located on this track. Remember that the records are in sequence. Can a record with a key lower than the one in the track index possibly be anywhere else?

As the second track is filled, the key of the last record stored on this track is added to the track index. The same thing happens on the third track, the fourth track, and so on.

On a disk, several surfaces are usually stacked on a single spindle, with one access mechanism holding the read/write heads that access all the surfaces. One position of the read/write heads thus accesses not one but several tracks, one on each surface. The set of tracks accessed by one position of the read/write heads is called a **cylinder**. When you read from or write to a disk pack, the access mechanism is first moved over the proper cylinder. Once the access mechanism is positioned, the proper read/write head is turned on, thus allowing the device to access a specific track. The cylinder represents the proper location of the entire access mechanism; the track defines which of the several heads on the access mechanism will be activiated.

As all the tracks in a given cylinder are filled with data, the key of the last record added to the cylinder is placed on a **cylinder index**. A new track index referencing the tracks in the second cylinder is then created, and the process continues. As a track is filled, an entry is made in this second track index; eventually, when the entire cylinder is filled, a second entry is made on the cylinder index, a third track index is created, and the process continues. Note that there is one track index for each cylinder in the file.

Since the file is created sequentially, it can be retrieved sequentially. The fact that indexes have been maintained allows individual records to be accessed randomly as well. ISAM is a very flexible data management technique.

Direct access is achieved by searching the indexes. First the cylinder index is searched, from the beginning. If the key of the desired record is greater than the key recorded in a given cylinder index entry, the record cannot possibly be on this cylinder, as the index entry is the key of the *last* record stored. Thus we move on to the next cylinder index entry. As soon as we encounter an index entry greater than or equal to the key of the desired record, however, we know that we have located the proper cylinder. Now it's on to the cylinder's track index.

A similar argument can be made for the track index. If the search key is greater than the track index entry, the record cannot be on that track. The track containing the record must be represented by the first track index entry having a key higher than or equal to the search key. If the record isn't found on this track, it simply cannot be on the file.

There is one very serious problem with indexed sequential files. They are created sequentially, with records simply written to the next available disk location. No unused space is left between records. If, later, it is necessary to add a record to the file, what happens? There is no place to put it. Instead, it must be placed in an **overflow** area. Overflow records are not where they are supposed to be. They can be retrieved, but retrieval tends to be quite inefficient. In fact, when the number of overflow records exceeds about 5% of the file, it becomes necessary (or at least highly desirable) to recreate the file. We will ignore the details of indexed sequential overflow; you should, however, remember that space must be set aside to hold these overflow records on the disk file.

CREATING AN INDEXED SEQUENTIAL FILE

An indexed sequential file is easy to create in COBOL. The real complexities are restricted to job control language, and are usually the concern of an experienced programmer. Our discussion of indexed sequential file creation will be followed by a brief optional section on job control and the physical nature of an ISAM file.

Let's use a specific example to illustrate. Our objective is to create a file of customer information containing the following fields:

positions	contents
1-8	customer number
9-25	customer name
26-40	street address
41-50	city
51-52	state
53-57	zip code
58-62	order number for unshipped customer order
63	status (0=pending;1=in process;2=finished)
64-67	date of last update
68-71	expected ship date
72-76	dollar volume last year (thousands)

Numerous applications are anticipated for this file. It will, of course, be used in addressing bills and advertising. Another nice feature is the ability to prepare advertising for only a selected set of customers—all those with the same zip code or all those who represented over $10,000 in sales last year, for example. The address portion of the record can be used to prepare lists of potential customer contracts for the sales department. Another planned use is in handling customer requests for order status where, for example, the customer calls and asks for the expected shipping date of a given order; with the data in this file, a clerk can simply ask for the record to be displayed on a terminal and pass the information along to the customer.

An existing file of this customer information is maintained on punched cards. The file consists of roughly 3000 records. Our objective is to copy these records to disk, maintaining an index showing the location of each. We plan to use the indexed sequential access method.

Some Basic ISAM Rules

Before beginning to create an ISAM (indexed sequential access method) file, the programmer should be familiar with a few basic ISAM rules. First, the file must be created in sequence. This implies that the input records to be used in creating the file must first be sorted. In other words, file creation is almost always done by a system of programs: a sort followed by file creation.

The fact that the file is created sequentially allows for the sequential retrieval of the records. To support direct access, indexes are maintained. This implies that the programmer must clearly identify the key field in the record format.

As is the case with almost any file, the records on an ISAM file are subject to change. New records are placed on an overflow area. Deleted records are not actually erased. Instead, the constant HIGH-VALUE is placed in the first character position of the record as it is stored on disk, clearly marking the record as being deleted. This implies that the first character of each ISAM record must be set aside to hold a deletion flag, and that this first position can be used for no other purpose.

An out-of-sequence record will be recognized as an invalid key; thus the programmer must code an INVALID KEY clause as part of the WRITE statement that creates the file. Later, we will encounter other uses for the INVALID KEY option in retrieving the records on an ISAM file.

The ENVIRONMENT DIVISION

In the ENVIRONMENT DIVISION the programmer describes each file accessed by the program though a series of SELECT and ASSIGN clauses. For an ISAM file (Fig. 16.1) the programmer codes

SELECT file-name ASSIGN TO DA-I-name

with the file name and the external names being defined as before. An ISAM file must be created on a direct access device; thus the device class DA (for direct access) must be coded. The file organization is indexed sequential; thus the I (for indexed).

COBOL Coding Form

SYSTEM: CUSTOMER
PROGRAM: CREATE MASTER
PROGRAMMER: DAVIS & FISHER
DATE: 3-15-79
PUNCHING INSTRUCTIONS — GRAPHIC: ∅ PUNCH: ZERO
PAGE 1 OF 3

```
IDENTIFICATION DIVISION.
PROGRAM-ID.  CRISAM.
AUTHOR.      DAVIS & FISHER.
REMARKS.     THIS PROGRAM CREATES AN INDEXED SEQUENTIAL
             CUSTOMER MASTER FILE FROM PUNCHED CARDS.
ENVIRONMENT DIVISION.
CONFIGURATION SECTION.
SOURCE-COMPUTER.  IBM-370-148.
OBJECT-COMPUTER.  IBM-370-148.
INPUT-OUTPUT SECTION.
FILE-CONTROL.
    SELECT CARD-CUSTOMER-MASTER    ASSIGN TO UT-S-CARDMAST.
    SELECT ISAM-MASTER-FILE        ASSIGN TO DA-I-ISAMMAST
        ACCESS MODE IS SEQUENTIAL
        RECORD KEY IS ISAM-CUSTOMER-NUMBER.
```

Fig. 16.1: *The ENVIRONMENT DIVISION entries for creating an indexed sequential file.*

Two other clauses are needed to access an indexed sequential file. The first is an ACCESS MODE clause. The programmer must code

ACCESS MODE IS SEQUENTIAL

to create an ISAM file. Why? Haven't we already defined the file as having an indexed organization? Yes, but an indexed sequential file can be accessed either sequentially or randomly. While the file organization is indexed sequential, that only defines the way the records are physically stored on disk. How the records are to be accessed (read or written one at a time) is something else, and must be specified through an ACCESS MODE clause.

The final clause (Fig. 16.1), the **RECORD KEY** clause, is used to specify the field within the description of the ISAM record that will be used as the key. Records must be in sequence (ascending order) by this key field. The key will be used by the system in creating track and cylinder index entries.

The DATA DIVISION

An indexed sequential file must, as is the case with any file, be defined in the FILE SECTION of the DATA DIVISION. The FD entry is much like that of earlier chapters. Blocking is permitted; however, we have chosen not to block our records (Fig. 16.2). The label record must be standard, but we have always used standard labels in creating a tape or disk file, so there is nothing new here.

It is permissable on a sequential or direct access file to have variable length records—a student's academic history, for example, would tend to be quite small as a freshman, but considerably longer as a senior. Variable length records cannot be stored on an indexed sequential file. Only fixed length records are permitted; to emphasize this fact we have coded (Fig. 16.2)

RECORDING MODE IS F.

The ISAM record description is identical to the input record except for one thing. Remember how the first character position of an ISAM record is used to hold a deletion flag? In Fig. 16.2, the first character position is called ISAM-DELETE-FLAG, and will be used to hold the constant **HIGH-VALUE** for any records that, in the future, are deleted from the file.

The PROCEDURE DIVISION

The PROCEDURE DIVISION for creating an indexed sequential file can be seen in the program listing (Fig. 16.3). The program is very simple. It begins by opening the sequential input and indexed sequential output files. Then it's on to the mainline loop, where input records are read, moved to the output area, and written to the ISAM file until all records have been processed. Finally, the files are closed and the program ends.

Two instructions are worth special consideration (Fig. 16.3). Note that, after reading an input record and moving the data to the output area, the constant

COBOL Coding Form

SYSTEM	CUSTOMER		PUNCHING INSTRUCTIONS	PAGE 2 OF 3
PROGRAM	CREATE MASTER		GRAPHIC Ø	CARD FORM #
PROGRAMMER	DAVIS & FISHER	DATE 3-15-79	PUNCH ZERO	

```
       FD  ISAM-MASTER-FILE          LABEL RECORD IS STANDARD
                                     BLOCK CONTAINS 1 RECORDS
                                     RECORDING MODE IS F.
       Ø1  CUSTOMER-MASTER-RECORD.
           Ø5  ISAM-DELETE-FLAG            PIC X.
           Ø5  ISAM-CUSTOMER-DATA.
               1Ø  ISAM-CUSTOMER-NUMBER    PIC 9(8).
               1Ø  ISAM-CUSTOMER-NAME      PIC X(17).
               1Ø  ISAM-CUSTOMER-ADDRESS   PIC X(15).
               1Ø  ISAM-CUSTOMER-CITY      PIC X(1Ø).
               1Ø  ISAM-CUSTOMER-STATE     PIC XX.
               1Ø  ISAM-CUSTOMER-ZIP       PIC X(5).
               1Ø  ISAM-ORDER-NUMBER       PIC 9(5).
               1Ø  ISAM-ORDER-STATUS       PIC 9.
               1Ø  ISAM-DATE-OF-UPDATE     PIC 9(4).
               1Ø  ISAM-SHIP-DATE          PIC 9(4).
               1Ø  ISAM-PAST-BUSINESS      PIC 9(5).
```

Fig. 16.2: *The DATA DIVISION for an ISAM file.*

```
     1                          3.00.40        OCT 21,1978

00001              IDENTIFICATION DIVISION.
00002                 PROGRAM-ID. CRISAM.
00003                 AUTHOR.     DAVIS & FISHER.
00005                 REMARKS.    THIS PROGRAM CREATES AN INDEXED SEQUENTIAL
00006                             CUSTOMER MASTER FILE FROM PUNCHED CARDS.

00008              ENVIRONMENT DIVISION.
00009                 CONFIGURATION SECTION.
00010                    SOURCE-COMPUTER.  IBM-370-148.
00011                    OBJECT-COMPUTER.  IBM-370-148.

00013                 INPUT-OUTPUT SECTION.
00015                 FILE-CONTROL.
00016                    SELECT CARD-CUSTOMER-MASTER  ASSIGN TO UT-S-CARDMAST.
00017                    SELECT ISAM-MASTER-FILE      ASSIGN TO DA-I-ISAMMAST
00018                       ACCESS MODE IS SEQUENTIAL
00019                       RECORD KEY IS ISAM-CUSTOMER-NUMBER.
```

Fig. 16.3: *A listing of a program to create an indexed sequential file.*

```
2          CRISAM         3.00.40        OCT 21,1978

00021              DATA DIVISION.
00022              FILE SECTION.
00023                FD  CARD-CUSTOMER-MASTER        LABEL RECORD IS OMITTED.
00024                01  CUSTOMER-SOURCE-RECORD.
00025                    05  I-CUSTOMER-SOURCE-DATA.
00026                        10  I-CUSTOMER-NUMBER    PIC 9(8).
00027                        10  I-CUSTOMER-NAME      PIC X(17).
00028                        10  I-CUSTOMER-ADDRESS   PIC X(15).
00029                        10  I-CUSTOMER-CITY      PIC X(10).
00030                        10  I-CUSTOMER-STATE     PIC XX.
00031                        10  I-CUSTOMER-ZIP-CODE  PIC X(5).
00032                        10  I-ORDER-NUMBER       PIC 9(5).
00033                        10  I-ORDER-STATUS       PIC 9.
00034                        10  I-DATE-OF-UPDATE     PIC 9(4).
00035                        10  I-SHIP-DATE          PIC 9(4).
00036                        10  I-PAST-BUSINESS      PIC 9(5).
00037                    05      FILLER               PIC X(4).

00039                FD  ISAM-MASTER-FILE    LABEL RECORD IS STANDARD
00040                                        BLOCK CONTAINS 1 RECORDS
00041                                        RECORDING MODE IS F.
00042                01  CUSTOMER-MASTER-RECORD.
00043                    05  ISAM-DELETE-FLAG         PIC X.
00044                    05  ISAM-CUSTOMER-DATA.
00045                        10  ISAM-CUSTOMER-NUMBER  PIC 9(8).
00046                        10  ISAM-CUSTOMER-NAME    PIC X(17).
00047                        10  ISAM-CUSTOMER-ADDRESS PIC X(15).
00048                        10  ISAM-CUSTOMER-CITY    PIC X(10).
00049                        10  ISAM-CUSTOMER-STATE   PIC XX.
00050                        10  ISAM-CUSTOMER-ZIP     PIC X(5).
00051                        10  ISAM-ORDER-NUMBER     PIC 9(5).
00052                        10  ISAM-ORDER-STATUS     PIC 9.
00053                        10  ISAM-DATE-OF-UPDATE   PIC 9(4).
00054                        10  ISAM-SHIP-DATE        PIC 9(4).
00055                        10  ISAM-PAST-BUSINESS    PIC 9(5).
```

Fig. 16.3: *Continued.*

```
3          CRISAM        3.00.40        OCT 21,1978

00057          PROCEDURE DIVISION.
00058               OPEN INPUT  CARD-CUSTOMER-MASTER
00059                    OUTPUT ISAM-MASTER-FILE.

00061          ISAM-FILE-CREATE-LOOP.
00062               READ CARD-CUSTOMER-MASTER
00063                    AT END GO TO END-OF-JOB.

00065               MOVE I-CUSTOMER-SOURCE-DATA TO ISAM-CUSTOMER-DATA.

00067               MOVE LOW-VALUE              TO ISAM-DELETE-FLAG.

00069               WRITE CUSTOMER-MASTER-RECORD
00070                    INVALID KEY GO TO END-OF-JOB.
00071               GO TO ISAM-FILE-CREATE-LOOP.

00073          END-OF-JOB.
00074               CLOSE CARD-CUSTOMER-MASTER.
00075               CLOSE ISAM-MASTER-FILE.
00076               STOP RUN.
```

Fig. 16.3: *Continued.*

LOW-VALUE is moved to the ISAM-DELETE-FLAG field. LOW-VALUE is a constant; it is, as the name implies, the precise opposite of HIGH-VALUE. If HIGH-VALUE is found in the first character of a record on an ISAM file, it means that the record has been deleted. It is possible that, just by chance, HIGH-VALUE might be in the memory location allocated to the first character of the record. By moving LOW-VALUE to this field before writing the record, the programmer controls the value in the delete flag field and makes certain that records flagged as being deleted are not accidently added to the file.

Associated with the WRITE statement is an INVALID KEY clause. If a record is out of sequence by the RECORD KEY field, an INVALID KEY is recognized. Our response to this condition will be to terminate the program.

The Physical Nature of an ISAM File (Optional)

How exactly is data stored on an indexed sequential file? Where is the index found? What about the overflow area? A basic understanding of the physical nature of an ISAM file can help the programmer to both answer these questions and understand some of the seemingly strange job control language parameters that must be coded.

There are three parts to every ISAM file: the index area, the prime data area, and the overflow area. Space must be set aside to hold each. Perhaps the easiest way to visualize such a file is by assuming that each of the areas is found on a separate physical disk pack or volume (Fig. 16.4). It is possible to create an ISAM file in this way. More realistically, the three areas will be found on the same volume with, for example, cylinders 10 through 12 holding the index, 13 through 100 holding the prime data area, and 101 through 110 being set aside for overflow. To use the correct technical term, each physical region is called an extent.

At the other extreme, a single extent (a single set of contiguous cylinders) can be used to hold the entire file (Fig. 16.5). Let's assume that there are 20 tracks in each cylinder. An example of a single-extent ISAM file might have the first two cylinders set aside for the index, with two tracks on each of the remaining prime data cylinders used for overflow.

Other configurations are possible. The index can be given its own extent, with the prime data and overflow areas sharing a region. The index and prime data areas can be combined, with overflow being handled separately. It is through job control language that the physical nature of a file is described to the system. The broad range of choices available for an ISAM file does make ISAM job control a bit confusing, but as long as you keep a physical picture of what we are trying to create firmly in

Fig. 16.4: *An ISAM file spread over three separate volumes.*

Index   Prime   Overflow
           data
           area

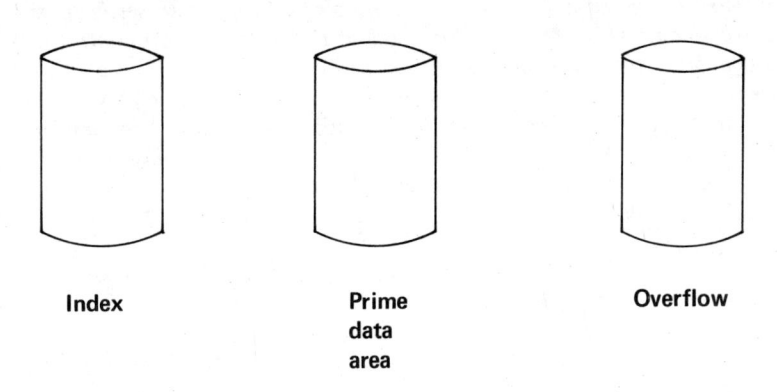

Fig. 16.5: *An ISAM file created as a single extent on a single volume.*

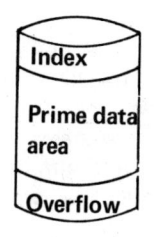

Index

Prime data area

Overflow

mind, you should have little difficulty understanding the discussion of ISAM job control that follows.

Job Control for Creating an ISAM file (Optional)

By far the easiest approach to creating an ISAM file is to set it up as a single extent (Fig. 16.5). Before coding the necessary job control language, let's stop for a minute and consider exactly what it is we are about to do. A series of cylinders are to be set aside to hold our file. Normally, the first few will be used to hold the index. On each of the remaining cylinders, one or more tracks will be allocated to the overflow area; the other tracks make up the prime data area. A control card to create such a file is shown in Fig. 16.6.

Each parameter has been coded on a separate line. The first line identifies the file, using the same name (ISAM) we used within the program as part of the ASSIGN clause. Continuing with the first line, the DD defines this as a data definition card, and the DSNAME=CUSTFILE provides a name for the physical file.

In the second line we indicate that the file is to be stored on a 3330 disk pack; a different system may well use a different model number. In line three, a specific 3330 disk volume, one with the name MIAMI3, has been identified. We want our file placed on this specific pack, and no other volume will do. Line four identifies this as a new (about to be created) file, and indicates that the file is to be cataloged at the end of the job.

The SPACE parameter of line five contains a few new subparameters. We are asking for a total of 10 cylinders, and want the first two tracks of each set aside for an index. Look carefully at the numbers coded within the inner set of parentheses. Two commas separate the 10 and the 2. The 2 is thus found in the third position, and represents the number of tracks in each cylinder that are to be set aside to hold the index.

There is another subparameter within the space parameter: CONTIG. It simply means that we want the ten tracks of our file allocated as a contiguous extent; in other words, we want ten adjacent tracks. Note again the use of two commas. Without getting into unnecessary details, there are other SPACE subparameters that we have chosen not to code, and the extra commas represent their absence. The need for such i-dotting and t-crossing sometimes makes job control language seem much more complex than it really is.

The final line of Fig. 16.6 contains a DCB or data control block. Within the parentheses, DSORG=IS must be coded. The OPTCD subparameter is used to define certain optional support features that the

Fig. 16.6: *A DD card to create a single-extent ISAM file.*

```
//ISAM     DD    DSNAME=CUSTFILE,
//               UNIT=3330,
//               VOL=SER=MIAMI3,
//               DISP=(NEW,CATLG),
//               SPACE=(CYL,(10,,2),,CONTIG),
//               DCB=(DSORG=IS,OPTCD=LY,CYLOFL=3)
```

Fig. 16.7: *The job control cards needed to create a three-extent ISAM file.*

```
//ISAM3    DD    DSNAME=CUSTFILE(INDEX),...............
//         DD    DSNAME=CUSTFILE(PRIME),...............
//         DD    DSNAME=CUSTFILE(OVFLOW),.............
```

> *programmer wants to utilize. The "L" means that the delete feature is to be used; the "Y" calls for cylinder overflow. Finally, CYLOFL=3 clearly indicates that three tracks on each cylinder are to be set aside for overflow.*
>
> *If the programmer wants to spread the file over more than a single disk extent, one job control language card must be coded for each physical segment of the file. Consider, for example, the three extent approach described in Fig. 16.4. The job control language for creating this file would consist of three DD cards (Fig. 16.7). The first DD card names the file (ISAM). Following the DSNAME is the word INDEX, indicating that this particular card defines only the index.*
>
> *The second DD card does not have a name field; thus the name is the same as that of the first card—ISAM. The keyword PRIME indicates that this card defines the prime data area. Finally, the third DD card defines the overflow area (OVFLOW). Additional parameters must, of course, be coded in each card; such detail is beyond the scope of this book.*

REORGANIZING AN INDEXED SEQUENTIAL FILE

In Chapter 17, we will consider a number of applications calling for adding records to and deleting records from an indexed sequential file. Adding a new record implies an overflow condition, as no space is set aside for expansion during the process of creating an ISAM file. Since an overflow record is not where it really should be, the process of retrieving an overflow record is relatively inefficient.

When records are deleted from an ISAM file, the constant HIGH-VALUE is moved into the first character of the record. The record still exists on the disk file, however. It still takes up space. Wasted space is another form of inefficiency.

As a result of these two problems, it is, with very few exceptions, necessary that an indexed sequential file be reorganized on a regular basis. How can this **reorganization** be achieved? Through a very simple two-step process. First, the indexed sequential file is read sequentially and copied to tape or disk. When an ISAM file is read sequentially, overflow records are processed in order by key without regard for their physical location; in other words, an overflow record looks just like any other record. Also, deleted records (HIGH-VALUE in the first character) are skipped. The result is a straight sequential file with records that had been placed on an overflow track now occupying their proper position and deleted records missing.

Now it's time for the second step. The file creation program developed in this chapter is simply run over again, with the newly created sequential file as its input. The result is a brand new ISAM file with no deleted records taking up space and no records on the overflow area.

What is involved in reading an ISAM file sequentially? Essentially, it's much like reading any sequential file. Physically, the file was created using ISAM; thus the ASSIGN clause must reference DA-I-name. A RECORD KEY clause, must be attached to the SELECT, and, although ACCESS MODE IS SEQUENTIAL will be assumed by the system, it is probably a good idea to add this clause if only for documentation.

In the DATA DIVISION, don't forget that the first character of the record will be the deletion flag. In the PROCEDURE DIVISION you will be reading the file sequentially; thus an AT END clause (rather than an INVALID KEY clause) is called for.

Many business organizations take advantage of ISAM file reorganization to perform an additional function. By copying the complete file to magnetic tape and then using this tape to recreate the file, a very accurate and up-to-date **backup** copy of the file is created. After reorganization has been completed, the tape can be stored in a safe place; later, should a disaster destroy the master file on disk, the most current tape can be used to recreate the file once again.

SUMMARY

The chapter began with a discussion of the use of indexes in everyday life. The general idea of an indexed approach to direct access was then established. Since maintaining an index can become difficult, most programmers prefer to use a standard indexed file support system, rather than maintaining an index themselves.

Next we turned our attention to IBM's indexed sequential access method (ISAM). The key ideas of track indexes, cylinder indexes, and overflow were discussed. Using the indexes, it is possible to retrieve records directly.

The problem to be solved in this chapter was the creation of a customer master file using the indexed sequential technique. After describing the problem, we discussed those characteristics of an ISAM file that impact our COBOL code. In the ENVIRONMENT DIVISION, the ASSIGN clause must refer to DA-I-name. ACCESS MODE and RECORD KEY clauses are also needed; the file is created sequentially, and the key is used in building the indexes. In the DATA DIVISION, our primary concern was with the deletion flag, the first character in the record. Records must be fixed length. An INVALID KEY clause must be attached to the WRITE instruction in the PROCEDURE DIVISION; an out-of-sequence record is recognized as an invalid key.

An optional section on the physical nature of an ISAM file and the job control language needed to create a file followed the discussion of COBOL implementation. The chapter ended with a brief description of the ISAM file reorganization application.

KEY WORDS

backup	index	overflow
cylinder	indexed sequential	RECORD KEY clause
cylinder index	ISAM	reorganization
HIGH-VALUE	LOW-VALUE	track index

EXERCISES

1. Explain the basic idea of using an index to support direct access..

2. Explain how IBM's indexed sequential access method can be used to directly access a record. Explain how the track and cylinder indexes are used.

3. Why is an overflow area needed on an ISAM file?

4. Explain how records are deleted from an ISAM file.

5. Why must the records be in sequence when creating an ISAM file?

6. Why must an ISAM file be reorganized at regular intervals?

7. Explain how the three primary regions of an ISAM file are physically structured on disk.

8. Payroll has been used as an example in several places throughout the text. Generally, the input record to the payroll program has contained the hourly pay rate and other personal information. Realistically, this is very unusual; more often, the personal information is kept on a personnel file which is accessed as part of the payroll preparation program.

    Write a program to create a direct access file of personal information. Include the following fields for each employee:

positions	contents
1-9	employee number
10-25	employee name
26-40	street address
41-50	city
51-52	state

positions	contents
53-57	zip code
58-60	department
61-64	hourly pay rate (99V99)
65	marital status
66-67	number of dependents

Use the indexed sequential (or other indexed) technique.

9. An airline reservation system has at its base a direct access file containing flight information. The key to accessing this file is generated from the name of our airline (TTA for Tree Top Airlines), the flight number, and the date; the key TTA377120380, for example, identifies Tree Top Airlines flight 377 leaving on December (12) 03, 1980.

   You are to write a program to create a direct access file of flight information. Each record should contain

positions	contents
1-12	the key as described above
13-25	city of departure
26-37	city of destination
38-40	capacity of airplane
41-43	number of seats currently sold
44-46	number of seats available

   Tree Top Airlines schedules 20 flights per day. Company policy is that flights for the next 30 days are to be kept on the direct access master file.

10. Several local libraries have gotten together to set up an interlibrary loan system. The basic idea is to create a direct access file of all the books in each library. Several research projects conducted at each of the participating schools have created a need for such a cooperative system.

    Write a program to create this file. Access will be by the Library of Congress number. Input cards for creating the file have been keypunched using the following fields:

positions	contents
1-15	Library of Congress number

16-30	author
31-50	title
51-60	publisher
61-65	year published
66-70	libraries where found.

Each library is identified by a single letter—right now, A-G are used. If the book is found in none of the libraries, this field is blank; if the book is found in more than one, each letter is listed, as in ACDG, which designates four different libraries. Roughly 10,000 volumes are to be cataloged in our interlibrary system.

Would you use the division/remainder method or an index technique in creating this file? Why? Would the fact that a Library of Congress "number" usually contains nonnumeric characters influence your choice in any way.

Write a program to create this file; you might limit the file to 100 records for testing purposes.

17

Indexed File Processing

OVERVIEW

An indexed sequential customer master file was created in Chapter 16; in this chapter we will develop programs to access and to update this file. The first application deals with the problem of answering requests for status information on a customer order. The objective is simply to obtain information; no changes are made to the file conttents. The second program will update the master file, and will include procedures for adding, deleting, and changing a record.

The chapter ends with a brief discussion of the reasons for using direct rather than sequential access. The strengths and weaknesses of two approaches to direct access (the use of an algorithm and the indexed sequential technique) are also explored.

QUERY APPLICATIONS

In a business environment, it is often necessary to know the current status of some operation or some phase of the business. Production might need the current stock balance of a critical raw material. Sales might need information on the current inventory balance of a given product, so that the decision to promise or not to promise immediate delivery can be made. Customers often want to know the status of their orders. Management might want to know if given customers have consistently paid their bills.

To the non-computer person, such applications are akin to asking the computer specific questions, such as, "What is the present stock on hand for part number 123456?". In computer terminology, such questions are called queries, and programs designed to deal with such queries are called **query** handling routines. Basically, programs falling in this general class are designed to accept input transactions in either a loosely or tightly formatted form. They then interpret these queries, access the necessary data files, and produce a response to the initial question. On some systems, the query is entered through a terminal and the response is sent back to that terminal, usually in a matter of seconds. On other systems, the query is prepared in punched card form and submitted to the computer, with a printed response printed and returned perhaps an hour or so later.

The ability to query a computer implies data **accessability**. Although it is possible to implement such applications using sequential files, a query capability normally implies direct access.

Although a program to implement a flexible, general-purpose query system is well beyond the scope of this book, we can illustrate how a simple direct access file retrieval routine might work. Using the indexed sequential customer master file created in Chapter 16, we will design a program to answer a customer request for information on the status of an order.

What is the Status of My Order?

Have you ever ordered a new automobile, or a replacement part for your old car, or a household appliance, or a textbook that for some reason wasn't available at the beginning of the term? Day after day, you waited, and still nothing happened. Weren't you tempted to approach the salesperson and ask, "Where is it?"?

Business people are people too. Business orders are sometimes delayed. Even when an order is not late, the customer may want to be reassured that it is still "on schedule". Providing exactly this kind of assurance is the purpose of the program we are about to write.

We'll assume, once again, that our organization has installed remote card readers and printers in each sales office. When a customer calls the office to inquire about the status of an order, the office manager takes the message and promises to call back shortly. A card is keypunched with the proper customer identification number, and this data card, along with a few control cards, is read into the central computer over standard telephone lines.

Within the computer, the input card is read and the customer number is used to search the indexed sequential file for the customer's record. Relevant information is extracted from this record and used to build an output message which is sent back to the sales office.

Back in the office, the message is printed on the remote printer. The office manager can now call the customer and pass along the good (or bad) news. Basically, that's all there is to the application.

WRITING THE ORDER STATUS PROGRAM IN COBOL

To many people, the indexed sequential technique seems a very complex way of accessing data. Actually, an application such as this one is *much* simpler than the master file update of Chapter 13. All that is necessary is to read one input record, extract the search key, read one record from the indexed file, and then write one line of output. What could be simpler? Although it really isn't necessary, a flowchart of the program has been prepared (Fig. 17.1).

Let's turn our attention to the files; we should know the format of each input or output record before beginning to code. One input record will come from the remote card reader. This record identifies the customer for whom information is desired. The customer number is to be punched in columns 1-8, and the date (mmddyy) is to be in columns 9-14.

It will be necessary, of course, for the program to access the indexed sequential customer file. The format of the records in this file was defined in Chapter 16; the records contain

positions	contents
1-8	customer number
9-25	customer name
26-40	street address
41-50	city
51-52	state
53-57	zip code
58-62	order number for unshipped customer order
63	status (0=pending;1=in process;2=finished)
64-67	date of last update (mmdd)

Fig. 17.1: *The basic logic of the customer status program.*

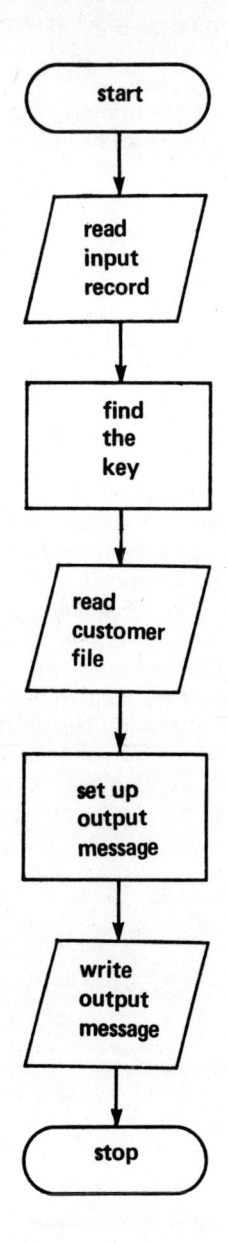

68-71   expected ship date (mmdd)

72-76   dollar volume last year

The final output of the program will be a printed line or a series of lines describing the status of the customer order. Perhaps the simplest thing to do would be to dump or copy the data record, exactly as it appears on the master file, to the printer, allowing the sales clerk to make whatever interpretations are necessary. We must remember, however, that sales people are not technical people. They have little or no interest in learning about the special codes used to conserve space on a mass storage device, as that is not their job. Sales wants to know the status of the job, and they want to know in clear, easy to interpret English. The programmer who cannot provide such service will very quickly cease to be a practicing professional programmer.

It is essential that the programmer or the systems analyst get direct user involvement in the planning of such things as the proper format for an output message. The real objective of this application is to help sell products. Programming efficiency is important, but not at the expense of this primary objective. Programming is a service function.

Direct user involvement is essential. The user, in this case, the sales department, must be asked such questions as, "What information do you need?", and "How would you like to see this field displayed?". The programmer may, of course, offer suggestions, but the user must be allowed to define the requirements. The program is, after all, designed to support the user.

After very careful consideration, a report format similar to that shown in Fig. 17.2 might be agreed upon. Sales will almost certainly want the customer identified by name. The expected ship date is probably the most important piece of information in the entire report, especially given the purpose of the application. Dates must, of course, be displayed in human readable form—the sales clerks are, after all, not technical people. The order status must be spelled out; again because so few sales people are technically trained, the code used to represent status on the master file is unacceptable.

Finally, the printers found in each of the sales offices are not the standard 133 character devices encountered in earlier chapters. Instead, small, inexpensive 80-character line printers have been installed. The output line for the program is thus 80 characters long.

Accessing an Indexed Sequential File Randomly

In accessing a direct access file, the first step was to move the relative track address and the logical search key of the desired record into the ACTUAL KEY field. Random access of an ISAM file is even easier. Rather than using the ACTUAL KEY, we use a field called the NOMINAL KEY. The NOMINAL KEY has only one part—the logical search key. In our example we will be accessing a customer master file by the customer number. We will therefore move the desired customer number into the NOMINAL KEY field and then issue a READ instruction. Essentially, that's all there is to it.

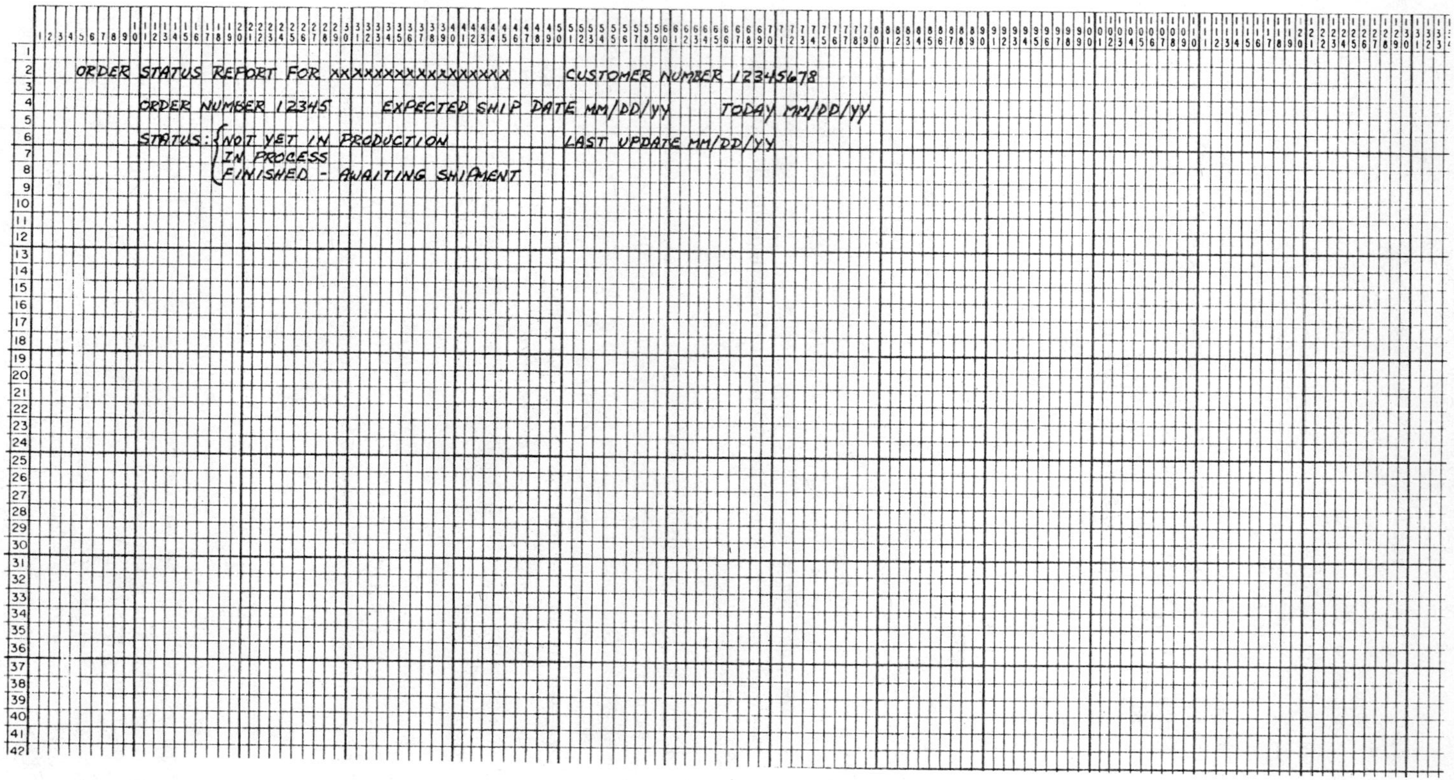

ORDER STATUS REPORT FOR XXXXXXXXXXXXXXXXX   CUSTOMER NUMBER 12345678

ORDER NUMBER 12345   EXPECTED SHIP DATE MM/DD/YY   TODAY MM/DD/YY
                                 LAST UPDATE MM/DD/YY
STATUS: {NOT YET IN PRODUCTION
         IN PROGRESS
         FINISHED - AWAITING SHIPMENT

Fig. 17.2: *The Format of the Output Message for the Customer Status Report.*

A listing of a program to support our query application is shown in Fig. 17.3. Look first at the ENVIRONMENT DIVISION. Associated with the SELECT clause for the ISAM-CUSTOMER-MASTER are four clauses, the ASSIGN, ACCESS MODE, NOMINAL KEY, and RECORD KEY. The first two should be familiar. The NOMINAL KEY and the RECORD KEY are both needed to support direct access.

The NOMINAL KEY must be defined in the WORKING-STORAGE SECTION (Fig. 17.3). The RECORD KEY, as was the case in the file creation example of Chapter 16, must be defined as part of the indexed sequential record in the FILE SECTION of the DATA DIVISION. The NOMINAL KEY is used to search the file. Following the input operation, the NOMINAL KEY and the RECORD KEY must match; if they don't (in other words, if the desired record is not on the file), an INVALID KEY is recognized. Incidently, deleted records that still exist on the file will not be ignored when the ACCESS MODE IS RANDOM; they will be made available to the program in response to a READ instruction. Thus the programmer should test for HIGH-VALUE in the first character position. It is only when ACCESS MODE IS SEQUENTIAL that deleted records are ignored.

The only potentially confusing part of this program involves handling dates. On the customer master file, dates are stored as a two-digit month and a two-digit day, with no year indicated. Given that our production cycle is only about 3 or 4 months, the year is always "last" year, "this" year, or "next" year, so there is no need to store the year on the file.

Customers, however, want to know the year, and sales insists that we print it. How can we, as programmers, possibly tell what the correct year must be? By using a little logic.

There are two dates listed on the master file: a "date of last update" and an "expected ship date". The "date of last update" can be no later than today; in other words, this date must be either today or some day in the past. The "expected ship date" can be no earlier than today or the product would have been shipped already; in other words, this date must be either today or some day in the future.

The key to identifying the year is the month. On the "date of last update" (which may be in the past) if the month is greater than the present month (today is March 4, while the update is December 23) then the correct year is last year. If the month is less than or equal to the current month, then the year must be this year. Where does the current date come from? It's part of the input card record. As an alternative, many systems make available a special instruction that allows the programmer to access the current system date.

On the "expected ship date", which must be either today or in the future, a recorded month less than the current month (today is November 15, while the expected ship date is February 10) must represent a day in the next year. If the master file month is greater than or equal to the current month, then the year must be this year.

Using these tests as a basis for determining the proper year, the date is formatted into a mm/dd/yy form prior to printing, making it easy to read.

```
  1              3.01.06      OCT 21,1978
00001        IDENTIFICATION DIVISION.
00002           PROGRAM-ID.   ISQUERY.
00003           AUTHOR.       DAVIS & FISHER.

00005           REMARKS.      THIS PROGRAM GENERATES A CUSTOMER ORDER STATUS
00006                         REPORT IN RESPONSE TO A QUERY FROM A SALES
00007                         OFFICE. THE QUERY IS SUBMITTED IN PUNCHED CARD
00008                         FORM. STATUS INFORMATION IS OBTAINED FROM THE
00009                         INDEXED SEQUENTIAL CUSTOMER MASTER FILE. A
00010                         REPORT IS GENERATED AND SENT TO THE PRINTER.

00012        ENVIRONMENT DIVISION.
00013           CONFIGURATION SECTION.
00014           SOURCE-COMPUTER. IBM-370-148.
00015           OBJECT-COMPUTER. IBM-370-148.
00016           SPECIAL-NAMES.   C01 IS NEW-PAGE.

00018           INPUT-OUTPUT SECTION.
00019           FILE-CONTROL.
00020              SELECT SALES-OFFICE-QUERY    ASSIGN TO UT-S-QUERY.
00021              SELECT ORDER-STATUS-REPORT   ASSIGN TO UT-S-REPORT.
00022              SELECT ISAM-MASTER-FILE      ASSIGN TO DA-I-ISAM
00023                                           ACCESS MODE IS RANDOM
00024                           RECORD KEY IS ISAM-CUSTOMER-NUMBER
00025                           NOMINAL KEY IS CUSTOMER-SEARCH-KEY.
```

Fig. 17.3: *A listing of a program to prepare customer status reports from the data on an ISAM file.*

```
   2        ISQUERY        3.01.06      OCT 21,1978

00027          DATA DIVISION.
00028          FILE SECTION.

00030          FD  SALES-OFFICE-QUERY    LABEL RECORD IS OMITTED.
00031              01  QUERY-TRANSACTION.
00032                  05  Q-CUSTOMER-NUMBER    PIC 9(8).
00033                  05  Q-DATE.
00034                      10  Q-MONTH          PIC 99.
00035                      10  Q-DAY            PIC 99.
00036                      10  Q-YEAR           PIC 99.
00037                  05  FILLER               PIC X(66).

00039          FD  ISAM-MASTER-FILE      LABEL RECORD IS STANDARD
00040                                    BLOCK CONTAINS 1 RECORDS
00041                                    RECORDING MODE IS F.
00042              01  CUSTOMER-MASTER-RECORD.
00043                  05  ISAM-DELETE-FLAG     PIC X.
00044                  05  ISAM-CUSTOMER-NUMBER PIC 9(8).
00045                  05  ISAM-CUSTOMER-NAME   PIC X(17).
00046                  05  ISAM-CUSTOMER-ADDRESS PIC X(15).
00047                  05  ISAM-CUSTOMER-CITY   PIC X(10).
00048                  05  ISAM-CUSTOMER-STATE  PIC XX.
00049                  05  ISAM-CUSTOMER-ZIP    PIC X(5).
00050                  05  ISAM-ORDER-NUMBER    PIC 9(5).
00051                  05  ISAM-ORDER-STATUS    PIC 9.
00052                  05  ISAM-DATE-OF-UPDATE.
00053                      10  ISAM-LAST-UPDATE-MONTH   PIC 99.
00054                      10  ISAM-LAST-UPDATE-DAY     PIC 99.
00055                  05  ISAM-SHIP-DATE.
00056                      10  ISAM-SHIP-MONTH  PIC 99.
00057                      10  ISAM-SHIP-DAY    PIC 99.
00058                  05  ISAM-PAST-BUSINESS   PIC 9(5).

00060          FD  ORDER-STATUS-REPORT   LABEL RECORD IS OMITTED.
00061              01  STATUS-REPORT-LINE       PIC X(133).
```

Fig. 17.3: *Continued.*

```
     3        ISQUERY         3.01.06        OCT 21,1978

00063            WORKING-STORAGE SECTION.
00064                77  CUSTOMER-SEARCH-KEY    PIC 9(8).

00066                01  STATUS-REPORT-LINE-1.
00067                    05  FILLER             PIC X(4) VALUE SPACES.
00068                    05  FILLER             PIC X(24)
00069                                       VALUE 'ORDER STATUS REPORT FOR '.
00070                    05  SR-CUSTOMER-NAME   PIC X(17).
00071                    05  FILLER             PIC X(5) VALUE SPACES.
00072                    05  FILLER             PIC X(16) VALUE 'CUSTOMER NUMBER'.
00073                    05  SR-CUSTOMER-NUMBER PIC 9(8).
00074                    05  FILLER             PIC X(6) VALUE SPACES.

00076                01  STATUS-REPORT-LINE-2.
00077                    05  FILLER             PIC X(10) VALUE SPACES.
00078                    05  FILLER             PIC X(13) VALUE 'ORDER NUMBER '.
00079                    05  SR-ORDER-NUMBER    PIC 9(5).
00080                    05  FILLER             PIC X(5)  VALUE SPACES.
00081                    05  FILLER             PIC X(19)
00082                                       VALUE 'EXPECTED SHIP DATE '.
00083                    05  SR-SHIP-DATE.
00084                        10  SR-SHIP-MONTH  PIC 99.
00085                        10  FILLER         PIC X     VALUE '/'.
00086                        10  SR-SHIP-DAY    PIC 99.
00087                        10  FILLER         PIC X     VALUE '/'.
00088                        10  SR-SHIP-YEAR   PIC 99.
00089                    05  FILLER             PIC X(5)  VALUE SPACES.
00090                    05  FILLER             PIC X(6)  VALUE 'TODAY '.
00091                    05  SR-CURRENT-DATE.
00092                        10  SR-CURRENT-MONTH PIC 99.
00093                        10  FILLER         PIC X     VALUE '/'.
00094                        10  SR-CURRENT-DAY PIC 99.
00095                        10  FILLER         PIC X     VALUE '/'.
00096                        10  SR-CURRENT-YEAR PIC 99.
00097                    05  FILLER             PIC X(3)  VALUE SPACES.
```

Fig. 17.3: *Continued.*

```
   4        ISQUERY         3.01.06         OCT 21,1978

00100              01   STATUS-REPORT-LINE-3.
00101                   05 FILLER              PIC X(10) VALUE SPACES.
00102                   05 FILLER              PIC X(8)  VALUE 'STATUS: '.
00103                   05 SR-MESSAGE          PIC X(28).
00104                   05 FILLER              PIC X(4)  VALUE SPACES.
00105                   05 FILLER              PIC X(12) VALUE 'LAST UPDATE '.
00106                   05 SR-LAST-UPDATE.
00107                      10 SR-LAST-MONTH    PIC 99.
00108                      10 FILLER           PIC X     VALUE '/'.
00109                      10 SR-LAST-DAY      PIC 99.
00110                      10 FILLER           PIC X     VALUE '/'.
00111                      10 SR-LAST-YEAR     PIC 99.
00112                   05 FILLER              PIC X(10) VALUE SPACES.

00114              01   ERROR-MESSAGE.
00115                   05 FILLER              PIC X(10) VALUE SPACES.
00116                   05 E-CUSTOMER-NUMBER   PIC 9(8).
00117                   05 E-BAD-NUMBER        REDEFINES E-CUSTOMER-NUMBER
00118                                          PIC X(8).
00119                   05 FILLER              PIC X(5)  VALUE SPACES.
00120                   05 E-MESSAGE           PIC X(24).
00121                   05 FILLER              PIC X(33) VALUE SPACES.
```

Fig. 17.3: *Continued.*

```
    5       ISQUERY       3.01.06       OCT 21,1978

00123           PROCEDURE DIVISION.
00124               OPEN INPUT    SALES-OFFICE-QUERY
00125                    INPUT    ISAM-MASTER-FILE
00126                    OUTPUT   ORDER-STATUS-REPORT.

00128           RESPOND-TO-QUERY.
00129               READ SALES-OFFICE-QUERY
00130                   AT END GO TO END-OF-JOB.

00132               IF Q-CUSTOMER-NUMBER IS NOT NUMERIC
00133                  THEN MOVE 'CUSTOMER NUMBER INVALID' TO E-MESSAGE
00134                       PERFORM ERROR-ROUTINE
00135                  ELSE NEXT SENTENCE.

00137               IF Q-DATE IS NOT NUMERIC
00138                  THEN MOVE 'DATE IS INCORRECT' TO E-MESSAGE
00139                       PERFORM ERROR-ROUTINE
00140                  ELSE NEXT SENTENCE.

00142               MOVE Q-CUSTOMER-NUMBER TO CUSTOMER-SEARCH-KEY.
00143               READ ISAM-MASTER-FILE
00144                   INVALID KEY MOVE 'RECORD NOT FOUND' TO E-MESSAGE
00145                               PERFORM ERROR-ROUTINE.
00146               IF ISAM-DELETE-FLAG IS EQUAL TO HIGH-VALUE
00147                  THEN MOVE 'RECORD DELETED FROM FILE' TO E-MESSAGE
00148                       PERFORM ERROR-ROUTINE
00149                  ELSE NEXT SENTENCE.

00151               PERFORM SET-UP-LINE-1.
00152               WRITE STATUS-REPORT-LINE FROM STATUS-REPORT-LINE-1
00153                   AFTER ADVANCING NEW-PAGE.
00154               PERFORM SET-UP-LINE-2.
00155               WRITE STATUS-REPORT-LINE FROM STATUS-REPORT-LINE-2
00156                   AFTER ADVANCING 2 LINES.
00157               PERFORM SET-UP-LINE-3.
00158               WRITE STATUS-REPORT-LINE FROM STATUS-REPORT-LINE-3
00159                   AFTER ADVANCING 2 LINES.
00160               GO TO RESPOND-TO-QUERY.

00162           END-OF-JOB.
00163               CLOSE SALES-OFFICE-QUERY.
00164               CLOSE ORDER-STATUS-REPORT.
00165               CLOSE ISAM-MASTER-FILE.
00166               STOP RUN.
```

Fig. 17.3: *Continued.*

```
6        ISQUERY        3.01.06        OCT 21,1978

00168            SET-UP-LINE-1.
00169                MOVE ISAM-CUSTOMER-NAME    TO SR-CUSTOMER-NAME.
00170                MOVE ISAM-CUSTOMER-NUMBER  TO SR-CUSTOMER-NUMBER.
00171            END-SET-UP-LINE-1.
00172                EXIT.

00174            SET-UP-LINE-2.
00175                MOVE ISAM-ORDER-NUMBER     TO SR-ORDER-NUMBER.
00176                MOVE Q-MONTH   TO SR-CURRENT-MONTH.
00177                MOVE Q-DAY     TO SR-CURRENT-DAY.
00178                MOVE Q-YEAR    TO SR-CURRENT-YEAR, SR-SHIP-YEAR.
00179                MOVE ISAM-SHIP-MONTH TO SR-SHIP-MONTH.
00180                MOVE ISAM-SHIP-DAY   TO SR-SHIP-DAY.
00181                IF ISAM-SHIP-MONTH IS LESS THAN Q-MONTH
00182                    THEN ADD 1 TO SR-SHIP-YEAR
00183                    ELSE NEXT SENTENCE.
00184            END-SET-UP-LINE-2.
00185                EXIT.

00187            SET-UP-LINE-3.
00188                IF ISAM-ORDER-STATUS IS EQUAL TO 0
00189                    THEN MOVE 'NOT YET IN PRODUCTION' TO SR-MESSAGE
00190                    ELSE IF ISAM-ORDER-STATUS IS EQUAL TO 1
00191                        THEN MOVE 'IN PROCESS' TO SR-MESSAGE
00192                        ELSE IF ISAM-ORDER-STATUS IS EQUAL TO 2
00193                            THEN MOVE 'FINISHED - AWAITING SHIPMENT'
00194                                 TO SR-MESSAGE
00195                            ELSE MOVE 'STATUS UNKNOWN' TO SR-MESSAGE.
00196                MOVE ISAM-LAST-UPDATE-MONTH TO SR-LAST-MONTH.
00197                MOVE ISAM-LAST-UPDATE-DAY   TO SR-LAST-DAY.
00198                MOVE Q-YEAR                 TO SR-LAST-YEAR.
00199                IF ISAM-LAST-UPDATE-MONTH IS GREATER THAN Q-MONTH
00200                    THEN SUBTRACT 1 FROM SR-LAST-YEAR
00201                    ELSE NEXT SENTENCE.
00202            END-SET-UP-LINE-3.
00203                EXIT.

00205            ERROR-ROUTINE.
00206                MOVE Q-CUSTOMER-NUMBER TO E-CUSTOMER-NUMBER.
00207                WRITE STATUS-REPORT-LINE FROM ERROR-MESSAGE
00208                    AFTER ADVANCING NEW-PAGE.
00209            *
00210            ** * * * * * * * * * * * * * * * * * * * * * * * * * * * **
00211            ** NOTE: IF AN ERROR HAS BEEN DETECTED, IT MEANS THAT WE ARE **
00212            **       FINISHED PROCESSING THE CURRENT TRANSACTION. THUS   **
00213            **       WE GO BACK TO THE TOP OF THE MAINLINE TO BEGIN THE  **
00214            **       PROCESSING OF THE NEXT TRANSACTION OR QUERY.        **
00215            ** * * * * * * * * * * * * * * * * * * * * * * * * * * * **
00216            *
00217                GO TO RESPOND-TO-QUERY.
00218            END-ERROR-ROUTINE.
00219                EXIT.
```

Fig. 17.3: *Continued.*

What Might Go Wrong?

Looking beyond the basic program structure, error conditions must be handled. The first step in error handling is error recognition. What could possibly go wrong? The sales person might make an error in preparing the query. If the error is just an incorrect customer number, we'll catch it as an INVALID KEY. Other errors are even more obvious. What if, for example, the customer number field on an input record contains non-numeric characters? A match will not be found; why should we waste our time searching the file? A NUMERIC class test will thus be run on the input customer number.

Some errors cannot be detected by the program. For example, what if the sales clerk were to submit the number of the wrong customer? The field would pass our NUMERIC test. A search of the file would yield a record. A report would be generated and sent back to the sales clerk. The clerk, hopefully, would then read the customer name field and realize that an error had been made. There is simply no way to automatically detect such errors; a data processing axiom is "garbage in, garbage out."

Once an error has been identified, it must be communicated to the nontechnical salesperson in easy to understand fashion. Each error is different. Some are the sales clerk's fault and can be corrected and resubmitted; others are beyond his or her control. A series of error messages and the error-handling logic can be seen in the program listing (Fig. 17.3).

UPDATING THE CUSTOMER MASTER FILE

The customer master file contains the following fields:

customer number	order number
customer name	order status
street address	date of last update
city	expected ship date
state	dollar volume last year
zip code	

What changes can be expected on this file?

Customer names do change; in fact, there are highly paid consultants who specialize in creating attractive and attention-getting names for business concerns. Customer addresses can change too, and an address change affects four of the fields in the master record. The order number, order status, date of last update, and expected ship date fields can be expected to change frequently. The final field, dollar volume last year, will change annually.

Additions and deletions can be expected, too. Every business concern hopes to gain new customers, and ours is certainly no exception. No firm likes to lose old customers, but it does happen.

Records can be added. Records can be deleted. The content of existing records can change. In spite of the fact that we are now dealing with an indexed sequential file, there is not a great deal of difference between updating the customer master file and updating the direct access product master file of Chapter 15.

Operating Procedures

In Chapter 15, the individual responsible for making changes to the product master file was required to keypunch a card for each change. The transaction type—ADD, DEL, or MOD—was punched into this card. In another field, the initials of the person authorizing the change provided identification.

The problems associated with updating the indexed sequential customer master file are similar. The same kinds of transactions are still possible. A change can still affect any of the fields in the record. Accuracy and control are every bit as crucial. Thus, a similar set of procedures is called for.

The basic input transaction to the customer file update program will be a punched card with the customer file fields appearing in the same order as they do on the master file. These fields take up the first 76 columns, leaving only four for the transaction type and the authorizing initials. Clearly, the initials will consume three, leaving only one for the transaction type. We'll use A for an addition, D for a deletion, and M for a transaction to modify an existing record.

The Basic Structure of the File Update Program

Examine the basic functions that must be performed in updating this master file. First, a transaction must be read. Within the program mainline, the transaction type must be clearly identified and the proper routine performed to add, delete, or modify a record. Once the transaction has been handled, the next transaction can be read and processed.

Within the ADD routine, the value of each of the fields can be edit-checked, a new master file written, and the necessary log entries prepared. A change to an existing record involves reading the master file, identifying those fields that are to be changed, checking and moving the affected fields, writing the master file record, and preparing log entries. A deletion involves reading the master file, moving the constant HIGH VALUE into the first character position, and writing the master file record back to disk.

Sound familiar? It should. The basic structure of the customer master file update program, at least to the level of the three primary routines, is identical to that of the product master file update program. Does this surprise you? It shouldn't. Why should the basic functions be any different? The objective, update a file directly, is, after all, exactly the same. Here you see still another value of the modular approach to program development. By following a careful, step-by-step approach, it is possible to develop solutions that are applicable to an entire class of problems, rather than solutions that are restricted to a single use.

The details, housed in secondary routines, will, of course, differ from program to program. Since our file is indexed sequential, we will be using the NOMINAL KEY rather than the ACTUAL KEY. Edit routines must be designed to check the contents of specific fields. The actual meaning of a particular type of error will vary with the application. But the basic flow of the program remains the same.

Too many programmers insist on treating each problem as something new, designing highly customized, made to order solutions. In the days when computers were very expensive and programming was (relatively) cheap, this approach may have made sense, but it no longer does. Really good programmers develop generalized solutions to a variety of problems, and then use these solutions over and over again, changing the details to meet the unique needs of a specific problem. (It resembles the automobile industry, where a basic product can be customized by changing such details as color, engine size and accents.) The result is efficiency, in the truest sense of the word.

Updating an Indexed Sequential File

Since the task of updating an indexed sequential file is much like updating a direct file, we can use the solution developed in Chapter 15 as a model. A copy of the modular flowchart of the direct access master file update routine is reproduced for reference as Fig. 17.4. The complete listing of our new indexed sequential master file update program is shown in Fig. 17.5.

Let's start with the ENVIRONMENT DIVISION (Fig. 17.5). Four files are listed: the input transaction file, a print file for error messages, a log tape file, and the master file. Note that ACCESS MODE, RECORD KEY, and NOMINAL KEY clauses are associated with the indexed sequential file.

Now, we'll move on to the DATA DIVISION. Note that the deletion flag is the first character in the ISAM file description. The detailed formats of the log tape and the error files are specified in the WORKING-STORAGE SECTION; several different formats are possible. The NOMINAL KEY is, of course, defined in WORKING-STORAGE.

In the PROCEDURE DIVISION, note that the type of access specified for the ISAM master file in the OPEN statement is I-O (Fig. 17.5). This means that the file is to be opened for both input and output; in other words, there will be cases when we will want to read and then rewrite the same record.

Look at the program mainline, and compare the code of Fig. 17.5 to the flowchart of Fig. 17.4. The flowchart was developed in Chapter 15 to solve a different problem, but the flowchart logic and the coded logic are remarkably similar.

Fig. 17.4: *A modular flowchart of the direct access master file update.*

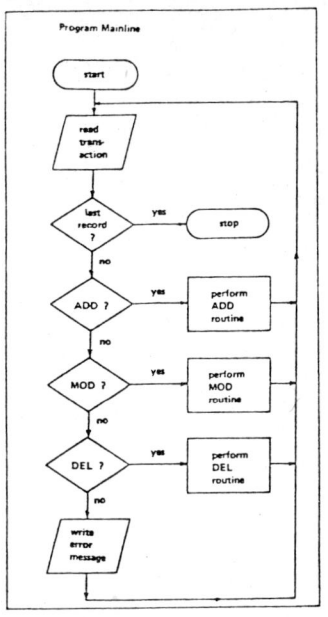

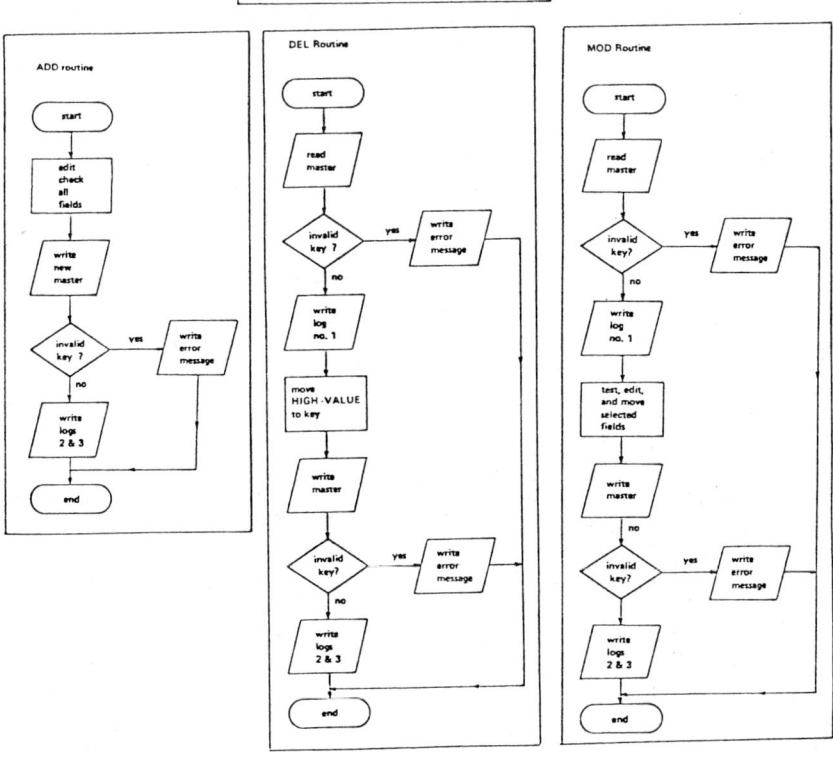

```
     1                  3.01.34       OCT 21,1978

00001        IDENTIFICATION DIVISION.
00002          PROGRAM-ID. ISUPDATE.
00003          AUTHOR.     DAVIS & FISHER.

00005          REMARKS.    THIS PROGRAM UPDATES THE INDEXED SEQUENTIAL
00006                      CUSTOMER MASTER FILE. INPUT IS IN THE FORM OF
00007                      PUNCHED CARDS; EACH CARD REPRESENTS ONE CHANGE:
00008                      AN ADDITION, DELETION, OR MODIFICATION OF ONE
00009                      MASTER FILE RECORD. ALL TRANSACTIONS WILL BE
00010                      LOGGED TO MAGNETIC TAPE


00012        ENVIRONMENT DIVISION.
00013          CONFIGURATION SECTION.
00014            SOURCE-COMPUTER. IBM-370-148.
00015            OBJECT-COMPUTER. IBM-370-148.
00016            SPECIAL-NAMES.   C01 IS NEW-PAGE.

00018          INPUT-OUTPUT SECTION.
00019          FILE-CONTROL.
00020             SELECT TRANSACTION     ASSIGN TO UT-S-TRANS.
00021             SELECT LOG-TAPE        ASSIGN TO UT-S-LOG.
00022             SELECT MESSAGE-FILE    ASSIGN TO UT-S-SYSOUT.
00023             SELECT ISAM-MASTER-FILE ASSIGN TO DA-I-ISAM
00024                                ACCESS MODE IS RANDOM
00025                                RECORD KEY IS CUSTOMER-NUMBER
00026                                NOMINAL KEY IS CUSTOMER-SEARCH-KEY.
```

Fig. 17.5: *A program to update the ISAM customer master file.*

```
00028              DATA DIVISION.
00029              FILE SECTION.

00031              FD  TRANSACTION      LABEL RECORD IS OMITTED.
00032               01  TRANSACTION-RECORD.
00033                   05 T-MASTER-RECORD-DATA.
00034                      10 T-CUSTOMER-NUMBER     PIC 9(8).
00035                      10 T-CUSTOMER-NAME       PIC X(17).
00036                      10 T-CUSTOMER-ADDRESS    PIC X(15).
00037                      10 T-CUSTOMER-CITY       PIC X(10).
00038                      10 T-CUSTOMER-STATE      PIC XX.
00039                      10 T-CUSTOMER-ZIP        PIC X(5).
00040                      10 T-ORDER-NUMBER        PIC 9(5).
00041                      10 TEST-ORDER-NUMBER     REDEFINES T-ORDER-NUMBER
00042                                               PIC X(5).
00043                      10 T-ORDER-STATUS        PIC 9.
00044                      10 TEST-STATUS           REDEFINES T-ORDER-STATUS
00045                                               PIC X.
00046                      10 T-DATE-OF-UPDATE      PIC 9(4).
00047                      10 TEST-UPDATE           REDEFINES T-DATE-OF-UPDATE
00048                                               PIC X(4).
00049                      10 T-SHIP-DATE           PIC 9(4).
00050                      10 TEST-SHIP-DATE        REDEFINES T-SHIP-DATE
00051                                               PIC X(4).
00052                      10 T-PAST-BUSINESS       PIC 9(5).
00053                      10 TEST-PAST-BUSINESS    REDEFINES T-PAST-BUSINESS
00054                                               PIC X(5).
00055                   05 TRANSACTION-TYPE         PIC X.
00056                   05 T-AUTHORIZATION          PIC XXX.

00058              FD  ISAM-MASTER-FILE      LABEL RECORD IS STANDARD
00059                                        BLOCK CONTAINS 1 RECORDS
00060                                        RECORDING MODE IS F.
00061               01  CUSTOMER-MASTER-DUMMY.
00062                   05 DELETE-FLAG              PIC X.
00063                   05 CUSTOMER-NUMBER          PIC 9(8).
00064                   05 REST-OF-RECORD           PIC X(68).
00065              FD  LOG-TAPE              LABEL RECORD IS STANDARD
00066                                        BLOCK CONTAINS 1 RECORDS.
00067               01  LOG-ENTRY                   PIC X(100).

00069              FD  MESSAGE-FILE      LABEL RECORD IS OMITTED.
00070               01  CONFIRMATION-MESSAGE.
00071                   05 C-CUSTOMER-NUMBER        PIC 9(8).
00072                   05 C-BAD-CUSTOMER           REDEFINES C-CUSTOMER-NUMBER
00073                                               PIC X(8).
00074                   05 FILLER                   PIC X(5).
00075                   05 C-MESSAGE                PIC X(20).
00076                   05 FILLER                   PIC X(47).
```

Fig. 17.5: *Continued.*

```
    3         ISUPDATE         3.01.34         OCT 21,1978

00078             WORKING-STORAGE SECTION.
00079                 77  CUSTOMER-SEARCH-KEY      PIC 9(8).

00081                 01  CUSTOMER-MASTER-RECORD.
00082                     05  ISAM-DELETE-FLAG         PIC X.
00083                     05  ISAM-MASTER-RECORD.
00084                         10  ISAM-CUSTOMER-NUMBER   PIC 9(8).
00085                         10  ISAM-CUSTOMER-NAME     PIC X(17).
00086                         10  ISAM-CUSTOMER-ADDRESS  PIC X(15).
00087                         10  ISAM-CUSTOMER-CITY     PIC X(10).
00088                         10  ISAM-CUSTOMER-STATE    PIC XX.
00089                         10  ISAM-CUSTOMER-ZIP      PIC X(5).
00090                         10  ISAM-ORDER-NUMBER      PIC 9(5).
00091                         10  ISAM-ORDER-STATUS      PIC 9.
00092                         10  ISAM-DATE-OF-UPDATE    PIC 9(4).
00093                         10  ISAM-SHIP-DATE         PIC 9(4).
00094                         10  ISAM-PAST-BUSINESS     PIC 9(5).

00096                 01  TRANSACTION-COPY .
00097                     05  TRANSACTION-AS-ENTERED   PIC X(80).
00098                     05  TC-MESSAGE               PIC X(20).

00100                 01  MASTER-FILE-COPY.
00101                     05  RECORD-AS-ON-FILE        PIC X(77).
00102                     05  MF-MESSAGE               PIC X(23).
```

Fig. 17.5: *Continued.*

```
    4       ISUPDATE       3.01.34       OCT 21,1978

00104           PROCEDURE DIVISION.
00105               OPEN INPUT  TRANSACTION
00106                    OUTPUT LOG-TAPE
00107                    OUTPUT MESSAGE-FILE
00108                    I-O    ISAM-MASTER-FILE.

00110           FILE-UPDATE-MAINLINE.
00111               READ TRANSACTION
00112                   AT END GO TO END-OF-JOB.
00113               IF T-AUTHORIZATION IS EQUAL TO SPACES
00114                   THEN MOVE ' UNAUTHORIZED' TO TC-MESSAGE, C-MESSAGE
00115                        PERFORM ERROR-ROUTINE
00116                   ELSE NEXT SENTENCE.
00117               IF T-CUSTOMER-NUMBER IS NOT NUMERIC
00118                   THEN MOVE ' CUST NUMBER ILLEGAL'
00119                             TO TC-MESSAGE, C-MESSAGE
00120                        PERFORM ERROR-ROUTINE
00121                   ELSE NEXT SENTENCE.
00122               IF TRANSACTION-TYPE IS EQUAL TO 'A'
00123                   THEN PERFORM ADD-ROUTINE THRU END-ADD-ROUTINE
00124                   ELSE IF TRANSACTION-TYPE IS EQUAL TO 'D'
00125                       THEN PERFORM DELETION-ROUTINE THRU END-DELETION
00126                       ELSE IF TRANSACTION-TYPE IS EQUAL TO 'M'
00127                           THEN PERFORM MODIFY-ROUTINE THRU END-MODIFY
00128                           ELSE MOVE ' ILLEGAL TRANS TYPE'
00129                                   TO TC-MESSAGE, C-MESSAGE
00130                                PERFORM ERROR-ROUTINE.
00131               GO TO FILE-UPDATE-MAINLINE.

00133           END-OF-JOB.
00134               CLOSE ISAM-MASTER-FILE.
00135               CLOSE LOG-TAPE.
00136               CLOSE MESSAGE-FILE.
00137               CLOSE TRANSACTION.
00138               STOP RUN.
```

Fig. 17.5: *Continued.*

```
    5       ISUPDATE       3.01.34       OCT 21,1978

00140     *
00141     ** * * * * * * * * * * * * * * * * * * * * * * * * * * * * * **
00142     ** NOTE:  THROUGHOUT THIS PROGRAM WE WILL BE USING THE READ    **
00143     **        INTO AND WRITE FROM FORMS OF INPUT AND OUTPUT WHEN  **
00144     **        WORKING WITH THE MASTER FILE. THE INTO AND FROM OP- **
00145     **        TIONS WORK WITH DATA DEFINED IN THE WORKING-STORAGE **
00146     **        SECTION. WITH A REGULAR WRITE OR REWRITE, THE DATA  **
00147     **        IS IN THE FILE SECTION; AFTER OUTPUT IT IS NO LONG- **
00148     **        ER AVAILABLE TO THE PROGRAM. WORKING-STORAGE DATA   **
00149     **        IS AVAILABLE UNTIL THE PROGRAMMER CHANGES IT. SINCE **
00150     **        WE WANT TO LOG CHANGES TO THE MASTER FILE AFTER THE **
00151     **        CHANGES HAVE BEEN MADE, AND SINCE LOGGING REQUIRES  **
00152     **        ACCESS TO THE MASTER FILE RECORD, WE MUST WORK WITH **
00153     **        THE DATA IN WORKING-STORAGE.                        **
00154     ** * * * * * * * * * * * * * * * * * * * * * * * * * * * * * **
00155     *
00156         ADD-ROUTINE.
00157             PERFORM EDIT-CHECKS.
00158             MOVE LOW-VALUE              TO ISAM-DELETE-FLAG.
00159             MOVE T-MASTER-RECORD-DATA   TO ISAM-MASTER-RECORD.
00160             MOVE T-CUSTOMER-NUMBER      TO CUSTOMER-SEARCH-KEY.
00161             WRITE CUSTOMER-MASTER-DUMMY FROM CUSTOMER-MASTER-RECORD
00162                 INVALID KEY MOVE ' ADD UNSUCCESSFUL'
00163                                 TO TC-MESSAGE, C-MESSAGE
00164                             PERFORM ERROR-ROUTINE.
00165             PERFORM LOG-TRANSACTION.
00166             PERFORM LOG-NEW-MASTER.
00167         END-ADD-ROUTINE.
00168             EXIT.

00170         DELETION-ROUTINE.
00171             MOVE T-CUSTOMER-NUMBER TO CUSTOMER-SEARCH-KEY.
00172             READ ISAM-MASTER-FILE INTO CUSTOMER-MASTER-RECORD
00173                 INVALID KEY MOVE ' RECORD NOT FOUND'
00174                                 TO TC-MESSAGE, C-MESSAGE
00175                             PERFORM ERROR-ROUTINE.
00176             PERFORM LOG-OLD-MASTER.
00177             MOVE HIGH-VALUE TO ISAM-DELETE-FLAG.
00178             REWRITE CUSTOMER-MASTER-DUMMY FROM CUSTOMER-MASTER-RECORD
00179                 INVALID KEY MOVE 'UNSUCCESSFUL REWRITE'
00180                                 TO TC-MESSAGE, C-MESSAGE
00181                             PERFORM ERROR-ROUTINE.
00182             PERFORM LOG-TRANSACTION.
00183             PERFORM LOG-NEW-MASTER.

00185         END-DELETION.
00186             EXIT.
```

Fig. 17.5: *Continued.*

```
  6       ISUPDATE       3.01.34      OCT 21,1978

00188         MODIFY-ROUTINE.
00189             MOVE T-CUSTOMER-NUMBER TO CUSTOMER-SEARCH-KEY.
00190             READ ISAM-MASTER-FILE INTO CUSTOMER-MASTER-RECORD
00191                 INVALID KEY MOVE ' RECORD NOT FOUND'
00192                              TO TC-MESSAGE, C-MESSAGE
00193                          PERFORM ERROR-ROUTINE.
00194             PERFORM LOG-OLD-MASTER.
00195             PERFORM SET-UP-NEW-RECORD.
00196             REWRITE CUSTOMER-MASTER-DUMMY FROM CUSTOMER-MASTER-RECORD
00197                 INVALID KEY MOVE 'UNSUCCESSFUL REWRITE'
00198                              TO TC-MESSAGE, C-MESSAGE
00199                          PERFORM ERROR-ROUTINE.
00200             PERFORM LOG-TRANSACTION.
00201             PERFORM LOG-NEW-MASTER.
00202         END-MODIFY.

00204             EXIT.


00206         EDIT-CHECKS.
00207             IF    T-ORDER-NUMBER   IS NOT NUMERIC
00208                OR T-ORDER-STATUS   IS NOT NUMERIC
00209                OR T-DATE-OF-UPDATE IS NOT NUMERIC
00210                OR T-SHIP-DATE      IS NOT NUMERIC
00211                OR T-PAST-BUSINESS  IS NOT NUMERIC
00212                   THEN MOVE ' DATA ERROR' TO TC-MESSAGE, C-MESSAGE
00213                        PERFORM ERROR-ROUTINE
00214                   ELSE NEXT SENTENCE.

00216         END-EDIT-CHECK.
00217             EXIT.


00219         ERROR-ROUTINE.
00220             MOVE TRANSACTION-RECORD TO TRANSACTION-AS-ENTERED.
00221             WRITE LOG-ENTRY.
00222             MOVE T-CUSTOMER-NUMBER TO C-CUSTOMER-NUMBER.
00223             WRITE CONFIRMATION-MESSAGE AFTER ADVANCING 1 LINES.
00224         *
00225         * ** * * * * * * * * * * * * * * * * * * * * * * * **
00226         * ** NOTE: FOLLOWING THE LOGGING OF ANY RECORD, WE ARE  **
00227         * **       FINISHED WITH THE RECORD WE HAD BEEN PROCESSING.**
00228         * **       THUS WE RETURN TO THE TOP OF THE MAINLINE TO **
00229         * **       BEGIN THE PROCESSING OF THE NEXT RECORD.     **
00230         * ** * * * * * * * * * * * * * * * * * * * * * * * **
00231         *
00232             GO TO FILE-UPDATE-MAINLINE.

00234         END-ERROR-ROUTINE.
00235             EXIT.
```

Fig. 17.5: *Continued.*

```
7         ISUPDATE      3.01.34      OCT 21,1978

00237              SET-UP-NEW-RECORD.
00238                  IF T-CUSTOMER-NAME IS EQUAL TO SPACES
00239                      THEN NEXT SENTENCE
00240                      ELSE MOVE T-CUSTOMER-NAME TO ISAM-CUSTOMER-NAME.
00241                  IF T-CUSTOMER-ADDRESS IS EQUAL TO SPACES
00242                      THEN NEXT SENTENCE
00243                      ELSE MOVE T-CUSTOMER-ADDRESS TO ISAM-CUSTOMER-ADDRESS.
00244                  IF T-CUSTOMER-CITY IS EQUAL TO SPACES
00245                      THEN NEXT SENTENCE
00246                      ELSE MOVE T-CUSTOMER-CITY TO ISAM-CUSTOMER-CITY.
00247                  IF T-CUSTOMER-STATE IS EQUAL TO SPACES
00248                      THEN NEXT SENTENCE
00249                      ELSE MOVE T-CUSTOMER-STATE TO ISAM-CUSTOMER-STATE.
00250                  IF T-CUSTOMER-ZIP IS EQUAL TO SPACES
00251                      THEN NEXT SENTENCE
00252                      ELSE MOVE T-CUSTOMER-ZIP TO ISAM-CUSTOMER-ZIP
00253                  IF TEST-ORDER-NUMBER IS EQUAL TO SPACES
00254                      THEN NEXT SENTENCE
00255                      ELSE IF T-ORDER-NUMBER IS NUMERIC
00256                          THEN MOVE T-ORDER-NUMBER TO ISAM-ORDER-NUMBER
00257                              ELSE MOVE ' DATA ERROR' TO TC-MESSAGE, C-MESSAGE
00258                                  PERFORM ERROR-ROUTINE.
00259                  IF TEST-STATUS IS EQUAL TO SPACES
00260                      THEN NEXT SENTENCE
00261                      ELSE IF T-ORDER-STATUS IS NUMERIC
00262                          THEN MOVE T-ORDER-STATUS TO ISAM-ORDER-STATUS
00263                              ELSE MOVE ' DATA ERROR' TO TC-MESSAGE, C-MESSAGE
00264                                  PERFORM ERROR-ROUTINE.
00265                  IF TEST-UPDATE IS EQUAL TO SPACES
00266                      THEN NEXT SENTENCE
00267                      ELSE IF T-DATE-OF-UPDATE IS NUMERIC
00268                          THEN MOVE T-DATE-OF-UPDATE TO ISAM-DATE-OF-UPDATE
00269                              ELSE MOVE ' DATA ERROR' TO TC-MESSAGE, C-MESSAGE
00270                                  PERFORM ERROR-ROUTINE.
00271                  IF TEST-SHIP-DATE IS EQUAL TO SPACES
00272                      THEN NEXT SENTENCE
00273                      ELSE IF T-SHIP-DATE IS NUMERIC
00274                          THEN MOVE T-SHIP-DATE TO ISAM-SHIP-DATE
00275                              ELSE MOVE 'DATA ERROR' TO TC-MESSAGE, C-MESSAGE
00276                                  PERFORM ERROR-ROUTINE.
00277                  IF TEST-PAST-BUSINESS IS EQUAL TO SPACES
00278                      THEN NEXT SENTENCE
00279                      ELSE IF T-PAST-BUSINESS IS NUMERIC
00280                          THEN MOVE T-PAST-BUSINESS TO ISAM-PAST-BUSINESS
00281                              ELSE MOVE 'DATA ERROR' TO  TC-MESSAGE, C-MESSAGE
00282                                  PERFORM ERROR-ROUTINE.

00284              END-NEW-RECORD-SETUP.
00285                  EXIT.
```

Fig. 17.5: *Continued.*

```
8       ISUPDATE        3.01.34       OCT 21,1978

00287        LOGGING-ROUTINES SECTION.
00288        LOG-OLD-MASTER.
00289            MOVE CUSTOMER-MASTER-RECORD TO RECORD-AS-ON-FILE.
00290            MOVE ' OLD MASTER READ'      TO MF-MESSAGE, C-MESSAGE.
00291            WRITE LOG-ENTRY.
00292            MOVE ISAM-CUSTOMER-NUMBER    TO C-CUSTOMER-NUMBER.
00293            WRITE CONFIRMATION-MESSAGE
00294                AFTER ADVANCING 1 LINES.

00296        LOG-TRANSACTION.
00297            MOVE TRANSACTION-RECORD TO TRANSACTION-AS-ENTERED.
00298            MOVE ' SUCCESSFUL'       TO TC-MESSAGE, C-MESSAGE.
00299            WRITE LOG-ENTRY.
00300            MOVE T-CUSTOMER-NUMBER   TO C-CUSTOMER-NUMBER.
00301            WRITE CONFIRMATION-MESSAGE
00302                AFTER ADVANCING 1 LINES.

00304        LOG-NEW-MASTER.
00305            MOVE CUSTOMER-MASTER-RECORD TO RECORD-AS-ON-FILE.
00306            MOVE ' NEW MASTER WRITTEN'   TO MF-MESSAGE, C-MESSAGE.
00307            WRITE LOG-ENTRY.
00308            MOVE ISAM-CUSTOMER-NUMBER    TO C-CUSTOMER-NUMBER.
00309            WRITE CONFIRMATION-MESSAGE
00310                AFTER ADVANCING 1 LINES.

00312        END-LOGGING-ROUTINES.
00313            EXIT.
```

Fig. 17.5: *Continued.*

The ADD-ROUTINE

A comparison of the flowchart and the program listing will also illustrate great similarity in the routines to add a record to the file. Of course, there are differences in coding rules. When a record is added to an indexed sequential file the NOMINAL KEY field must be set to the value of the key of the record being added. An INVALID KEY will be recognized if the key to be added matches the key of a record already in the file.

The DELETION-ROUTINE

Once again compare the flowchart with the program listing; the routines to delete a record are also identical. There are, of course, coding differences. The NOMINAL KEY must be set to the value of the customer record to be deleted before a READ instruction can be executed. If a record with the specified NOMINAL KEY is not found during the READ instruction, an INVALID KEY error is recognized—you cannot delete a record that does not exist on the file.

The fact that an ISAM record has been deleted is indicated by the presence of HIGH-VALUE in the first character position. It is the programmer's responsibility to move the critical value into the deletion flag. Once this has been done, the record can be written back to the ISAM file; a future attempt to read the record will encounter the HIGH-VALUE and know that the record has been deleted.

Writing a record back to an ISAM file requires the use of a new output instruction. **REWRITE**. As the name of the instruction implies, REWRITE is used to write a previously read record back to a direct access device, replacing the old versions of the record with the new, modified version. The NOMINAL KEY and the RECORD KEY must match when a REWRITE is executed, otherwise an INVALID KEY is recognized. If the NOMINAL KEY cannot be found on the ISAM file, an INVALID KEY is once again the result.

The MODIFY-ROUTINE

Once again, the flowchart (Fig. 7.4) and the program listing (Fig. 17.5) show the logical equivalence of modifying a direct access record and an indexed sequential record. Record deletion, the topic we have just finished covering, is a special case of record modification; thus we will encounter nothing new in this routine. The sequence still calls for the setting of the NOMINAL KEY, a READ instruction, and a REWRITE instruction, with the necessary data editing, data manipulation, and transaction logging sandwiched in between.

The transaction log routine and the various error processing routines should present little trouble as you read the program.

WHY DIRECT ACCESS?

The last four chapters have concentrated on the direct access of individual records. Earlier we considered sequential access, with every record in a file processed in a fixed order. Some applications call for direct access; others seem to dictate sequential access. What are the characteristics of an application that make it direct rather than sequential?

Sequential file processing normally involves reading or writing an entire file. In a sequential master file update, it costs about the same to read the old master and create a new one no matter how many transactions must be processed. What if there are only a few? It might be cheaper to process them one at a time rather than all together, suggesting the use of direct rather than sequential access.

Perhaps an example would help. Let's say that we have a deck of punched cards, each containing one individual's name and address. The cards are in alphabetical order. What is the easiest way to change one individual's address? The answer should be obvious: Select that individual's card, change it, and replace the corrected card in the deck. That's not sequential file processing. Would anyone seriously consider reading the old master file one record at a time, merging the transactions file (a single record) with it, and creating a complete new master file? No. Why not? Because it's so much easier to select and change the single record. Not only easier, but less expensive.

Consider still another example using the same deck of address cards. Imagine that you have been assigned the task of addressing a letter to a customer. Chances are that you would simply go to the address file, pull the needed card, type the correct address, and replace the card—direct access. On the other hand, what if you were assigned the task of preparing addressed envelopes for an advertising brochure to be sent to every individual on the file? The one-record-at-a-time approach is no longer reasonable. Instead, you would almost certainly use a computer program to read each of the cards, in turn, and print a mailing label, later pasting the completed labels to envelopes (special printer forms with peel-off labels are available).

What is the difference between these two applications? In data processing terminology, the difference is the level of **activity**. If a file is highly active, a significant percentage of the records on that file must be updated or otherwise accessed each time the application program is run. On a file with low activity, only a few records must be processed at one time. Sequential file processing is most efficient (from a cost point of view) on highly active files; direct access is most efficient when processing files with relatively low activity.

Most banks use a program similar to the sequential master file update application of Chapter 13 for updating checking accounts on a daily basis—checking accounts tend to be quite active. Compare the level of activity on your checking account with that of your savings account; almost certainly, activity on the savings account will be much lower. Have you ever been in a bank or savings and loan office that processed your savings account deposit or withdrawal through a terminal? Your account is probably stored on a direct access file. Why won't simple sequential batch processing do in this case? For reasons of security and control, the master file must be updated at least daily, and there is not enough activity to justify a daily, sequential master file update.

Let's look at another application where sequential file-processing just won't do, this time for quite different reasons. Our national air defense system is computer coordinated. Information on regularly scheduled flights, non-scheduled charter or private flights, the weather, and wind conditions, is kept in a massive "data base". Radar, ground spotters, airborn units, and sea installations constantly feed current information to the system. If an unidentified aircraft is spotted, an attempt is made to identify it, starting with calculations to determine, for example, if a known flight might have been blown off course and ending with the dispatching of interceptors and the alerting of responsible personnel.

There is no way an operation of this type can run sequentially. Imagine insisting that we wait until "5:00pm" to determine the identity of the aircraft because "5:00pm is the scheduled time for our sequential run". By 5:00pm, Chicago might not be there. Even were we to try to find the one or two needed records on a sequential file, there would be delays. We might be lucky and find that the desired record is the first one on the tape. On the other hand, it might just as easily be the very last record on the tape. On the average, half the tape would have to be searched before the correct record could be found and, on applications such as air defense, such delays are intolerable. Direct access is essential.

Air defense is an extreme example of a system requiring rapid retrieval of specific records. Consider, as another example, an air reservation system similar to the ones run by most modern commercial airlines. A ticket agent, using a terminal, requests a reservation for a customer. The information is sent to a central computer which checks the status of the desired flight and, in a matter of seconds, confirms or rejects the reservation. Transactions are processed one at a time, an almost certain clue that direct access is used. Why?

Most airlines are private organizations in business to make money. What if you, as a customer, were to approach "Tree Top Airways" to request a reservation on the next flight to New York and were told to wait until one half-hour before flight time (when the sequential reservation program is run) for confirmation? While waiting, you walk across the aisle to the ticket agent for "Kamikaze Airlines" who gives you an immediate, firm reservation on a flight leaving only a few minutes after the "Tree Top" flight. Which airline are you going to choose? Ignoring any qualitative differences, you'd probably select the "sure thing" over the "come back later" response. Although there are other reasons for putting a reservation system on-line, such as minimizing the impact of no-shows and handling a last-minute rush, it's basically done for competitive reasons. Airline customers have come to expect rapid response on reservation requests, and the airline that cannot provide this service will lose customers. Thus the one-transaction-at-a-time, direct access mode of operation is called for.

Numerous other examples could be cited. Basically, direct access is used either because the nature of the application makes one-record-at-a-time processing less expensive than sequential processing (the activity factor) or because the need for rapid **response time** makes sequential access, with its inherent time delays, unacceptable.

DIRECT VS. INDEXED SEQUENTIAL ACCESS

The level of activity and the need for response time are criteria commonly used to choose between sequential and direct access. Suppose that we have chosen direct. We have considered two techniques for direct access, one using the division/remainder method and the other using an index. Which technique is better?

Once again the answer will depend on the nature of the specific application. It is difficult, for example, to use a computational technique such as the division/remainder method when the key can contain alphabetic characters. Although it is possible to convert letters to numbers via an algorithm, non-numeric keys usually dictate an indexed approach.

A major problem with indexed sequential files is that as the number of additions and deletions increase, accessing the file becomes less and less efficient. If a significant number of such changes is expected, a file is said to be highly **volatile** The indexed sequential approach should be avoided on volatile files.

Perhaps the major problem with the algorithm approach to direct access is the generation of synonyms. If the randomizing rule (the divisor in the division/remainder method, for example) is not very carefully selected, the result can be a significant percentage of synonyms leading to very inefficient data access. How can the "correct" algorithm be selected? That is a good question; unfortunately there is no good answer. Mathematical techniques do exist, but few business data processing installations are equipped to deal with sophisticated mathematics on an everyday basis. More often than not, the "easy to understand" indexed technique is the first choice, unless high volatility or some other characteristic of the application clearly calls for an algorithm approach. The second choice is often a simple division/remainder technique using the total number of records or the number of tracks required by the file as the divisor. Should the simple algorithm prove unacceptable, it is probably time to call in a consultant who specializes in developing direct access algorithms.

A growing trend in business data processing is the use of a commercially available **data base management** package. The basic idea of data base management is to collect all the data resources of an organization into a single, integrated data base and then to provide a software monitor, the data base management system or DBMS, to control access. While the details of data base management are beyond the scope of this book, we can comment briefly on the impact such systems have on the COBOL programmer. Essentially, the programmer can ignore the details of input and output—the fact that the file may be sequential, direct, or indexed sequential is no longer relevant. Instead, all input and output requests are made , using a consistent format, through the data base manager. Programs thus gain a measure of data independence and, from the standpoints of documentation, program debug, and maintenance, this is highly desirable. The future promises only growth for the data base approach.

SUMMARY

The chapter began with a discussion of query applications. A specific example of a query problem, obtaining customer order status, was then described, and we turned our attention to writing this program in COBOL. The need for user involvement was emphasized. The instructions needed to randomly access an indexed sequential file were developed. Error handling routines were shown to be an essential part of the program.

We then considered the problem of updating an indexed sequential file. Operating procedures were first established. The basic logic of the program was seen to be similar to that of the direct access file update routine developed in Chapter 15. The details of ISAM file processing were then considered, with the only new instruction being REWRITE.

The chapter ended with a discussion of why direct access might be chosen over sequential access for a given application; a low level of activity and a need for rapid response time were shown to be two common characteristics of a direct access application. We then considered some of the strong and weak points of the algorithm and indexed approaches to direct access.

KEY WORDS

accessability	data base management	query	REWRITE
activity	I-O	response time	volatility

EXERCISES

1. What is a query?

2. Why is user involvement so important in planning a solution to a problem such as the order status application of this chapter?

3. Explain the steps involved in using the COBOL language to randomly access an indexed sequential file.

4. Why did we begin our discussion of the customer master file update application by describing the operating procedures?

5. Why do you suppose that the program to update a direct access file and the program to update an indexed sequential file are so similar?

6. How does the level of activity affect the choice of direct or sequential access?

7. How does the need for rapid response affect the choice of direct or sequential access?

8. How does the programmer or systems analyst choose between an algorithm approach such as the division/remainder method and an indexed approach to direct access?

9. Exercise 8 in Chapter 16 asked you to create a direct access file of personnel information. Earlier in the text, you wrote several programs based on the payroll application. Select the most current payroll program as a starting point. Eliminate the hourly pay rate from the input record. Modify the program to read the input record and, using the employee number as a key, look up the related personnel record in the personal file, getting the hourly pay rate from this source.

10. We need a master file update program for the personnel master file. New employees are constantly being hired and old employees retire, quit, or are fired. Present employees change their names and addresses. They shift to new departments, and get raises. They get married and have children. The rate of change, while substantial, is not really adequate to support a sequential master file update, so a direct access master file update routine is called for. Write the program.

11. Write a program to allow a reservation clerk to get information on the number of seats currently available on a given Tree Top Airlines flight. Use the file described in exercise 9 of Chapter 16.

12. Write a program to allow a reservation clerk to update the flight information file. The clerk should report the flight number and date (in the form defined as the key for this file), a code indicating if this is a request for a new reservation or a cancellation of an old one, and the number of seats involved. The program should adjust both the "number of seats currently sold" and the "number of seats available" to reflect this change. Don't forget that the number of seats actually sold may not exceed the capacity of the airplane; be prepared to generate a message indicating that not enough seats are available.

13. Every day, flights that have already departed become obsolete and must be deleted from the system. New flights, now only 30 days in the future, must be added to the file. Write a program to accept as input the "to be deleted" date and the "to be added" date, and make the necessary changes. Assume that one flight will be added for each flight deleted; everything but the date will be the same for the new flight. For all new flights, set the number of seats sold equal to zero and the number of seats available equal to the capacity of the airplane.

14. Exercise 10 in Chapter 16 set up a file of books by their Library of Congress numbers. Additions are frequently made to this list; occasionally deletions are made. The only modification that is considered to be important is the addition of the letter code of an additional library which has obtained a copy of the book. Write a program to update this file.

15. Prepare a simple program to handle a query to the interlibrary loan system. The input record will consist of a Library of Congress number. The output will consist of a message saying either we have it or we don't, followed by the name of the author, the title, and the code letters for the libraries that actually have the requested books if catalogued.

Appendix

Appendix A: The IBM 029 Keypunch

BASIC IDEAS

The whole point of keypunching is to convert the characters printed on a source document into a pattern of punched holes on a card. Each column of a card holds one character of data; the hole pattern within the column determines which character it is. The keypunch is designed to be used much like a typewriter, with the operator depressing keys on a keyboard; the only difference is that the characters are punched into a card rather than printed on a sheet of paper.

The keyboard (Fig. A.1) is similar to a typewriter keyboard. There are, however, a few differences. To the experienced typist, the most obvious difference is the position of the digits 0 through 9; rather than being located across the top of the keyboard, they are gathered into an adding machine-like group just beneath where your right hand would normally be positioned. This is intentional, the experienced operator soon learns to enter numeric data with one hand, using the other to depress the numeric shift key or to track the data on the source document. Another difference between a typewriter and a keypunch is that there are no lowercase letters on a keypunch; every letter is a capital letter.

Above the keyboard in Fig. A.1, you should be able to see a series of switches. Those are called the control switches or the selector switches; they are used to control the operation of the keypunch. More about these switches later.

Let's step back a bit and take a look at the whole keypunch (Fig. A.2). The on/off switch is located near the bottom right, underneath the keypunch proper. The keyboard sits atop a table-like ledge. Behind the keyboard are the card-feed and punching mechanisms. A card moves from the card hopper (at the right), down into the card bed, through the punching station where it is punched and, continuing its movement to the left, into the card stacker; look for each of these basic positions in the diagram of Fig. A.2.

Normally, the contents of each card column are printed at the top of the card. This is for the convenience of the keypunch operator or other individual who wishes to verify the cards visually; the computer needs only the holes.

LOADING CARDS

Before using a keypunch, it is necessary to have a supply of blank cards in the card hopper. To place cards in the hopper:

1. push the pressure plate at the rear of the card hopper back until it catches;

Appendix A

Fig. A.1: *The keyboard of a keypunch.*

Photo courtesy of International Business Machines Corporation.

Fig. A.2: *A keypunch.*

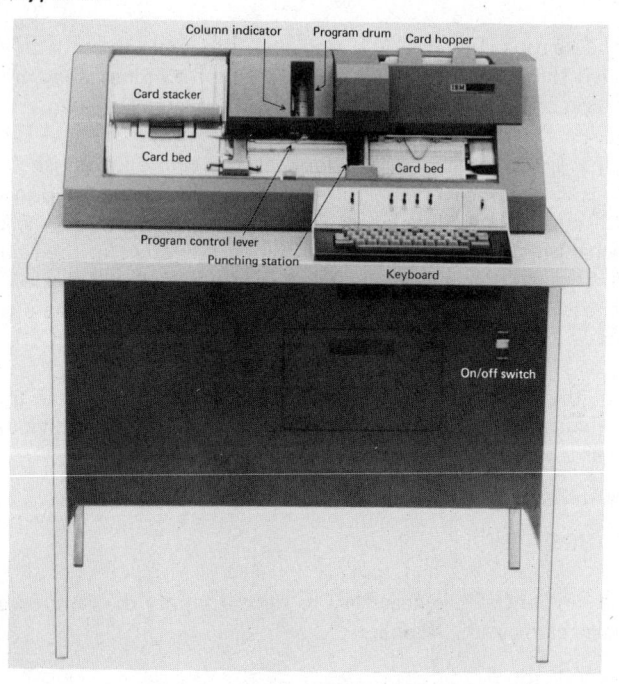

Photo courtesy of International Business Machines Corporation.

2. grab a stack of cards;

3. fan through the cards to loosen any that might be stuck together;

4. use the edge of the keyboard to straighten and align the cards in the deck;

5. look at the edges of the cards and remove any that look nicked or warped (they can jam the machine);

6. place the cards in the hopper 9-edge (bottom) down and with the printing facing you;

7. release the pressure plate.

You are now ready to begin punching.

BASIC KEYPUNCH OPERATION

Most beginners are concerned with punching a series of cards; thus our basic operating steps are designed around a "multiple card" assumption. The on/off switch is located at the bottom right of the machine, underneath the ledge; turn the machine on. As you begin, all the control switches at the top of the keyboard should be flipped up. One, the CLEAR switch, won't stay up; don't worry about it.

The first step in the keypunching operation is to move a card from the card hopper to the punching station. The following two steps achieve this objective:

1. depress the FEED key (it's a blue key, near the right edge of the keypunch in the second row down from the top);

2. depress the FEED key again.

The first feed operation feeds one card from the card hopper down to the card bed. The second feed operation moves the first card into the punching station and feeds a second card.

You are ready to begin punching data into a card. Each keystroke causes one character to be punched, with the character being printed at the top of the column; after punching, the card automatically advances to the next column, where another character can be punched. Alphabetic characters and any symbols located on the lower half of a key can simply be punched; numeric characters and symbols on the upper half of the key must be punched while the NUMERIC key (bottom left of keyboard) is being held down.

An extremely useful aid to the keypunch operation is the column indicator, a small red indicator, which can be viewed through the window near the center of the keypunch (see Fig. A.2). This marker indicates the card column that is about to be punched.

Appendix A

After completing the punching of a single card, hit the REL key; it's in the top row, near the right edge. The REL key causes the card which has just been punched to be released from the punching station, the second card to be moved to the punching station, and a third card to be fed from the card hopper to the card bed. The "just punched" card now rests near the center of the card bed, where it can be visually checked (if desired) by the keypunch operator.

A second card can now be punched. When all the data has been keyed, the card is released; at this time, the first card moves to the card stacker, the second card (the one just punched) moves from the punching station, the third card moves to the punching station, and a fourth card is fed. This process is continued until all the cards have been punched. By flipping up the CLEAR switch at the top right of the keyboard (Fig. A.1), you can move all cards on the card bed to the card stacker, and the job is finished.

Basic Operations: A Summary

1. Load cards.
2. Turn keypunch on.
3. Flip all control switches up.
4. Feed first card.
5. Feed a second card.
6. Punch the card.
    a For numbers, hold down NUMERIC button.
    b For alphabetic characters, just keypunch.
    c Check column indicator for position.
7. When finished with card, depress REL key.
8. Visually check card.
9. Go back to step 6 and punch another card.
10. When finished, flip up CLEAR switch.

DUPLICATING A CARD

Programmers and keypunch operators often find it desirable to duplicate all or part of a card. Assume that you have just finished keypunching a card. Hit the REL key, moving this card to the middle position on the card bed and moving a second card to the punching station. Now, hold down the DUP key (top row, just to the right of center). You will get a column-by-column copy of the first card.

Appendix A

If only a portion of a card is to be duplicated, the DUP key can be "tapped," causing one column at a time to be copied; the column indicator can be used to determine which column will be punched next. If several consecutive columns, 1-25, for example, are to be duplicated, the DUP key can be held down until the column indicator shows that you are "getting close," at which time you can shift to a one-column-at-a-time mode of duplication.

PUNCHING A SINGLE CARD

To punch a single card, the AUTO FEED switch should be flipped down. This turns off the automatic card feed feature, meaning that no additional cards will be fed when the REL key is depressed.

Hit the FEED key, feeding one card to the card bed. Now hit the REG key (it's just below and slightly to the right of the FEED key); this moves the card to the punching position. Now you can punch this card. When you are finished, flip the CLEAR switch and retrieve the card from the stacker.

CORRECTING AN ERROR

Every keypunch operator makes errors. It's very frustrating to have to re-punch an entire card just because one character is incorrect, especially when you know that the process of rekeying the card may well produce additional errors. Don't. Take advantage of the DUP feature.

Start by turning the automatic feed feature off (flip the AUTO FEED switch down). Feed one card. Now, take the card containing the error and slip it into the center position of the card bed; if you look closely (Fig. A.2), you'll see a set of small openings at the top and bottom of the plastic card guides which provide an ideal path for slipping the card in. Once the card containing the error has been successfully inserted into the center position, hit the REG key; both cards should move into place. Carefully check and note the number of the card column containing the error. Using the column indicator as a guide, duplicate (DUP key) over as far as the column containing the error. Type the correct character or characters in the column(s) to be corrected and then duplicate the remainder of the card. Use the CLEAR switch to move both cards to the output stacker, visually check the new card for accuracy, and throw the error card away.

CORRECTING AN ERROR: A SUMMARY

1. Turn AUTO FEED off.

2. Feed one card.

3. Slip the error card into the center position.

4. Hit the REG key.

Appendix A

5. Make sure you know which column contains the error.

6. Duplicate over to the error column.

7. Punch the correct character or characters.

8. Duplicate the remainder of the card.

9. Flip the CLEAR lever.

ADDING A CHARACTER OR CHARACTERS TO A CARD

Beginners, be they programmers or keypunch operators, often make the error of simply forgetting to punch one or more characters; this often happens with the period at the end of a COBOL statement or the semicolon at the end of a PL/I statement. Assuming that sufficient blank columns exist on the card, characters can be added without duplicating the whole thing.

Start by slipping the card to which characters are to be added into the rightmost position of the card bed; again, a convenient set of guides is provided for this purpose. Make sure the card lies flat on the card bed, and then hit the REG key. Now, simply space over to the desired column (using the column indicator as a guide), type the desired character or characters, and flip the CLEAR switch.

PROGRAM CARDS

The work done by a keypunch operator is often very repetitive, involving the punching of thousands of cards all having the same format. By using a program card, the operator can:

1. automatically cause the keypunch to shift into a numeric mode, thus eliminating the need to depress the NUMERIC key while entering digits;

2. automatically duplicate selected fields;

3. automatically skip several columns, thus eliminating the need to skip one column at a time using the space bar.

The use of a program card saves keystrokes.

Program cards are prepared on a keypunch, using the following codes:

Code	Meaning
blank	Designates start of a manual numeric field; i.e., starts automatic numeric shift
0	Start of automatic duplication
1	Start of a manual alphabetic field

Appendix A

11	Start of an automatic skip field
12	Used to define the length of a numeric field
A	Used to define the length of an alphabetic field

To cite an example, let's say that you've been assigned the task of punching several thousand cards all having the following format:

Columns	Contents
1-9	Social Security number
10-20	Blank, unused
21-35	Customer name
36-50	Name of our firm; constant for all cards

We have a numeric field, a string of 11 consecutive unused columns, an alphabetic field, and a constant field that can be duplicated. A control card for this job (Fig. A.3) would contain:

1. A blank in column 1 marking the beginning of a numeric field.

2. Ampersands (&) in columns 2-9, indicating the length of this field. The ampersand (&), an uppercase P, is represented as a 12-punch.

3. An 11-punch (a minus sign) in column 10, marking the beginning of an automatic skip field.

4. The letter A in columns 11-20, marking the length of this skip field.

5. A 1 in column 21, marking the beginning of the customer name field (it's alphabetic).

6. The letter A in columns 22-35, indicating the length of this field.

7. A 0 in column 36, marking the beginning of an automatic duplication field.

8. The letter A in columns 37-50, indicating the length of this field.

9. An 11-punch in column 51 (the rest of the card is to be automatically skipped.

10. The letter A in columns 52-80, taking us to the end of the card.

Program cards should be prepared one at a time. Switches are to be set as follows:

1. AUTO SKIP off (down).

2. AUTO FEED off.

3. PRINT off.

Appendix A

4. LZ PRINT off.

5. PROGRAM switch to ONE.

USING A PROGRAM CARD

In order to use a program card, the card must first be mounted on the program drum, which can be found behind the little window near the top center of the keypunch. Refer to Fig. A.2; the program drum is right above the column indicator. If you have access to a keypunch, lift the cover to get a better look.

Toward the left of the program drum is a set of starwheels that read the hole pattern on the program card. A switch, the program control lever, can be found just beneath the program drum area. This switch controls the starwheels. In the off position, the starwheels are up; in the on position, the wheels are down, contacting the program drum.

To insert a program card, turn the starwheels off and pull the program drum cylinder straight up; it should slide off the spindle with very little effort. Inside the drum is a lever called the clamping strip handle; turn it away from you (counterclockwise) to open the clamping strip. Slide the 80-edge of the card in under the clamping strip, making sure that the program card is straight; then turn the clamping strip handle back toward you, locking the card into place. Roll the card around the drum, making sure that it is straight and smooth; if you are inserting the card correctly, you should be able to read the printing on the card. Insert the 1-edge of the program card under the clamping strip, and turn the clamping strip handle toward you as far as it will go, thus locking the card into place. Replace the program drum on the spindle, engage the starwheels, and you are ready to go.

Fig. A. 3: *A keypunch program card.*

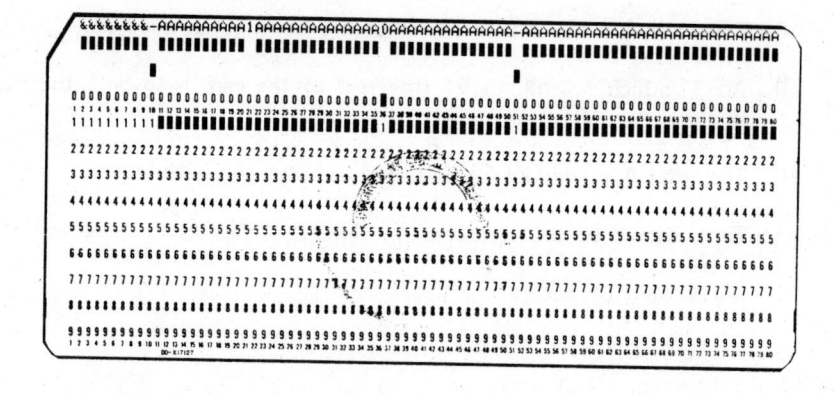

Appendix A

Two Programs on the Same Card

Another problem sometimes faced by the keypunch operator is the job for which cards must be punched to one of two different formats. Rather than having the operator change control cards each time the format changes, two different programs can be punched into the same card, one in the top six rows and the other in the bottom six rows. The program select switch (PROG SEL) allows the operator to indicate which of these two programs should be in control; ONE is for the top program and TWO is for the bottom program.

OTHER FEATURES

One switch we have not yet mentioned is the one labeled PRINT. This switch turns the printer on or off. Certain applications call for the punching of confidential information (a wage rate, for example); such information might well be punched with the printer off.

Another feature sometimes used by professional keypunch operators is left zero punching. Let's say that we have a numeric field five columns long. What if the number 8 is to be punched? Using all five columns, the operator would punch 00008.

Using the left zero feature, the operator would simply punch the digit 8 and hit the LEFT ZERO key. The data, rather than being punched directly into the card, is placed in a buffer; when the LEFT ZERO key is depressed, nonsignificant zeros are added to the left and the card field is punched automatically. The left zero feature requires the use of a program card. The LZ PRINT switch is used to control printing when this feature is used.

The AUTO SKIP DUP switch controls another special feature. This one allows the operator to automatically duplicate a card up to the column containing an error. A keypunch operator, like a typist, often senses that an error has occurred as soon as the wrong key is depressed. The automatic skip duplication feature allows the operator to automatically duplicate the card over to this point, correct the error, and continue punching.

Appendix B: DOS Job Control and File Linkage:

ENVIRONMENT DIVISION CONSIDERATIONS: the ASSIGN clause.

general format: ASSIGN TO symbolic-class-device-organization

symbolic name: Under DOS, all physical devices are assigned a 6-character symbolic name. Standard assignments include:

name	meaning
SYSRDR	input unit for job control statements
SYSIPT	input unit for application programs
SYSPCH	unit for punched card output
SYSLST	unit for printed output
SYSLOG	unit for operator messages
SYSLNK	disk extent for linkage editor input
SYSRES	system residence area (operating system)
SYSCLB	private core-image library
SYSRLB	private relocatable library
SYSSLB	private source statement library
SYSREC	disk extent for error logging
SYS000–	other units—installation dependent
SYSmax	

One of these symbolic names must appear as the first field following the ASSIGN TO.

class: three device classes are valid on an IBM computer. They are:

DA for mass storage, usually disk or drum.

UT for utility, which can mean any of the standard system input or system output devices, magnetic tape, or sequential files on disk,

Appendix B

> UR for unit record equipment.

> The device class must be the second field.

device: defines the physical device. Typical devices include:

> 1442R for the 1442 card reader
>
> 1442P for the 1442 card punch
>
> 1403 for the 1403 printer
>
> 2501 for the 2501 card reader
>
> 2520P for the 2520 card punch
>
> 3330 for the 3330 disk system
>
> 2400 for the 2400 tape drive series.

> The list of valid devices will vary from installation to installation.

organization: the physical organization of the records on the file. Valid organizations include:

> S for sequential files,
>
> D for direct access files,
>
> I for indexed sequential files.

Note that the indexed sequential organization is not an ANSI COBOL standard; indexed sequential is an IBM-only file organization.

Examples:

> input from a 2501 card reader:
>
> > SELECT filename ASSIGN TO SYSIPT-UR-2501-S.
>
> output to a 1403 printer:
>
> > SELECT filename ASSIGN TO SYSLST-UR-1403-S.
>
> input to or output from a 2400 tape drive:
>
> > SELECT filename ASSIGN TO SYS007-UT-2400-S.

Appendix B

input to or output from a direct access disk file:

SELECT filename ASSIGN TO SYS011-DA-3330-D.

Note: in the last two examples, SYS007 and SYS011 were assumed to be the symbolic names assigned to these specific devices.

JOB CONTROL LANGUAGE:

The JOB statement: The functions of the DOS JOB statement are to separate and identify jobs. The general form of the JOB card is as follows:

// JOB jobname accounting-information

The slashes must be coded in columns 1 and 2. Column 3 must be blank. The word JOB must be coded; it can begin in any position after column 3. A job name field must be coded to provide the program with a unique name which may consist of from 1 to 8 alphanumeric characters; any name will do, although many computer centers have imposed local standards. Accounting information is optional.

The EXEC statement: The function of the EXEC statement is to identify the specific program to be loaded and executed. The general form of this statement is:

// EXEC program-name

Once again, the slashes must be coded in columns 1 and 2, and column 3 must be blank. Blanks also separate the key word EXEC from the program name.

The ASSIGN statement: Every physical device on an IBM computer system is assigned a unique, 3-character (hex) address identifying the channel number and the device number; a visit to an IBM computer center should reveal these physical device addresses which are normally posted in clear view of the computer operator. Under DOS, each symbolic device name (SYSxxx) is assigned to a specific physical device. On occasion, it becomes necessary to temporarily change this assignment (for example, the assigned tape drive is busy but another drive is free). Such reassignments can be made by coding an ASSIGN statement:

// ASSGN symbolic-name,physical-address

For example, if SYS007 is to be temporarily reassigned from the standard device to device 182, the card

// ASSGN SYS007,X'182'

Appendix B

would achieve this reassignment. The slashes must be coded in columns 1 and 2. Column 3 must be blank. Blanks also separate the keyword ASSGN from the specification of device reassignment.

Note: the reassignment is only temporary. The symbolic name reverts to the standard system assignment at the end of the job. The ASSIGN statement does not affect the device assignment for any other job.

The Linkage Editor: As with any system, programmer source statements cannot be directly executed by a computer running under DOS; instead, the source statements must be compiled to machine-level code. Normally, there is a third step involved as a linkage editor program finishes preparing what is called a load module, a set of code that can be loaded and executed on a computer.

In discussing program preparation in the text, the linkage editor program was simply mentioned and not really explained. Not all computer manufacturers use the linkage editor, with many housing its functions within the language compiler programs. On an IBM system running under OS or a VS operating system, an EXEC statement can refer to a cataloged procedure which includes the linkage editor references, allowing the programmer to effectively ignore this program. Under DOS (although a limited version of the cataloged procedure is available on newer versions) the programmer must code an EXEC card for *each* job step including the linkage editor; thus the programmer must be at least aware of its existence.

The linkage editor is executed in response to the job control statement:

    // EXEC LNKEDT

In preparation for the linkage editor step, the programmer must tell the compiler that the use of the linkage editor is contemplated. This is done by placing an OPTION statement before the EXEC statement identifying the compiler, as in:

    // OPTION LINK

    // EXEC COBOL.

Examples:

To compile only:

```
// JOB  jobname
// EXEC  COBOL
       source deck
/*
/&
```

To compile, link edit, and execute:

```
// JOB  jobname
// OPTION  LINK
// EXEC  COBOL
       source deck
/*
// EXEC  LNKEDT
// EXEC
       data cards
/*
/&
```

Notes: the /* card identifies the end of a card file. The /& card identifies the end of the job. The last EXEC card

```
// EXEC
```

contains no job name; it identifies the load module most recently created by the linkage editor.

SORT/MERGE UTILITIES:

A version of the sort/merge utility program is available in most DOS installations. Although the precise code may vary from installation to installation, the job control statements illustrated below are typical:

Appendix B

```
// JOB  SORT1
// ASSGN    ⎫
            ⎬   ASSGN statements for the input,
            ⎪   output, and sort work files as
            ⎪   needed.
// ASSGN    ⎭
// TLBL
// DLBL     ⎫
            ⎪   TLBL (tape label), DLBL (disk
            ⎪   label), and EXTENT (define loca-
            ⎬   tion of a file on a disk pack) as
            ⎪   needed in support of input, output,
            ⎪   and sort work files.
// EXTENT   ⎭
// EXEC SORT
    SORT FIELDS=(start,length,type,order)
      RECORD    logical and physical record description
      INPFIL    description of input file
      OUTFIL    description of output file
      OPTION    options on output
      END       marks end of control cards
/*
/&
```

Appendix C

COBOL Reserved Words

Source: This collection of COBOL reserved words was taken in part from *IBM OS Full American National Standard COBOL* (IBM No. GC28-6396). Reproduced by permission from International Business Machines Corporation.

IBM AMERICAN NATIONAL STANDARD COBOL RESERVED WORDS

ACCEPT	CHANGED
ACCESS	CHARACTER
ACTUAL	CHARACTERS
ADD	CLOCK-UNITS
ADDRESS	CLOSE
ADVANCING	COBOL
AFTER	CODE
ALL	COLUMN
ALPHABETIC	COM-REG
ALPHANUMERIC	COMMA
ALPHANUMERIC-EDITED	COMP
ALTER	COMP-1
ALTERNATE	COMP-2
AND	COMP-3
APPLY	COMP-4
ARE	COMPUTATIONAL
AREA	COMPUTATIONAL-1
AREAS	COMPUTATIONAL-2
ASCENDING	COMPUTATIONAL-3
ASSIGN	COMPUTATIONAL-4
AT	COMPUTE
AUTHOR	CONFIGURATION
	CONSOLE
BASIS	CONSTANT
BEFORE	CONTAINS
BEGINNING	CONTROL
BLANK	CONTROLS
BLOCK	COPY
BY	CORE-INDEX
	CORR
CALL	CORRESPONDING
CANCEL	COUNT
CBL	CSP
CD	CURRENCY
CF	CURRENT-DATE
CH	CYL-INDEX

Appendix C

CYL-OVERFLOW	EMI
C01	ENABLE
C02	END
C03	END-OF-PAGE
C04	ENDING
C05	ENTER
C06	ENTRY
C07	ENVIRONMENT
C08	EOP
C09	EQUAL
C10	EQUALS
C11	ERROR
C12	ESI
	EVERY
DATA	EXAMINE
DATE	EXCEEDS
DATE-COMPILED	EXHIBIT
DATE-WRITTEN	EXIT
DAY	EXTENDED-SEARCH
DE	
DEBUG	FD
DEBUG-CONTENTS	FILE
DEBUG-ITEM	FILE-CONTROL
DEBUG-LINE	FILE-LIMIT
DEBUG-SUB-1	FILE-LIMITS
DEBUG-SUB-2	FILLER
DEBUG-SUB-3	FINAL
DEBUG-NAME	FIRST
DEBUGGING	FOOTING
DECIMAL-POINT	FOR
DECLARATIVES	FROM
DELETE	
DELIMITED	GENERATE
DELIMITER	GIVING
DEPENDING	GO
DEPTH	GOBACK
DESCENDING	GREATER
DESTINATION	GROUP
DETAIL	
DISABLE	HEADING
DISP	HIGH-VALUE
DISPLAY	HIGH-VALUES
DISPLAY-ST	HOLD
DISPLAY-n	
DIVIDE	I-O
DIVISION	I-O-CONTROL
DOWN	ID
DYNAMIC	IDENTIFICATION
EGI	IF
EJECT	IN
ELSE	INDEX

Appendix C

INDEX-n
INDEXED
INDICATE
INITIAL
INITIATE
INPUT
INPUT-OUTPUT
INSERT
INSPECT
INSTALLATION
INTO
INVALID
IS

JUST
JUSTIFIED

KEY
KEYS

LABEL
LABEL-RETURN
LAST
LEADING
LEAVE
LEFT
LENGTH
LESS
LIBRARY
LIMIT
LIMITS
LINAGE
LINAGE-COUNTER
LINE
LINE-COUNTER
LINES
LINKAGE
LOCK
LOW-VALUE
LOW-VALUES
LOWER-BOUND
LOWER-BOUNDS

MASTER-INDEX
MEMORY
MERGE
MESSAGE
MODE
MODULES

MORE-LABELS
MOVE
MULTIPLE
MULTIPLY

NAMED
NEGATIVE
NEXT
NO
NOMINAL
NOT
NOTE
NSTD-REELS
NUMBER
NUMERIC
NUMERIC-EDITED

OBJECT-COMPUTER
OBJECT-PROGRAM
OCCURS
OF
OFF
OH
OMITTED
ON
OPEN
OPTIONAL
OR
OTHERWISE
OUTPUT
OV
OVERFLOW

PAGE
PAGE-COUNTER
PERFORM
PF
PH
PIC
PICTURE
PLUS
POINTER
POSITION
POSITIONING
POSITIVE
PREPARED
PRINT-SWITCH
PRINTING
PRIORITY

Appendix C

PROCEDURE	SA
PROCEDURES	SAME
PROCEED	SD
PROCESS	SEARCH
PROCESSING	SECTION
PROGRAM	SECURITY
PROGRAM-ID	SEEK
	SEGMENT
QUEUE	SEGMENT-LIMIT
QUOTE	SELECT
QUOTES	SELECTED
	SEND
RANDOM	SENTENCE
RANGE	SEPARATE
RD	SEQUENTIAL
READ	SERVICE
READY	SET
RECEIVE	SIGN
RECORD	SIZE
RECORD-OVERFLOW	SKIP1
RECORDING	SKIP2
RECORDS	SKIP3
REDEFINES	SORT
REEL	SORT-CORE-SIZE
REFERENCES	SORT-FILE-SIZE
RELEASE	SORT-MODE-SIZE
RELOAD	SORT-RETURN
REMAINDER	SOURCE
REMARKS	SOURCE-COMPUTER
RENAMES	SPACE
REORG-CRITERIA	SPACES
REPLACING	SPECIAL-NAMES
REPORT	STANDARD
REPORTING	START
REPORTS	STATUS
REREAD	STOP
RERUN	STRING
RESERVE	SUB-QUEUE-1
RESET	SUB-QUEUE-2
RETURN	SUB-QUEUE-3
RETURN-CODE	SUBTRACT
REVERSED	SUM
REWIND	SUPERVISOR
REWRITE	SUPPRESS
RF	SUSPEND
RH	SYMBOLIC
RIGHT	SYNC
ROUNDED	SYNCHRONIZED
RUN	SYSIN

Appendix C

SYSIPT	UNIT
SYSLST	UNSTRING
SYSOUT	UNTIL
SYSPCH	UP
SYSPUNCH	UPON
S01	UPPER-BOUND
S02	UPPER-BOUNDS
	UPSI-O
TABLE	UPSI-1
TALLY	UPSI-2
TALLYING	UPSI-3
TAPE	UPSI-4
TERMINAL	UPSI-5
TERMINATE	UPSI-6
TEXT	UPSI-7
THAN	USAGE
THEN	USE
THROUGH	USING
THRU	
TIME	VALUE
TIME-OF-DAY	VALUES
TIMES	VARYING
TO	
TOTALED	WHEN
TOTALING	WITH
TRACE	WORDS
TRACK	WORKING-STORAGE
TRACK-AREA	WRITE
TRACK-LIMIT	WRITE-ONLY
TRACKS	WRITE-VERIFY
TRAILING	
TRANSFORM	ZERO
TYPE	ZEROES
	ZEROS
UNEQUAL	

Appendix D

COBOL Ready Reference

OVERVIEW

This book is designed to be a textbook, and not a reference manual. As your skill in programming increases, you will encounter a growing need for a ready guide to the proper syntax of a specific instruction. The purpose of this appendix is to provide just such a ready reference guide. The source of much of this material is IBM publication No. GC28-6396, *IBM OS Full American National Standard COBOL*.

THE IDENTIFICATION DIVISION

The IDENTIFICATION DIVISION must be the first division in a COBOL program. Its purpose is to identify the program, and it consists of a series of paragraphs which provide documentation. Allowable IDENTIFICATION DIVISION paragraphs are

```
IDENTIFICATION DIVISION
    PROGRAM-ID        program-name
    AUTHOR            comment-entry
    INSTALLATION      comment-entry
    DATE-WRITTEN      comment-entry
    DATE-COMPILED     comment-entry
    SECURITY          comment-entry
    REMARKS           comment-entry
```

The PROGRAM-ID paragraph must be coded. A program name can be composed of from 1 to 30 alphabetic or numeric characters and the hyphen (the hyphen cannot begin or end the name). Since the program name serves to identify the program to the computer system, certain system consideration often take precedence over the COBOL standards; thus it is strongly advised that you follow local standards in selecting program names. The PROGRAM-ID paragraph must be the first paragraph in the division.

All other IDENTIFICATION DIVISION paragraphs are optional, although, once again, local standards may require the programmer to code one or more of them. Standard COBOL calls for the paragraphs to be coded in the order given above; many versions of COBOL will accept them in any order. A paragraph ends when a period is followed by another paragraph name or by the ENVIRONMENT DIVISION.

The DATE-COMPILED paragraph is a bit unusual, in that the comment coded by the programmer will be replaced by the current system date as the program is compiled.

Appendix D

THE ENVIRONMENT DIVISION

The ENVIRONMENT DIVISION describes the environment in which the program is designed to run, listing such things as the computer system and necessary input and output devices. The basic structure of the division is

    ENVIRONMENT DIVISION.
        CONFIGURATION SECTION.
            SOURCE-COMPUTER paragraph
            OBJECT-COMPUTER paragraph
            SPECIAL-NAMES paragraph
        INPUT-OUTPUT SECTION.
            FILE-CONTROL paragraph
            I-O-CONTROL paragraph

CONFIGURATION SECTION

The CONFIGURATION SECTION is used to describe the computer system for which the program was designed. The SOURCE-COMPUTER paragraph names the computer for which the initial source program was written; the OBJECT-COMPUTER paragraph names the computer on which an object-level program was produced—note that they could differ. Both paragraphs are treated as comments. To the professional programmer, a particular model of computer implies a number of very specific characteristics and, knowing this information, the programmer can be reasonably sure of the key modifications that will have to be made if the program is to be revised for use on a different machine.

The SPECIAL-NAMES paragraph allows the programmer to define certain mnemonic names that will be used throughout the program to stand for key functions. For example,

    SPECIAL-NAMES.
        C01 IS TOP-OF-PAGE.

was used in several text examples to tie a mnemonic name to carriage control channel 01 on the printer. If several different entries are made in the SPECIAL-NAMES paragraph, it is important to remember that the period should not be coded until the end of the entire paragraph.

INPUT-OUTPUT SECTION

The INPUT-OUTPUT SECTION provides a link between each program input and output file and the physical device associated with the file. There are two paragraphs within this section. The FILE-CONTROL paragraph is where the file/device links are

Appendix D

defined. The I-O-CONTROL paragraph is used to define certain special techniques, and was not covered in the text.

Key clauses within the FILE-CONTROL paragraph include:

```
FILE-CONTROL.
    SELECT Clause
    ASSIGN Clause
    RESERVE Clause
    FILE-LIMIT Clause
    ACCESS MODE Clause
    PROCESSING MODE Clause
    ACTUAL KEY Clause
    NOMINAL KEY Clause
```

The SELECT clause is used to name a file. An ASSIGN clause assigns the file to an external device or medium. Typically, at least when dealing with sequential files, these two clauses are all that is needed, as in

SELECT CARDFILE ASSIGN TO UT-S-SYSIN.

Under IBM's full operating systems, the general form of an ASSIGN clause is

ASSIGN class-organization-name.

Valid classes include DA for a mass storage device such as disk or drum, UT (utility) for such devices as the standard system input and output devices, magnetic tape, and sequential files on disk, and UR for unit record files. Valid organizations include S for sequential and D for direct; although it is not an ANSI standard, I for indexed sequential is often used on IBM computers. The name must be the DDNAME on a DD job control language card. The precise format of the ASSIGN statement will vary by machine type and manufacturer, so check your local standards carefully. The proper format for an ASSIGN statement on an IBM DOS system can be found in Appendix B.

Typically, the SELECT and ASSIGN clauses work together, with one set defined for each file accessed by the program. The other clauses, used to define certain additional functions or features associated with a given file, are attached to a SELECT... ASSIGN set.

The RESERVE clause is used to modify the number of buffers assigned to the file. The clause

RESERVE 2 ALTERNATE AREAS

for example, asks for two buffers in addition to the one required for basic I/O (total of 3). The FILE-LIMIT clause serves as documentation only; it identifies the logical beginning and ending of a file on disk or drum, and is rarely used. The ACCESS MODE clause indicates how the records on the file are to be accessed; the word MODE is optional. Valid clauses include

Appendix D

ACCESS MODE IS SEQUENTIAL

and

ACCESS MODE IS RANDOM

If not coded, SEQUENTIAL is assumed. The PROCESSING MODE clause

PROCESSING MODE IS SEQUENTIAL

serves only as documentation. Finally, the ACTUAL KEY clause:

ACTUAL KEY IS data-name

identifies the DATA DIVISION field that holds the actual key for a direct access file. The ACTUAL KEY is composed of two parts, a relative track address and a search key. Normally coded in the WORKING-STORAGE SECTION, the actual key field often takes the following form:

```
01   THE-ACTUAL-KEY.
    05 RTA   USAGE COMPUTATIONAL   PICTURE S9(5) SYNC.
    05 SEARCH-KEY   PICTURE X(15).
```

The search key will, of course, vary with the application.

The NOMINAL KEY clause is used to identify the search key that will be used to randomly access an indexed sequential file. The NOMINAL KEY field must be defined in the WORKING-STORAGE SECTION. Only the logical search key, a customer identification number, for example, is required to access an indexed sequential file.

The NOMINAL KEY is also used in accessing a direct file when relative record addresses are used. For a direct file, the NOMINAL KEY must contain the relative record number, and not the logical search key.

Three clauses can be coded within the I-O-CONTROL paragraph. The RERUN clause is used to specify that checkpoints are to be taken. The SAME clause specifies that two or more files are to share the same input or output area. The MULTIPLE FILE TAPE clause, used only for documentation, indicates that a given tape reel contains more than one file. Since these clauses (or, more to the point, the data processing techniques behind them) are a bit advanced, we will refer the interested programmer to a reference manual.

The DATA DIVISION

All data to be processed by a COBOL program must be described in the DATA DIVISION. Standard COBOL divides the DATA DIVISION into three sections: the FILE SECTION, the WORKING-STORAGE SECTION, and the REPORT SECTION.

Appendix D

FILE SECTION

In the FILE SECTION, the programmer must provide a description of each externally stored file (using an FD entry) and of each sort file (using an SD entry). The following clauses can be coded as part of an FD entry:

>FD file-name
>>**BLOCK CONTAINS Clause**
>>**RECORD CONTAINS Clause**
>>**LABEL RECORDS Clause**
>>**VALUE OF Clause**
>>**DATA RECORDS Clause**
>>**REPORT Clause**

The BLOCK CONTAINS clause can be used to identify the number of records or characters contained in a physical block of data as stored on a file. The clause

>BLOCK CONTAINS 10 records

identifies a block with 10 logical records, while

>BLOCK CONTAINS 350 CHARACTERS

identifies a block with 350 characters of data. By coding

>BLOCK CONTAINS 0 RECORDS

the programmer allows the computer system to supply the actual blocking factor for the file from the label of an *existing* file when the OPEN instruction is executed.

The RECORD CONTAINS clause is treated as a comment, since the actual number of characters in a record is determined by counting the number of positions defined in the record description. The LABEL RECORDS clause is used to define the type of label used on the file—there are both standard and user-defined labels. Typically, the programmer will code

>LABEL RECORD IS STANDARD
>
>LABEL RECORDS ARE STANDARD
>
>LABEL RECORD IS OMITTED

or

>LABEL RECORDS ARE OMITTED.

Appendix D

Note that there is no difference between the singular and plural forms of this clause—they are equally valid. The LABEL RECORDS clause *must be* a part of each FD entry. User labels are quite complex; thus we will refer you to a good reference manual for questions concerning user labels.

The VALUE OF clause is treated as comments, as is the DATA RECORDS clause. In the DATA RECORDS clause, the programmer can list the name of each record associated with the file, as in

DATA RECORDS ARE RECORD1, RECORD2, RECORD3.

In a file with several record formats, this can be a valuable aid to documentation.

The REPORT clause is associated with the report writer feature; see a reference manual.

The FD entry is terminated by a period.

Following the FD entry come a series of data description entries. Normally, the data description begins with a level number and a data name, as in

    01 SAMPLE-RECORD ...

      05 PRIMARY-FIELD-1 ...

        10 SECONDARY-FIELD-1 ...

        10 SECONDARY-FIELD-2 ...

      05 PRIMARY-FIELD-2 ...

The level numbers identify the relationship between various fields, with lower numbered fields potentially subdivided into one or more higher numbered fields. Data names consist of from 1 to 30 alphabetic or numeric characters and the hyphen; at least one character must be alphabetic. The data name FILLER can be used to identify any unreferenced field.

The general format of a data description is shown below.

$$\text{level number} \quad \begin{Bmatrix} \text{data-name} \\ \text{FILLER} \end{Bmatrix}$$

    REDEFINES Clause
    BLANK WHEN ZERO Clause
    JUSTIFIED Clause
    OCCURS Clause
    PICTURE Clause
    SYNCHRONIZED Clause
    USAGE Clause
    VALUE Clause

Appendix D

A REDEFINES clause allows the programmer to assign alternate names to a field, or to use the same memory space for two different fields. Our most common application of this clause was to redefine a numeric field as alphanumeric to allow a test for blanks to be performed without risking program termination. A typical set of code might be

> 05 A PIC 999.
>
> 05 B REDEFINES A PIC XXX.

Now, B can safely be compared with SPACES.

The BLANK WHEN ZERO clause, as the name implies, sets a data item to all blanks whenever its value is zero. The JUSTIFIED clause is used to override the positioning of data in a nonnumeric field. Normally, following a MOVE or other data repositioning instruction, data in a nonnumeric field is left justified. Coding the clause

> JUSTIFIED RIGHT

overrides this convention.

An OCCURS clause is used to set up a table. Since a detailed description of this clause could prove very long, we will simply refer you to the textbook explanation which can be found in Chapter 8; see the index for a specific page reference.

The PICTURE clause is used to describe, character by character, the contents of a given data field. The clause

> PICTURE XXX

defines, for example, a 3-character alphanumeric field, while

> PICTURE IS 999

is a 3-character numeric field. Long fields can be defined by using a repetition factor, as in

> PIC X(120)

which defines a 120 character alphanumeric field.

Various edit characters can be used in a PICTURE clause. The valid symbols and their meanings include:

symbol	meaning
A	alphabetic character (A-Z and the blank character)
X	alphanumeric character (anything)

Appendix D

9	numeric character
V	implied decimal point
S	implied sign
B	position where a blank is to be inserted
Z	zero suppression
0	position where 0 is to be inserted
,	position where comma is to be inserted
.	position where decimal point is inserted
+ − CR DB	sign symbols for edited output
*	floating asterisk—check protect symbol
$	floating dollar sign

We refer you to a reference manual for questions involving complex editing.

The SYNCHRONIZED clause causes a data item to be aligned on a word boundary in main memory. It is often used with the USAGE clause, as in

05 A PIC 99V9 USAGE COMPUTATIONAL SYNCHRONIZED.

Data items are normally assumed to be

USAGE DISPLAY

which means that they are stored in a coded or external form. Normally, before arithmetic can be performed on such DISPLAY items, they must be converted to a numeric form. By using the clause

USAGE COMPUTATIONAL

the field is defined to hold pure numeric data, which can be used in arithmetic without conversion. Attaching a SYNC or SYNCHRONIZED clause to the item further improves efficiency by aligning the item on a word boundary.

Normally, COMPUTATIONAL is defined only for items in the WORKING-STORAGE SECTION, although data can be stored on tape, disk, or another magnetic medium in COMPUTATIONAL form. In standard COBOL, the precise form of COMPUTATIONAL data is whatever form of numeric data is most efficiently processed on the computer in question; on an IBM System/360 or System/370, for example, COMPUTATIONAL data is stored in pure binary form. There are other forms of computational data. Again using IBM as an example, the following computational types are defined for the System/360 and System/370 computer series:

field type	internal data format
COMPUTATIONAL	pure binary (halfword or fullword)
COMPUTATIONAL-1	floating-point
COMPUTATIONAL-2	double precision floating-point
COMPUTATIONAL-3	packed decimal

COMP is an acceptable abbreviation.

The VALUE clause can be used to assign an initial value to a field, as in

    05 A PIC 99 VALUE IS 0.

or

    05 B PIC XX VALUE IS SPACES.

The VALUE clause, if used in the FILE SECTION, is treated as comments by many compilers, although such use is technically illegal in standard COBOL.

THE WORKING-STORAGE SECTION

The FILE-SECTION defines all data stored outside the computer. In the WORKING-STORAGE SECTION, all internal data items must be defined. This includes such commonly used fields as arithmetic and logical work fields, fields to hold intermediate results, and headers. Basically, all the information described under "data descriptions" above remains valid in this section. In addition, a few new entries are possible.

A field with the level number 77 can be used to define an independent work field that is not part of any data structure. Level-77 entries must normally be coded first in the WORKING-STORAGE SECTION. Other special level numbers, 66 for items or structures described by a RENAMES clause and 88 for conditional variables, are also legal; for details, we refer you to a reference manual.

The VALUE clause has meaning only in the WORKING-STORAGE SECTION.

THE REPORT SECTION

The REPORT SECTION is used in support of the COBOL report writing feature. Basically, this feature allows the programmer to define a report format in a manner similar to the RPG language. In the FILE SECTION, the fact that the report feature is being used is described through the REPORT clause, which lists the name of each

Appendix D

report associated with the FD entry. For each report listed, an RD entry must be specified in the REPORT SECTION.

The report feature is rarely used; thus, we refer you to a reference manual for additional details.

SORT FEATURE CONSIDERATIONS

When the COBOL sort feature is used, the regular input and output files must be defined by using FD entries, just as though they were being processed by a program not using the sort feature. The purpose of the SD entry is to define the sort work files. Although a sort routine may use several different files, only one SD entry must be coded for each sort. Do not code such clauses as LABEL RECORDS or BLOCK CONTAINS as part of the SD. On an IBM machine, although a SELECT and ASSIGN clause must be associated with each SD entry, the external name (last subfield in the ASSIGN) is treated as comments, meaning that any name will do.

THE PROCEDURE DIVISION

The PROCEDURE DIVISION houses the logical instructions to be executed by the program. The instructions are grouped into sections, within sections into paragraphs, and within paragraphs into sentences; the period must be coded at the end of a section name, a paragraph name, or a sentence.

In this section, the various COBOL statements will be presented in alphabetic order.

ACCEPT

The ACCEPT statement is designed to input a small amount of data from the operators's console or another input device. The general form of the statement is

> ACCEPT identifier.

or

> ACCEPT identifier FROM mnemonic-name.

The "identifier" must be either a data name defined in the DATA DIVISION or the special register TALLY. If the second operand is not coded, many systems assume that the operator's console is called for.

In standard ANSI COBOL, the mnemonic name must be defined in the SPECIAL-NAMES paragraph of the ENVIRONMENT DIVISION. Many versions of COBOL (including IBM's) allow the input device to be designated by such names as SYSIN (for the system input device) or CONSOLE (for the operator's console) without defining these names in the SPECIAL-NAMES paragraph.

The ACCEPT statement actually implies that the functional equivalent of the following three instructions will be executed: OPEN/READ/CLOSE. Great care must be taken when using the ACCEPT statement to access a file later to be accessed by a READ statement. To be safe, it is strongly advised that all necessary ACCEPTs be coded early in the housekeeping paragraph, with the OPEN instruction for the mainline input file being coded later.

ADD

The function of the ADD statement is to find the sum of two or more numbers. There are two basic forms of the instruction. In the first form

$$\text{ADD iden-1 iden-2 } \ldots \text{ TO iden-n.}$$

one or more data fields or numeric constants are added to a receiving field. A typical example would be

$$\text{ADD 1 TO COUNTER.}$$

or

$$\text{ADD VALUE TO ACCUMULATOR.}$$

The second general form of the instruction is

$$\text{ADD iden-1 iden-2 iden-3 } \ldots \text{ GIVING iden-n.}$$

This instruction adds a series of data fields or numeric constants and places the results in the "GIVING" field. In each case, only the last field, the one following the GIVING or the TO, is changed; all other fields retain their initial values.

A ROUNDED option can be used to obtain an answer rounded to the precision specified in the DATA DIVISION. If, for example, the variable C were defined with a PICTURE clause of 99.9, the instruction

$$\text{ADD 1.55 1.53 GIVING C.}$$

would compute and store the value 3.0 in C, while

$$\text{ADD 1.55 1.53 GIVING C ROUNDED.}$$

would compute and store 3.1.

Another commonly used option is the ON SIZE ERROR option. It is possible that a sum exceeding the maximum value that can be stored in an identifier can be generated by an ADD instruction. The ON SIZE ERROR option allows the programmer to take corrective action when such problems occur, for example

$$\text{ADD A B GIVING C ON SIZE ERROR PERFORM FIX-ROUTINE.}$$

Appendix D

ALTER

The ALTER statement is used to change the target of a GO TO statement. It is little used; we refer you to the COBOL reference manual for your computer.

CALL

The CALL statement links a COBOL program to a subprogram (external) written in COBOL or some other language. The general form of the instruction is

        CALL program-name USING iden-1 iden-2 iden-3 . . . .

The identifiers following the USING are the parameters being passed to the subprogram; their order must match the order specified within the subroutine.

CANCEL

On some systems, it is possible to assign space to a subprogram only when that program is actually needed. The CANCEL statement releases that space after the main program no longer needs the subprogram. Refer to the COBOL reference manual for exact formats and limitations on use.

CLOSE

The CLOSE statement terminates processing on the named file or files, performing such functions as writing an end-of-data marker and requesting the rewinding and unloading of tapes. In general, the instruction is coded as

        CLOSE file-name.

or

        CLOSE file-name-1 file-name-2 . . . .

Special options are available for performing unusual magnetic tape or mass storage operations; these include REEL, UNIT, NO REWIND, and LOCK. As is our usual practice with little-used options, we refer you to a COBOL reference manual for details.

COMPUTE

The COMPUTE statement allows the programmer to code complex mathematical operations in a single instruction by writing the functional equivalent of an algebraic expression. Variables and numeric constants, coupled with the arithmetic operators for addition (+), subtraction (−), multiplication (*), and division (/), and, on some systems, exponentiation (**), can be formed into a single expression representing the equivalent of several COBOL statements. For example, the three statements

Appendix D

ADD A B GIVING C.

MULTIPLY C BY 14 GIVING D.

SUBTRACT D FROM E GIVING F.

Can be coded as a single COMPUTE statement, as in

COMPUTE F = E − ((A + B) * 14).

FORTRAN programmers will find this instruction familiar. Many COBOL installations, however, do not allow its use simply because extremely complex and difficult to follow code can be generated. For example, consider the readability of the 3-step set of instructions as contrasted with the COMPUTE statement illustrated above. Detailed rules for constructing COMPUTE statements can be found in the COBOL reference manual for your system.

COPY

The COPY instruction is not executed by the computer. Instead, it is a message to the COBOL compiler that previously written source code is to be copied from a source statement library and added to the source program before (or during) compilation. The general form of the instruction is

COPY library-name.

Since the use of this statement can vary significantly from installation, check your reference manual carefully.

DISPLAY

The function of the DISPLAY statement is to allow the programmer to write a small amount of data on some output device. It is commonly used for communicating with the operator, as in

DISPLAY 'ENTER CURRENT DATE' UPON CONSOLE.

The general form of the instruction is

DISPLAY literal-1 or identifier-1 UPON mnemonic-name.

Any number of literals or data fields may be displayed. Under standard ANSI COBOL, the mnemonic name must be defined in the SPECIAL-NAME paragraph in the ENVIRONMENT DIVISION. Many computer manufacturers allow a number of pre-defined mnemonic names to be used; IBM, for example, allows CONSOLE to represent the operator's console, SYSPUNCH to represent the system output device (for punched cards), and SYSOUT to represent the system output device for printed output.

The DISPLAY instruction implies that the functional equivalent of the three instructions OPEN/WRITE/CLOSE will be executed. Be very careful when using the DISPLAY statement with reference to files that will later be written.

DIVIDE

As the name implies, the DIVIDE instruction supports a divide operation. There are two general forms. The first

DIVIDE A INTO B.

replaces the second operand, in this case B, by the quotient. The second general form

DIVIDE A INTO B GIVING C.

or

DIVIDE B BY A GIVING C.

places the quotient into the third field (C) without changing the first two. Either numeric fields or numeric constants may participate in the divide, but the receiving field must be a variable.

The ROUNDED and ON SIZE ERROR options can be used with a DIVIDE; see the ADD instruction for an explanation. Another common option is the REMAINDER option. In the instruction

DIVIDE A BY B GIVING C REMAINDER D.

the remainder is placed in a field named D and can be used in later processing.

ENTRY

This statement defines an entry point in a COBOL program or subroutine; a CALL statement can then refer to this entry point. The general format of the instruction is

ENTRY literal-1 USING iden-1 iden-2 . . . .

the identifiers following the USING are the named of the fields or constants being passed to the routine; the sequence in a CALL statement must match this sequence.

EXAMINE

This statement allows the programmer to count the number of occurances of a character or to replace a character with another character. One general form is

Appendix D

$$\text{EXAMINE identifier TALLYING} \begin{Bmatrix} \text{UNTIL FIRST} \\ \text{ALL} \\ \text{LEADING} \end{Bmatrix} \text{literal-1}$$

REPLACING BY literal-2.

If, for example, the instruction

EXAMINE A TALLYING ALL SPACES.

is coded, the field named A will be tested, character by character, and a count of the number of blanks encountered will be maintained in the special register TALLY. The LEADING option, if used in this example, would result in a count of the number of blanks encountered until the first non-blank character. The UNTIL FIRST option would count the number of non-blank characters until the first blank was encountered.

If the REPLACING option is used, the first literal is replaced by the second literal; for example, the statement

EXAMINE A TALLYING ALL SPACES

REPLACING BY ZEROS.

would result in a count of the number of blank spaces encountered and the replacing of each blank by a zero.

The other form of the instruction simply drops the counting function. Its general form is

$$\text{EXAMINE identifier REPLACING} \begin{Bmatrix} \text{ALL} \\ \text{LEADING} \\ \text{FIRST} \\ \text{UNTIL FIRST} \end{Bmatrix} \text{literal-1}$$

BY literal-2.

The EXAMINE statement is very useful in editing input data. In particular, it can allow certain nonnumeric characters (such as a blank) to be replaced by valid numeric characters in preparation for a numeric test.

EXIT

The EXIT provides an end point for a procedure or series of procedures. We have used this statement as the final statement in a secondary routine, giving it its own paragraph name. The EXIT statement must be preceeded by a paragraph name, and must be the only statement in that paragraph.

Appendix D

EXIT PROGRAM

Can be used to mark the end of a called program.

FORMAT CONTROLS FOR COMPILER LISTING

The programmer can control the printing of a compiler listing by inserting an EJECT statement for a new page or one of the instructions SKIP1, SKIP2, or SKIP3 to have the listing space 1, 2, or 3 spaces respectively. These instructions are neither executed by the computer nor printed by the compiler. They must be coded between columns 12 and 72 of the coding form.

GOBACK

The GOBACK instruction returns control from a called subroutine back to the main or calling program.

GO TO

This instruction transfers control to the first instruction in the named section or paragraph; for example,

$$\text{GO TO TOP-OF-MAINLINE.}$$

transfers control to the instruction immediately following the paragraph named TOP-OF-MAINLINE. Modern programming practice suggests that the use of the GO TO statement be kept to a minimum.

A second form of the instruction

$$\text{GO TO proc-1 \quad proc-2 \quad proc-3 \ldots}$$

$$\text{DEPENDING ON identifier.}$$

transfers control to the first section or paragraph if the value of the identifier is 1, to the second if the value is 2, and so on. This is not a commonly used option in COBOL; in fact, many installations prohibit its use.

IF

The IF statement is the basic conditional statement in COBOL. The general rule is

$$\text{IF condition THEN} \begin{Bmatrix} \text{statement-1} \\ \text{NEXT SENTENCE} \end{Bmatrix} \text{ELSE} \begin{Bmatrix} \text{statement-2} \\ \text{NEXT SENTENCE} \end{Bmatrix}.$$

Appendix D

For a full description of conditions, we refer you to Chapters 5 and 7, or to a COBOL reference manual.

MOVE

The MOVE statement copies data from one field or literal to one or more other fields without changing the first field. The general form of the instruction is

$$\text{MOVE} \begin{Bmatrix} \text{identifier-1} \\ \text{literal} \end{Bmatrix} \text{TO} \quad \text{iden-2} \quad \text{iden-3} \ldots .$$

For example, the instruction

> MOVE SPACES TO PRINT-LINE.

transfers the space character to the PRINT-LINE, while

> MOVE A TO B C D.

copies whatever is found in the field called A to fields B, C, and D.

The CORRESPONDING option allows a number of fields to be moved at one time. It is common, for example, for several fields from an input record to be moved without change to the output record. If the fields are defined using the exact same names in both the input and output record, the instruction

> MOVE CORRESPONDING A TO B.

will result in the transfer of each lower numbered field within A to a field within B having the same name. We have not used this option within the text.

MULTIPLY

The MULTIPLY statement supports multiplication, for example

> **MULTIPLY A BY B GIVING C.**

ROUNDED and ON SIZE ERROR options can be coded; see the ADD instruction for details.

NOTE

The NOTE statement allows the programmer to insert comments into the program. We have not used this statement, taking advantage of the fact that our compiler allows a comment to be identified by an asterisk (*) in column 7.

Appendix D

OPEN

The OPEN statement marks the beginning of processing on the named file or files. Typical functions of the OPEN include checking or creating labels, completing necessary internal linkage blocks, and filling the first set of buffers on an input file. The general form of the instruction is

OPEN INPUT file-name **OUTPUT** file-name I-O file-name . . . .

Any number of files can be opened in a single statement, although we have consistently coded the OPEN for each file as a separate instruction. Either INPUT, OUTPUT, or I-O must preceed each file name; I-O implies a direct access file that may be used for input, output, or both within the program.

PERFORM

The PERFORM statement allows the program to branch to a subroutine or procedure and then return. The first form of the instruction is

PERFORM procedure-1 **THRU** procedure-2.

The THRU is optional. When this instruction is executed, control passes to the first named procedure, eventually returning to the instruction following the PERFORM.

A second form of the instruction is

PERFORM procedure-1 **THRU** procedure-2 n **TIMES**.

where "n" may be a data field or a numeric constant. This form of the instruction causes the named procedure or procedures to be executed repeatedly a specified number of times.

A third form is

PERFORM procedure-1 THRU procedure-2 UNTIL condition.

This form of the instruction calls for the repetitive execution of the procedure or procedures, with execution continuing, in a loop-like fashion, until a terminal condition is met. It must be noted that the condition is tested before execution of the procedures begins. If the terminal condition should occur during execution, that cycle will be completed. If, for example, the terminal condition is set by an end of file condition and if that condition is encountered as part of the secondary routine, all instructions in the routine will be executed before the condition is again tested.

The fourth general format looks quite complex, but is really relatively simple.

Appendix D

PERFORM procedure-name-1 THRU procedure-name-2

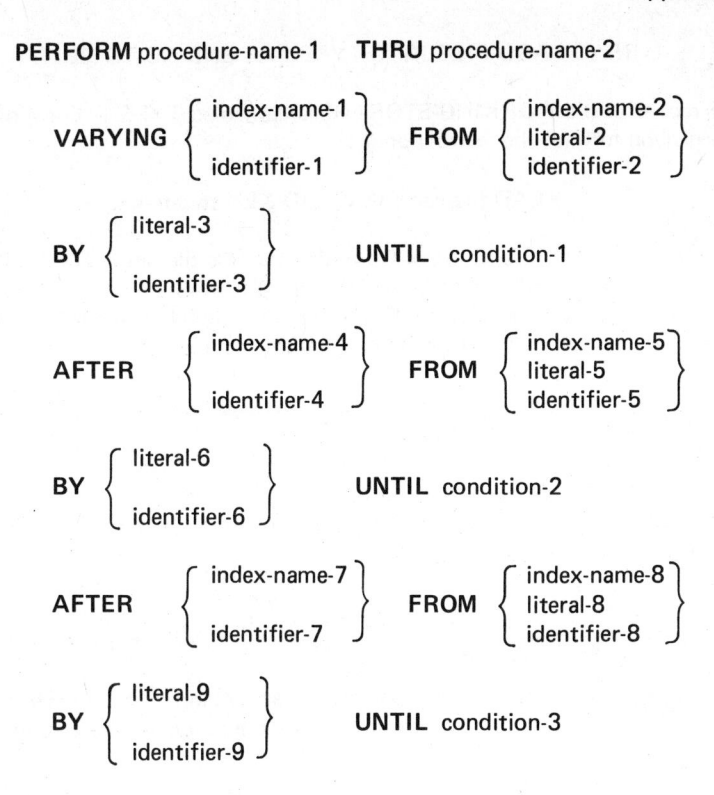

VARYING $\left\{\begin{array}{l}\text{index-name-1}\\ \text{identifier-1}\end{array}\right\}$ FROM $\left\{\begin{array}{l}\text{index-name-2}\\ \text{literal-2}\\ \text{identifier-2}\end{array}\right\}$

BY $\left\{\begin{array}{l}\text{literal-3}\\ \text{identifier-3}\end{array}\right\}$ UNTIL condition-1

AFTER $\left\{\begin{array}{l}\text{index-name-4}\\ \text{identifier-4}\end{array}\right\}$ FROM $\left\{\begin{array}{l}\text{index-name-5}\\ \text{literal-5}\\ \text{identifier-5}\end{array}\right\}$

BY $\left\{\begin{array}{l}\text{literal-6}\\ \text{identifier-6}\end{array}\right\}$ UNTIL condition-2

AFTER $\left\{\begin{array}{l}\text{index-name-7}\\ \text{identifier-7}\end{array}\right\}$ FROM $\left\{\begin{array}{l}\text{index-name-8}\\ \text{literal-8}\\ \text{identifier-8}\end{array}\right\}$

BY $\left\{\begin{array}{l}\text{literal-9}\\ \text{identifier-9}\end{array}\right\}$ UNTIL condition-3

For example, the instruction

    PERFORM TEST-PARAGRAPH

        VARYING N FROM 1 BY 1

        UNTIL N = 25.

tells the computer that it is to perform the paragraph named TEST-PARAGRAPH. A field named N is to be initialized to 1. Each time the paragraph is performed, the value of N is incremented by 1. This process is to continue until N is equal to 25. The two AFTER options allow the programmer to specify as many as two additional indexes or identifiers which are to be varied in similar fashion after the first limiting condition has been met.

READ

The READ instruction transfers one input record from a physical device or from an internal buffer into the program. For sequential files, the instruction is coded

    READ file-name AT END statement.

An INTO option may be used; for example,

Appendix D

READ CARD-FILE INTO TYPE-1 AT END GO TO QUIT.

reads a record into a WORKING-STORAGE area named TYPE-1. For a direct access file, the general form of the instruction is

READ file-name INVALID KEY statement.

The INTO option can also be used. On a direct access file, an ACTUAL KEY clause must have been specified in the ENVIRONMENT DIVISION; a NOMINAL KEY is needed for randomly accessing an ISAM file. An OPEN statement for the named file must have been executed before any READ is executed.

RELEASE

When using an input procedure as part of the SORT feature, the RELEASE statement is used to transfer a record from the input procedure to the sort operation. Refer to the COBOL manual for your system.

RETURN

When using an output procedure as part of the sort feature, the RETURN statement is used to transfer sorted records from the sort operation to the output procedure.

REWRITE

The REWRITE statement is used to copy a just-read record back to an ISAM or direct file. Its format is similar to that of the WRITE statement.

SEARCH

The SEARCH statement looks up a value in a table. The general form of the instruction is

SEARCH table-name

VARYING name-1

AT END statement-1

WHEN condition-1 statement-2

WHEN condition-2 statement-3

The table-name may not itself be subscripted or indexed; in other words, you may not code SEARCH TABLE-1 (INDEX-1). In the DATA DIVISION, there must be both an OCCURS clause and an INDEXED BY option. The VARYING option allows an index

Appendix D

other than the one controlling the referenced table to be varied. The AT END clause specifies what is to be done if the entire table has been searched without success. As many as two WHEN options can be coded; should either condition be met, the specified statement associated with the condition will be executed—usually a GO TO, PERFORM, or NEXT SENTENCE.

An alternative form of the instruction is

SEARCH ALL table-name

AT END statement-1

WHEN condition-1 statement-2.

The basic difference is that the SEARCH ALL calls for a binary search rather than a serial search. When using this form of the instruction, the entries in the table must be in either ascending or descending order, and the reserved word ASCENDING or DESCENDING must be attached to the OCCURS clause.

SET

The SET statement is used to initialize or change the value of an index. For example,

SET INDEX-1 TO 5.

SET INDEX-2 UP BY 1.

SET INDEX-3 DOWN BY 1.

SORT

The SORT statement allows the programmer to implement the COBOL sort feature, providing the information needed to control the sort operation. The general form of the instruction is

$$\text{SORT file-name-1 ON} \begin{Bmatrix} \text{DESCENDING} \\ \text{ASCENDING} \end{Bmatrix} \text{KEY data-name-1} \dots$$

$$\text{ON} \begin{Bmatrix} \text{DESCENDING} \\ \text{ASCENDING} \end{Bmatrix} \text{KEY data-name-2} \dots \dots$$

$$\begin{Bmatrix} \text{INPUT PROCEDURE IS section-name-1} \quad \text{THRU section-name-2} \\ \text{USING file-name-2} \end{Bmatrix}$$

$$\begin{Bmatrix} \text{OUTPUT PROCEDURE IS section-name-3} \quad \text{THRU section-name-4} \\ \text{GIVING file-name-3} \end{Bmatrix}$$

Appendix D

The file name must be defined in an SD entry in the DATA DIVISION. The programmer must specify either ASCENDING or DESCENDING order for the sort. Following KEY, the data name or names of the field or fields on which the records are to be sorted must be coded. Note that it is possible to perform a sort on more than one level, with the most significant key listed first, the secondary key second, and less significant keys following in order of their significance. For example,

SORT FILE1 ON ASCENDING KEY A B C . . .

defines a 3-level sort. Following execution of this instruction, the file will be in sequence by field A. All records having the same value in field A will be sorted by field B. Within those records having the same value in field B, the sequence will be by field C. Here, A is the primary sort field, B is the intermediate key, and C is the minor key.

The second ON . . . KEY option allows a secondary key to be sorted in an order opposite that of the primary key. For example,

SORT FILE1 ON ASCENDING KEY A

ON DESCENDING KEY B . . .

would designate a primary sort on key A, with records being placed in ASCENDING order. Within the set of records having the same value for key A, the sequence would be DESCENDING by key B.

Records can be supplied to the sort routine by using either a USING option or an INPUT PROCEDURE. Records can be returned from the sort routine by using either a GIVING option or an OUTPUT PROCEDURE. The GIVING/USING combination is the easiest to use, requiring the programmer to simply name the input and/or output file. An example of this form of the sort is

SORT FILE1 ON ASCENDING KEY A

USING FILE2

GIVING FILE3.

In this example, FILE2 and FILE3 must be defined as FD's in the DATA DIVISION. Do not open files when using this form.

When using an INPUT PROCEDURE and/or an OUTPUT PROCEDURE, the programmer must supply the instructions to open, read and/or write, and close the files. Records are passed to the sort routine by using a RELEASE statement; the RETURN statement is used to return sorted records to the OUTPUT PROCEDURE. In effect, the programmer supplies a subroutine for handling input and/or output, and this subroutine is essentially performed under control of the SORT statement. The advantage is that the programmer can implement any needed data manipulation operations; the disadvantage of this approach is greater complexity.

Appendix D

It is legal to mix a USING option and an OUTPUT PROCEDURE or an INPUT PROCEDURE and a GIVING option.

STOP

The STOP statement halts program execution. Generally, the programmer will code

STOP RUN.

at the end of his or her program. Another option is to code

STOP literal.

where the literal is any numeric or nonnumeric literal constant. This form temporarily halts program execution, the literal is communicated to the operator, and operator intervention is required to resume program execution. Since unnecessary operator intervention is to be avoided (for one thing, it makes operators angry), the use of the "temporary halt" form of the STOP instruction should be avoided.

SUBTRACT

The SUBTRACT instruction, as the name implies, implements subtraction. The first form of the instruction,

SUBTRACT X FROM Y.

is similar to the first form of the ADD instruction. More than one field can participate, as in

SUBTRACT A B C FROM D.

Numeric constants can also be used.

A second form of the instruction

SUBTRACT A FROM B GIVING C.

or

SUBTRACT A B FROM C GIVING D.

is similar to the second form of the ADD instruction. In both cases, ROUNDED and ON SIZE ERROR options can be coded.

WRITE

The WRITE statement transfers one record of data from within the computer to an output device (or to a buffer for eventual transfer to an output device). For sequential files, the general form of the instruction is

   WRITE record-name FROM identifier.

The FROM is optional; if coded, it implies that the record will first be moved from WORKING-STORAGE and then written. An AFTER (or BEFORE) ADVANCING clause can be used to control line spacing on the printer, as in

   WRITE record-1 AFTER ADVANCING 2 LINES.

or

   WRITE record-2 BEFORE ADVANCING NEW-PAGE.

In the second example, a mnemonic name, defined in the ENVIRONMENT DIVISION, was used. Normally, once an ADVANCING option has been used, all sebsequent WRITEs to that file must use the ADVANCING option.

For a direct access file, the general form of the instruction is

   WRITE record-name FROM identifier

   INVALID KEY statement.

The FROM is, once again, optional. An ACTUAL KEY field must have been described in the ENVIRONMENT DIVISION (ACTUAL KEY clause) and defined in the DATA DIVISION before direct access can be used. The NOMINAL KEY clause is used for randomly accessing an indexed sequential file.

Before a WRITE statement can be executed, the file must have been opened. Note also that, in COBOL, we read files but write records.

Index

Index

A-section of coding form 30, 32, 34, 35, 42, 47
access arm (or access mechanism) 224, 391
access method 223
ACCESS MODE 399, 451, 471, 480, 523, 524
ACCEPT 530, 531
accessability 466
accumulator 6, 20
accuracy 218
activity 491
ACTUAL KEY 399, 404, 405, 410, 412, 469, 480, 523
ADD 55, 56, 531
AFTER ADVANCING clause 58, 110
algorithm 5, 84, 156, 178, 285, 286, 395, 396, 398, 404
ALPHABETIC class test 238
alphanumeric character 44
alphanumeric literal constant 108
ALTER 532
arithmetic and logical unit 9, 12
ASCENDING KEY 272
ASSIGN 36, 42, 71, 523

asterisk (edit character) 321
AT END clause 54, 55
AUTHOR 34, 521

backup 439, 461
B-section of coding form 30, 32, 34, 36
binary search 190
block 223, 234, 264
BLOCK CONTAINS clause 42, 224, 250, 399, 525
blocking 223, 234
branch 55
break point 93 (see also control break)
business data processing 28
BY 58

CALL 532
CANCEL 532
card reader 11, 12
carriage control 109, 110
character 20, 35, 42, 44, 46
class (ASSIGN clause) 36
class test 238

CLOSE 59, 69, 241, 250, 532
COBOL 21
COBOL coding form 29 - 31, 64
COBOL sort (see sort feature)
COBOL statement 29, 30, 32 (see also statement)
COBVCG 68, 69
column header 104, 105
command language 66, 67, 227, 250
comment 30, 168
compilation process 64, 65
compiler 64 - 66, 74
complex condition 97
compound condition 97, 238, 239
COMPUTATIONAL 404, 528, 529
COMPUTE 532, 533
computer 8 - 14
condition 93, 97, 166
conditional branch 55
CONFIGURATION SECTION 35, 110, 522
constant 52, 53, 105, 108, 109
continuation line 29, 57
continuation of a statement 57
control break 287, 288, 319, 321, 345
control unit 9, 12
COPY 533
CR edit characters 332
cylinder 226
cylinder index 447, 448

data 12, 14, 19, 20
data base management 493
data cards 73, 74
DATA DIVISION 32, 36, 42 - 48, 51, 52, 55, 73, 89, 98, 105, 118, 524 - 530
data edit (see edit checking)
data format 86, 88, 89, 139, 140, 526
data name 44 - 47, 52, 526
data processing 12
data structure 44, 108, 183
DB edit characters 332
DCB parameters, JCL 458, 460
DD statement, JCL 69 - 72, 74, 228 - 231
deblocking 223
debug 138, 139, 158
decimal point 20
decimal point (PICTURE) 47
default 399

detail line 284, 285, 319, 321, 324, 332, 337
detail record 89, 109
detailed logic 156
direct access 390 - 419, 424 - 441, 446 - 461, 466 - 493
direct access devices 390, 391
direct access file update 424 - 441, 478 - 493
direct access techniques 395 - 399
disk 12, 224 - 227, 230, 234, 258, 391, 392
DISP parameter, JCL 228, 230
DISPLAY 302, 533
DIVIDE 58, 534
division/remainder method 395, 397 - 399, 404, 405, 410
divisions of a COBOL program 30 - 32
documentation 19, 28, 32, 138, 160
dollar sign ($) PICTURE 146
DOS job control 509 - 514
drum, magnetic 391
DSNAME parameter, JCL 228, 230, 458

edit character 47, 98, 99, 104
edit checking 220, 221, 231 - 250, 282, 302, 426
EJECT 310
ELSE 97, 98
end-of-data logic 17
end-of-data marker 17, 72, 74, 330
END-OF-PAGE 112
end-of-job logic 286, 292, 362
ENTRY 534
ENVIRONMENT DIVISION 30, 32, 35 - 38, 51, 89, 110, 522 - 524
error (compilation) 79
error handling 295, 297, 362, 412
error message 76 - 80
EXAMINE 534, 535
EXEC statement 68, 69, 72, 74, 227
EXIT 118, 535
EXIT PROGRAM 536
external name (ASSIGN clause) 36

FD entry   42, 44, 51, 525, 526
field   35, 42, 44 - 47, 52, 53, 108
field name   (see data name)
file   35, 42, 44, 51, 392
FILE-CONTROL   35, 36, 522, 523
file description   (see FD entry)
file name   36, 42, 46
FILE SECTION   42 - 47, 89, 98, 105, 109, 118, 525 - 529
FILLER   45, 46, 108, 109, 526
first record processing   362
floating dollar sign   146
flowchart   14 - 19, 28, 48, 50, 54, 86, 87, 157, 159, 166, 181, 182, 330

GIVING   56, 58
GIVING (sort option)   272
GO BACK   536
GO TO   55, 536
GO TO, a cautionary note   55

header   104, 105, 108, 109, 112, 284, 285, 294, 319, 321, 324, 327, 332, 337, 363
HIGH-VALUE   241, 428, 449, 451, 471
housekeeping functions   54, 93
hyphen   32, 34, 35, 47

IDENTIFICATION DIVISION   30, 32 - 34, 89, 521
IF   93, 97, 98, 157, 161 - 168
IF...THEN...ELSE block   97, 98, 161 - 168
implied decimal point   45, 46, 48, 53, 99
implied sign (S)   99
index   187 - 194, 201, 396, 397, 446
index area   456
INDEXED BY   188
indexed file   397, 446 - 461, 466 - 493
indexed sequential access method   446 - 461, 466 - 493
information   12
INVALID KEY   404, 412, 449, 456, 478, 490
input   9, 11, 12, 14, 20, 86
INPUT (OPEN)   51
input device   12, 21
INPUT-OUTPUT SECTION   35, 522, 523
input procedure (sort)   274, 276
instruction   9, 12, 52, 53

interblock gap   223
intermediate data file   220 - 227, 231, 234, 258
internal sort   (see sort feature)
interrecord gap   223
ISAM   (see indexed sequential access method)
ISAM file update   478 - 493
I-O   480
I/O device   35 - 38, 66, 69, 86
I/O device linkage   35 - 38, 69, 70

JCL   (see job control language)
job control language   66 - 73, 227 - 231, 250, 265 - 268, 458 - 460
job deck   74 - 76
job name   67
JOB statement   67, 68, 72, 74, 227
job step   227

key (or logical key)   260, 358, 395 - 397, 404, 447, 448
keypunch   29, 30, 64, 499 - 507

label   224
LABEL parameter, JCL   228
LABEL RECORD clause   44, 226, 525, 526
last card indicator   54
last record processing   292, 327, 330, 362
level number   44, 526
level-01 entry   (see 01-level entry at end of index)
level-77 entry   (see 77-level entry at end of index)
line number   76
linkage editor   65
listing   76 - 81, 310
literal constant   52, 53, 108
loop   6, 55
LOW-VALUE   241, 456

magnetic tape   12, 222 - 224, 228, 258, 390, 391
mainline   93, 112, 118, 136, 138, 146, 158, 160, 178, 204, 294, 302, 327, 332, 337, 358
maintenance   138, 160

major break   319, 324
manual solution   5 - 7, 16
master file   86, 258 - 261, 352 - 379
master file update   259 - 261, 352 - 379
memory   8, 12, 14
minor break   319, 324
modular flowchart   364, 366, 367
modular programming   113 - 119, 136 - 146, 150, 158, 160, 204, 289, 294, 345
module   136, 138, 150
MOVE   52 - 54, 57, 105, 118, 537
MULTIPLY   58, 537
Murphy's Law   291

nested IF statements   161 - 168, 172
new master file   354
NEXT SENTENCE   118
nine PICTURE   (see 9-PICTURE at end of index)
NOMINAL KEY   405, 469, 471, 480, 490, 523, 524
NOTE statement   168, 537
numeric character   44
NUMERIC class test   238, 239, 337, 478
numeric field   53

OBJECT-COMPUTER   35, 522
object module   65, 72
OCCURS clause   183 - 185, 187, 190, 194, 527
old master file   353
ON ASCENDING KEY   272
OPEN   51, 69, 241, 538
organization (ASSIGN clause)   36
output   9, 11, 12, 20, 88, 89
OUTPUT (OPEN)   51
output device   12, 14, 21
output procedure (sort)   274, 276
overflow   396, 398, 448
overflow area   456

page controls   112 - 118
page header   (see header)
paragraph   32, 35, 48, 51
paragraph name   32, 34, 45, 54
PERFORM   113 - 119, 138, 150, 158, 160, 201, 330, 378, 538, 539
PERFORM...UNTIL   378
period   35, 48, 54, 168

PICTURE clause   44, 46, 47, 53, 74, 88, 89, 98, 99, 108, 140, 146, 527, 528
planning   5 - 7, 14 - 21, 84 - 89, 119, 134 - 140, 157 - 160, 286 - 297, 321 - 330, 354 - 367, 408, 410, 419, 428
primary key   319, 324
prime data area   456
printer   11, 12, 20, 109, 110
printer spacing chart   105, 109, 321, 354
problem definition   4, 5, 134
PROCEDURE DIVISION   32, 48 - 59, 93, 112, 161, 530 - 544
processor   8, 9, 12
program   8, 12, 14, 21
program development process   4 - 21
PROGRAM-ID   32, 34, 521
program name   34
proof totals   84, 88, 89
psuedo code   86, 157
punched card   11, 20

query   466

RANDOM (ACCESS MODE)   399
random access   390
range test   238, 239
READ   54, 55, 58, 69, 539, 540
read/write head   222, 224, 391, 392
record   35, 42, 44 - 47, 139, 223, 258, 390
RECORD KEY   451, 471, 480
record name   44, 46
RECORDING MODE   451
REDEFINES   195, 198, 302, 430, 526, 527
relative address   391 - 395
relative record   393, 394 - 396, 405
relative sector   392
relative track   392 - 394, 396, 398, 399, 404
RELEASE   276, 540
REMAINDER   404
REMARKS   34, 89, 521
reorganization (ISAM file)   460, 461
report   104, 105

report generation 261
REPORT SECTION 529, 530
reserved word 34, 46, 52, 57, 515 - 519
response time 492
RETURN 540
REWRITE 490, 540
right justified 332
ROUNDED option 168
rules for COBOL word 34
rules for data name 44
rules for file name 36
rules for paragraph name 44

S PICTURE (see sign)
SD-entry 269, 271, 272, 530
SEARCH 190, 540, 541
secondary key 319, 324
secondary storage 262
section 32, 35, 48
SECTION 46
section A of coding form 30, 32, 34, 35, 42, 47
section B of coding form 30, 32, 34, 36
sector 226, 391
SELECT 36, 42, 51, 69, 71, 523
self documenting nature of COBOL 28, 30
sentence 32, 48, 54, 168
sequence checking 291, 295
SEQUENTIAL (ACCESS MODE) 399
sequential file 258, 259, 261, 358 - 379, 390
serial search 190
SET 187, 541
sign (S-PICTURE) 99, 332, 404
skeleton mainline 138, 140 - 147, 150, 178, 204
SKIPn 310
sort 260 - 276, 282, 321
sort control card 266
sort feature 269 - 276, 530
SORT statement 261, 269, 272, 541, 542, 543
sort utility 261 - 268, 321
sort work files 266, 269, 530
sort/merge 262, 264, 321
SORTD procedure 265 - 268
SOURCE-COMPUTER 35, 522
source module 65
SPACE parameter, JCL 230, 458

SPACES 57
SPECIAL-NAMES 110, 522
spooling 42
STANDARD label 226
start-of-job logic 286, 291, 327, 362
statement 32, 48, 51
STOP RUN 59, 543
stored program 12, 14
structure (see data structure)
structured programming 119, 136, 150
structured walkthrough 7
subroutine or subprogram 161, 261, 269
subscript 184 - 187
SUBTRACT 56, 57, 543
summary line 89, 93, 109, 284, 285, 319, 321, 324, 327, 330, 332, 345
summary report 352
summary totals 84
switch 239, 377
switch setting 239, 241
SYNCHRONIZED 404, 528
synonym 396
system of programs 227, 261, 276, 282, 319

table file 198, 201
table handling 178 - 211
table initialization 194 - 203
table look-up 166 - 168
temporary file 234, 258
terminal 11
test data 146, 147, 286, 353, 354
testing 146 - 150, 158
THEN 97, 98
TO option 52
top-down approach 4, 150
track 224, 226, 258, 391, 392
track index 447, 448
transaction 259, 319, 356 - 358, 427
transaction file 260, 353, 354
transaction log 425, 427

unconditional branch 55
UNIT parameter, JCL 228, 230
USING (sort option) 272

551.

utility program 261

V PICTURE 45, 46
VALUE clause 108, 109, 194, 529
VARYING option on PERFORM 201
VOL parameter, JCL 228, 458
volatile file 493

warning 79
word (COBOL) 34
work field 47, 53, 88, 89, 140, 160
WORKING-STORAGE SECTION 47, 48,
    89, 105, 109, 118, 160, 529
WRITE 58, 69, 110, 544
WRITE FROM 118, 332, 337

X PICTURE 44, 46, 47, 53

yes/no logic 9

zero divide 297
zero supression (Z PICTURE) 99, 104
ZEROS 53

01-level entry 44
9 PICTURE 44, 46 - 48, 53
77-level entry 48